WITNESS TO REVOLUTION

WITNESS TO REVOLUTION

THE ADVOCATE REPORTS ON GAY AND LESBIAN POLITICS, 1967–1999

EDITED BY CHRIS BULL

alyson books
los angeles | new york

MANUFACTURED IN THE UNITED STATES OF AMERICA.
COVER DESIGN BY BRUCE ZINDA.

THIS TRADE PAPERBACK ORIGINAL IS PUBLISHED BY ALYSON PUBLICATIONS,
P.O. BOX 4371, LOS ANGELES, CALIFORNIA 90078-4371.
DISTRIBUTION IN THE UNITED KINGDOM BY TURNAROUND PUBLISHER SERVICES LTD.,
UNIT 3 OLYMPIA TRADING ESTATE, COBURG ROAD, WOOD GREEN, LONDON N22 6TZ ENGLAND.

FIRST EDITION: JUNE 1999

99 00 01 02 03 **a** 10 9 8 7 6 5 4 3 2 1

ISBN 1-55583-465-5

LIBRARY OF CONGRESS CATALOGING-IN-PUBLICATION DATA
  WITNESS TO REVOLUTION : THE *ADVOCATE* REPORTS ON GAY AND
LESBIAN POLITICS, 1967–1999 / EDITED BY CHRIS BULL.
    ISBN 1-55583-465-6
    I. GAY RIGHTS—UNITED STATES—HISTORY. 2. GAY LIBERATION
MOVEMENT—UNITED STATES—HISTORY. 3. HOMOSEXUALITY—UNITED STATES.
4. ADVOCATE (LOS ANGELES, CALIF.) I. BULL, CHRIS, 1963–   .
II. ADVOCATE (LOS ANGELES, CALIF.)
HQ76.8.U5W584 1999
305.9'0664—DC21   99-19724 CIP

TO THE MEMORY OF
ADVOCATE EDITOR DEVON CLAYTON
1961–1996

ACKNOWLEDGMENTS

I would like to thank the following people who were instrumental to the completion of this collection: John Gallagher for suggestions and advice; Gerry Kroll for encouraging its start; Scott Brassart for skillfully seeing it through to completion; Mark Thompson for command of *Advocate* archives; Hans Johnson and Trudy Ring for indispensable editing. Sam Watters made it possible and Judy Wieder stuck by me throughout. Jim Schroeder ably edited many of my own articles included in this anthology.

Contents

PART TWO. Liberation: Building a Movement (1976–1981)

PART THREE. Health Crisis: AIDS and Backlash (1982–1988)

PART FOUR. Sex, Religion, and Politics: From Antigay Initiatives to the White House (1989–1999)

Introduction

The story was frighteningly ordinary. Plainclothed Los Angeles Police Department officers pushed their way through the crowd at a popular nightclub, ordered the bartender to unplug the jukebox, and instructed the hapless patrons to remain where they were. The officers then arrested ten men, leading them away in handcuffs and charging them with "lewd conduct." Their behavior had been anything but lewd. Their only crime was congregating at a bar catering to gay men. After their release the men were left to grapple with fallout from their arrests, which often included publicity in the local news, lost jobs, and family rejection.

Dick Michaels was furious. The energetic young gay writer watched with growing frustration as similar incidents took place across the city and country. Michaels belonged to a local homophile organization, Personal Rights in Defense and Education, which sought to end the bar raids, and believed the group's struggling newsletter could play an important role in the fight. Thus Michaels and his partner, Bill Rand, launched *The Los Angeles Advocate,* a broadsheet illicitly mimeographed in the basement of CBS's Los Angeles affiliate and distributed at gay bars for 25 cents, primarily to alert other men to police harassment and the raids that had become ubiquitous in gay social life. "Vice Raid Silver Lake Bar," declared the inaugural September 1967 issue. Subsequent issues carried articles like "Anatomy of a Raid" and "L.A. Cops, Gay Groups Seek Peace." The political and social climate was so uniformly hostile toward gays that sources—and even reporters—usually protected their identities by remaining anonymous or using pseudonyms.

It was an auspicious time in America. Less than two years would elapse before a dramatic series of disturbances took place following a raid on the Stonewall Inn, a Greenwich Village gay bar that would eventually come to symbolize the birth of the modern gay liberation movement. The civil rights movement was in high gear. Feminism was gaining steam. Martin Luther King Jr. and Robert Kennedy, both of whom would be assassinated the following year, shared visions of an open, inclusive society. And gay lib, as the gay rights movement was known, was a motley crew of energetic but disconnected activists and organizations in need of a unifying voice. Michaels, in addition to his warnings to bargoers, thought he could provide that platform.

Michaels believed that conventional journalism with a pro-gay slant would benefit not just gay people but the rest of society as well. The mainstream press was certainly not providing such a view. The two *Times*—Los Angeles and New York—generally raised the topic of homosexuality only to attack it. THE LOS ANGELES ADVOCATE, as Michaels dubbed it in capital letters, would not merely champion the gay cause, it would be a monthly newsletter devoted to anything that was "important to the homosexual—legal steps, social news, developments in the various organizations." Michaels also wanted a lively publication befitting the colorful and courageous men and women he would chronicle: "*The Advocate* will present a generous portion of feature material to entertain, to inform, and perhaps to provoke."

And entertain, inform, and provoke it did. Early editions juxtaposed the sexual liberationist fervor of the times with serious news reporting. The front page of the August 1969 edition, for instance, carried a report on the appointment of gay rights foe Warren Burger as chief justice of the Supreme Court. Next to it was a story about the ejection of a young Hollywood model, Jamie Brooks, from an International House of Pancakes for wearing transparent pants over nothing but a jockstrap. A "certain amount of derriere cleavage was visible through the white fishnet knit trousers," the story revealed, followed by what is surely one of the all-time great editor's notes: "[His ass showed.]." A large photo of Brooks's posterior made sure readers would not overlook the article.

Michaels could not have imagined just how provocative *The Advocate* would become. Paging through the magazine's voluminous archives, located at its current headquarters in Los Angeles, is to enter a world stranger than fiction. The nearly 800 issues contain more twists and turns than a Katherine V. Forrest thriller and more pathos than a Greek tragedy. Thirty years of *The Advocate* have seen right-wing arsons, fiery protests, serial killers preying on gay men, tumultuous legislative battles, chilling court decisions, a terrible plague, and the fire-and-brimstone of preachers filled with hatred.

The cliché—the more things change, the more they remain the same—is borne out by *The Advocate*. The contents of the July 21, 1970, edition of the newspaper, for instance, could just as well have appeared in a 1998 edition. There were reports on a Los Angeles gay pride parade; a commitment ceremony for two young women conducted by Troy Perry, the pastor of the Metropolitan Community Church; an increase in public sex arrests in San Francisco; and how "military policies toward homosexuals defy any rational analysis."

But *The Advocate* is not only the story of gays, lesbians, and their adversaries. It is the story of contemporary America. It is the story of how the institutions of family, church, government, business, and marriage have reacted and adapted to gay demands for justice and equality. The issue that arises continually concerns the extent to which homosexuals are allowed to openly participate in these institutions. That tension, unique to gay politics, is what makes reading *The Advocate* mesmerizing.

The magazine has both chronicled and inspired those changes, and this book is an attempt to provide an accessible record of that complex symbiosis. Thirty years and three publishers after Michaels, *The Advocate* is a glossy, full-color, national newsmagazine that covers everything from same-sex marriage to the military. Bar raids are largely a thing of the past, but reports of discrimination, harassment, and worse continue to fill the pages

Still, America is a better place. There are now openly gay members of Congress, ten states and dozens of municipalities with bans on antigay discrimination, dozens of openly gay Administration officials, and a president who, flawed though he may be, regularly condemns homophobia.

Despite the angry rhetoric of antigay activists, it's impossible to come away from this history of the magazine without the impression that the nation is a far more civilized place than when the publication began, and not just for gays and lesbians. Opponents fail to countenance the contributions that gay people have made not just to themselves but to society as a whole. In less than half a century, gays have created a sprawling infrastructure of business, civic, religious, political, cultural, and athletic organizations that enrich and enliven the nation beyond measure. These accomplishments and the struggle to create them have been painstakingly recorded in *The Advocate.*

Chris Bull
April 1999

[PART ONE]

THE AWAKENING: PRE- AND POST-STONEWALL RIOTS
(1967-1975)

By the early 1970s the political establishment was beginning to take notice of the fledgling movement. In the August 16, 1972, issue, Rob Cole reported on the attempt by a spokesman for Democratic presidential candidate George McGovern to distance the liberal senator from one of the first unequivocally pro-gay statements from a national candidate. "I hope for the day when we do not need to specify that 'Liberty and Justice for All' includes blacks, Chicanos, American Indians, women, homosexuals, or any other group," McGovern said. "ALL means ALL."

Despite such progress, gay life sometimes resembled a war zone. In the August 1, 1973, edition, the newspaper reported that an arson fire at the Up Stairs, a popular New Orleans gay bar, had killed 32 men. A photo depicted the charred body of a man frozen in place trying to escape the fire through a window. (The arson remains unsolved.) The same issue carried a photo of the Rev. Ray Broshears, a Metropolitan Community Church minister in San Francisco, brandishing a shotgun after announcing the formation of the "Lavender Patrol" to combat "teenage attacks on homosexuals."

The newspaper was not without reports of victories, some of them historic. The January 16, 1974, edition reported, in "Sick No More," that the American Psychiatric Association's board of trustees had voted 13–0 to remove homosexuality from its list of mental illnesses. Psychiatrists had studied the lives of gays and lesbians and found no evidence of pathology. The decision had far-reaching ramifications, effectively placing the scientific establishment on the side of gays and lesbians. Critics, however, noted that the change came only after years of lobbying from gay activists, and they refused to countenance the science underlying the vote.

As the feminist saying went, the personal was political. Four years earlier, the July 21, 1970, issue had carried a report on a medical-journal article by gay rights foe Charles Socarides asserting that homosexuality is a mental illness. Socarides, the article said, believed that homosexuality "derive[s] from a 'faulty sexual identity' caused by a 'pathological family constellation' composed of a domineering, crushing mother," and an "absent, weak, or rejecting father." In one of the great ironies of American politics, 26 years later *The Advocate* reported that President Clinton had appointed one of Socarides's children, Richard, to be White House liaison to gays and lesbians. Richard Socarides became one of the highest-ranking openly gay officials in the nation's history.

HAPPY BIRTHDAY TO US (Editorial)

September 1967

We are born. And like all infants, we are and will for a time be clumsy, awkward, full of innocence, and perhaps even a little ugly—except, of course, to our parents. Any new newspaper faces a precarious existence. With few staff members and even fewer dollars, *The Los Angeles Advocate*'s chances of survival would be rated by experienced journalists as somewhere around zero. Yet, we've decided to stumble ahead with this venture because, we feel, *The Advocate* can perform a very important service as the newspaper of the homophile community—a service that should be delayed no longer.

Homosexuals, more than ever before, are out to win their legal rights, to end the injustices against them, to experience their share of happiness in their own way. If *The Advocate* can help in achieving these goals, all the time, sweat, and money that goes into it will be well spent.

Even at the start, a newspaper must have an outlook, a set of concepts, an image of what it is and what it is not. Let's begin with what *The Advocate* is not. It is not a magazine. It is in no way a competitor of the many fine and interesting magazines published by homosexual organizations in Los Angeles and elsewhere. We regard them as colleagues, not rivals, and urge all homosexuals to continue to buy and to read those publications. As a newspaper, *The Advocate*'s main purpose is to publish news that is important to the homosexual—legal steps, social news, developments in the various organizations—anything that the homosexual needs to know or wants to know.

The only opinions that will appear in the news stories will be those attributed to people involved in the particular news items. All other opinion will be confined to signed columns. Furthermore, *The Advocate* welcomes all shades of opinion from all responsible individuals and groups in the homophile movement. We want this newspaper to be a forum. Different ideas, we believe, often result in better ideas. At the same time, *The Advocate* will present a generous portion of feature material to entertain, to inform, and perhaps to provoke. We do not intend to be deadly dull.

These are ambitious aims. It will be a long time before the Advocate rivals the prestigious *L.A. Times* or the lusty, scrapping *L.A. Free Press*. Until it does, we must depend a great deal on our friends in the various organizations and on our readers to keep us posted on what is going on around town. We exist to serve you, but we cannot do it well without your help.

THE WORLD IS MY ASHTRAY

by Dick Michaels

September 1967

The August 18 issue of *Time* magazine carried a review of Judy Garland's most recent stint at New York's fabled Palace Theatre. The writer uses up a great deal of space discussing the near fanatic adulation of Judy's audiences, then notes, "Curiously, a disproportionate part of her nightly claque seems to be homosexual. The boys in the tight trousers roll their eyes, tear at their hair and practically levitate from their seats," particularly when Judy sings you-know-what. Without reading further, we imagined a senior associate assistant managing editor of *Time* reading his reporter's fresh copy, then shouting across the room, "Get a couple of headshrinkers on the phone. Find out why the queers like Judy so much."

Sure enough, so help me Henry Luce, right in the next paragraph we find out. We gravitate toward superstars, one Doc says, because "these are people they can idolize and idealize without getting too close to. In Judy's case, the attraction might be made considerably stronger by the fact that she has survived so many problems; homosexuals identify with that kind of hysteria." Says another Manhattan psychiatrist, "Judy was beaten up by life, embattled, and ultimately had to become more masculine. She has the power that homosexuals would like to have, and they attempt to attain it by idealizing her."

Back in the *Time* office, we imagined again, Brilliant Young Reviewer is sitting in the office of the SAAME (the one that yelled before). The Big One speaks, cigar clenched firmly between teeth, smoke curling lovingly around each word, "Good work, Grimsby! You really dug into the nitty-gritty and sent it flying up the flagpole."

"Thank you, Miss Lovelace," replies Brilliant Young Reviewer, rolling his eyes, tearing at his hair, and levitating gracelessly from his seat.

ANATOMY OF A RAID

by David S. (as told to Dick Michaels)

July 1968

There was nothing very unusual about the Yukon—nothing to make it stand out from dozens of other small gay bars. It was just a neighborhood beer bar on Beverly Boulevard a few blocks west of Vermont. As in any neighborhood place, most of the customers during the week were regulars who lived nearby. The bar usually wasn't jammed until Friday and Saturday nights and for the Sunday afternoon "beer bust." Even then, it took only about 35 people to make a mob in the Yukon. So, as I say, there was nothing unusual about the place—that is, not until that Friday night near the end of March 1966.

The Yukon's greatest asset was its manager and regular bartender, Tommy. He was a blond, good-looking young man with a nice body and an infectiously happy personality. He probably still is, I guess. I say "was" only because I haven't seen him in almost two years. Tommy had been running the bar since it opened some six months earlier. He worked hard to build up the business and was proud of how much he had accomplished in that time.

It is true that whatever success the Yukon had was due directly to Tommy's great personality and his ability to project friendliness and fun in all directions. In a gay bar, the bartender is the most important fixture. The amount of beer I drank while cruising Tommy would float the Queen Mary.

Although he made it a fun place, Tommy ran a tight bar, in the sense that he never allowed any hanky-panky that would endanger the bar's license or its customers. He was quick to warn people when they got a little out of hand but did it in such an expert way that there was never any bad feeling afterward.

On that fateful Friday, I had picked up my love that time, Larry, at about 7 o'clock, when he was off work. We went to the Yukon and drank beer for an hour or so. Several friends we hadn't seen for a while wandered in, and it looked like it was going to be a good, fun night at the Yukon. We went to dinner and got back to the bar about 10:30. By then the place was crowded, and there was a lot of laughing and cruising around as there usually is among friends. There were several people I hadn't seen before, but it too was normal on a crowded night.

Tommy was breaking in a new bartender; I think it was his first or second night. The new boy was behind the bar, and Tommy was sitting at the bar with some friends. He stayed in that same place the whole night. Whenever he went to the men's room, he always stopped along the way to chat and joke with some of the customers he knew well.

Larry and I sat at the north end of the bar. Behind us was the pool table, which took up most of the space between the bar and the rest rooms. The jukebox, always loud at the Yukon, was blaring away as usual. Occasionally, I got up and moved about talking with friends for a few minutes, but most of the time I drank and I sat in the same place, talking earnestly.

At one point, about 12:30 A.M., Tommy was passing by and stopped to talk to me. After we talked a few minutes, I saw that he wasn't paying attention but was looking over my shoulder toward the door. I turned and saw several uniformed policemen coming in. Two plainclothesmen were with them. One of them, whom we later referred to as Hooknose, yanked the jukebox cord and ordered the lights turned on. The other, who chewed gum steadily, just stood around.

Hooknose announced, "We're going to make a few arrests. Just stay where you are. Anyone who runs will be shot." No one ran. He went behind the bar, checked the license, stared closely at the label on the bottle of Champale, then came back out, and went about his fun task of picking victims.

I'm not sure where he started, but I think it was with two boys dressed in cowboy garb, who were obviously not cowboys. He then picked George, who was standing at the bar to Larry's right. Each tap on the shoulder was punctuated with "You're under arrest." At one point he stopped to count on his fingers. He seemed to be figuring out how many people the cars outside could take.

Then he went back to his grim business. He skipped over Larry. My back was to Hooknose. I felt the dreaded tap and turned. "You're under arrest."

I walked out to the street. Several more uniformed cops were standing around. Five or six black-and-white cars lined the curb. I was put into the backseat of one of them. Others came out, usually two at a time handcuffed together. Two of these were put in the back of the car with me. Two cops sat in front.

I found out later that Tommy, during the arrests, went up to the Gum Chewer and said, "I'm the manager; what's going on here?" Gum Chewer arrested him, the only arrest he made that night. "What for?" Tommy demanded. "You'll find out," was the reply. Again, when Tommy was being put into a car outside, he asked one of the uniformed cops what was going on. The answer he got from the cop should be chiseled on the front of police headquarters, "Who know what those bastards are up to!"

Altogether they took 12 people out of the Yukon that night—about a third of the patrons. They took us to the Hollywood station. There, we assembled first in a small room just inside the back door. Hooknose wasn't there. In fact, we never saw him again for the rest of the night. This is important in the light of his later testimony at one of the trials.

Gum Chewer, still chewing, advised us of our "rights" as we stood in a circle. Then as we passed through a door into the cell area, he pointed to each and said "lewd conduct," except for one who was charged with being drunk. We were all put into one small cell. Then Gum Chewer called us out one by one and talked to each for a minute or so. When my turn came, we stood a half dozen feet from the cell as Gum Chewer pointed toward the cell. "See that boy in the blue shirt?" It was Lee; I've know him for years but never had sex with him in any form. "You humped him," the Man said. I told him I didn't know what he was talking about. He tried to ask several other questions ("Are you a homosexual?" "Where do you work?" "Do you have a security clearance?"), but I clammed up.

That's pretty much the way it went for each one. Lee was accused of groping someone sitting next to him, and that guy was charged with rubbing legs with Lee. Tommy was supposed to have groped one of the "cowboys."

They took us all downtown in a police bus for booking. Gum Chewer came along. We sat on a bench in front of a line of booking windows. Three of them were manned, I think, and as one became vacant, one of us was called up to it. Gum Chewer sat on an iron railing at the end of the line of windows. When one of the booking officers asked who the arresting office was, G-C gave the name of the other vice officer, the one who disappeared right after the raid.

When I was booked, I answered the questions about name and address but balked at where I worked. "That's not necessary, is it?" I asked, not knowing what they were really entitled to know. "You don't have to say a damn thing," he snapped back, obviously irritated. Probably to get even, when he took the contents of my pockets, he kept all my cigarettes and all the money except one dime, even though the booking slip itself says that you have a right to make two phone calls, not just one. I found out latter that some fellows were left with only matches and others with cigarettes and no matches. It figures that sadism can take very subtle forms too.

After that there was a lot waiting in little rooms as the cops took mug shots and fingerprints of each person. I couldn't understand how some of the guys arrested with me could joke around and laugh. Maybe it was just a nervous reaction. I was worried—worried about my job and some personal matters that this arrest could make worse. I was silent most of the time and didn't feel like talking to anyone.

One young Canadian boy was in a state of near panic. He was so frightened that the cop trying to take his fingerprints was having a rough time. The boy couldn't relax his hand enough. The cop threatened to knock him on his ass if he didn't relax. That just made things worse. The hassle went on for what seemed a long time.

All of us eventually would up in one large cell, each waiting for a bail bondsman. Tommy got out first and seemed reluctant to leave while we were all still there. When the bondsman sent by Larry arrived for me, I had no trouble convincing him that I was solvent. I asked him to see about getting Lee and some of the others out, but Lee wasn't working at the time, and those guys don't like to take chances.

It was past 4 A.M. when I finally left the jail. The bondsman drove me to my apartment, but just as we got there, I remembered that my car was still parked at the Yukon. I asked him to take me there, less than half a mile away. He was irritated. I was irritated, tired, scared, and depressed. And I still am whenever I think about that night.

An interesting incident less than a week later illustrates once again the low opinion that uniformed officers have of the vice squad. A straight bar owned by the owner of the Yukon was burglarized one night. When the police were investigating this the next day, the owner brought up the subject of the two vice cops who led the raid on the Yukon. The reaction of one uniformed cop was devastating: "Those two! They're the type—well, if they weren't on the force, we'd be looking for them."

"GOD LOVES ALL:" BOLD NEW CHURCH WELCOMES GAYS

by A.B.T.

February 1969

Thumbing through *The Advocate* a while back, quickly scanning a few articles and ads, my eyes came to a screeching halt for a moment. There, in a medium sized ad was one for a church! It included a rather striking picture of the pastor, a Rev. Troy Perry of the Metropolitan Community Church in Huntington Park. I read the ad, thought, *That's different,* and went on to another page.

A few weeks later, on a Tuesday night, I just happened to stop by that swinging bistro, the Little Club, to see its show, "I've Got A Secret." One contestant particularly stumped the panel, but not me. There on the stage was one with a real secret, Reverend Perry. After listening to some of his answers and to some of his later remarks, I was impressed enough to find out what this church was like—me, who hadn't darkened the door of a house of worship in years!

I was impressed. And after the services Reverend Perry consented to an interview. Before we get into the questions and answers, perhaps a little more of the church and its minister. First of all—Reverend Perry...quick statistics run as follows: Born in Tallahassee Fla., 28 years ago, he now stands 6 feet 1 inch, weighs 176 pounds (give or take a few)...black hair with almost hypnotically intense hazel eyes...speaks with a soft Southern accent...divorced...father of two sons. He attended seminary in Illinois...pastored in Florida, Illinois, and California...spent two years in the U.S. Army in Germany...been back in Los Angeles for a year.

The church was founded in October of last year, after many months of soul-searching. The first service in his home was attended by only 12 people. In the few months of its existence, it has grown. The church now has its own chapel (rented) that seats about 150. The congregation is composed of people from various religious groups (Catholics, Protestants, Jews, and even some Buddhists).

The services are ritualistic, but simple, with a little fundamentalist fire thrown in, particularly in the sermon. Reverend Perry's messages are always to the point, however. Taking a clue from the Episcopalians, they rarely exceed 20 minutes...but there is a hell of a lot more fire than the Anglicans have.

Also important—for late sleepers—the services start at 1:30 P.M. so folks like you and me who have been kept up late on Saturday night with a sick friend(!) can still make it.

Anyway, enough of the background. Let's get to the questions. I tried to be as concise as possible; to ask questions that the average homosexual would like to ask.

There was one question uppermost in my mind so that was the one I started off with...

Reverend Perry, is the Metropolitan Community Church a gay church?

No. Not if you mean is it a church only for homosexuals. We invite anyone who wishes to attend church. If we were a church for gays only, we would be guilty of the same sin that most churches are when they exclude the homosexual community from their groups.

Well, let me put my question a bit differently. Are any of your church officers gay?

Some are, some are not. I really feel that you should ask them.

I see. Then the membership of your church is primarily gay.

I believe so. Our church was organized to fill a need for religion which exists in the Greater Los Angeles homophile community. We organized with the hopes of reaching those people who cannot or will not attend church because of the attitudes of other religions concerning homosexuality. Most gays feel very strongly in God, but most churches simply refuse to let them worship him.

You don't believe homosexuality is sinful, then, as most churches believe?

Of course not! God made all of us. He loves a homosexual as much as any of his children. I was reared in a Pentecostal Church environment. I was taught that anyone could "walk with God" …and he with them. To this day, I still have that closeness with God. I feel him always in my life, even though I myself am a homosexual.

That's interesting. Tell me, how else does the Metropolitan Community Church differ from most of the established churches?

There are only two things that set our church apart from the so called "established churches":

1. We do accept homosexuals, *as well as anyone else who* feels the need of God's love, into the full membership in the Body of Christ, the church.

2. Our church believes in and advocates the legalization of homosexual marriages.

Do you mean that you want to see the laws changed, so that two men or two women can be married as a man and woman are now?

That's right. I feel so strongly about it that I do perform marriage ceremonies for gays.

You mean that if I fell in love and wanted to marry a guy, you would do it?

Yes, if you were *really* in love.

I did, and we are.

In that case, both of you come to my home tomorrow night for counseling, if you'd care to.

Thank you, we will. Do you perform a religious ceremony and pronounce them man and wife?

No. I conduct a marriage ceremony and pronounce them married in the sight of God. I do not pronounce them "man and wife," because they are not that. I don't ask, "John, do you take George to be your wedded wife?" Rather, I ask, "John, do you take George to be your wedded *spouse?*" There is a difference.

Are these marriages legal?

Yes, in the sight of God. This I truly believe. In the sight of the civil code they are not yet so.

How serious are these people who come to you to be married?

Quite serious, I hope. Although some people who have come to me have not been ready, I have felt. However, the ones I *have* married have been quite serious.

First, I require that any couple who comes to be married to have been together at least six months. Second, I counsel with them to make sure they understand the importance of their decision. One couple was so serious about their wedding that both of the men had their parents attend the ceremony.

Well, let me ask you this… Do you find a lot of people attend your church for cruising?

[*Laughing*] An understandable question. But the answer is, well, not really. There are many other places better for cruising. Most of the homosexuals who attend our church come to worship God. After church services we do have a coffee hour, and at that time one can meet new friends and visit old ones. However, I do not feel that it is used for the purpose you asked about.

Reverend Perry, there are many questions I would like to ask you, but time and space don't permit it at this time, so I have one last questions. What do you preach?

First: Love… "Thou shalt love the Lord thy God with all thy Heart, with all thy Soul, and with all thy Mind. Thou shalt love thy neighbor as thyself."

Second: Have faith in God and yourself. Always believe in God and always believe in you. Be at peace with yourself, and you will always be at peace with the world. I always tell my congregation, "Look *above* the circumstances!"

OVEREXPOSED MODEL CAN'T SEE OVEREXPOSED FILM

August 1969

Sunday, June 15, was an unusual day for Hollywood model Jamie Brooks. Within less than half an hour, he was invited not to return to a restaurant where he had just had lunch and then was refused admittance to a movie theater on Hollywood Boulevard.

No—Jamie isn't a militant Black Panther or even a menacing Blue Meanie. But he did happen to be wearing his brand-new see-through bell-bottom pants.

Of course he was also wearing a jock strap to protect both his modesty and his legality, but a certain amount of derriere cleavage was visible through the white fishnet knit trousers. [His ass showed. —Ed.]

The manager of the International House of Pancakes on Sunset Boulevard near Highland didn't see Jamie when the youth first came in, he said when he indicated that Jamie was no longer welcome. If he had, Jamie wouldn't even have gotten lunch. Company policy, he explained.

Assistant manager Richard Hileman at the Vine Theatre did see him, however, before Jamie could get through the door. Protecting something other or other, Hileman would not let the slender young blond enter.

It mattered not to Mr. Hileman that the movie playing at the Vine, *Romeo and Juliet*, features a scene in which Romeo is not only bare-assed, but bare all over. Romeo, of course, slept with a girl—in that scene anyway.

A couple of hours later, fellow model Johnny Johnston, wearing see-throughs much like Jamie's, bought a ticket at the Vine Theatre in order to test the newly discovered policy. By this time, Mr. Hileman had taken refuge in his office, according to Johnston, and he refused to appear even though Johnston asked the box-office girl to make sure that he could enter. She assured him that he could.

Contacted a few days later by this newspaper, Hileman at first agreed to discuss the matter if a reporter would appear at the theater when he was on duty. A few minutes later, he phoned back to say that the manager had ordered him not to discuss the matter. He would not even confirm that the incident had occurred.

Said to be the latest rage in fashions, see-through pants are still seldom seen in public—not even on Hollywood Boulevard. A breakthrough of sorts was made on the night of the Academy Awards presentations, however, when Barbra Streisand wore a pair of very see-throughs, thereby winning her an Academy Award and at the same time making her the owner of the most famous behind since Anthony Quinn's.

POLICE RAID ON N.Y. CLUB SETS OFF FIRST GAY RIOT

by Dick Leitsch
(originally printed in *New York Mattachine Newsletter*)

September 1969

The first gay riots in history took place during the predawn hours of Saturday and Sunday, June 28–29, in New York's Greenwich Village. The demonstrations were touched off by a police raid on the popular Stonewall Inn, 53 Christopher St. This was the last to date in a series of harassments that plagued the Village area for the last several weeks.

Plainclothes officers entered the club at about 2 A.M., armed with a warrant, and closed the place on grounds of illegal selling of alcohol. Employees were arrested and the customers told to leave. The patrons gathered on the street outside and were joined by other Village residents and visitors to the area.

The police behaved, as is usually the case when they deal with homosexuals, with bad grace, and were reproached by "straight" onlookers. Pennies were thrown at the cops by the crowd, then beer cans, rocks, and even parking meters. The cops retreated inside the bar, which was set afire by the crowd.

A hose from the bar was employed by the trapped cops to douse the flames, and reinforcements were summoned. A melee ensued, with nearly a thousand persons participating, as well as several hundred cops. Nearly two hours later, the cops had "secured" the area.

Even Waiters' Tips

The next day, the Stonewall management sent in a crew to repair the premises, and found that the cops had taken all the money from the cigarette machine, the jukebox, the cash register, and the safe, and had even robbed the waiters' tips!

Since they had been charged with selling liquor without a license, the club was reopened as a "free store," open to all and with everything being given away rather than sold.

A crowd filled the place and the street in front. Singing and chanting filled Sheridan Square Park, and the crowds grew quickly.

At first the crowd was all gay, but as the weekend tourists poured into the area, they joined the crowds. They'd begin by asking what was happening. When they were told that homosexuals were protesting the closing of a gay club, they'd become very sympathetic, and stayed to watch or join in.

One middle-aged lady with her husband told a cop that he should be ashamed of himself. "Don't you know that these people have no place to go and need places like that bar?" she shouted. (Several hours later, she and her husband, with two other couples, were seen running with a large group of homosexuals from the night sticks brandished by the Tactical Police Force.)

The crowds were orderly and limited themselves to singing and shouting slogans such as "Gay Power," "We Want Freedom Now," and "Equality for Homosexuals." As the mob grew, it spilled off the sidewalk, overflowed Sheridan Square Park, and began to fill the roadway. One of the six cops who were there to keep order began to get smart and cause hostility.

A bus driver blew his horn at the meeting, and someone shouted, "Stop the bus!" The crowd surged out into the street and blocked the progress of the bus. As the driver inched ahead, someone ripped off an advertising card and blocked the windshield with it. The crowd beat on the sides of the (empty) bus and shouted, "Christopher Street belongs to the queens!" and "Liberate the street."

'Screw you' Look

The cops got the crowd to let the bus pass, but then the people began a slow-down-the-traffic campaign. A human line across the street blocked traffic, and the cars were let through one at a time. Another car, bearing a fat, gouty-looking cop with many pounds of gilt braid chauffeured by a cute young cop, came through.

The fat cop looked for all the world like a slaveowner surveying a plantation, and someone tossed a sack of wet garbage through the car window and right on his face. The bag broke, and soggy coffee grounds dripped down the lined face, which never lost its "screw you" look.

Another police car came through Waverly Place and stopped at the corner of Christopher. The occupants just sat there and glared at the crowd. Suddenly, a concrete block landed on the hood of the car, and the crowd drew back. Then, as one person, it surged forward and surrounded the car, beating on it with fists and dancing atop it. The cops radioed for help, and soon the crowd let the car pass.

Christopher Street from Greenwich to Seventh Avenue had become an almost solid mass of people—most of them gay. No traffic could pass, and even walking the few blocks on foot was next to impossible. One little old lady tried to get through, and many members of the crowd tried to help her. She brushed them away and continued her determined walk, trembling with fear and murmuring, "It must be the full moon; it must be the full moon."

Wants Cops to Behave

Squad cars from the fourth, fifth, sixth, and ninth precincts had brought in a hundred or so cops who had no hope of controlling the crowd of nearly 2,000 people in the streets. Until this point, the crowd had been, for the most part, pleasant and in a jovial mood. Some of the cops began to become very nasty and started trouble. One boy, evidently a discus-thrower, reacted by bouncing garbage can lids neatly off the helmets of the cops. Others set garbage cans ablaze.

A Christopher Street merchant stood in the door of her shop and yelled at the cops to behave themselves. Whenever they would head in her direction, she'd run into the shop and lock and door.

The focus of the demonstration shifted from the Stonewall to "the Corner"—Greenwich Avenue and Christopher Street. The intersection, and the street behind it, was a solid mass of humanity. The tactical police force arrived in city buses. One hundred of them disembarked at the Corner, and 50 more at Seventh Avenue and Christopher.

"Save Our Sister"

They huddled with some of the top brass that had already arrived, and isolated beer cans, thrown by the crowd, hit their van and cars now and again. Suddenly, two cops darted into the crowd and dragged out a boy who had done absolutely nothing. As they carried him to a waiting van brought to take off prisoners, four more cops joined them and began pounding the boy in the face, belly, and groin with nightsticks. A high, shrill voice called out, "Save our sister!" and there was a general pause, during which the "butch"-looking "numbers" looked distracted.

Momentarily, 50 or more homosexuals who would have to be described as "nelly" rushed the cops and took the boy back into the crowd. They then formed a solid front and refused to let the cops into the crowd to regain their prisoner, letting the cops hit them with their sticks, rather than let them through.

(It was an interesting sidelight on the demonstrations that those usually put down as "sissies" or "swishes" showed the most courage and sense during the action. Their bravery and daring saved many people from being hurt, and their sense of humor and "camp" helped keep the crowds from getting nasty of too violent.")

The cops gave up on the idea of taking prisoners and concentrated on clearing the area. They rushed both ways on Greenwich, forcing the crowds into Tenth Street and Sixth Avenue, where the people circled the blocks and reentered Christopher. Then the cops formed a flying wedge and, with arms linked, headed down Greenwich, forcing everyone in front of them into side streets. Cops on the ends of the wedge broke off and chased demonstrators down the side streets and away from the center of the action.

"Up Your Irish Ass"

They made full use of their nightsticks, brandishing them like swords. At one point a cop grabbed a wild Puerto Rican queen and lifted his arm to bring a club down on "her." In his best Maria Montez voice, the queen challenged, "How'd you like a big Spanish dick up your little Irish ass?" The cop was so shocked he hesitated in his swing, and the queen escaped.

At another point, two lonely cops were chasing a hundred or more people down Waverly Place. Someone shouted out that the queens outnumbered the cops and suggested catching them, ripping off their clothes, and screwing them. The cops abandoned the chase and fled back to the main force for protection.

The police action did eventually disperse the crowds, many of whom abandoned the cause and headed to the docks for some fun. By 2:30, nearly two hours after the bus had been delayed, the area was again peaceful. Apart from the 200 to 300 cops standing around the area, it looked like an unusually dull Saturday night.

Then at 3 A.M. the bars closed, and the patrons of the many gay bars in the area arrived to see what was happening. They were organized, and another attempt was made to liberate Christopher Street. The police, still there in great numbers, managed to break up the demonstrations. One small group did break off and attempt to liberate the IND subway station at Sixth Avenue and Waverly Place, but the police went in and chased everyone out.

By 5:30 A.M., the area was secure enough that the TPF police were sent home, and the docks were packed tight with homosexuals having the times of their lives. After all, everything was perfectly "safe"—all the cops were on "the Corner"!

Only Four Injured

In all, 13 people were arrested on Saturday morning—seven of them employees of the Stonewall. Four more were arrested on Sunday morning, and many more were detained, then released. Apparently, only four persons were injured—all of them cops. Three suffered minor bruises and scratches and one a "broken wrist" (it was not specified whether it was the kind of "broken wrist" that requires a cast, or the kind that makes it noisy to wear a bangle bracelet).

Sunday night saw a lot of action in the Christopher Street area. Hundreds of people were on the streets including, for the first time, a large "leather" contingent. However, there were never enough people to outnumber the large squads of cops milling about, trying desperately to head off any trouble.

The Stonewall was again a "free store," and the citizenry was treated to the sight of the cops begging homosexuals to go inside the bar that they had chased everyone out of a few nights before.

Inasmuch as all the cops in town seemed to be near The Corner again, the docks were very busy, and two boys went to the Charles Street station house and pasted "Equality for Homosexuals" bumper stickers on cop cars, the autos of on-duty cops, and the van used to take away prisoners.

One of the most frightening comments was made by one cop to another, and overheard by a Mattachine Society of New York member being held in detention. One said he'd enjoyed the fracas. "Them queers have a good sense of humor and really had a good time," he said. His "buddy" protested, "Aw, they're sick. I like nigger riots better because there's more action, but you can't beat up a fairy. They ain't mean like blacks; they're sick. But you can't hit a sick man."

N.Y. GAYS: WILL THE SPARK DIE?

by Lige Clark and Jack Nichols

September 1969

The Sheridan Square revolt has had some amusing, baffling, and disturbing aftermaths. With our ears to the ground, we've been able to feel some of the vibrations, and in a few cases, we've been present when new social experiments were taking place.

Local newspapers picked up the uprising and played it to the hilt. The *Daily News*, as usual, made fun of the gay community, referring to the rioters as "queen bees," and so forth. The *New York Post*, on the other hand, was somewhat more sympathetic, and *The Village Voice* carried two front-page photographs and two articles describing the events which led to the outbreak.

After the young people rioted, the prophet of the new age, Allen Ginsberg, walked amid the rubble, inspecting the Stonewall and commenting on the changed appearances of the gay clientele as contrasted with those of ten years ago. "They no longer have that 'wounded' look," he said. Ginsberg took well to the concept of 'gay power' and identified himself as a homosexual. "It's time we did something to assert ourselves," he mused. "After all, we do comprise 10% of the population."

Gay Groups Disagree

Various homophile groups, somewhat at odds with each other over strategy, passed out leaflets during the days following the riots. Craig Rodwell's HYMN (Homophile Youth Movement) called for an end to Mafia control of the gay bars and suggested a two-front struggle on the part of the homosexual community; one to remove police harassment, and the other to boycott Mafia establishments.

Other homophile leaders felt that an attack on the Mafia was not pertinent or expedient and that it was the police who were primarily to blame for the incident. A new consciousness seemed to sweep through the bar crowds, and the Stonewall management passed out hundred of buttons reading EQUALITY FOR HOMOSEXUALS. For the first time in New York's history, numerous young people wore these buttons unashamedly onto the streets.

The Homophile Youth Movement received telephone threats to sabotage its bus trip to the homophile picket at Independence Hall on July 4. Whether the threats came from incensed Mafiosi is unknown. Callers said that they would run the bus off of the road, and leader Rodwell decided to arrange for a police escort out of the city.

Mattachine Active

Dick Leitsch of the New York Mattachine Society worked to gain support for his organization in the days following the riot. Mattachine leafleteers saturated Greenwich Village with invitations to two functions geared to keep the revolution going.

The first was an all-gay night at the Electric Circus, the nation's foremost psychedelic discotheque located in the heart of the East Village. "If you are tired of gay bar raids, come to the Electric Circus," said pamphlets. The management of the Circus, obviously hungry for some new business, opened their arms to the homosexual community. At our suggestion, Randy Wicker was chosen as the "gay militant" who would speak to the assembled homosexuals.

On Sunday, July 6, the Circus was filled with a large crowd of hip youngsters, most of whom were gay. The live acid-rock band blared forth a medley of tunes, and the crowd responded with great enthusiasm. Randy Wicker was scheduled to speak at midnight. Straight couples mingled with gay, and no one seemed offended or upset.

At midnight Wicker, wearing an American flag shirt and striped blue-and-white bell-bottoms, mounted the platform to sound a note of gay militancy. He had spoken only a few words, however, when a violent fight broke out in the back of the room, started by one dissident and deranged straight fellow. He plunged through the crowd, swinging wildly at everyone in his path, and jumped up onto the platform where he was finally subdued by Electric Circus bouncers and escorted from the hall forcefully, while he shouted, "Damned faggots! Goddamned faggots!"

Impact Lost

The social experiment, which had started so successfully, had been besmirched. In spite of the fact that the Circus had longed for a gayer crowd, it remained to be seen whether or not homosexuals would feel welcome in an atmosphere where violence festered. The impact of Wicker's speech was lost on those who became concerned with helping those slugged in the melee.

The Mattachine next called upon young activists to join the society members at Freedom Hall for an all-out discussion of what could be done to correct police abuse.

Over two hundred young people gathered at the hall and decided to hold a rally in Washington Square on July 16. Following the riots, a number of New York's foremost underground papers carried lengthy news items and editorials on "gay power."

There have been some who are worried about outside groups who are offering to help the gay community and to channel its energies towards causes which have nothing to do with homosexuals. Extremists of various sorts have been trying to capitalize on their own causes by leading the new revolutionaries down their own paths. Most of the young people who met at Freedom Hall rejected such outside intervention.

BITCH FIGHT OF THE YEAR: BUCKLEY VERSUS VIDAL

by Lyn Pedersen

October 1969

Aficionados of classic bitch fights shouldn't miss the William Buckley–Gore Vidal scrap in *Esquire*'s August and September issues. More fastidious readers will wish to keep their distance, for each contestant, normally suave and sophisticated, ends up well covered with that which hit the fan.

The antipathy between the conservative political columnist and the liberal novelist was a long time building. Conjecture as to which could be the bitchiest has made them hot numbers on TV's talk shows.

While Vidal has written openly about homosexuality (*City and the Pillar, Myra Breckenridge*), certified hetero Buckley merely displays the outward mannerisms commonly attributed to homosexuals. Their potshotting at one another at their respective families and political allegiances, has become bitter and showy.

Explosive Combination

When the American Broadcasting Company chose to combine them last summer as commentators on the national political conventions, the expected fireworks were not long coming. Vidal characterized the GOP as sick. Buckley said that a man who could write pornography like *Myra Breckenridge* (which he had not then read) must be *really* sick. Vidal replied that he'd drawn the character of Myra from Buckley himself—"passionate but irrelevant."

While arguing about the Chicago police riot, Vidal called Buckley a "crypto-Nazi." Buckley blew his cool entirely: "Now listen, you queer...I'll sock you in the goddamn face and you'll stay plastered!"

All this in front of 10 million viewers! It might have been more convincing had Buckley, whose manner is rarely described as "butch," threatened to *slap* Vidal's face. Buckley added that he'd been in the infantry in the last war. Vidal denied that Buckley was in the infantry or fought in the war at all.

Their debate had then been going for two weeks. Afterward, ABC kept them in separate rooms. Buckley screamed that he never wanted to see Vidal again. Vidal said he'd never wanted to see Buckley in the first place.

Why Faggotty?

Buckley's nine ponderous pages in the August *Esquire* are well worth reading. In the piece, titled, "On Experiencing Gore Vidal," he began by bitching that *The East Village Other,* an underground paper, had labeled his reasoning as "faggot logic." Buckley couldn't understand why a paper heavy on homosexual advertisements would label him faggotty—and be so nasty about it.

He gave a lengthy account of his experiences with Vidal, tracing the growth of their mutual dislike. It was a story of innocence beset. Typical was a telegram he'd meant to send to Jack Paar in 1962 after Paar had elicited anti-Buckley comments from Vidal:

"Please inform Gore Vidal that neither I nor my family is disposed to receive lessons in morality from a pink queer. If he wishes to challenge that designation, inform him that I shall fight by the laws of the Marquis of Queensbury. He will know what I mean. W.F. Buckley Jr."

For any reader not knowing what that means: The Marquis of Queensbury, author of the standards rules of boxing and father of Lord Alfred Douglas, sent such an insulting note to his son's intimate friend. Wilde sued for libel, and the trials ruined him.

Vidal objected to "Noel Parmentel's" review, in Buckley's magazine, of Vidal's play, *Romulus*. Vidal, the reviewer claimed, "evinced an interest in homosexuality equaled only by the editors of *One*."

Against Vidal's claims that sexual diversity was implicit in classical writings, Buckley said: "Nonsense, as it happens. E.g., Aristophanes, who mocked Plato's homosexuality; Juvenal, who stigmatized the Greek-aristocratic homosexuality; Catullus, who found Caesar's bisexuality...ridiculous and disgusting." (Vidal's indicated closer familiarity with these classical writers.)

"Fingers Trembled"

Buckley lamented having let Vidal upset him badly on TV. ("My pulse was racing, and my fingers trembled as wave after wave of indignation swept over me.") He got even by dissecting *Myra*, proving to his own satisfaction that it was not a nice book. Though Buckley's argument was self-pitying, supercilious (always), and sometimes tedious, it seemed to this reader that he had adequately disposed of Vidal and had cornered the coveted title of "Superbitch" until the September issue of *Esquire* came out with Vidal's succinct and devastating answer.

Time magazine, no mean entry itself in the field of bitchiness, felt that Vidal had struck the lowest blows.

Claiming that he had intentionally prodded Buckley into revealing, before that vast audience, that he was utterly cuckoo, Vidal gave quite a different account of the history of their feud:

"Buckley begins his tirade with, I should have thought, a most dangerous quotation from *The East Village Other*.... The implication is plain. The writer thinks that Buckley is a faggot. He is not alone. Norman Mailer even shouted the word "fag" at Buckley during a Les Crane taping: it was cut from the show.... Now Buckley's private life should be a matter of no concern to *The East Village Other* or even to that vivacious compendium, *The Homosexual Handbook,* whose listing of well-known degenerates includes...William F. Buckley...which is why it seems to me odd that someone himself suspect should be so quick to smear others as 'queers'."

Not a Propagandist

Noting Buckley's habit of describing persons he disapproves of—including Robert Kennedy—as mincing, lisping, or epicene, Vidal quotes Paul Newman as having called Buckley a "male c★★t!"

Denying Buckley's charge that he is a propagandist for homosexuality, Vidal says: "I am not an evangelist of anything in sexual matters except a decent withdrawal of the state from the bedroom. There will, of course, always be morbid twisted men like Buckley, sniggering and giggling and speculating on the sexual lives of others."

Before landing his heaviest blow, and while discussing the RFK assassination, Vidal wrote one utterly idiotic paragraph, made worse by his boast of researching things: "I said that I thought it significant that Sirhan was brought up in Pasadena, a city rich in anti-Jews, anti-blacks, anti-poor. In fact, Orange County, California, is one of the strongholds of the virulent Right Wing. Now obviously, Pasadena is not solely responsible for making Sirhan do what he did, but it was certainly a contributing factor. You cannot live unaffected in a community where so many tote guns and talk loudly about how this Commie and that Jew and that nigger ought to be shot. Needless to say, Buckley defends Pasadena."

We hope that while defending Pasadena, Buckley managed to put it back in the heart of Los Angeles County, where is has always been. Vidal's description of this town is pure fantasy.

Incident Resurrected

In conclusion, Vidal cited police and newspaper accounts of a 25-year-old incident in Sharon, Conn., when a church was desecrated after one of its members had sold a house to a Jewish family. Buckley and brothers were arrested and convicted of smearing honey and feathers, and scattering obscene pictures around the church.

Vidal also quoted *The New York Times*, speaking of Buckley more recently: "Those instincts are fear, ignorance, racial superiority, religious antagonism, contempt for the weak and afflicted, and hatred for those different from oneself."

Buckley, who had not been at any time reluctant to slander Vidal, promptly sued *Esquire* for a million for expanding Vidal's campaign of vilification against him. He also sued the publishers of *The Homosexual Handbook,* but withdrew that action when they apologized and promised to delete his name from future editions.

RAID VICTIM IMPALED ON FENCE

by Leo Louis Martello

May 12, 1970

The near-death of a young man who leaped or fell from the second floor of a New York police station has once again galvanized New York City's gay community—just as the Stonewall raid did last year.

The youth was impaled on a metal fence outside the station, and it took the combined efforts of the fire department and a surgical team to remove the fence from his body. At last reports he was still in critical condition.

The tragedy topped several eventful days that started with the Gay Activists Alliance picketing New York City Hall to protest job discrimination, harassment of homosexuals, and recent raids and arrests at bars and baths. They were met in force by New York's finest and forcibly prevented from entering City Hall.

Barricades were set up; police manned the steps; and there was lots of shoving and pushing. Finally, three delegates were given permission to meet with the mayor's counsel, Michael Dontzon, as Mayor Lindsay was in Buffalo.

Gay activists carried such signs as POLICE ON GAY SPREE WHILE MUGGERS GO FREE and POLICE: PROTECT THE PUBLIC...FORGET OUR PRIVATES. Other signs said REPRESENTATION NOT OPPRESSION, EQUALITY FOR HOMOSEXUALS, GAY IS GOOD, and END JOB DISCRIMINATION AGAINST HOMOSEXUALS.

The press and photographers were there snapping away, taking notes, with stories appearing in the *New York Post, Women's Wear Daily, Long Island Press,* and a front-page photo-story in the Spanish paper *El Diario.* News coverage appeared on many stations, including WCBS, WINS, WBAI, and WABC-TV.

Make Demands

When GAA's three representatives were given permission to enter City Hall, they found it closed from the inside. Plainclothesmen stopped President Jim Owles, Arthur Evans, and Joseph Stevens from entering. They were permitted to meet with Michael Dontzon. Prior to this Evans shouted, "It seems that City Hall is only closed to homosexuals today."

Dontzon requested that no photos be taken and asked that Arthur Irving not record what was said on his portable tape recorder. The three GAA delegates discussed the constant harassment of the Continental Baths, the subway pay toilets, repeal of the sodomy laws, fair employment practices, the Carol Greitzer petition (which was still being circulated outside), taxation without representation, the hundreds of thousands of gay votes, and that it was about time the mayor's office opened up channels of communication and dialogue with the gay community.

Michael Dontzon told the press later, "I listened, said I'd look into the matter and see what I could do." He told the GAA delegation that police had stopped plainclothes entrapment of gays in New York, that they have stopped hiding behind screens in public toilets, and that the mayor was sensitive to gay problems without any preconceived prejudices.

All the picketers were GAA members, with the exception of two female observers from Gay Liberation Front. Reactions of the lunchtime crowd were generally good, with a few uptight exceptions, notably one Catholic priest who was asked to sign the petition for the civil rights of homosexuals. He refused, saying, "They're immoral." When challenged on this, he made a hasty retreat.

Reaction Came Fast

All told, it was a successful action participated in by about 30 demonstrators. That night the GAA discussed future and frequent actions to "keep the heat on." Coverage was very good. But the reaction came faster than anyone anticipated!

At 5:00 A.M. Sunday, the police raided an after-hours bar called the Snakepit. They arrested 167 persons. One of those arrested jumped or fell from the second-floor window of the Charles Street police station and ended up impaled on an iron picket fence.

Six 14-inch-long prongs pierced his thigh and pelvis. The cops couldn't lift him off the fence without injuring him further. The fire department's Rescue Company No. 1 was called. They sawed off the section of the fence, and both were taken to St. Vincent's Hospital. The operation was done with an electric saw. They cut off the crossbar and were able to ease out the iron prongs.

The operation took two hours and was performed by firemen and completed by a surgical team of doctors. Lieutenant Leddy of the fire department's rescue company said, "It's a very tiring and brain-wearying job, trying to pull spikes out of a man's interior."

The victim was variously identified as Vito, then Diego, then Alberto Vinales, who is still in critical condition. News of the raid, the arrests, and the impalement spread fast.

The charges against the Snakepit were that it was illegally operating after hours. Four of the employee were charged with violations of the Alcoholic Beverage Control Board laws, while the patrons were charged with "disorderly conduct."

Distribute Flyer

Prior to the raid on the Snakepit, two other after-hours places were raided though no arrests were made. News of what happened had also spread like wildfire. An emergency session of GAA was called immediately, and from noon Sunday, March 8, a phone-in was staged, plans made, circulars written, ideas discussed. The apartment of Jim Owles and Marty Robinson was jam-packed with angry, determined gays. A recently acquired secondhand mimeographing machine broke down. Fortunately, one of the girls had access to the Daughters of Bilitis duplicator. About 3000 of the following were run off and distributed in the bars and on the streets:

GAY ACTIVISTS ALLIANCE

"Snakepit" Raided, 167 Arrested...

One boy near death at St. Vincent's

Police raided The Snakepit at corner of Bleecker & West 10th last night...167 were arrested and given summonses for disorderly conduct. One boy either fell or jumped out of the precinct window, landed and was IMPALED on a metal fence!

ANY WAY YOU LOOK AT IT...THAT BOY WAS PUSHED! WE ARE ALL BEING PUSHED.

Fighting Gays and any of you who call yourselves human beings with guts...STAND UP TO THIS HORROR!

Gather at Sheridan Square tonight, March 8 at 9:00 P.M., to march on the Sixth Precinct.

Stop the Raids! Defend your Rights!

There will be a DEATH WATCH VIGIL at St. Vincent's immediately after the protest.

We must all come. There is only the truth to guide us.

That night almost 500 gays gathered and marched to the Sixth Precinct shouting, "Say It Loud...Gay Is Proud," "Gay Power," and "Stop the Killings." Busloads of Tactical Patrol Force police, hundreds of cops, countless plainclothesmen had encircled the area.

GAA members had worked diligently all day attempting to contact the gay community, including officers of any other gay groups that could be reached. One of those arrested was a GLF member. Among those groups participating in this action sponsored by GAA were the GLF and members of Homosexuals Intransigent. The GLF brought its banner. Both groups had marshals to supervise the march and to keep people on the sidewalks.

The marchers were met at the Charles Street 6th Precinct by a barricade of cops with plainclothesmen interspersed throughout the crowd (easily recognized). They shouted slogans, made their demands, protested the harassment and possible death of the impaled boy, and made it clear that whether he was physically pushed or whether he jumped in panic, the fact remains that he was psychologically pushed by oppressive laws and an oppressive society.

After this confrontation, the crowd marched to St. Vincent's Hospital. The shouting stopped voluntarily out of respect for the boy and other sick patients. The Death Watch Vigil began. Reverend

Weeks of the Church of Holy Apostles said a public prayer for the boy's recovery.

After this the crowd attempted to hold a vigil march around the hospital, and they were stopped by the cops. Finally they did so on the other side of the street. From there, they marched to and through Greenwich Village's Gay Street, up through Christopher to reconvene at the Sheridan Square Park.

Two L.A. Girls Attempt First Legal Gay Marriage

July 21, 1970

The first marriage in the nation designed to legally bind two persons of the same sex was performed in Los Angeles June 12.

Two young women, Neva Joy Heckman and Judith Ann Belew, pledged their troth "until death do us part" in a simple double-ring ceremony conducted at their home by the Rev. Troy D. Perry, pastor of Metropolitan Community Church.

The occasion lent fresh significance to the minister's traditional admonition, "What God hath joined together, let no man put asunder."

A legal test of the marriage is expected.

The rites were conducted under a provision of California law that allows a common-law marriage to be formalized by a church ceremony and issuance of a church certificate when the couple have been together two years or more. Neva and Judith had been together just over two years.

Issuance of the certificate by MCC completed the law's requirements. No marriage license is required under this provision, bypassing Los Angeles County Clerk William G. Sharp, who said recently that he would not issue such a license to persons of the same sex "under any circumstances."

The law does not specify that marriage partners must be of the opposite sex. Sharp based his stand on common-law presumptions of the nature of the marriage bond and on what he considered to be the expressed intent of the "whole law."

Office of Husband and Wife

The law does require that the couple be asked if they accept each other as husband and wife. Reverend Perry, therefore, had Neva make this altered version of the vow:

"I, Neva, take thee, Judith, to be my wedded *spouse*, to have and to hold from this day forward, for better and for worse, for richer and for poorer, in sickness and in health, to love and to cherish, according to God's holy ordinance, *to serve in the office of husband* until death do us part, and thereunto I give thee my troth."

Judith made the same vow except to say "wife" instead of "husband."

Instead of declaring them husband and wife, Rev. Perry pronounced "our sisters, Neva and Judith," to be "living in the offices of husband and wife."

"Only This Rapport..."

The ceremony was conducted before a simple white screen decorated with two small birds and flanked with tall candelabras. "Bo" Siewert, vice president of the Los Angeles chapter of the Daughters of Bilitis, stood up with Neva; Reverend Perry's mother, Edith Perry, with Judith.

Poet William J. Margolis read from his works a poem that included the line, "We are too many, and only this rapport can make us one."

Reverend Perry opened the ceremony by asking divine blessings on the union. "Given them to your power and your glory, oh Lord, as they live together from this day forward in the holy state of matrimony."

Judith wore a long-sleeved street-length gown of white chiffon over white rayon, with an empire waist, lace at the cuff and neck and six rows as a bib on the bodice. Her veil was a simple bow with three layers of netting. White pumps completed the ensemble. She carried a bouquet of white carnations and a single white orchid.

Neva wore a black waistcoat over formal white slacks and shirt with black neck band.

Sixteen guests, friends of the couple and well-wishers, were present. Two movie companies, one British and one American, filmed the ceremony for possible television use.

In a short interview after the ceremony, Judith said the couple hoped to adopt a baby.

Asked if it had taken any courage on their part to decide to get married, Neva replied, "That's a difficult one to answer." Judith merely smiled.

Both said they had had no last-minute doubts.

They were asked what they looked forward to now.

"Being together and being accepted as a married couple," said Neva.

"Do you think you will be accepted?" she was asked.

"I feel that a lot of people will have their own personal opinions, and we don't want to change those opinions," Neva replied. But she went on to say she thought many would accept them.

They said they planned to file a joint income tax return this year.

Reverend Perry, asked if he thought the marriage was legal, cited the state law. "It is lawful," he said.

Reverend Perry said he had no immediate candidates for a second wedding, but his lover, Steve Jordan, caught the bride's bouquet. The relationship of the two has not yet been formalized.

SOCARIDES WARNS OF HOMOSEXUAL EPIDEMIC

July 21, 1970

New York psychiatrist Charles Socarides, addressing the nation's physicians in the May 18 issue of *The Journal of the American Medical Association,* writes that "homosexuality is a form of mental illness" and constitutes " a major health problem" of "epidemiological proportions."

Socarides, a member of the psychiatry department of the Albert Einstein College of Medicine in the Bronx, N.Y., is widely known for his commentaries on "sick" homosexuals, and in his article says that "at least one-third of life-long exclusively homosexual patients can become exclusively heterosexual," presumably by taking his "cure."

He has appeared on both nationwide and local television and was a member of the panel on homosexuality brought together for *Time*'s cover issue on the subject last fall. His current article is a summation of his views concerning homosexuality.

Since he believes that homosexuality is a medical problem and all homosexuals should therefore be considered medical patients, Socarides concludes that "only in the consultation room does the homosexual reveal himself and his world. No other data, statistics, or statements can be accepted as setting forth the true nature of homosexuality. All other sources may be heavily weighted by face-saving devices or rationalizations or, if they issue from lay bodies, lack the scientific and medical background necessary to support their views."

He also writes that since homosexuality is a medical problem, the homosexual should not be subject to legal restrictions on activities that are done in private with consenting adults; however, "any change in the legal code should be accompanied by a clear-cut statement as to the nature of obligatory homosexuality, its diagnosis as a form of mental illness, and a universal declaration of support for it s treatment by qualified medical practitioners."

He said that use of the word "lesbianism" to describe female homosexuality is "an attempt to romanticize and minimize it." Observing that homosexuality in women is discussed less frequently than in men, he finds that women may, in fact, be worse off than their male counterparts—"loss of a homosexual partner can lead the bereft female homosexual to severe depressions and suicide with greater frequency than in the male."

Socarides considers homosexuality to derive from a "faulty sexual identity" caused by a "pathological family constellation" composed of a "domineering, crushing mother," and an "absent, weak, or rejecting father." He sees a high incidence of paranoia in overt homosexuals as a result of the "medical fact that overt, obligatory homosexuality is either a fixation or regression to the earliest stages of ego development."

He tosses a bouquet of nettles when he bleakly states that "not all homosexuals or perhaps even a majority, display the 'absence of conscience' mechanism so characteristic of the so-called psychopath."

Of the "homosexual revolution," he says that talk of homosexuality as a variation of normality is "naive, not to say grounded in ignorance." He also mentions colleges "pressured" (by whom he doesn't say) into permitting gay organizations on their campuses and thereby "lending tacit approval" to these groups.

He asked his audience of doctors, when taking sexual histories, "to respond with interest and compassion to efforts of the patient to communicate his shame and despair in the guilty revelation so demeaning and injurious to pride."

Concluding, he hopes that the subject of homosexuality will become a challenge to "the great resources and medical talent of the United States."

GET 'EM IN, THROW 'EM OUT: MILITARY POLICIES ON GAYS MAKE NO SENSE

by Rob Cole

July 21, 1970

You're gay and you get a draft notice. Or you're already in the military and want out.

Now what?

The first situation divides into two: You want to serve, or you don't. At first glance there would seem to be no problem for those who want to serve. But these are the ones who often wind up on the inside wanting out and worrying about ways and means.

But let's start with that draft notice.

It leads to a preinduction physical, and that leads to what can often be an embarrassing question for those who want to serve and a long, frustrating, and eventually losing battle for those who don't.

In the first instance, if you're gay and don't say so on the preinduction questionnaire, you are liable to court-martial and dishonorable discharge for fraudulent enlistment (Title 10, U.S. Code, Section 856, Article 83). Prosecutions under this rule are uncommon—there are less stringent measures, of which more later, but it's there, hanging over you, usable at the discretion of authority if your sexual proclivities come out later.

Officially, the Armed Forces don't want you if you're a bona fide "sexual deviant." Army Regulation 635-89, for example, says homosexuality "appreciably limits the ability of an individual to function effectively in a military environment" and therefore renders him "unfit for military service and impairs the morale and discipline of the Army." Other services have similar regulations.

Not on Your Ankh

So all you have to do to stay out is say you're gay when you're called in for the once-over? Not on your ankh.

The odds are, you won't be believed, especially if you're a butch type. According to a spokesman for the Armed Forces Entrance and Examining Station in Newark, N.J., you must bring a letter from your psychiatrist, certifying your "condition." Or if you fail to bring such a letter, you are examined by three civilian psychiatrists attached to the station. (The fact is, you may be examined anyway, despite that certificate from your psychiatrist. The military is extremely suspicious of anyone who seeks to avoid its embrace.)

If, said the spokesman, the stations psychiatrists accept you as gay, you are automatically deferred. If not, in you go.

The rule of thumb is, you're straight unless you can prove otherwise—at least, until you're actually in the service.

"We've have some weird ones come in here," said the Newark station spokesman. "Some come in claiming to be card-carrying members of a 'homo' society; several arrived dressed in women's clothing, and some carry on as effeminately as possible to impress us."

Many of these were inducted anyway.

"However, it's on a discretionary basis," said Don Slater of the Homosexual Information Center in Los Angeles. "The policy is not uniformly applied. It can't be uniformly applied because there is no possible test of whether a man is telling the truth when he says he's gay."

HIC, which has an enviable record in helping gays stay out of the service, advises simply making the claim and sticking with it, without trying to prove it.

"We have not lost a man to the service since November of 1967," said Slater, "because we stopped giving proof. The man's word is his authority in this case. We don't offer any proof. There is none. If you can offer proof that you're gay, then somebody else can offer proof that you're not.

"So we don't support words anymore, and we've never lost in consequence. We've backed them down."

What this all boils down to is that if you're going to say you're gay in order to stay out of Indochina, you better have a lot going for you, especially a strong organization like HIC or one of the other group around the country that help homosexuals with this sort of thing.

A horrible example of what can happen is the case of Lawrence Ostroff of Los Angeles. Ostroff did all the right things, *except* get help from an organization at the beginning. At his induction physical in Los Angeles on November 12, 1968, he said he was a homosexual and presented documentary evidence. He was inducted anyway. Two weeks later, he visited an Army psychiatrist, who subsequently reported, "A review of this subject's history of homosexual activity gives no reason for this examiner to disbelieve his statements. The subject gives a history consistent with a diagnosis of homosexuality."

Ostroff was promptly contacted by military intelligence agents, who asked him for the names and addresses of other males with whom he had had sex. They said they would contact these persons to verify his claim. Of course, those who backed him up could be prosecuted on sodomy charges.

Ostroff refused to give any names and challenged the Army's right to hold him on the ground that he had been illegally inducted.

Off to Vietnam

He was promptly ordered to Vietnam.

At this point, he asked HIC for help.

The upshot was, an administrative hearing was set up for the reluctant draftee under Army Regulation 635-206. This procedure, which is just short of a court-martial, is often used by the Army to get rid of those it considers to be not worth the effort to make into soldiers.

It provides for "discharge because of misconduct, fraudulent entry, conviction by civil court, or absence without leave, or desertion." In practice, the other reasons cited are usually handled under other rules, leaving misconduct.

However, Ostroff had a mail fraud charge pending against him in a civilian court, for which he was convicted in December of 1969. The U.S. Supreme Court and the Court of Military Appeals had thrown the regulation into question by parallel rulings earlier in the year that civilian convictions could not be used as a basis for military prosecution. But the conviction was brought up anyway.

On April 22 the hearing was held by a board of officers at Fort MacArthur in Oakland, Calif. Ostroff was ordered separated from service under AR 635-206, *not* for homosexuality. His discharge papers read "Undesirable."

The reluctance of the military to apply its official policy on homosexuality may be due to reports that requests for deferment on this ground are increasing by leaps and bounds.

There are no hard statistics to go on—or at least none that are available. A spokesman for the Hollywood draft board told *The Advocate* flatly, "This is not a matter of public information." Other news media have been equally unsuccessful for the most part. However, that examining station in Newark, mentioned earlier, and several of the local New Jersey boards became sufficiently exercised about the situation recently to admit that there had been a "definite" increase in the number of males seeking deferment for psychological reasons, including homosexuality, drug addiction, and bed-wetting.

This posed a crisis.

"The framers of this policy [on homosexuality] assumed," said Slater, "that only a small number of draftable youths would be lost to the Armed Services because of it. They could not imagine that a straight-looking homosexual would be willing to confess his secret aberration, even under penalty of perjury."

When the number of claims of homosexuality began to rise in 1968 and 1969, said Slater, a secret directive was sent by the Pentagon to local draft boards instructing them to draft all masculine-appearing persons, even though they did claim homosexuality.

As a result said Slater, though the number of claims of sexual deviancy may be up, the number of actual deferments for this reason are down.

The ironic thing is that, although the draft board may not believe you're gay, your superiors, once you're in, are very likely to. This doesn't mean they will help you get out, at least not without scars. Noncoms and even commissioned officers often seem to have the idea that by clamping down hard on any sign of homosexuality, they can "make a man out of that goddamned queer."

"It's a great handicap to be serving at the same time the company commander knows that you're gay," said Slater. "And he does know. This record [your disallowed claim for deferment] follows you, because they say, 'Let's watch this guy. He looks beefy enough. He looks as if he could serve.'

"But you're constantly under scrutiny, under surveillance, and it's a very unpleasant situation."

Many gays have, of course, found paradise in military service. The tales of those shipboard, base camp, or South Sea Island orgies trail almost every gay veteran of every war the United States has ever been in. Even allowing for a bit of exaggeration, there's plenty of gay life on the other side of those camp gates. But it exists side by side with some of the most entrenched antihomosexual prejudice to be found anywhere.

How Many Ask Out?

How many go into service, with or without previous claim of being gay, and later try to get out on grounds of homosexuality?

Here again, statistics are soft, at best. Some sources say this is becoming more and more common, especially with rising disaffection with the Vietnam War being added to other reasons why a man might insist he's gay to get out.

But as Ostroff's case indicates, insisting you're gay probably won't be enough. Army Regulation 635-212, which generally deals with discharges for medical reasons, also provides for administrative discharge for any individual who shows "evidences of homosexual tendencies, desires, or interests, but is without overt homosexual acts."

Discharge may be honorable, general, under honorable conditions, or dishonorable, in such instance qualified as "for unfitness" or "for unsuitability."

AR 635-212 also says, "Personnel who voluntarily engage in homosexual acts, irrespective of sex, will not be permitted to serve in the Army in any capacity, and their separation is mandatory."

Danger

What is a "homosexual act?"

Title 10 U.S. Code, Section 926 Article 125(a) (Uniform Code of Military Justice) says, "Any person subject to this chapter who engages in unnatural carnal copulation with another person of the same or opposite sex or with an animal is guilty of sodomy. Penetration, however slight, is sufficient to complete the offense."

Article 125(b) goes on to say: "Any person found guilty of sodomy shall be punished as a court-martial may direct."

Title 10, U.S. Code Annotated, Section 856, Article 125, sets out the maximum penalty for sodomy: "Dishonorable discharge, forfeiture of all pay and allowances, confinement at hard labor not to exceed five years."

Obviously, to get out the easy way under AR 635-212 or its equivalent for the other services, you've got to prove yourself without getting down to the nitty-gritty.

At Their Mercy

In practice, you are at the mercy of your immediate superiors. As in Ostroff's case, it's largely up to them whether you will be permitted to opt out at all, faced with a bad conduct discharge, or allowed to take the lesser evil of 635-212.

According to a spokesman for the Army Advocate General's Office in Los Angeles, "separations because of homosexuality are usually general discharges under honorable conditions, which is almost the same as an honorable discharge, except that there are certain benefits that you can't get from the Veterans Administration."

To get back to the area of statistics, the Washington Office of the Assistant Secretary of Defense told *The Advocate* there were 1,542 discharges for homosexuality under AR 635-212 and comparable regulations of the other services in 1969, against 1,671 in 1968. If the number of applications is, indeed, rising, resistance must be stiffening.

The Office of the Assistant Secretary broke down its figures into two columns, headed "Homosexual tendencies (Unsuitability)," for which it listed 446 discharges in 1969 against 552 in 1968, and "Sexual Perversion (Unfitness)" for which it listed 1,096 in 1969 and 1,119 in 1968.

The breakdown and choice of headings may indicate that if you want that discharge under honorable conditions, you may have to walk a very narrow line in demonstrating you're gay.

If You Don't Want Out

Another irony is that it's apparently a lot easier to get kicked out if you don't want to be than if you do.

A case in point is former Air Force Staff Sgt. Richard G. Burchill (Sgt. X) who fell under the scrutiny of that Service's Office of Special Investigations when they somehow got hold of a friend's letter (*The Advocate,* May 26).

Burchill, who had intended to make the Air Force his career, furnished about 30 names of other alleged gays under threat of criminal prosecution coupled with a promise he could stay in the service if he cooperated. Before the investigation got well under way, 55 military personnel and 76 civilians were involved. Burchill was ousted anyway. The fate of the others remains to be seen.

There is a great deal of dispute over what effect a discharge involving homosexuality is likely to have on a man's future.

Ostroff got a job almost immediately on discharge. Burchill sought a job with a defense contractor and was turned down.

A prospective employer cannot see the official record and thus cannot determine the specific reason for a discharge without the written permission of the applicant. But obviously, the mere fact of being refused a look at the record may be enough to prejudice a prospective employer.

GAA Zaps *Harper's Magazine*

December 8, 1970

NEW YORK CITY—The Gay Activists Alliance staged a peaceful all-day sit-in at the New York offices of *Harper's Magazine* October 27 to protest an article by Joseph Epstein in the September issue in which homosexuals were described as "condemned to a state of permanent niggerdom among men."

GAA president Jim Owles came away with the impression that *Harper's* publisher William S. Blair had agreed to print a statement of policy in an upcoming issue "in support of the goals of the GAA, and disassociate themselves from Mr. Epstein's article."

Blair, however, flatly denied that he had agreed to publish anything. "Indeed, no," he told *The Advocate.* "What I said was that we would be willing to write a letter to the GAA saying that we have disagreements about the wisdom of publishing that particular piece. I hope that they don't think this happens because we, personally, are against the civil rights of homosexuals, or fail to recognize that they are treated harshly and should not be.

"But that's far from a statement of policy to be published in the magazine. It's a statement signed by me making clear, I hope, that our decision to publish that article was not because we in any way want to denigrate homosexuals."

There was an agreement," said Owles. "He gave us his word that there would be a policy statement in an upcoming issue of *Harper's*."

"The magazine as such doesn't take policy positions," said Blair. "It never has. Never endorse candidates for public office, for example. It's not that kind of thing."

Despite the dispute over the policy statement, however, both the GAA and the magazine's editors agreed that the sit-in had been productive.

"There was an exchange," said *Harper's* managing editor Robert Kotlowitz. "And those things are always valuable."

"It went very smoothly," said Owles. "We had 50 or 60 people, and we moved in there about 9:00 A.M. and started confronting the staff. It was not a violent or heavy scene or anything like that. They brought in coffee and doughnuts; we rapped with the editors and with the staff and told them our feelings toward the article. We spent the whole day talking with the publisher and the other people in charge.

"We got very good coverage in the media. We were picked up on at least three television stations and about five radio stations, and it went very good."

He said he thought the demonstration would make other magazines think twice about running such articles.

"I think we served notice that they can expect similar affairs any time such an article on homosexuality is printed."

Kotlowitz saw the matter a bit differently.

"The point of view that we expressed was a description of the function of the magazine and how it operates, and how a piece like that fits into the magazine.

"I think they read the article as a polemic against homosexuality, which it was not. It was a very personal expression of certain discoverable prejudices by a liberal, white, heterosexual male."

Epstein said in the article that he thought "homosexuals cursed, and I am afraid I mean this quite literally, in the medieval sense of having been struck by an unexplained injury, an extreme piece of evil luck, whose origin is so unclear as to be, finally a mystery. Although hundreds have tried, no once has really been able to account for it."

Dismissing Freud, Dr. David Reuben, Dr. Edmund Bergler, and the Mattachine Society, and looking askance at Gore Vidal, whom he calls "a veteran propagandist for homosexuality," Epstein suggests that the best explanation for the emergency of homosexuality in American in the "swinging Sixties" and '70's is that "the *zeitgeist* has never been more encouraging of hedonism in all its forms, homosexuality among them. One takes one's kicks where they are to be had. The swinging Sixties offered a large selection. Smoke it, swallow it, eat it, wallow in it, screw it, kick it, stomp it to death, and never mind what 'it' is—such appear to be the principal exhortations of the last decade."

Laws against homosexuality "are barbarous, not to say illogical: When committed by consenting adults, homosexuality is a crime without a victim, and for this reason alone, the onus of criminality surely ought to be lifted," he writes. "Perhaps the audacious and unguent Gay Liberation Movement will bring about the abolishment of these laws—and one can only say more power to them."

Acceptance Out

But however wide the public tolerance of homosexuality may become, he writes, "between public tolerance and private acceptance stretches a wide gap, and private acceptance of homosexuality, in my experience, is not to be found, even among the most liberal-minded, sophisticated, and liberated people."

"Why can't I come to terms with it?" he asks. Is it fear of the latent homosexuality in myself, such as is supposed to reside in every man, that makes this impossible? Do I secretly envy homosexuals, not their sexual pleasure, but their evasion of responsibility, for despite all that I have thought about homosexuality, I am still not clear about whether homosexuals are truly attracted to men or are only running away from women and all that women represent: marriage, family, bringing up children."

"One can tolerate homosexuality," he concludes, "a small enough price to be paid for someone else's pain, but accepting it, really accepting it, is another thing altogether. I find I can accept it least of all when I look at my children. There is much my four sons can do in their lives that might cause me anguish, that might outrage me, that might make me ashamed of them and of myself as their father. But nothing they could ever do would make me sadder than if any of them were to become homosexual. For then I should know them condemned to a state of permanent niggerdom among me, their lives, whatever adjustment they might make to their condition, to be lived out as part of the pain of the earth."

Equal Time

Kotlowitz said the article "drew a strong emotional response, both in letters from readers and from people who wanted to do some kind of piece on the subject."

The GAA, in literature handed out at the sit-in, said it had asked for "equal time for the gay community, in the form of an article of rebuttal," which it said as the only thing that "could alleviate the damage *Harper's* had done."

But it said the magazine "refused to publish any of a series of articles submitted by GAA, and refused to commission an unprejudiced article from other sources…"

"I think," said Kotlowitz, "we've had something like three submissions since the piece appeared, all of which have been rejected because they were not good enough, not for substantive reasons."

He said it had been pointed out to the GAA demonstrators "that we do not sit down and decide to publish a piece on homosexuality, as a contribution to the subject for the year. I mean, the magazine deals in serious discourse on an ongoing basis. It's a subject we return to fairly often, and we will constantly go back to. Nor does the piece in any way represent an editorial point of view. I think that was not understood by the alliance before they were up here."

Owles said, "We went down to show them that they had a moral responsibility as a liberal institution to print articles that were not oppressive to homosexuals. An article like Mr. Epstein's was clearly oppressive."

MCC IS HOME: OVER 1,000 ATTEND DEDICATION SERVICE IN LOS ANGELES

by Rob Cole

April 13, 1971

"They say miracles are past."—Shakespeare

On March 7, 1971, Metropolitan Community Church of Los Angeles proved that Shakespeare was premature.

On that date, the church founded October 6, 1968, by a dozen diehard optimists to serve a class of people largely rejected by—and rejecting—Establishment religion, dedicated its first permanent home in a majestic service attended by standing-room-only crowd of over 1,000 persons.

The eyes of the world were not exactly riveted on the event. California governor Ronald Reagan and Los Angeles city councilman Thomas Bradley sent best wishes but regretted that they were unable to attend. KNBC television covered it on a local telecast the next day. *Time* magazine reportedly had a correspondent on the scene. But the city's two major dailies apparently ignored it.

But it was an historic occasion nevertheless, the culmination of the greatest outpouring of energy, money, devotion, and faith the gay world has ever seen.

"Not since the Apostolic church, which followed the death and resurrection of Jesus Christ, has there been anything on the face of the earth like this," said assistant pastor John Hose, his voice trembling with emotion.

Splendor and Cracked Plaster

The long-delayed dedication service was held with permanent seating still to be installed in the sanctuary—the congregation sat on folding chairs from Abbey Rents. Ancient wooden lathing showed like bare bones through cracked and fallen plaster in many areas of the half-century–old building at 2201 S. Union near downtown Los Angeles.

But in the main auditorium, Christ gazed from one of a pair of two-story–high stained-glass windows on an altar gleaming with brass and gold under a red velvet canopy, and the congregation sat under a huge brass colonial chandelier donated by a church member.

Deep-pile green carpeting, dark paneling, and rich fabric wall coverings glowed in the soft light from other stained glass windows in the church offices and a completed lounge.

Many of the church's members worked every spare moment for weeks to get the building ready for dedication. The congregation as a whole has had to dig deep to even begin to pay for it all, and many of the furnishings and fixtures were extra gifts from members and well-wishers.

The building cost $55,000, with repairs and renovation expected to run about $20,000. By dedication day, renovation costs had topped $35,000 and were still climbing.

Only two weeks before dedication day, church officials were engaged in a frantic search for an additional $15,000 loan. Conventional lending agencies had turned them down. At the last moment, the parents of a church member put up the money. This last loan put the total debt on the church at $60,000.

And Still They Came

But on the morning of March 7—a crisp, sunny, unusually smog-free day in Los Angeles— none of that seemed important. Expecting a big turnout, the church had issued tickets to its 500 members, 66 associate members (called "friends"), special visitors, and a couple of hundred others, and advised them to show up between 9:30 and 10:30 A.M., when the doors would be opened to the general public.

The L-shaped sanctuary will seat about 850, with a little crowding.

By 10:15 every available seat was filled, and people were already standing. By the time services started, a little before 11 A.M., ushers had counted a total of 1,012.

Among them were several ministers and many members of other churches and missions in the expanding Fellowship of Metropolitan Community Churches; representatives of gay organizations in the Los Angeles area and elsewhere; ministers from unrelated churches, including

Bishop Mark Harding of the Old Catholic Church in Denver; and Dr. Evelyn Hooker, head of the National Institutes of Mental Health task force that recommended liberalization of laws on homosexual activity.

Hooker and Edith Perry, mother of MCC pastor Rev. Troy Perry, received standing ovations.

"It's been a long, hard road," said MCC music director Willie Smith, who opened the service by singing "The Impossible Dream" from *Man of La Mancha*.

He said Reverend Perry, who started MCC to give homosexuals a church where they could feel they belonged, "had the faith, and he had the vision. He had the dream that this would come true, and the dream is not fulfilled yet. This is barely the beginning."

"Our seats may be temporary," said Hose, "but our faith in Jesus Christ and our knowledge of the love that God has for us and all mankind, is permanent, as is this house of worship for Metropolitan Community Church....

"I bid you welcome in the name of Jesus Christ."

"This is the culmination of two and a half years of work and hope," said the Rev. Richard Ploen, minister of education. "It is a time of thanksgiving, a thanksgiving to Almighty God that we can meet together, that we can help others, that we have a home that we can call our own."

Perry, in his sermon, traced the wanderings of MCC from its founding in his living room in the Los Angeles suburb of Huntington Park, to the clubhouse of that town's Women's Club, to the downtown Embassy Auditorium, to the First Methodist Church, and finally to its last temporary home, the Encore Theatre in Hollywood, where it remained for a year and a half through the generosity of owner Louis Federici.

Recalling the frustration of the Israelite king David, whose dream of raising a temple had to wait for realization by Solomon, his successor, Perry said there had been times when he wondered if he would ever live to see MCC in a building of its own.

But now that the dream had been realized, he had a warning for the congregation: "A building, a church doesn't make.... If we get so wrapped up in this building and unwrapped in God, we'll fail, like so many other churches have....

"But if we look to him...we *shall* overcome. And we *shall* run the race with prejudice, and we *shall* see the end of this thing."

The service was enhanced by the church's combined chancel and gospel choirs, 49 voices strong, backed by organ, brass, and percussion, which gave a powerful performance of the "Entrata Festiva" processional by Flor Peters and the old church hymn, "God of Our Fathers," among several other works and gospel songs.

IDAHO SEX REFORM: ADULT CONSENT LAW ADOPTED; NATION'S THIRD

June 22, 1971

BOISE, Ida.—This rugged western state whose capital, Boise, was convulsed by what has become widely known as a "homosexual witch-hunt" in 1955 and 1956 has become the third state in the nation to wipe laws dealing with private homosexual behavior off its law books.

The state's new penal code, signed into law by Democratic governor Cecil D. Andrus on March 18, eliminates all penalties for private homosexual acts between freely consenting persons 16 years old and older and reduces solicitation for homosexual acts where no money is involved to a petty misdemeanor carrying a 30-day penalty.

Under the old law "the infamous crime against nature" was punishable by not less than five years in prison. One defendant in the mid-'50s scandal got life.

The new code goes into effect on January 1, 1971, following Connecticut's sex law reform, which takes effect in October. Illinois, the pioneer state in homosexual law reform, abolished its old law in January 1962.

At least one other state, Colorado, is expected to abolish its laws against private homosexual acts this year, and Oregon and Hawaii may follow suit.

One of the principal architects of the Idaho reform was former state Republican senator William Roden, who was a deputy prosecutor in the office of Ada County (Boise) prosecuting attorney Blaine Evans during the witch-hunt.

Roden now calls the witch-hunt, which was detailed by former *Time* and *Newsweek* editor John Gerassi in the 1966 best-seller *The Boys of Boise,* "a very unfortunate situation" and indicates that he would have pursued it with less vigor if he had been prosecutor.

Initiated by Legislature

The new code is the result of a study initiated by the legislature itself in 1967, when an interim subcommittee of the Legislative Council was appointed to explore a possible need for a general penal code revision.

Rode, then in his fourth term, was chairman of the subcommittee. When he chose not to run for reelection two years ago, he was retained as a consultant to the subcommittee and did the drafting that led to the final bill.

The former Boise senator told *The Advocate* the new code was substantially the same as the Model Penal Code of the American Law Institute, which has been used as a guide for most penal code revisions considered by state legislatures. Its provision making "loitering to solicit deviate sexual relations" a petty offense has been widely criticized by advocates of homosexual law reform and was deleted in the Illinois reform and in the measure now awaiting the signature of Colorado governor John Love.

Rep. Clyde Keithly (R–Nampa) served as floor sponsor for the legislation embodying the new code, which the House passed 42–25 on February 26. Keithly is chairman of the house judiciary rules and administration committee, the code's official sponsor.

The senate passed the measure March 9 by a vote of 23–11.

Roden, now an attorney in private practice, said that "the basic area of controversy" in both houses was the sex provisions of the code.

"I personally favor the provisions," he said. "I think our present laws as we have them in Idaho are rather archaic, and I frankly don't care to see the so-called crimes against nature made criminal."

The Boys of Boise, which the *Harvard Law Review* called "a chilling account of the influence on the police and judiciary of an hysterical and largely ignorant public," wasn't discussed in debate on the sex provisions of the code, Roden said.

Basic Provisions

These are the basic provisions of the code, as set forth by assistant attorney general Martin Ward, that pertain to homosexual acts:

Eliminates the original "infamous crime against nature" provisions in the law and substitutes these, under what will become Title 18, Chapter 9:

"18-903. (1.) DEVIATE SEXUAL INTERCOURSE BY FORCE OR IMPOSITION. A person who engages in deviate sexual intercourse with another person or who causes another to engage in deviate sexual intercourse commits a felony of the second degree if (1) he compels the other person to participate by force or by threat of imminent death, serious bodily injury, extreme pain, or kidnapping to be inflicted on anyone, or (b) he has substantially impaired the other person's power to appraise or control his conduct by administering or employing without knowledge of the other person drugs, intoxicants, or other means for the purpose of preventing resistance, or (c) the other person is unconscious, or (3) the other person is less than 12 years old. Deviate sexual intercourse means sexual intercourse *per os* or *per annum* (Mouth or anus) between human beings who are not husband and wife and any form of sexual intercourse with an animal.

"(2.) BY OTHER IMPOSITION. A person who engages in deviate sexual intercourse with another person, or who causes another to engage in deviate sexual intercourse commits a felony of the third degree if (a) he compels the other person to participate by any threat that would prevent resistance by a person of ordinary resolution, or (b) he knows that the other person suffers from a mental disease or defect which renders him incapable of appraising the nature of his conduct, or (c) he knows that the other person submits because he is unaware a sexual act is being committed upon him.

"18-904. CORRUPTION OF MINORS AND SEDUCTION. A male who has entered sexual intercourse with a female not his wife, or any person who engages in deviate sexual intercourse or causes another to engage in deviate sexual intercourse is guilty of a felony of the third degree if (a) the other person is less than 16 years old and the actor is at least 4 years older than the other person, or (b) the other person is less than 21 years old and the actor is his guardian or otherwise responsible for the general supervision of his welfare, or (c) the other person is in custody of law or detained in a hospital or other institution and the actor has supervisory or disciplinary authority over him."

In Idaho length of sentence is indeterminate, and the judge has considerable discretion in setting penalties. The new codes sets 30 years as a maximum for a second-degree felony and 15 years as a maximum for a third-degree felony.

TED KENNEDY SAYS HE'S FOR GAY RIGHTS

by Guy Charles

December 8, 1971

NEW YORK CITY—U.S. senator Edward M. (Ted) Kennedy (D-Mass.) says that if elected president, he would be willing to issue an executive order—if "necessary"—to ensure "basic rights" of homosexuals.

Kennedy was questioned amid a busy round of speechmaking here November 16 by Bruce Voeller, chairman of the Gay Activists Alliance State and Federal Affairs Committee.

"Would you, as chief executive, order the federal government to cease discrimination against homosexuals—in all its branches—by the issuance of an executive order?" Voeller asked.

Kennedy said he felt all citizens should be allowed to exercise their rights as guaranteed under the constitution and that if an executive order were the necessary first step, then he felt it was a necessary and compulsory move to take to ensure those rights.

Defense Department and other security procedures that deny homosexuals the right to work gainfully in their profession and as committed Americans should be ended, Kennedy urged. He said he would support any such measure that may be taken.

Voeller's questions were posed at the St. Regis Hotel on Fifth Avenue following an anniversary dinner honoring Rep. William F. Ryan (D-N.Y.).

At the dinner Kennedy strongly supported amnesty for "all young men" who have found themselves in prison or "gone to Canada or elsewhere" in order to avoid the war.

Continuing, he stressed the necessity of a Supreme Court "where the judges are selected for their dedication to Constitutional principles, instead of one where the agents of justice see their task as the avoidance of Constitutional restraints."

Approached on the issue of Intro 475, Kennedy felt he could not state his opinion at that time for lack of knowledge of the exact content of the bill—as well as the fact that it is essentially a local bill.

However, he requested that a copy of the measure be sent to him so he could study it.

Intro 475, the Clingan-Burden-Scholnick-Weiss bill pending in the New York City Council, would afford homosexuals protection against discrimination in employment, housing, and public accommodations.

Kennedy deferred comments on other homosexual rights issues, saying that he did not have time to comment but would reply at a later date.

SENATOR MUSKIE DODGES ISSUE

December 8, 1971

NEW YORK CITY—At a special seminar conducted by New York University at Gould Auditorium, on the Bronx Campus, the principal speaker, Sen. Edmund Muskie (D-Maine), was only slightly shaken by an interruption of a local Irish Republican group asking for an embargo on any type of aid to Britain. He was visibly shaken when a member of the Gay Activists Alliance approached him on leaving the stage and asked him, "What do you think of equal rights for homosexuals?"

The brusque reply was, "I haven't thought about them."

Muskie, current front-runner for the 1972 Democratic presidential nomination, had given a speech assailing President Nixon and his administration on Vietnam policies and answered questions from a panel consisting of Martha Peterson of Barnard College, Bill Salterfield, a columnist for a local black newspaper, and David Conliffe, an undergraduate student at NYU. Then Muskie was rushed off to see a group of senior citizens in two lounges on the second floor.

Hall Offen, the GAA member, pursued the Muskie entourage into the lounges and finally confronted Muskie with the questions, "What are your opinions on the repeal of sodomy laws? If you were elected would you approve an executive order to end discrimination in the federal government?"

Visibly shaken and without an answer, the senator managed to say that sodomy laws were the state governments' worry. He would not reply to the second question but hurriedly left the room.

He was met by a group of GAA demonstrators, who had been leafleting. Among them were Dr. Bruce Voeller and his three children, one of whom handed a leaflet to Muskie, which was accepted and immediately dropped when Muskie realized the source was a homosexual group.

The demonstrators immediately surrounded Muskie, and he was whisked into a waiting car, having lost his smile and a little bit of patience.

"Marriage Is an Evil That Most Men Welcome"

by Rob Cole

March 29, 1972

Despite widespread derision even in the gay world, many homosexuals continue to seek church weddings and to press with more and more determination for legal sanction of their unions.

Remarks like "Who was the bride?" and "Which one wore the veil?" are shrugged off with growing impatience by two general classes of gays: those who feel that legal acceptance of their unions will confer many practical benefits and those to whom it is a matter of morality or religion.

The strongest objection to such marriages seems to come from those who call them an aping of a heterosexual practice which demeans what they view as an emerging gay life-style.

Over the years many gay marriages have gotten newspaper publicity from time to time of the "Would you believe this?" variety. But even the news stories are playing it straighter and straighter, though the underlying motivation for running such stories probably continues to be more to entertain readers than to inform them of a serious event.

Originally even the participants tended to treat the whole thing as an elaborate joke. Ceremonies were performed in bars with bartenders doubling as ministers, and in many cases one of the participants wore the clothing of the opposite sex in complete mimicry of a heterosexual marriage.

These days ceremonies are being performed in churches by ordained or licensed ministers of many denominations. The couples are sober and serious, and cross-dressing has almost totally disappeared for male couples, although in lesbian unions one woman often still wears male attire.

At Metropolitan Community Church in Los Angeles, some 150 such weddings have been performed. The simple double-ring ceremony includes a communion service. The word "spouse" is used instead of "husband" and "wife," and instead of vowing to stay together "until death do us part," the couple commit themselves to the union "as long as there is love."

The church requires that candidates for marriage have been together six months or longer before the ceremony will be performed.

At New York's Church of the Beloved Disciple, the word "marriage" is not used. Church pastor Father Robert Clement performs ceremonies of "holy union." He and his longtime lover, John Noble, were united in such a ceremony last July 18, performed by the Rev. Troy Perry, pastor of MCC/LA.

Many MCC ministers around the nation also avoid using the word "marriage." And in mainline churches where such ceremonies are performed, the ministers often prefer to say merely that they are "blessing" a union. Where religion and morality motivate their actions, participants may profess themselves satisfied with these circumlocutions.

But couples such as Jack Baker and Mike McConnell of Minneapolis will be satisfied with nothing less than full parity under the law with heterosexual unions.

They and at least two lesbian couples have embarked on a long legal battle to back the law down on the issue. The U.S. Supreme Court has been asked to hear the Baker-McConnell case, but whether it does or not, or whichever way it rules, it appears obvious that the legal fight will continue.

Michel Girouard and Rejean Tremblay, the two French-Canadian entertainers whose marriage February 26 brought the latest big publicity splash, may have found a legal compromise that will prove acceptable to some couples.

They signed a "contract of union" that is neither strictly a marriage contract nor the business partnership used by many gay couples to try to solve the problems of joint ownership of property, bank accounts, insurance, and inheritance.

Whether this makes them, as their lawyers claim, the first legally married homosexual couple in Canada may be argued by many.

Baker and McConnell consider themselves the first legally married homosexual couple in the United States. But their claim is based on a marriage license obtained last August by the ruse of having McConnell adopt Baker and Baker then change his name to Pat Lyn McConnell, which does not reveal his sex. When the ruse was discovered, authorities called the license invalid, but it has yet to be subjected to a full legal challenge.

The couple's original legal fight, to be married in a fully recognized same-sex union, is still going on.

Actually, the distinction of being the first legally wedded gay couple in the United States may belong to two young women, Neva Joy Heckman and Judith Ann Belew, who were married by Reverend Perry in Los Angeles on June 12, 1970. Their wedding and a high percentage of the other gay marriages performed by MCC ministers in California may be legal because of a quirk in California law. But a court test has yet to be made.

The gay rush to the altar may continue to confound straights and fellow gays alike, but there seems to be little doubt that there are going to be more and more such marriages and a good bet that eventually the legal barriers will fall.

Way back in the fourth century B.C., a Greek comedy writer named Menander cracked, "Marriage is an evil that most men welcome."

Maybe it all means that gays and straights are not so different after all.

FIRST IN NATION: RIGHTS LAW IN SAN FRANCISCO

by Don Jackson

April 26, 1972

SAN FRANCISCO—This city apparently is going to be the nation's first to prohibit discrimination based on sexual orientation.

The board of supervisors, the governing body of the city and county of San Francisco, voted ten to one April 3 for a long-stalled amendment adding the words "sex and sexual orientation" to the administrative code. The code already bans discrimination on the basis of race, religion, and ancestry by firms doing business with the city.

The amendment requires the signature of Mayor Joseph Alioto to become law. The measure's principal sponsor, supervisor Dianne Feinstein, told *The Advocate* she didn't know whether Alioto will sign it or not. "However, the measure did pass by a ten-to-one vote," she pointed out, "and it only takes a two-thirds majority, or eight votes, to override the mayor's veto."

Mrs. Feinstein said she was pleased with the passage of the amendment. "I think it's a substantial step into the 1970s," she added.

Jim Foster of the Society for Individual Rights, whose organization was one of the initiators of the measure, said he was "ecstatic."

Similar acts have been proposed elsewhere, most notably in New York, where the proposed anti-discrimination ordinance Intro 475 has become a hard-fought issue. Down the San Francisco peninsula at San Mateo, the San Mateo County Human Relations Commission endorsed a request to the Board of Supervisors March 16 for an ordinance change almost identical to that approved by the San Francisco board. The San Mateo board has yet to act on the request.

The Advocate contacted Feinstein March 21, after supervisor Robert E. Gonzales—another of the amendment's sponsors—told the March 20 meeting of the Gay Activists Alliance that it was up to Feinstein to get the bill out of committee, where it had been stalled since last August.

In the March 21 conversation, an *Advocate* reporter mentioned Intro 475 and commented that Feinstein would have to hurry if she wanted her bill to become the nation's first law prohibiting discrimination against homosexuals.

Feinstein said she did want San Francisco to be first, and that she would bring the measure up for a vote "very soon."

Too Vague

Supervisor John Barbagelata, who cast the only nay vote, complained that the language of the measure was too vague.

"There's a lack of standards here," he told the board. "Does this ordinance apply to dogs as sexual partners, or does it just mean two consenting adults?"

Feinstein responded by adding the word "human" to the amendment. In an interview with *The Advocate* the next day, Barbagelata said, "I'm not against the legislation or its intent. I just feel it should have been less vague."

He said he had two objections to the bill: "Firstly, there is no provision defining sexual partner, there is no legal definition of sexual orientation. Does it mean sex between men and small boys? Sex with animals? Secondly, as it is written, the provision must be included in all contracts and subcontracts with firms that do business with the city and county. It will create confusion, as the contractors and subcontractors will not know if they are complying with the law or not on account of the vagueness."

Barbagelata went on to say "Sodomy and oral copulation are felonies in California. Can a county ordinance supersede state law?"

As amended, the measure defines sex as "the character of being male or female," and sexual orientation as "the choice of human sexual partner according to gender."

Archbishop Opposed It

The only organized opposition to the amendment came from the Roman Catholic Church. Archbishop Joseph T. McGucken sent a letter to the board of supervisors stating his opposition to the measure.

Copies of the archbishop's letter were distributed to members of the board of supervisors by Barbagelata immediately before the measure came up for vote.

Ironically, the Catholic Commission on Social Justice endorsed the change in the ordinance last year. Father Jean Boyle, who then headed the commission and is now director for justice and peace of the National Federation of Priests Councils, recently reaffirmed his support of antidiscrimination legislation for gays.

Barbagelata furnished *The Advocate* with a copy of the archbishop's letter. It carried the letterhead of the Archdiocese of San Francisco and is signed "Joseph T. McGucken, Archbishop of San Francisco."

It reads as follows:

"In answer to your inquiry of this date as to whether I approved the motion passed by the Archdiocesan Commission on April 21, 1971—namely, 'The Commission on Social Justice urges the addition of the category "sexual orientation" to the San Francisco City and County anti-employment discrimination ordinance'—may I inform you that I did not approve this motion."

Proposed in 1969

The antidiscrimination legislation was proposed to the city's Human Rights Commission in the fall of 1969 by Larry Littlejohn, then president of SIR; Del Martin, then with the Daughters of Bilitis; and the National Organization for Women.

Although the commission's employment committee recommended no action, the commission as a whole voted after a heated session the following March 12 to endorse the legislation for passage by the board of supervisors.

The board, however, took no action until Foster, SIR's political committee chairman, successfully urged Feinstein to formally introduce an amendment to the administrative code.

In addition to Feinstein, who was then board president, and Gonzales, supervisors Terry A. Francois and Robert Mendelsohn endorsed the amendment.

The board's social services committee held public hearings but wound up tabling the amendment. There the matter rested, despite expressions of support from clergymen and others, until Feinstein revived the measure this spring.

Although the measure will not apply to firms not doing business with the city and county, Foster said that what he thought "is important here is that we have firmly established the principle that employment discrimination will not be based on sex or sexual orientation.

"We have gotten ourselves an implement, or a tool, to go after bigger fish. If the City of San Francisco can do it, why can't the state of California do it? If the state does it through the Fair Employment Practices Commission, why can't the federal government do it?"

THESE COPS ARE GAY AND PROUD

May 9, 1973

NEW YORK CITY—As citizens, most gays probably regard police as necessary to an orderly society, but as homosexuals practicing their own lifestyle, many come to regard cops as their natural enemies. There is no doubt about that there are gay policemen, but how many can be open about it?

In the light of all this, a recent development on the New York police force has to be nothing short of a mind-blower.

Since early January, two up-front gay men from Brooklyn Heights have been serving their neighborhoods two or three nights each week as auxiliary policemen. They wear uniforms, carry nightsticks and handcuffs, patrol, direct traffic, and do everything regular police do except carry pistols. (Auxiliary police are not armed in New York City.)

One of the two gay auxiliaries, 30-year old Jerry Hoppe, said a friend they met on patrol "told me we so wrecked his mind that he couldn't think for two days. Another person we ran into the Promenade literally could not talk to us. Fifteen minutes later, walking back, the only thing he could say was, 'Oh, my God, I don't believe you; oh, my God. I don't believe you.'"

Auxiliary police—citizen volunteers doing their bit to combat burgeoning crime—are becoming a familiar part of the American scene. They help ease the manpower bind faced by many police departments without a corresponding drain on the city budget, since auxiliaries usually serve—as in New York—without pay. Often they must furnish their own uniforms and—where allowed—weapons. In New York uniforms are provided by the department, but the volunteer has to buy his own badge for $5.

Auxiliaries are sometimes resented by regular officers to the point where they find themselves subjected to harassment and even arrest, according to a recent *Wall Street Journal* survey. But other regular officers accept and welcome the auxiliaries, and more and more police departments are organizing such adjuncts.

Service as an auxiliary is often a stepping stone to the regular force, a fact that adds significance to the acceptance of the two Brooklyn Heights men. Most of the opposition to Intro 475, the gay rights bill so long stalled in a city council committee, has centered on whether homosexuals should be allowed to become teachers, firemen, and policemen.

The beachhead in Brooklyn Heights is a small one, and there is enough potential opposition in the department to make one of the two gay men reluctant to accept publicity at this stage of the game. He agreed to allow use in this story only of his last name and the academic label "Dr." to which he is entitled.

However, police officials meeting with representatives of the New York Mattachine and Gay Activists Alliance in City Hall on February 22 reportedly pledged that the department "would not discriminate" against a known gay applicant to the regular force "provided he passed the physical and civil service tests." No gay applicants to the regular force have made themselves known, but two other gays are currently in training as auxiliaries.

The first of the gay men to join the auxiliaries in Brooklyn Heights was "Dr. Jarman." A six-foot, 180-pound 31-year-old, he first came into contact with police officers at the 84th Precinct station at 72 Poplar St. while serving as chairman of the community relations committee of the Gay Alliance of Brooklyn.

"We were planning a dance at Spenser Memorial Church," he recalls. "We were going to serve beer, and many people kept telling us we needed a license. We know we couldn't possibly get it in the time allowed.

"I went in and talked to Patrolman Murphy, the 84th Precinct's community relations officer. I explained the situation, gave him an idea what the movement was about, the character of the people involved, and the names of our committee chairmen—we had no officers at the time—some of whom he already knew."

Jarman said he told Murphy that GAB had heard some straight people might harass the dance. Murphy "told us to go ahead, called in some other officers and told them to be aware, to keep alert, to keep a lookout. He then gave us a phone number to call in case people did come in and harass us."

This was at a time when the Daughters of Bilitis center in the East Village was being harassed by police, Jarman noted. "Their dances had been raided and some members taken to jail for serving beer at their social functions."

"We didn't intend to put up with that kind of trouble," he added. "I belong to the local Democratic organization, the West Brooklyn Independent Democrats, and I am an officer of the Township Association, a nonpartisan community group seeking to have Brooklyn Heights incorporated as a separate entity in New York City. Other members of GAB belonged to the Brooklyn Heights Trade Association, the Rotary Club, various churches, and so on. We felt that we could therefore raise pressure in the community if we were hassled.

"But we weren't hassled that night," he said with a smile. "The police came by to make sure everything was all right, told us they would be riding around the block, and if we needed their help, to call on them. We felt we had been treated well.

"Patrolman Murphy called in late summer to inquire about the general attitude of gay people toward their local police department. Some gay community people had complained of harassment by straights on the Promenade. There was some hustling and minor drug trafficking there, and one guy had been cut in the neck by some would-be muggers. Because of this, the police would sometimes run people off the Promenade after midnight, saying it was legally closed. Some gays had apparently been offended by this.

"Patrolman Murphy asked if the police were protecting gay people. Were they visible to us when we needed them? Were they sympathetic and understanding when we complained? My response was 'Yes, I feel we have been treated well.'"

Suggested Joining

During the course of their conversation, Murphy suggested to Jarman that he might be interested in joining New York's two-year-old auxiliary police force as an open gay.

Murphy reportedly noted that Mayor John Lindsay had recently issued an executive order banning discrimination against homosexuals in city employment and that Police Commissioner Patrick Murphy and others had been pressing for minority representation in every possible area of the police department.

"If it would work anywhere in New York," Jarman commented, "it would work in Brooklyn Heights."

The next day Jarman went to the 84th Precinct and talked for three hours with patrolman Robert Ferrintino, who coordinates the auxiliary police for that precinct.

Ferrintino, after discovering Jarman taught information science at Polytechnic Institute, was active in numerous community groups, and did not appear to be "antipolice," seemed delighted he had applied.

"Most auxiliary policemen do not have top educational backgrounds," Jarman notes. "I explained to Ferrintino that I thought the auxiliary police was one way the community could exert some control over the regular police department. I think he realized my connections with community groups would get police department spokesmen into organizations which wouldn't ordinarily invite them because of their antipolice prejudices. Finally he asked me to fill out an application.

Thought He Knew

"I assumed all along he had been informed I was gay because it had been suggested to me that I go down and speak to him personally," Jarman recalls.

"One of the questions on the application was 'Why do you want to join the auxiliary police department?'" he continued. "So, I wrote something to the effect that: 'I want to demonstrate that a mature and responsible homosexual is able to work side by side with an institution like the police department, which in the past may have been looked down upon by gays as a persecutor of their lifestyle. I want to demonstrate that a gay person can work with, cooperate and still maintain the dignity of his life-style and respect of his community and the respect of the police department.'

"When he picked up the form and looked at it, he practically fainted," Jarman relates. "He thought I was joking. I told him I wasn't joking, that I was serious. Then he said, 'So what. It's none of my business what you do in your own private life.'

"From that day to this, he has not, in my opinion, treated me differently from any other member of the auxiliary police department. In early January he appointed me to the review board of the 11th District as an out-front gay. The board reviews candidates who apply to become auxiliary policemen. They try to balance the review boards by having one black, one Puerto Rican, one caucasian, and so on. I was asked to play a double role as caucasian and homosexual."

Training Course

Extensive training has become mandatory for auxiliary policemen in most areas. New York City's program consists of a 10-week course, given one night a week for four hours: five weeks of law, one of Red Cross, one in self-defense, one in techniques of handcuffing a suspect, one review session, and finally a test. The instruction is also supplemented monthly by separate seminars.

New York auxiliary policemen are authorized to make arrests but at the present time do not issue summonses or parking tickets. However, this may be changed in the near future. While patrolling, auxiliaries carry walkie-talkies, and the regular officers in patrol cars around the area are alerted that they are on duty.

Armed ambushes on uniformed offices early this year caused Commissioner Murphy to suspend auxiliary officers from patrolling in uniform, fearing they would become targets for snipers, but this restriction was lifted a few days later.

Keeping an Eye Out

Jarman and Hoppe say they became acutely aware of how closely the regular forces kept an eye out for them while returning home after an evening's patrol.

A woman rushed up saying that someone was attempting to break into a parked automobile around the corner. Hoppe and Jarman dashed around the corner and across the street, where they found an obviously intoxicated man on his knees limply pulling on the locked door of an empty car and mumbling, "Help her out of the car. A woman is in there calling for help. Got to help her out."

"But weren't there 90 seconds," Hoppe relates, "when a patrol car rushed up. They were aware that we were out there frisking a man. Either they saw a couple cops running across the street or someone called them."

Hoppe, 30 years old, six feet tall, and 180 pounds, is the very image of a neighborhood policeman. A production coordinator for a heavy industrial equipment manufacturer, he joined the auxiliary police at Jarman's suggestion. Sometime the two end up patrolling together.

"While patrolling," Hoppe said, "if we meet someone we know, we say, 'Hi, how are you?'

If someone we know is on the other side of the street, we might even cross over to say hello."

Some Just Laugh

While a frequent reaction has been shock and disbelief, some of his friends just laugh, Hoppe says. "They've seen me here, they've seen me there. They've seen me doing this, they've seen me doing the other things. And then to see me in uniform, they think it's hilarious at first."

Jarman says it is usually Hoppe's friends who react that way, and that such reactions are rare. He finds such an attitude offensive and recalls nearly arresting someone for harassment when that person continued to behave in a way that Jarman felt did not reflect proper respect for the uniform.

Jarman lives with a lover and meets fewer people than Hoppe, who is an extrovert and more of a partygoer.

"I am very straight except for the fact that I like guys," Jarman says. He thinks this is why people usually react differently to him as a cop than they do to Hoppe.

"People who know me, straight and gay, are hostile," he says with a trace of resentment. "I think they feel I am some sort of traitor. Some won't even speak to me when I am in uniform."

And yet, he says, "I'm openly gay at the university where I work. I'm the representative from my department to the American Association of University Professors and have fought for our contract to ban discrimination against sexual orientation.

"I've been supported, defended, encouraged, loved, and respected by my colleagues," he reflects, "until the day I brought Patrolman Ferrintino over and let it be known now I was an officer. Then I got a lot of hostility from everyone."

Some of the comments he has received, he says, include: "Anybody who wears a uniform and loves guns is a masochist or a sadist at heart." "You really want to have authority and lord it over people." "You really have a fetish for uniforms."

Reactions of regular police officers, Jarman and Hoppe agree, range from naive lack of awareness to friendly or humorous acceptance.

During training, they said, all sections of the law had been explained in great detail until the instructor came to the section titled, "Misdemeanor to loiter for lewd or lascivious behavior." They he tried to pass over it very quickly.

But Jarman spotted the word "pervert" in the notes and asked what it was supposed to mean. "What is a pervert?" he pressed. "What does 'lewd behavior' mean? What does it mean, 'propositioning'? How can we tell what that means?"

There was total silence in the room, he recalls. "Everyone knew exactly what I was trying to get at. I forget exactly what he [the instructor] answered. It was something like, 'When a man is after another man and he tries to make him.' Something crazy like that. And he looked at me as if to say,

'You know damn well what I mean.' But he was trying so desperately hard not to be offensive. He was fully aware that we were gay."

New York City has 5,000 auxiliary policemen. But the 84th Precinct in Brooklyn Heights was one of the last to organize an auxiliary force, and even now it has only about 30 auxiliary officers.

"That's because it is a liberal community," says Jarman, "which is not antigay but *is* anticop. The Heights lacks large numbers of blacks and Puerto Ricans, also—the two groups which have been most attracted to the auxiliary police."

One of Hoppe's duties, especially, has helped give him an idea of the reaction of the regulars in the 84th Precinct to him and Jarman.

"Our duties vary," he explained, "although we mainly patrol. But I've worked the switchboard, where we're in touch with all the patrol cars in the precinct. It's not like working an office switchboard. You have to make decisions like which calls to answer first. And in doing that, we've gotten compliments from lieutenants on down."

"I think the 84th Precinct has the most unusual group of cops in the city," Jarman adds. "Many of them are well-educated. Most of them are on the liberal side. Maybe that's why they're there. I don't know."

He says he's never had an unpleasant incident and that contacts with other officers, regular or auxiliary, have always been cordial, friendly, and cooperative.

"There's a spirit of the people who wear blue," Jarman says. "I see it. I don't care if you're auxiliary or regular. We belong to the police department. We're their fellows, and they take care of their fellows."

Jarman and Hoppe both want to rise in the ranks of the force. They put it two or three nights weekly, double the requirement of auxiliaries of one night's service weekly. Jarman had his eye on sergeant, but it may be several months before he can complete the required training.

But both want to continue participating in the community by taking patrol duty, which would limit how high they can go. When he reached the rank of lieutenant, an officer becomes almost a full-time administrator.

They note that numerous candidates for political office are proposing that the auxiliary police be expanded to aid more directly in the city's war on crime. Many have proposed paying the auxiliaries hourly wages. Congressman Ed Koch (D-N.Y.) has proposed expanding the auxiliary force on a one-to-one ratio with the regular force, which would give the city 32,000 auxiliaries.

Jarman was asked if he might be tempted to give up his university position to become a career police officer.

"No, I wouldn't," he replied. "Teaching is my life."

"A PART OF OUR SOULS WAS IGNITED..."

by Martin St. John

August 1, 1973

In a rare show of national gay togetherness, memorial services were conducted throughout the United States the weekend after the holocaust at the Up Stairs bar in New Orleans.

Ironically, the closest thing to a nationwide gay observance heretofore was the celebration in many cities of Gay Pride Day the last Sunday in June, the day the tragedy occurred.

Gay historian Jim Kepner, speaking at the Los Angeles service, expressed what seemed to be a common feeling among the mourners everywhere when he said, "Inescapably, for each of us, a part of our souls was ignited, and a part charred, in the Up Stairs bar last Sunday..." He then went on to rebuke the millions of gays who ignored the services, "to whom this awful massacre seems no more personal than any news report of anonymous peasants dead in China of flood or famine."

Most of the services were conducted on Sunday, July 1—which gay leaders had sought to designate as a national day of mourning—in San Francisco, Los Angeles, New York, San Diego, and in New Orleans.

Some 500 persons crowded into the San Francisco Metropolitan Community Church. Over 400 attended Los Angeles MCC services, 250 mourners turned out in New Orleans. Some 125 were at an ecumenical service in New York, and 120 attended San Diego MCC services.

In San Francisco gay political activist Jim Foster—a director of three organizations—was guest speaker. He said that his sense of outrage was not directed so much at the people responsible for the fire as it was "toward the climate of ignorance, hate, and fear that exists in this country that allows this kind of thing to happen."

"A memorial service," he asserted, "is not as important as a living memorial—a determination that we must go out of this church tonight and work to end arbitrary, discriminatory law enforcement and to establish more viable social service opportunities for our less fortunate brothers and sisters."

Foster urged all to "determine that the sacrifice in New Orleans is met with our own sacrifice in terms of time, effort, and money."

The Rev. James Sandmire, who conducted the service, said, "Many people are oppressed, but we are the only group that is oppressed because we want to love."

He said that for 2,000 years, homosexuals have been called "sinful" and "sick" and that this has caused people to "look upon us as lonely, alienated, emotionally immature, and mentally unbalanced.... Those who died in the New Orleans fire were simply eating and drinking together in a spirit of fellowship. They were people relating to one another."

The entire congregation then joined hands over their heads for the popular MCC hymn, "I Am Not Afraid Anymore."

Also at the service were San Francisco sheriff Richard Hongisto and John Molinari, a member of the board of Supervisors.

Hongisto later expressed his concern to *The Advocate* that all of the fires at gay places in the past year be properly evaluated. "I believe that there should be a close evaluation of the circumstances surrounding all of these fires to determine who is responsible and whether or not they are related."

The crowd in San Francisco was considerably swelled by other Northern California MCC members and clergy.

In Los Angeles over 400 jammed into the parking lot at the HELP Center for a memorial service.

The service started with a prayer by the Rev. June Norris, associate pastor of Los Angeles MCC.

Jerry Small, vice president of Beth Chayim Chadashim, a Metropolitan Community Temple, then read the traditional Jewish Prayer of Mourning, in the original Aramaic.

This was followed by a choral offering from the choir, "Peace, Be Still."

Deacon Bill Thorne of Los Angeles MCC read a passage from the New Testament, and Morris Kight, president of the board of the Los Angeles Gay Community Services Center, addressed the group on "A Sense of Community Through Love."

The Rev. Lee Carlton, pastor-elect of Los Angeles MCC, gave a condolence address, followed by speakers from throughout the community. These included the Most Rev. Mikhail Francis Itkin, C.L.C; Rick Reyes, Greater Liberated Chicanos; James Kepner, president of ONE Inc.; Jeanne Cordova, staff coordinator, the *Lesbian Tide;* Maxine Feldman, gay feminist singer; Mina Robinson, director emeritus, GCSC; and Dr. Evelyn Hooker, clinical psychologist.

The Rev. Troy Perry, just returned from New Orleans, who had earlier broken into tears at the sight of the familiar faces at the service, delivered the memorial address.

Filmmaker Pat Rocco then sang what is believed to be the last song shared by the group at the Up Stairs before the fire—"United We Stand," which was their customary closing song.

A weeping Kight and Mr. Perry then joined in lighting 30 votive candles—one for each person killed in New Orleans.

The congregation then sang "We Shall Overcome" before communion.

Father Itkin, bishop-abbot of the Evangelical Catholic Communion: Community of the Love of Christ, called for the creation of a society where such a disaster as happened in New Orleans would not be repeated.

"Our brothers and our sisters, whose tragic deaths we mourn tonight, must not be allowed to have died in vain. To simply mourn them this night and then forget the struggle is not only to betray their memory, but also to betray ourselves and the faith we claim to profess..." he asserted.

"In closing," Itkin said, "I'd like to again quote from Joe Hill, a union organizer martyred by the state of Utah. In his will, the closing words are: 'Don't mourn—organize.'"

Reyes issued a call for compassion and understanding, for love and brotherhood.

"New, Terrible Witch-burning"

Kepner, after blasting what he called the apathy of most gays towards the New Orleans tragedy, went on to say this:

"We—each of us—knew those who became faggots for a new and terrible witch-burning. We knew those who met their deaths piled promiscuously in such a hopeless mass of flesh that individual identification was near impossible, knew them through the universality of the gay experience," he said.

"Inescapably," Kepner asserted, "for each of us, a part of our souls was ignited, and a part charred, in the Up Stairs bar last Sunday, as those 29 bodies were so mangled together as to become one flash, one angry flame of revolutionary love, which no fire department will ever extinguish, nor any newspaper blackout ever hide from public view, though it may take us a year—as with Watergate—to bring it to full public attention."

"We have still only half learned that liberation is more than the right to have drag balls and consentual adult sex. We are only barely learning—and in that, Up Stairs bar was far ahead of other New Orleans bars—that gay love is a wider, deeper commitment than the mere search for sex thrills and partners. And we must find ways to live as those 29 died—forged so closely together in the flames of our shared oppression and our love that no man can put us asunder...."

"If their death does for nothing, then it will have been our souls that were charred beyond recovery in that barroom inferno," Kepner concluded.

Cordova called for the New Orleans dead to be remembered, along with other gay martyrs, each year on the anniversary of the fire—Gay Pride Day.

Maxine Feldman sang "Angry Athis," her gay folk song, which declares, "I hate not being able to hold my lover's hand, except under some dimly lit table, afraid of being who I am."

"Our Worst Fears"

Robinson followed, reading a poem, "New Orleans, 1973," by her companion, Sharon Raphael, which declared, "Our worst fears can come true, that we can die in any circumstance, at any moment, as prisoners of the dark, and as seekers after liberation. Let us not forget what we might best remember: That we, too, are the survivors of New Orleans: of our worst fears and greatest dreams."

She also read a poem by Lenore Kandel, "First, They Slaughtered the Angels."

Hooker read, "Do Not Go Gentle into That Good Night," a poem in villanelle form by the late Dylan Thomas, whose lines of repetition are: "Do not go gentle into that good night," and "Rage, rage against the dying of the light."

In New Orleans 250 persons—including persons who had escaped from the fire or been slightly injured in it—turned out for the memorial service held July 1 at St. Mark's United Methodist Church.

The Rev. Paul Breton, Northeast District coordinator for the MCC Fellowship, started the service with a prayer, followed by a reading of "a whole list of telegrams from all over the country and London, England," by Lucian Baril, worship coordinator for the New Orleans MCC.

Morty Manford, special delegate to New Orleans from the New York Gay Activists Alliance, expressed condolences on behalf of the national gay community.

Perry preached the eulogy, the central theme of which was developed around "United We Stand," which the congregation sang after prayer.

Manford, following the prayer, told the mourners that "the church calls us sinners, psychiatrists say we're sick, the police call us criminals, the capitalists call us subversive, and the communists say we're decadent."

During the final hymn, Perry interrupted the organist to announce that cameras from local television stations and The [New Orleans] Times-Picayune were waiting outside, and a side exit was available.

"Nobody went out the side door," Breton noted.

In New York the Church of the Beloved Disciple held a memorial service, conducted by the Right Rev. Robert M. Clement, its pastor, as part of its regular Sunday service. The parish also donated $25 from its own funds, Father Clement said, upon hearing the news of the fire.

The evening service of New York Metropolitan Community Church was given over to an ecumenical service.

The Rev. Roy Birchard, MCC pastor: the Rev. Howard Well, assistant MCC pastor; the Rev. Robert Carter of Dignity; and Clement conducted the memorial service.

A member of the Gay Synagogue in New York delivered a prayer at the service, Clement said.

Brother Kristian Caron delivered a message of condolence from the Church of the Holy Apostles, an Episcopal church which works closely with the gay community.

Susan Day, a local activist, delivered another message of condolence, calling for the memory of the New Orleans victims to be kept alive, and Jay Friend, a member of the Metropolitan Gay Community Council, delivered an appeal for blood and money for the victims.

Over $300 was raised for the fire fund, Clement said.

Freedom

In San Diego the service was conducted by the Rev. John Hose, vice moderator of the MCC Fellowship, as part of the regular Sunday evening service of the MCC there. The theme of the service was "Freedom."

Mr. Hose said $40 was taken up in a "love offering" for the New Orleans victims.

In Long Beach, Calif., some 110 persons attended a memorial service July 1, according to the pastor, the Rev. Robert Cunningham. A member of the church, Hugh Cooley, was among those who died in the fire, Cunningham said.

Across the nation in Miami, three MCC memorial services were conducted—one just after the fire on June 25 and two on July 1. Sixty attended the first service, conducted by the Rev. Herb Hunt, an MCC exhorter, and 45 attended an evening service July 1.

Media Response

Crouch reported that the media in Miami had been very active in its support of the memorial effort. "We had the story all day Sunday on two of our television stations, both of our papers, and three of our radio stations."

As a result, he said, three heterosexual churches, not connected with MCC, "have donated blood and sent 25 pints each to the victims."

He said the services were very simple, with a flower-decked altar, and over $916 was collected for the memorial fund.

In Washington, D.C., 100 turned out for the memorial services mid afternoon on July 1.

The service was conducted by "Brother John," the pastor of the Washington MCC, who was joined by the Rev. William Moremen, the pastor of the First Congregational Church, where MCC holds its services, and the Rev. Walter Ziffer, pastor of Concordia United Church of Christ.

The Rev. Rick Weatherlee, assistant MCC pastor, said a cross section of the gay community had attended the service. "We managed to get bar owners, drag groups, bike club members, and all sorts of people there," he said.

The service's offering resulted in $207 for the memorial fund, Mr. Weatherlee said.

In Boston, the Rev. Larry Bernier, pastor of the Boston MCC, was joined by the Rev. Don McGaw, the Rev. Nancy Wilson, and the Rev. Penny Perrault, all of the Boston MCC.

Perrault reported that the memorial service started "with a mourning theme, with a death theme, and then finished up with a resurrection theme."

Fifty-five persons turned out for a June 30 service, she said, and the Sunday regular service July 1 was also conducted as a memorial service.

In Salt Lake City the Rev. Richard Groh, pastor of the MCC, and Virgil Scott, chairman of the board of deacons, conducted the memorial service July 1.

God's Plan

Groh said that the service centered around "expressing our loss, but our faith in God that the church would rise again, that there are no mistakes or accidents in God's master plan.

"We believe this," he said. "We believe that if this has happened, if God has allowed it to happen, then he's going to bless us for it in some way. We did take a memorial offering that amounted to $214."

"Approximately 40 people" turned out for the service, he said.

At the Denver Metropolitan Community Church—no longer a member of the Universal Fellowship—the Rev. Ron Carnes and the Rev. Robert Darst conducted a memorial service during the regular Sunday evening worship service July 1.

Some 80 persons attended the service. The Denver church reported that its deacons were collecting a memorial offering for the New Orleans victims.

In Milwaukee, where an MCC mission has been discontinued, about 65 persons attended a July 1 service at the Church for All People, conducted by the Rev. Bill Parish, pastor of the church, and the Rev. Wilbur Cain, a Lutheran minister and a leader of the Council on Religion and the Homosexual in Milwaukee.

In Sacramento the Rev. Bob Wolfe conducted an MCC memorial service June 27, attended by 40 people, according to the Rev. Freda Smith, assistant pastor of the Sacramento MCC.

She said the theme of the service was "that we don't understand everything," but "we are so grateful that the people [who died] were with us for a while, and we praised God for the fact that we'd had them and they were part of us all growing together."

NEW ORLEANS TOLL 32; ARSON EVIDENCE CITED

by Bill Rushton

August 1, 1973

NEW ORLEANS—With the death toll in the Up Stairs bar fire up to 32, new evidence of arson has been unofficially reported here, but authorities continue to be tight-lipped. Several persons have been questioned in connection with the fire, but there were no suspects in custody as of July 12.

General community reaction to the tragedy has continued to range from mild hostility to total apathy, but on a more positive note, a new gay activist group has been formed.

The last deaths in the blaze were those of Larry Stratton, 24, and Luther Boggs, 47. Both died in Charity Hospital, Stratton July 12 and Boggs July 10. The others perished at the time of the blaze.

Four bodies remained unidentified as of July 12.

Among the confirmed deaths was that of George C. "Mitch" Mitchell, 36, a Metropolitan Community Church exhorter and former assistant pastor, who escaped from the burning building and then fought off firemen to reenter it in an effort to rescue his lover, Horace Broussard, 26. His body was found over Broussard's.

Eight persons remained hospitalized, five in "grave" condition, two in "critical" condition, and one in "serious" condition.

The arson evidence came from sources close to the management of the Up Stairs, who now say that a can of Ronson lighter fluid was found in the stairwell of the bar after the fire. The report would seem to back up eyewitness accounts of fire being seen on the bottom three steps of the stairway moments before the building erupted in flames.

Fire department spokesmen expressed initial surprise at the report, saying that evidence of that nature has not been officially determined.

It is possible that some evidence in the case is being kept confidential, however, and a spokesman insisted that as large or larger an effort is being devoted to this case compared with the Ralt Center fire disaster, which preceded it.

High-Level Silence

Meanwhile, there was a strange silence on the part of the city's leadership. At City Hall the Human Relations Committee said it had sent a private note to the chief of police deploring public remarks attributed by the press to Maj. Henry Morris, chief of detectives of the New Orleans police department.

Morris was quoted as calling the Up Stairs a "hangout for thieves and homosexuals." A police spokesman later said that the attribution was false, but apologized to gay leaders anyway.

No plans for a public statement have been made, said a spokesman for the rights unit, and no representatives had been sent to either of two memorial services held for the victims of the fire the week before.

Churches Also Silent

The local Roman Catholic archdiocesan human relations committee said that it had seen no reason to issue any sort of statement on the matter and had no plans to issue one now.

The Roman Catholic archbishop of New Orleans also has issued no statement and had no explanation to offer.

The priest who answered the chancellery office's telephone let long pauses of silence separate our questions and made no real reply to any of them—all this despite the fact that at least one Catholic—an ex-Jesuit scholastic from New Orleans' Loyola University—had been one of the 32 people now dead as a result of the fire.

Only one spokesman from the Protestant clergy stepped forward to join the mourners. That was the Rev. Finis Crutchfield, the Methodist bishop of Louisiana, who personally authorized memorial services at St. Mark's Methodist Community Center on North Rampart Street the Sunday following the blaze (July 1) and stayed there to attend services with the pastor of the church.

Services were held at St. Mark's after several churches refused to permit the use of their facilities.

The Metropolitan Community Church of Greater New Orleans declined to identify the refusing churches to newsmen and would only praise Bishop Crutchfield.

There were other reports, however, that the Episcopal bishop of Louisiana had ordered the services not to be held in any of the Episcopal churches approached.

Other public officials reacting—or not reacting—to the blaze included the governor's office, which declined to make a statement, and New Orleans mayor Moon Landrieu.

Just back in town from Europe and holding his first press conference July 11, Landrieu said that he considered any loss of life a problem for the city. As for the subdued nature of community reaction to the "homosexual" angle of the tragedy, Landrieu said, "I'm just as much concerned about that life as any other life" and "I'm not aware of any lack of concern in this community over the loss of those lives."

Individual Expressions of Concern

Despite the silences, however, a number of positive, largely individual expressions of concern have begun to surface.

Visitors to New Orleans's Charity Hospital the night of the fire were greeted by an entire emergency wing cleared out for their convenience.

The social worker at the hospital who arranged for the space also persuaded the dietary department to provide coffee.

The police officers and staff involved in the "dispassionate" handling of the emergency were absolutely "noncondemnatory," she said.

The principal problems came from hysterical parents suffering from poor communications with reclusive sons, whom the parents feared might be among the victims of the blaze.

The coroner's office had 12 "possibilities" still left July 12 on the list of "candidates" for bodies number 13, 18, 23, and 28, most of them phoned in from wives and parents as far away as California and Michigan.

One of the largest floral arrangements sent to St. Mark's for the service had been hand-wired by French Quarter flower vendor Jo Ann Clevenger, who also operates several "straight" bars in the Quarter.

The Young Democrats at the Louisiana State University branch in New Orleans issued a statement supporting the national day of mourning called by gay leaders July 1 and urged "complete rewriting and enforcement of state and local fire codes."

The Up Stairs Players, a group of actors who had been meeting and performing at the Up Stairs prior to the tragedy, have been invited by the Salt and Pepper Lounge, a "straight" bar, to present a Crippled Children's Hospital benefit show originally scheduled for June 30 at the Up Stairs.

Perhaps the most significant development has been the founding of a Gay People's Coalition (GPC) with its second meeting July 10.

Several committees, contact persons, and telephone numbers for gay services have been announced.

A listing in the New Orleans telephone directory under the title "Gay Switchboard' has been approved by South Central Bell Telephone Co. and will be announced shortly.

Committees also are being formed to work with city agencies, media, legal problems, gay parents, and other problems, and full committee reports will be published soon in a French Quarter community newsletter.

Yet there still remains considerable paranoia on the streets, fed by the following ugly incidents:

• Almost as soon as some people began placing flowers at the door of the Up Stairs the Monday after the blaze, some other people began removing them.

One man, seeing this, didn't like it and stood guard by the door, telling people to leave the flowers alone.

• The first Saturday night in the French Quarter after the fire, uniformed and plainclothes police officers were placed outside three gay bars that had received threatening phone calls. The calls materialized in the aftermath of crank calls phoned in to local television stations and reported to the public on only one of them.

Patrons of the guarded bars subsequently reported that the police harassed them. The crowds in the bars were generally one third to one half their usual Saturday night size.

• Meanwhile, in front of the candle- and flower-strewn "People's Shrine" at the Up Stairs entrance, a woman watering the flowers was arrested by police for "obscenity against a police officer" after failure to "move on."

The following Monday afternoon her case came before civil district court and was dismissed because arresting officers failed to appear.

No Morals Arrest

Police have made no arrests on any "homosexual" or other "morals" charges in New Orleans in the last two years, and none of their records comment on alleged clientele of nightspots where arrests are made.

Sgt. Frank Hayward, police information officer, says the department has no record of any arrests at the Up Stairs—for thievery or anything else.

Community trust in the police department, however, has not been aided by the Up Stairs incident and the subsequent lack of any new official developments in its quietly proceeding investigation.

Some complaints have been made, for instance, about a group of "thugs" from the 100 block of Royal Street, near the Up Stairs, led by a man identified only as "Chucky," who reportedly went through the Quarter collecting "donations" for the fire victims and then pocketing the proceeds.

Those reports were not being forwarded to the police because of fear of reprisal from the thugs and for fear of inaction on the matter by the police, complainants said.

But the worst case of paranoia of all came from initial reports that were later determined to be untrue that four of the 32 dead had been secretly buried in a local pauper's cemetery.

The New Orleans Parish coroner's office produced the names of the four paupers buried in the cemetery and the bodies of the victims remaining in order to disprove the reports.

SICK NO MORE

January 16, 1974

WASHINGTON, D.C.—The 20 million homosexuals in the United States achieved a sort of instant "cure" as the American Psychiatric Association removed homosexuality from its list of psychiatric disorders.

The action came December 15 in a 13–0 vote of the association's board of trustees, meeting at its headquarters here. Two members abstained, and four were not present at the time of the vote.

The board also passed a resolution urging repeal of all state and local sodomy laws and deploring discrimination against gays.

Dr. Robert L. Spitzer, a member of the APA's Task Force on Nomenclature, said homosexuality was removed because the APA decided it does not fit the two criteria of mental disorder: that it either "regularly cause emotional distress or regularly be associated with generalized impairment of social functioning."

Sexual Orientation Disturbance

In place of homosexuality as such, the APA inserted a newly defined disorder, which it labeled "sexual orientation disturbance."

This was defined as follows: "This category is for individuals whose sexual interests are directed primarily toward people of the same sex and who are either disturbed by, in conflict with, or wish to change their sexual orientation. This diagnostic category is distinguished from homosexuality, which by itself does not necessarily constitute a psychiatric disorder. Homosexuality per se is one form of sexual behavior and, like other forms of sexual behavior which are not by themselves psychiatric disorders, is not listed in this nomenclature of mental disorders."

Spitzer, who drafted the two resolutions adopted by the board, said the statements did not mean the APA feels homosexuality is "normal" nor that it is "as desirable as heterosexuality."

"Many people will interpret this to mean we're saying it's normal," he noted. "We're not saying that; we're also not saying it's abnormal. The terms normal and abnormal are not really psychiatric terms."

Historic Step

Leaders of several gay organizations noted the limitations of the APA move but nonetheless hailed it as an historic step.

"We have won the ball game," announced Ronald Gold of New York, who helped spur the APA to action by cornering Spitzer and convincing him to reconsider his own attitude toward homosexuality. "No longer can gay people grow up thinking they're sick. They know they're not, and now finally the American Psychiatric Association has agreed with us."

Although several other professional organizations have in recent years adopted policies that homosexuality is not sick, the psychiatrists' association was the most important nut to crack. The APA nomenclature is generally regarded as the official definition of mental disorders.

Frank Kameny, head of the Mattachine Society of Washington, who for years did battle with psychiatrists over their nomenclature, termed it "one of the major bulwarks of support of the patterns of discrimination" in such fields as criminal law, civil service employment and private employment, the armed forces, and security clearance systems.

Spitzer himself acknowledged this in his position paper outlining the reasons for the change. "We will be removing one of the justifications for the denial of civil rights to individuals whose only crime is that their sexual orientation is to members of the same sex. In the past, homosexuals have been denied civil rights in many areas of life on the ground that because they suffer from a 'mental illness,' the burden of proof is on them to demonstrate their competence, reliability, or mental stability."

Dr. Alfred M. Freedman, president of the APA, who made the announcement of the change at a press conference, said it is also likely to have effects in the training of new psychiatrists. Pressure within the profession that has kept "a sizable group of homosexual psychiatrists" in the closet should begin to disappear, he said.

Gay leaders, holding their own press conference in APA headquarters immediately after the APA officials ended theirs, generally agreed that the APA was simply recognizing what many gays have known all along—that gays can be as happy and healthy as anybody.

"I don't feel any healthier today than I did yesterday," said Jean O'Leary of Lesbian Feminist Liberation in New York. "But," she added, "I realize this is an historic decision that will have a lot of implications for society, especially, as far as I'm concerned, for lesbian mothers who will no longer be judged unfit mothers on the basis of their homosexuality."

Tom Smith, a member of the National Gay Task Force in New York who works with city agencies to help provide social services to gays, said his job would be a bit easier now. He also noted that the move would encourage black gays like himself to be as proud of their gayness as they are of their blackness.

Barbara Gittings, head of the task force on homosexuality of the American Library Association, noted that the APA did not act until it felt the pressure of organized gays. "If we had left it up to the APA to come up with something like this, it would have taken at least another 30 or 40 years," she commented.

Only for Gays

Several gays objected to the fact that the new category, "sexual orientation disturbance," applies only to homosexuals who are bothered by their orientation. One of the newsmen at the press conference, William Hines of the *Chicago Sun-Times,* pressed Freedman about that.

Hines: "Is there a similar category that might be called sexual orientation disturbance—heterosexuality? What if somebody's uptight about being heterosexual? He needs some help, too, right?"

Freedman: "There is no such category at the present time."

Hines: "Why?"

Freedman: [*Long pause*] "Uh…the…uh…for those categories the…uh…specific disturbances would be the primary diagnosis… We look upon this as a developing and changing conceptualization of what has heretofore been an ambiguous area, and this is one step that has been taken in this direction. That further changes may take place as we gain further knowledge in these areas, I think, is to be expected."

Call for Law Changes

The APA's call for repeal of sodomy laws and for enactment of gay civil rights laws was considered just as important as the change in the nomenclature.

Dr. Howard J. Brown, former New York City health commissioner and now chairman of the National Gay Task Force, commented, "This is tremendously important. As we who are activists go to state legislatures and the Congress, or to city councils, or as we go to the courts, we are going to have the various health organizations joining with us as advocates. We'll have the psychiatric association, the American Medical Association, and most public health organizations."

Three Parts

The "Position Statement on Homosexuality and Civil Rights," which the board adopted unanimously with one abstention, has three parts:

(1) It "deplores all public and private discrimination against homosexuals in such areas as employment, housing, public accommodation, and licensing," and urges that "no burden of proof of...judgment, capacity or reliability...be placed upon homosexuals greater than that imposed on any other persons."

(2) It "supports and urges the enactment of civil rights legislation at the local, state, and federal levels that would offer homosexual citizens the same protections now guaranteed to others on the basis of race, creed, color, etc."

(3) Finally, it "supports and urges the repeal of all discriminatory legislation singling out homosexual acts by consenting adults in private."

Illinois, Colorado, Connecticut, Hawaii, Oregon, and Delaware have already repealed sodomy laws, and similar repeals will take effect this year (1974) in Ohio and in North Dakota in 1975. Five other states are considering repeal, and in New York and Pennsylvania, homosexual behavior has been reduced from a felony to a misdemeanor.

Social Change

The APA's change in nomenclature has it roots in a general softening of social stigmas, APA officials said. Dr. John Spiegel, professor of social psychiatry at Harvard University, noted that homosexuality has always been included in psychiatry's list of disorders for as long as there has been a list, about 80 or 90 years.

Its elimination from the list, he said, brings up "the question of the function of labeling and social control. Society finds ways of controlling behaviors it defines as problems. The original way of controlling homosexuality was to define it as a criminal act." Defining it as a sickness was originally considered an advance, Spiegel said.

Now, he continued, there is a "recognition within the profession that the behavior called homosexuality no longer needs to be defined as a social problem."

APA chairman Freedman also said the dropping of homosexuality arose from progress in the profession. "We have new knowledge and new information and new thinking and these are certainly reflected in a changing field," he commented.

Spitzer, however, said it wasn't just a matter of "new knowledge." In fact, he admitted, psychiatry was "wrong all along" about homosexuality.

In his position paper supporting the change, Spitzer contended: "Clearly homosexuality, per se [by itself], does not meet the requirements for a psychiatric disorder since...many homosexuals are quite satisfied with their sexual orientation and demonstrate no generalized impairment in social effectiveness or functioning.

"The only way that homosexuality could therefore be considered a psychiatric disorder would be the criterion of failure to function heterosexually, which is considered optimal in our society and by many members of the profession.

"However, if failure to function optimally in some important area of life as judged by either society or the profession is sufficient to indicate the presence of a psychiatric disorder, then we will have to add to our nomenclature the following conditions:

"Celibacy (failure to function optimally sexually);

"Revolutionary behavior (irrational defiance of social norms);

"Religious fanaticism (dogmatic and rigid adherence to religious doctrine);

"Racism (irrational hatred of certain groups):

"Vegetarianism (unnatural avoidance of carnivorous behavior):

"Male chauvinism (irrational belief in the inferiority of women)."

Far from being a disorder, Spitzer argued, homosexuality "is one form of sexual behavior. Our profession need not now agree on its origin, significance, and value for human happiness when we acknowledge that by itself it does not meet the requirements for a psychiatric disorder. Similarly, by no longer listing it as a psychiatric disorder we are not saying that it is 'normal' or as valuable as heterosexuality."

Some Opposition

Despite Spitzer's attempts to leave the way open for some psychiatrists to continue to treat homosexuals they feel are "bothered by, in conflict with, or wish to change their sexual orientation," some die-hard homophobes apparently were unhappy with the nomenclature change.

There were reports that Dr. Charles W. Socarides, a New York psychiatrist who is known for his homophobic tendencies, is circulating a petition among APA members in an attempt to bring the nomenclature change up for reconsideration at the APA's general membership meeting in Detroit in May.

Socarides did not respond to several phone messages. It was not known whether he was likely to obtain the needed 200 signatures (the APA has a membership of 20,000).

But Ron Gold of the National Gay Task Force said he was unconcerned. "My comment is, good. The more anybody talks about, the better," Gold said.

"And," he added, "the more absurd it seems for people to vote about whether 20 million people are sick."

WOMEN'S RAGE SPLITS APA PANEL

June 19, 1974

DETROIT—Two separate factions of gay activists came to this convention city to confront members of the American Psychiatric Association and ended up in a confrontation with each other.

The controversy that developed centered around a panel discussion that had been scheduled by the APA as a regular part of the convention program to explore the topic "Homosexuality: Where do we go from here?" It was intended to help provide direction for the psychiatric profession in the aftermath of its nomenclature change on homosexuality.

But a delegation of radical lesbian feminists mounted the stage in mid program, took over the microphones, and apparently brought the direction-finding exercise to a halt with their protest over what they consider sexist considerations toward women.

The originally scheduled panelists were Dr. Robert Spitzer, a New York member of APA's nomenclature committee who has pushed for the policy change; Dr. Richard Pillard, pro-gay psychiatrist from Boston; Bruce Voeller of the National Gay Task Force; Barbara Gittings of Philadelphia, head of the American Library Association Task Force on Homosexuality; and Frank Kameny of Washington's Mattachine Society.

But to the demonstrators who challenged them, Voeller, Gittings, and Kameny represented the professional gay Establishment in somewhat formalized relationships with the APA, while the protesters considered themselves representatives of grassroots gay militancy—especially on behalf of women, who, they argued, were being ignored in the convention program.

The result was a dramatic demonstration of differences between what might be called established gay leaders, on the one hand, and gay activists with a more radical, anti-Establishment perspective, on the other. Many of the psychiatrists for whom the panel was intended were not present to witness the result, since most walked out when the lesbians began their takeover attempt.

The lesbians who attempted the takeover were participants in a gay mental health counterconvention held in Ann Arbor, Mich., the same week as the APA gathering. More than 120 participants in the Ann Arbor conference, both men and women, had agreed to let lesbians speak for them, on the ground that men had traditionally assumed that role in the gay movement, while women had often been relegated to an "invisible" status.

The counterconvention on the campus of the University of Michigan was sponsored by the Gay Awareness Women's Kollective and the Gay Liberation Front of Ann Arbor and attracted participants primarily from the Midwest, though some came from other parts of the country.

A few hours before the start of the scheduled APA panel, delegates from the Ann Arbor conference met with the panel members and demanded that the men withdraw, leaving the panel with Barbara Gittings and four women from the Ann Arbor contingent.

Two of the men, Voeller and Pillard, agreed to withdraw, but the others declined. Panel moderator Dr. Kent Robinson, a psychiatrist from Towson, Md., asked the Ann Arbor representatives to accept a compromise, permitting women to have three of the five seats on the panel.

After a brief caucus, the Ann Arbor participants agreed that three fifths of a loaf was acceptable, as Robinson and Spitzer had forecast that no psychiatrist would remain in the audience if the panel were changed entirely from its original format, but that most would stay if there were only a partial change.

The women from the Ann Arbor conference who had demanded a completely lesbian panel said their motivation was not merely statistical juggling. "Our experience is that if men have an option, they will not listen to us. We can no longer afford to give people the option of ignoring us," they said.

As part of the "compromise," it was agreed that Spitzer and Robinson would contact the APA convention office and attempt to secure a room so that an all-lesbian panel could be presented two nights later.

The originally scheduled gay panel began on time, with Spitzer, Kamen, and Gittings presenting their prepared remarks. Then two of the lesbians from the Ann Arbor conference, Rachel Kamel of Ann Arbor and Joan Nixon of Bloomington, Ind., presented a speech prepared cooperatively by women who had attended the Ann Arbor session.

As they ended their speech, Kamel said, "We've been pretty nice so far. Starting from now, we're defining what happens in this workshop. I want to see all the lesbian sisters up on the stage, right now." Between 20 and 30 lesbians came and stood in a line on the stage behind the speakers' table.

"And as our next move, I want to see these men off the stage," she said. Spitzer and Robinson protested, with Spitzer saying he would not carry out the plan to schedule an all-lesbian panel because "we made an agreement, and you violated it." As Spitzer tried to address the audience, one of the women took the microphone away from him and began singing, "Any woman can be a lesbian."

Audience Protest

A young man from the audience, saying he was in sympathy with the women's aims but disagreed with them as a matter of "revolutionary tactics," urged them not to eject anyone and to "at least let everybody speak."

One of the women replied, "I was ejected from my position, and I'm now jobless because I'm a lesbian. All I'm asking them to do is go out into the hall."

Confronted with demands that he step down, Kameny sat firmly in his place and replied, "I was chosen to be here, I was invited to be here, and I'm going to remain here."

As he spoke, one of the women took the microphone Kameny was using off the table. After a brief but vehement discussion among the women, Nancy Wechsler, a lesbian who was formerly a militant member of the Ann Arbor city council, gave the microphone back to Kameny.

"We accepted a compromise," Wechsler said. "It was a democratic decision that we made as a group of lesbians, and gay men were there. I don't like to see gay people denying other people their civil rights and going against decisions that we made democratically."

Men, Men, Men

At this point most of the nearly 100 psychiatrists in the room had filed out, leaving only a handful of psychiatrists in the room with about 80 gays and 20 or 30 other spectators. When a male psychiatrist took the podium and spoke of the needs of transvestites and sadomasochists without mentioning lesbians. Kamel said she and some of the other lesbians were leaving also. Asked to stay, she replied, "For what? So we can hear men talking to men about men? No, thank you."

"I had hoped that by bringing women up on the stage, we could establish a different kind of interaction, a different tone for this meeting. I had hoped we could start to have people honestly talking to people with the object to learn about lesbianism," she said.

"But I can see that the people here—most of them—are chiefly interested in keeping their rational discussion, keeping their polite discussion, keeping their parliamentary procedure. I can't relate to that any more," Kamel concluded.

Follow-up Rap

Although some of the lesbians left at that point, many others stayed and took part in an open and wide-ranging discussion from the floor. Some of it focused of the action of the lesbians. Voeller said he thought it was "a shame" that the action had caused most of the psychiatrists to leave and that many subjects did not get discussed during the evening. But other comments were addressed to the subject of the panel discussion: What the psychiatrists should be doing now.

Wechsler suggested that psychiatrists should acquaint themselves with gay liberation literature, participate in gay liberation demonstrations if they themselves are gay, refer gay patients to gay counselors "if you don't know what it's like to gay," and give immediate support to patients who tell them they are gay.

In the earlier prepared remarks of the panelists, many other suggestions were made. Among them:
• Kameny urged that homosexuality be taken from under the "magnifying glass" of psychiatric research and that homophobia be put there instead. "Instead of Dr. (Irving) Bieber studying 106 homosexuals and their family backgrounds, let us have studies of 106 homophobes and their family backgrounds. Perhaps we could start with Dr. Bieber and Dr. (Charles) Socarides and 104 others," Kameny said, referring to two psychiatrists well known for their theories that homosexuality is a pathology.
• Several participants, both on the panel and in the audience, suggested that psychiatrists could benefit from contact with gay organizations. Kameny noted that "a whole parallel series of facilities and services" have been started by and for gay people because the psychiatric and medical professions were failing to meet many needs of gay people. He said these facilities "will continue, but that doesn't mean we can't use help from psychiatrists as long as they are acceptable to us."
• There were several suggestions that psychiatrists admit they really don't know too much about homosexuality. Gittings urged the psychiatrists, "You should start phasing yourselves out as authorities on homosexuality. You must start saying, 'My being a doctor does not mean I know about homosexuality.' Better, you should say, 'Psychiatry deals with problems in living, and homosexuality is not a problem.'"

Male-Defined

The speech by the lesbians representing the Ann Arbor conference argued that lesbians and women are "invisible" because they are "given no identity as people. We are constantly told to define ourselves as mistresses, wives, daughter, mothers—all in relation to men."

They contended that "psychiatrists further this isolation and nonidentity by convincing women to adjust to men."

They proposed an alternative "feminist therapy," which, they said, "does not imagine that it can solve women's problems. Rather, it concentrates on helping us to know and understand ourselves, helping us find our strengths, so that we can better fight our oppression."

The lesbians' speech also contained an attack on what they saw as the political power of psychiatrists. "By deciding what is sane and what is pathological, you decide who has civil rights and who does not; who may be employed and who may not; who may love and who may not."

Another dramatic encounter took place several hours before the APA panel, when Frank Kameny visited the open rap session that the Ann Arbor conferees were holding for psychiatrists who wanted to talk with them. Kameny told the radicals he thought the speech prepared by the lesbians, which had been printed and distributed in advance, was concerned mostly with what he considered exclusively women's issues and did not deal primarily with what he considered to be strictly gay issues.

Joint Force

A political chasm soon made itself apparent between Kameny and the radical gay men and women, who asserted that there were important connections between the two movements, and that gay people, both men and women, should concern themselves with both.

"There's no division. This is not the '50s any more," asserted one of the radical men.

"They are still separate issues—'50s, '60s, '70s, or '90s," rejoined Kameny.

The radicals seemed to consider Kameny a representative of a sort of elite Establishment within the gay community. "I find very interesting the ease with which you divert your efforts from fighting the people out there to fighting your own people," Kameny said at one point after he had been under attack for "middle-class attributes" such as wearing a suit and dealing with middle-class professional associations like the APA.

"You're not our people," one of the radicals countered. "You are their lackey."

"Gay Is..."

The Ann Arbor counterconference had as its theme, "Gay is mental health." It featured workshops on why gays are committed to mental hospitals; forms of therapy such as peer counseling; how gays can relate to nongay radical movements; the "politics of drag;" and "the politics of coming out."

There were several workshops for women only, including one on lesbian and feminist action projects around the country and one titled "Radical Feminist Biology and Her-story."

BOY RAPED ON TV SHOW STIRS PROTEST

by David Aiken

September 11, 1974

NEW YORK—*Marcus Welby, M.D.*, the television series which a year and a half ago enraged gays with a segment showing a distressed married man being counseled to suppress his homosexuality in order to "deserve the respect" of his son, has again prepared a show likely to incur gay wrath.

The forthcoming segment is appropriately titled "The Outrage." It tells of a boy who is forcibly raped by his junior high school science teacher. In the original script the boys suffers from inflammation of the intestinal wall, but he is ashamed and refuses to tell who attacked him.

He relents only when relatives convince him that he is still "a man" and need not feel ashamed.

Despite changes by ABC network officials in charge of program standards, gay leaders fear the show will be broadcast this fall with its basic plot intact and that it will reinforce the myth that child molesters are homosexuals.

National Threat

Although filming of the show was completed in early August, no date has yet been announced for its broadcast. Gays in New York and Los Angeles are preparing to call for a nationwide protest demonstration against ABC if changes in the story do not satisfy them.

Ronald Gold, communications director for the National Gay Task Force in New York, has filed a complaint with the Television Code Authority of the National Association of Broadcaster, an industry panel which sets voluntary broadcasting standards.

A line of dialogue assuring the boy's angry father that the attacker was not a homosexual but a "guy with several mental and emotional problems" was written into the script by ABC.

But Gold wrote to the code authority that this should be viewed "in the context of a plot that specifically reinforces false images of gay men as child molesters," and "could in no way prevent 'The Outrage' from being used to defeat civil rights measures now pending in many cities throughout the country."

Script Review

Gold received the script from ABC in early July in compliance with an agreement by all TV networks to submit scripts dealing with homosexuality for comment by the Gay Media Task Force, of which Gold is a member.

Gold said he told Richard Gitter, an executive in the programs and standards office at ABC's New York headquarters, that the script was entirely unacceptable and should not be produced.

After hearing nothing from ABC for two weeks, Gold said, he called back and learned that shooting had already started. He then began phoning gay organizations around the country, asking that they call ABC and protest.

An impasse apparently developed between Gold, who insisted that the show be scuttled, and the network's vice president for programs and standards, Alfred Schneider, who said he would agree to changes but not to canceling the segment.

Cross-Country

Gold then stepped out, and negotiations with ABC were taken over at each end of the continent—in New York by Morty Manford, president of New York's Gay Activists Alliance, and by GAA's press liaison, Maurice Rosen; and in Los Angeles by Morris Kight, a founder of the Gay Community Services Center.

Kight dealt with the producers of the program at Universal Studios in Hollywood, where the show was being filmed, while the New York activists talked with Schneider.

As a result of this two-way pressure, the network ordered several additional changes in script in an attempt to eliminate dialog that overtly conveyed the image of homosexuality.

ABC's Schneider said that in the most important change, "nothing remains" of the section showing attempts to convince the youth that he is still "a man" despite the attack. In its place, he said, is a section dealing with the "emotional problems of how a boy deals with an assault of whatever nature."

Counseling Urged

His parents are advised to have him obtain "counseling" to help him "approach his peers" after "having had something done" to him, Schneider said.

Also eliminated is a scene showing the junior high school teacher picking up another young boy and beginning to seduce him. Instead, other characters allude to the fact that another child has been brought to the hospital with signs of being molested, although they don't specify whether the victim is a boy or a girl, Schneider said.

A number of other small changes have been made in dialogue, including elimination of a line spoken by the boy's father calling the attacker "a pervert" and exclaiming that "they ought to put all those creeps—every last one of them—in jail."

Schneider said that "as far as I'm concerned, we have done everything reasonable and fair under the circumstances." But Manford said he would wait for a screening of the completed film before deciding whether to organize further protests.

Contingency Plans

"If they show it to us and it does not fulfill our worse fears, we'd be willing to hold back action," he said. "If it does fulfill our worst fears, we'll try to talk them out of showing it. If we are unable to talk them out of showing it, we'll prepare to mobilize."

Noting that ABC had not yet confirmed that it would show gays the finished film before it was broadcast, Manford added, "If they refuse to show it to us, then we will feel that they have closed doors to reasonable discussion. At this point our knowledge and sense of the program suggests that it would be devastating to our movement, and we would then mobilize."

Meanwhile, Manford said, he would attempt to "keep the doors open at ABC," and Schneider said he had told Manford that "our doors are open."

Manford noted, however, that Schneider showed him a press release already prepared by ABC which, he said, they were ready to issue "at the first sign of a big stink." In the release, the network points to the changes it has made in the program and claims that the show is not antigay but is "a sensitive handling of a problem faced by many people," Manford said.

Stockton Helffrich, director of the Television Code Authority, said ABC had agreed to show the program to him before it is broadcast. He said he would try to determine whether the program had "a tendency to stereotype" gay people, and "if not, does it think in terms of human dignity as far as the content involved."

He said he had not asked to see the script, because "we don't want to establish the risky business of prior restraint."

NOBLE WINS: FIRST OPEN GAY IN LEGISLATURE

by Allen Young

December 4, 1974

BOSTON—It became official on Election Day: Elaine Noble was chosen by a vote of 1,772 to 1,172 to become the first up-front lesbian state representative in the history of the United States.

Noble's margin of victory over her only opponent, Joseph Cimino, an independent, was comfortable in every precinct, while in the precinct that includes Boston University, she won by a two-to-one ratio.

Pizza was the main item on the menu as Noble's campaign workers, supporters, friends, and neighborhood people gathered on election night for a joyful victory party in the Queensbury Street office of the Committee to Elect Elaine Noble. And as an indicator of the support and good feelings within the Back Bay-Fenway community that chose her, the pizza man down the street *made* the pizza, but since his oven was broken, the pizza man up the street *baked* the pizza.

Noble's supporters were so confident of her victory that they had printed up buttons with the legend I WORKED FOR REP. ELAINE NOBLE in lavender and white, not unlike the pre-election buttons, which said, ELECT ELAINE NOBLE.

Two days later, when this reporter interviewed Noble, the first subject the victorious candidate brought up was not gay rights but revenue sharing. "I've had to learn everything about revenue sharing," she explained. "A guy from the 'little city hall' is coming down to a meeting tonight to talk to neighborhood people about how federal money will be spent around here, and I think he's a bit too friendly with local slum landlords and real estate agents. I have to be smarter than him tonight."

Not One-Issue Candidate

While Noble was well-known throughout the district (Suffolk-6) and the city as a lesbian-feminist and gay rights activist, she has dealt with all of the issues relevant to her constituency, especially housing and the problems of the elderly.

"I had no business running if I wasn't going to approach it that way," Noble said.

Of course, working for gay rights legislation will be a big part of Noble's work in the forthcoming session of the Massachusetts house of representatives. She expects to cosponsor several bills with Barney Frank, who introduced them on behalf of gay organizations for the last two years.

While gay people inside and outside of Noble's district were generally enthusiastic about her approach to politics—that of a gay activist concerned about *all* social issues—the straight media focused narrowly on her lesbianism.

A postelection wrap-up by the United Press International reporter, datelined Washington, D.C., for example, dealt with the importance of the 1974 election for women nationally and referred to Noble as "a lesbian running on a gay liberation rights ticket." Ironically, the words *lesbian* or *gay liberation rights* appeared on none of Noble's campaign literature.

Postelection Challenge

Noble's lesbianism has nonetheless not gone unnoticed. One member of the Governor's Council, an anachronistic body that the governor-elect, Michael Dukakis, plans to do away with, threatened to attempt to prevent Noble from taking her seat. This council member, Patrick "Sonny" McDonough, is and old-time Boston politician who has said that since Noble is a lesbian, she commits felonious acts and therefore is not morally fit to serve in the house. The council has the formal duty of seating elected state representatives.

Informed sources said it was unlikely that McDonough would get anywhere with his plans, since the powerful speaker of the house, David Bartley, as well as governor-elect Dukakis believes that Noble should take her seat routinely.

In addition, Frank said that if Noble is denied her seat because of her sexual activities, he will ask that seats be denied to any representative who has committed illegal sexual activities. Massachusetts "crimes against nature" statutes, like those in many states, outlaw anal and oral intercourse whether the partners are homosexual or heterosexual.

Hard-Fought Primary

Noble won the election last September. She faced no Republican opposition, but the "independent" candidate, Joseph Cimino, 31, took the election more seriously than some had anticipated.

Cimino, part-owner of a singles' bar called Daisy Buchanan's, worked hard at defeating Noble and apparently had a lot of money to spend. According to a report in Boston's weekly *Gay Community News,* he even offered $1,000 to Dukakis if Dukakis would endorse him instead of Noble. Dukakis turned down the offer and reaffirmed his support for Noble on the grounds that she won the primary "fair and square," according to *Gay Community News.* Later Cimino took out a full-page ad in a Boston weekly to denounce those who accused him of this bribe and to deny the charges, but a reporter for *Gay Community News* said that Dukakis's representatives confirmed the story.

One possible explanation for Cimino's intense interest in seeing Noble defeated lies in the traditional complex relationship between politics and whiskey in Boston.

First of all, one of Cimino's business partners is an old law school chum, James McDonough, who is the son of Patrick McDonough (the council member who decried Noble's lesbianism). Also, Cimino has business ties with the Vara brothers, owners of the popular gay bars the Other Side and Jacques.

The Vara brothers reportedly were furious with Rep. Barney Frank, Elaine Noble's friend and supporter, for his role in encouraging the Bay Village Association, a neighborhood group, to press for action against the Other Side and Jacques for contributing to noise and crime in the neighborhood. It has been suggested that the Vara brothers encouraged Cimino's candidacy as a way of getting even with Frank and his friends, including Noble. Significantly, Cimino chose not to run in the September primary, but rather to wait until November and to appear as an independent on the ballot.

But now that the voters have had their say, such machinations are over, at least for a while, and Elaine Noble has to get on with the business of being a state representative.

A former Emerson College instructor in speech, Noble said that she hopes to get a seat on the education committee. She has been concerned with the public school situation in Boston and specifically with the vitriolic opposition to busing as a method of achieving integration.

Noble laments the fact that "people who aren't racist in Boston never get covered by the media."

She recently won an award "in appreciation, from the children of Boston," given by the Citywide Education Coalition. This group, consisting of parents, teachers, citizens, and students, is "committed to working for quality education," and it has been outspoken in favor of integrated schools and against the sometimes violent and usually overtly racist opponents of busing.

Noble, who is 30 years old, expects to devote herself full-time to the responsibilities of her office. "I'm pretty sure that I'll be sworn in on January 3, at the beginning of the new legislative year," she said, "but, you know, I'm not sure how much I make!"

INSPIRED BY ELAINE NOBLE: LEGISLATOR COMES OUT

by Howard Erickson

January 1, 1975

MINNEAPOLIS—After two years of working with the gay movement, quietly at first but edging closer and closer to the spotlight, a Minneapolis legislator has come out publicly.

"State Sen. Allan Spear Declares He's Homosexual," read the six-inch headline December 9 on page 1 of *The Minneapolis Star*, Minnesota's largest newspaper.

In granting the interview that comprised the lengthy, sympathetic news article, the portly, 37-year-old Spear became either the nation's first or second elected official, depending on the criteria used, to come out publicly. Spear told *The Advocate* that the victory November 5 of Elaine Noble, an up-front lesbian who was elected to the Massachusetts legislature, helped him make up his mind. "When she won, it made me feel a little less lonely," Spear said. Noble doesn't take office until January, but she is undeniably the first legislator to be elected *after* letting it be known she is gay. Spear is the first to proclaim himself gay while already established in office.

Spear was elected to the Minnesota senate in November 1972 from a district that includes the 43,000-student University of Minnesota campus where he's on the faculty as well as a large blue-collar neighborhood in northeast Minneapolis. The district is heavily Democratic-Farmer-Laborite in its voting habits, which helped DFLer Spear.

Before he ran he made a point of telling close friends and campaign workers that he's gay—and that he wouldn't deny it if it came up during the campaign. It didn't—even though Spear is convinced that his opponent, Alderman John A. Cairns, knew he was gay, (Cairns, now a practicing lawyer, is national chairman of the Ripon Society, a liberal Republican group.)

Spear also said, "Everyone around the Capitol [in St. Paul] and the politically active people know it anyway," and that his gayness was the regular subject of gossip. "I wanted to stop the tittering. There's nothing to be ashamed of. Nobody should have to talk about it on back stairways," he said.

Spear was one of the founders and in June was elected cochairman of the Minnesota Committee for Gay Rights, an organization of nearly 2,000 $10-a-year members that seeks to mount a broad-based program for educational and legislative goals.

Earlier, during the 1973 legislative session, Spear kept in regular contact with gay lobbyists for antidiscrimination and consenting-adults sex bills, but he felt bitterly he had to keep silent during a gay rights debate on the senate floor. "I don't want to go through that again," he said. "I felt lousy."

In 1975 Spear intends to work actively and speak out for the bill as a gay senator.

Felt Obligation

Spear said he also felt an obligation to other gay people to come out. Many straights think of gays as exotic creatures in far-off cities, he said. "They don't think about it happening in their family or among their friends.

"It's a time when gay people are beginning to emerge from their closets," Spear told the *Star*. "Gay people are not confined to the classic gay professions. They're in politics, in teaching, in business, in everything you can imagine. It's important for gay people struggling with their own identities. They need all kinds of role models."

Although regularly permitting *The Advocate* to quote him as a gay senator, Spear resisted coming out further out of a concern, he said repeatedly, that he would become known solely for being gay, overshadowing his views on housing, education, taxes, gun control, and the myriad other issues that the legislature faces.

Thus, although he was the main speaker at the Minneapolis gay pride week rally in Loring Park last June, speaking pretty clearly as a gay person, Spear discouraged suggestions that national TV networks be alerted to the rally and invited to cover his speech. Major Twin Cities news media virtually ignored the rally and march, but a neighborhood newsletter, the *Loring Community Crier,* did report that Spear is gay. KSJN-FM Radio, reporting a Committee for Gay Rights press conference in May, broadcast Spear's extensive comments that left little doubt that he was gay. It was after that press conference, Spear said, that *Star* subeditor Deborah Howell offered to write his "coming-out" story whenever he was ready.

What About Reelection?

Spear concedes that coming out may affect his prospects for reelection in 1976, but he has been careful to observe party loyalty within the DFL party that dominates the district. He made a point of openly supporting conservative DFLer Chester Durda for county prosecuting attorney in November at a time when many gay and civil liberties DFLers jumped to support Republican Gary W. Flakene, a liberal who has steadily backed gay rights.

"It's a pretty sophisticated district. In some areas people will be upset [to learn I'm gay]," Spear said, "but I think most of the people in my district are concerned with issues and my performance as a senator, which I think has been decent," he told the *Star*.

"I have served the district as well as I can. Primarily, I am a representative of that district. Quite secondarily, I am a spokesman for gay rights."

Ideologically Spear is liberal, almost radical in the opinion of some. He has been active in civil rights causes and the peace movement, and the local Americans for Democratic Action chapter ranks him as the most liberal of the 67 state senators.

Indeed, to win the DFL endorsement for the senate in 1972, Spear pledged to introduce a bill to specifically permit same-sex marriages—not to win gay delegates' votes "but to prove how radical I was," Spear said later.

Today he describes himself as a moderate in the gay movement, calling gay marriage no "burning issue," but quickly affirming to the *Star* that gay people should have the same rights as heterosexuals.

Spear told *The Advocate* that he does not expect to introduce gay rights bills in 1975, however. He announced that senate majority leader Nicholas Coleman, whose district includes the St. Paul gay ghetto, has reversed an earlier decision and agreed to be chief sponsor of a gay antidiscrimination bill once again. Coleman was the main backer of a limited gay rights bill that squeaked through the Senate but was defeated in the house in 1973.

In addition to his legislative service, Spear is an associate professor of history at the university, where he specializes in Afro-American history. He holds a Ph.D. from Yale University and in 1967 wrote the book *Black Chicago: The Making of a Negro Ghetto, 1890-1920*.

Like Peoria, Ill., native Dr. Howard J. Brown, whose coming-out was reported on page 1 of *The New York Times* in October 1973, Spear is a native of the Corn Belt. He was raised in a small town in Indiana, the son of a traveling salesman, and was 13 years old when he first "knew what my attractions were."

"But it was too horrible a thing to admit," he told the *Star*. He had no one to talk to about it, so he consulted library books. The only book available were on abnormal psychology, yet "I never felt I was sick."

Later, in Minnesota, he had no gay friends in the Twin Cities and went to gay bars only when out of town. He dated women, became serious about a few, he said.

Told Parents

Last Christmas he came out to his parents, who are retired and live in Mexico. "I never thought I could tell them," he said, and they were just as shocked as he expected. But he found them much more sensitive than he expected, too:

"Mama said a lovely thing. She said that it used to be that such a thing would have been horrible. More recently, she said she would have felt sorry for someone who was sic, but 'Allan,' she said, 'I don't think you're sick.'"

Today Spear owns a three-bedroom home in a quiet neighborhood near the campus, where he lives alone. The *Star*'s news report was picked up by national wire services, and Spear's home telephone started to ring regularly as soon as the afternoon newspaper reached the newsstands, with congratulations from friends and inquiries from other journalists.

Gay activist J. Michael McConnell called Spear's decision "delightful" and predicted it would "give us more power at the legislature next year."

Jack Baker, elected student body president at the university 3½ years ago, praised Spear for taking "a fantastic step, both for himself personally and for the gay movement."

Noting that Minnesota has three other legislators who are gay—two of them completely isolated from the gay movement—Baker said, "Having gays in public office is of limited value unless they're seen, unless they can stand as a symbol both to the gay community and to the world."

Said Spear, citing his personal history of activism in civil rights efforts on behalf of other minorities, "It took me a long time to realize that *I'd* been oppressed by society's attitude, and now I want to do something about it."

[PART TWO]

LIBERATION: BUILDING A MOVEMENT (1976–1981)

The December 4, 1974, issue of *The Advocate* announced that the magazine had been sold by Dick Michaels and Bill Rand to David Goodstein, a San Francisco businessman and activist. The publication had come a long way in seven years. Michaels and Rand had begun the upstart publication with less than $200 worth of capital, a circulation of 500, and $24 worth of advertising. With no office for the first year, Michaels and Rand wrote, edited, folded, and collated the newspaper on Michaels' dinning room table. Seven years later circulation exceeded 37,000, and each issue generated thousands of dollars in advertising revenue. Michaels believed that *The Advocate* filled a void left by the virtual blackout of gay news in the mainstream press.

Goodstein set out to raise *The Advocate*'s profile. John Preston, who would go on to become a well-known writer, was named editor. Goodstein moved the publication to San Mateo, Calif., and began publishing in nonglossy magazine format. To increase sales, he featured a steady stream of hunks on the cover—gay actor and porn star Cal Culver was the first. Goodstein also gave the magazine a New Age bent, affixing the logo "Touching Your Lifestyle" to the cover and starting "*The Advocate* experience," a self-help retreat based on EST, Werner Erhard's cultish spiritual program.

Goodstein beefed up the reporting. One of his most important hires was Randy Shilts, not long out of the University of Oregon. In the August 13, 1975, issue of *The Advocate,* the ambitious young reporter made his debut in the magazine with "Candy Jar Politics—The Oregon Gay Rights Story," the first of many articles Shilts would write for the magazine. Typical of Shilts's work are a prescient April 21, 1976, report on a startling increase in venereal diseases among gay men, and a January 12, 1977, piece chronicling his own debilitating bout with hepatitis to illustrate the danger the disease posed to sexually active gay men.

As the right wing began formally organizing against gay rights, *The Advocate* hired its first full-time female reporter, Sasha Gregory-Lewis, to expand its coverage of women's issues and chart the rise of conservatism. Gregory-Lewis was among the first to recognize that fund-raisers like Richard Viguerie were enlisting previously dormant right-leaning fundamentalist and evangelical Christians to add firepower to the conservative movement. Gregory-Lewis accurately predicted that this unlikely coalition would create a potent political force.

It was this antigay organizing that created the advance-and-backlash cycle that has come to characterize gay politics—gay inroads followed closely by antigay measures, and vice versa. The December 4, 1974, issue, for instance, reported that Elaine Noble was elected to the Massachusetts legislature as an out lesbian. Less than one month later the magazine reported that Allan Spear, a highly regarded Minnesota state representative, had revealed he was gay. These advances created a backlash, evidenced by the April 20, 1977, cover proclaiming "Save Us From the Anita Nightmare." The activism of former beauty queen Anita Bryant, the magazine explained, had sparked a wave of antigay ballot measures across the country, many of them successful.

Bryant's success, however, awakened a gay giant. "The success of [Bryant's] hysterical 'Save Our Children' campaign in Dade County resurrected a slumbering activism and converted apathy to anger and action," Shilts wrote optimistically. "It inspired spontaneous demonstrations…in the streets of New York, Los Angeles, Chicago, Houston, New Orleans, San Francisco, and other major cities. It gave birth to a host of new organizations and programs to counter the threat of an antigay backlash. It elicited support from national leaders, organizations and the press. And it opened many closet doors. As one observer put it, 'The radicals aren't the only ones being radical anymore.'"

Like inexperienced reporters everywhere, Shilts made his share of mistakes. An unintentionally hysterical two-part series in December 1977, "Life Among the Heterosexuals," depicted the nuclear family as awash in child abuse, wife beating, and gay bashing. "Shirley was only four years and when her stepfather started to fondle her," began his first report, "Child Sexual Abuse." "It was touching, gentle touching at first. Then the touching turned to petting—and the petting turned to intercourse." A 1978 article, "The Polyester Plot," resorted to crude caricatures of religious conservatives: "They may be funny to look at—they wear tacky polyester suits and make tacky polyester comments—but there are about 50 million of them."

Tragedy struck with the November 27, 1978, slaying of openly gay San Francisco supervisor Harvey Milk and mayor George Moscone by disgruntled former supervisor Dan White. When White was given a lenient sentence, protesters rioted throughout the city, burning dozens of police cars and damaging government buildings in what became known as the "White Night Riots." In chronicling the aftermath of the double assassination, *The Advocate* gently reminded readers that Milk had preached Gandhian passive resistance. "I don't think anyone should turn to violence," Milk said.

Robert I. McQueen, who replaced Preston as editor, made Larry Bush the magazine's first Washington correspondent. In an example of the unique ability of the gay press to hold leaders accountable for their antigay rhetoric, in the April 15, 1982, issue Bush profiled Terry Dolan, founder and president of the National Conservative Political Action Committee, a powerful right-wing group that used antigay fund-raising appeals to raise millions. Bush prodded Dolan into an apology of sorts: "I truly regret that we ever put something into print that would ever question the morality, the patriotism of another person. That's totally inappropriate." But Dolan dodged questions about his own homosexuality, an open secret until his AIDS-related death in 1986.

MILK GETS CANNED BUT KEEPS ON RUNNING

by Sasha Gregory-Lewis

April 7, 1976

San Francisco's gay power exercise in mainstream reformist politics is showing unprecedented results this year: Three openly gay people have been appointed to important city commissions; the sheriff has hired an openly gay deputy; the city finally enforced its gay rights ordinance against the local arm of Ma Bell. Even the police chief is supporting gay rights, as are most of the city's elected officials.

This gay power exercise has taken too long, some people feel. Its results, they charge, are unsatisfactory, its politics tainted.

One of the people who isn't happy with this political exercise is Harvey Milk, a gay camera store owner who, casting himself in the role of the little guy fighting the big political machine, is making his third bid for elective office in as many years.

This time, after two unsuccessful bids for the city's board of supervisors, Milk is challenging Arthur Agnos, experienced politico and longtime aide to assembly speaker Leo T. McCarthy, in the Democratic primary race for the state assembly.

Milk's experience in government is recent and brief. He served about two months on the city's permit appeals board as the first gay person appointed to a city government slot by recently elected Mayor George Moscone. The appeals board job was viewed as a grooming position by many city politicos, including, reportedly, Mayor Moscone himself. Milk was to show his stuff and get his name in the public view, so the story goes, in preparation for a shoo-in victory in the 1977 supervisoral race.

Milk, however, didn't see the slot as a grooming job. Says Milk, "If anything, it was really to get me out of the way while they groomed someone else." Milk notes, however, that the appeals board is important to the gay community because it is a court of last resort for businesses and others who must apply for permits to sometimes insensitive city departments. The board's decisions may only be overridden by the board of supervisors.

When Milk announced that he was thinking of running for the assembly seat (on the same day that Agnos formally announced his candidacy), Moscone, in a statement that caused a flurry of controversy in the local media, said that he would kick Milk off the board because he didn't think Milk could do a good job on the board and run for public office at the same time.

Milk responded that elected officials don't resign from their positions when campaigning and that he saw no reason why he couldn't run for the assembly and keep his board position.

When Milk filed for the race March 12, Moscone removed him from the board, replacing him with Earl Rick Stokes, a gay attorney with no immediate political ambitions. Milk then demanded that Agnos resign from his appointive position on the city's Commission on the Aging and from his position as McCarthy's aide. Agnos then revealed that he had tendered his resignation from the commission before announcing his candidacy. Agnos also said he was resigning from his post in McCarthy's office.

Milk also demanded that Agnos pay back the salary he had earned as McCarthy's aide since announcing his intention to run for the assembly seat. Agnos replied that he had no intention of turning back any of his salary because "I haven't campaigned on state hours."

Although Milk is short on experience in public office, he is a tireless campaigner, having rounded up some 53,000 votes in the 1975 supervisoral race, bringing him into the position of first runner-up to the reelected incumbents.

Milk, praising himself on his campaign, says that he was able to bring out his 53,000 votes with the infinitesimally small campaign war chest of $10,090, $2,500 of which came from his own pocket. He says he can win the much more costly assembly race on a mere $30,000.

Despite the fact that Milk has been able to get impressive numbers of votes from the community at large, he has never been a favorite in the organized gay community: "I didn't have much support from any organized [gay] media or any organized political force, gay or straight.

"I am not a stereotype politico," Milk explains. "I think from the streets…therefore I don't play the political game and therefore I'm an outsider as far as the politicians go.

"I'm not controllable. I wouldn't be anybody's puppet.," Milk says, explaining comments that mainstream gay political activists don't trust him.

Milk admits that he doesn't play by the "rules," which he contends don't work fast enough: "I demand my slice of the pie now." Milk views the city's gay rights ordinance, the state's consenting sex bill, and other signs of gay rights progress as "crumbs. I don't care if crumbs are better than we've had before. Bull. If they give you a crumb, they can take that crumb away. But if they give you freedom, it's pretty hard to take that away," says Milk, who defines freedom as the absolute end of discrimination.

Milk charges that the reason a state gay rights law did not pass in the 1975 California legislature was that Speaker McCarthy and Ways and Means chair John Foran (whose seat Milk and Agnos are contesting while Foran makes a bid for the state senate) didn't work hard enough to get it through: "Do you mean that the two most powerful people in the state house cannot get anything they want passed through the assembly? They can, but they have to pay the price for it," Milk claims. "They do not want to pay that price for gay rights. They are not willing to pull all the strings; they aren't willing to go all the way."

While Milk blames the assembly leaders for not making enough deals, exerting enough pressure, and calling in enough due bills, he claims that were he in office, he wouldn't make political deals. "I wouldn't sway my vote for somebody else's vote for something I didn't believe in.

"I may not get anything passed that way," Milk admits, "but maybe I could set an example… Maybe I could make them all just a shade more honest."

Milk, noting the contradiction between his demands for other legislators to use their deal-making power and his refusal to make deals, says that he would use media pressure to help get his legislation through.

Milk also has another basic difference with the gay reformist political model. Gay San Franciscans have spent years developing a "gay vote," taking and receiving credit for using the gay vote to bring pro-gay people into top city offices.

Milk doesn't believe that a gay vote exists.

"There's a myth in San Francisco about the gay vote," Milk explains, "a myth about the number of gays in San Francisco, a myth in San Francisco about the gay precinct. I live in a 'gay precinct,' and if 20% of the voters are gay here, then that's high," he claims.

Ironically, Les Morgan, political pollster and analyst most responsible for documenting the gay vote, recently predicted that an openly gay person will be able to win elective office in the city in the near future.

Milk did not run a gay campaign in the last supervisoral race. He didn't hide his affectional preference, but he didn't publish it in his literature, either. He was able to get endorsements and support from a variety of nongay groups, including the construction workers' union, a Chinese publication, and several neighborhood groups. (Most of these groups haven't yet announced who they'll be backing in the assembly race.) Fourteen thousand of his 1985 votes came from the conservative Sunset district. Although the Sunset district isn't in his assembly district (supervisoral races are at-large), Milk contends that the efforts which brought out the Sunset vote will bring out the vote in the nongay precincts of his assembly district.

Milk counts on what he describes as the vote-getting power of his personal appearances at candidates' nights and in-person, dogged campaigning.

Milk's supporters, he says, "cut across every conceivable line. They voted for me partly to get rid of the incumbents, but more because they heard me at candidates' nights."

Milk's biggest issue in the 1975 race was "the direction the city was going. If you liked the way the city was going, then you voted for the incumbents.... If you didn't like what you were getting for your [tax] dollar, if you didn't like the Manhattanization, then you didn't vote for the incumbents."

At issue in this race, according to Milk, will be his fight against what he calls the political machine running the city.

Members of this machine, Milk charges, are Mayor Moscone, Congressman John Burton, and Speaker McCarthy, all of whom, along with other Democratic heavyweights, have endorsed Agnos.

Despite the fact that Milk doesn't campaign as a "gay candidate," he explains that he entered politics because "it's time that we had a gay person in office."

He sees his campaigns as opportunities to "build the bridges. If I can be accepted by the hard-hat construction worker, that's going to help gay people."

Milk, who is down on the organized mainstream gay movement, charging that it is part of the machine, feels the movement is dominated by "those who have the most money [who think it's enough] to show you can do it [be a successful gay person]. That's not what the gay movement is about," Milk says, explaining that he doesn't "do anything politically without three people in mind: 1) a 15-year-old girl in San Francisco who told me that because she is an up front gay she was to be denied her high-school diploma, 2) Steven, 17, who just 'turned gay' and is terrified of what will happen if his parents find out; who called me to say he'd seen me talk, that he was watching me, 3) the 14-year-old in Des Moines, Iowa, or some other small town, who is terrified of coming out.

"That's what the gay movement is about. So that 15-year-old kid can walk down the street relaxed and free," says Milk.

The June 8 primary race between Milk and Agnos is developing into a bitter one, one which Milk already describes as being like "guerrilla warfare."

Milk expects that, despite the antipathy of the organized gay community to him, and despite the fact that Agnos is marshaling not only support from heavyweights by from gay heavyweights as well, he will get some gay votes in his assembly bid from those who believe, as he does, that it is time that a gay person is elected to office.

Meanwhile, the city's reform-minded gay politicos contend, as Jo Daly of the city Human Rights Commission, that Milk's opponent, Agnos, has been a longtime "supporter of gay rights and a friend of the gay community. He has been a voice for us in the capital. I just think we should support people who have supported gay issues."

A Closet Full of Loneliness

by Randy Shilts

They hold some of the most respectable positions in society. They serve on civic committees, manage businesses, hold public office, and teach Sunday school.

Yet overnight any one of them could become a social outcast. Fear gnaws at them daily. They must always conceal a secret that could cost them their jobs, their homes and, for some, their families.

So they lead double lives. They often meet in clandestine rendezvous. They correspond through anonymous post office boxes. Many use pseudonyms. Above all, they must constantly guard against the one slip that might cost them so much.

They are gay professionals. Many of them are in hiding.

Faced with social intolerance on one side and almost omnipresent threat of discrimination on the other, this large segment of America's 20 million gay people must constantly conceal their homosexuality. And the price, in terms of human anguish, is huge.

Elizabeth Stanton, a 26-year-old grade-school teacher in a small town on the Oregon coast, is such a person. (Throughout this article, names have been changed and identities concealed to protect the gay interviewees.) "If those parents knew I was gay," Stanton says, "they would damn near tar and feather me to get me out of town." So every morning she puts on a heterosexual mask when she goes to work. At night she returns home to write love poems to her friend, a 23-year-old education senior at Oregon State University.

"I lead a completely double life," says the tall, imposing Stanton. "When I get into my car in the morning, it's like I put on a stone-lead cast. I have to be careful that it doesn't get out. I feel totally, irrevocably repressed. I hate it. But then I remember that I have to make my paycheck."

Stanton started having gay relationships in the relaxed, liberal atmosphere of her college days at the University of Oregon. She led a free and open life there until a teaching job in the coastal logging town forced her to assume a heterosexual facade.

It hasn't been easy. To keep herself from being suspected, she finds herself flirting with men. A married teacher frequently visits her home. He can't understand why she doesn't use the pill. He makes passes at her and then accuses her of being frigid when she will not be seduced. She listens casually as colleagues casually talk of dykes and faggots. Since taking the job, she has begun seeing an analyst.

While she initially laughs at the child-molester stereotype, she says it causes most parents' objections to gay schoolteachers. Like most myths, however, it is a stereotype more easily created than destroyed. For now she must content herself to eagerly count the hours until she moves to a larger city where she can have the anonymity that will allow her to be herself.

With this to look forward to, she is more fortunate than Ed Hoover, a 58-year-old federal administrator in a major Northwest city. Hoover keeps his homosexuality a secret not only from his colleagues and friends but from his wife and family. Only a few months away from retirement, Hoover not only fears for his job, but for the prominent social position he has gained through years of leadership in civic affairs and professional organizations.

Hoover says he has known of his homosexuality since he was ten years old. He fled to heterosexual matrimony after a disastrous affair with a married man over 20 years ago. "I figured if this is what it (being gay) was like, I didn't want any part of it. So I tried to trick myself into thinking I was heterosexual," Hoover says. "I tried for 19 years, and then it came to the point that I decided I should have something I wanted for a change."

So at age 53 Hoover decided to resume gay relationships on the side. For fear of straight associates spotting him, Hoover avoided both the city's gay bars and relationships with local people. In an adult bookstore one day, he spotted *The Advocate* and noticed the large classified section. He promptly got a post office box under a pseudonym and began writing.

"In the first year I corresponded with about ten guys. One thing led to another until I had correspondence with 60 to 70 people," says the short, graying executive rather gleefully. "None of them are from around here. They write, we arrange something, and then meet in a motel room when they come through town. It isn't that I prefer this. It's just safer this way."

These clandestine liaisons have not always run smoothly. An 18-year-old last year responded to one of Hoover's ads and asked to visit him. "I didn't want anything to do with an 18-year-old," Hoover says. "I wrote and told him so. Well, the next thing I get is a letter from his folks, who found out about his post office box. They threatened me, saying they knew I was a married man who worked for the government. They said they could make things very difficult for me. For days after that I was so nervous I couldn't go to work. Every time the phone rang, I went into a panic."

Nothing ever came of these threats, but he still worries.

While Hoover says he would lead an open lifestyle if he had his life to do over again, he does not see any alternative to his present double life.

The marriage route is a common disguise for homosexuality. A survey recently conducted by the Indiana University Institute for Sex Research showed that 35% of the lesbians interviewed had been or are married, while one in five gay men had walked the aisle of matrimony. The researchers added that most of their sample group were drawn from the active gay subculture and that the actual percentages probably are far larger.

But the problems of hiding go deeper than involvements in dishonest relationships. According to Michael Maharis, a 37-year-old Seattle psychiatrist who counsels a primarily gay clientele, the tension of the deception manifests itself in alcoholism and sometimes suicide. Maharis points to himself as a case in point.

"For years I told myself 'I'm not gay. How could I be gay? I'm not effeminate, abrasive, and all those other things gays are supposed to be,'" says Maharis, a former administrator of a federal education program. "I didn't know any other gay people who had responsible positions. So I just ignored my sexuality and lived a monastic life. I threw myself into my work, gunnysacked my feelings of confusion, and swept it all under the carpet. I ended up with a bleeding ulcer and a high liquor bill."

After going into private practice, a situation that allowed him to be more open with himself and his friends, Maharis found that many others were in the same position.

"A lot of people I know and work with are in the gray zone where they are gay but either refuse or are afraid to admit it. They're living in an emotional vacuum. They know they can't make it with women, but they're not about to try it with a man. These people are countless," Maharis says. "Many are not even in touch with what's prompting their anxiety of feelings of emptiness."

Maharis says that the emptiness takes its toll.

"When people feel they do not have a legitimate outlet for their sexuality and cannot meet their basic human need for gaining respect within a society by being what they are—not by being what they pretend they are—they look for ways to escape. Alcohol and drugs are two popular ways."

And sometimes the escape takes even more permanent forms. He recalls one college roommate who seduced him one night in their dorm room. Some time later, the ex-roommate stormed into Maharis's office insisting Maharis had been the seducer. Maharis says the former liaison later admitted his aggressive role, and within ten hours of the conversation, the friend drove in front of a cement truck and was almost killed. Maharis considers this accident, by a person who had never received so much as a traffic ticket, a suicide attempt. Nor is this the only gay person who Maharis says considered suicide because of social and psychological pressure.

In his own practice, Maharis says he knows of three people who have committed suicide because of fear of job loss due to homosexuality. Beyond these extreme manifestations, Maharis thinks the day-to-day anxieties of a double life are themselves damaging.

"The price is huge, astronomical," Maharis insists. "It's a price of living without a sense of self-worth, without a sense of honesty, without a sense of being in touch with who you are."

And because of this, Maharis, like many others, is beginning to be more open about his homosexuality to his friends, colleagues, and family.

"Being open has been a great relief," Maharis adds. "It was like I've been walking around all my life with 50 pounds—make that 100 pounds—on my shoulders. Now it's gone, and I feel a lot freer because of it."

Other gay professionals are banding together in groups such as Seattle's Dorian Society or San Francisco's Golden Gate Business Association. Some are forming caucuses in their own professional organizations where they can nurture better attitudes toward gay people in their professions' attitudes and policies.

Others are simply going it alone in an open lifestyle. Jim Willard, for example, is a 32-year-old public affairs producer and television personality for a network television station in a major West Coast city. His station knows he's gay and doesn't mind as long as it isn't public knowledge, a situation the employers feel would threaten the station's credibility.

"It's a lot more effort to cover up and always worry about being caught than it is to be just who you are," says the producer, who was once married himself. "If people know about you, you don't have to laugh at the queer jokes, you don't have to try to be something you're not. The newsroom here has become a lot more sensitive to gay problems now that they know and work around a gay person."

Willard is also quick to separate those who would actually be fired for their homosexuality from those who use discrimination as an excuse to avoid the less tangible social stigma attached to gay

people: "A lot of people who never would be fired use the whole discrimination thing to hide behind just because they're afraid that people won't like them anymore. There's a difference between
genuine fear and simple cowardice."

Despite this factor, however, most professions offer plenty of deterrent to any practitioner who
wants to be gay and proud.

The stories of discrimination even extend into sports, as athletes still remember the case of "Big"
Bill Tilden—a man generally considered to be the greatest tennis player who ever lived. When
Tilden's homosexuality became public knowledge in the late '40s, after two prison terms stemming
from bathroom busts, Tilden found that no meets would accept his entries and no tennis player
would play with him. Sports observers agree that if that profession's attitudes have changed since
then, they've only changed for the worse.

This discrimination perpetuates a vicious circle in our society. As long as it persists, most gay professionals will be afraid to come out of hiding. And as long as most gay professionals stay covert, the
deeply embedded myths about gay people will not change. Until the society sees that they are
taught, insured, and operated on by gay people, they still will see our huge minority as a lunatic
fringe of hairstylists and bathroom dwellers.

Until these more profound attitudes change, a massive part of America will remain silent and in hiding.

THE REPUBLICANS: EMBRACING HOMOPHOBES
AND GAY RIGHTS BACKERS—A FRESH LOOK
AT THE GRAND OLD PARTY

by Sasha Gregory-Lewis

October 6, 1976

Gay activists, entrenched in the Democratic, Socialist, or Libertarian camps, have virtually ignored the
first major party that endorsed the Equal Rights Amendment, that embraced Abraham Lincoln and
produced the first black U.S. Senator since 1880; but the growing number of Republican politicians
who support gays rights suggests that the GOP might be fertile ground for the seeds of gay liberation.

While the party's neurotics and homophobes were busy grabbing headlines (Ronald Reagan, S.I.
Hayakawa, and Los Angeles police chief Ed Davis, all noted homophobes, began their careers, in-
terestingly, in the Democratic Party), a fairly large number of civil rights–oriented Republicans were

introducing and supporting gay rights legislation. It is time, some of these Republican civil rights backers say, for gay people to scratch the surface of the radical right patina and take a closer look at the Grand Old Party.

Says Bob Jones, a pro-gay Republican mayor trying to unseat Leo Ryan, one of California's homophobic Democratic members of Congress, "With benign neglect, we would have a one-party system. If that party is the Democratic Party, then the Democrats can take gay people and anyone else for granted. There's nothing better to check the abuse of power than competition.

"Gay people should certainly work both sides of the fence."

Says Duke Smith, openly gay aide to Republican California state senator Milton Marks, "By not paying attention to the Republicans, we're closing the doors on ourselves."

Citing his state's toss-up U.S. Senate race between homophobe Hayakawa and Democrat John Tunney, Smith says, "What if Hayakawa is elected? We haven't even tried to reach him. We have no openings to him. He can go ahead and say we're sick and should be put in prison, and if he's elected, we won't even be able to get in the door to see him. Where will we be then?"

Who Are They?

Who are the pro-gay Republicans?

There are a handful in nearly every state. Some of them are liberals, some are considered crackpots, some are Republicans in name only, and others are die-hard conservatives:

• California Congressman Paul N. (Pete) McCloskey, a liberal, best known to gay people as the sole Republican to cosponsor federal gay rights legislation.

• Less well-known, Congressmen Joel Pritchard (Washington) and James M Jeffords (Vermont), who have announced that they favor federal gays rights legislation.

• In the U.S. Senate, Texan John Tower, a conservative Republican heavyweight; and Massachusetts liberal Edward Brooke, the first black member of the upper house since 1880. Both have gone to bat for gay people.

• Governors Daniel Evans (Washington), Robert D. Ray (Iowa), and Otis R. Bowen (Indiana), who supported their states' penal code revisions, complete with sodomy repeal sections.

• Alaska governor Jay S. Hammond, whose Equal Employment Opportunities Commission says it is looking into protecting gay people against discrimination.

Pro-gay Republicans proliferate at the state level:

• California, which couldn't have passed its consensual sex legislation without support from four Republican state senators.

• Hawaii, which cleared a gay rights bill through its lower house with the support of more than half of its Republican legislators.

• Oregon, which nearly passed a similar bill with backing from a third of the state's elected Republicans.

• Massachusetts, whose Republicans often seem to be stronger rights supporters than do many of the state's Democrats.

• Texas, where a Republican has cosponsored reform of the state sodomy law.

• Maryland, where a Republican joined two Democrats in sponsoring gay rights bills.

• Kansas, where a sodomy-reform measure sponsored by a Republican passed the state senate with Republican as well as Democratic support.

And occasionally, when asked, Republicans trying to unseat Democratic incumbents will pledge to support gay rights: Bob Jones, running for Congress in San Mateo County, Calif.; E.C. Armesto and Frank Diaz-Silveira, running for seats in Florida's lower house.

What Motivates Them?

State senator Marks, California's Senate cosponsor of sex-law reform, and New York state senator Roy M. Goodman could perhaps have been expected to support gay rights proposals—their constituencies embrace liberal-to-radical urban denizens—but what about Republicans like state Senator Howard Way, hailing from California's farm belt?

Way, who has his Republican parallels in other states, was one of four California Republican senators to favor sex-law reform. His reasoning on the issue was simple, and very "Republican:" "My reason for voting for it is that government has no business sticking its nose into what goes on in private between consenting adults," he told *The Advocate*.

"The decision was easy," Way recalled, but was not without its constituent opposition: "You should have seen the mail. I really heard it from some Christian groups, you'd better believe it. I represent the 'heart of the Bible Belt,' and there was even talk of a recall movement."

The recall movement did not develop. "It's strange," explains Way, "but in politics, if you take a stand on a controversial issue and then explain your reasoning, people respect you for being willing to take a stand, to have the courage of your convictions. This is true even if there is a lot of emotion at the time and people are upset. The vote would not have been much of an issue in a re-election campaign. [Way is retiring.]

"It's the wobblers, those who try to always straddle the fence—trying not to take positions that will alienate anybody—that end up with ulcers and a public image that their spines are like spaghetti."

Candidate Jones, trying to woo traditional Democrats unhappy with Congressman Ryan's style of representing them as well as keep loyalist Republicans in line, echoes Way's statements, saying he's "finding out that people are responding positively when you're honest with them on issues where there's disagreement.

"There is no political risk in being honest with people," Jones says, adding that he welcomes gay support in his campaign.

Jones's support of gay rights is also very "Republican." "It is to our society's benefit to uphold the Constitution, the right to privacy and freedom of speech. I'm dedicated to individual freedom. We need to cut down on government controls. We must make some effort to free the people!"

Ironically, it is the issue of less government that causes some Republicans to oppose federal measures to end discrimination. Says Republican U.S. representative Barry M. Goldwater Jr.: "These rights [to be free from discrimination based on sexual preference] are already protected by the Constitution." But when conservatives are faced with evidence that gay rights are not, in truth, protected in the United States today, they sometimes begin to shift toward legislation that would do the job, as did Texas congressman John Tower, who angrily reacted with a pro-gay statement to news of gay Air Force Purple Heart recipient Leonard Matlovich's discharge earlier this year.

The Ford Record

Although the Republican Party has not announced a position on gay rights (neither have the Democrats), an amazing amount of changes have passed quietly through the two-year-old administration of President Gerald R. Ford.

The most sweeping reform was last year's revision of the U.S. Civil Service guidelines to ban discrimination on the basis of sexual orientation. The revision, in the works for years, directly affects the lives of many thousands of gay people.

Security clearance guidelines have been unofficially changed so that gay civilians can get clearances—another policy revision quietly emanating from the Ford administration.

When overt discrimination outside of the military establishment has been publicized, like that uncovered in the Job Corps, Ford appointees have been quick to end it.

Immigration and naturalization policies have been loosened.

And it was a Ford-appointed Supreme Court justice who opposed the majority ruling that sodomy laws are constitutional.

What Can Be Done?

Support for gay rights by Republicans has had benefits that aren't at first apparent. Republicans can be critical to important legislation, as California, Oregon, Hawaii, Kansas, and Idaho have learned; but they can also be played off against Democrats with some success.

Republican support for controversial issues like gay rights can be used to give the issue an aura of respectability, as Texans saw in the case of liberal Democratic member of Congress Barbara Jordan's meeting with gay activists. Jordan earlier this year got caught on a live radio show by a gay rights question. She fumbled it miserably, saying gay people don't face real discrimination.

Following the show, gay activists turned up at her office for a chat. Frankly, she told them, she didn't think that supporting gay rights could do her any good politically. It was too liberal and controversial an issue, she said. But when Texas gay people mentioned that conservative Republican senator John Tower had written to support federal gays rights legislation, Jordan, after momentary disbelief, began to change her position.

Even such Democratic liberals as U.S. senator John Tunney have privately observed that more Democrats would be willing to cosponsor a gay rights bill if it has some respectable, conservative Republicans as authors. Sen. Alan Cranston was more blunt about it: When conservatives (i.e. Republicans) move to pick up the ball on a federal gay rights bill, he will also.

Many Democrats in Congress would like to see Republicans carrying the gay rights bill. Almost all who've commented on it privately swear that having the bill carried by Rep. Bella Abzug is almost certainly its death knell.

If gay people want to see the Democratic Party endorse gay rights in its platform, tongue-in-cheek Democratic politicos comment, they should get the Republicans to do it first. The remark, in view of the history of the two major parties' roles in the Equal Rights Amendment's battle for party endorsement, might have more merit to it than is at first apparent.

Far removed from the game of political strategy is a much more compelling reason for getting gays rights off the ground in the Republican Party: "Republicans are a significant part of this country. We can't afford to ignore them," concludes Duke Smith.

How It's Done

"The beauty of it," says Bob Jones, "is that politics is the same in the Republican Party as it is in the Democratic Party.

"Gay people," Jones says, "should do two things" to begin to have some clout in the GOP: "Get involved in the political process and back candidates you can trust."

The issues, suggests Jones, that gay people can use as wedges into the GOP are simple, Republican issues—the party standbys: "The right to privacy and freedom of speech. The constitutional issues."

BE IT EVER SO VIOLENT: THERE'S NO PLACE LIKE HOME

by Randy Shilts

December 28, 1977

The gavel sounds. Another Congressional committee is called to investigate violence on television. Legislators query an assortment of television producers and writers about the nightly parade of prime-time mayhem. After appropriate huffing and puffing—accompanied by a stream of indignant press releases to hometown newspapers—the gavel sounds again, and the solons adjourn their investigation until the next session.

Meanwhile, an institution that is host to a far greater portion of American violence goes unexplored. It is a criminal turf on which some 2,500 women were murdered in 1973 alone, according to FBI statistics. It is a dangerous arena that is responsible for over one in five police fatalities. It is an institution that so ensnares its victims that they often can only escape with the help of elaborate "underground railways" reminiscent of the slave era.

The waiters clear up the last of the $50 plates as the candidate mounts the podium. The crowd claps enthusiastically as he talks of law and order. Like candidates throughout the United States, he hammers away at what are perceived to be the major threats to our domestic tranquillity—crime in the streets, robbery, rape, and terrorism.

But he says nothing of the social institution in which an estimated 1 million youngsters are annually battered and starved—sometimes even killed. Nothing is said of he criminal arena in which an estimated 1.4 million children each year are threatened with knives and guns while another 2.2 million are beaten.

Indeed, even the staunchest supporters of law and order say nothing about the American institution that is home to more violent crime than any other social setting. That dangerous and violent institution is the heterosexual nuclear family.

A Litany of Terror

. While sundry leaders of religion and politics call upon the American people to preserve the family from the alleged threat of homosexuality, they leave a more profound question unanswered: Can the heterosexual family be saved from itself? The litany of statistics emerging from recent studies on family violence indicates such salvation may be far off.

Item: According to FBI statistics, there is more violence in the home than on the streets. Violence occurs in an estimated 60% of American families.

Item: Studies indicate that as many as one half of American wives have been beaten by their husbands at some point.

Item: According to research by University of Rhode Island sociologist Richard Gelles, nearly 1.4 million children between the ages of three and 17 have been threatened by a knife or gun—held by one of their parents. Parents of another 2.2 million children acknowledge having "beaten up" their children. Gelles cautions, however, that these figures may be conservative.

Item: In further studies on a statistically standard sample of nearly 1,200 American families, Gelles found that at least 63% experienced a violent episode with children in the last year. Nearly half the parents acknowledged pushing and shoving their children in the past year. Twenty percent admitted hitting their children while another one in ten said they have thrown, kicked, bitten, or punched their children with a fist in the past 12 months. Again, these figures may be conservative.

Item: A conservative estimate puts the number of children physically abused or neglected last year at 1 million. Of these, approximately 30% suffer permanent injury. About 5,000 die. Authorities warn, however, that the great proportion of child abuse remains unreported.

Item: Police agencies throughout the United States report that they receive more calls for help in cases of domestic violence than for all street crimes combined.

Item: According to one estimate, a wife is beaten by her husband every 30 seconds. In 1973 approximately 2,500 murders were committed in the home.

"Everybody's rising up in defense of the family lately," comments Del Martin, president of the San Francisco Commission of the Status of Women and author of *Battered Wives,* one of the first books on the subject. "I'm just wondering what kind of institution they're trying to idealize."

From Neglect to Murder

The institution being researched in growing numbers of studies on domestic violence is hardly the blissful family so reverently characterized in *Father Knows Best* and *The Donna Reed Show.* Research now shows that wife battering, physical child abuse, child neglect, and incest are far more commonplace than anyone ever imagined. But the statistical abstracts from the research sometimes obscure the human side of these problems—and the devastating impact the high proportion of family violence has on our society.

Barbara Flaherty, coordinator for the Los Angeles County Child Abuse Program, has seen that side of human suffering for the two decades in which she has worked with children's services agencies. Last year some 43,000 children were referred to her agency alone for investigation of child abuse—yet she worries that this represents a minority of the physically abused children in her county. "The issue of child abuse has only recently been raised," she says. "We're just getting past our first big barrier—convincing people that the problem was there."

Experts argue over causes of physical child abuse. They have found that abuse occurs at all socioeconomic levels, in all ethnic groups, and to children of all ages. Abuse happens to both planned and unplanned children—with the planned child often getting worse abuse if he or she doesn't live up to parental expectations.

Parents sometimes appear to project their own fears and insecurities onto the child. One Southern California social worker, for example, recalls one set of parents who brutally beat their eight-year-old son because they were intimidated by the child's high intelligence.

Abuse sometimes has bizarre psychological overtones. In one Portland Ore., case, a young man brutally beat his two-year-old stepson in the genitals for many months. The child was the product of the first marriage of the stepfather's wife—and therefore the victim of the man's feelings of sexual inadequacy.

Physical abuse is sometimes the parents' last resort in a tardy attempt to assert control over the child. "We have a lot of teens who are abused," says Flaherty. "Some parents never have established control over the child, and when the adolescent moves toward independence, the parents try to break them down."

Researcher Gelles corroborates this point with his finding that the age of 17 is a particularly dangerous time to be in a heterosexual family. Gelles's research found that more than one in four of the young people surveyed had experienced violence in the last year at home. One in ten suffered physical injuries requiring medical attention.

Wives and Children: The Violent Connection

Often, the abuse comes in the form of mere neglect. "The extreme is the case of the parent who just doesn't feed the baby and allows it to starve to death," says Flaherty. In milder cases the parent may simply ignore a baby for days—leaving social workers to find infants trapped in a crib filled with fecal matter.

Such neglect can often be attributed to lack of education about parenting. "For all the time schools spend on academic subjects, there are no lessons on how to have or take care of a baby," says Flaherty. "You just get pregnant and it's there."

A more basic factor is that child batterers themselves tend to come from physically abusive families. Thus, the abuse follows the family from generation to generation.

This is not the only statistical connection researchers have uncovered about domestic violence. Most authorities in the area of family violence say there appears to be a connection between wife battering and child battering.

"I don't have any statistics, but I know that they do occur together," says Los Angeles County's Flaherty. "If a woman is beaten and frustrated, for example, she can very easily take out that frustration on the child."

The wife-battering problem similarly is one that is carried from generation to generation. One Long Beach, Calif., social worker recalls the story of a child who grew up in a home in which her mother was frequently pistol-whipped by her husband. The daughter went on to marry a man who in turn beat her—until he eventually killed her.

"Often the girls in a battered wife family figure out early that their role is to be a victim," says author Del Martin, co-coordinator of the battered wives task force of the National Organization for Women. "It then just continues from generation to generation."

Like the subject of physical child abuse, the topic of wife battering only recently has come out of the closet of hidden social issues. While the child abuse problem, however, met with swift legislative action for mandatory reporting laws, those active in the wife-battering cause have had a tougher time getting remedies.

Government agencies traditionally have been more a part of the problem than of the solution. Law enforcement officers are reluctant to get involved with domestic altercations—often for reasons of self-preservation. Police intervention in husband-wife fights is responsible for 22% of police fatalities, according to the FBI.

The failure of the criminal justice system to get involved with wife beating has left the battered woman at the mercy of her husband. Workers in that area can recite tale after tale of police inaction in domestic fighting—and its often fatal consequences.

In one Long Beach case, for example, a husband would tie, gag, and then beat his Asian wife for days on end—though he would take occasional breaks to watch television football games. When the wife called police, the husband calmly explained that his wife was a "psycho," under mental health care. The police later claimed they couldn't understand the wife's complaints because of her accent.

In a more famous case, the wife of a professional football player once called police after a particularly brutal beating from her quarterback husband. The awestruck officers spent the bulk of their visit talking football with the husband, ignoring the wife's pleas for help.

"It's the same all the time," says Del Martin. "The police come after the fighting. The husband comes on like nothing serious has happened. The wife, however, is hysterical because she's been beaten—but the cops don't understand that and just view her as another hysterical woman."

In New York and Oakland, Calif., women's groups have filed suits against the police departments because of the agencies' reluctance to help battered women. The New York suit cites one case of a man whose fingers literally had to be pried from his wife's throat by neighbors. The police then came, said there was nothing they could do, and left.

In such scenarios the woman stays trapped in a nightmare existence. She frequently must stay in the home because she has no skills or means by which to support herself. If she has children, the idea of leaving home is almost inconceivable. Husbands often will go to such extremes as keeping any money away from the wife so she can't make an escape.

In many cases the wives do not consider leaving the home because their socialization has given them no alternative to the wife/mother role. Marjorie, a woman who anonymously works with battered wives in Southern California, says that out of every 100 calls she gets from battered wives, only one or two callers eventually work up the courage to run away. "These women have no context in which to live their lives without men," she says. "So they just stay and take it."

Feminist groups in some areas have established shelters for battered wives and are pushing for the creation of more. Yet these shelters can't begin to cope with the large numbers who need refuge. In San Francisco, for example, the battered wives facility has room for only 30 women.

Even when women do escape to these shelters, they often are pursued by vindictive husbands or private detectives. Marjorie says she maintains secret hiding places for women who have left their homes. That practice is not unusual. Says Del Martin: "Sometimes it's best to get the woman out of the state in order to protect her from her husband. We have an underground railway going for these women—like the one for slaves in 19th-century America."

Such escapes are rare, however, as the women who most need such assistance are often unaware of such alternatives. Given this, many women simply murder their husbands. Martin recalls one lecture she gave on wife battering in Lincoln, Neb., where she met a woman who had spent six years in jail for killing her husband. Says Martin: "She told me it was the only way she could get out of the situation, nobody would help her."

Women sometimes take other desperate options. One New York woman took her husband to court five times on battery charges. Five times the court did nothing. The woman then killed herself.

As with the problems of rape, incest, and child abuse, the basic task before activists in the battered wives field is education. "For years the emphasis has always been on the victim—what did she do to provoke it?" says Martin. "Now we're trying to get people to see this for what it is: criminal violence."

Legislative solutions now are in the works. A bill sponsored by Rep. Barbara McClusky (D-Md.) would establish training for Vista-like volunteers to work with family violence. The bill also would establish a national action center with a toll-free number for domestic crises. A bill authored by Rep. Lindy Boggs (D-La.) would establish emergency centers for women throughout the United States. Neither the Boggs nor the McClusky legislation, however, has seen substantial Congressional action—and any major pushes do not seem forthcoming.

A major part of the problem lies in the sheer ugliness of the issues. While opposing violence on television or crimes in the street is not unlike endorsing motherhood, politicians have a much harder time dealing with issues of family violence that have such far-reaching implications on the institution of the heterosexual nuclear family. The fact that such problems are inherent in the contemporary model of the heterosexual family is undeniable, according to many authorities.

This is particularly true in the wife-battery problem, says Martin. "You've got to take a look at the institution of marriage and see the context in which the battery takes place," she says. "The woman is really in a master-slave relationship. Men are supposed to be dominant; woman are supposed to be passive. It's all a setup for abuse."

The roles of both wife and children as chattel for men also has contributed to the problem. Martin sees irony in the recent outbursts of antigay activity that spread antigay prejudice in the name of preserving the heterosexual family.

"Would you want your child grown up in one of these homes?" she asks. "I think the heterosexuals need to clean up their act before they get down on us."

THE POLYESTER PLOT: A CONSPIRACY OF BELIEF

by Randy Shilts

March 8, 1978

Editor's note: Three American cities may soon face Miami-like referendums over the issue of gay civil rights, as religious fundamentalists in St. Paul, Minn., Wichita, Kan., and Eugene, Ore., have filed petitions initiative to repeal those cities' gay rights ordinances. The Advocate *dispatched Ranch Shilts to the Midwest to examine the repeal drives in Wichita and St. Paul. The following is his report.*

I. The Polyester Conspiracy (and Other Tales of Fear and Loathing in the Bible Belt)

The piano strikes a simple C chord. "Open your books to hymn 21," says the man in the umber leisure suit. The sea of brightly colored polyester jackets rustles as the congregation of Wichita's Glenville Bible Baptist Church rises.

"Yesterday, today, forever, Jesus is the same.

All may change, but Jesus never—

Glory to his name."

The tall, handsome Rev. Ron Adrian takes the pulpit and stares at the audience, which is homespun in every way—except for the decidedly synthetic attire. The group has braved subzero wind chills of a January Kansas night to catch up on the local news, and the reverend—who doubles as chairman of Concerned Citizens for Community Standards—isn't going to let them down.

Graying beehives bob throughout the church when Reverend Adrian announces it's time to make up the coming week's prayer lists. The young Smithson girl has the flu and could use some kind words to the Almighty—and indeed, young Ms. Smithson's name appears on tablets throughout the church. Brother Taylor's uncle in Haven, Kan., meanwhile, has a tumor and could use some good words from the people at Glenville—and pens move to add Brother Taylor's uncle's name to prayer lists.

Prayers also need to be directed for Mark Sheffler, who has broken a leg doing his farm chores; young Johnny Johnson, who is about to start his second term at Oklahoma State University, and for the Allen family, who has just lost a grandmother. Scores of beehives nod sadly as they jot down the Allen family's misfortune while a polyester rustle rises from the men impatiently recrossing their legs.

Here I am in the center of all the fear and loathing the Bible Belt could muster, and the most colorful copy I can gather concerns Brother Taylor's uncle's tumor. The God presiding over the Glenville Bible Baptist Church seems less an angry Jehovah ready to smite sodomites than a cosmic CPA, keeping track of prayer debits and credits on some celestial pocket calculator.

But to the denizens of Glenville Bible Baptist Church, he is, if nothing else, a personal God who would personally listen to each prayer, noting both donor and recipient. It is a personal, even anthropomorphic, vision of God as an entity with all-seeing eyes, all-hearing ears, powerful hands, and one hell of a temper—as gay activists learned the hard way last September.

"Homosexuals want to adopt children, pervert them, and send them back into the mainstream of our society," read a statement from the Concerned Citizens for Community Standards, an antipornography organization that shifted into the anti–gay rights leadership role when the Wichita City Commission started considering a gay rights ordinance in July. "Can you [the city commission], with one whisk of your pens, cast away the tenets of family sanctity that made this nation both good and great in the sight of God?"

The controversy over the gay rights ordinance is engendering Wichita's biggest showdown between good and evil since former Wichita sheriff Wyatt Earp faced a band of gunslinging outsiders during the cattle drive of 1872. Like Earp, the contemporary polyester armies of good stand ready to shoot it out with the outside forces of social change—and they look like they're going to win.

"If God spared not the angels that sinned or the ungodly world during Noah's day, or even Sodom and Gomorrah, what makes us think God will spare our country, which is reaching the nadir of moral degeneracy?" asks the Reverend Adrian.

Such arguments come off as nearly reasonable when compared to other opposition statements to gay rights at the early September city commission hearing at which the gay rights ordinance was approved. At one point a damnation-minded Kansas citizen cited facts about homosexuality from both Leviticus and the *National Enquirer,* which may prove to be one of the few times in which the two publications have been given equal credence.

Citations from neither publication, however, carried that day, and the Wichita city commission voted 3–2 to pass an ordinance banning discrimination in housing, public accommodations, and employment. It was a piece of legislation that remains stricter than anything on law books of San Francisco, New York, or Los Angeles,

Not to be outdone by a bunch of clamorous gay activists, the Concerned Citizens took their campaign door to door with a petition to repeal the laws. After all, Wichita's Sedgwick County is part of the string of Midwestern farm counties known as the Bible Belt. It didn't take Concerned Citizens long to find out why the *National Enquirer* and the Bible are respectively the best-selling newspaper and book in the United States: People believe them. And they weren't about to buy some big-city line about granting equal rights to the very corrupted souls that had Sodom and Gomorrah buried under a holocaust of fire and brimstone.

Within weeks Concerned Citizens had collected some 40,000 signatures. These aren't shoddy results, considering that Wichita has only about 100,000 voters to start with and that the city's last general election drew only 38,000 of them. Concerned Citizens needed only 10,000 signatures to get on the ballot. The Reverend Adrian says the group actually has 50,000 signers, but decided to turn in only 40,000 for brevity.

In St. Paul the Rev. Richard Angwin of the Temple Baptist Church nods his head approvingly as I relate greetings from his old friend, the Rev. Ron Adrian. He admits embarrassment that his friend has collected almost six times the signatures that Temple Baptist's small cadre of petition gatherers was able to muster in its fight to repeal St. Paul's gay rights ordinance.

"We're all in a conspiracy," jokes the Rev. Angwin. A conspiracy? The eyes of gay activists throughout the United States brighten up when I mention that the leaders of the Wichita and St. Paul repeal drives are old friends. The idea of their possible collusion is enough to titillate the most sublimated persecution complex, and gay activists aren't noted for doing a good job at sublimating their persecution complexes.

But Reverend Angwin *is* joking about a conspiracy, though to some extent, the polyester forces of God are involved in a conspiracy to undermine gay rights efforts, if not throughout the entire nation, then at least in St. Paul and Wichita. It is not, however, a conspiracy evolved from a clandestine cell block of neo-Righters plotting the overthrow of a nation. If any conspiracy exists, it is a conspiracy of belief.

The born-again Christian movement represents one of the most significant cultural trends of the decade. They may be funny to look at—they wear tacky polyester suits and make tacky polyester comments—but there are about 50 million of them. That's what the Gallup organization estimated when it found that one in four Americans said they had been "born again." These religious fundamentalists *believe* the world rapidly is going to hell in a handbasket—for further details, read Revelation—and the advance of gay rights merely represents the final straw.

Their motive for action is simple and powerful: Their all-powerful, vengeful God will surely smite the moral decadence of a perverted nation. If you want to be among the unsmitten, then you'd better raise your voice against the ungodly sodomites. An all-seeing, all-hearing God will note this on his pocket calculator, and when the Judgment Day comes, you won't have to worry about your leisure suit melting in hell.

Sound outlandish? Not to the countless fundamentalists who can quote scripture to back up their contention that gay rights is merely part of the preordained conquest of the world by the Antichrist.

Gay activists understandably prefer to outline the argument along less theological lines. "I consider all discrimination to be a moral issue," says Steve Endean, cochair of the National Gay Task Force and a leader of the Minnesota Committee for Gay Rights, the organization that is gearing up for the St. Paul election. "But this is not a moral issue, but one of human rights."

The Reverend Angwin doesn't see it that way. "The question is whether this society is going to pray to God or pray to freedom," he says, comfortably citing a half-dozen Bible passages indicating that Leviticus does take precedence over the newfangled concepts of freedom inherent in gay rights ordinances.

"This is all part of a universal struggle between good and evil. Everywhere—even in your own heart—is this struggle between the moral and immoral. The two forces can just never get along," he says. The stuffed mallard on the small refrigerator near the pastor's desk looks on impassively as the Reverend Angwin takes a final swig of ginger ale and concludes, "No issue typified the struggle between good and evil better than this gay rights thing."

II. From Cowtown to Gaytown—The Rec Room Conspiracy

For the gay side of the ordinance controversies, the tale is told less in terms of good vs. evil than in nuts-and-bolts politics of civil rights. All of which raises the fundamental question that gay activists throughout the United States have asked ever since last September: How in the hell did Wichita ever pass a gay rights ordinance in the first place?

The gears started moving nearly two years ago when Kate Millett came to talk to Wichita feminists and shocked a room full of Wichita's most political women by saying that lesbians should go public. "Everybody thought she was crazy, but it started people thinking," says Nita Marks, treasurer of the Homophile Alliance of Sedgwick County.

Others, meanwhile, were thinking along the same lines, and a number of gay people—notably a young social worker named Robert Lewis—got involved in the 1977 election campaigns for Wichita's five-member city council. These gay people merged with a community activist group and distributed some 120,000 pieces of campaign literature for the two most liberal city council candidates.

Lewis, meanwhile, became one of the four or five advisers closest to candidate Garry Porter—which is not a hard task when only four or five hard workers are needed to win Wichita. Lewis soon earned his political pull via hours of envelope stuffing, shopping center leafleting, and phone calling—mundane tasks to be sure, but the stuff of which political success is made.

Midway during the campaign, fledgling gay activists like Marks and Lewis organized the Homophile Alliance of Sedgwick County. Yes, *homophile*. "We used that term because we thought that here in Wichita nobody would know what it meant and we could just quietly slip our programs through," admits current HASC codirector Geri Dunnell. The group began meeting in the recreation room of the town house subdivision in which a number of the new activists lived. The quiet strategy worked at first: HASC sent out a questionnaire to all city council candidates. The number one question: Do you support an ordinance prohibiting discrimination on the basis of sexual orientation?

Armed with these results, HASC distributed leaflets throughout the city's four gay bars and took to registering voters. The final election tallies put two liberal backers of gay rights on the city council and gave a new sense of political efficacy to Wichita's gay community. "For the first time, gay people here felt they had some effect in the political process," says Lewis. "That meant a lot to people."

In early July, just four weeks after the Dade County, Fla., election, HASC made its first overture and asked the city council to pass an ordinance banning discrimination on the bases of marital status and sexual orientation. The news swept through the city's fundamentalist community faster than an August twister on the Kansas prairie. The city's significant Baptist population—made up of Okies who escaped the 1930s dust bowl for jobs in the area's agribusiness and aircraft industries—mobilized, and the previously deserted city council meetings became standing-room-only affairs.

What emerged were two irreconcilable world views as the polyester conspirators of belief battled the rec room conspirators of civil rights. Gay rights opponents quoted from the Bible as gay rights proponents quoted the Constitution. God's law versus freedom's laws.

Wichita mayor Tony Cosado—a onetime Cuban refugee who clings to Kansas conservatism with a convert's zeal—spoke for opponents. "We don't move very fast here in Kansas, and if people don't like that, they can move to San Francisco, where they might be better off," he still says.

On the other side was Garry Porter, who grew up in Columbus, a Kansas farming town of 2,000. He still recalls the talk that spread through the stands when his high school basketball team took the floor. The team actually had a Jewish player, quite a novelty in rural Kansas. Of course, this was not as scandalous as another local team that had a black player. "I think I learned a lot about prejudice then," he says.

The debate between the two sides roared for nearly seven hours as all tried to sway the commissioner in the middle, Jack Shanahan. In the end Shanahan cast his lot for gay rights, using Biblical metaphors to back his position. "Though they err," he said, "they are people—and they have a right to work, live, and eat some place. And I'm not sure I'm the one to cast them into the wilderness."

Within weeks Anita Bryant was in town leading an anti–gay rights rally. The hundreds of pro-gay pickets who gathered outside marked the largest demonstration in the history of Kansas. Bumper stickers appeared on the chrome bumpers of God-fearing Chevys throughout Kansas: FROM COW-TOWN TO GAYTOWN—THANK GARRY, CONNIE, AND JACK.

The petition drive, spearheaded by enraged congregation members from the city's Baptist churches, set out door-to-door. Billboards throughout Wichita urged citizens to sign.

All the politicians from both sides of the issue agreed: They'd never seen anything that got the normally staid citizens of Wichita so riled up. Even the fluoridation issue, scheduled for the same special election ballot as the gay rights referendum, failed to engender this special brand of fear and loathing in the Bible Belt.

The passage of gay rights in Wichita had pushed a button that activated heretofore latent political energy. Like the two best-known protagonists of Kansas folklore, Dorothy and Toto, the fundamentalists of Wichita had the eerie feeling they weren't in Kansas anymore.

III. Fear and Loathing in St. Paul

In the main sanctuary of Temple Baptist Church in St. Paul runs a digital scoreboard of sorts, a scoreboard that ticks off the world's death rate. The Reverend Angwin of Temple Baptist has thought a lot about death—both of the body and of the soul—ever since he was "born again" 13 years ago while flying 30,000 feet over Iowa in a company jet.

After experiencing his personal salvation, Angwin left the ranks of Wichita's bustling aircraft industry executives and joined the ministry. He now ministers to the relatively small community of fundamental Baptists who have left the South for the blue-collar jobs and tract homes of St. Paul. Angwin is a charismatic leader for the repeal forces—with a measured speech, casual demeanor, and deliberate charm not unlike that of Jimmy Carter.

"I have to admit that I never heard of the ordinance until a few months ago," says Angwin of the gay rights ordinance that was passed in July 1974. The way Angwin tells the story, the gay rights matter came up at a small Bible group he regularly attends. All agreed that repeal was in order, and Angwin was chosen to spearhead the drive.

Gay activists tell the story differently. They say Angwin's interest was sparked by Minnesota state senator Mike Manning, the Bryant-designated leader of Minnesota's antigay crusade. According to gay activists, Miami and Minnesota antigay honchos chose to challenge the St. Paul ordinance because they felt that St. Paul represented the most vulnerable turf of all the big cities that endorsed gay rights.

No matter whose version lies closer to the truth, the St. Paul drive has proved less dramatic than the Wichita controversy. According to gay activist Steve Endean, the necessary signatures were gathered by pairs of Temple Baptist parishioners who would walk conservative east St. Paul neighborhoods and ask one question: Do you want your children to be taught by an overt homosexual?

Those who didn't were asked to sign the petition. The 50 to 75 couples who circulated petitions, according to Angwin's estimate, also made sure that all signers were duly registered to vote. By mid January Angwin and a handful of parishioners were standing in the St. Paul city recorder's office handing in 7,100 signatures they had gathered to put an initiative on the ballot—a figure that represented 20% more signers than were needed to ensure a late-April gay-rights election.

The challenge comes to a gay community that has neither the funds nor the organization to wage a major electoral battle. Until a few weeks ago, the anti-initiative efforts were being organized by Steve Endean, who lives in Minneapolis. Indeed, much of the original lobbying for the St. Paul ordinance came from Minneapolis activists.

Added to this relative inactivity of St. Paul gay people is the fact that Minneapolis is home to one of the most unusual gay groups in the United States, the Target City Coalition. *Unusual* may not be the right word. In a movement in which a small number of kooks seem able to gather an amazing amount of press, the Target City Coalition—led by former University of Minnesota student body president Jack Baker—must take an award for being the most stoned-out, off-the-wall, bona fide crackpots yet to appear in the gay rights cause.

Target City made its splash at last year's Twin Cities gay pride parade by wearing uniformed attire and signing "Tomorrow Belongs to Me"—that charming little ditty sung by Nazi youth in *Cabaret*. When Target City leader Jack Baker didn't like the way things were going in Minnesota legislative hearings on a gay rights bill two years ago, he and a group of transvestites held a press conference in the men's room of the state capitol. That act obliterated any chances of gay rights passage in that session. Such unpredictable behavior has left mainstream gay activists biting their fingernails over what Target City will do as a showdown in St. Paul nears.

Gay rights proponents, however, say they have some demographics on their side. St. Paul perhaps is the quintessential ethnic, liberal Northern city, as its German Catholics and Scandinavian Lutherans long have provided a blue-collar backbone for Minnesota's own brand of progressive liberalism. They come from a much more practical and common-sense stock than the Bible-thumping Baptists and wigged-out Cuban reactionaries of Miami.

St. Paul's liberalism, however, is rooted in the ideology of the working class with a much larger dose of social conservatism than St. Paul's sibling city across the river, Minneapolis. Minneapolis, for example, has elected the only openly gay person ever to serve in a state senate in the United States. St. Paul, meanwhile, recently voted to outlaw strip bars and pornography shops. Antiabortion forces have found strong support in ethnic St. Paul neighborhoods.

The strength of such social conservatism—coupled with the strong antigay teachings of the Catholic Church—could prove fertile ground for gay opponents, if properly cultivated by the fundamentalists. The Reverend Angwin, for example, says he expects a statement of support from local Archbishop John Roach.

Steve Endean, however, says that such an endorsement won't happen because the Baptists have yet to thaw the traditionally cold feelings between Catholics and fundamentalists. "They could have organized large numbers of antigay Catholics," says Endean. "If they had, we would be in a lot more trouble than we are now."

But the fundamentalists still haven't made that outreach, while the newly organized St. Paul Citizens for Human Rights have gathered a list of endorsers that looks like a "who's who" of St. Paul's Democratic Farm-Labor Party bigwigs. Endean also expects endorsements from the League of Women Voters, the Urban League, Black Ministerial Alliance, and B'nai B'rith.

The fact that the ordinance existed for four years without raising much fuss will also aid the gay side, activists hypothesize. "In Miami the Save of Children people could spell out a list of horror stories about what would happen if the gay rights law went into effect—things about child molestations and all that," says Endean. "Here they can't do that because we've had the law for fours years and none of it has happened."

In a disco along the Hennepin Avenue strip of Minneapolis gay bars, a gay patron sums up the overriding Twin Cities gay feeling about the St. Paul repeal drive: apathy. "I don't care what happens either way," says the St. Paul schoolteacher. "I had my job before they passed the ordinance—I'll have it after they repeal it. It won't affect me."

IV. Dolly Parton and the Domino Theory

Late last year the Homophile Alliance of Sedgwick County surveyed a selected percentage of Wichita voters about how they would vote on a gay rights ordinance. The results indicated that not one precinct in Wichita would vote to endorse gay rights.

If all the strategizing and maneuvering for gay rights in St. Paul is successful, "We might have an even crack at winning," says state senator Allen Spear.

Though gay activists in both Wichita and St. Paul are busily donning smiling faces, they frankly worry that the question is not whether they will lose but by how much. They understandably are taking the issue to the courts in an effort to head off gay rights elections.

In Wichita HASC will ask the federal courts to stop the election, using a California supreme court precedent that threw out the referendum repeal of California's open housing law a decade ago. The connections are somewhat tenuous, but it's the best argument HASC can find.

In St. Paul gay forces hope they can avert a gay rights vote by persuading the city council not to accept initiative petitions. Under St. Paul's charter ordinances are repealed via referendums that must be filed within 45 days of enactment. New ordinances are adopted through initiatives. Fundamentalists, trying to repeal a four-year old ordinance, have avoided these charter provisions by creating an initiative to enact a new civil rights law—without the gay rights clauses. Gay rights proponents argue that this breaks the spirit, if not the letter, of the charter.

Activists in both cities are counting on these tactics to work and see them as their last hope, since the national gay community seems to be reluctant to give either the moral or financial support needed to wage a costly electoral battle.

The executive committee of the National Gay Task Force, for example, recently turned down Endean's request that the NGTF organize a national "referendum fund" to raise money for all the cities facing referendum battles. Gay publications that raised a large amount of the Dade County battle war chest, meanwhile, are refusing to lend their support for raising money for Midwestern gay groups.

The scores of gay activists who streamed in and out of the Miami media spotlight last year aren't going to St. Paul or Wichita this year. Midwestern gay organizes are grumbling that the national gay leaders are less concerned about the gay rights cause then about grabbing their own media aggrandizement—aggrandizement they won't find in the less publicity-ridden battlegrounds of Wichita and St. Paul.

HASC in Wichita has only $900 in its treasury, not enough to publish even one citywide brochure. Its only hope is in a current attempt to get Dolly Parton—who is to Midwestern gays what Barbra Streisand is to their East Coast counterparts—for a fund-raiser. In St. Paul the gay rights proponents have had to borrow their office space.

"Very few cities can raise the kind of money needed to run a campaign on their own," says Endean. "If the people in San Francisco, New York, and Houston think that progress will keep going forward when city after city repeals, they're full of shit."

Robert Lewis in Wichita sees a domino effect emerging. "If these people are able to win in Miami, then Wichita, St. Paul, and Eugene, what makes the big-city people think they're going to stop? It's only a matter of time before they start feeling their political power and go after the big cities. Who will stop it then?"

The Reverend Angwin also foresees a domino pattern. "I have no doubt whatsoever that we will win because America is just tired of the direction it's been going in."

The battle lines are basic, concludes Angwin. "It's as simple as right versus wrong," he says. Virtually everybody involved on both sides of the issue agrees.

A CITY GRIEVES GOOD MEN SLAIN

by Scott Anderson

January 11, 1979

San Francisco mayor George Moscone, a longtime friend of gay people, and openly gay supervisor Harvey Milk were gunned down in their city hall offices November 27 in what was apparently an act of political vengeance.

Police charged former supervisor Dan White, who had resigned from his post less than three weeks earlier, with two counts of murder and with illegal firearms possession. At the moment of the mayor's death, board of supervisors president Dianne Feinstein because acting mayor, and she was later confirmed as mayor until next November.

Mayor Moscone was a longtime friend of the gay community (see story) and had campaigned vociferously against Proposition 6. Supervisor Milk was the city's first openly gay official (see story) and was at the time of his death one of only two up-front elected gay politicians in the country. Already emerging as a leader of gay people at the national level, Milk was acknowledged by President Carter as "a leader of San Francisco's gay community, who kept his promise to represent all constituents." Milk left behind several tape recordings, one of which named candidates he favored and opposed to succeed him as supervisor.

Reactions to the murders came from stunned friends and colleagues of the two men. They were both remembered universally as activist politicians who listened with compassion to their constituents. President Carter said, "In every conversation with Mayor Moscone, I always knew that the people of San Francisco and California were uppermost in his mind and heart. He was a good and kind man, and he will be sorely missed. As supervisor, Milk had come to be widely regarded as a symbol of the aspirations of gay people to participate openly in mainstream politics and in society at large."

Charles F. Brydon, cochair of the board of the National Gay Task Force, called Milk "an important, visible leader to our community and an example to everyone of the humanity of gay people." Mayor Dianne Feinstein said of the murdered supervisor, "The fact of his homosexuality gave him an insight into the scars which all oppressed peoples wear. He believed that no sacrifice was too great a price to pay for the cause of human rights." Gerry Parker II, chair of the California State Democratic Party gay caucus, said, "Harvey Milk epitomized the idealism and courage of the great freedom fighters in American history. Harvey's persistence gave new hope for all Americans, both gay and nongay." Even Milk's political adversaries remembered him with admiration. State senator John Briggs, who debated milk several times in the course of the controversial Proposition 6 campaign, said that despite their political differences, "I came to develop a respect for Harvey as a man who pursued that in which he fervently believed, though I thought he was wrong. There are many demagogues in this world, and he was not one of them."

The two liberal leaders were honored by a massive outpouring of grief unprecedented in city history. They both lay in state beneath the city hall rotunda on November 29 as thousands of San Franciscans filed past the closed caskets to pay their respects. Various memorial services throughout the week honored the dead officials. On November 27, the evening of the shootings, more than 25,000 people carrying candles marched silently from the heavily gay Castro area—part of District 5, which Milk represented—to city hall to pay tribute to the slain supervisor. A Tuesday afternoon service packed Temple Emmanuel-El, where Milk was commemorated by fellow Jews and other friends. An interdenominational service Thursday drew an overflow crowd to the Opera House, where Milk was warmly remembered by aides and fellow politicians. According to his wishes, Milk was cremated and his ashes scattered at sea. He is survived by a brother, Robert Milk, 51, a Long Island, N.Y., salesman.

A Wednesday rosary and Thursday mass were said for Moscone, followed by a private interment at the Holy Cross Cemetery. Moscone is survived by his widow, Gina, and their four children.

The accused, Dan White, resigned his supervisor job November 10, saying he could not support his wife and infant son on the $9,600 annual half-time salary. Five days later, after family and friends had offered him financial support, White asked for the job back. While city attorneys examined the legality of reinstating White, the mayor, responding to complaints from White's constituents, decided to name someone else to the post. Meanwhile, Milk lobbied against retaining White.

Moscone was killed in his inner office during a private meeting with White, just 30 minutes before a press conference at which the mayor planned to name Don Horanzy, a neighborhood activist and political unknown, to success White. Police allege that after shooting Moscone, White crossed city hall and shot Milk. White had gained access to city hall by telling a building engineer he had lost his keys. After leaving city hall White turned himself in at a police station, where later he reportedly confessed to the killings.

White, 32, represented District 8 in south San Francisco, a largely working-class area with sizable minority populations. During his campaign for supervisor in 1977, White emphasized his sympathy for those who believed San Francisco's white middle class was losing ground to minority groups. "I am not going to be forced out of San Francisco by splinter groups or radicals, social deviates, incorrigibles," one campaign brochure said. White was the only one of 11 supervisors to oppose the city gay rights bill that Milk had lobbied for and which Moscone signed into law. White, a Vietnam veteran and former policeman and fireman, campaigned for supervisor on an anticrime platform. At a meeting last year of the Northern California Coalition for Handgun Control, White had spoken out for strict regulation of private weapons.

If convicted, White might fact the death penalty under the provisions of Proposition 7, which became law when voters overwhelmingly approved it November 7. The law invokes capital punishment for "special circumstances," which include assassination of public officials. The murder charges against White, brought by San Francisco district attorney Joseph Freitas, state that he killed the men "in retaliation for and to prevent the performance of [their] official duties."

The week before his death, Harvey Milk had issued a press release calling for a march on Washington, D.C., next summer to dramatize the need for national gay rights legislation. Supporters of Milk pledge to carry on his work in organizing the march. Ann Kronenberg, a close aide to the supervisor and his campaign manager, received a standing ovation when she spoke of "completing Harvey's dream. The time is now."

MILK: UP-FRONT AND COMMITTED

by Lenny Giteck

January 11, 1979

For a long time it looked as though Harvey Milk was destined to become the gay Harold Stassen. Milk first ran for the San Francisco board of supervisors in 1973 when, sporting a moustache and long ponytail, he declared, "I stand for all those who feel that the government no longer understands the individual and no longer respects individual rights." He was defeated.

He ran for supervisor in 1975, calling for a program to bring San Francisco government "back to the people who actually live in the City." He was defeated again.

In 1976 Milk ran for the California state assembly; to his dismay, a number of gay leaders supported his heterosexual opponent, Art Agnos. Milk had just been appointed to the city board of permit appeals by Mayor George Moscone. When he decided to run for the assembly, the mayor fired him from his new post. Milk then went on to lose the election—two defeats for the price of one.

So when Milk ran for the San Francisco board of supervisors in 1977 and *won,* victory was sweet indeed. Even detractors had to admire his persistence and determination. Said the exultant candidate: "I understand the responsibility of being gay. I was elected by the people of this district, but I also have a responsibility to gays—not just in the City, but elsewhere."

Milk never lost sight of that responsibility. During his year in office, he submitted a landmark gay rights ordinance to the board of supervisors. The measure—which moved to end antigay discrimination in jobs, housing, and public accommodations—was passed by the board and signed into law by Mayor George Moscone. Supervisor Dan White, the alleged assassin of both Milk and Moscone, cast the only dissenting vote.

Milk and San Francisco police chief Charles Gain met with representatives of the gay community and urged homosexuals to report antigay harassment or violence to the police department. Milk also met with gay people in the South of Market area about a rash of arson there.

He fought to have the board of supervisors grant Phyllis Lyon and Del Martin, longtime lovers and lesbian activists, a certificate of honor for "25 years of living together, of working together, of collaborating together; 25 years as leaders and pioneers against bigotry." The two women received the award.

At this year's gay pride parade Milk spoke forcefully about the need for gay people to come out of the closet. He called on President Carter to come to California and speak against the Briggs initiative.

Milk—along with San Francisco State University speech instructor Sally Gearhart—debated John Briggs on television. He went to Chicago to campaign for a gay candidate running for a seat in the Illinois house of representatives.

But Milk also realized that a gay public official had to deal with a whole range of issues. In doing so he felt he could help straight citizens learn to trust and respect gay people. Noted Milk, "I'm showing people here that gays are involved with taxes, and dog shit, and Muni, and everything else. So that people say, 'Hey, you know it doesn't matter if a person is green with six heads.'"

Milk was neither green nor six-headed, but he did involve himself with everything from taxes to public transportation. He proposed that the board of supervisors reexamine San Francisco's city government and its thousands of municipal codes. After the Jarvis-Gann property tax cut was passed, he urged San Francisco to adopt legalized gambling as a way of raising revenues. He was active in debates over the construction of the Yerba Buena convention center and proposed improvements at the San Francisco airport.

And yes, Milk was involved with the issue of dog shit. He authored a bill to force dog owners to clean up after their pets "did it" in the streets. The bill was passed by the board of supervisors and signed by Moscone. Milk went out to demonstrate his technique for picking up dog deposits. He reportedly conducted the demonstration with synthetic droppings and then, in full view of the media, accidentally stepped in the real thing.

Nobody laughed louder than the supervisor himself; despite his deeply felt convictions and political fervor, Milk never lost his sense of humor. On the contrary, he had a quick smile and an easygoing friendliness with people. It was one of the reasons he took the bus to city hall each morning.

"Riding Muni is one of the best ways I can keep in touch with people," Milk said. "A lot of the people on the bus recognize me and either wish me well or complain about how the city is being run. Besides, meeting people for just a 25-cent Muni fare is one of the biggest campaign bargains around."

Milk entered politics relatively late in life; he was 43 years old when he first ran for the board of supervisors. He decided to become politically active out of anger over the Vietnam War and the Watergate scandal: "I finally reached the point where I knew I had to become involved or shut up."

Born in the village of Woodmere, N.Y., Milk was the second son of a Jewish family. His father was in the retail clothing business. Milk graduated from Albany Teachers College in 1951. It was during the Korean War, and he became a Navy deep-sea diving officer on a submarine rescue ship in the Pacific. In 1953 the Navy discovered his homosexuality, and Milk was dishonorably discharged.

The discharge prevented Milk from pursuing his teaching career, so he worked for insurance and brokerage firms, He also helped produce several Broadway musicals and plays. In 1969 he moved to San Francisco and became a securities analyst with a large company. However, his position was abolished following a merger. It was then that he came out of the closet.

"It wasn't a difficult transition," Milk recalled. "In fact, it was easier than I expected, almost like a weight had been lifted off my back. I realized I no longer had to lead a double life with double standards."

Milk opened a popular camera shop in the Castro area. A month before his death, he closed the store for the last time; it was losing money because he was devoting so much time to his job as supervisor.

As San Francisco's first openly gay supervisor, Milk came to symbolize the gay community's determination to be part of the political process. His very presence in City Hall forced all San Franciscans to acknowledge that gay people play a vibrant, important role in the life of San Francisco.

The slaying of Milk brought forth an unprecedented display of sorrow and affection from San Francisco's gay population. It was perhaps an indication of how much the man had grown during his year in office.

In the end, Milk—the gay Harold Stassen—was called a gay Martin Luther King Jr.

MOSCONE: A PASSION FOR PEOPLE

by Scott Anderson

January 11, 1979

George Moscone was a politician who fought passionately for his convictions without alienating his opponents. Even those who disagreed with him liked the charming, unprepossessing man. He was remembered in the week following his death as a warm, generous, and compassionate man capable of tough arm-twisting on issues he was committed to. He was also remembered as the person who integrated gay people into the political process—both in San Francisco and statewide—to an unprecedented degree.

"George realized that the most important thing was to make everyone see that gay people are like everyone else," recalled grief-stricken Jim Foster, an openly gay Democrat and longtime Moscone ally. For George Moscone, says Foster, being gay was not an issue. "George used to say, 'If they're the best people I can find, I don't care if they're gay.'"

Moscone believed that the key to acceptance of gay people lay in putting them in visible positions where they could be seen doing a good job. He appointed openly gay people to head various city commissions, and the gay community enjoyed unprecedented access to the mayor's office. Moscone also had several gay people working within his administration.

One of them was Bill Cook, a senior adviser to the mayor on health and the arts. "I was probably the first open gay staff person in this kind of position," Cook says. "George was very supportive of me. He didn't want me to be a 'gay liaison.' He wanted me to do a good job. That meant a lot more to me than just being his 'in-house gay.'" Cook came out to the mayor in 1977 during discussions of the annual gay parade. "George was basically my catharsis," Cook recalls. "I was having a lot of problems dealing with my sexuality, and he was just incredibly supportive of me personally. He just wanted you to be who you were."

This sort of personal touch never disappeared from Moscone's manner. During his years in the California state senate, 1966–74, he remained committed to people-oriented issues. His legislative successes included decriminalization of marijuana, a school lunch program for needy children, and financial disclosure for elected officials. He also worked for bilingual education and strengthening the state Department of Consumer Affairs. A year after his first election, fellow Democrats chose Moscone for their majority leader, a post to which he was reelected three times.

One of Moscone's most important actions affecting gay Californians was his agreement to sponsor the senate version of the consensual adult sex bill, which Willie Brown had introduced in the state assembly. After being approved by the lower chamber, the bill faced a 20–20 deadlock in the senate. Using his powers as majority leader, Moscone had the senate chamber locked until Lt. Gov. Mervyn Dymally could fly to Sacramento from Denver to cast the deciding vote. It was that kind of commitment that inspired loyalty in his followers and admiration for his tenacity even in his opponents.

At the state level Moscone lent support to gay figures who wanted to organize politically. "No one is more responsible for the existence of the state Democratic gay caucus than George Moscone," declares *Advocate* publisher David Goodstein. "He took us [gay Democrats] *everywhere* and rammed us down the throats of those politicians he had to." When a planned dinner with gay leaders for state senators found no takers, Moscone did some cajoling to produce a dozen legislators at the event.

After he became San Francisco mayor in 1975, Moscone appointed openly gay Jo Daly to the Human Rights Commission. By consecutively naming three gay commissioners to head the Board of Permit Appeals (Harvey Milk, Rick Stokes, and David Scott), Moscone in effect created a permanent gay seat on the board. Even when he faced a bitter recall vote, Moscone never abandoned the people and the issues he thought were important.

Earlier this year Mayor Moscone signed into law a city rights ordinance protecting gay people from discrimination in housing employment, and public accommodations. And when his close adviser, Don Bradley, was asked to head the No On 6 campaign, Moscone encouraged him to do so, despite the potential peril for Moscone's own political career. Moscone himself campaigned openly against Proposition 6 and in behind-the-scenes maneuvers convinced many other politicians to oppose it. "George was willing to take an unpopular position and put his name and prestige behind, knowing he would face a lot of hostility," says Jim Foster. "He was always available and always willing."

An End to the Silence About Suicide

by Eric E. Rofes

August 9, 1979

Although the subject of suicide in the gay community has been pushed into the closet, suicide is a gay issue.

Suicide is an important and unfortunate part of our history as gay people. The pressure on homosexuals before the gay liberation movement drove an untold number of gays to take their lives because of intense feelings of depression, alienation, and hopelessness. Suicide has been one response to the overwhelming oppression and shame that society has forced on gay people.

While some activists see suicide as a vestige of the pre-Stonewall gay sensibility that will decrease with the growth of gay pride, lesbians and gay men have not stopped taking their lives. Suicide remains a part of the contemporary gay experience, and it will not go away simply by being ignored. Only by bringing the subject of suicide out into the open and confronting the fact that many gay people *do* kill themselves will we as a community continue to develop resources and techniques for coping with it.

Gay People and Suicide: The Statistics

The actual number of suicides in any population is difficult to determine, and finding accurate statistics for suicides among gay people is virtually impossible. Annual figures from the U.S. Department of Public Health place the total number of suicides in the country at approximately 30,000. Assuming homosexuals make up one tenth of any given population (and that the rate of suicide for gays is the same as for nongays), one could estimate the annual number of suicides by lesbians and gay men to be near 3,000. Suicide experts agree, however, that the 30,000 figure is probably quite low; some place the total number at about 150,000—or about 15,000 gay suicides.

One reason suicide statistics are so unreliable is that interpretations vary as to what exactly constitutes a suicide. Some coroners require that a suicide note be found before a death is certified a suicide, although fewer than 30% of the confirmed suicides involve such notes. Other types of deaths, such as car crashes, especially single car crashes, or drug overdoses, are a matter of subjective interpretation.

The gay suicide rate is a subject of great debate among sociologists and researchers. Antigay crusaders frequently cite high suicide rates among gay people in an attempt to prove that homosexuality is a deviant, ill-fated lifestyle. Tim LaHaye, in his book *The Unhappy Gays,* writes, "One writer claims that 50% of the suicides in American can be attributed to homosexuality…the suicide rate among the homosexual community is 12 to 14 times greater than that of the straight community." LaHaye does not document the source of this information.

On the other hand, gay people have too often refused to acknowledge that suicide has been and continues to be an issue plaguing their community. As early as 1951, in his landmark book *The Homosexual in America,* Donald Webster Cory defensively wrote, "Few suicides are homosexuals and few homosexuals commit suicide. Perhaps homosexuals are so accustomed to the slings and the arrows of a life in which they have buffeted from one difficulty to another that they find it easy to accept a philosophical approach to the torments of human existence." Cory does not cite statistics either.

In their recent Institute for Sex Research study, *Homosexualities,* Alan Bell and Martin Weinberg include several charts of statistics for suicide attempts. The source of the statistics was a study made in the San Francisco area almost ten years ago. Of the gay men in the study, almost 20% reported at least one suicide attempt, while under 3% of the heterosexual men reported attempting suicide. The statistics increased to almost 25% in the lesbian study group, while straight women reported only half that number of incidents. (In general, women attempt suicide more often than men, but men complete suicide at a much higher rate.)

In their new book, *The Gay Report,* Karla Jay and Allan Young note that 40% of the gay men and 39% of the lesbians surveyed answered affirmatively to the question, "Have you ever attempted or seriously contemplated suicide?" Of these people who had attempted or considered taking their lives, 53% of the men and 33% of the women felt that the attempt was directly related to their homosexuality.

Although some statistics are ambiguous, it does seem clear that lesbians and gay men frequently experience stressful situations that lead them to consider taking their own lives. It is not yet clear, however, whether the past ten years of the gay movement have created a climate where fewer gay people become desperate and unhappy. We might expect one of the effects of increased gay pride and openness to be a decrease in self-destructiveness and depression among gay people. As one woman who works with an international suicide prevention network put it, "The gay rights movement is certainly helping to make more people happier with themselves."

The Causes of Suicide

People kill themselves for a variety of reasons. Four basic types of suicides are listed in the literature put out by San Francisco Suicide Prevention: 1) Relief suicide: people seeking relief from pain or anxiety, or suffering from terminal diseases; 2) Surrender suicide: people who have severe problems in relationships—feeling lonely, depressed, hopeless, rejected; 3) Sociocultural suicide: people who are attempting to make a political statement, merge with a deity, perform a ritualistic suicide; 4) Psychotic suicide: people suffering from schizophrenia, delusions, hallucinations.

While people of any sexual orientation commit suicide for reasons in these categories, gays are greater risks in certain types of suicide. Sidney Abbott and Barbara Love begin their book *Sappho Was a Right-On Woman* with the statement "Guilt is at the core of the lesbian's life experience." This guilt is shared by all gay people and reinforced by a homophobic society. Such guilt can lead a person to violence and, as Abbott and Love go on to show, self-destructive acts:

> Suicide is the ultimate violence to oneself. It is the most extreme reaction to guilt, a final solution. The machinations of guilt take over the personality and mete out a punishment more severe even than society would wish. Can heterosexual society comprehend the agony a lesbian has gone through who conceives of death as the only solution?

> Every lesbian knows of women who have taken this final route out beyond their peripheral and despised position in society to nothingness. Gay women may attempt suicide as a desperate cry for help. Emotional and psychological pressures have become too much to bear alone. They may have tried to ask their parents to hear them and may have paid a professional listener (therapist), and still felt they were not heard. Instead of destroying unjust laws and attitudes, they destroy themselves. Alone they feel helpless and fear life more than death.

> While some people can cope comfortably with feelings of hatred directed at gay people and the repression involved in living a double life, other people internalize their

guilt and are filled with self-hatred. These people are at risk in the category of relief suicide; their pain and anger may lead them to attempt to "end it all" in order to stop living with overwhelmingly painful feelings.

For gay people who are not out to their family, friends and work associates, the fear of exposure is great and often leads to tremendous fear and distress. Historically this distress has probably been a cause of many gay suicides. In *Gay American History* Jonathan Katz reports several incidents of lesbians and gay men who, when faced with exposure to their family or their community, took their own lives. Katz cites Magnus Hirschfeld's study *Homosexuality in Men and Women,* published in 1914, which quotes a "Uranian" (homosexual) scholar from Colorado:

> Four years ago there was an engineering student here who was carrying on with boys
> in the YMCA building; he was arrested and taken to the police station, where he killed
> himself with a revolver. He was the son of a professor.

While the fear of exposure was a tremendous issue *before* the gay liberation movement, many gay people *still* believe they must lead their lives quietly and avoid exposure at any cost. In *The Gay Report* a man writes, "I have lived in total fear of my company, friends, or family learning of my homosexuality. I have lived with complete guilt related to my actions. In late 1973 I attempted suicide by drowning." As long as there are gay people in the closet, suicide will be prompted by the fear of exposure.

Richard Pillard, associate professor of psychiatry at Boston University's medical school, believes that another factor in gay suicides is the lack of support in our culture. "There just isn't the support system available to gay people that straight people have," says Pillard. "If you're a married straight person and you get into trouble, you've got parents, family, your church, your job; society stands ready to take care of you as one of its own. Gay people generally don't have that." While Pillard thinks this situation is changing with the growth of gay organizations, service groups and churches, most gay people are still "pretty much isolated."

Isolation is intensified if a person has been single for a long time. Hugh Crell, a hot line staffer at Suicide Prevention in San Francisco, reports that most of the calls received are from single people. "So many gay men are single," Crell says. "They're isolated and have difficulty relating to others. I don't think gay men kill themselves because they're gay but because they're single."

High-Risk Factors in the Gay Community

While experts have assumed for a long time that gay people are a high-risk group, there is not enough statistical evidence to prove or disprove this assumption. Within the gay population, however, certain groups are more likely to commit suicide than others.

Coming Out: Dr. Richard Pillard, who has counseled many lesbians and gay men at Boston's Homophile Community Health Services, has found that a gay person is very susceptible to feelings of anxiety and depression during the coming-out period. "Right around the coming-out time, people may feel euphoric for a while but then become depressed, feeling the loss of a socially approved identity. The process of coming out has to be more than just telling people you're gay. After that there's a lot of work to do. The notion of giving up the idea of oneself as straight and realizing, 'Now I'm different...now I'm an outcast,' and *really* dealing with it leads a lot of people to depression."

For some gay people, coming out is a difficult and painful process every step of the way. As one respondent to *The Gay Report* survey wrote, "During my first years of coming out I considered suicide often enough not to be frightened by it. I knew how I would do it. There were times that acknowledging my homosexuality was so painful that suicide seemed an alternative."

The Loss of a Lover: The death or departure of a lover is difficult for people of any orientation. The emotional distress and pain of breaking off a relationship can be overwhelming enough to affect even the most stable people.

The situation may be compounded if one is gay. Sally Casper, codirector of the Boston branch of the Samaritans, a befriending service and intervention suicide network, says, "For a closeted gay person who has lost his or her partner, there's no sympathy from coworkers or friends or family. A loss that's socially not recognized cuts the person off from the normal channels for mourning and getting over it. Loss of a lover is a normal problem that can happen to everyone, but it might be worse for gay people." Having to hide or deny one's grief because one is in the closet can lead to intense feelings of alienation and sorrow.

Holidays: There are conflicting studies on whether or not more people commit suicide during the holidays, particularly at Christmas. Experts agreed, however, that people are more likely to recognize feelings of isolation, loneliness, and unhappiness during a period when many other people are publicly celebrating with friends and loved ones.

For a gay person, holidays can be an extremely difficult time. Since many gay people are estranged from their families or have deliberately distanced themselves from their parents and siblings, traditional holidays can heighten their awareness of being "different." A group of friends or a lover can certainly be a good substitute for one's family, but if one should find oneself alone on Christmas Eve, it can be a deeply depressing situation.

A Samaritans Hotline staffer in Boston reports that last Christmas Eve, the first eight calls she received on the overnight shift were from gay men who had spent the entire day in bars and were lonely, depressed, and desperate. A lesbian who has been suicidal for long periods of time says, "On the first Christmas Eve that I was no longer with my lover, I realized how unhappy I had been since we broke up. Not having the holidays with her made me very depressed and, for the first time, I consciously thought about ending it all."

Gay Youth: Ten years ago, in her book *Ann Landers Talks to Teenagers About Sex,* Landers wrote, "Most of the boys [with gay feelings] who write are tortured with guilt and self-hatred. They live on the razor's edge, terrified that someone may learn they aren't 'like everybody else.' Many who write are so ashamed of their physical desires for members of their own sex that they speak of suicide. One 17-year-old Chicago boy wrote, 'If I can't get cured, I would rather kill myself than be a pansy all my life.'"

Of the gay people who had attempted suicide in the Bell/Weinberg study, over 50% had first attempted suicide when they were 20 years old or younger. Homosexuality as a factor in depression and suicide among young people led youth service programs to call on gay professionals for advice and assistance. The Massachusetts Committee for Children and Youth, a youth advocacy agency coordinating a statewide educational program on youth suicide, has made efforts to assure that gay people were included as members of its board because of the committee's assumption that there is a high rate of suicide among gay youth.

Youth suicide may well be the most unfortunate type of suicide because so often the death could have been prevented had the young person's perspective on the situation been altered. Many young people who have never acted on their gay feelings might attempt suicide without realizing that there are places where gay people can openly live and work. For many young people, the societally caused self-hatred and shame, and the secrecy associated with "different" forms of sexuality, combine to bring them to the brink of suicide.

Older Gays: As mentioned earlier, the risk of suicide increases with a person's age. Older people may experience feelings of depression relating to ill health, loneliness, and fear of death. Older gay people experience the same difficulties that all the elderly face. Many gay people jokingly say they're going to kill themselves when they turn 40, claiming, "There's nothing worse than being old and gay." If a person places all of his or her value in physical attractiveness, body condition, and health, middle and old age may indeed be difficult periods to cope with.

Enduring a lover's death is doubly hard when the relationship has lasted many years. F.O. Matthiesson, Harvard professor and author of the landmark study of American literature *American Renaissance,* committed suicide in 1950 as he neared the age of 50. His lover of 20 years, artist Russell Cheney, had died five years earlier. Matthiesson's suicide note stated, "I am exhausted…I can no longer believe that I can continue to be of use to my profession and my friends." Despite his explanation in the note, Matthiesson seems to have been gripped by painful feelings of alienation and aimlessness after Cheney died. Ten years earlier, while institutionalized in McLean Hospital, a mental sanitarium outside Boston, Matthiesson wrote in his journal:

"Towards the end of my session with Dr. Fremont-Smith he dwelt on the danger of fear, and perhaps intuitively introduced the fear of the death of someone you loved. At once I raised the question of whether I could face life without Russell…"

—*Rat & the Devil: Journal Letters of F. O. Matthiesson and Russell Cheney*, edited by Louise Hyde—pp. 246-47

The loneliness and isolation Matthiesson imagined in a life without his lover led him to experience feelings of depression and suicide that many older gays may feel after the loss of a long-term lover.

Alcoholics: Alcoholics are a high-risk group for suicide. One hot line staffer in New York reports that many of the calls he's received from suicidal gay people involve alcohol abuse. One suicidal alcoholic lost his job in a manufacturing firm, not because he was gay but because he drank. A lesbian from Miami who had attempted suicide twice says, "I know that I'm most dangerous to myself when I've had too much to drink. The first time I slashed my wrists was after I'd spent a night at the bar, feeling sorry for myself. By the time I got home I was too sloshed to control myself or even realize what was going on. I was so desperate and so drunk that I lost control."

Valerie Waidler of San Francisco Suicide Prevention notes, "Particularly for the male homosexual, I think we see a very high frequency of alcohol and drug abuse with depressed callers. Alcohol is used as a tension reliever, yet it really exacerbates the tension. A lot of social interaction for gay men occurs in the bars. We get people calling us who are trying to cope with feelings of loss, yet using drugs to cope with these feelings often increases them. Alcohol is a sign of self-destructive behavior."

For many recovering alcoholics, the struggle is difficult and can become overwhelming. If success in fighting alcoholism seems remote, some people choose to kill themselves rather than continue the fight.

Suicidal Lifestyles: Certain people who have dangerous lifestyles might be considered to be unconsciously suicidal. A man who has a very dangerous occupation or is turned on only by anonymous sex with straight men might be seeking trouble without being consciously aware of his suicidal tendencies. People who routinely mix alcohol and pills or drink heavily and then drive are not clearly making a suicide attempt, yet they are exhibiting suicidal behavior.

It is this group of people—who might be inviting danger while not actually making a clear suicide attempt—that has no place in suicide statistics. While it would be an exaggeration to say that all men who are interested in S/M are heading toward confrontation with suicide, the element of risk and danger, an important part of the S/M scene, makes it vital that these men explore their conscious or unconscious feelings of suicide.

Preventing Gay Suicide

Most people who experience distress intense enough to cause suicidal feelings need immediate help. If they are at the peak of crisis, hospitalization may be necessary until they feel less desperate.

For some people, speaking to a counselor or calling a hot line is enough to prevent them from hurting themselves. Even if the person is able to get through the time of crisis without taking his or her own life, the risk of suicide is not over. Any person who comes close to attempting suicide should seriously consider entering some kind of therapy.

Dr. Richard Pillard suggests that gays who are in need of counseling find a counselor who is comfortable with gay people. Most urban areas have a gay-oriented counseling service that can provide psychiatrists, psychologists, and social workers, many of whom are gay themselves. If a gay-oriented service is not available, many of the gay churches can refer people to suitable counselors. For rural gays and gay people in small towns, it may be difficult to find a sympathetic counselor, but it is still important.

Hugh Crell suggests to gay people feeling suicidal,

> Have a long talk with yourself or with a suicide prevention volunteer and examine the root causes of your unhappiness. That isn't as easy as it sounds. So often it is so muddled that it is difficult to tell cause from effect, action from reaction. Soul searching is painful but, in the long run, repression of feelings is more so. Repressed feelings do not go away. They lurk inside and grow stronger. It's like leaving the fire on under a pressure cooker. You risk blowing the lid off.
>
> If alcoholism or drug abuse is making your life miserable, for God's sake, don't accept it as an inevitable consequence of homosexuality. Get into a rehabilitation program. Some of the happiest gay people around are members of Alcoholics Anonymous or Narcotics Anonymous. If you are lonely, take advantage of the many healthy opportunities to meet people. Knights in shining armor do not come pounding on strangers' doors. Neither are they found perched on barstools night after night. If meeting people is too threatening an experience for you, get into counseling with a good psychologist to discover why. (Knights in shining armor are occasionally found in group therapy sessions.)

Hot lines can be another good source of befriending or counseling for suicidal gays. The Samaritans Hotline carefully screens its phone volunteers for homophobic attitudes and trains them about gay concerns. Sally Caspar explains that "Volunteers need to know that gay people can be just like people who are not gay. A person's homosexuality doesn't have to be an issue; the emotions are often the same. We also make sure that our volunteers don't have the idea that homosexuality is a stage of 'incomplete emotional development.' That's a clear put-down."

When Hugh Crell is answering phone calls at the San Francisco Hotline, he sees his primary job as listening to the caller. Many suicidal people have a hard time sharing their feelings, and when they finally muster the courage to divulge information to a phone volunteer, the volunteer must be attentive. "Volunteers act as pressure valves if the person will tell us what's on their mind," Crell says. "Just by confiding their feelings, they can experience a good degree of relief." Crell tries to direct people to mental health programs for counseling. If a caller is in an emergency situation, the center may also attempt a rescue.

Some gay callers are hesitant to identify themselves as gay. Asking if a person is gay can be awkward for a staffer and can also cause stress for the caller. Sally Caspar says, "If a caller is being very careful to avoid pronouns, right away I'm alerted that the lover they're talking about is possibly of the same sex. Sometimes, in that situation, I'll say, 'How did you meet him or her?' If they're gay, it conveys that it would be acceptable to me and people tend to open up more."

While counseling may aid an individual to overcome his or her feelings of depression and self-hatred, the larger issues concerned with gay suicide need to be confronted at a societal level. The circumstances that make lesbians and gay men fear exposure must be eliminated. Gay people must be protected from discrimination at their jobs, in housing and education, and with their children. The gay community, with its vast and diverse resources, must continue to develop alternatives to traditional social patterns, alternatives that foster healthy and supportive relationships between gay people. While this process may be dangerous and difficult, it is an important step toward a positive self-image that allows a person to become whole.

As Valerie Waidler says, "I truly believe that people decrease the risk for suicide if they can come out and express their feelings so that great feelings of pain and hopelessness don't get turned against themselves. Coming out with feelings has to be a liberating action. I can only see it as a positive experience for all people."

THE THIRD MAN'S THEMES: GAY RIGHTS AND SOCIAL EVOLUTION—JERRY BROWN: THE CANDIDATE TAKES FUTURE STOCK

by Lenny Giteck and Scott Anderson

March 20, 1980

Newsweek called him "the apostle of future shock in American politics—a Zen-schooled, '60s-bred original who has flouted all the conventions of his craft and still won every office he has sought except, in 1976, the Presidency."

One Carter aide has said, "He's like a jellyfish. You may burn your hand a little picking him up, but when you hold him up to the sunlight you can see right through him."

He is Jerry Brown, 42-year-old governor of California and, once again, candidate for the presidency of the United States. To his admirers, Brown is a political visionary who will usher in a New Age of environmental consciousness, fiscal responsibility and alternative energy. To his detractors, he is a political opportunist and trend follower whose multicolored rhetorical pyrotechnics are all show and no substance. To most Americans, Brown remains—despite his years in the public eye, despite the scores of articles and countless speeches—a riddle wrapped in an aphorism inside a buzzword.

But one thing is certain: On the issue of gay rights, Jerry Brown is without rival. He has supported equal rights for homosexuals longer, more consistently, and more vociferously than any other major American leader. In 1978 Brown opposed the anti–gay teachers initiative, Proposition 6, and began naming gays to state commissions. In 1979 he signed an executive order banning antigay job discrimination in California government. He also appointed an openly gay man superior court judge. His presidential campaign has been run by David Mixner and Peter Scott, gays who own a Los Angeles–based public relations firm. Brown has relied heavily on gay financial support in order to qualify for federal matching campaign funds in 20 states, and he's attended numerous private and public gay fund-raisers—one at a gay bar in Washington, D.C.

Despite all that, there are some people who view Brown's support of gay rights as a desperate attempt to create *some* sort of national constituency. And they're not alone in questioning the depth of Brown's commitment to issues. J.D. Lorenz, a staff assistant in Brown's 1974 gubernatorial campaign and former director of the California Employment Development Department, has written a damning book titled *Jerry Brown: The Man on the White Horse*. In it Lorenz quotes Brown as saying exultantly of one of his law-and-order campaign commercials, "That ad has six buzzwords in it. I sound tough, and I haven't proposed anything the liberals can criticize me for. In fact, I haven't committed myself to do anything at all."

Brown strongly favors the development of new and renewable energy sources, space exploration, combating environmental pollution, and decentralizing political power. He opposes reliance on nuclear energy and reinstatement of the draft. Insisting the United States can no longer police the entire world, Brown advocates the creation of well-armed regional alliances to resist Soviet expansionism. He had almost single-handedly injected phrases such as "less is more," "planetary realism," and "era of lowered expectations" into American political parlance. Says Brown of his vision for the United States, "What I'm offering the people in this country is not just another personality to replace President Carter, but rather the opportunity to bring American into a new age, whereby we are more self-reliance, more frugal, more just and more understanding of the diversity within our own country and the diversity within the Third World."

All very nice. Nevertheless, the governor has had difficulty shaking his image as a "flake;" he has been a frequent target of Garry Trudeau's wit in the *Doonesbury* cartoon strip. Brown's much ballyhooed trip to Africa with singer Linda Ronstadt and his earlier misguided trip to New Hampshire have only damaged his presidential prospects. So have Ted Kennedy's entry into the race and Jimmy Carter's rise in popularity because of the crises in Iran and Afghanistan. (It may be premature to count Brown out of the race; he made surprisingly a strong showing in the recent Maine caucuses.)

Still, for gay people, Jerry Brown—no matter how deep his commitment to the cause—may be the brightest hope. Because of that, *The Advocate* recently interviewed the candidate at his Los Angeles home. Here is what he had to say:

Ted Kennedy has called for a plank in the Democratic Party platform in support of gay rights, and President Carter has also made some pro–gay rights statements. If gay people focus politically on the gay issue, why should they vote for you?

My views in favor of a gay rights plank in the Democratic Party platform, my actions in signing a state executive order banning discrimination based on sexual orientation, my appointment of a gay man to be a superior court judge in Los Angeles, and the participation of gays in my presidential campaign have all motivated President Carter and Senator Kennedy to take more advanced positions on gay issues than they would have otherwise. My positions on gay issues derive from my strong commitment to individual rights and to broadening the base of participation in government. I believe my track record in appointing women and minorities—and more recently in specific actions regarding gay rights—stands stronger than either of my two opponents'.

Gays have been particularly vulnerable to discrimination in the FBI, the CIA, and the State Department. What would a Brown administration do about that?

I start with the premise that discrimination based on color, creed, sex, and sexual orientation has no place in our government. Myths and stereotypes that create an atmosphere if intimidation and discrimination with reference to gays should not be allowed to continue in hiring and promotion in the agencies that you mentioned.

The "reasoning" behind such antigay discrimination is that, supposedly, homosexuals can easily be blackmailed.

A heterosexual who does certain things—perhaps has an affair with somebody else's wife—is certainly subject to blackmail. Such a person is not thereby prohibited from serving in the U.S. government. In recent years the whole issue of homosexuality has come out of the shadows. The greater candor regarding gay issues is eroding the whole basis—if there ever was one—for blackmailing gays. Since being gay is not something people have to be ashamed of or have to conceal, there's no reason its exposure should be an occasion for blackmail. Our thinking about this should be revised accordingly.

Another area where there have been problems recently, one which has received a lot of media attention, has been homosexual foreigners who've been stopped at our borders and refused entry. The Justice Department recently ruled that U.S. Immigration must enforce the 1952 law lumping homosexuals together with psychopaths. As president, what would you do about that policy?

I would seek a reinterpretation of that law, if it were legally justifiable. If it were not, I'd seek congressional change. To me, the point that has to be communicated to Americans is that we respect people as individuals, not as stereotypes. Gender identify is something many people now believe begins prior to birth or early in life. Whatever it turns out to be is not something that ought to be the occasion of shunting people into the backwaters of society. While our knowledge continues to evolve and our interpretations develop, we should assert the basic First Amendment and 14th Amendment rights that have been claimed by blacks, by women, by the elderly, by Hispanics—and by gays.

How would a presidential executive order on gay rights work?

I would sign an executive order banning discrimination based on sexual orientation similar to the one I signed in California, and it would be enforced by the appropriate civil service authorities within the federal government.

How seriously is a "gay vote" seen by politicians in this country?

There's definitely an emerging awareness of it in California. There may be an emerging awareness in a few other places, but I would not say it has been diffused throughout the 50 states.

The issue in California has been more politicized because of the Proposition 6 campaign. And here is the irony: Even though gay rights legislation is defeated in various cities and states, what has been a taboo subject becomes more familiar and more acceptable because it's placed in the realm of political debate. For that reason I believe this issue is gaining grater visibility and gay rights greater acceptability all across the country. It's just a matter of time.

Do most politicians perceive that there's a risk attached to supporting gay rights?

I would say so, but my view is that it's time to build a new governing coalition based on the realities of the world as they're going to be, not as they have been. What may seem to be a risk in 1980 will be recognized over time as part of the evolution of our society.

We're witnessing a resurgence of fundamentalist Christian groups, many of which are vocal in their opposition to gay rights. How powerful will these groups become?

It's hard to me to assess that. I do think there is a spiritual revival occurring in this country, and maybe even in the entire world. The gross materialism that has been the driving force in the recent American past is giving way to what I believe is an awakening sense of the primacy of spiritual values. As part of that awakening there is a renewed fundamentalism, but I don't think true spirituality can exclude individuals based on their sexual orientation. The religious texts on which the great religions are based have to be penetrated for their essence. When they are, the predominant sentiment will be a toleration and a respect for people quite different from some narrow crusade against gays.

What kind of debate did you and your staff have about the advisability of going to the fund-raiser you attended at a gay bar in Washington?

Very early on we asked Mixner and Scott to work with us. I've been going to various gay groups discussing the issue, seeking political and financial support, and the affair in Washington was just in that general context. There really wasn't that much discussion about that particular event.

Were there negative political repercussions?

There are a number of people who view this issue with fear and loathing—not to say insecurity—and therefore they react negatively. The fact that there's negative reaction to my attending and supporting the gay rights fund-raiser in Washington, D.C., is not all that much different to some of the reaction to my opposition to nuclear power, my appointment of Jane Fonda to the Arts Council, or a number of other controversial appointments and actions I've taken. I see my role as breaking new ground along the lines that this society must develop.

When you speak of a negative response to your appearance at the fund-raiser, what are you referring to specifically?

Some people say it's harder to raise money. People say, "Why is Brown doing that? Why does he put so much emphasis on that?" But they say that about the other things I do too. I've thought through the issue, and I believe my position is defensible and right. I think the justice of the case will be communicated over time.

What needs to be done to ensure the passage of gays rights legislation in California?

The individual legislators have to know that there are people in their districts who care very much about this, and the subject has to be discussed, analyzed, argued about—and ultimately accepted.

Have you worked with members of the California legislature toward that end?

Yes. My office has been actively involved. My persuasive powers are open to some question in the legislative arena. But we did work actively both this year and the year before.

What do you think happened with state senator Joseph Montoya, who cast the deciding vote against a gay rights bill in January?

This is an issue that remains invisible unless it's brought to certain people's attention. It's controversial, and the general rule of politics is if something is controversial and you can avoid it, you should. That is only overcome when a group is able to effectively assert the legitimacy of its claim to legislative representatives. I do see that as a matter of time.

There was a lot of media coverage of your so-called "flip-flop" on Proposition 13. At the time, you said it was obvious the people wanted the measure enforced and that you were therefore obliged to enforce it. What if it becomes clear that a majority of Americans oppose civil rights guarantees for homosexuals?

I've said in my campaign that I'm going to push legislation banning discrimination based on sexual orientation. If I become president, I will follow through on that. I will urge Congress to accept these proposals. Obviously, if the constituency is not in the country, the Congress will resist. The president can lead, can teach, can set priorities, can urge, but the President operates within a context of beliefs and pressures. The country has to change along with the occupant in the White House.

You were raised as a devout Catholic and trained for the priesthood. What was the process you went through in changing your views on the gay rights issue?

Obviously, based on my training and my upbringing, gay rights was not something that I'd normally select as a political issue or just naturally conclude was a righteous cause. But through my own political experience in Sacramento, the contacts I've made through the California Democratic Council, and my own reading—particularly during the No On 6 campaign—I came to understand the issue better. As I encountered more people who made the case for gay rights, I saw it in a light that I'd never see it in before—as part of the evolution of society and the assertion of individual rights. In that context, my own thinking has developed and matured to the point where it is now.

The possibility that you yourself might be gay has been bandied about for some time. What do you think about that?

I don't think too much about it. I recognize that in seeking the presidency, one's life in all its dimensions becomes fair game for scrutiny, argument, gossip, and analysis. I accept that, and that's about it. I feel really strange having to describe or defend my personal identity, and I generally try to focus on my past records and what I conceive to be a viable future for the country. So if people want to ask me questions about my sexual identity, I'll tell them.

Have you been asked outright?

Yes. Some people say "Are you gay?" and I say "No, I'm not." Sometimes they're embarrassed to raise the subject. It's an interesting phenomenon that more and more of our lives is being opened up to discussion. While on the one hand I think we should have a zone of privacy to allow us to flourish and develop, I also think increasing candor will probably create a healthier society.

Do you see your being a bachelor as a problem for becoming president?

No. People said it was important to be married in order to run for governor of California. I ran successfully twice. When people begin to examine the marriages of politicians or even look at the quality of their personal relations, they find that the intensity and emotional absorption of senators or governors or presidents or would-be presidents is such that there will be a little more hesitation and humility in giving politicians advice about whether or not to get married as a precondition for seeing higher office.

If you don't get the nomination this year, are you going to try again in 1984?

I believe that my chances this time are much better than most people assume, that the Democratic nomination may become a two-person race very quickly, that the times definitely require a challenge, that the incumbent is enjoying a certain mesmerized popularity the facts don't justify, that over the course of the next several months there's a good opportunity to run a successful challenge. But I recognize that my candidacy is an uphill battle.

A CHILL WIND FOR GAY RIGHTS

by Larry Bush and Richard Goldstein

July 9, 1981

When the Connecticut Life Insurance Company released a national poll it commissioned in April, the fears of many gays after last fall's elections were confirmed: The American public is more willing than ever to make connections between private religious beliefs and public policy.

The study, which has since passed into the stock lore politicians draw on when making legislative decisions, held an ominous warning: "The danger lies in the opening for a divisive leader to mobilize large numbers in the service of a partisan campaign to blame the nation's troubles on one or another group labeled 'immoral.'" It should come as no surprise that the report's authors found homosexuals the most likely group to serve as such a foil.

The Connecticut Life Insurance study comes at a time when religiously oriented political groups are making startling gains in Congress (in 1980 they helped elect between 20 and 30 senators and representatives), and in the White House (where numerous appointments acknowledged the importance of this constituency). The study is careful to note that the best known of these groups, a registered political lobby called Moral Majority Inc., did not initiate the shift in public attitudes, nor can it direct the political expression of this search for absolute values.

But as groups like Moral Majority stumble about locating issues that can place them in the forefront of American politics, gays face a new reality of backlash and even violence. Hardly a month passes without more evidence that gays are selected—and sometimes preferred—targets. In Chicago a rape watch is maintained by the local gay newspapers following a series of attacks on gay men. In San Francisco Community United Against Violence reports attacks on gay people have risen 30% since the publicity about an antigay political drive, on top of a 400% rise since last year's airing of the CBS News documentary *Gay Power, Gay Politics*. Political reality is altering the prospect that gays can live peaceably in a pluralistic society.

The campaign against homosexuals isn't a casual aspect of the new right's agenda; its the one issue on which it can get a broad constituency to agree. The 40 million Americans who say they have been born again vary in political ideology and part company on a number of dogmatic points. But when it comes to homosexuality, they share an overwhelming consensus. Only 3.5% of fundamentalists would like to take sodomy laws off the books. Among all Americans, a 1979 Harris survey reported, 70% feel that sodomy between consenting adults should be legal.

"We hadn't originally intended to use the gay issue," says Gary Jarmin, a prominent evangelical organizer and formerly a paid advocate for the Unification Church and the governments of Rhodesia and Taiwan. "We were working on school prayer, but then we found that almost everybody was unaware of Jimmy Carter's support for the gay rights plank [in the 1980 Democratic party platform]. That is an issue which symbolized a drastic departure from Christian morality. Christians debate among themselves over school prayer, but when it comes to homosexuality, it is so clearly wrong that to find a born-again president supporting gay rights is a real eye-opener. That's when we really got the 'ohs' and 'ahs' and gasps."

To target Jimmy Carter, the fundamentalist right took an issue that hadn't been mentioned in the presidential debates and made sure the faithful knew where the president stood on it. "President Carter's platform carries his pledge to cater to homosexual demands," ran the sound track on one commercial. "The choice November 4 involves moral issues. Carter advocates acceptance of homosexuality. Ronald Reagan stands for the traditional family."

Reagan himself has been silent on gay rights since the day he took the oath of office with his hand on a Bible open to a verse chosen by fundamentalists. But the silence is about to be broken, at least in the Republican-dominated Senate. On June 17 the new right's most ambitious attempt to codify its ideology, the Family Protection Act, was introduced. This omnibus legislation claims to "counteract disruptive federal intervention into family life, and to encourage restoration of family unity, parental authority, and a climate of traditional morality." It would accomplish this, in part, by forbidding federal funding of programs that "inculcate values or modes of behavior which contradict the demonstrated beliefs and values of the community" or educational materials that "tend to denigrate or diminish traditionally understood role differences between the sexes."

The Family Protection Acts also stipulates that "no federal funds my be made available to any public or private individual, group, foundation, commission, corporation, association or any other entity which presents homosexuality, male or female, as an alternative lifestyle or suggests that it can be an acceptable lifestyle."

The Congressional Research Service, a government agency that reviews the impact of proposed legislation, has issued the following analysis of the Family Protection Act: "The condition on federal funding that would be imposed is sweeping. No person who was a homosexual or who even intimated that homosexuality might be an 'acceptable' lifestyle could receive any federal funds under such programs as Social Security, welfare, veteran's programs, or student assistance. Similarly, any organization that indicated that homosexuality might be an acceptable lifestyle would be ineligible for any government assistance."

The chilling effect such a statute would have on politicians, journalists, researchers, and social activists who support gay rights is incalculable. And the bill raises an even more ominous prospect: How do you tell who is homosexual? Is it anyone who has ever had a homosexual experience? Is it anyone who is seen in a gay bar, found in possession of gay literature, or accused of befriending a known homosexual? (Such evidence can and has been introduced in military courts to justify the expulsion of servicemen and women charged with harboring homosexual "tendencies, desires, or interests.") Or is this law actually designed to punish those who refuse to conceal their homosexuality?

"We oppose any effort by homosexuals to flaunt their perversion," says the Moral Majority in a full-page ad that ran last March in major newspapers, including *The New York Times*. But just what constitutes "flaunting"? Is it cruising, holding hands, or simply petitioning for equal treatment under the law? In some states laws against "sexual imposition" are used to deny charters to gay political groups. Under the Family Protection Act, anything that acknowledges the existence of homosexuality—or the reality of gay oppression—would be subject to scrutiny by the state.

This backlash does not intend to abolish homosexuality, only the homosexual's capacity to be visible and seek a redress of grievances. "We will never end homosexuality, or any sin for that matter, on this earth," says Jerry Falwell. "But we can make it easier for politicians and all citizens to do right rather than wrong."

Gary Potter, the president of Catholics for Christian Political Action and a framer of the Family Protection Act, has a less felicitous interpretation of what this law would accomplish: "There will be no satanic churches, no more free distribution of pornography, no more abortion on demand, no more talk of rights for homosexuals. When the Christian majority takes control, pluralism will be seen as evil and the state will not allow anybody the right to practice evil."

The most frightening aspect of the repression waiting in the wings is the unwillingness of liberals to speak out before it becomes law.

In the months since last fall's conservative sweep, the Gay Rights National Lobby has done an admirable job of keeping support high for a congressional gay rights bill. This session's version of that bill has 47 cosponsors to date. But the list does not include two representatives who pledged to be there: Jim Weaver, reelected to his seat despite a campaign against his gay rights stance; and Ron Wyden, who defeated a gay rights bill sponsor with the pledge that he would be an even stronger advocate. Both had made it clear that despite their victories, the 1980 election sent them an unmistakable message.

That message was also heard by the Select Commission on Immigration and Refugee Policy. After two years of public hearings, it had become a foregone conclusion that the commission would urge Congress to drop the archaic immigration law banning suspected homosexuals. But when the commission met to make its final recommendations in January, the repeal of an antigay law was considered explosive. "This could blow the commission out of the water," argued Democrat Romano Mazzoli, chair of the House immigration panel. Among the absentees at the hearing was Sen. Ted Kennedy, who had pledged during his presidential campaign to win repeal of the law he helped strengthen in 1965, when he floor-managed a more explicitly antigay provision.

Even among the liberal committee members present, no word was raised to question statements that overt discrimination was a legitimate public policy. Immigration reform remains alive, thanks to the commission staff's efforts to draft a modernized code, but congressional sources say its only chance is to be kept out of the spotlight.

Liberal and moderate support for gay rights evaporated altogether last summer when it was put to the test on a roll call vote regarding the Legal Services Corporation. An amendment denying funding for gay rights cases was defeated in a voice vote but overwhelmingly passed after Georgia Democrat (and current John Birch Society board member) Larry McDonald insisted his colleagues go on the record. Fancy footwork by the Gay Rights National Lobby kept this year's version of the Legal Services bill from taking an even more restrictive direction after an amendment was proposed that would have gutted the agency's new directive banning discrimination against gay employees. That fight may yet resurface on the floor of Congress.

Accepting gay rights as civil rights is something the prestigious Leadership Conference on Civil Rights has been unable to do. In 1977 application for membership by the National Gay Task Force was turned down because the conference, which includes representatives of major black organizations, the National Organization for Women, and the Anti-Defamation League, was "unable to reach a consensus and therefore unable to act favorably." When NGTF sought to reapply this year, the conference's director warned, "I do not know whether a consensus is achievable now."

Even so prominent a supporter of gays rights as New York City mayor Ed Koch is signaling a shift. Koch's first official act had been to sign an executive order banning discrimination against gays in city hiring. With gay rights once again before the city council, Koch has said he will not take on its opponents as he would racists or anti-Semites, out of "respect" for "religious sentiments." Antigay attitudes are "a matter of conscience," according to Koch.

In the professions, where there was once considerable support of gay rights, there is now widespread indifference, if not retrenchment. The National Education Association has backed off a case involving the rights of gay teachers in Oklahoma; the American Bar Association has rejected a proposal to support repeal of the antigay immigration law; and even the American Bar Association has rejected a proposal to support repeal of the antigay immigration law; and even the American Psychiatric Association, one of the most potent allies of gay rights, is facing a reactionary push. "The possibility of a reversal [in the APA's position that homosexuality is not an emotional disorder per se] cannot be dismissed," writes Ronald Bayer in his newly published study, *Homosexuality and American Psychiatry*. "To diminish the likelihood of such an outcome will take powerful resistance on the part of a well-organized gay community and its psychiatric allies."

What gays and their allies face is a public policy debate taking place for the most part behind closed doors, where opponents of gay rights are setting the terms. Gays can take little comfort from the fact that no laws have been introduced calling for federal agents to stone homosexuals to death in a reprise of Old Testament morality. It is quite enough that the "guidelines" being followed by the Reagan administration would dismantle much of the gay community and place in jeopardy its claim to status as a minority group.

"No one is advocating the invasion of the private life of any individual," Ronald Reagan told interviewer Robert Scheer during the 1980 campaign. "I think Pat Campbell [sic] said it best in the trial of Oscar Wilde. She said, 'I have no objection to anyone's sex life as long as they don't practice it in the streets and frighten the horses.'"

Many gays were assuaged by Reagan when he opposed the Briggs initiative. "Individual rights has long been a hallmark of conservative philosophy," says Duke Armstrong of San Francisco's Concerned Republicans for Individual Rights. "With a little nudge from us, the new administration will quietly honor its commitment."

Individual rights do not, however, include laws banning discrimination on the basis of sexual orientation in housing and employment. As for the right to sexual privacy, in his interview with Scheer, Reagan said he would not have signed a consenting adults bill as governor of California because "in the eyes of the Lord" homosexuality is "an abomination."

The conservative argument against gay rights legislation is much the same as its arguments against federal funding for abortions and affirmative action. But the consequences of a laissez-faire policy toward homosexuality are not. Not only would such a policy remove federal funding of gay health clinics, legal programs, and community outreach centers, but it would leave highly discriminatory practices intact and give states and municipalities the right to bolster these practices through local ordinances. A good example of how laissez-faire can work against gays will soon be provided by Christian Voice. It is pressing for a provision that would cut off federal funds to every school district that did not expressly forbid the hiring of homosexuals, unless every parent gives his or her written consent for homosexuals to teach. In effect antigay forces are claiming a veto over human rights.

It is a mistake to think the Christian right has already achieved that power. Its success so far has been not so much in exercising a veto as in preventing discussion. When gays and their allies have broken through the silence, some achievements have been gained.

In March, for example, a bill to halt "the teaching of homosexuality" at state colleges in Arkansas was stopped after a black Little Rock legislator, Irma Hunter Brown, rose to protest. In Maine a state gay rights bill was narrowly defeated, but not before antigay bigots went into full cry and nearly destroyed their credibility. As a result, Maine gays believe they stand a good chance of getting a bill passed in the future. In Illinois a gay rights bill failed in the state legislature on May 14, as it had in 1977. But its sponsors were buoyed by the private support of many legislators in a sharply more conservative session.

The American Civil Liberties Union, which refused gay rights cases in the 1950s, remains in the forefront of the battle and boasts open gays on its national board and many of its local boards. Major religious organization, from the National Council of Churches to the Lutheran Council, have joined with NOW, National Women's Political Caucus, American Psychological Association, Americans for Democratic Action, and the ACLU in affirming their support for gay rights legislation.

The Gay Rights National Lobby organized a 75,000-member constituent network to deter antigay bills and issued alerts on antigay Congressional proposals. It also orchestrated opposition to antigay Reagan nominees. But it anticipates little time for pushing a positive gay agenda. Its best hope is that the claim of gays to equal protection under the law will spark a reaction to various antigay proposals (an anti-antigay backlash, if you will).

The National Gay Task Force, which put considerable energy into lobbying federal agencies in the year before the election, has made no announcements of similar meetings since Reagan took office. After officials took steps to undo several pro-gay Carter initiatives, NGTF codirector Charles Brydon was quoted in the gay press as accepting those setbacks with no protest. A letter to a member of Congress suggesting that a pro-gay bill was an "emotionally charged issue" and that no bill should be introduced "now or in the foreseeable future" shook local gay political clubs in San Francisco as well as California Democratic Council's gay caucus and clubs and leaders in New York City, Miami, Louisiana and Texas. In the uproar that followed, the NGTF letter was withdrawn, and Task Force leaders and board members promised that a June meeting would provide new and clearer directions.

"The one truly dark cloud in the otherwise sunny sky smiling over Ronald Reagan's election concerns the Moral Majority," writes conservative spokesman Norman Podhoretz, no friend of consensual sodomy. "On issues like abortion and homosexuality, even many people who voted for Reagan, let alone those who did not, are genuinely worried about a wave of bigotry and repression; it is indeed in discussion of these matters that the word fascism has come up…

"Nevertheless, even among [liberals] one senses…a feeling, almost, of relief at the thought that now at least a line will be drawn to keep things from going further than they already have gone. The liberal culture of recent years has been unable to draw any such line, even when in its heart of hearts it may have wanted to…Absolutist only in its moral relativism, how could it stand against the encouragement (as opposed to the tolerance) of homosexuality, or object when the number of abortions began to exceed the number of live births? Unable to do these things for itself, the liberal culture may not be altogether averse to having the dirty work done by others, while of course deploring and disclaiming any responsibility."

There is nothing inevitable about the antigay backlash. It can be nipped in the bud if liberals and moderates recognize that faggots are being used to fuel a fire that will engulf them as well. Though gays will be among the first to bear the brunt of this repression, in the long run women, children, racial minorities, and their allies of all religious persuasions—or none—will suffer as well. All are pariah groups that emerged in the recent era of respect for pluralism to demand full participation in society. The antigay backlash forges those links into a chain.

As of now, the entire dialogue has shifted to the right. Discretion and repression are what is being debated. Gay liberation has nothing to do with it.

[PART THREE]

HEALTH CRISIS: AIDS AND BACKLASH (1982–1988)

Like all newsmagazines, *The Advocate* had occasional lapses. As longtime arts and features editor Mark Thompson, who shepherded much AIDS reporting, has pointed out, it was largely silent during the early days of the AIDS epidemic, addressing the topic only to question a connection between the disease and gay men. Randy Shilts had departed for the *San Francisco Chronicle*, depriving the magazine of an aggressive reporter eager to cover the disease. (Shilts would go on to write the classic AIDS book *And The Band Played On.*) *The Advocate*'s first major coverage did not appear until

March 18, 1982, eight months after *The New York Times,* itself under criticism for ignoring the burgeoning health crisis, ran an article, "Rare Cancer Seen in 41 Homosexuals."

The magazine eventually got around to covering the epidemic. In a two-part series, "Is Our
'Lifestyle' Hazardous to our Health?" Nathan Fain, a New York journalist, focused on promiscuity in
an age before condom use became the norm. "The sexual athlete has become the object of concern,"
the introduction to one piece read. "The complexity of these men's lives fascinates researchers. The
variety of sex and drugs over the last ten years is to some the equivalent of a medical trip to the moon.
Now Ground Control, awed and worried, is trying to catch up. It is rare to find a doctor who has
taken that lunar step alongside his patients, but such doctors do exist. And they are worried."

Mostly, however, the editors plowed blithely ahead with stories like "Celebrating 15 Years" of *The
Advocate,* which appeared in the October 14, 1982, issue. In a self-congratulatory column, Goodstein
praised his magazine's "professional standards of journalistic truth" without once mentioning the disease. A year before the column was published, Brent Harris, the magazine's associate editor, had died
of GRID, as AIDS was known at the time.

Fain contributed another first-rate piece, "Coping With a Crisis," in the February 17, 1983, issue.
The now famous cover featured three towel-clad men in a bathhouse posing as "see no evil, hear
no evil, speak no evil." Goodstein nevertheless maintained his denial. In an August 18, 1983, editorial, he opined that "The only subject most gay men discuss these days is AIDS. This is understandable; all of us are frightened of dying. It also is boring. There are other matters of concern with
which we have to deal," citing a California gay rights bill as among those concerns. (Victor Fain,
Nathan Fain's father, declined to grant permission to reprint several of his son's early AIDS articles.
Thus, they are not included in this volume.)

Goodstein died June 22, 1985, of complications from cancer surgery. A drawing of his smiling
face graced the October 1, 1985, cover. Before his death Goodstein tapped Niles Merton, a Los Angeles businessman, to take the reins. Merton made few changes in the magazine's editorial direction and focused instead on transforming *The Advocate* into a money-making venture.

On October 21, 1985, shortly after his prison release, Dan White committed suicide. "Dan
White: Suicide as Justice?" *The Advocate* asked, leaving little doubt as to the editor's answer. Some
rejoiced openly: "With so many of our friends and lovers dying, this is the happiest obituary I've
ever read," one San Francisco resident was quoted as saying. "Maybe that's a terrible way to look
at it. But justice prevails in its own way."

As the decade wore on, AIDS became a permanent part of America's landscape. The disease
brought out the best and worst in Americans. On one hand there was an outpouring of sympathy
for gay men and the enormity of their loss, often from unexpected sources. On the other there were
right-wingers like Paul Cameron, a discredited antigay researcher who sought to take political ad-

vantage of the epidemic. Cameron published a series of pamphlets such as "Homosexuality and the AIDS Threat to the Nation's Blood Supply." He called for the execution of homosexuals and the quarantine of everyone with AIDS. "There would by no AIDS epidemic in the West if the laws of Moses had been followed," he declared.

But Cameron was nothing compared to the Supreme Court. The gay movement was dealt a stunning setback June 30, 1986, when the high court handed down *Bowers* v. *Hardwick,* a 5–4 decision upholding Georgia's antiquated sodomy law. The five-member majority compared gay sex to "adultery, incest, and other sexual crimes," stating that the prohibition on homosexuality had "ancient roots." The court's inexplicable decision sparked protests across the country and a new gay militancy, all covered in the pages of *The Advocate.*

AIDS activism was also taking off. An article by Darrell Yates Rist, "Sexual Slander: Why Gays Should Stop Taking the Blame for AIDS and Start Fighting Back," appeared in the May 13, 1986, edition, setting the stage for ACT UP and the 1987 March on Washington.

As *The Advocate*'s reputation as the gay publication of record solidified, its access to national politicians improved. The May 10, 1988, issue featured an interview with Jesse Jackson, whose surprisingly strong showing in the Democratic presidential primaries was due in no small part to strong turnout among urban gay voters. Jackson returned the favor by making gay rights a regular part of his appeals at a time when even liberal politicians still hesitated to use the word in public. In the interview Jackson movingly described his friendship with Keith Barrow, a gay man who died of AIDS. Barrow, the son of a prominent civil rights leader, had baby-sat for Jackson's kids. Jackson also spoke about growing up in an African-American neighborhood. Gays "were just a part of the community of people," he said. "I think that is what is important to understand."

Also on the electoral front, the magazine's September 26, 1989, edition reported that openly gay congressman Barney Frank suffered a setback when Stephen Gobie, a male prostitute, went public with the story that Frank had paid him for sex and then hired him as a personal assistant. The magazine predicted that the revelation might cost Frank his career. Today, however, he is one of the most powerful and highly regarded members of the House, regularly quoted in the magazine and other national media outlets. As *The Advocate* noted in 1998, Frank went on to become the second-ranking Democrat on the House judiciary committee, which would sit in judgment of President Clinton's sex scandal.

While the magazine had moved a long way in seriousness from stories about fishnet-clad Hollywood models, it retained an element of "beefcake" reporting. A 1989 cover story profiled porn star Jeff Stryker. Other stories, including, "Risky Business: Sex for Sale in the Age of AIDS," and "What's a Nice Boy Like You…? Why Clean-Cut Men Do Sex Videos," examined aspects of the sex industry.

INSIDE FALWELL COUNTRY: A GAY COMMUNITY IS GROWING RIGHT ON MORAL MAJORITY'S DOORSTEP

by Jere Real

February 18, 1982

In my age, we laughed at queers, fairies, and anyone who was thought to be a homosexual. It was a hideous thing and no one talked about it, much less ever confessed to being a homosexual. Now they are coming out of the closet.... That frightens me because when they come out of the closets, they are a much larger group than we expected.
                        —*The Rev. Jerry Falwell, in his book* How You Can Help Clean Up America

On a quiet summer evening last August in Lynchburg, Va., the Rev. Jerry Falwell, television evangelist and founder of the Moral Majority, stepped to the pulpit of his Thomas Road Baptist Church and once more began to yell, "Queer!"

His target was a local college professor who had written about the minister and the Moral Majority. Said the preacher: "Some of the most militant enemies of Jerry Falwell and this ministry are militant homosexuals. I think of a homosexual right here in this town—at least he's accused of that by some of his colleagues. He's an instructor...a teacher, often writing about me and so on. I've held back on him, but in a few weeks I'm going to change that.... He started in on me when I joined the Dade County referendum in 1977. He's been against me ever since.... Well, the fact is that we're disturbing his little bird's nest. He wants to live a perverted, immoral lifestyle and one day be respectable."

Falwell regularly attacks gay people, so that aspect of his diatribe was not new. What was more interesting was the minister's emphasis on the idea of "respectability." Respectability has become almost a fetish for the Virginia evangelist since his Moral Majority played an important part in the 1980 national elections. Falwell wrote several articles last year, each time trying to suggest that his extremist organization is, ultimately, a responsible and reasonable group. The déclassé son of a bootlegger, Falwell the television evangelist has achieved national notoriety (if not popularity) in the past two years, but in his native state he remains something of a social pariah. After all, as novelist William Faulkner once noted admiringly, Virginia is a state where people are so busy "being snobs" they leave everyone else alone. Not Falwell. He considers everyone's business his own.

Falwell is, in effect, the Virginia version of Faulkner's calculating and aggressively ambitious Flem Snopes. Realizing that, one understands his moralistic posturing, his extremist positions, and his intemperate rhetoric. Falwell—even with his financial success and public recognition—remains an outsider in his native state. This is largely because he has built his success, as did Alabama's Gov. George Wallace, on appeals to ignorance and fear.

Falwell's views on human sexuality are especially narrow and outmoded. His local radio attacks in Virginia and recent fund-raising mailings denouncing gays (sent out in envelopes marked like those for pornographic mailings) show he is as homophobic as ever. Falwell may try to appear "moderate" on network talk shows ("I'm not opposed to civil rights for homosexuals; I'm just opposed to homosexual marriages"), but the minister really has no respect for anyone's sexual privacy unless it meets his standard of "one man for one woman."

Well, times are changing—even in Falwell's Virginia. Until recently, the state had been a huge sexual closet. In the Old Dominion that closet may have had Chippendale style and a lock of polished brass, but nonetheless it contained a massive amount of sexual hypocrisy. Two trends are developing today. For one thing, a recent poll disclosed that Falwell was one of the least-trusted public figures in Virginia. Also, there is now emerging throughout the state, from northern Virginia to Richmond to Norfolk, yes, even to "Falwell Country" in central Virginia, a positive, creative, and public gay community that may in time offset the negative image of homosexuals that Falwell and Co. have tried to perpetuate.

Virginia's sex laws remain antiquated. Unlike neighboring West Virginia, the state does not yet have a consenting adults sex law, and any attempts by Virginia's general assembly to pass one would meet, naturally, with Falwell's organized opposition (just as happened in nearby Washington, D.C., last fall). But laws, like individuals, cannot predict or determine human sexual selection. And the homosexual community of Falwell Country is as varied, if not yet as open, as anywhere else in the nation. Central Virginia's gays are a cross section of everyday people—married and single; men and women; white and black, Latino and Asian. Their occupations are equally diverse. In Falwell's own backyard are gay doctors, architects, lawyers, bartenders, teachers, grocers, restaurateurs, pharmacists, auto mechanics, musicians, ministers, professors, tax consultants, theater operators, college students—even police officers. There are also businesspeople: from corporate executives to small store owners, from short-order cooks to construction company owners, from computer specialists to church organists.

Yet all of these live in an environment where Falwell and his 16,000-member Thomas Road Baptist Church regularly carry on antigay broadcasts and pamphleteering. A recent fund-raising appeal by Falwell raises the false specter of gays attacking children:

> Your hometown may be next!...
>
> This is why we must stop the homosexuals dead in their tracks—before they get one step further toward warping the minds of our youth!... We must not...let these perverted, immoral individuals influence our naive, innocent children! If the gays win this battle, it will mark one of the blackest days in the history of our nation! The time for us to attack is now!... The enemy is in our camp!

Such violent and emotionally exploitive fund-raising letters overlook the fact that there is now in Falwell's hometown a healthy, active gay community—as well as a guilt-ridden, hidden one among his own followers.

The first sign of the active community came recently as Lynchburg and Roanoke newspapers announced the formation of the Blue Ridge Lambda Alliance, the first such group for central Virginia outside a major college campus (both the University of Virginia in nearby Charlottesville and Blacksburg's Virginia Tech have gay student groups). The Blue Ridge group—led by gays from several cities and towns—was created to help foster a positive public image for gay people in the region.

Already it has moved toward that goal. Its first major project was the Gay Helpline Telephone Service, staffed by men and women trained to help in personal crises and ready to refer callers to doctors, lawyers, rescue squads or mental health services in the area. Several fund-raising events have been staged to finance the help line, including a $25-a-plate dinner.

BRLA also plans an educational program for the straight and gay communities. To that end, BRLA members invited veteran gay activist Franklin Kameny to speak on the history of the gay rights movement in America. About 100 people attended the meeting, a high-water mark for gay activism in Falwell territory. Kameny told the group: "All I have to do is come to Lynchburg and see this group here to realize that we are not going to go away, we are not going to be defeated; we are going to continue to move forward and advance."

BRLA has also begun to test Virginia's conservative political waters. The organization recently sent candidates for governor and other state offices a survey of questions on attitudes toward the state's sodomy laws and toward the restrictive alcoholic beverage control laws (state regulations specify that homosexuals cannot be served liquor). None of the candidates polled responded to the questionnaire, according to a Lynchburg attorney prominent in the BRLA leadership.

Although political parties and candidates are ignoring the fledgling gay movement throughout the state, there is growing concern over the impact of Falwell's supporters on Virginia elections. The state Republicans saw their party caucuses swollen by Moral Majority members in the past year. Nevertheless, when the minister announced on election eve that he was voting Republican, the next day—for the first time in 12 years—a Democrat was elected governor by a stunning margin. The state's GOP is still trying to sort out the meaning of Falwell's endorsement.

Currently, Republicans in Falwell's Lynchburg base are split over the possible candidacy for city council of Falwell's employee Harry Covert, the editor of the *Moral Majority Report*. Covert's paper regularly attacks gays, even to the point of gloating over the firing of gay college professors. Covert has recently tried to put distance between himself and the Moral Majority, claiming that any candidacy of his would be "as an individual," not as a Moral Majority man. So far, Lynchburg's Republicans have not been convinced by Covert's protestations. Virginia's GOP is no staunch ally of gay people, but it has begun to wonder if Moral Majority backing may not be something of a mixed blessing.

Covert has stressed that he is interested in local issues, but that did not keep him from using his newspaper columns to attack the Washington, D.C., sex law reform bill as "a perverted act" that would legalize bestiality and convert the nation's capital "into the Sodom and Gomorrah of the world."

If Covert runs, it seems likely that he will be opposed by BRLA and other gays both directly and indirectly. The leadership of BRLA is, after all, a very pragmatic group. One of the principal figures in the new organization is area businessman Douglas Deaton, 38, who operates the Black Rock Market in the Wintergreen resort area not far from Lynchburg. He also runs another business aimed strictly at a gay clientele, a gay guest house, The Mists, near Wintergreen's ski area. Deaton has provided the 16-room house in Lynchburg's older residential area that serves as a BRLA meeting place, coffeehouse and home of the help line.

Another man active in BRLA is a religious fundamentalist who says he was baptized, ironically enough, in Falwell's Thomas Road Baptist Church some years ago. Gary Bird explains that he left that church because of its antigay positions and its narrow outlook toward other religious groups. "They have the view that they are right and everyone else is wrong," he says. "That simply isn't Christianity as I understand it." Bird is now interested in the fundamentalist gay group Evangelical Outreach, headquartered in Atlanta.

A third BRLA spokesman is Roanoke's Bill Hammond. Talking about BRLA's goals and the media in the region, he says the group will "show a positive image of homosexuality in this area. The help line is just our first such activity. We want to erase the stereotypes that have been around for a number of years."

Although local newspapers in Roanoke and Lynchburg carried news of BRLA's activities, ABC affiliate WSET in Lynchburg did not. And in December, after initially agreeing to carry a public service message for the help line, WSET failed to run the announcement when weatherman Charles Middleton—who each night sports a boutonniere for some civic cause—refused at the last minute to wear one for the BRLA help line. WSET's news director, Roger Wellman, said the station had no policy against news of gay organizations; however, the receptionist for the station, who schedules public service announcements, said, "When we agreed to do the help line announcement, we did not know it was a gay activist group."

Local television may still be uncomfortable with gay news, but Roanoke's gay disco, the Park, is planning a fund-raiser for the help line. Although gays in central Virginia are within easy weekend range of social spots in Washington, D.C., and neighboring North Carolina (Raleigh, Durham, or Greensboro, for example), the Park in Roanoke is the major gay entertainment center. Opened three years ago by two owners known to everyone as Ed and Del, the Park is a duplex private club with an annual membership fee plus a regular door admission. Both floors and the main dance area are operated Wednesday, Friday, Saturday, and Sunday, with the first-floor bar and a small dance area open other nights.

"About a thousand persons are here each weekend," one owner boasted recently. Amid the Park's rustic decor, flashing traffic signals and indoor trees with tiny white lights, area gays mingle with gay students from colleges in Lynchburg and Roanoke; from Washington and Lee University, Radford University, and Virginia Tech; and from Virginia Military Institute.

Gay men dance together and gay women socialize in the Park's easygoing ambience. There the moralist fulminations of Lynchburg's well-known evangelist are ignored. The Park regularly features special shows by performers from gay entertainment centers like Washington or Atlanta.

(The atmosphere of the Park is in marked contrast to the social environment of Falwell's Liberty Baptist College, his staunchly fundamentalist school where social life is totally regulated. Dress, dating, and other social conduct are dictated by a rigid fundamentalist book of regulations ironically entitled "The Liberty Way." First-year LBC students cannot single-date, and no dancing or moviegoing—except for occasional Disney or religious films shown on campus—are allowed.)

Both the social life and the business activity of gay people in the area dramatically refute Falwell's frequent assertion that gays are always unhappy:

> Where in the world did somebody get the word *gay* to describe homosexuals? I have never met a happy homosexual. There's no such thing as a happy homosexual. Why? Because when you're living a perverted lifestyle, when you're going against the grain, against the rules, against nature, it just automatically brings guilt and shame and unhappiness and lack of fulfillment. That is always true. The unhappiest people in the world are homosexual people.

Certainly Falwell would like to see homosexuals unhappy. At his Liberty Baptist College, the minister has a counseling center where his message of shame, guilt, and denial of sexuality is reinforced. As Falwell tells his congregation:

> Do you know why homosexuals—lots of them—come to Lynchburg to get help at our counseling center? Because they know we love them; and because we love them, we tell them that what they are doing is wrong. A good doctor would never mislead you about your condition. A good minister or a good Christian would never tell you that sin is right.

That policy is followed by counselors at Falwell's center. Ron Hawkins, associate director of the center, explains that some homosexuals do come to Lynchburg for counseling at LBC. "They come from all over the country. I'm surprised at how far some do come." He adds that in their hometowns many avoid talking about their sexual problems because they fear people they know would learn of their homosexual tendencies.

Hawkins reports that about "one or two persons a week" are counseled about homosexuality. "A ballpark figure would be about 50 or so a year." Some of these are in the student population at Falwell's college. "Some have had homosexual experiences. With others, it's simply a matter of thoughts they've had about it, but they come wanting counseling about these thoughts. You know, they wonder if they might be homosexual."

What is the approach of counselors at Falwell's center? "We would try to reorient the person," Hawkins explains, "to try to reestablish a heterosexual lifestyle…to move out of homosexuality and into a different form of sexuality." He readily admits this is not always easy, since "many times, sexual behavior is so deeply embedded," and adds: "It is not possible to move into heterosexuality for some time." Hawkins says all the counselors at the center will "at some point give a biblical evaluation of the person's problem…. Oh, yes, we would advise them that homosexuality is not an appropriate lifestyle. If we weren't biblical, we wouldn't be working for Jerry."

One former LBC student who went through the antigay counseling program offers a different view of the counseling: "It's more like brainwashing than anything else," says the ex-member of Falwell's Youth Ministry. "They tell you that homosexuality is wrong, that you must ask God to forgive you, and that you must pray a lot." He explains that there were fixed times each day for him to pray about his sexuality. "They had this schedule of prayer and scripture readings they gave you to correct your thinking. Why, I'd be getting up early in the mornings to read scripture and pray about my sexual thoughts."

The LBC counselors also suggested to him, somewhat obliquely, that he should "spend more time with girls" so as to overcome his homosexual leanings. "The main thing with their counseling," he adds, "is that homosexuality is a sin and that God did not intend you to be that way. They made you feel as if you were worthless and degraded."

The former student (who says he is now quite happy with his homosexual lifestyle) knew from age 14 that he was gay. But because he went to a fundamentalist church—with a minister who was a graduate of Falwell's LBC—the boy too entered LBC. "I tried to overcome my sexual feelings by getting involved in all kinds of religious activity and work. But eventually, I just couldn't handle my sexual feelings any longer. So I went to the college counselors." He began the counseling when he was 17. He claims there were a number of gay students at Falwell's college, all trying to cope with their real sexual identity. "Ultimately, what they offer you there is an asexual life…or, in some cases, marriage." He says that he knew many gay students who eventually married. "They still know what they want, and they are miserable."

There are other indications that while there is a healthy, well-adjusted gay community in Falwell Country, there is also a lot of closeted homosexuality within Falwell's own organization and activities. Some time back, Falwell's Thomas Road Baptist Church helped finance a short "born-again" movie about convicts becoming Christians. The film, titled *39 Stripes*—with torture, whippings and beatings that would have delighted an S/M fancier—was premiered at Falwell's church. Falwell personally introduced cast members to his congregation. A short time later, one of the actors was at a gay disco in Roanoke. There he was quite pragmatic about his association with the Falwell endeavor: "I wasn't the only gay working on that film," he said. "The money was good." He hesitated, then added: "You know, those people really don't know what's going on all around them."

In the final analysis, what is evident in central Virginia is two differing approaches to life and to human sexuality. Falwell, for all his rhetoric about the Christian life with Christ as the ultimate role model, does not practice what he preached. He surrounds himself with all the material comforts the American dream can summon—expensive suits, fancy cars, travel in private jets, an imposing house (surrounded by a high wall and numerous security guards). Indeed, Falwell has achieved the same luxurious lifestyle through his evangelism that Hugh Hefner and Bob Guccione have attained through their magazines, those "smut" magazines Falwell so dearly loves to criticize.

In a sense, Falwell's house is symbolic of his outlook; it is welled-in, isolated from his neighbors, protected, guarded—a closed world. By contrast, the BRLA meeting place and coffeehouse, only a few miles away in the same town, is open, receptive, and friendly; there is no pretension there.

Falwell and his Moral Majority philosophy are really something of a contradiction in a state that still values its Jeffersonian heritage. Virginians—snobs though they may be at times—have traditionally valued privacy and individualism more than meddling religiosity. Furthermore, Virginians have always placed higher value on "being a gentleman" than on being "respectable" in any bourgeois sense. Because of that, gays in Virginia may take heart: There is a growing awareness among thinking Virginians that Falwell is no gentleman—and never will be.

A SPY INFILTRATES A FALWELL DINNER

by Scott Tucker

February 18, 1982

Editor's note: Last fall, when Philadelphia gay Democratic activist Scott Tucker heard Jerry Falwell was coming to town, he decided to meet the man face-to-face. Tucker, his lover, Larry, and some of their friends put on fundamentalist drag and infiltrated a Falwell dinner and rally. Here's what happened to them.

On the evening of November 3, we drive to the Marriott Hotel, and Larry jumps out to get the demonstration rolling. I stay in the car as night falls, keeping my eye on the Kona Kai Polynesian

Restaurant, where I am to meet my fellow conspirators. Plainclothes and uniformed security is evident everywhere in the hotel and parking lot. One guard must have noticed the QUESTION AUTHORITY bumper sticker on our car, because he hovers nearby and tries to get a glimpse of my face. When my group arrives, I manage to sneak by him as soon as he has turned his back. I am irritated by having to play this little cat and mouse game.

Our group, all dressed properly for the event, gathers while the other demonstrators (numbering 500 at their peak) begin marching and changing "1-2-3-4: We Don't Want Your Holy War! 2-4-6-8: Falwell Preaches Christian Hate! They Say No Choice—We Say Pro-Choice!" The dozen of us who are undercover feel as though we are walking into the lion's den. There in the hotel lobby stand hundreds of Moral Majoritarians, and most of them look like just plain folks in their Sunday best. Not many black people, lots of people holding Bibles, lots of polyester and JESUS FIRST lapel pins. We proceed to a large anteroom full of hundreds more people. Doors lead into the cavernous banquet hall.

We had ordered reservations through the mail (for free, by the way) and are hoping there will be no incident. We mill about in the crowd for nearly a half hour. One couple with cheerleader charm strikes up a conversation, asking us if we've seen "the gays and the feminists outside." I say no, we haven't, but Falwell must be used to *them* by now. One lesbian in our group, being quite fluent in fundamentalism (her parents have been supporters of Falwell for years), converses calmly and at some length. We do our best to submerge ourselves in the fellowship of the crowded room.

I am just beginning to breathe easily when I overhear a certain litany—"niggers, commies, queers"—delivered with the sotto voce aplomb of a salesman. The speaker is in his mid 30s, athletic-looking, smiling but intense; his listener is a man much the same. I eavesdrop: "Oh, sure, the '80s are gonna be 10 times worse than the '60s, no doubt about it. Like I said, the niggers, commies, and queers are gonna get out of hand. And anyone who doesn't stock up on weapons is just a fool. There's gonna be riots at home and maybe a war with Russia, you never know. Anyone who doesn't stock up on food and clothing and medicine is just a fool. You gotta have guns to defend what you've got. Look, it's simple logic..."

I step into the men's room to take a nervous leak. When I return and mill around some more, I overhear yet another survivalist. If the first man had a youthful, paramilitary style, the second seems grandfatherly and high-minded. Soberly he explains to two older women that Jesus will provide worldly goods in time of trouble, that the great battle of Armageddon is surely upon us, but that Good will triumph over Evil, etc. I suddenly wanted to be in Machu Picchu or in the Alhambra, or in the back room of the Mineshaft—anywhere else in the world. I am struck firsthand and forcibly by the fact that many of these Moral Majoritarians are very much like, for example, my grandparents: decent folks, really, and yet.... My grandmother on my father's side is a devout Christian Scientist. I haven't seen or spoken to her in a decade, though she adored me as a child. Might she hold significant common ground with Falwell today?

Falwell has captured a swell of populist discontent, but populism needn't be either democratic or progressive. No doubt most fundamentalists are decent people, but even decent people are capable of colluding in abominations. Falwell, in his own language, says something similar about "secular humanists"—that we are dupes of the devil, either allowing sin to flourish or sinning ourselves. Both sides are past the point of conciliation or dialogue. There is, in fact, no "misunderstanding." An open political fight is inevitable and necessary.

Finally we are allowed to file into the banquet hall, with security making spot checks of our reservations. The specific occasion is "The Friends of Liberty Dinner," a public boosting for one of Falwell's ventures, the Liberty Baptist College, "where new generations are trained to carry on the work of Christ" and so forth. Almost as soon as our group has seated itself at a big round table, a security guard comes over to ask us what our religious affiliations are. (Are we giving off a telltale scent?) The lesbian fluent in fundamentalism gives likely answers, and the guard withdraws, though men with walkie-talkies keep a steady eye on us.

The meal is edible, but how to describe the water torture of the next two hours? Falwell inveighing against "the feminists, the abortionists, the homosexuals who threaten the Traditional Family." (And of course he's right, we do.) Falwell declaring, "There has always been a struggle between the temporal, material world and the eternal, spiritual world. On Judgment Day, when we may look forward to meeting our maker, we'll leave the world to the liberals." (Collective chuckle.) At one point Falwell asks all the ministers and pastors in the audience to rise, and a formerly Jewish, transsexual member of the Metropolitan Community Church stands up from our table to be counted among them.

As we are finishing dessert, a dozen Liberty Baptist College Choir members introduce themselves one by one. I'm Jane/John Doe from Lynchburg, Va., and I major in so-and-so.... The six women are dressed in floor-length, powder-blue gowns, and all but one have elaborate Farrah Fawcett hairdos. The men wear dark suits, and one, a pretty blond with divine dimples, reminds me of an old flame. I have sodomite fantasies while the choir sings the dreariest hymns. Next comes a slide show projected on three screens, "We've Come This Far by Faith." As well as being a guided tour of Liberty Baptist College, it is a cult-of-personality show: Jerry the fearless evangelist, Jerry the family man, Jerry hobnobbing with Phyllis Schlafly and Sen. Jesse Helms.... Drip, drip, drip...

At the end the lights come up again, and I feel like a deep-sea diver with the bends. Falwell begins delivering another homily. Like Reagan, he comes across really homey and folksy, a wolf in sheep's clothing. While he speaks I glance across the room and catch sight of Larry standing in a doorway, and I feel a surge of comfort and courage when we exchange smiles. Shortly after, our group signal to each other that we have seen and heard what there was to be seen and heard. (The homilies sure heated up after the news media left the banquet hall: Is Falwell cultivating a new cool for the press?) We rise from the table, and from our pockets and purses we unravel squares of cloth with slogans like THE MORAL MAJORITY IS NEITHER.

First there are stunned stares, and perhaps certain survivalists expect us to pull out submachine guns next. Nothing of the kind: This is a silent witness. Currents of muttering pass through the hall, and security guards rush from all corners to grab us and hustle us out the door. The guy I saw in the parking lot is among them, as well as an enthusiastic volunteer from one of the tables. Falwell expresses his regret that "there are people among us who do not have Jesus," adding, "They will be escorted from the hall, and volunteers will pray with them outside. Jesus loves you." As the last of us is shoved out of the room, Falwell makes some appropriate remark, followed by appropriate laughter. My lover, wearing a JESUS FIRST pin, proceeds to shame the security guards for having pushed and twisted the arms of cooperative people. One guard sheepishly says to me, "I'm sorry I pushed you." I am heading toward the door to get some fresh air, and the guard adds, "In fact, I'm sorry I *touched* you!" A young woman from the choir cranks up a smile and repeats like a talking doll, "God bless you, God bless you…"

We regroup outside the hotel and talk to the press. What, finally, was the point of it all? Symbolic action and acts of silent witness have a modest yet significant purpose. They make it clear we are capable of varying tactics, including restraint. There is a time and place for aggressive and passionate resistance, but we wanted to walk out of the lion's den unpawed. Speaking for myself, I wanted to know and deal with my enemy face-to-face instead of frowning at newspapers and the TV screen.

Each of us may choose a different way, time, and place to "draw the line," but the advancing right must meet a collective challenge. The Moral Majority and other reactionary forces have cast a shadow of fear of the lives of millions. I can only say I feel stronger now.

NEW RIGHT LEADER: TERRY DOLAN

by Larry Bush

April 15, 1982

The offices of Washington power brokers are often fabulous affairs: Senators treasure chandeliered hideaways just off the Senate floor more than they do committee assignments, and lawyers and lobbyists regularly write off Oriental rugs as a business expense. Such status symbols are particular favorites among the conservative set who occupy the key power niches in Washington these days.

The offices of Terry Dolan, founder and president of the National Conservative Political Action Committee, the wealthiest such outfit in the country, are an abrupt change in that landscape. His organization overflows a warren of four or five office areas on an unfashionable lower level of the high-rise across the Potomac River from the political center he watches. Boxes and computer print-outs are scattered helter-skelter. In sum, it has all the charm of a command center during the height of battle.

Still, someone has found time to hang three pictures that do appear to have some permanence. Two are on the wall outside Dolan's office, 19th-century political cartoons that portray long-dead politicians fighting over long-dead issues. Only their spirit of intense partisanship, supported by the reality of 19th-century political machines and bosses, makes them an appropriate touch here. Inside Dolan's office, a third poster is displayed: Soupy Sales huckstering for some product or other. It is a perfect fit for Dolan's operation: the marriage of old-fashioned, sock-it-to-'em politics where the deals are cut far from the public eye and modern media hype.

In 1980 Dolan used these methods to help defeat four U.S. senators who had long stood as monuments of American liberalism (George McGovern, Frank Church, Birch Bayh, and John Culver) and helped put the U.S. Senate under Republican leadership for the first time since Dwight Eisenhower's first term of office. Dolan helped elect the most conservative president since Herbert Hoover left office, with a mandate to reverse a generation of liberal government. And in 1980 Dolan was 30 years old.

This year NCPAC walks into the 1982 elections with the top standing for expenditures in political campaigns: $7.5 million last year alone. In 1980, with about the same budget, Dolan gave a parsimonious $250,000 to candidates he favored; $2 million went into "independent expenditures" to defeat the ones he wanted out of office. This technique allows friends to benefit without directly taking the heat for the claims made in NCPAC campaigns. It is a technique that has put Dolan squarely on the top of the liberals' list of enemies.

Recently, when *The Advocate* spoke with liberal political action committees to assess their commitment to gay civil rights as part of a liberal agenda, a frequent answer was that the liberals would be putting their energies into countering Dolan's influence; by extension, this would benefit the cause of gay civil rights. That was a somewhat disingenuous response in many cases, since liberals have their own reputation for balking at gay civil rights issues. Still, as these groups were quick to point out, Dolan's campaign contributions have given new muscle to those members of Congress who are quickest to introduce repressive legislation and to force votes that treat gays unfairly.

Many gay conservatives have been left between a rock and a hard place in the current sorting out of liberals from conservatives. The conservative leaders they would identify with on many issues make them feel definitely unwelcome (one has only to see how gay Republican clubs have been treated, even at California state gatherings). At the same time, liberal positions on everything but gay civil rights appear to be more than gay conservatives can tolerate.

In places where conservative gays gather—from the Republican wing of the Houston Gay Political Caucus to San Francisco's Concerned Republicans for Individual Rights—much solace has been taken in the statements of the small but influential number of conservative politicians and spokesmen who have taken note of gay civil rights. It is no longer unheard-of for even very conservative Republicans to state publicly that discrimination against gays should not be fostered by the government or even to attack the "morality" campaigns of the Moral Majority as a violation of the conservative conscience. Certainly, the leading figure in this regard is President Reagan himself, whose opposition to the 1978 Briggs initiative in California, which would have barred gays from jobs in the public school system, is well-known in gay circles. During the 1980 campaign, Reagan reiterated those 1978 sentiments, issuing a campaign statement that opposed "intolerance and discrimination" based on sexual orientation and adding that homosexuality "should have no bearing on the private sector or government hiring." A little-noted fact during that 1980 primary campaign was that most of the leading Republican candidates took similar positions, including former Texas governor John Connally, Howard Baker, and George Bush.

From time to time conservative columnists William Safire and James L. Kilpatrick have also opined that gay civil rights is an issue they can support, and to some extent, conservative public officeholders have gone beyond the rhetoric of rights to act on their statements. Rep. Robert Livingston, the indisputably conservative Republican from New Orleans, took the floor during the D.C. sexual assault reform bill debate to argue fervently that it was an unacceptable abuse of the law to continue government intrusion into private lives. Rep. Henry Hyde (R-Ill.), the nationally prominent congressional leader of the antiabortion movement, made a valiant effort to limit the scope of Rep. Larry McDonald's (D-Ga.) amendment to curtail gay access to the legal services program.

Conservative gays may well take satisfaction in such speeches, but so far they have been unable to take much comfort from them. The reality is that the rise to power of the conservative movement in Washington, both in terms of the number of elected officials and the perception by members of Congress of conservatives' campaign strength, has made gay civil rights demonstrably less popular than before.

Despite President Reagan's campaign statements opposing intolerance, he failed to include a reform of the antigay immigration exclusion when he introduced his comprehensive immigration reform bill. The White House was also silent when the D.C. sexual assault reform bill was being debated. Most recently, President Reagan announced that he intended to appoint a devoutly antigay fundamentalist to the U.S. Civil Rights Commission. An uproar ensued in which the candidate's intolerance of gays was a central theme. When asked about this, President Reagan skated by the issue with no response.

In Congress the situation has been even more apparent. Conservatives have led the fight to use gays as a special target in a game of hardball. This has been so severe that even many on the conservative side of the aisle privately call the attacks "mean spirited."

But the conservative movement is in fact many movements, appearing united only to those at the opposite end of the spectrum. Within conservative ranks, there are the Moral Majority and other Christian activist groups that have no qualms about using federal authority to further their moral vision; there are also libertarian groups that view government authority with horror.

Terry Dolan and his NCPAC are not merely one manifestation of the conservative movement: They are the point company in the war. Dolan's shaping of the issues; his choice of candidates to back as well as those to oppose: and, not least, the alliances he makes with other right-wing groups all give him an unrivaled position at the top of the conservative campaign apparatus. Whether the political process will be used to bait gay civil rights concerns or whether it will lead to at least a small area of agreement will be hugely influenced by the position Dolan, his group, and his candidates take.

Dolan, a personable man with considerable charm, can often be found in front of microphones, issuing a statement of conservative purpose and political intent, but he rarely makes time for private, in-depth interviews. Dolan's role is more one of behind-the-scenes strategist, and he is not anxious to blaze new trails in conservative philosophy. At least part of that seems motivated by his desire to save the conservative alliance, which stretches from the Moral Majority to the libertarian wing, from breaking into disarray.

When he did sit down to talk at length about gay civil rights concerns with *The Advocate,* it was clear that Dolan's own conservative views mark a sharp break with many in his alliance and, indeed, are radically different from views held by some of the people he has elected to office. He is adamantly opposed, for example, to permitting the government to discriminate on the basis of sexual orientation, whether it be at the federal level or in local school districts. He thinks conservative strategies that scapegoat citizens in order to build a fund-raising base are counterproductive and objectionable; indeed, Dolan apologizes for a fund-raising letter for his own organization that did just that. At the same time he is a radical advocate of the free-market system, arguing that laws such as the 1964 Civil Rights Act are "irrelevant" and that the penalty for discrimination should be levied by the marketplace, not by legislation or government authority.

Dolan is also aware of how unwelcome gay conservatives have felt in his own movement, which may explain in part why he granted the interview.

"I would say there is as much personal animosity toward gays in the liberal movement as there is in the conservative movement," Dolan said in the interview. The contribution of a visible gay community, Dolan said in answer to a question, has been to change the perception that gay rights is a liberal issue. The presence of openly gay people, according to Dolan, has forced "a recognition that sexual preference is irrelevant to political philosophy."

In Dolan's mind, conservatism has been inconsistent in its handling of social issues, including gay rights. Conservatism is forgetting its own traditions.

"I think conservatism ought to be focusing on a consistent philosophy, and to date I think it has not been thoroughly consistent," Dolan said. "The philosophy, I think, is a philosophy of freedom. What is going to advance individual freedom?... At home you have that question, and it not only relates to the economy—and I think the economy is the most important issue, by the way—but it relates as well to areas of social life, morality, social issues."

"We talk about social issues, and, in fact, the conservative position on social issues has been in the past, and I hope will continue to be, that the government has no business in setting any social agenda from Washington, D.C.," Dolan explained. "There is, in fact, a logical inconsistency—at least to my mind there is. If we conservatives believe the government has no right to regulate our economic life, then it *certainly* has no right to regulate our private life, except to the point where we do harm to each other."

Dolan, however, draws a sharper line between the close limits he would set on government's power to set social policy, and the wide latitude he would allow individuals and businesses to act without regulation, whether for economic or social reasons.

"The government should not hire somebody based on sex, sexual preference, size, ethnic background, religion, race," Dolan said flatly. "The government should not be using any part of its taxing ability, hiring ability, or ability to pass out money to enforce what they feel to be socially desirable goals, whether it is heterosexuality or homosexuality. Both will survive with or without the government, and we don't need the government telling us which is good."

That line of reasoning, which had led Dolan to oppose the Moral Majority's position calling for the veto of the D.C. sexual assault reform bill, in this interview led him to consider legislation barring the government from using its offices or powers to discriminate against gay citizens.

Would Dolan support such a law? "Absolutely, absolutely. As a matter of fact, if there isn't a law, there ought to be a law."

When Dolan reflects how such a law might affect the military, which claims it has the right to discriminate against gays, he hedges only slightly by arguing that homosexuality might be considered a factor, but not an absolute bar.

"The military and defense have a right to take into consideration factors that would relate to national security," Dolan said. "Now, I cannot see how a private in the U.S. Army or a sergeant in the U.S. Army would have any real problems with national security."

But the military's central position, that gays should be barred because other armed forces personnel are intolerant, does not go down well with Dolan. "Same thing with blacks, I guess. What the military are saying is that somebody can't be in the armed services if they're different, and that argument doesn't end.

"Because I happen to be on the short side and I am discriminated against, I don't want protection because I'm short, and I don't want the government telling me that even if I can do a job, they don't want me to do a job because they have some artificial quota, or because they make the judgment that short people aren't good enough…. I don't think you ought to have a blanket rule that says eliminate them.

"I have said consistently that I am never surprised by the lunacy of the United States government, which is why I am against giving it power. And I am against giving it power to oppress gay people just as much as I am against given it power to protect gay people. The day you recognize that it can protect gays, you also recognize that it can do anything it wants to them at the same time. The oppression of minorities in America or in the workplace does not come primarily from religious leaders or big business, it comes from government. There's the Nazis and the way they treated Jews or gay people or a lot of other people they happened not to like."

Dolan argues that the government's power to discriminate should be strictly limited at the local level as well, including the hiring of schoolteachers. "In the final analysis," Dolan said, "you hire somebody to teach. If a teacher comes in drunk or comes in advocating the election of Barry Goldwater to the presidency of the United States or says 'I'm a homosexual and I want everybody to know why' and everything else, he's not teaching.

"But does that mean the government should go in and say, 'OK, we want to ask you this whole series of questions'; or more pernicious, say, 'We want to ask you if you are a homosexual.' Because that says we are establishing a hierarchy of what's good and what's bad." He dismisses the argument that conservatives should use a "community standards" approach that would apply governmental morality under any circumstances.

"First of all, let me qualify this by saying any society, any community, has the right to set its own moral standards," Dolan said. "I have no problem with that; I fully agree with the Supreme Court's decisions on pornography [that express that principle]. But the question comes down to: Should they? And I think that's what I'm dealing with."

"Some of my friends say, 'That's terrible. Our children would be corrupted, and so on and so forth.' The answer is, 'No, they wouldn't.' Because when that child comes home and doesn't do what he or she is told, it's the parents' responsibility. The child isn't my responsibility, it isn't the pornographer's responsibility, and it certainly isn't the government's responsibility. It's parents' responsibility. And if they can't put up with the woes of life in the 1980s, then they're not doing a very good job of being parents."

Dolan extends that argument to include the right of the gay community to be visible whenever and wherever it wants through its institutions, including gay bars in local neighborhoods. No zoning prohibitions, he argues, should prevent that. Nor does he see a visible gay community as a threat to the American family or to family values.

"No, I don't," Dolan said. "But I can understand how some other people would, and the answer becomes, 'Well, tell your children not to pay any attention to it.' Tell your children to stay away, and if they don't, crack 'em on the butt. That's how you do whatever you need to do to make sure they obey. And that to me is the most traditional family values, which is to respect what your parents say and do it."

Where government has used its authority to "protect" citizens from homosexuality, Dolan said, the result has been to make a fraud of the law. The penthouse restaurant in his own office building, for example, is currently advertising itself as a good investment for a gay bar. The problem, however, is that Virginia has legislated that no alcoholic beverages may be served to homosexuals in the state.

"My guess is that there are gay bars all over the state of Virginia," Dolan said. "So there is a law on the books that some politician can enforce if he chooses to. Of course it makes a fraud of the law."

Dolan is also opposed to a current congressional proposal drafted by his new Christian right allies that would use the federal government to impose moral standards to their liking. "See, one of the reasons I get a little bit upset, and why I get into a little bit of trouble with my friends over there [new Christian right allies], is that I honestly believe morality is too important to leave to the government," Dolan said. "Everything the government touches, it screws up."

In some of its provisions, the family protection act, which Dolan says is vastly improved over its original version, also crosses over a line that Dolan wants respected. "Here's one I disagree with," Dolan volunteered. "I understand there is a provision that says if a local school board provides birth control devices to minors, they have to notify the parent. And it they don't, then they lose all federal funds. Now, I happen to think parental notification is a heck of a good idea and it ought to be done. At the same time, I don't think it's up to the federal government, the United States government, to tell the people in Dubuque, Iowa, what kind of standards they should establish for parental relations with children.

"The same would apply to homosexuals. If you're saying New York City can't have any money if it gives any to homosexuals, sure, that's ridiculous. I do not believe in federal blackmail, whether it's in the form of liberals saying you have to have bilingual education, or you have to bus, or it's conservatives saying you have to outlaw adultery. I don't think there are any grounds for that, and as a consistent conservative, I think that's really the best position we ought to take."

Dolan added that Senator Jepsen's office is sending him assurances that the rewrite of the antigay provision is "very strict and clear." When the Congressional Research Service's analysis was cited to challenge Jepsen's interpretation, however, Dolan responded, "You're right, there are some real problems with that."

But while Dolan feels that conservatives should be a watchdog with a bite when it comes to governmental authority, he thinks government should not serve a similar role in dictating to individuals or the private sector. For Dolan, the government is the oppressor, its control so insidious that the only solution is to tear it out at the roots.

"The first thing you've got to do is get the U.S. government out of the way," Dolan said, "because it is the biggest violator of personal freedom in this country." This has led Dolan to oppose federal civil rights laws.

"I have consistently opposed laws, passed by the federal government primarily, for the protection of any group, whether it's blacks or gays or women or fat people or short people. As a matter of principle, I don't think the government should be in the business of guaranteeing rights. The rights that need to be guaranteed already exist in the Constitution and in the 14th Amendment; and those are access to courts and the protection of life, liberty, and property," Dolan said, editing the Declaration of Independence's guarantee to "life, liberty, and the pursuit of happiness."

"As a matter of fact," Dolan continued, "there are a number blacks, including Thomas Sowell [the Reagan administration's outside conservative economic adviser] and others, who maintain that the 1964 Civil Rights Act had nothing to do with the growth of 'civil rights' in the South, that in fact was coincidental with the occurrence of the remarkable growth in the economy. That is the factor that has given blacks what they need in the South. I think there is a certain amount of evidence for that."

"I think the '64 Act is irrelevant," Dolan added. "I don't want to see the federal government mandating anything. I think the Voting Rights Act, for example, is absolutely silly.... If it is successful, then why do we need to keep it for another 10 to 15 years? By and large, I oppose all types of federal laws and federal power, with the exception of defense expenditures, and that would apply to the Civil Rights Act of 1964." Later, on reflection, he clarified his position by saying that the 1964 law was important in overturning discriminatory state and local laws, calling the Jim Crow laws "pernicious" and their repeal at the federal level necessary.

"Individuals have a right to discriminate," Dolan concluded. "I believe that. And businesses have the right to discriminate. I would apply that to gay people," he said, his philosophy in a nutshell.

Since there are likely to be gay people who subscribe to that same position, what accounts for their near-complete invisibility and overt rejection by conservative groups?

"First of all," Dolan said, "I think everybody ought to be conservative. Gays ought to be conservative because in the final analysis they've got to earn a living too. There is a certain amount of misunderstanding between conservatives and a lot of separate groups, special-interest groups. I don't know what you would call gays."

Just as he thinks Jewish groups consist of liberals who happen to be Jewish, Dolan regards gay groups simply as liberals who happen to be gay.

Dolan cites as an example a gay contingent in the 1981 Solidarity March against Reagan's budget cuts. "They presented themselves as spokesmen for gay America. They created the impression that this is what all the gays in American wanted. The same thing with blacks; the same thing with Jews, as I mentioned."

"At the same time," Dolan admitted, "I think that some of the rhetoric that some of my friends in the right have used on gay activism has been excessive."

Dolan will not criticize any new Christian right group by name ("I am not in the business of criticizing conservative organizations. If I did criticize them, it would certainly be off the record. I have never said anything nasty about another conservative, even if I think what they did was wrong"), but he did take a few tentative steps toward criticizing the use of inflammatory antigay materials to raise funds to appeal or to volunteers.

"I don't think it's fair," Dolan began. "Let me start off from my bailiwick. I don't think it's smart politically to turn off a section of people who probably agree with you on a good number of issues, because of one single issue, unless you feel very strongly about it." Even then, Dolan gave the impression of seeing some hypocrisy in the new Christian right's focus on homosexuality. "My guest is that people in the new Christian right are very upset about adultery, but they probably don't want adulterers, people who have participated in adultery, voting against their candidates, because my guess is that they would certainly lose. Any more than the people who have ever lied, blasphemed, participated in any of the things the Bible lists as elements of sinfulness. So from a political point of view, I don't think it makes much sense."

"Even from a philosophical view," Dolan added after a pause, "I don't think it makes much sense to raise an issue unless you feel strongly enough about the issue and are going to do something about it. To the degree that people are raising the issue to do nothing more than to make money off it, I don't think that's very appropriate."

"I agree with most of the things the Christian right does," Dolan said, seeking to clarify, "but I have difficulty with a number of the logical consequences of what they say. This is a good example." Asked if one of the logical consequences of antigay rhetoric is to create an atmosphere that encourages antigay violence, Dolan responded: "I'm sure it does."

When Dolan is presented with his own fund-raising appeals, which say gay activities are a threat to moral values, he is quick to apologize for the letters and promises such a tactic will never be repeated.

"I truly regret that we ever put something into print that would ever question the morality, the patriotism, of another person," Dolan said. "That's totally inappropriate. We don't need things like that to win, and if we did, we wouldn't use them."

Much of what Dolan says in the interview is candid, a rigorous examination of conservative thought as it applies to the concerns of gays and lesbians. He is relaxed almost to the point of confidentiality. Off the cuff he shoots in, "Have you ever been to a Republican meeting? Ugliest women in America. No, no, that's not true. The second ugliest women in America. The ugliest are at Democratic conventions. My guess would be that most political organizations tend to attract—to be charitable—an interesting group of people. I don't know why that is, but it's the nature of politics in America. They are not what I would call normal people. I presume that can be proven by certain data. In fact, I know it has in a couple of cases."

Notwithstanding Dolan's candor, the key question is whether his philosophy will be reflected in the candidates he chooses.

"We never support anybody who is 100% in agreement with my philosophy," Dolan said. "I'd love to see it, but it has never happened. And, in the final analysis, the people we elect, on a scale of 1 to 100, would fit in the 85 bracket in terms of working for a system that would guarantee freedom, whether that's here in America or overseas."

When Dolan is asked which member of Congress is closest to his own philosophy, he says he has no idea, then suggests perhaps Rep. Ron Paul (R-Tex.), a conservative libertarian from Houston. But despite Paul's occasional statements against government-sanctioned discrimination, he has voted down the line with Christian Voice—where he serves on the advisory board—on every gay-related issue. That fact resulted in a major protest against Paul's selection as a keynote speaker at this year's California Libertarian Party fund-raising banquet, and gay protests were strong enough to make the dinner lose money.

Such distinctions are not lost on Dolan, who said near the end of the interview that perhaps questioning potential candidates about their stance on gay civil rights would help distinguish the varieties of conservatives who seek his backing.

"We have a very extensive questionnaire, which is going through rewriting right now," Dolan said. "But there isn't a candidate who is eliminated because of his position on one particular issue....I'm not going to say, 'Do you think the government should be in the business of guaranteeing or denying civil rights?'" Dolan seems to shift in mid sentence. "That question may or may not be in there in the latest thing; as a matter of fact, it might be an interesting question. But we cover all fields." Asked if a better question might not be whether a candidate favored ending government-sanctioned discrimination, Dolan says, "Interesting question."

"We might put it in. I am very serious about finding out where our candidates are. That might be a very telling question."

Dolan's response hangs in the air for a moment. The discrepancy between his views of a consistent conservatism and the actions of those he helps elect calls to mind a recent observation by Sam Smith, a veteran Washington *Tribune* writer and political voyeur, about other political games in town: "While politics may make strange bedfellows, a sufficient number of people wise up the next morning."

AIDS: MYSTERIES AND HIDDEN DANGERS

by John Rechy

December 22, 1983

The only fact about AIDS is that it exists. It is probably fatal, but not enough time has elapsed to determine that, extending needed hope to patients. Beyond that fact, assertions range from reasonable conjecture to cruel fabrication. Suspected, even invented, horrors pour out as facts from a hostile press in gloating obituaries on our sexuality; some of our own publications borrow these assumptions; too many homosexuals accept them. Caught in this rampage of conjecture, we are endangered by another illness, the exhumation of guilts and self-hatreds we insisted were buried forever. This may go on killing us even after a cure for the diagnosed illness is found.

A homosexual in a Hollywood store cackles, "Know what gay stands for?—'Got AIDS Yet?'" In a New York bar one man screeches at another, "Bitch! I bet you've got AIDS!" Accusing him of being "responsible" for present dangers, a heavyset man savagely pummels and kicks a slender, shirtless homosexual cruising the Silver Lake turf of Los Angeles. But this time the attacker is not a heterosexual thug—he too is homosexual.

AIDS commands our lives. Every homosexual has contracted a form of it, in fear, suspicion. And accusation.

Cruelly, viciously, a homosexual writer asserts in *The Village Voice* that AIDS patients lurk in darkened doorways. However genuinely motivated, a homosexual reporter in San Francisco provides two journalists of doubtful credentials the flimsy basis for *California* magazine's violent accusation that homosexuals are hiding the danger of AIDS. Instead of questioning the spurious allegations, several homosexual newspapers carry those spewings as facts. In the boredom-of-it-all tone that afflicts that magazine, a *Christopher Street* columnist writes: "And so the recent comparison of the behavior of pigs infected with African swine fever virus—pigs observed to lick sperm up from the floor, to fornicate with each other—and male homosexuals is not merely darkly amusing, it is quite accurate."

Time magazine crows: "The flag of gay liberation has been lowered...and many do not regret it."

A homosexual gets knifed on a Santa Monica bus by a man screaming: "Diseased pervert!"

It is not a time for rashness or bravado, but for care and responsibility. No *definite* proof exists that the syndrome is transmitted sexually. But empirical evidence is too strong to allow us *not* to accept that conclusion. The possible alternative is too high for gambling. We are left to cope simultaneously with equal evidence that at least in part we are reacting to conjectures by an antagonistic press.

For more than two years we demanded attention be paid to our crisis. Instead, we were exposed to another of the "opportunistic" diseases of AIDS, sensationalized journalistic indictments that assumed a tone of cursing litany: "gay plague…pansexual excess"—*Time* magazine; "if AIDS is the penalty for promiscuity, the sentence of death is awfully high"—Morton Kondracke, Washington, D.C., syndicated columnist; "difficult for many straight to avoid the conclusion that nature or God is punishing homosexuals…as told by the Bible itself"—*Newsweek*.

Even "good heterosexuals" find bonds with Jerry Falwell. In one of the meanest articles—its prejudices are masked as "intellectual concern"—Jonathan Lieberson in *The New York Review of Books* applauds homosexuals who have "become 'twice born,' despising their former promiscuous selves." The self-avowed "liberal" *New Republic* finds in AIDS a "metaphor" symbolizing "the identity between contagion and a kind of desire."

Chilling in their lack of compassion, these journalistic assaults have in common the rank stench of repression, a note of harrowing triumph in the authentication of bigotry. They attempt to make AIDS patients accountable for their illness—much as blacks have been blamed for their poverty, women for rape, Jews for the Holocaust. AIDS affirms Susan Sontag's powerful observation: "Nothing is more punitive that to give disease…a moralistic meaning."

On a hot afternoon in Beverly Hills, a slightly effeminate man waits for his bus in the shade of a park. A man identifying himself as a cop orders him out: "We don't want queer disease."

What justifiable anger the men who have AIDS must feel to be plundered by these outrages, some by our own. In televised interviews, in photographs, or as they join marches, they convey a humbling courage to be learned from: Their dignity is intact even after the constant clawings by ignorant inquisitors into every aspect of their lives. Their determined faces leave an indelible image. These men have experienced the cruelest and bravest of all comings-out.

"Keep fighting and scratching," says AIDS patient and Gay Olympics gold medal winner Doug MacDonald, urging "a special amount of heart and hope."

Hidden dangers: The emergence of a pressurized generation of once-healthy homosexuals branded by assumptions of mutual contagion: murderous lovers. Impotence, alcoholism, addiction, suicide. If old guilts are entrenched as new ones, the return to institutions of our oppression: religion, psychiatry, the tenets of repressive politics. Darker closets more difficult to break out of because we are helping to shut the doors.

What outlet for a young man just coming out, what of him, with eager yearnings, when his first contact may be fatal? As the projected period of incubation is extended without evidence—from months to years—how will living under lingering sentence of death affect every single area of endeavor among homosexuals?

A psychological time bomb, its forms of implosion and explosion another unpredictable aspect of AIDS.

"Sure we had raids, arrests, jailings, but we kept on living, and fully—and having sex; if nothing else,

that got us through," says a middle-aged man. "What now?"

Ralph Ellison said black men are invisible to white men. AIDS confirms that homosexuals are equally so to heterosexuals; to priests, ministers, rabbis who tried to "convert" us; to psychiatrists who tried to "cure" us; "sociologists" who tried to "change" us by condoning punishment; politicians who saw us only at their fund-raisers.

Ignored: our many voices, the vicissitude of our vastly complex sexuality. Even some doctors assume "husband-wife" couplings. How, then, can they draw sound conclusions about our complicated sexual modalities?

We are not blameless in perpetuating sexual untruths. In often trying to be "acceptable" to heterosexuals, we hid some of our richest individualities, including our sexual profligacy. Because our sex was forbidden harshly and early by admonitions of damnation, criminality, and sickness, sexual profligacy became—not for all of us but for many more than we claim—an essential, even central, part of our lives, our richest form of contact, at times the only one. Because our profligacy questioned their often-gray values, the enemies of desire supported our persecution. With AIDS their sexual envy was avenged: The illness was "created" by promiscuity! they exulted.

But was it?

Promiscuity occurred virtually as often before the late '60s as after; the literature of those times confirms that unequivocally. It merely shifted to safer locations, and there was wider knowledge of it. Then why now? Confusion itself is an integer in the riddle of AIDS, but the effects of its mere awareness are definite.

Two men go home together. They strip. Cocks rise in ready desire. (Will he be the one who kills me, the one I kill?) They press sealed lips, trying to awaken softening cocks.

We prevailed over torturing inquisitions, concentration camps, jailings, registration as "deviants," aversion therapy. Then in 1969 a few courageous transvestites, male and female, resisted arrest at the Stonewall Inn, other homosexuals rioted, and gay liberation was officially born. Then it all changed! Instantly! We paraded, chanted prideful slogans, linked hands!

And left the unjustified, heterosexually imposed but now powerfully absorbed guilts in the darkest closets of ourselves.

Mean bars proliferated. We ritualized fantasies of punishment without exploring origins. Discarded: "fats, femmes, trolls"! Banished: defiant "stereotypes"! The young exiled the now-old fighters—and cut themselves off from a heritage of endurance. Older homosexuals who qualified as "hunks" were granted extensions on their sexual passports—too often to act as punishing "daddies" instead of as needed, experienced guides through still-mined territory.

Yes, there was courage, abundant courage. We vanquished Anita Bryant, crushed the Briggs amendment. In prideful triumph, we thrust our vast energy outward as anger, and we overcame again.

Why—now—the threatening chaos, the blind meanness turned against our own? Because the rallying crises of our immediate past had demanded no introspection. The enemy was outside, identifiable. AIDS, with its mysteries, tapped our unjustly inherited guilts where we had left them unexplored:

Inside.

Men cruise behind a closed bar in San Francisco's Mission District. Recklessly a car speeds along a darkened street. A man, alone, yells: "AIDS! AIDS! AIDS!" A Paul Revere of indeterminate allegiance.

The heterosexual press proposes monogamy, celibacy. We add the feasible: condoms, the silly: "dating," know-your-partner, organize a closed circle of sexual friends (how will sudden monogamy, impromptu "closed circles," or hours of conversation protect against a syndrome with no symptoms until it is on the verge of illness?) and the desperate: "phone sex"! ("Everyone Is Touchable by Telephone!" chimes one ad.) Pornography! Its stars sacrificial lambs—performing dangerous acts to be experienced vicariously and safely by others? Masturbation! Untouchables even to each other. Immunological repression.

Two men walk along an East Village New York street. It is hot, humid. One man coughs. The other faces a sudden enemy: "Are you sick?!" Automatically, the first one examines the glands at the sides of his neck.

We have become knowledgeable in the viral theory and the immunity-overload theory. The first—progressively strengthened—claims a new virus struck us first; the second—clung to by those who judge us—claims we have been so pillaged by diseases through promiscuity that our immune systems collapsed. Some suggest that biological experimentation conducted on men not likely to bear children might have unleashed the syndrome. Unthinkable? Yes—as unthinkable as experiments with LSD on unsuspecting soldiers, the sterilization without consent of black women, syphilis left deliberately unattended among black men, the effects of pollutants stirring new diseases—like AIDS?

"Releasing New Bacteria Into Air Called 'Ecological Roulette' "—Front-page headline, Los Angeles Times, *September 15, 1983.*

Theories made no difference when we knew someone with AIDS.

At a book signing, I see a tall, handsome, slenderly muscular man who appears familiar. As he moves closer, I recognize him. He looks better than ever, slimmer. Only afterward do I remember a fierceness in the dark eyes—after he has told me that tomorrow he begins treatment for Kaposi's sarcoma. The slenderness is illness in transition.

1. Why is no emphasis placed on the supposedly small group of AIDS patients euphemistically described as those "with no ascertainable risk factors"—that is, heterosexuals—when their very "exceptionality," and its reduced variables, might produce significant clues, even answers? Similarly, why are Haitians being removed from the "high-risk" category, especially since there is a higher incidence of AIDS among Haitian than non-Haitian women—a factor that might provide leads to the

origin of the illness? Is there an intent to zero in on homosexuals only?

2. Are "bisexuals" included in the 70% grouping of homosexuals with AIDS? If the syndrome is as contagious as asserted, why have so few heterosexual men contracted it from the women who have had intercourse with those "bisexual" men? Is this claim of "bisexuality" a forced extension of definition to contain an unexplained heterosexual group, larger than implied?

3. Since the '60s and '70s saw the proliferation of "promiscuity" among heterosexuals, why have their immunological systems been spared under the overload theory, when they have been attacked by illnesses as powerful and prevalent as herpes?

4. If the receiver of sperm in both anal and oral sex is more susceptible than the ejaculator, does this not make the latter the carrier of the hostile agent? If so, from whom acquired?—someone already "inseminated" by another "carrier"? Since most homosexuals shift in sexual activity, as receivers and ejaculators, are not deductions about *individual* sex acts at best equivocal? Might there not be here another buried bias—that the penetratee is weaker, i.e., more "female," than the penetrator?

5. How is it possible for "authorities" to attribute to sudden reduction of sexual activity the fact that projections of cases doubling every six months have proven incorrect, if the period of incubation of AIDS is believed to be as long as years? It would take an equally long time to reflect any changed behavior. Is it possible that the projections—withdrawn, then reasserted—are only speculative, inflammatory?

6. How does the often cited "control sample," in which AIDS patients reputedly had an average of 60 sexual contacts yearly as compared with the control group's 25, *necessarily* indict "promiscuity"? In that sample did one of those patients have only five contacts (far fewer than the average control) while another had 115; did another have only one while two others had 120 and 59 respectively? Those uneven combinations all produce an average of 60. If only *one* of the patients had fewer than 25 partners, the deductions are at least arguable.

7. How can *any* period of incubation be proposed when there is no certainty that the syndrome is viral? And how is a period of incubation projected if the "overload" theory is applied? Since AIDS reputedly only allows opportunistic diseases to infect, would not the incubation period be determined by the assaulting agent?

None of these questions lessen the gravity of the syndrome; surely some have logical answers. But too many assumptions originate not from the Centers for Disease Control but from dubious "authorities" inflaming hatred, panic—and that interferes drastically with achieving a cure.

At a dinner party for homosexuals in New York, one man recounts his recent sexual conquests, ignoring—as his listeners pretend to, with mirthless laughter that hardly shifts the candles' flames—the invisible presence in the room, in our lives. There is a telephone call for the man narrating exploits. When he returns, the phone rings again. The host stands over it, lifts it with his back to the others. He is wiping the mouthpiece before he answers.

To ask for evidence for every conclusion; to question each in our own press, not just convey it as fact; to insist that our own doctors be involved in all research into our complicated sexual patterns and that there be homosexuals in every official group dealing with AIDS; to provide highly refined, intelligent, *realistic* counseling (not psychojargon and grimly cheery clichés) based on awareness of the deep seriousness of the problems of men suddenly and traumatically deprived of once-abundant sex; to prepare for a time when the illness ends and the metaphor of contagion remains strengthened; boldly to face that our guilts—stirred anew—will not disappear without powerful, even painful exploration; to recognize that those guilts have their roots in heterosexual totalitarianism; to realize that we have been struck not by judgment but by illness: Might that help release us from the threatening association of homosexual sex with death?

A young man whom I love and who loves me called me from New York, where he lives: "Our whole world has changed, but theirs moves on as if nothing had happened," he expresses the horror of unconcern. He tells me he has chosen to be abstinent. I feel rage at the pervasive lack of compassion that exists for him, for others. There is nothing I can say to him, not in contradiction, modification nor affirmation of his decision. "I don't want to die," my beloved friend has already said, "there's so much I want to accomplish." It is a time when even advice is dangerous.

Weekends, after the bars closed, dozens of homosexuals would gather in the mutedly lighted area of parking lots and garages off Santa Monica Boulevard. Men lined walls of buildings, others drove in cars along alleys. Paired off, some rode away or walked into heavy shadows.

The men still gather on weekends, but fights erupt too easily. Several of the youngest men are painted—not effeminately, less "punk" than boldly assertive in the glow of fire-yellow street lights. Radios in parked cars are turned up. And these men who would once come here to cruise and connect for sex instead keep raising the volume of their radios as if to throttle the sound of their own bruised laughter, and in that lot off Santa Monica Boulevard, in the darkest hours of night and early morning, they drink and smoke grass—and they dance, clap, twist their bodies. There is the atmosphere of dead euphoria, of despair flailing to find its shape in a dance tinged with danger and defiance and deep, deep sorrow.

S.F. Judge Closes Ten Gay Baths, Sex Clubs

by Ray O'Loughlin

November 13, 1984

In an effort to stop the spread of AIDS, San Francisco superior court judge William Mullens grant-ed a temporary restraining order on October 15 that closed the city's six remaining bathhouses and four remaining gay sex clubs.

There was to have been a hearing on October 30 to determine if the businesses are to be closed permanently.

Mullens also granted a partial restraining order prohibiting sexual activities in two gay movie the-aters and two gay bookstores.

In his ruling Mullens said there was "ample evidence" to conclude that AIDS is "a rampant epi-demic" transmitted by sexual activity, and that closing the bathhouses and sex clubs "puts some kind of brake on the spread of the disease." He called the baths "a real and present health menace."

In an unusual move, Mullens refused even to hear arguments on civil liberties questions from sev-eral attorneys. He rejected applications from the American Civil Liberties Union, the Bay Area Lawyers for Individual Freedom, and Bay Area Physicians for Human Rights to file friend-of-the-court briefs presenting the constitutional issues in question.

Expressing his dismay at Mullens's refusal to consider the constitutional issues more thoroughly, attorney Tom Steel, who represents the Northern California Baths Association, said he feared that "if private sexual activity between consenting adults can now be regulated in one location, it can be regulated anywhere." Steel said his clients would obey the court order nonetheless.

Randy Stallings, former president of the Alice B. Toklas Lesbian and Gay Democratic Club, told *The Advocate*, "It seemed to me that the judge couldn't distinguish between low-risk sex and high-risk sex. He only heard gay sex and disease."

Declaring the AIDS epidemic worse in San Francisco than anywhere else in the United States, Dr. Mervyn Silverman, the city's public health director, issued an order on October 9 closing 14 commercial gay sex establishments in the hope of curbing the spread of the disease. By noon that day six bathhouses, four sex clubs, two gay movie theaters, and two gay bookstores were shut down by health inspectors. Within hours, however, most reopened for business.

According to attorney Steel, Silverman's order was not based on his emergency quarantine pow-ers as expected, but on a local nuisance abatement ordinance.

Steel told *The Advocate*, "This is an unprecedented use of the health director's closure powers.

Normally, quarantine powers are used against infected premises, which is not the case here. No one has said the infectious agent is in the buildings."

The surprise defiance by the owners left it to the city to back up its action with a court order. The city took the case to court and received the ruling in its favor on October 15 from superior court judge Mullens. Following the judge's decision, the gay establishments were again closed—and they remain so as of this writing.

At a news conference Silverman announced he now had "solid medical evidence" linking the gay sex shops to the spread of AIDS. He said he had sent health inspectors—actually, specially hired undercover private investigators—into 30 businesses to observe the facilities and the behavior occurring in them. Inspectors reported they saw sexual activities believed to transmit AIDS taking place at 14 establishments. At 16 others no high-risk sexual acts were observed. The report has been described as explicit and graphic.

With more than 700 diagnosed cases of AIDS in San Francisco as of October 5, Silverman said the city now had the highest per capita incidence of the disease in the nation. He characterized the 14 operations where high-risk sex was observed as profiteering from "the community that made them rich."

In a strongly worded statement, Silverman labeled them "establishments which promote and profit from the spread of AIDS," and said they "demonstrate a blatant disregard for the health of their patrons and of the community."

Calling AIDS a "universally fatal" sexually transmitted disease, Silverman said: "The places that I have ordered closed today have continued in the face of this epidemic to provide an environment that encourages and facilitates multiple unsafe sexual contacts, which are an important factor in the spread of this deadly disease."

When dangerous activities continue to take place in commercial settings, he said, "the health department has a duty to intercede and halt the operation of such businesses."

Silverman denied he was interfering with civil liberties, saying that his order affected only public businesses and had no application to private behavior.

Silverman's move to close the bathhouses is the latest round in 1½ years of turbulent wrangling over the role of the baths in the AIDS epidemic.

SHOULD THE BATHHOUSES BE CLOSED?

by Peter Freiberg

February 8, 1985

For almost a century they have been "safety zones"—havens, as gay historian Allan Berube says, where gay men "could be sexual and affectionate with each other." When police harassment eased up in the post-Stonewall period, the baths blossomed, becoming a symbol, to some, of "sexual liberation." Nevertheless, they were virtually unknown to the nongay public.

But today, in the era of AIDS, gay bathhouses are being thrust into the public eye—most noticeably in San Francisco, where a front-page dispute rages over the city's efforts to close the baths on the grounds they help spread AIDS through multiple-partner, high-risk sexual activity.

At the same time news media in cities across the country have been carrying wire-service stories on San Francisco's actions—and the reaction of the gay community. Gay baths, while still largely invisible, are moving out of the shadows.

So far the closure controversy has not become an issue for public debate in cities other than San Francisco—not even in New York. In most places the number of AIDS cases is so small compared with San Francisco and New York that, as Michigan gay activist David Piontkowsky says of his state, "No one has really brought the baths up at all."

Nevertheless, what happens in San Francisco could affect other cities. Stan Berg, owner of a bathhouse in Indianapolis and managing director of the Association of Independent Gay Health Clubs, flatly predicts: "If the San Francisco clubs are allowed to be closed...there will probably be a dozen cities around the country...that will file suit to close their bathhouses. I'm sure my city is going to be one of them."

This possibility generates diverse reactions within the gay community. Virtually all gay leaders have opposed government closure as an intrusion on civil liberties. Organizations of gay doctors insist there is no medical evidence to justify closure. An argument frequently voiced—by leaders of New York's Gay Men's Health Crisis and others—is that the baths are a "red herring," diverting attention from more important priorities, such as government funding for safe-sex education.

Nevertheless, many gay activists admits they would love to see the baths close for lack of business. A few urge that the government ban sexual activity in bathhouses. Many more say the baths should be pressed to change their environment to discourage unsafe sex acts with multiple partners and to educate their patrons about safe sex.

In New York the Coalition for Sexual Responsibility is seeking meetings with bathhouse owners, and eventually with other sex establishment operators, to urge them to make changes. Some critics say that in New York and elsewhere, these owners—and much of the gay leadership—have been acting like ostriches, hoping the issue will go away.

Recently Stephen Caiazza, who heads the New York Physicians for Human Rights, a gay group, stunned activists with a blunt letter in which he, speaking as an individual, declined to get involved in negotiations with bath owners.

"I feel it impossible for me to have any role in negotiating with the bathhouses short of presenting a demand for their immediate closure and their continued closure during the AIDS crisis," Caiazza wrote.

"AIDS will not go away if the baths close. The incidence will continue to climb geometrically. But it is medically undeniable that if the baths close, some lives, how many we do not know, will certainly be saved. And as a physician, my primary and ultimate duty is to save lives regardless of how many or how few lives I am dealing with."

In an interview Caiazza, who treats many AIDS patients, said, "As far as I'm concerned, right now the only good bath is a closed bath."

The baths issue involves three major facets, all of them interrelated: health, civil liberties, and political ramifications.

Although much about AIDS remains a mystery, there is general agreement that the more sexual partners an individual has, the greater the danger of developing AIDS. There is also widespread acknowledgment that certain sexual acts—among them rimming; swallowing semen, urine or feces; engaging in anal intercourse without a condom—are high-risk activities that increase the chances of contracting AIDS.

The question that sparks sharp disagreement is whether closing baths (as well as back rooms and other commercial sex establishments) would reduce the incidence of AIDS.

In New York the city health department has opposed closure as ineffectual. Task forces set up by local governments in Los Angeles and San Diego have also recommended against closure.

While urging individuals to avoid places "in which there is opportunity for multiple sexual contacts and/or partners," the Los Angeles City/County AIDS Task Force concluded: "Closure would have no significant health impact inasmuch as the conduct which leads to infection can move to other locations and occur anywhere."

Neil Schram, a gay doctor who headed the Los Angeles task force, maintains closure would send a "wrong message to the gay male community that if they don't go the bathhouses, there is no risk of developing AIDS."

Dennis McShane, president of the Bay Area Physicians for Human Rights, a San Francisco gay group, says that while baths can "serve as a source of unsafe sex, so can your own bedroom."

The crucial factor, McShane stresses, is not the location but the activity, "the high-risk sexual behaviors that are the effective means of transmitting the disease."

BAPHR strongly opposes closure. McShane says, "Our goal is education to allow people to make a decision that will be applicable no matter where they find themselves."

Rodger McFarlane, executive director of New York's GMHC, contends that the baths are a "red herring...I'm not saying anonymous sex in the establishments that promote those things is good, but massive public education is the biggest need."

McShane believes closure simply drives the allegedly small proportion of gay males who patronize the baths to other locales—parks, rest areas, and the like.

But Michael Callen, a New York AIDS patient who is one of the most outspoken critics of the baths, retorts, "You'll never make it impossible for gay men to have unsafe sex, but you can make it a lot more difficult."

Callen opposes government closure at this point but demands changes in the baths. "What the baths [and back rooms] sell is the opportunity to have an unlimited number of partners." That behavior, Callen says, is far less likely if men meet in bars or social settings.

Jim Fouratt, a New York gay activist, says the commercial sex establishments "provide a safe place" that encourages anonymous sexual activity.

"You cannot have the same number of partners in a public rest room or a park. Does this mean that if people stop going to them [the baths] the AIDS will disappear? I don't think so, but it certainly will lower the amount of exposure."

Fouratt criticizes gay leaders for not urging gay men strongly enough to stop going to the baths. When GMHC held fund-raising benefits at the Mineshaft, a Greenwich Village back room, Fouratt commented: "It blew my mind. What are you saying to the general public, that it's OK to go there?"

Paul Popham, president of GMHC's board, says, "I'm sure there are [GHMC] volunteers that didn't approve. But because the Mineshaft does a benefit for us doesn't mean we're condoning what goes on downstairs [in the backroom].... The city allows them to stay open. Should GMHC set itself up as the judge of whether they should close?"

Relatively few gay activists have called outright for closure—at least for now. But on all sides of the issue, there is criticism that many bathhouse owners have been irresponsible—and concern is growing.

In New York the New York State AIDS Advisory Council recently agreed, on Callen's recommendation, to set up a subcommittee to look into the baths issue.

Callen believes that since the baths are businesses, the state has legitimate authority to regulate them, though he would prefer that the bath owners make changes on their own. Callen was instrumental in forming the Coalition for Sexual Responsibility, which is trying to meet with owners of commercial sex establishments.

A list of requests to be made to the owners includes the hanging of safe sex posters in prominent places; making safe sex brochures always available; holding forums on AIDS; providing condoms to customers; eliminating glory holes; turning up the lights; allowing the coalition to monitor the facilities; making free venereal disease testing available.

The coalition itself has not discussed what to do in the event the bath owners refuse to cooperate. But Callen says that such a refusal, in light of "compelling" medical evidence that closure would significantly reduce the number of AIDS cases as well as a failure by the gay community to mount an adequate educational campaign, would lead him to support government closure in New York.

Whether the baths—and their patrons—have changed during the AIDS crisis is a subject of dispute. In New York there are reports that some baths have resisted any changes, even refusing to put up safe sex posters. Claims that business is up, down, or stable cannot be verified.

Bruce Mailman, managing partner of the St. Marks Baths, maintains that he had implemented virtually all the coalition's recommendations on his own before the group was formed.

According to Mailman, business at the St. Marks remains down 30% to 40% from its pre-AIDS crisis high, despite report from some patrons that business is booming.

Moreover, Mailman asserts, "The baths have become a much more social place. I think there's a lot of looking a lot of talking a lot of masturbation, and very little else."

In Indianapolis Stan Berg says business at the Body Works is the best since he opened it eight years ago. He claims that bathhouse is clean, provides literature on AIDS, sells condoms (although virtually no one buys), and puts up posters.

"Every time I put the safe sex poster up, somebody tears it down," says Berg. "Obviously there's a group of people who don't want to hear about AIDS." Three of the four orgy rooms have been eliminated, according to Berg, to discourage group sexual activity.

Berg guesses that 50% of his patrons "do not engage in any kind of sexual activity." Those who do have sex, he says, have fewer partners.

Jack Campbell, a shareholder in many of the Club Baths, states that in the 17 Sun Belt baths he manages directly, "We have brightened up the clubs. They're more like regular health clubs." He says gymnasiums have been installed (where possible), orgy rooms eliminated, condoms provided free, and safe sex posters put up.

But others maintain the Club Baths, like many others, have a long way to go. One recent patron at the Washington, D.C., Club Bath said the orgy room remained—and was active, no safe sex posters or brochures were available, and no condoms were in sight. "It was business as usual," said the customer. "You wouldn't know there was an AIDS crisis."

Campbell declares that although he is a shareholder in the Washington baths, he is not its manager. He recently hired Richard Berkowitz, a gay authority on safe sex, as a consultant for the clubs Campbell manages.

If some baths are making changes, a major motivation is fear of government closure. Many gay activists who oppose closure say they have no great fondness for the baths: Their concern is that government action will set a precedent for other interventions.

Opposing forced closure, the National Gay Task Force warned that "personal behavior should not be regulated by the state, which historically has been an instrument of our oppression."

The statement reflected a fear that other institutions where gays meet could be closed. Los Angeles's Schram goes so far as to say, "To argue for closing bathhouses is essentially to argue for outlawing sex between two men."

BAPHR's McShane, opposing what he calls the Big Brother approach, says, "Our role…is to educate people about good health factors, but you can't force them to do it." He favors pressure on the baths to encourage safe sex there, but he concludes the decision is ultimately up to the individual.

New York's Fouratt does not support government closure—for now—but says, "I think the people who put civil liberties over health are saying, 'You can fuck yourself to death.'"

Caiazza, also in New York, warns that the gay community itself must close the baths—or face much greater threats to civil liberty. "If we do not [close them]," Caiazza cautions, "others will step in in our place, claiming we are incapable or unwilling to do the job. My fear is that using this excuse, they will not stop with the baths, but proceed to impose further sanctions on gays in other, unrelated, areas. The possibility of a terrible backlash is very real. Witness Houston."

In reality the baths were barely mentioned by antigay groups in their successful campaign against Houston's protections for gay employees (although AIDS was brought up a great deal). And NGTF Washington representative Jeff Levi reports that thus far the baths issue has had no impact on his AIDS lobbying.

However, the right-wing, antigay columnist Patrick Buchanan has already called for closing the baths as AIDS "incubators." If grim predictions of up to 40,000 more AIDS cases within the next two years prove correct, the question of commercial sex establishments will inevitably heat up—placing the main responsibility on the gay community for shedding light and taking responsible action on a complex, tinderbox issue.

DAN WHITE: SUICIDE AS JUSTICE?

by Charles Linebarger

November 26, 1985

Dan White, the convicted murderer of San Francisco's mayor George Moscone and the city's first openly gay supervisor, Harvey Milk, committed suicide October 21. According to San Francisco police, White, a 39-year-old former city supervisor, firefighter, and policeman, connected a hose from the exhaust pipe of his wife's 1973 Buick Le Sabre to the passenger compartment. With garage doors closed, he died of carbon monoxide poisoning. White's body was discovered by his brother, Tom.

Police captain Michael Lennon paraphrased one of White's suicide notes as saying, "I'm sorry you have to find me this way, and I'm sorry for the problems I've caused. Dan." Contents of other notes have not been released.

Dan White was born in Long Beach, Calif., in 1946 but was raised in San Francisco's working-class Ingleside district. After graduating from public high school in 1964, he attended San Francisco's City College for one month before dropping out to join the police department. White resigned from the police department twice before trying his hand at the fire department in 1974.

Then in November 1977, in San Francisco's first district election, he was elected supervisor from District 8. Those elections also brought the first openly gay man, Harvey Milk, to the board of supervisor. Milk was elected from District 5, a rapidly changing part of the city, which includes the gay-populated Castro district. (One of White's campaign brochures had stated in part, "I'm not going to be scared out of San Francisco by splinter groups of radicals and social deviates. There are thousands and thousands of frustrated, angry people such as yourselves, waiting to unleash a fury that will eradicate the malignancies which blight our city.")

Within a year the mercurial White had resigned his supervisoral seat, claiming that he couldn't support his family on supervisor's salary. Several days after his November 10, 1978, resignation, White changed his mind and wanted his seat back. But the politically liberal Mayor George Moscone refused to reappoint him.

On November 27, the day Moscone planned to name someone else to White's former seat on the board of supervisors, White walked into the mayor's office and killed Moscone with four bullets—two in the chest and two in the head. White then walked down the hall and told supervisor Harvey Milk he wanted to talk to him. Milk followed White into his office and was killed with five bullets—three in the chest and two in the back of the head.

White's three-week trial became notorious for the defense's use of the so-called "Twinkie defense," or a diminished capacity in judgment by reason of depression resulting from the excess consumption of junk food. White was convicted of voluntary manslaughter and sentenced to a maximum of seven years in prison, with time off for good behavior.

The city exploded. In what became known as the White Night riots, a crowd of 5,000 angry citizens descended on City Hall, attacking the ornate facade of the building, breaking the glass doors and pulling away their cast-iron grillwork. Thirteen squad cars were set on fire. By the end of the night, 160 people—including 59 policemen—had been injured.

White was paroled from prison January 6, 1984, after serving five years and one month. Exactly one year later, he was released from parole. Reports had him living in Los Angeles and New Jersey, but he was seen walking with his wife in the Ingleside section of San Francisco, and nerves remained on edge throughout the city, particularly in the gay community. Many felt that the book had not finally closed on the White case and that a last act had yet to be played. So it was not surprising that there was something akin to relief across the city when the White case was finally laid to rest.

Like most of San Francisco, Castro Street took the news of White's death calmly. A news film truck was parked in the small Harvey Milk Plaza above the Castro Muni Station, and TV anchorpeople and film crews roamed the Castro's two-block length looking for news. It was hard to find.

The manager and cook of the Castro Street Café erased the specials from the chalkboard sign outside the restaurant and wrote in a special greeting, "Dan White is dead/suicide. Happy Birthday Scott Smith. Can of beer 85 cents." A fresh copy of the day's paper with its screaming red headline, "Dan White Dead," was taped to the window of an ice cream parlor.

Bob Wright, who was selling newspapers at the corner of Castro and 18th streets, commented on White's death by saying, "With so many of our friends and lovers dying, this is the happiest obituary I've ever read. Maybe that's a terrible way to look at it. But justice prevails in its own way." A passerby interjected, "I know, isn't it nice," and another said, "Praise the Lord."

"It's still sinking in," commented Scott Smith, Milk's former lover. "White was a symbol of homophobia. And what he did was a manifestation of things that are still happening, even in our own city. Two years ago, when he got out of prison, AIDS was just hitting the community and our priorities suddenly changed drastically. Dan White got put back in a little cubbyhole in our minds because we had something more important to deal with. It's easy to forget Dan White, but we won't forget George or Harvey."

Robert Epstein, producer of the Academy Award-winning documentary *The Times of Harvey Milk* (which will be televised nationally November 13 on PBS), commented that White's suicide was "very much in keeping with his character—that of a petulant adolescent. Obviously it was an admission of great guilt. I guess he finally saw the film!"

Supervisor Harry Britt, an openly gay associate of Milk's who was appointed by Mayor Dianne Feinstein to fill Milk's seat on the board of supervisors, responded to the news of the suicide by saying he felt he had just "come out of a very bad movie that I wished I hadn't gone to: You're glad you're out, but you don't feel good either. The pain of the injustice of the Dan White verdict has been appeased a great deal by this. He has performed the act of punishment that the court failed to perform.

"The response of the gay community has been pretty restrained," Britt continued. "If it had happened five years ago, people would have been more willing to wish death on Dan White. We're a different community today because of the AIDS epidemic. We just have other things on our minds besides Dan White. We have other things to deal with. But this has closed a chapter on what happened."

Mayor Dianne Feinstein, who replaced Moscone immediately after the assassinations, talked to reporters at a crowded news conference on the afternoon of the suicide.

"I am very sorry to hear that Dan White has taken his life," said Feinstein. "My sympathy goes to his widow, Mary Ann, his children, and his family, who have suffered very much. This latest tragedy should close a very sad chapter in the city's history."

Jim Rivaldo, a close friend of Milk's who had worked on Milk's last three political campaigns, said, "I think most people have a place in their heart to forgive people who go crazy and do terrible, violent things. But [White] never acknowledged causing anybody any pain. He never said he was sorry, and he wasn't punished. Now, by his death, we see that he did suffer and was, in effect, punished by what he did, even though the legal system wasn't able to do it."

HIGH COURT UPHOLDS SODOMY LAW

by Dave Walter

August 5, 1986

When the Supreme Court effectively ruled that gay people have no constitutional right to engage in same-gender sexual relations, the gay legal activists who had kept a close watch on *Hardwick* v. *Bowers* reacted with shock and then outrage. But it was not the ruling itself that angered them so; rather, it was the blatantly homophobic opinion that accompanied the decision.

The high court's 5–4 ruling on June 30 upheld Georgia's sodomy law and stated that there is no fundamental right to engage in homosexual sodomy. But the justices in the majority went even further, comparing gay sex to "adultery, incest, and other sexual crimes" and pointing out that society's prohibitions against gays have "ancient roots."

"I was really stunned by the opinion," said Joe Tom Easley, an attorney, legal scholar, and cochair of the Lambda Legal Defense and Education Fund. "I thought there was a 60–40 chance we would win. But what I was absolutely astounded at was the vehemence of the majority's opinion and the transparent hostility and bitterness toward gay people that the opinion represents. I cannot think of any opinion in the history of the Supreme Court that I can remember reading where the court has been as vitriolic and hostile toward any segment of the American public."

"It's clear they went beyond the issues in the case," said Abby Rubenfeld, LLDEF's legal director. "This purported use of history, that's an interesting way of interpreting the Constitution—to say that discrimination that existed for centuries justifies continued discrimination."

Gay leaders predict that the Supreme Court decision will directly result in increased expressions of homophobia. "It has the ability to generate a great deal of discrimination—even violence—against gay people all across the country," said Easley. "It puts the stamp of legitimacy on homophobia and comes from one for the most powerful and venerable institutions in American life."

Acknowledging the high court ruling as the worst defeat ever for the gay rights movement, gay leaders say they are both worried and hopeful about the impact the decision will have on the gay community itself. On the downside is the crushing blow the decision represents for gay people in general and the likelihood that many gays will prefer the safety—or convenience—of the closet. "The atmosphere it creates for gay men and lesbians is terrible and terrifying," said Rubenfeld. "It certainly doesn't encourage people to come out. It really shows how powerless we are as a community."

Nan Hunter, director of the Lesbian and Gay Rights Project of the American Civil Liberties Union, observed that the court ruling comes during an "era of backlash" against gays and others. It appears as the new right continues its ascendancy, as the federal courts become more filled with conservative judges, and as the gay community continues to reel from the AIDS crisis. In fact, the decision was handed down only one week after the Justice Department said that people who are perceived to be contagious for HIV can be fired from their jobs. "It's enormously damaging to us, absolutely, there's no question about it," said Hunter. "But I also think there will be a political response to it that will prove to be one of our major sources of energy in years to come."

"At its worst the *Hardwick* case could represent the turning point that would be the end of the highwater mark of the gay rights movement," said Easley. "But it could be the Stonewall of the '80s that will energize gays, that will cause us to get out there and say, 'No, we're not going to take it anymore,' and mobilize us to fight. It could be a watershed either way. We could turn down a bad road or a good road."

Gay leaders say that because the Supreme Court decision is so offensive, it will have the effect of spurring into action gay people who have until now not become involved in gay rights efforts. "This is like hitting people over the head with a hammer and saying, 'It's time to get serious about our lives,'" said Vic Basile, executive director of the Human Rights Campaign Fund. Gay rights organizations have received a flurry of calls from angry gays asking what they can do to help out in light of the ruling.

Furthermore, many nongays are also upset by the high court's ruling. "I think there will be greater sympathy as a result of this decision," said Hunter. "The decision in a sense brings out into the open the degree of contempt that exists for our community. And that kind of official expression of contempt is something many people feel uncomfortable with." That Justice Harry Blackmun was so eloquent and forceful in his dissent from the majority, Hunter added, will not be lost on the public at large.

Basile predicted that widespread disgust at the Supreme Court's action will result in new support for gay rights efforts from outside the movement: "It will help to do for us what we thus far have been unable to do for ourselves, which is to form a broader coalition with people—whether gay or straight, black or white—who can't help [but] see the egregiousness of this decision. I think we will find support from people who we didn't expect to find support from."

Basile hopes some of that support will come from the U.S. Senate, which reviews nominations of federal judges. He said HRCF will increase its focus on judicial appointments and will seek to help elect to the Senate candidates supportive of liberal judges.

The National Gay and Lesbian Task Force, meanwhile, plans its own political response to the Supreme Court ruling. According to Jeff Levi, NGLTF's executive director, the organization will work with state groups to develop strategies for repealing sodomy laws in the District of Columbia and the 24 states that still have such laws on the books. "It will require more resources, and it will be a challenge," Levi remarked, "but the court has thrown down the gauntlet, and we have to respond."

Gay legal activists agree that challenging sodomy laws through the political system is urgently needed because *Hardwick* will result in the continued and possibly increased use of sodomy laws to justify antigay court decisions—even in non–sodomy-related cases. Sodomy laws have, for example, been cited frequently as a basis on which to deny custody of children to gay parents. "They are used to support the argument that gay people are habitual lawbreakers," comments Hunter. "The sodomy laws are really the last refuge of homophobes."

Currently there are federal challenges to state sodomy laws in Arizona, Louisiana, and Minnesota; challenges have been filed in state courts in Missouri and Nevada.

The Ad Hoc Task Force to Challenge Sodomy Laws, a national organization made up of individual attorneys and various legal groups, was scheduled to meet in mid July to reevaluate the current court challenges and to map strategy for the future. Rubenfeld predicted there will be a shift from federal to state court suits. "Traditionally the federal courts have been the forum to which minority groups go to have their rights protected," she observed. "It is so ironic that this Supreme

Court has basically cut us off from federal courts. So we're left to going into state courts to protect our rights."

Legal activists anticipate the Supreme Court decision will have a mixed impact on state courts, which decide cases on state—not federal—constitutional grounds. Some courts, they say, will exercise their independence from the high court and ignore the federal ruling: others will find the Supreme Court opinion persuasive and use it in reaching decisions.

Hunter insisted that the federal courts, meanwhile, will not be abandoned. "We're not going to cede that route to the other side, not without a lot more fighting," she commented. "As bitter as this blow is, there are still a lot of cases to be fought and won in the federal court system."

Some legal activists said there would be little point in taking another gay-related case to the Supreme Court, given the *Hardwick* decision. But Leonard Graff, legal director of National Gay Rights Advocates, disagreed: "I can understand why people are not too anxious to go back to the Supreme Court. But there is a certain statement in going forward, which is to say, 'We're not going to cower in the corner for 20 years until we have a new court. We're going to keep on filing new suits. We're going to still be there battling away.' Eventually we will prevail."

"I think our movement will continue and we will regroup and move forward," said Rubenfeld. "There is a right to privacy and it does encompass private consensual sex (among gays). This was a political decision. It's important for them to know politically that we're not going to go away."

Gay leaders concede that rights victories are going to be won only with great difficulty and, in some cases, after many years. But they vow that the homophobes ultimately will be defeated. "We have to remember that they don't understand us as well as we understand them," NGLTF's Levi told a rally outside the Supreme Court. "And every time they knock us down, whether it's the Justice Department or the Supreme Court or Anita Bryant in the '70s—we come up stronger than ever before."

SUPREME COURT DECISION SPARKS PROTESTS: "NEW MILITANCY" SEEN IN ANGRY DEMONSTRATIONS

by Peter Freiberg

August 5, 1986

Enraged by the U.S. Supreme Court decision upholding the right of states to ban private, consensual gay sex, thousands of New York City gays took to the streets for two angry, militant demonstrations: a traffic-stopping Greenwich Village sit-in, followed three days later by a massive protest march during the July 4 Liberty Weekend celebration.

The demonstrations—the biggest by New York gays since the 1970s and the largest of several held around the country in opposition to the Supreme Court ruling—began with an evening rally by more than 1,000 people July 1 at Sheridan Square in Greenwich Village—a location that only two days before had been thronged by thousands of exuberant participants in the gay pride parade and Christopher Street Festival. After 90 minutes of speeches denouncing the decision, activist Buddy Noro told the crowd to sit down in the middle of Seventh Avenue South and stop traffic.

The protesters obliged, with police detouring traffic during the sit-in. But when organizers attempted to end the sit-in after almost a half hour, the crowd refused, instead surging east along Christopher Street to Sixth Avenue. Chanting "1-2-3-4, civil rights or civil war" and singing "We Shall Overcome," the protesters moved to the intersection of Sixth Avenue, 8th Street, and Greenwich Avenue. There the sit-in resumed, blocking traffic for 3½ hours until the last remaining demonstrators dispersed at 12:30 A.M.

It was during the sit-in that some participants called for a demonstration to "disrupt" the July 4 celebration, which was to be attended by President Reagan and Chief Justice Warren Burger. Even while the sit-in was taking place, a flier was mimeographed that called for gays to "show our rage" by snarling subways and disrupting traffic.

On July 4 6,000 chanting, singing, placard-carrying people marched from Greenwich Village to the federal courthouse downtown to Battery Park at the tip of Lower Manhattan, where hundreds of thousands of people were enjoying the Liberty Weekend festivities.

At one point the July 4 march came close to exploding into violence when protesters were met at Wall Street by helmeted police officers carrying nightsticks and standing behind hastily erected wooden barricades. The marchers were told that they could not proceed en masse to Battery Park, where they wanted to hold a rally.

While some in the crowd shouted "To Battery Park" and "Civil rights or civil war," Gina Alvarez, an activist with the Coalition for Lesbian and Gay Rights, urged the marchers to sit down in the street (which was closed to traffic) and to avoid a confrontation with police.

"Do you want to see your brothers and sisters hurt?" she shouted through a bullhorn. "We don't want a riot. Liberty, not blood."

Any possible violence was averted when Darrell Yates Rist, an activist with the Gay and Lesbian Alliance Against Defamation, told police that the protesters would go "one by one and two by two" to Battery Park rather than as a group. Many marchers then circumvented the barricades and proceeded downtown to Battery Park—holding aloft such signs as MISS LIBERTY? YOU BET I DO, LADY LIBERTY, LIGHT THE TORCH FOR US TOO and PRIVACY: A BASIC AMERICAN RIGHT.

"We have a message for Burger, we have a message for Falwell, we have message for Reagan," shouted Rist when the crowd regrouped in Battery Park. "The message is, 'We've had enough and we're not going to take it anymore.' "

With the Statue of Liberty in view, gays pointed their fingers and shook their fists in the statue's direction as they repeated the angry chant they had used earlier when they massed at the steps of the federal courthouse in Foley Square: "Shame, shame, shame, shame..."

Both the July 4 rally and the traffic-stopping demonstration by more than 1,000 people the night of July 1 made it apparent that the Supreme Court decision infuriated many New York gays more than has anything else in recent years—particularly as it was handed down on the eve of the Liberty Weekend extravaganza extolling the rights and freedoms supposedly enjoyed by all Americans.

Nor was the gay community's anger mollified by the news, disclosed on July 3 and publicized at the rally the next day, that right-wing homophobes had failed to gather enough signatures to put the recently enacted New York City gay rights law on the November ballot for a referendum vote.

The fury of the participants, some of whom had never before been involved in gay organizations or protests, led one longtime activist to predict a resurgence of grassroots organizing.

"What I've seen," said Jim Owles, a founder of the defunct Gay Activists Alliance in New York, "makes me feel more than ever that there's a time again for a new militancy in the gay and lesbian community."

But other activists, noting that street rallies alone would not overcome the impact of the Supreme Court decision, urged the protesters to get involved in the nitty-gritty work of donating money and volunteering time to organizations working to increase the legal and political clout of the gay community.

"We have to demonstrate that the court was wrong in its implicit analysis that this [community] is a politically powerless group," said Nan Hunter, director of the American Civil Liberties Union's new Lesbian and Gay Rights Project.

Some speakers emphasized that a key to changing public attitudes is for gay people to come out in far greater numbers than they have so far—at work and to their families and friends.

CLGR activist Andy Humm said, "We have to create the atmosphere in our community that encourages people to come out rather than [one that] tells people to stay in the closet and enjoy it." Humm added that he hoped the protests, aside from allowing gays to vent their anger, would show the marchers that "if they can go down to Battery Park in front of thousands of people, they can certainly come out to their families and office [workers], and that's where it's at."

While the demonstrations in New York City drew the largest crowds, protests held in other cities were equally spirited:

• In Washington, D.C., 175 gays and their supporters marched July 2 in a circle in front of the

Supreme Court, where they heard National Organization for Women president Eleanor Smeal portray the decision as an act of "neo-fascism."

• In San Francisco the Associated Press reported that 600 gays gathered on June 30, just hours after the decision was announced, to protest what gay lawyer John Wahl called "the day that will live in infamy."

Pat Norman, a lesbian city official who is running for the board of supervisors, said, "Today, all rights to privacy have been revoked by the U.S. Supreme Court. I am outraged."

• In Cincinnati the AP quoted gay rights activist Rick Buchanan as telling 200 cheering, applauding gay people gathered at City Hall, "We are a gentle, angry, loving people and we are not going to give up our rights. We will not go back into the closet."

Activist Ted Good called for volunteers to participate in lobbying campaigns aimed at getting legislators in Kentucky to repeal that state's sodomy law and to make sure that Ohio, which repealed its sodomy law in 1974, does not reenact one.

• In Dallas some 500 supporters of the Dallas Gay Alliance rallied near city hall. After expressing opposition to the Supreme Court decision, they marched to the Lone Star Gas Company to protest what they charged were the company's discriminatory hiring policies against people with AIDS.

The July 4 march in New York was seen by thousands of people, some of whom made clear their antigay feelings. One gay man was attacked while the march was still in Greenwich Village—he suffered a broken cheekbone, while two gay men were reportedly slightly injured in scuffles.

At Battery Park and elsewhere in Lower Manhattan, some spectators booed and screamed, "Fuck gay rights." But the majority of people watched the march bemusedly, and some bystanders cheered and applauded. "I think it's great," said Valeria Bambushew. "My sister's a lesbian, and I support her. My whole family's very supportive."

One speaker at the July 4 rally, Mark Green, who is seeking the Democratic nomination in New York for the U.S. Senate, warned the crowd that gays would not be able to negate the impact of the Supreme Court decision by themselves, just as blacks needed white support to get civil rights legislation in the 1960s. "Get allies, get allies," he urged.

N.Y., PA., MASS.: IMPACT OF RULING UNCLEAR

by Peter Freiberg

August 5, 1986

New York State attorney general Robert Abrams and gay legal activists said they did not expect the Supreme Court's decision, which upheld the right of states to pass sodomy laws, to resuscitate New York's law, which was declared unconstitutional by the state's highest court.

Of the 26 states that have struck down sodomy laws, New York is among three—Pennsylvania and Massachusetts are the others—where it was done judicially, not legislatively.

As a result there was some fear that the Supreme Court decision might invalidate the 1980 ruling by the New York State Court of Appeals. The Supreme Court said that private, consensual gay sex was not protected by the U.S. Constitution; the New York court ruling was based in part on the federal constitutional right to privacy.

But Thomas Stoddard, executive director of Lambda Legal Defense and Education Fund, a national gay legal rights organization, noted that the New York State Court of Appeals had also ruled the state sodomy law invalid because it applied only to unmarried people.

"Most likely the law is still unconstitutional," said Nathan Riley, a spokesman for Abrams. "One of the reasons offered by the state's highest court for striking down the law was that there was no rational basis for distinguishing between married and unmarried couples. Thus the court concluded that the New York statute denied its citizens the equal protection of the law."

Riley said that Abrams may soon issue a formal opinion on the status of the New York sodomy law. In a statement issued following the U.S. Supreme Court's ruling, Abrams said: "This decision, by a bare 5-4 majority, is a gross invasion of the privacy rights of all Americans....The New York Court of Appeals'...decision remains in effect unless the court reverses its own decision."

According to Stoddard, the Pennsylvania supreme court's declaration that the sodomy law is a violation of the state constitution will be unaffected by the U.S. Supreme Court ruling. In Massachusetts, he said, the state's supreme judicial court never invalidated the sodomy statutes but rather issued an opinion in 1974 stating that they were unenforceable.

Kevin Cathcart, executive director of Gay and Lesbian Advocates and Defenders, a Boston-based legal rights group, was quoted in the *Boston Herald* was saying that while the Massachusetts court decision makes prosecution of gays unlikely, "the fact that laws like this are on the books leaves open potential for abuse.

"The [U.S.] Supreme Court ruling does not recriminalize sodomy—it only makes [sodomy laws] more difficult to get rid of," Cathcart said. Nevertheless, he added that he hoped to see the Massachusetts sodomy law challenged within the next year.

New Lineup of Justices More Antigay: Reagan Nominates Rehnquist, Scalia to Fill Empty Seats

by Dave Walter

August 5, 1986

As devastating as the Supreme Court decision in *Hardwick* v. *Bowers* is, gay legal activists say they do not regret that the case ended up at the high court. After all, they assert, it might have been worse had the case been decided by what will be—pending Senate approval—the Rehnquist court.

President Reagan's nominations of William Rehnquist to replace retiring Chief Justice Warren Burger and of Antonin Scalia to be a new associate justice are generally expected to result in the court's becoming more conservative, and predict gay observers, more solidly antigay.

Rehnquist, a 62-year-old Nixon appointee, voted with the majority in *Hardwick* but did not write the majority opinion or a concurring opinion. He did, however, pen some thoughts about gay rights in February 1978, when he objected to the court's decision not to hear *University of Missouri* v. *Gay Lib,* a case centering on the school's refusal to recognize a gay student group.

"The issue in this case is the extent to which a self-governing democracy, having made certain acts criminal, may prevent or discourage individuals from engaging in speech or conduct which encourages others to violate those laws," Rehnquist wrote. "Expert psychological testimony...established the fact that the meeting together of individuals who consider themselves homosexual in an officially recognized university organization can have a distinctly different effect from the mere advocacy of repeal of the state's sodomy statute. As the university recognized, this danger may be particularly acute in the university setting, where many students are still coping with the sexual problems which accompany late adolescence and early adulthood."

Scalia, 50, distinguished himself as an antigay jurist in 1984, when he joined fellow U.S. Court of Appeals judge Robert Bork in a scathing attack on gays. In *Dronenberg* v. *Zech* Bork asserted that there is no constitutional right to engage in gay sex and that the Navy could not be required "to treat heterosexual conduct and homosexual conduct as either morally equivalent or as posing equal dangers to the Navy's mission."

Abby Rubenfeld, legal director of the Lambda Legal Defense and Education Fund, predicted that the Rehnquist-Scalia combination will not bode well for gays. "I think we're in for tough times in terms of the Supreme Court," she said. "[Rehnquist] will be more aggressive than Burger was and much more of a scholar—and he is much more of a committed conservative. And so is Scalia. The ideological balance doesn't change...but the reality is, they're adding a very persuasive spokesman for conservative judicial philosophy and changing to a chief justice [a judge] who's aware of the power he'll have—and will use it."

"Burger's problem was that he was not a consistent right-winger on the court," said Nan Hunter, director of the Lesbian and Gay Rights Project of the American Civil Liberties Union. "He voted all across the middle from the right. One does not expect Scalia to deviate from the right."

Leonard Graff, legal director of National Gay Rights Advocates, predicted that Rehnquist might become more moderate in order to win opinions marked by greater consensus—and therefore win more favorable treatment in the history books. But regarding gay-related issues, added Graff, Scalia will be "as bad, if not worse" than Burger.

Gay legal activists agree that the best hope gays have is for a scenario in which the pro-gay Supreme Court justices—Harry Blackmun, William Brennan, Thurgood Marshall, and John Paul Stevens—remain on the court until a liberal president is elected and is provided with the opportunity to appoint several new justices. But that still would not necessarily mean gays could breathe a sigh of relief. "Because of the new appointment of Scalia and the presumed life expectancy of the more conservative members of the court, at best you're going to see a very fractured court for a long time," said Hunter. "That's the best we have to hope for. At worst, the court will shift in a very dramatic way to the right. And then we're going to be in very serious trouble."

Of the pro-gay justices, all but the 66-year-old Stevens will be in their 80s before Ronald Reagan is even out of office. Meanwhile, the three conservatives (Rehnquist, Scalia, and Sandra Day O'Connor) are 63 or younger; Byron White, the conservative moderate who wrote the antigay decision in *Hardwick,* is 69; Lewis Powell, who joined the antigay majority in the case, is 79.

IN THE JUSTICES' OWN WORDS...

by Dave Walter

August 5, 1986

Following are excerpts from the majority opinion, written by Justice Byron White, who was joined by Chief Justice Warren Burger and Justices Sandra Day O'Connor, Lewis Powell, and William Rehnquist:

Striving to assure itself and the public that announcing rights not readily identifiable in the Constitution's text involves much more than the imposition of the Justice's own choice of values on the States and the Federal Government, the Court has sought to identify the nature of the rights qualifying for heightened judicial protection. In *Palko* v. *Connecticut*...it was said that this category includes those fundamental liberties that are "implicit in the concept of ordered liberty," such that "neither liberty nor justice would exist if [they] were sacrificed." A different description of fundamental liberties appeared in *Moore* v. *East Cleveland*...where they are characterized as those liberties that are "deeply rooted in this Nation's history and tradition..."

It is obvious to us that neither of these formulations would extend a fundamental right to homosexuals to engage in acts of consensual sodomy. Proscriptions against that conduct have ancient roots... Sodomy was a criminal offense at common law and was forbidden by the laws of the original 13 States when they ratified the Bill of Rights.... In fact, until 1961, all 50 states outlawed sodomy, and today, 24 States and the District of Columbia continue to provide criminal penalties for sodomy performed in private and between consenting adults.... Against this background, to claim that a right to engage in such conduct is "deeply rooted in this Nation's history and tradition" or "implicit in the concept of ordered liberty" is, at best, facetious.

Plainly enough, otherwise illegal conduct is not always immunized whenever it occurs in the home. Victimless crimes, such as the possession and use of illegal drugs, do not escape the law where they are committed at home.... And if respondent's submission is limited to the voluntary sexual conduct between consenting adults, it would be difficult, except by fiat, to limit the claimed right to homosexual conduct while leaving exposed to prosecution adultery, incest, and other sexual crimes even though they are committed in the home. We are unwilling to wind down that road.

Following are excerpts from the dissenting opinion, written by Justice Harry Blackmun, joined by Justices William Brennan, Thurgood Marshall, and John Paul Stevens:

This case is no more about a "fundamental right to engage in homosexual sodomy, as the Court purports to declare...than *Stanley* v. *Georgia*...was about a fundamental right to watch obscene movies, or *Katz* v. *United States*...was about a fundamental right to place interstate bets from a telephone booth. Rather, this case is about [quoting former Justice Louis Brandeis] "the most comprehensive of rights and the right most valued by civilized men," namely "the right to be let alone."

Like Justice [Oliver Wendell] Holmes, I believe that "it is revolting to have no better reason for a rule of law than that it was laid down in the time of Henry IV. It is still more revolting if the grounds upon which it was laid down have vanished long since, and the rule simply persists from blind imitation of the past...." I believe we must analyze respondent's claim in the light of the values that underlie the constitutional right to privacy. If that right means anything, it means that, before Georgia can prosecute its citizens for making choices about the most intimate aspects of their lives, it must do more than assert that the choice they have made is an "abominable crime not fit to be named among Christians."

Only the most willful blindness could obscure the fact that sexual intimacy is "a sensitive, key relationship of human existence, central to family life, community welfare, and the development of human personality...." The fact that individuals define themselves in a significant way through their intimate sexual relationships with others suggests, in a Nation as diverse as ours, that there may be many "right" ways of conducting those relationships, and that much of the richness of a relationship will come from the freedom an individual has to *choose* the form and nature of these intensely personal bonds.

Following are excerpts from the dissenting opinion, written by Justice John Paul Stevens, who was joined by Justices William Brennan and Thurgood Marshall:

Society has every right to encourage its individual members to follow particular traditions in expressing affection for one another and in gratifying their personal desires. It, of course, may prohibit an individual from imposing his will on another to satisfy his own selfish interests. It also may prevent an individual from interfering with, or violating, a legally sanctioned and protected relationship, such as marriage. And it may explain the relative advantages and disadvantages of different forms of intimate expression. But when individual married couples are isolated from observation by others, the way in which they voluntarily choose to conduct their intimate relations is a matter for them— not the State—to decide. The essential "liberty" that animated the development of the law in [previous] cases...surely embraces the right to engage in nonreproductive, sexual conduct that others may consider offensive or immoral.

Although the meaning of the principle that "all men are created equal" is not always clear, it surely must mean that every free citizen has the same interest in "liberty" that the members of the majority share. From the standpoint of the individual, the homosexual and the heterosexual have the same interest in deciding how he will live his own life, and more narrowly, how he will conduct himself in his personal and voluntary associations with his companions. State intrusion into the private conduct of either is equally burdensome.

REAGAN'S GAY SEX SCANDAL

by Tim Brick

November 25, 1986

Ronald Reagan might have captured the presidency 12 years sooner were it not for a gay witch-hunt that involved the top levels of his California administration and broke his presidential momentum. Campaign chronicler Theodore White wrote, "The scandal all but shattered Reagan's self-confidence, as well as his confidence in his fellow men."

Twenty years later reverberations are still being felt. The rumors and innuendos could hobble another presidential aspirant, conservative New York congressman Jack Kemp, who was serving as an athletic adviser to Reagan at the time of the brouhaha.

The controversy that rocked Sacramento reveals a lot about the style and substance of our current president and about his attitude toward gays. It also serves as a fascinating study of the role of homophobia in politics—then and now.

By 1967 the jockeying for the 1968 presidential election was already intense. Democrats were still united behind Lyndon Johnson, but several Republicans, anxious to redeem their party from the humiliating Goldwater defeat of 1964, had begun to make their moves. Governors Rockefeller and Romney were maneuvering for position. Richard Nixon had been resurrected from the political grave sealed by his defeat by Edmund G. "Pat" Brown in the 1962 California gubernatorial election.

But from out of the West a new figure ambled forth to enter the presidential casting call. Ronald Reagan, the amiable actor and Boraxo salesman who had snatched up the conservative mantle of Barry Goldwater, had walloped that same Pat Brown in the 1966 election for governor of California.

Within ten days of his victory, Reagan assembled his closest confidants at his Pacific Palisades home for a discussion of his biggest role—the presidency.

The strategy was set. A meticulous time line was devised, and key aides were assigned to execute it. By the summer of 1967, Reagan's game plan was well advanced. As a dutiful "noncandidate," interested only in raising money for the Republican Party, Governor Reagan had been touring the country preaching the conservative creed.

As the national press corps turned its attention to the latest California novelty, a controversy split Reagan's staff. The issue: How intently should Reagan pursue the presidency in 1968? The governor's top aide, who had directed the gubernatorial campaign, was a "dove" advocating a go-slow approach to the presidential drive. Press secretary Lyn Nofziger, a tough right-winger who went on to become director of political affairs in the Reagan White House, was a "hawk."

The debate went on for months. Then Nofziger spotted an opening. It came in the form of a tip from Washington. Rumor had it that Reagan's top aide, a man so powerful that journalists were now referring to him as "Governor," was a homosexual. (Due to the murky nature of the allegations and the investigation that followed, and out of respect for the privacy of individuals involved, news accounts in 1967 and subsequent recountings have refrained from citing the names of "suspects"—with the exception of Jack Kemp.)

Other Reagan advisers balked at the rumors, but Lyn Nofziger, a ferocious infighter, decided to take action. Together with Arthur Van Court, a former detective from Los Angeles who was now Reagan's body guard and travel secretary, the press secretary developed a plan to document the allegations. Other Reagan aides, such as current Attorney General Edwin Meese and former Secretary of the Interior William Clark, were brought in on the plan, although the governor was apparently unaware of the investigation until much later.

Van Court enlisted the help of private investigators and friends on the Los Angeles police force to systematically check out the reports.

As usually happens in such witch-hunts, jealousy, rumors, and snide remarks were blended into a stinking stew that stained the inquisitors as much as the subjects. Rumors of secret trysts and Lake Tahoe orgies at a cabin owned by the top aide and athletic adviser Jack Kemp were circulated. Quickly, other Reagan staffers and consultants were added to the list of the accused. The investigation ballooned into a far-reaching search for a "homosexual ring" at the top levels of the Reagan administration. Two top Reagan administration officials, athletic adviser Kemp, two sons of a Republican state senator, and a member of a California campaign management firm were fingered by the witch-hunters.

The suspects soon became aware of the surveillance. At one point the chief suspects tried to elude the snoopers in a high-speed chase on a California highway. Among the Reagan staff the probe was the subject of jokes, but California's chief executive still knew nothing about it, even though by now the investigation involved a major part of his top staff.

Reagan already was notorious for the distance he maintained from the everyday functioning of government, but other motives as well led the investigators to keep him in the dark. Some aides feared that Reagan, coming from a Hollywood purportedly more tolerant of homosexuals, would not believe the reports. Others wanted to be absolutely sure of the facts before alerting him.

While the investigation satisfied Nofziger's suspicions, it failed to turn up conclusive proof. The two major suspects were known to have shared motel or hotel rooms in San Diego, San Francisco and Sacramento, but Van Court's efforts to record the "orgies" on tape failed. No arrest records or other types of hard evidence were discovered.

Because of the volatility of the issue and the suspects' awareness of the probe, the homosexual hunters wanted to wrap it up quickly. On a hot late August day in Sacramento, Nofziger, Meese, Clark, Van Court, and other staffers held a secret meeting. They decided the time had come to present the evidence to California's chief executive.

Reagan had retreated to the stately Hotel del Coronado in San Diego, 500 miles south of Sacramento. Clad in pajamas and robe, he was surprised early the next morning when 11 top aides and associates paraded into his room. Without a word, they handed him a report of the investigation. Reagan read it and turned pale. In a classic Reagan non sequitur, he reportedly exclaimed, "My God, has government failed?" He remarked that the action he must take was obvious. The next day the governor set the report on his top aide's desk without saying a word. The official resigned at a press conference the following Monday. (He is now a high-powered private attorney, married and with children, in Los Angeles.)

Staff members held their breaths hoping that capital reporters wouldn't perceive the real reason for the resignation. Ironically, most commentators saw the sack as another indication of developing presidential momentum.

Though Reagan and his leading staffers were gleeful that the media had missed the story, they were terrified of how damaging the revelations could be to his presidential hopes. Tension in the governor's office was intense. Morale among the Reagan team had been shattered by the traumatic investigation and now by the swirling rumor mill. "It was a heart transplant where one wasn't replaced and where the operation was performed with a dull knife," according to one of the investigators. "The trauma was so severe that the patient—the governor's office—went into a state of shock for four months. And the governor cut himself off from a lot of things that he shouldn't. The governorship went into receivership."

Finally Nofziger cracked. Trying to defuse widespread rumors and angered that the former aide still claimed influence with the governor, Nofziger leaked the story to three savvy California political reporters. Two Reagan staff members had been dismissed as homosexuals, he told them. Then, on board the SS *Independence* sailing to the 1967 National Governors' Conference in the Virgin Islands in late October, Reagan's press aide swore three other national reporters to secrecy and filled them in. Since the people involved had already left the Reagan staff, these reporters considered the matter closed. None of them wrote or broadcast about it, although a mysterious entry was contained in the "Periscope" column of *Newsweek* on October 30: "A top GOP presidential prospect has a potentially sordid scandal on his hands. Private investigators he hired found evidence that two of his aides had committed homosexual acts. The men are no longer working for the GOP leader, but the whole story may surface any day."

Then October 31 syndicated columnist Drew Pearson broke the story. After a long career as America's premiere muckraker, Pearson had just slammed Connecticut senator Thomas Dodd for improprieties. Now he set his sights on the man leading what he saw as an attempt by the far right to take over the Republican Party and the United States.

Pearson led off his October 31 column: "The most interesting speculation among political leaders in this key state of California is whether the magic charm of Gov. Ronald Reagan can survive the discovery that a homosexual ring has been operating in his office."

That morning Ronald Reagan, who had just returned from a fund-raising trip through several Midwest and Southern states, held a regularly scheduled news conference. The first question: "Governor, is there any truth to a published report that a homosexual ring has been uncovered among your administration?"

Reagan replied with characteristic clarity: "No, there is no truth to the report, and I know where the report comes from. I was informed last night, while most Californians won't see it, because I think that's the best clue to the veracity of the report—is the fact that as far as we know most of the major papers are refusing to run the Drew Pearson column in which it appears."

Pearson's column was regularly picked up by 530 papers nationally, but no major California paper carried the hard-hitting exposé, which charged that Ronald Reagan had investigated reports that members of his staff were engaged in homosexual activities but had not dismissed the individuals involved until they came under suspicion of being moderate in their politics.

Pearson claimed that Reagan, on learning of the rumors, had appointed security aide Arthur Van Court to investigate. "Van Court," according to the article, "came up with tape recordings of a sex orgy which had taken place at a cabin near Lake Tahoe, leased by two members of Reagan's staff. Eight men were involved. This event apparently took place while the governor was meeting with Nevada governor Paul Laxalt regarding joint concerns about the lake."

Reagan's defense consisted of denial and denunciation. "Drew Pearson has been sort of riding on my back for a number of years, long before I ever got into this business, back when I was just making speeches along the banquet trail. Pearson has devoted columns to me, and I'd like to say now three presidents of both parties have called Drew Pearson publicly a liar. And to my knowledge none of them has ever seen fit to retract that opinion. I certainly have never seen anything that would justify my disagreeing with those three presidents on that score. Drew Pearson shouldn't be using a typewriter and paper. He's better with a pencil on outbuilding walls."

Pearson, who had little sympathy for conservatives *or* gays, wrote in the famous column: "The press has treated him with consideration equaled only by their treatment of General Dwight D.

Eisenhower. The question is whether he will get the same treatment regarding the homo ring.

"The case is significant," the column continued, "first because Reagan was critical when President Johnson was faced with a similar situation in the campaign of 1964 and dropped his assistant (Walter Jenkins) after he became involved in a homosexual affair. Johnson acted immediately. Reagan, on the other hand, waited for about six months."

At the news conference Reagan's anger flared when he was informed that the *San Francisco Chronicle* had printed an article similar to Pearson's that morning. "Well, then someone violated what I've been told they were going to do," the governor retorted, "but I can only say that I'm not going to dignify Drew Pearson by even attempting to answer anything as scurrilous and as ridiculous as the report. And I think that—I myself wonder how respectable newspapers can continue to carry the column of a man who has done what he's done, and this is about the lowest, this is stooping to destroy human beings, innocent people, and there is just no sense in getting into that kind of contest with him."

Reagan reacted vehemently to a reporter's suggestion that he had extracted an agreement from California papers not to publish the Pearson column. His fist came down on the rostrum with a bang. "I didn't extract—wait a minute, come on, I didn't extract any agreement," he shouted, red-faced. "I simply said that at the time that this—I was notified of this, I was told that the major newspapers of California were not going to run this column."

The governor than outlined his screening process for state appointees, which entailed "doing the utmost to check them out completely and thoroughly."

"In your investigations have you ever uncovered or discovered a homosexual?" a reporter asked.

"No," Reagan replied.

"Are you calling Drew Pearson a liar?"

"I'm saying that in the experience of the stories, including the one that he printed about me during the primary—it's my turn again, he seems to have gotten back around to me again, but in every experience that I have had with regard to stories involving me, there has been no truth and he's a liar."

"How about in this case?"

"He's lying."

Pearson's column reported that communications director Lyn Nofziger had told reporters aboard the SS *Independence* that two Reagan aides had been dropped on morals charges.

"He's here, and you can ask him directly," the governor said of Nofziger. "I am prepare to say that nothing like that ever happened. Want to confirm it, Lyn?" Nofziger, standing on the sidelines, raised his hands and said, "Confirmed."

Bodyguard Van Court was standing at Nofziger's side. Asked about the surreptitious tape recording allegedly made by Van Court, Reagan replied, "I'm familiar with what Mr. Pearson said, and again

I say there is absolutely no truth in it. You want to ask him—Art?" Van Court replied: "Complete fiction."

Following the news conference, *The New York Times, The Washington Post, Time,* and *Newsweek* all confirmed that Nofziger had indeed told reporters that two staff members had been dismissed as homosexuals. Tom Wicker reported in *The New York Times* that one journalist asked Nofziger directly why a former member of the Reagan staff had left. "The press secretary replied that the man in question was a homosexual," according to Wicker. Nofziger, when asked why he would give out such information, replied that, since the deposed aide had been spreading the word that he was still influential with Governor Reagan, "some members of the governor's staff had decided to give the facts when asked about the former aide."

Drew Pearson, who claimed he had evidence of his charges, called for an investigation of the apparent contradictions. The "Sacramento credibility gap," according to the columnist, existed because Governor Reagan "delayed six months in getting rid of the offenders" and Nofziger "belatedly sought to create the impression that the Governor had acted promptly."

Pearson challenged Reagan to back up his denials with a libel suit and rushed back to California for a confrontation. Reagan, in turn, warned the muckraker that he had better not spit on the sidewalk while he was in California.

On November 8, the *Washington Star* editorialized: "The black mark on Reagan's record is not that he hired such men, or that he was slow in firing them. Where he stumbled was in his histrionic denial and in calling Drew Pearson a liar when he must have known Pearson's article was factually correct. The motivation of the extraordinary performance is not easily discerned."

At a press conference on November 10, Reagan reiterated that he had no evidence and refused to explain the contradictions between his statements and Nofziger's. When reporters confronted Nofziger as to whether he had briefed reporters, the press secretary replied, "I'm not saying anything on that."

Some of the most revealing insights into Governor Reagan's attitudes toward homosexuals came in early December when he traveled to Yale to deliver a seminar on government. Students were both fascinated and distressed by the newest phenomenon from California. At a news conference on his arrival, the first question fired at the governor threw him off balance. A senior from Los Angeles asked if there was any place for homosexuals in government. The governor swallowed hard, paused, and then replied, "Well, perhaps in the Department of Parks and Recreation." Undeterred by the disarming witticisms the nation now expects from Reagan, the student journalist pressed on. "Shouldn't homosexuality be legal?" Reagan hesitated. "Do you believe homosexuality should remain illegal?" the student asked. "Yes, I do," the governor replied. "It's a tragic illness, a neurosis, and I wish for a cure and for good health." Another student journalist asked which other illnesses should be illegal. The governor did not reply.

The national media continued to roast Reagan about the inconsistencies, but Reagan simply refused to respond. Their interest slowly faded, but the effects on Reagan and his presidential drive were lasting. The novice governor demonstrated a pattern that has characterized his political life. When emotionally difficult and complex problems arise, Reagan distances himself. As the weeks drew on, he increasingly turned for support and advice to the millionaire backers known as his Kitchen Cabinet. They all realized he had delegated too much authority, but the crisis led him even further away from the everyday workings of the governor's office.

"From this blow," Theodore White wrote in *The Making of the President 1968,* "the Reagan campaign never recovered." The scandal, according to White, "all but shattered Reagan's self-confidence, as well as his confidence in his fellow men."

The Sacramento imbroglio demonstrates several major elements of Reagan's political style. The homogenized view of people, the overdelegation of authority, the skill at distancing himself from impropriety and scandal, and the ability to deflect criticism with homey charm are all characteristics that America has come to know.

The flap is particularly revealing of Reagan's attitudes toward gays. The governor's embarrassed denials were not so much directed as saving the good names of the men who were spied upon as at protecting his political reputation. He accepted the accusations without even discussing them with his top aide and the others involved. The presumption of guilt and the dread of political fallout was so overpowering that, on the basis of jealous smears and a politically motivated inquisition, he was willing to expel the man who had directed his gubernatorial campaign, the person who was considered his closest confidant. The accused lost their careers and were forever stigmatized by allegations for which Reagan repeatedly claimed there was no substantiation. Ironically, the "substantiation" came from his own press secretary, who initiated the witch-hunt and then leaked the story to reporters.

The self-serving squeamishness and the traumatizing effects of the Sacramento scandal didn't end in 1967. Despite his attempts to ignore homosexuals, gay-related issues have continued to haunt Ronald Reagan. Changing societal attitudes and now AIDS have ensured that.

Once, in 1978, when Reagan issued a pivotal statement opposing the Briggs initiative in California—which would have barred homosexual teachers from classrooms—it even appeared that Ronald Reagan had grown.

But since then Reagan's personal queasiness has been formalized into callous federal policies on gay and lesbian rights in general and AIDS funding in particular.

Prohibitions on job discrimination have been dismissed as "efforts to obtain governmental endorsement of homosexuality."

Fear of contagion justifies discrimination against people with AIDS, according to the Reagan Justice Department—despite substantial medical documentation that such anxieties are unfounded.

And Reagan appointees to the Supreme Court guarantee that homosexual acts of intimacy will not be afforded constitutional protections.

Ronald Reagan and his policies have been devastating to gay men and lesbians. But it all becomes easier to understand when you realize the deep roots of Reagan's homophobia.

THE NEW YORK TIMES VERSUS GAY AMERICA: ALL THE (HETEROSEXUAL) NEWS THAT'S FIT TO PRINT

by George De Stefano

December 9, 1986

It was billed as "the biggest gay event of all time": a performance of the Ringling Brothers and Barnum and Bailey Circus to benefit the Gay Men's Health Crisis. On the evening of April 30, 1983, some 18,000 gay men, lesbians, and their friends filled Madison Square Garden in New York for "The Greatest Show on Earth"—and even for those with low tolerance for clowns, animal acts, and high-wire acrobats, it was a great night at the circus.

The New York and national media didn't need to be told that the sold-out circus benefit was a news worthy event. There was, however, one significant gap in the otherwise thorough press coverage: *The New York Times*. Except for a small preview item in the "New York Day by Day" column, the *Times* ignored the biggest AIDS fund-raiser to that date and an unprecedented social event in the city's gay community.

There was shock, incomprehension, and outrage among gay New Yorkers. How could the most influential newspaper in its city, the nation, and arguably the world, decide that such an important event was not news fit to print?

To many veteran *Times* watchers, the failure to report the circus was consistent with the paper's history of slighting the gay community. The *Times* had rarely acknowledged that New York's gay male and lesbian population was an integral part of the city's social, cultural, and political life, and that its concerns and activities were worthy of more than meager and infrequent attention.

And in 1983, two years into the AIDS crisis, gay discontent with the *Times* was exacerbated by the paper's coverage of the epidemic. Although the first report in the mainstream media of the condition that was to be named acquired immune deficiency syndrome appeared in *The New York Times* ("Rare Cancer Seen in 41 Homosexuals," July 3, 1981), coverage thereafter had been spotty. In all of 1982, the *Times* printed only five AIDS stories, two of them dealing with transfused blood as a route of infection and one about the disease among Haitian immigrants. Poisoned Tylenol and the deaths of prize Lipizzaner stallions got front-page coverage in 1982, but "the paper of record" didn't think AIDS demanded comparable treatment. In *The Normal Heart,* Larry Kramer's 1984 play about the early years of the epidemic, crusading activist Ned Weeks proclaims *The New York Times* (along with the city's mayor) "the biggest enemy gay men and women must contend with in New York."

The failure to cover the GMHC circus benefit was the last straw for a group of gay activists. They wrote to *Times* chairman Arthur Ochs "Punch" Sulzberger and requested a meeting with him to discuss that particular journalistic lapse as well as the general quality of gay coverage. If the *Times* refused their request, they would call for a gay boycott of the paper. Sulzberger demurred, but Sydney Gruson, *Times* corporate vice chairman, agreed to an off-the-record meeting with Andrew Humm, representing the Coalition for Lesbian and Gay Rights; Virginia Apuzzo, then the executive director of the National Gay Task Force; and veteran activists David Rothenberg and Richard Failla (now a New York civil court judge).

"The meeting was really 'Homo 101,'" recalls Apuzzo. "We had to walk him through the fundamental things, including the use of the word *gay* and a community's right to define itself." (Despite some recent signs of change, the *Times* continues to bar the use of *gay* unless it is part of a proper name or a direct quotation.)

"We outlined all our complaints and criticisms," says Rothenberg, "with the quantity and quality of the AIDS coverage being perhaps the main item on our agenda."

Rothenberg also told Gruson that *Times* reporters who were gay feared that their careers would be stalled if their homosexuality became known. Their closeted status, argued Rothenberg, compromised their journalism because it made them unwilling to "volunteer their sources and contacts in the [gay] community."

The four gay leaders thought that the meeting was generally successful. Gruson was receptive to their criticism and agreed with some of it. He conceded that the failure to cover the circus was a blunder. No change in the gay nomenclature policy was forthcoming, although when Gruson consulted his dictionary he discovered, to his chagrin, that *gay* was indeed an accepted synonym for *homosexual.* But most important, the meeting opened lines of communication with the *Times,* an institution that had been indifferent, even hostile, to the gay community.

However, Andy Humm "still felt that the *Times* deserved a razzing," and the Coalition for Lesbian and Gay Rights went ahead with plans for a boycott. CLGR held a demonstration outside the *Times* offices on West 43rd Street and organized a mail protest that Humm says resulted in more than 700 angry letters and postcards being sent to the paper.

Further meetings were arranged between *Times* and gay leaders—minus Humm, who had disclosed the off-the-record meeting with Gruson to a *New York Post* reporter. Humm says he spoke to the press because he "felt an obligation to report to the [gay] community that a dialogue had been opened" with the *Times*. He was furious with his colleagues for agreeing to his exclusion from subsequent sessions because "it means that CLGR, a grassroots organization, would not be represented."

Apuzzo, Rothenberg, and Failla subsequently met, on separate occasions, with *Times* editorial writers, the national and metropolitan editors, and with executive editor A.M. Rosenthal. (On November 1, A.M. Rosenthal stepped down as the *Times'* executive editor, after directing news coverage at the paper for 17 years. He did not respond to the request for a comment for this piece. His successor is Max Frankel, former editor of the editorial page. Rosenthal will remain influential at the *Times* as associate editor and columnist.) "We decided that we would not simply criticize," says Rothenberg, "but we'd go in there to propose stories the paper should cover." The suggested stories included Gay Men's Health Crisis and its support services, the 1983 national convention of the Parents of Lesbians and Gays, and the increased involvement of gay and lesbian activists in electoral politics. Before the year was out, all three stories were covered.

On June 16 and 17 the *Times* published its first front-page AIDS coverage. In two lengthy articles, reporters Michael Norman and Dudley Clendinen examined the impact of AIDS on the gay male and lesbian communities. Norman surveyed gay professionals, social scientists, political activists, writers, and businesspeople to discover how the epidemic was changing "the basic patterns of male homosexual life." Clendinen examined the fear of AIDS that was rampant in the gay community, instances of discrimination against persons with AIDS, and the rise of gay volunteer services designed to cope with the epidemic.

In December a major feature on GMHC appeared on the front page of the *Times* metropolitan section. In chronicling the birth and growth of GMHC, a "sophisticated social service organization with growing political power," reporter Maureen Dowd presented a moving account of incredible suffering and heroism. There were also some condescending observations about AIDS generating "a new maturity among homosexuals," but in fairness to Dowd and the *Times,* several of the gay men interviewed for the piece offered the self-flagellating quotes that informed the reporter's conclusions.

Three years later—after the meetings with gay leaders, after the scathing attacks against the *Times* in *The Normal Heart,* the boycott threat and the constant vigilance by gay *Times* readers who wrote letters and made phone calls—the powers that be at West 43rd Street seem to have discovered that yes, there is a community out there worthy of inclusion in the journalistic orbit of *The New York Times.*

The quality and frequency of gay-related coverage has markedly improved, say even many of the *Times'* toughest critics.

"The paper has made enormous strides in the past couple of years," says Andy Humm. "I don't pick up the *Times* and get outraged much these days."

"There's been a quantum leap during the past three years in coverage of issues ranging from [antigay] discrimination to AIDS," says Thomas Stoddard, executive director of Lambda Legal Defense and Education Fund in New York. "We should recognize the improvement and praise the *Times* for its new sensitivity."

"The coverage has improved so dramatically that the gay community, in New York and nationwide, should have few arguments with the paper," says Ronald Najman, former media director with the National Gay and Lesbian Task Force.

A quick inventory of the *Times'* recent record justifies much of the praise. Feature articles have reported the rise of gay political power in West Hollywood, Calif., the growing numbers of gay elected officials and candidates for political office, and a trend among middle-class gay men and lesbians toward suburban living. Coverage of AIDS has improved and diversified; in addition to the frequent medical stories, there are more articles exploring the social and political dimensions of the epidemic. These include: a shattering account in the *Times'* Sunday magazine of how AIDS had devastated the lives of several gay men, written by gay journalist and author George Whitmore; a front-page feature on the efforts of the gay male community to educate its members about "high-risk" sexual behavior; a story on GMHC's legal assistance program; and an interview with the Broadway cast of *As Is*, William Hoffman's celebrated play about AIDS.

The *Times* has also shown a new sensitivity to the civil liberties issues the AIDS epidemic has raised. An editorial that appeared late last year deplored attempts to "seek out and segregate those exposed to AIDS," claiming that such measures portend "a new apartheid."

The *Times* also gets high marks for its handling of the three most important stories of 1986 involving the legal rights of gay people. Andy Humm credits that paper's reporting of the bitter, drawn-out, but ultimately successful struggle to get the New York city council to pass Intro 2, the gay civil rights bill. He says the bill's passage was aided by the *Times'* decision to print the a measure's entire text (homophobes had repeatedly misrepresented its contents in their antigay propaganda) and by running two editorials supporting the measure.

Last February, a month before the city council passed Intro 2, the *Times'* editorial writers requested a meeting with David Rothenberg, Lambda Legal Defense's Tom Stoddard, and Lee Hudson, Mayor Ed Koch's liaison to the gay male and lesbian community, to discuss the legislation and why it was needed. "The fact that they requested the meeting and wanted our input was very remarkable," says Stoddard.

When the Justice Department ruled last June that federal employers could legally fire employees whom they believed might "spread" AIDS, a *Times* editorial called the decision cruel and unwarranted. Once again the editorial board sought gay input while formulating its position; in this case members met with Lambda spokesperson Nancy Langer.

The *Times'* coverage of the U.S. Supreme Court ruling that upheld the Georgia sodomy law was "by far the best of any paper in the United States," says Tom Stoddard. The paper's editorial denounced the high court decision as "an offense to American society's maturing standards of individual dignity."

How much credit can gay activists take for the improvement in *Times* coverage?

"We've budged them a bit, but the meeting [between gay leaders and *Times* editors] didn't have squat to do with it," insists Larry Kramer.

Others acknowledge that "changing times" may have influenced the improvement as much as community protest.

"Like other media, *The New York Times* has come to see our issues as it hasn't before because they just can't be ignored anymore," says Tom Stoddard.

But current and former *Times* editors say criticism from the gay community definitely made an impact. His 1983 meeting with Apuzzo, Rothenberg, and Failla helped executive editor Rosenthal "become aware of the concerns of the gay community and its feeling that we weren't giving fair coverage," says *Times* assistant managing editor Craig Whitney. "It was a policy decision to take into account the concerns [expressed by the community] and to resolve to do better."

"The *Times* has caught up a bit as the gay community has become more open and vocal," says a former editor and columnist.

Critics say, however, that the improvement has been constrained by the paper's essential conservatism.

Articles about the ways gay men are coping with AIDS focus almost exclusively on critics of "promiscuity," those in the community who express the most contempt for what is called the "fast-lane gay lifestyle of the Seventies." Feature stories in the *Times* give the unmistakable and simplistic impression that there are "good gays"—those who've abandoned their wicked ways and feel appropriate remorse—and "bad gays," the unrepentants who still champion rampant gay male sexuality.

Last year in an investigative feature article titled "Sex and *The New York Times*," *Forum* magazine's Eric Nadler speculated that the *Times* has devoted more attention to AIDS because "in the current reactionary social climate…articles on the wages of sin are in."

The *Times* has difficulty seeing male homosexuals as anything other than "AIDS victims," charges Wayne Morse of the Gay and Lesbian Alliance Against Defamation. "Almost everything they've printed connects us with disease. They haven't done much else but AIDS coverage."

The paper's conservatism comes out also in its view of which gay people are worthy of coverage.

"*The New York Times* still tends to equate 'gay' with white, male, and middle-class," says Tom Stoddard. Accordingly, there has been no coverage of the emergence in recent years of Third World gay and lesbian activism. The paper ignored the International Conference of Black and White Men Together held in New York in July, even though the keynote speaker was Bayard Rustin, a veteran of the civil rights movement. (As one of the most conservative black political figures, Rustin would seem to be exactly the *Times'* kind of activist.)

"Black and Latin people are a myth and a mystery to the people who run the *Times*," says a former metropolitan editor. "Add to that homosexuality, a subject they also find distressing, and you get a good idea" of why nonwhite homosexuals rarely appear in the paper.

Village Voice press critic Geoffrey Stokes says the *Times* is hobbled by its "painfully deferential attitude towards conventional figures of authority." This stance colored the paper's handling of two recent major stories, both involving homosexuality and the Roman Catholic Church.

In 1984, after prominent Catholic laymen protested to *Times* corporation vice chairman Sidney Gruson, author John Cooney was forced to delete material about the homosexuality of Francis Cardinal Spellman from *The American Pope,* his biography of the powerful prelate, which was to be published by Times Books (a separate division from the newspaper). What had been four pages of reporting about Spellman's affairs with priests, altar boys, and laymen was reduced to an innocuous paragraph that mentioned widespread "rumors" of the cardinal's sexual exploits.

Last February, more than two years after the dawning of what Tom Stoddard calls the *Times'* "new sensitivity" to gay concerns, the paper gave admiring coverage to one of New York's most aggressive homophobes. In a front-page profile on John Cardinal O'Connor (who replaced the late Spellman), Joseph Berg wrote that the prelate "has brought a fresh assertiveness to the role of archbishop of New York."

The head of New York's Roman Catholic Archdiocese, Berger noted, has "made his views widely known on abortion, housing for the homeless, and other issues." Among those other issues graced by O'Connor's fresh assertiveness is homosexuality. An adviser to Mayor Ed Koch told Berger that the cardinal's vehement opposition to Intro 2, the gay civil rights bill, "May well have scared the hell out a few members of the city council." Berger, however, did not ask members of the gay community or supporters of gay rights what they thought of O'Connor.

This was too much for Charles Kaiser, a gay former *Times* reporter. He fired off an indignant letter to John Vinocur, the metropolitan editor, with copies to Berger and Allan M. Siegal, the reporter and news editor respectively. "To hundreds of thousands of New Yorkers, gays and straights alike, Cardinal O'Connor is a bigot, nothing more, nothing less," wrote Kaiser. "If this was 1956 instead of 1986, and Peter Kihss [a former *Times* reporter who covered the black civil rights movement] wrote a story about a cardinal in Mobile, Ala., and his efforts to block integration, don't you think the reaction of the NAACP would have been included?

"I fear," Kaiser concluded, "that we will all wait a long time before we see an 'Editor's Note' about this particular failure to be balanced." Kaiser never received a response to his letter.

A veteran of eight years at the *Times*, Kaiser, 35, joined the paper in 1971 as a stringer, became A.M. Rosenthal's clerk in 1973, and was a news reporter from 1974 until his resignation in January 1980. He tersely explains his departure from a newspaper many journalists would kill to join: "I was fed up with the bullshit." He also wanted to write a musical comedy.

"Over the past 15 years, the *Times* has done a third-rate job of covering the gay community and everything else in New York," he says. The quality of gay coverage "reflects how badly the paper reports the city as much as it does homophobia."

But how much does in-house bigotry—particularly at the top—affect what gets printed?

"There's no question that Rosenthal hates homosexuals and is an absolute fanatic on the subject," says Kaiser. "But from time to time, his news judgment overcomes his homophobia."

Kaiser illustrates his point with an anecdote about the *Times'* handling of an important gay story in 1982. Walter Mondale, the former vice president and then leading contender for the Democratic presidential nomination, was scheduled to speak at a fund-raising dinner held by the Human Rights Campaign Fund, making him the highest-ranking political figure ever to appear at a gay event.

"Middle-level editors spend a lot of time worrying about how to assign stories to conform to Rosenthal's prejudices," says Kaiser. Peter Millones, then the metropolitan editor, assumed that Rosenthal would not want the paper to cover Mondale's appearance. According to Kaiser, Millones sent a reporter to the dinner but told him not to file a story unless New York governor Mario Cuomo attended. "This was simply an excuse not to cover the story, not a legitimate news decision," says Kaiser. When the reporter called the city desk from the dinner to say that Cuomo had not shown up, he was absolved from writing a story.

"But Rosenthal had apparently been at home watching the TV news, and he saw the Mondale story," says Kaiser. "So he called the *Times* news desk and said, 'I assume there'll be a story about the gay dinner because Mondale was there.' A story was hastily put together, and it made the final edition." (The *Times* prints four editions; the final has the smallest press run.)

Another ex-*Times*man also maintains that Rosenthal's homophobia affects his relationship with individuals more than it does his news judgment. "Rosenthal's a very insecure man. Not violently homophobic, I don't think, but it certainly makes him distraught to learn that someone on his staff is gay."

"Gay reporters on the staff are very nervous," reports the ex-editor. They are definitely unwilling to talk on the record about their employer.

Assistant managing editor Craig Whitney says sexual preference is no obstacle to being hired or promoted by the *Times*. "I know of gay reporters who have been promoted or made foreign correspondents," he says.

"If it's known at the paper that you're gay, it won't necessarily ruin you," says Kaiser. "You can have almost any reporter's job, except London bureau chief and White House correspondent." He pauses briefly and considers. "You probably couldn't get to be managing editor, though."

Kaiser says that gay and lesbian reporters won't have problems as long as they're "discreet." And what constitute discretion? "There's a certain line which, if crossed, they'll bring you up on it. It's not articulated as policy. People figure it out by hints and clues."

One reason gay *Times*people might feel insecure is the lack of an antidiscrimination clause in the paper's contract with the Newspaper Guild. According to guild representatives, the *Times* has consistently resisted the inclusion of such language, despite its editorial stance opposing antigay discrimination. In contract negotiations with the guild, the *Times* has repeatedly maintained that it abides by the antidiscrimination provisions of existing local, state, and federal law. Now that New York has a citywide gay rights law, perhaps the *Times* will change its position when it negotiates a new contract with the guild early next year. Guild representatives say they will fight for a nondiscrimination clause during the contract talks.

It's difficult to gauge the effect the uncertain status of gay male and lesbian reporters has on the *Times'* coverage of gay news. More telling is the way the paper views the community. According to Whitney, the *Times* does not regard gay people as having minority status comparable to groups defined by race, ethnicity or class. "We never sat down and said, 'This is a specific community defined by its sexuality that we should cover,'" he says. The paper reports news "of interest to all readers, not only of specific concern to gays." Besides AIDS, these "general interest" stories include "civil rights, invasion of privacy, Supreme Court rulings."

Stokes argues that the *Times'* refusal to designate the gay community as a journalistic beat that reporters regularly "work" for stories is "a big part of what's wrong with their coverage." Stokes says that although the paper is capable of "individually brilliant efforts," its overall effectiveness is crippled by its unwillingness to recognize the legitimacy of the gay community.

Consistent and regular coverage could be ensured by assigning reporters to a gay beat, agrees Kaiser. The reporters need not be gay, just capable: "Quality should be the issue, not their sexual preference." But Rothenberg argues for openly gay and lesbian reporters. "The *Times* wouldn't have to do any recruiting," he suggests. "They could just hire from within."

The *Times'* current nomenclature policy is inseparable from its refusal to recognize gay people as a legitimate minority group. Activists argue that *homosexual,* the paper's preferred appellation, signifies only sexual behavior, while *gay* designates a social and political identity based upon sexuality. The other major New York dailies—the *Daily News, Newsday,* evenly the fiercely homophobic *New York Post*—routinely use the word *gay.*

"Self-definition is much more than a symbol," says Virginia Apuzzo. "It's a fundamental issue. We have the right to be called what we call ourselves."

"Fundamentally silly" is how Stokes characterizes the *Times'* aversion to *gay*. In his *Village Voice* column, he observed that the *Times'* recent decision to permit the use of the honorific *Ms.* may portend the acceptance of *gay* by the time the 21st century rolls around.

Most *Times* watchers say the policy came in response to an article that appeared in the paper's Sunday travel section 11 years ago. "The All-Gay Cruise: Prejudice and Pride" by freelance writer Cliff Jahr described a weeklong ocean cruise that took 300 gay men and lesbians from Fort Lauderdale, Fla., to the Yucatan and Guatemala.

Jahr's article had none of the *Times'* customary reticence about sexuality. He noted a shipboard romance between the closeted "young dean of women at a small East Coast college" and "a blonde ex-showgirl from Miami." The male voyagers were hardly inactive. "I've met three Mister Rights before lunch," one man crowed. Describing one afternoon's activities, Jahr wrote: "With spirits and libidos revived, there began an exchange of meaningful glances, the mating ritual called 'cruising.'" Jahr told of naked poker players, poppers ("a drug inhaled to rescue waning ardor") and an S/M fashion show, at which leatherclad models posed while the tape-recorded "moans and shrieks of someone being savagely whipped" echoed across the ship's deck.

It's hard to believe Jahr's article actually appeared in *The New York Times*. It was hip, sexy, funny, and stylishly written. It was also politically savvy. Jahr noted that for many of the passengers, the cruise was a respite from the oppression of closeted lives. There were no whiffs of disapproval of homosexuality, and the word *gay* appeared throughout the piece.

But publisher "Punch" Sulzberger was not pleased. "The shit really hit the fan over Jahr's story," says a former *Times* reporter. "Sulzberger was furious."

According to Eric Nadler's account of the episode in *Forum,* both travel section editor Robert Stock and then Sunday *Times* editor Max Frankel were "called on the carpet." Frankel was reportedly fired, then quickly rehired.

"The contretemps resulted in a new *Times* rule," wrote Nadler. "No longer would the word *gay* appear in Punch's paper."

But the no-gay policy may be weakening. A recent profile of Mario Cuomo in the Sunday magazine noted that the governor pleases liberals with "his support on such issues as gay rights." A news story that appeared in September cited Catholic opposition to "New York's gay rights law."

Other aspects of *Times* editorial policy have come under fire. Obituaries almost never acknowledge that gay people are survived by anyone other than blood relatives or legal spouses. Even long-term lover relationships go unmentioned. When Merle Miller died this year, *Newsday* reported that the openly gay author of *Plain Speaking* and *On Being Different* was survived by writer David Elliott; according to *Times,* Miller left no survivors. *Times* spokesman Leonard Harris admits that the paper does not customarily mention the lovers (or as he put it, "companions") of deceased gay persons in its obituaries.

Harris says that AIDS is given as the cause of death if medical authorities or survivors disclose the information or if the deceased person had wished it known.

Last year the *Times* published two virulently homophobic op-ed columns. In a polemic against the New York gay rights bill, Rabbi Yehuda Levin likened homosexuals to murderers. Conservative columnist William F. Buckley Jr. suggested that "AIDS carriers" be marked with an identifying tattoo as a means of "protecting" the public.

When asked why the *Times* would publish such commentary, Leonard Harris said the op-ed page was supposed to be "a platform for all views, even extreme and unpopular ones." But the *Times* does not publish anti-Semitic diatribes or blatant appeals to racism. Gay people, it seems, are the only group whose rights—and very existence—are open to debate in *The New York Times*. That we should be so vulnerable is hardly reassuring, despite whatever improvements have occurred in the overall quality of reporting and editorializing.

Not that all is basically well except on the op-ed page. Although the *Times* is doing a better job of covering AIDS, there are still lapses. The HTLV-3/HIV orthodoxy reigns at the paper; alternative theories about the epidemic get short shrift. Nor does the *Times* look closely at the performance of the Centers for Disease Control and other government health agencies.

"The *Times* hasn't subjected the federal response to AIDS to the same sort of scrutiny it gives the Challenger space shuttle disaster or [the nuclear power accident at] Chernobyl," says Apuzzo.

Moreover, the *Times*' unwillingness to create a "gay desk" means that the paper is not on top of such important stories as the increasing incidence of antigay violence, the birth and growth of New York's Lesbian and Gay Community Services Center, and the emergency of the Third World gay movement.

But *The New York Times*—lordly, arrogant and conservative—is not deaf to community protest; it can be moved, as recent history demonstrates.

Why is it important for the gay community to give feedback to the *Times*? Because the paper has inordinate power to validate issues and mass movements, and for better or worse, it sets the pace for the rest of the media, here and abroad.

"The *New York Post* is a pain in the ass," says Rothenberg. "But *The New York Times* affects our lives."

REP. BARNEY FRANK COMES OUT PUBLICLY AS GAY; SAYS MEDIA IS MAKING 1987 "YEAR OF THE CROTCH"

by Peter Freiberg

July 7, 1987

In a move hailed by gay activists as "courageous," Rep. Barney Frank has come out publicly as gay, joining fellow Massachusetts Democrat Rep. Gerry Studds and becoming the second openly gay member of Congress..

Frank, 47, ended—in a front-page interview published May 30 in *The Boston Globe*—years of internal wrestling over whether to publicly disclose his sexual orientation. His coming out differed markedly from that of Studds, who revealed his sexual orientation in 1983 in the wake of a congressional report that he had had sex 10 years earlier with a 17-year-old House page.

In an interview with *The Advocate,* Frank remarked that the controversy over Gary Hart's love life, which forced Hart to withdraw from the presidential race, and what Frank called the "unseemly" debate over the sexual orientation of Rep. Stewart McKinney (R-Conn.) following his death from AIDS, were key factors in Frank's decision to acknowledge being gay. He added that 1987 was turning out to be the "Year of the Crotch" in the media.

"I'd just as soon not have this feeling as I walk around that people are speculating about the most intimate details of my private life," he admitted. "But the political reaction has been generally good."

While Frank, a staunch liberal, appears assured of reelection next year—in a district that includes several suburbs, towns and the city of Fall River outside of Boston—the disclosure could have a negative impact on his prospects for a House leadership role.

Leaders of national gay organizations as well as Massachusetts gay groups expressed jubilation over Frank's decision. Vic Basile, executive director of the Human Rights Campaign Fund, observed that "he came out voluntarily…at a time when there is really so much fanatical hysteria about AIDS. To publicly say 'I'm gay, so what?' challenges people to look at his performance as a congressman who happens to be gay and who is not ashamed of it."

Basile, noting that Frank is widely regarded as an aspirant for a House leadership position added, "He's in a fairly secure district, and I doubt that he's going to have any problem with being re-elected. The question is how his colleagues are going to react. It's a very courageous act."

Frank's sexual orientation was known to many reporters as well as politicians and to at least some of his constituents. A strong supporter of gay causes, he gave numerous speeches to gay organizations, including some in which he virtually came out ("I'm a Johnny-no-come-out lately," he quipped to one group) but never crossed the line. He said it "wasn't certain" he ever would come out, and told the *Globe* that the major reason for his indecision was fear of how his constituents would react.

He acknowledged to the *Globe* that he was also influenced by gay leaders who "were saying to me, 'Well, you know you might be giving people the notion that you are ashamed of yourself,' and I'm not. I don't want people to focus on my sexual orientation, but I don't want to give credence to the notion that I'm feeling inferior or embarrassed…"

Frank told *The Advocate* that in his internal debate over whether to come out, "I wanted people to know because it might help to defeat some of the prejudice, and there was some advantage to somebody making his gayness known without it being associated with something unpleasant, whether AIDS or some law violation."

But he maintained he "didn't know how to go about volunteering it," because his conviction has been that "it was irrelevant…I couldn't announce it and then say it wasn't relevant."

In the wake of the controversies over Hart and McKinney, Frank related, "I finally decided…that the next time somebody asked me [if I was gay], I was going to say 'Yes, so what?' I needed to be asked, because I couldn't volunteer it…. A number of reporters knew I would say yes if asked."

Frank, who is now serving his fourth term in Congress, received 90% of the vote in an uncontested 1986 race. He faced his toughest campaign in 1982, when he ran in a new district whose lines had been severely altered by the state legislature; he was considered the underdog against Rep. Margaret Heckler, a Republican, but won with 59% of the vote.

"I expect to get reelected [in 1988]," Frank predicted, "but I think I'll have to work harder at the electoral aspects of the job than I have. I don't think I'll lose, but you never know."

Frank named another openly gay Massachusetts politician, Robert Ebersole, a Republican who is the elected Town Clerk of Lunenburg, as someone who had influenced the way in which Frank came out.

Ebersole stated that since coming out in 1984, he had several conversations with Frank about "coming out, how I did it in a way that I felt comfortable with. I tried to point out the burden that was lifted by coming out and how it improved…my outlook on life and my performance at work."

Will Hutchinson, president of the Boston Lesbian and Gay Political Alliance, said his only fear was that Frank might initially "steer away from gay and lesbian issues." Frank acknowledged his concern that voters might get a "distorted perception" that he was exclusively concerned with gay-related issues: "I've always been active on gay rights, and I will continue to be, but I have to guard against the perception that that's all I do."

HRCF director Basile noted that Frank has been "one of the most helpful and cooperative members of Congress in our struggle for our civil rights…. Now that he's come out, he has done the only other thing that was possible to help this community that he wasn't already doing."

THE MARCH ON WASHINGTON: HUNDREDS OF THOUSANDS TAKE THE GAY CAUSE TO THE NATION'S CAPITAL

by Peter Freiberg

November 10, 1987

With tears and laughter, anger and joy, several hundred thousand lesbians, gay men, and their supporters marches in Washington, D.C., on October 11 in a massive, emotion-filled demonstration to demand a federal war on AIDS and an end to homophobic discrimination.

There was disagreement on the turnout: The U.S. Park Police initially put the crowd at 50,000 but later revised the figure to 200,000, while march organizers raised their initial estimate of 500,000 to 650,000. But there was no disputing that the huge outpouring of people from all over the country made the march the largest gay rights demonstration ever assembled, dwarfing the first gay March on Washington in 1979 and marking a new milestone in modern gay history.

"This is indeed our day," an ebullient Harvey Fierstein, the actor and playwright, called out to the vast throng assembled on the Mall near the U.S. Capitol. "We have marched out of the closets... We are gay and lesbian, and we did this."

The march set off exactly at noon. Prominent gay activists and nongay supporters, including farm union leader Cesar Chavez and former National Organization for Women president Eleanor Smeal, led the way as they held a black-and-white banner reading NATIONAL MARCH ON WASHINGTON FOR LESBIAN AND GAY RIGHTS.

Directly in back of them were people with AIDS and ARC, most marching but about three dozen wheeled by friends, lovers, family members, and "buddies." Actress Whoopi Goldberg, looking somber in jeans and sneakers, wheeled an old friend, Jim Manness, for the entire march.

For five hours, an array of geographical, religious, sports, political, musical, and other groups, reflecting the diversity of American gay life, marched the two miles beginning at the Ellipse, past the White House on Pennsylvania Avenue, and over to the Mall.

They chanted, "What do we want? Gay rights. When do we want it? Now," "Money for AIDS, not war," "We are everywhere; we will be free," and "Two, four, six, eight! Being gay is really great!" They sang "America the Beautiful" and "We Shall Overcome." And they angrily pointed their fingers at the White House as they shouted, "Shame! Shame! Shame!" and "Increase AIDS funding. Americans are dying."

Form the stage near the Capitol, the huge throng appeared to stretch almost the dozen long blocks to the Washington Monument. The crowd held aloft a sea of pink and purple balloons, rainbow banners, placards, and signs—among them, I LOVE MY GAY AND LESBIAN FRIENDS, FIGHT AIDS, NOT PEOPLE WITH AIDS, THANK GOD I'M GAY, GET READY FOR THE GAY '90S, and simply LOVE, with a pink triangle substituting for the *V*.

Over and over, in speeches and interviews, marchers compared the event to the black civil rights marches of the 1960s. Many called the march, together with the planned civil disobedience action at the Supreme Court two days later, a watershed that showed how far the movement had come and how it was now prepared to move toward increased organizing and militancy.

"Get ready, America, we are coming forward in ever increasing numbers," Duke Comegys, a Los Angeles gay activist and cochair of the Human Rights Campaign Fund, told the cheering crowd. "We have become a tide of strength. Do not stand in our way. As we learn from the brave and courageous demonstrators at [the 1960s black civil rights demonstration in] Selma, Ala., we too must overcome.

"We do not ask for your acceptance. We *do* demand that we be left alone to live our lives as we wish. That is the true meaning of our Constitution, and make no mistake about it: We will not stop until we have achieved our freedom, our justice, and our pursuit of happiness."

Another speaker, Virginia Apuzzo, former executive director of the National Gay and Lesbian Task Force and now a New York State official, warned that the civil disobedience scheduled at the Supreme Court to protest the 1986 decision upholding state sodomy laws would be the first of many such actions in the fight against discrimination and for more funding for AIDS research and treatment.

"We vow to spend our dollars, our votes, and our nights in jail to make the violence and the injustice that stalk our lives vivid to our nation," Apuzzo said. "We're nobody's nasty little secret anymore."

Whether the march, huge as it was, would have any immediate political impact remains to be seen. Coverage of the demonstration was extensive, with major newspapers across the country giving it front-page play; in some cases, as with the *Philadelphia Inquirer,* it was the lead story. But gay activists maintained that the primary, immediate effect would be on the gay community itself, accelerating the sense of solidarity that has been building since the Stonewall rebellion.

It was clear that the vast majority of marchers felt exhilarated, even heady, over seeing so many openly gay men and women gathered in one place, marching under hundreds of different banners and placards but with the same goals in mind.

"My main reason for being here is just the spiritual revitalization of being where queers are in the majority," commented Michael Callen, a person with AIDS and activist from New York. "I've been telling everyone that this is going to be a watershed. They're going to have to take us seriously when they see how many of us are ready to take to the streets."

One foreign observer, Henk Krol, editor of a gay newspaper in Holland and one of at least 45 Dutch people who came to the United States for the march, marveled at the turnout.

"For this crowd, I have no words to describe it," he said. "I can't say it in English; I couldn't even say it in Dutch. It's too much. The people are so united, so together.... We know there are a lot of differences, but today it seems that everybody has forgotten a lot of the differences, and that feels very good."

Nicole Ramirez-Murray, a San Diego activist and a member of the March on Washington steering committee, drew laughs when he said, "This is the biggest damn family reunion I've ever been to."

For several days before the march, gay people had been pouring into Washington.

Some came to volunteer at the march committee's cramped offices. Others came to attend one or more of the six dozen events surrounding the Sunday march, among them: a two-day lobbying effort, in which hundreds of gay constituents met with members of Congress to seek support for the proposed federal gay rights bill and for more AIDS funding; a mass recommitment ceremony for gay couples; a moving memorial service for slain San Francisco supervisor Harvey Milk; and meetings and receptions held by a variety of groups.

On the subways and in the Dupont Circle neighborhood, a center of Washington gay male life, an almost partylike atmosphere prevailed. Thousands of gay people wearing buttons proclaiming they were here for the march and making sure they had at least a touch—and sometimes much more—of lavender color in their clothes crowded the Metro and the streets.

As they gathered at the Ellipse on the morning of October 11, meeting their marching contingents and listening to a speakers program organized by the people of color caucus of the March on Washington committee, many participants explained that they had been determined to come to the capital, regardless of financial or logistical problems.

Nancy Poage, a lesbian from Salt Lake City, said that at the '79 march, Utah was the only state not represented "because everybody was scared." This year 30 people came. "We're not afraid anymore," she observed. "They're going to have to start listening to us, even from Utah."

Like most gay people in Mormon-dominated Utah, Poage is closeted, but she observed that just participating in the march made her more determined to come out. "If I'm on television, I'm not going to worry about it. I figure, hey, it's time."

Near a Williams College banner, Katie Kent and Jon Sorenson held a banner reading PREPPY DYKES AND FAGGOTS—COME OUT! Kent, who was only 13 at the time of the 1979 march, said she and the other 35 Williams students at the march felt they were "making history here today."

"A lot of us came out at 15," she commented. "A lot of us have told our parents. We're prepared to live our lives completely out, so this [march] is essential for us."

Charles Barney, a New York activist, felt it was "really important to be here. It says to the USA, 'We're a group to be reckoned with; you can't avoid us anymore.'"

The New York and California contingents appeared to be the largest ones there. The New York AIDS service group Gay Men's Health Crisis alone brought 2,000 participants, according to reports.

But while large delegations from the two coasts were expected what was especially striking about the march was the extensive representation of cities between the coasts. Missouri participants came three days early to lobby their congressional representatives and said they believed the march would change things in their state.

"We're going to use this march as a jumping-off block to organize [in Kansas City]," explained Bill Todd. "Kansas City has no [gay] political vehicle right now." Another Kansas City resident, Ann Saunders, asserted, "There are a number of people who are firmly committed to going from this place to [forming] a political action coalition to work in Missouri on a local and county and state level."

Participants in the march seemed to be nearly equally divided between men and women, but the number of black marchers was very small. There also did not appear to be large numbers of heterosexual marchers. As always, members of Parents and Friends of Lesbians and Gays were well-represented.

Some nongay marchers had never been to a gay demonstration before. "I'm here to show support for gay people because they deserve the chance to express themselves and love whomever they want," commented Eleanor O'Brien, a 17 year old freshman from Earlham College in Richmond, Ind., and one of a number of straight students who joined their gay classmates in traveling to Washington from the Quaker-affiliated school.

Suzanne Crawford-Caves, whose son died of AIDS and who founded a Long Beach, Calif.–based group called Families Who Care, came to Washington primarily to seek more AIDS funding during the two lobby days that preceded the march. Long a supporter of gay rights, she said she had learned more about gay issues while in the capital and was marching to make clear her support for AIDS funding as well as for antidiscrimination laws.

"I came because my son's death has to mean something," she said. "He's gone, but it isn't too late for others."

In explaining the reasons for the huge turnout, march organizers noted that there was a much larger network of gay groups than eight years ago. "We knew this could happen," asserted Joyce Hunter, a New Yorker who was a cochair of the 1979 march and helped organize this one, "because we had so much support this time. In '79 it was very different."

Both Hunter and Steve Ault, a cochair of this year's march, emphasized that the AIDS crisis had created a sense of urgency within the community. Many gays have witnessed the death from AIDS of someone close to them, and Ault commented that these experiences accentuated the personal involvement of people in the march. Ault, who has participated in many antiwar and other marches, observed that this one was "unique" in that "each person coming here is someone who is incredibly linked to the whole event. People think that it is *their* march, not a march that they are going to. They have a very personal stake in this."

Some people had felt so strongly about getting people to the march that they contributed money through a Los Angeles-based group, A Time to Shine, to help bring a reported 150 people with AIDS to Washington. These and other people with AIDS expressed the conviction that it was important for them to be in Washington, that their presence could make a difference.

Cornell Britt, a wheelchair-bound person with AIDS from Newport News, Va., was accompanied to Washington by two of his buddies. "I think that I as well as others must take a stand," said Britt. "It was important for me to be here. It lets me know that people care. That makes me feel better, much better."

One of Britt's buddies, Troy Pay, noted that his lover was hospitalized with AIDS. "He couldn't be here, but he wanted me to come, so here I am," he said.

Another person with AIDS who came to the march was the leadoff speaker, Dan Bradley, an attorney and former head of the federal Legal Services Corporation. In a moving speech that brought tears to many who heard it, Bradley emphasized how "countless more of us now face illnesses, suffering, and death. At a time when our president fails to provide leadership, and in a time when our government does too little and too late, the gay and lesbian community has provided leadership, funds, and organizations to fight this threat to our very lives."

Bradley wept as he described a meeting with a Miami journalist friend in which he related what he wanted his obituary to read. Bradley said he told his friend simply to note that after a lifetime of oppression, fear, and struggle, he finally came to Washington, D.C., in 1982 and had the courage to say, "I'm gay and I'm proud."

Tears were a frequent sight during the march. Many marchers were shaken and crying when they visited the Names Project quilt that memorializes people who have died of AIDS. Whoopi Goldberg cried as she hugged and greeted people with AIDS seated in front of the stage; she said in an interview that 60 friends had died of AIDS, and in a later speech she accused President Reagan of not doing anything to help children with AIDS.

But if tears and reminders of illness and death were omnipresent—whether in announcements from the stage that someone had forgotten his AZT or in the sight of people with AIDS shivering so much that the city health commissioner had to provide blankets for them—the march and rally were no less infused with anger.

"Today we stand here as the largest minority in this country," shouted Robin Tyler, a lesbian comedian who organized the entertainment at the rally, "to say we are no longer asking for acceptance; we are demanding our civil rights.... To hell with the Hardwick decision, to hell with Bork, and to hell with the Reagan administration."

The march and rally had a clearly leftist tinge. Some conservatives had complained prior to the event about a too-broad agenda, but Ramirez-Murray, who noted he was the only Republican on the organizing committee, said it was up to gay Republicans to get more involved.

The choice of speakers also drew some private criticism from gay organizations, whose most prominent leaders were not invited to speak. But the decision to invite the Rev. Jesse Jackson, a Democratic presidential candidate, to address the crowd was widely praised after he gave a rousing speech demanding more federal action on AIDS and calling for an end to violence against gay men and women.

Jackson's speech, in which he urged gay people to stand with him at "election time" just as he had stood with them at the rally, raised the question of where the gay rights movement will go from here.

More and more openly gay people are getting involved in electoral politics, as reflected in the hundreds who lobbied their congressional representatives, and some of those who lobbied predicted they would soon begin to see political benefits. Many march participants also expressed the hope that their sheer numbers would boost gay political clout, but some national gay activists doubted this would happen quickly.

"I don't think it's going to affect what happens in Congress at all," asserted Leonard Graff, executive director of San Francisco-based National Gay Rights Advocates. Gay-supportive members of Congress, he said, already know how numerous gays are, while "the only thing our enemies see is a few hundred thousand queers on the Mall. I don't think our sheer numbers [at the march] will really change the way they're going to vote or speak out on the issues. It's mostly for ourselves that we're doing this."

Nevertheless, former NOW president Smeal emphasized the need for electoral involvement. "The importance of this march is to carry it on into the 1988 elections," she asserted during her speech.

Vic Basile, executive director of HRCF, called the march "the kind of morale boost that people need." He and other activists forecast that the march and its auxiliary events could lead to increased mobilization at the local level and more support for national groups.

"The march goes beyond symbolism," insisted San Francisco activist Cleve Jones. "It's an efficient, powerful way of getting our message across, and it will contribute to a much stronger organizing effort."

The day after the march, several hundred activists met in Washington to begin planning for a national lesbian and gay congress, which would convene for the first time in 1988 and at regular intervals thereafter. Ray Hill, a Houston activist who introduced the idea for the congress, said its purpose would be to give grassroots "input" to national groups such as the National Gay and Lesbian Task Force and to provide a forum for local groups to network. The congress, he insisted, would not compete with already existing national organizations.

Even the clear success of the march could not hide continuing weaknesses in the gay rights movement. While many activists were gratified at the apparently near equal numbers of lesbians and gay men, the relatively small number of black participants remains a cause for concern. More-over, the large majority of gays who are closeted—many of them because they fear discrimina-tion on the job—hampers the efforts of local and national activists to win civil rights protections that could reduce these fears and make it possible for many more to come out.

The next few months will provide insight on what the long-term effects of the march will be: whether the march and the civil disobedience in front of the Supreme Court reflect a new militan-cy in the gay community nationwide and whether the march was, as more than a few people called it, "our Selma." Many activists are convinced that they—and many thousands of others—left Wash-ington imbued with new confidence.

"I think the lasting impact will be on us," commented Tom McClain, a Detroit activist. "It will make us realize that when there are this many of us working together, we have the power to do things and to change things."

INTERVIEW: BARNEY FRANK

by Rick Harding

April 12, 1988

On May 30, 1987, Massachusetts Democrat Barney Frank became the first member of Congress to come out of the closet voluntarily. To political insiders and to many gays, Frank's acknowledg-ment—reported on the front page of *The Boston Globe*—came as no great surprise: He had revealed his orientation to some House colleagues and party leaders several years before.

Frank's sexuality had come under media scrutiny before, in 1986.

Conservative Robert Bauman—who had lost his congressional seat following his arrest in a scan-dal involving a young male prostitute—wrote in his autobiography that Frank had attended a Wash-ington, D.C., gay pride festival with a male companion.

"I was asked, 'Are you gay?' in connection with Bauman's book, and I didn't want to say yes in that context," Frank recalled in an interview with *The Advocate*. "I didn't want the stories to be: 'Here is this book about a man who has sex with people who are under the legal age, who—by his own admission—gets beaten up a lot, who is an alcoholic; and, oh, by the way, one of the people who is like him is Barney Frank.' No…that ain't me."

Frank said he had known for years that he would eventually come out publicly, and he chose the

May 1987 funeral of House colleague Stewart McKinney (R–Conn.), who had died of AIDS, to do it.

"I liked and respected Stew a lot, and I was depressed about having this kind of scuffle about whether he was or wasn't gay or bisexual. I didn't want that kind of debate to happen over me. I think I probably said at that point, 'OK, that's it.'"

Four months after he came out, Frank paid $7,000 for a poll to measure his constituents' reaction to his revelation. "The general finding was that, overwhelmingly, people in the district will judge me on how I do my job as a member of Congress and not anything else," he said.

Frank has proved increasingly popular with his constituents, with election vote results climbing from 52% in 1980 to 70% in '82, 74% in '84, and 89% in '86. Contributions to his campaign in 1987 were double those received in 1985, his most recent preelection year. And so far, state Republicans have not found anyone to oppose him in this year's elections.

Frank, 47, with what a colleague once described as a "staccato, rapid-fire Jersey–Bay State accent," has long been considered one of the most talented debaters in Congress. In 1984, following his second term in the House, the *National Journal's Almanac of American Politics* said that Frank "may very well have the deadliest wit in Congress.… [T]he abilities he has shown already on his feet and on the campaign trial make him one of the most formidable Democrats in the House." In the same year, the *Washington Monthly* magazine selected him one of the six best members of the House of Representatives.

Frank has been a strong supporter of gay rights throughout his terms in Congress and has been an active proponent of pro-gay legislation on the House floor.

Frank's personal style has changed markedly since he came to Congress. For years his rumpled appearance was something of a trademark; when he ran for reelection to the Massachusetts state legislature in the 1970s, his campaign posters stated unapologetically, NEATNESS ISN'T EVERYTHING. But in 1984 he dropped 70 pounds, got a new hairstyle, and began wearing stylish suits.

Frank spoke with *The Advocate* shortly after coming out and again late February.

The last time we talked, the comments you had received since you came out were mostly positive. Is that still the case?

Mostly. But there's been some partisan Republican reaction. Frank Wayne, the Republican state chairman of the county that makes up about a third of my district and third of Gerry Studds's district, said publicly that he's appalled to have two gay representatives and [that] we should both be defeated in disgrace.

Also, the executive director of the Republican state committee said, "We're going to attack Frank not on the fact that he's gay but on the assumption that because he's gay he's pursuing gay issues and, therefore, ignoring other issues to the detriment of his constituents."

Some Republicans are trying to find a way to use the issue against me while claiming they're not.

That's only a slightly more sophisticated form of bigotry. And that's not unique to gay people. They've tried to do that with blacks, with women, with Portuguese-Americans. As long as you're a member of a specific, identifiable group, they say you may care excessively about that group without regard to other people.

How will you handle that issue when it comes up in your reelection campaign?

My answer will be that I'm not working any differently now. Yes, I'm working on gay issues; I always have. My announcement clearly hasn't made any difference. The second thing is, I would ask them to give me examples of things I should be doing for my district that I'm not doing. They haven't got any answers. I'm not going to argue that I'm not working on gay rights issues—I am working on them, as I work on issues affecting a lot of minorities and on general issues as well.

I know that for every member of Congress, it's hard to decide which issues to focus on because there's only a limited amount of time. How do you decide what kind of balance you're going to strike? I've heard that you try to handle more issues than many members of Congress.

I work very hard at this job. I don't have a lot of outside interests, I mean outside of my job and my friends. It's not that I work all the time, but I don't like to travel that much, and I don't have a lot of other competitive things. And I think I have a terrific staff that works very well with me. They extend me, you might say.

One of the things that I like about this job is it's suited to my particular combination of strong and weak points. I don't have the powers of concentration that I would like to have. I was going to write a Ph.D. thesis, and I sharpened my pencils and made coffee and talked, and I never wrote one. I'm undisciplined. But here [in Congress], what would be a shortcoming in some lines of work is an advantage.

Today, for instance, I started out with a breakfast meeting with a guy who wants to run for Congress. I came back and did some constituent work in my office, then I went to a hearing with the new chairman of the Federal Reserve Board on monetary policy, then I went to a meeting on the *contras,* then I went to a meeting on the housing problem in my district. Some people are distracted by that. I'm not, so I can shift gears pretty quickly.

You have a reputation in Congress as being quite a fierce debater. One might assume that a person with the reputation would pull back a bit after going through an announcement such as yours, trying not to ruffle feathers for a little while. Has that been the case with you?

I'm not conscious of that, no. You don't want to ruffle feathers for the sake of ruffling feathers, but I am not conscious that there's been any change in the way I have done my job before or after June.

Do you hear prejudice—"fag" remarks—in the cloakrooms of Congress?

Not much. I did have a case where a liberal senator whom I admired made an antigay remark. And for two months I kept trying to get a private moment with him so I could object to that. When

I finally did, he apologized. He said, "Gee, I'm sorry it sounded that way." But people have been somewhat careful around me. I only heard the one.

Considering the stance that the Catholic Church has taken on gay issues, do you have any fears about the Catholic hierarchy in Massachusetts reacting to your coming-out?

No. The church, as I understand it, has been sort of careful to say, "We're dealing with this in our sphere, and we're not trying to get into yours." I've gotten the message from some clergy that they have a theological position on what I am doing, but they don't think it's a political issue.

Have you been getting a lot of feedback from gays?

Oh, yes, from the day I announced. I've gotten a lot of favorable feedback, and it's meant a great deal to me personally. It's a nice thing to have people say nice things to you and to have gay men and lesbians be so generous.

The increase in fund-raising—do you think a major portion of that has come from your gay supporters?

A lot of it has.

Some people, when they come out publicly, do it with this tremendous feeling of "My God, I finally did it and it feels great to be free!" What went through your mind?

I don't do feelings for publication. Feeling are private. I have this constant tension between what gets left private and what gets made public. I've got to keep my feelings private.

Since you came out, do you feel less constrained in what you can do? Do you feel that you can go to functions in your capacity as a congressman and have a male companion with you?

I've been doing that for a couple of years here in Washington and occasionally in Massachusetts. I probably still wouldn't dance with a male companion in public because I don't want to have a picture of me dancing in the papers. Anyway, I'm not that great a dancer.

Do you go to publicly identified gay places?

I go to bars all the time. And I went to D.C.'s gay pride day back in 1985. I go to Provincetown and had a house there for two weeks last summer. I've been living fairly openly, as much as I wanted to. I go to a gym in Boston that's predominantly gay, and I go to its affiliate down here. I had my picture taken by public television at the gay gym in Boston, and NBC filmed me at the gym here.

The Congressional Black Caucus sees its role as serving the needs of blacks all across the country. Do you see any kind of role like that for yourself with gays?

Yes, there's some of that. One of the things I can do that doesn't take up an enormous amount of my time is to refer people. I get letters from all over the country and phone calls from people who have problems. We can refer people to the Lambda Legal Defense and Education Fund or National Gay Rights Advocates or the National Gay and Lesbian Task Force. We do a lot of that.

Joe Martin, who works for me, is a gay man who's been active in gay community business. He was, I think, one of the first gay lobbyists in Massachusetts. It's not fair for my staff to take on the advocacy of individual cases. But we are able to help people by referring them to the people who do the work.

You were in Los Angeles recently and were quoted as saying that an openly gay candidate, Val Marmillian, should not run against liberal Democratic incumbent Anthony Beilenson for the 23rd District U.S. House of Representatives seat. In a previous interview with us you mentioned the importance of staying on good terms with your colleagues in the House. Will gay candidates be able to look to you for support when they run against House incumbents?

It depends on the incumbent. If it's an incumbent who's bad on the issues, sure. But if it's an incumbent who's good on the issues, I think it's a great mistake. One of the problems that liberals have in America is that we get outspent by conservatives. There is only a certain amount of money to go around. To spend hundreds of thousands of dollars on a race between two liberals seems to me to be a great mistake.

There's going to be a lot of important races in California this year. Spending a lot of time on which good liberal represents that district doesn't seem to me to be a very good use of resources.

It appears that the only hope that open gays might have of being elected is in liberal districts, and a lot of times they're going to run up against supportive incumbents....

Do you really think it's useful to have races where gay liberals run against straight liberals; where a substantial part of the time, energy, and money of the gay political community is spent; and if we succeed, we have no more votes in Congress? I don't think that makes any sense.

In fact, I have proposed to Vic Basile that a useful thing the Human Rights Campaign Fund could do would be to start looking at the parts of the country where it is reasonable to think that openly gay candidates can get elected, look at when the vacancies will come up, and begin a process to find a good gay candidate. Get some potential candidates identified for a state legislative seat, a city council seat, a congressional seat, or whatever, and begin working with her or with him on fund-raising so that when the day comes that the seat is vacant, the candidate will be ready.

But the notion that people should run against people with whom they agree is a terrible waste of time, energy, and resources. And, you know, seats come open.

Isn't the symbolism of having an openly gay person elected to Congress important?

It's important, but I don't think it's worth spending a lot of time and energy on. And you have this problem with incumbents. Do you want to say to them, "Listen, if you are a straight person, no matter how good you are on this issue, you should understand that you may be challenged by a lesbian or a gay man." I don't think that's a very useful lobbying strategy.

Turning to the gay political movement, we just had a very successful national march, and gay groups are getting more contributions than ever before. But gay rights issues have hit a few stumbling blocks recently, such as the amendment by Jesse Helms to censor most references to gays in federally funded AIDS education information. From your obviously unique perspective, what should the community be doing differently?

Nothing. Exactly what it's doing. Keep it up. I think there have been a lot of successes, the biggest of all being the absence of defeat, given the AIDS crisis and the demagogic response by some of the right-wingers.

I think a lot of people four years ago would have expected much more negative stuff to have happened. The Helms amendment, even in the form in which it was adopted, was obnoxious, although Helms is unhappy about the way it was trimmed…Beyond that, though, we have succeeded in defeating nearly all of the efforts to use AIDS as an excuse for repression, and I think that's a success.

Also, we got the gay section of the hate-crimes bill passed by a big majority of the judiciary committee. And in Massachusetts the gay rights bill passed both houses, although the senate president used his powers to keep the bill from going through. I think AIDS has slowed down progress, but it hasn't stopped it. The next thing is immigration, and I do think we're going to be able to get them to repeal the antigay immigration policies.

When I first came here, gay rights was kind of a "no way" issue—when it came up people would say, "No way, I'm not voting for this.…" People don't want to see it. Gay issues have now become, for most members, a tough issue. Democrats in particular understand that gay people are an important part of the constituency they want to appeal to—but that you have to deal with antigay discrimination if you want to put together that coalition.

So you wouldn't say the Helms amendment is indicative of what's to come in the House.

No. And it was not totally surprising either. I'd say if the comic books that he was giving out dealt with straight sex, the vote would have probably been about the same.

It appears that the level of AIDS funding is reaching the recommendations of experts. Is the gay community now spending too much effort on AIDS at the expense of other issues?

I don't think so. It may look that way in terms of what the press writes, but if you look at it, NGLTF [National Gay and Lesbian Task Force] has done very good work on the antigay violence issue. HRCF [Human Rights Campaign Fund] has been working closely with me on immigration. And there's a lot happening in local areas.

As far as a national gay civil rights bill, we're a long way away from that. But there's still a lot left on the AIDS agenda. Much of the work that gay groups are doing now on AIDS is really quite unselfish because gay men will not be the major beneficiaries of AIDS education anymore. The gay and lesbian community together have been a model of responsibility and caring in the area of AIDS. I wish the rest of the population was as up to speed on this.

You brought up the Massachusetts gay rights bill. A lot of gays in that state have criticized Michael Dukakis for what he did with that—they said he could have done more.

He could not have done more. They really don't know what they're talking about. The senate president has a lot of power, and I think he killed that bill because of his own prejudice. Massachusetts has an unusual legislature, where the Senate president has very, very strong powers, and he uses them in a very strong way. I disagree with Michael Dukakis's foster care policy—I think that's a bad policy. But he worked as hard as he could for the gay rights bill. It would not have gotten as far as it did without his support.

Are you supporting Dukakis for president?

Yes. But I'd have to say I think all the Democrats have pretty good positions on gay rights issues. And all the Republicans [have] terrible ones. That in itself is a sign of progress. Every Democratic candidate for president supports gay civil rights. Every Democratic candidate for president is opposing most of the bad stuff on AIDS. They all should be better, but there has been a lot of progress.

What are your future plans for office? Should we anticipate a race for the Senate?

I plan to stay right here. I like this job better than any other. The only other job in the world I'd rather have is the president's, and there's no chance of that whatsoever.

So you're writing off the presidency?

I'd done that even before I came out. There may be a Jewish president in my lifetime, but I don't think it will be me.

Is coming out going to affect your ascendancy in the House leadership at all?

If there was a chance for me to become a member of that leadership, coming out has undoubtedly diminished it. I don't know if there was a chance or not. There are a number of people who are qualified from whom the choice is made. And if you are particularly controversial and other people aren't, that's a good reason to bypass you.

If something happened and you lost your office, would you regret coming out?

No. I've reached the point in my life where it was the only thing to do. I might regret losing the office, but I wouldn't regret what I've done.

JESSE: PUTTING JACKSON INTO PERSPECTIVE

by Mark Vandervelden

May 10, 1988

The Rev. Jesse Jackson's quest for the Democratic presidential nomination—a race in which he rose from being a probable sure loser only six months ago to being the near front-runner at the midway point of the race—has put gay loyalties to the test and has unexpectedly upped the political ante for gay voters in 1988.

Consider: It was Jesse Jackson, alone among the Democratic contenders, who stood with the hundreds of thousands of people gathered for last October's March on Washington for Lesbian and Gay Rights and who called for more AIDS funding, sweeping civil rights protection for gays, and an end to antigay violence.

True, Jackson was the only candidate invited to address the rally (a point many gay Jackson supporters often conveniently forget), but his well-received remarks struck a responsive chord with activists.

"There are those who isolate differences, desecrate our humanity, and then justify their inhumanity, just as the Nazis did with yellow stars and pink triangles," Jackson told the rally. "It was not right in Nazi Germany, [and] it's not right in America."

Jackson also issued that day an impassioned appeal for gay support in his bid for the Democratic presidential nomination. "Today I stand with you," he declared. "Election time you stand with me. Together we will make a difference. Together there will be compassion and care and jobs and peace and justice."

Since then, no other candidate in the field—Republican or Democrat—has staked out a clearer or more comprehensive set of positions on gay civil rights and AIDS issues.

Jackson has appeared in other gay contexts. For example, he addressed a predominantly gay Metropolitan Community Church congregation in Minneapolis, visited a home for AIDS patients in Dallas, and, at press time, was scheduled to speak at New York City's gay community center. He has drawn gays into his campaign inner circle and has set up a full-time liaison between the campaign and grassroots gay activists.

Significantly, unlike some other candidates, Jackson doesn't exhibit any hesitation to use the word *gay* in public, even before audiences not particularly sympathetic to gay concerns. Earlier in his campaign, Jackson was referring to the march on Washington as "the AIDS march," but that grating habit appears to be broken.

Now that he is locked in a precinct-by-precinct tug-of-war with Massachusetts governor Michael Dukakis for votes and delegates—and very much in need of gay support at this point—Jackson has once again laid down a challenge to gay voters to, in effect, put up or shut up.

In an interview with *The Advocate,* Jackson said, "I know that I have done the right, constitutional, and moral thing by affirming a role for everybody in the quilt of humanity. So now the obligation is on gay and lesbian activists to be consistent. I have come forth with courage and consistency and clarity. I deserve support."

But winning gay support has not been as easy for Jackson as it might seem. For months now it has been clear that no Democrat will arrive at the convention in Atlanta this July with enough delegates in hand to secure the nomination outright. As the convention approaches, the high-stakes guessing game over who the nominee will be has many gay activists in a quandary over strategy.

"I think there is going to be a big fight over gay and lesbian issues and whether or not they will be included for discussion at the convention," said Randy Miller, Jackson's national constituency coordinator to the gay community. "We need to show that we can get the strength of the gay community behind one candidate and go into the Democratic convention being able to document the number of votes we delivered, all the work we did, [and] the amount of money we can raise in the gay community and be able to say to whoever the nominee is, 'Hey, look, if you really want to win, we've got a well-organized political system here, but here is our price for that.' We would say that to Rev. Jackson, [and] we would say that to Michael Dukakis.

"We need to be politically astute…but we also need to demand a price, our piece of the pie for our votes, just like every other constituency in the Democratic Party has done since time immemorial. We may very well be defeated, but I think we need to put up the fight."

In the view of some gay leaders, the best way to wage that fight is for gays to hedge their political bets. "I think the smart thing to do in the gay community is to spread our support around right now," said Vic Basile, executive director of the Human Rights Campaign Fund. "I think we can assure ourselves a place at the bargaining table if we can show our strength in all the campaigns.

"[Jackson] does deserve gay support. I think he has been very good on the issues. But Dukakis seems to be getting better on the issues and has a growing amount of gay support. So I think you have to read the tea leaves here. The winnowing process has begun, and we need to figure out who is going to wind up with the nomination. I think there is an awful lot at stake here. I think we need to play pragmatic politics."

Jackson supporters maintain that solid gay support for their candidate is pragmatic, considering his recent good fortunes and the undeniable fact that he will be a dominant political player at the convention.

"Whether or not Jesse wins the nomination, our support is critical to making Jesse as strong [a voice] as possible in the Democratic national convention and in the Democratic Party," said Pam David, national cochair of Lesbians and Gays for Jackson.

"He has committed himself to putting our issues out there [on the bargaining table] and supporting a full platform of lesbian and gay rights. He proved to us his support in 1984. He can have more clout going into the 1988 convention. We can beat back [Democratic Party chairman] Paul Kirk's attempt to keep the party platform dry, cut to the bone, and 'not catering to special interests,' i.e., people who have real needs."

Much At Stake For Gays

If pragmatism colors the thinking of gay would-be Jackson supporters, it is because of the enormous stake gays have in the outcome of the 1988 presidential election. For example:

• Whoever is sworn into the presidency on January 20, 1989, will set the tone and shape the agenda governing the nation's response to the worsening AIDS tragedy for the remainder of this century. The international implications of this are obvious and far-reaching. The lives of millions in the United States and beyond hang in the balance.

• Depending also on who ends up occupying the White House, the advancement of gay civil rights on the federal level will either proceed or remain stalled indefinitely. The success of gays' efforts to seek dignity and respect through the law hinges largely on the outcome of this November's elections.

• The future role of gays in the Democratic Party remains, at best, uncertain. Party chairman Kirk is known to view gays as a "special interest" liability to the party and has been outwardly indifferent to gay concerns. With the prospect that the party will be at odds over finding an acceptable nominee, the question arises: Who at the bargaining table can be counted on to speak most forcefully to gay concerns?

Gay voters have great potential to influence the outcome of the presidential contest. As Democratic hopefuls enter the final stretch of the primary season, each is courting the gay vote to one degree or another. Gay Democratic voters, if loyal to a single candidate, could play a decisive role in the outcome of a number of big state primaries, including Ohio, Pennsylvania, New Jersey, and California.

Within this context, and fearing a repeat of the ignominious defeat of the party's nominees in four of the last five presidential elections, gay Democrats, therefore, are seeking to avoid at all costs another humiliating electoral blowout at the hands of voters. Moreover, in the view of gay Democratic activists, another four to eight years with Republicans in power—cast in the same mold as the Reagan era—would be tantamount to disaster.

In fact, that scenario may be hard to avoid in any case. Some polls suggest that, even under the best of circumstances, all of the current crop of Democratic hopefuls—Dukakis, Sen. Al Gore (Tenn.), and Jackson—would face a tough go of it against the likely Republican nominee, Vice President George Bush. If Jackson gets the nomination, most political observers and public opinion polls agree, a Jackson-Bush face-off could turn into an unthinkable rout.

That is the rub for gay voters. There is no question that, on the basis of his clearly and consistently stated positions on gay issues alone, Jackson qualified for gay support. On the other hand, few cast their vote simply on the basis of a candidate's positions. Other factors—character, experience, and electability—all enter into voters' political equations.

Moreover, gays are anything but a homogeneous voting block; there are countless gay Republicans, for example, who find the Democratic Party, and Jesse Jackson in particular, anathema.

Many gays and nongays alike, who might otherwise be favorably disposed toward Jackson's politics, are still sitting on the sidelines in the belief that he cannot and will not win enough votes to take the nomination. He cannot win the nomination, their reasoning goes, not because he is black but because his views on economic and foreign policy are far afield of the Democratic, let alone the national, mainstream.

Jackson's base of support, while enthusiastic, is too small to win a national campaign. In spite of impressive gains in white support, he has yet to prove that he can draw better than a quarter of the white vote. Finally, Jackson's complete lack of experience in public office is unnerving to those who are unwilling to view the presidency as an on-the-job training program.

Tough Choice for Gay Democrats

The dilemma and challenge posed to gays by Jackson's candidacy is that it contains at once many of the gay community's highest hopes and aspirations and many of its deepest frustrations and fears.

The hope rests in Jackson's gift for sounding a passionate message that heals and empowers, a message for which many gays long. There is hope also that his achievement can be the nation's achievement, a sign that American society has moved toward greater reconciliation and understanding, a goal gays share with other minorities.

The fear and frustration reside in the harsh recognition that the poison of racism—the powerful, immoral counterpart to homophobia—may ultimately, and fatally, curse Jackson's candidacy.

For many undecided gay voters, those feelings of fear and frustration gnaw away at the point where one's most deeply held sense of ethics, morality, and idealism collides head-on with one's gut instinct for what can and must be done in a world where politics dominates. In the case of gays, that political world often works effectively to oppress.

In the final analysis, gay voters must look into their hears and make up their own minds, commented Jackson organizer Miller. "We are, in 1988, politically sophisticated enough to question the conventional wisdom we get from the straight community—that is, it is not the time for a black candidate for president—and start deciding on our own whom we will be supportive of.

"I think there is a basic issue of loyalty here. You stand by the friends who stand by you, and that is a bottom line for me."

The Interview

Advocate western regional news editor Mark Vandervelden talked with Jesse Jackson during a March 20 flight between campaign stops in California. Following are excerpts from the interview.

I'd like to go back to October 11 and the March on Washington for Lesbian and Gay Rights. As you were standing on the stage, looking out over that sea of faces, what struck you most about the political statement gays were making that day?

Well, the political statement is not what struck me the most. It was the humanity of the people, in unison, reaching out for human understanding; reaching out to be heard on one of the great health crises of our day…AIDS; reaching out for that most basic right, the right to be who one is.

And I remember, my only political thought was the absence of any other candidates there. It was during the period we were campaigning for Iowa, and I thought about how the other [candidates were] going through snowstorms to get to 40 people and 40 cameras. Here [were] 600,000-plus people, and [the candidates] were absent—threatened and intimidated. Therefore, that many people [were] being abandoned [because of] intimidation.

When you look at 600,000 people reaching out in that way, you cannot see them by sexual preference or by race or by sex or by religion; you just see people.

And the other thing that struck me acutely was—I think this is where I almost choked up—was when I saw the people in front of me who had contracted AIDS, who were dying but reaching out in their dying moments to make a statement—trying to make a statement to their families and friends, the U.S. Congress, and the president.

I saw some sitting there wrapped in blankets and sheets with their loved one, their parents holding them. Crying, some of them. Perspiring, some of them, with pneumonia. Others with death rattles in their throats. Weak, yet reaching out to humanity.

Immediately after I spoke, [I went] down there, embraced them, and let them know that I really cared as a human being and that I have no sense of reluctance or any shame in reaching out to suffering humanity seeking to be understood and seeking equal protection under the law.

How would you describe your own personal growth on the issue of gay and lesbian rights in the past decade or so?

Well, as we fought for, in the South, basic civil rights—the right to use public accommodations, the right to vote, equal housing, equal access to education—if you were black, no matter what your religion was, your sex was, [or] your sexual orientation was, you were certainly denied equal protection [because of] race.

The constitutional definition of blacks as three-fifths human was based upon race. To that extent, all black people had the same struggle to gain equal protection under the law, which applied, of course, to Hispanic people and Indian peoples as well. And…some of the people who were leaders, who were teachers, who were professionals, were gay or lesbian, and no one denied them their role in leading a demonstration, their right to go to jail, their right to risk their lives….

And so I grew up. I knew professionals, teachers, [and] musicians who were gay, and there was no witch-hunting on the matter. Though there was always a certain reluctance to promote one's gay or lesbian status, there was no witch-hunt on the question.

I think also [that] I take a fairly constructionist view of the Constitution, in the sense that citizens—civilians—should never be denied their civilian rights, and there is no room for one to be denied those rights based upon race, sex, or religion….

On a more human level, I've known gay and lesbian people all of my life—people [with] whom my family and I developed good human relations.... Some of my most brilliant teachers and some of my classmates were gay. They were just a part of the community of people. I think that is what is important to understand....

I remember, in later years, once this matter became a kind of important political issue, one of the young friends of my family, Keith Barrow, [the son of] Rev. Willie Barrow, who is the head of Operation PUSH now...was gay. Keith grew up with my children. Keith baby-sat for my children.... He was a friend of the family—and grew up singing [in] the choir I organized.

Then Keith contracted AIDS, which really brought my family face-to-face with AIDS as a killer disease. We watched the disease eat him up. I know the hospital costs of AIDS. I know the pain the family goes through...from shame to pain to cost.... And I watched his family go through the process. He came from a very strict religious background, but, you know, love covers all, and his parents and friends and pastor had to come to grips with his humanity.

There is almost no other disease that has been as politicized as this one....

Well, you know, there is a lot of room in the realm of the unknown to roam—a lot of room to operate. And people usually close the gap of the unknown by adopting some reasoning process to corner the market. Usually it is driven by the unknown: We are afraid of the unknown, we are ignorant of the unknown, [and] then we begin to hate objects of the unknown—we violently reject it. So a part of my view of life is to bring light to the unknown, to expose it, and to at least talk with people....

So I have simply made myself available to learn more, to be more compassionate, [and] to be more caring on a personal level. I mean, everybody is for research—and should be for more research. That's good. But my impression is [that] people who are in this predicament need human understanding.

Have you ever imagined what your reaction might be if you discovered that one of your own children might be gay?

Well, yeah. [None] of them is. But my position has always been with my children [that] whatever of life's circumstances greet them, I still love them.... And I urge my daughters not to get pregnant prematurely. If they do, [they shouldn't] panic, because I'm their father and Jackie's their mother—if they make A's in school, if they make F's, if they achieve what we call a profession or lose their way....

I don't want my boys to impregnate any young woman they will not marry. But if they do, it's my grandchild. I don't want my children on drugs, but if they do [them], they need not panic. They can come home; they're my children.

I can't be a part-time father [or] love them only when they give me gratification. Real love comes out in the low moments. You really must love people the most when they need it the most. People don't need much love when they've got a tail wind blowing. They need love when they are facing head winds and crosswinds.

Back in the 1950s and 1960s, blacks were largely dependent on their white liberal friends to take care of them, politically speaking. Gays in the 1980s are in a similar predicament, in the sense that they also have to depend on others—liberal friends—to take care of them. What advice would you give to gays seeking political empowerment in the '80s, drawing from the lessons that you learned from the civil rights campaigns in the 1960s?

Well, I'm not sure that we were dependent upon liberals to take care of us. I don't think that's accurate. Rosa Parks and Martin Luther King did not depend on liberals to initiate the bus boycott.

We have a sense of self-respect and a sense of self-determination. Some liberals joined it, which was welcomed, but it was not initiated by them. The students sitting down in Greensboro for public accommodations did not depend upon liberals to initiate it or carry it on.

Blacks…led the march to vote…. We had the good judgment to reach out for alliances…. Now, whether it is family farmers reaching out or abandoned workers or gays and lesbians, people who want their full rights must reach out for coalition and must have enough sensitivity in coalition to make sure [not only] that their interests are affirmed but that their interests converge with other people's interests…. When you reach out bigger than yourself, you get bigger than yourself.

One of the things, I think, that many gay activists believe has impeded their ability to participate in the efforts of other interests is the gay community's preoccupation with AIDS—and simple survival.

I don't think so. I think that… gays have rightly led that struggle [against AIDS] because gays and lesbians have been the disproportionate victims of it. But I think that if any group leads the struggle to increase consciousness about AIDS—if any group serves the nation by getting more research to end AIDS—it has served interests broader than itself because no one group has a corner on the AIDS epidemic.

But I submit to you that the idea of reaching out for an agenda bigger than yourself is always a way to grow. It's like you have to stretch and reach out to grow. When the blacks are preoccupied with the black agenda, Hispanics with the Hispanic agenda, Jews with the Jewish agenda, Arab-Americans with the Arab-American agenda, gays with the gay agenda, [and] women with the women's agenda, there is almost always the tendency on the part of other groups to pull back and let you go on your own way. But you can go but so far….

Do you think the Democratic Party is…prepared to accept your positions on such issues as gay rights at the moment?

The party is made up of its constituency groups that vote for it, so registered voters prepare the party to accept their collective views….

But [Democratic National Committee] chairman [Paul] Kirk essentially—

That's not the party.

He has essentially said there are not going to be party planks per se this time around; there is going to be only a generic statement of principles.

That has not been determined; that has been suggested.

So you still think that is open for discussion?

I'm sure I will be active at the platform committees.

Entering the final months of the campaign, it is very clear that no single candidate is going to walk in with sufficient delegate strength to walk away with the nomination on the first vote. Of all the gay civil rights issues that you have staked out a strong position on, is there one that stands out that you feel prepared to go to the mat on?

You know, let me tell you. What's fundamental about activists—be they gay activists or labor activists—the fundamental challenge is this: Shouldn't ideology drive you to stand with people who stand with you? If you say, "I am a gay activist, and Jesse Jackson has affirmed my [constitutional rights, and] Jesse Jackson has affirmed my person, and he was the only candidate at the rally October 11—but I will not vote for Jesse Jackson," then your conflict is not a sexual conflict at that point, it is an ideological contradiction. It is a political contradiction, and that is significant.

Why would workers… stand with somebody who would not stand and hold a picket sign? Why would farmers stand with someone who would not come to stop a farm foreclosure? Why would gay activists stand with somebody who would not stand with them October 11? Why would gay activists stand with someone who would not stand close to, talk with, [and] communicate with someone who was dying [of] AIDS?

I know that I had done the right, constitutional, and moral thing by affirming a role for everybody in the quilt of humanity. So now the obligation is on gay and lesbian activists to be consistent. I have come forth with courage and consistency and clarity. I deserve support.

Jesse Jackson on Gay Rights and AIDS

No other candidate seeking the presidency has spelled out his positions on gay rights and AIDS policy as clearly or as frequently as Jesse Jackson. Jackson has pledged nothing short of a full guarantee of civil rights for gays. In a series of strongly worded campaign issue briefs, Jackson has said he:

• Supports the gay rights bill pending before Congress that calls for an end to discrimination based on sexual orientation.

• Supports a presidential executive order banning antigay discrimination in the federal government, including the military.

• Opposes immigration policies that discriminate against gays,

• Has called for the repeal by legislative action of the U.S. Supreme Court's 1986 *Hardwick* decision, which upheld states' rights to regulate private sexual activity between same-gender consenting adults.

• Defends the rights of lesbians and gay men to child custody

• Wants gay couples to be afforded the same health care and other benefits accorded to nongay couples.

In line with other candidates, Jackson has called for increased federal funding for AIDS research, prevention, treatment, and care. Specifically, Jackson:

• Proposes a comprehensive national health program to meet the needs of all Americans.

• Favors an infusion of funds for AIDS hospice care for the terminally ill and social support for patients and their families.

• Has called for the boosting and enhancing of AIDS education efforts that include "discussion of explicit sexual practices and risk-reduction techniques."

• Has denounced mandatory HIV antibody testing, quarantines, and "other repressive measures."

• Backs an end to AIDS-related discrimination in employment, housing, education, and health care.

• Has called on the United States to take a more vigorous international role in combating AIDS.

THE NEW GAY ACTIVISM: ADDING BITE TO THE MOVEMENT

by Peter Freiberg, Rick Harding, and Mark Vandervelden

June 7, 1988

In Raleigh, N.C., a gay organization generated considerable media attention when it staged a kiss-in outside the offices of antigay U.S. senator Jesse Helms (R–N.C.).

In Maine a group twice picketed speeches by Massachusetts governor Michael Dukakis, a Democratic presidential candidate. The group charged that Dukakis's foster care policy, which effectively bars gays in Massachusetts from adopting children, inspired a similar proposal in the Maine legislature.

In Nashville, Tenn., a dozen gays were ejected from a presidential AIDS commission hearing after they disrupted testimony by antigay U.S. representative William Dannemeyer (R-Calif.). As Dannemeyer began to testify that AIDS represents God's punishment of gays, group members shouted, "We are not going to tolerate your stupidity."

High-Profile Tactics

All across the United States, gays and lesbians—fed up with the ineffectiveness of traditional lobbying tactics—are taking their case to the streets. High visibility is the goal, and groups are staging radical demonstrations that more often than not end up on the front page of newspapers or on the local news.

And in almost every case, the new organizations are dedicated either wholly or largely to direct political action.

"A lot of people feel that traditional lobbying and politics just aren't going to work," said Linda Royster, a Washington, D.C., activist and organizer of the city's new direct-action group, Out! "[Gays] are starting to feel that as long as we keep appearing in our three-piece suits and saying, 'Please sir, can I have my rights?' we just won't be effective."

The new era in gay activism may have reached a high point the week of April 29, when more than 30 new and established groups across the country staged a series of direct actions, including rallies, protests, and acts of civil disobedience.

The demonstrations resulted from a conference called by New York City's protest group AIDS Coalition to Unleash Power (ACT UP) during last October's National March on Washington for Lesbian and Gay Rights. The conference was meant to inspire organizations in other cities to conduct direct actions, and, in fact, it did spur the formation of a coalition called ACT NOW (AIDS Coalition to Network, Organize and Win), which sponsored the week's actions.

Almost every new or revitalized organization cited the national march and the AIDS crisis as playing major roles in its creation, but many were also inspired by specific local issues.

Mass Act Out, a Boston direct-action group, was formed in response to Dukakis's proposal to allow insurance companies to require HIV testing in Massachusetts in certain instances.

The Guilford (County, N.C.) Alliance for Gay and Lesbian Equality formed after Greensboro city police banned parking in a gay cruising area, and the Lawrence, Kan., Citizens for Human Rights came together to fight for a city gay rights ordinance.

To Break the Law—or Not

Just as the impetus for the groups' formations varies, so do their methods. New York's ACT UP, for instance, is the undisputed master of civil disobedience among gay organizations.

The group has staged dozens of direct actions and marked its first anniversary with a major civil disobedience action in March. More than 500 ACT UP members blocked rush-hour traffic in the city's financial district, chanting slogans critical of President Reagan. Police arrested more than 100 protesters.

But many of the new direct-action groups eschew civil disobedience. Sue Hyde, director of the Privacy Project of the National Gay and Lesbian Task Force, said she would worry about civil disobedience actions where only a few people are willing to participate.

"If there are only four of five people being arrested and the cops are nasty, there could be some real danger," she said. "I'd be really cautious about encouraging a situation like that."

Civil disobedience often is not needed to get press notice outside New York City, Hyde said. "In a lot of towns, ten gays picketing in front of city hall will be on the front page of the next day's newspaper."

Not every group uses direct action. Some use traditional lobbying, and others combine that with more radical techniques. But regardless of how they get their message across, it's clear that they do intend to make themselves heard. And those who have not yet chosen this line of protest say that they are ready to do so should the situation warrant it.

Making a Personal Commitment

Some of those participating in the new gay activism have been heavily involved in the movement for some time. But many others are either just starting to get involved or are heightening their commitments.

For Steve Busby of Boston, AIDS was the motivator. For Scott Turner of Iowa City, it was seeing teenagers yell obscenities at people leaving the gay bar where he worked. And for Cindy Hoffman of Pittsburgh, it was the march on Washington.

"One's sense of outrage at the way the federal government is handling this crisis [AIDS] is so strong that you feel you must act in some way," said Busby, a member of ACT UP/Boston. The organization is one of many around the country inspired by the New York ACT UP group.

The degree to which AIDS activates people seems to depend at least in part on how hard the epidemic has hit their own communities.

In the New York area, more people have been diagnosed than anywhere else—and it is not surprising that the first ACT UP chapter started there.

"Most of us have very close friends who have already passed away from this disease," said Troy Hoskins, an ACT UP/New Jersey member, as he left a Wall Street demonstration.

Such "frustration in a truly life-and-death situation radicalized people and makes them ready to become activists," noted Greg Herek, an openly gay assistant professor of psychology at the Graduate Center of the City University of New York.

Michael McFadden, an activist with two new Pittsburgh gay groups, compared the epidemic to the draft during the Vietnam War: "People got involved initially because they didn't want to go [to Vietnam], and then they started questioning the cause itself.

"AIDS has certainly [prompted] a lot of activity just because of the government's slow response to the crisis," he said, "but it's really made clear how we stand with the government and how we stand with society as a whole.

"We have to be active on behalf of AIDS, but we have to be active on behalf of the civil rights that are threatened by the backlash."

The March on Washington's Impact

For many people, the October 11 march on Washington, which included AIDS issues as part of its agenda, was an inclusive event reflecting a broad range of gay issues and demonstrated the community's anger, hope, and solidarity. The march's huge turnout surprised many people, but just as surprising has been its impact in the following months.

"Going to Washington was kind of a rejuvenation," said Cindy Hoffman, a member of a new group called Cry Out! in Pittsburgh. "I think, *My God, there's a lot of us.* When I got back to Pittsburgh, I wanted to get really involved on a local level."

Hoffman said that she had been involved in civil rights issues over the years but had gradually become "cynical and discouraged."

In many regions committees formed to organize local march participation remained in existence after the march to agitate around gay issues on a permanent basis.

"[If] you take North Carolina as an example, the march provided the excuse for organizations to start [forming] in places where they hadn't," said John D'Emilio, a history professor at the University of North Carolina at Greensboro and author of *Sexual Politics, Sexual Communities.*

"People didn't have to figure out what the first step [of the new organization] would be; it was getting people to Washington. But… having taken that step to do very visible organizing, it became natural to [take] the next step," he said.

Some observers view the increase in civil disobedience and demonstrations as part of a cycle many social movements have experienced.

"Early on, we were much more confrontational. As the [gay rights] movement progressed, we saw our leadership mature and try to work from inside," explained Jim Bussen, national president of Dignity/USA. "But we need both [methods]. We had gone to the point where there wasn't any sign of confrontational politics going on."

Plenty to Be Angry About

It was the radicals whose militancy in the early post-Stonewall years made it possible for "more Establishment things to occur" afterward, D'Emilio said.

The successes of major national groups like Human Rights Campaign Fund, the National Gay and Lesbian Task Force, legal organizations, and local groups helped create the climate in which a nascent militancy could take root.

At the same time, frustration and anger at recent defeats contributed significantly to the current activist upsurge. Those losses range from the U.S. Supreme Court's 1986 *Hardwick* decision upholding state sodomy laws to the defeat in many states of gay rights bills through the efforts of representatives of the Roman Catholic Church, fundamentalists, and homophobic conservatives. To date, Wisconsin remains the only state to have passed comprehensive antidiscrimination legislation.

D'Emilio drew a connection between the upsurge in militancy and the waning of the Reagan administration. "Especially in Reagan's first term, his success as a president in shaping a political agenda put so much of a damper on things. Gay direct action is just one more piece of a general thawing out that is occurring after this time of Reagan."

The impetus for gay organizing also came from outside the country, particularly from the Vatican. In 1986 Cardinal Joseph Ratzinger wrote a letter condemning same-sex orientation as a "tendency toward an intrinsic moral evil" and an "objective disorder."

The letter also called for the expulsion of Dignity, the gay Catholic group, from church facilities and urged bishops to oppose gay rights legislation.

"The Ratzinger letter galvanized the gay Catholic movement and Dignity as no other thing had," Dignity's Bussen said. "It's our Anita Bryant."

When the bishops started doing "the Vatican's dirty work" by evicting Dignity chapters, Bussen said, protests erupted across the country. Their scope surprised even Bussen.

In New York the Cathedral Project, a continuing protest that takes place every month at St. Patrick's Cathedral, has drawn extensive local media publicity and a church lawsuit. New York's Dignity chapter split over the use of confrontation.

As with ACT UP, the Cathedral Project's militancy may be emulated in other cities. Dignity/Hartford president Michael Michaud has urged gay Catholics to consider forming another local Catholic group that would "probably be more disruptive...to make a statement."

While AIDS, the Ratzinger letter, and other new issues are major factors sparking activism, traditional forms of discrimination and antigay violence have been crucial too.

Scott Turner, a leader of the Gay People's Union at the University of Iowa in Iowa City, says that after he saw gay bar patrons subjected to verbal abuse by passing teenagers, "I just felt there had to be something I could do to raise people's consciousness about gay people, about issues, in some little way.

"People are starting to stand up for their own rights," declared Turner. "They feel they don't have to be afraid anymore.... You're seeing people say, 'We're not going to deal with this anymore; we're going to make them understand.' It's very empowering."

Questions of Effectiveness

If it seems clear enough that the recent groundswell of gay activism has produced dramatic new forms of protest and a new sense of empowerment, it remains considerably less obvious whether the new activism has been effective in bringing about significant, long-term political change.

Even under the best of circumstances, measuring something as intangible as political effectiveness can be tricky business, explained openly gay U.S. representative Barney Frank (D-Mass.).

"When you have a complex political process where there are so many factors at work, it is very hard to measure in a lot of cases the specific effectiveness of any particular act or acts," he said. "I think, for example, that the march on Washington was an enormously significant event, but I can't sit here and tell you that it produced this, that, or the other. I can say that there [have] been a lot [fewer] oppressive [laws] adopted around AIDS than we had feared five years ago. The activism is a major factor in that. Every Democratic presidential candidate who was running this year was more pro-gray than [he] ever had been before, an the activism is clearly responsible for that," Frank said.

"The major thing that the new activism has done is [to make] the politicians... aware that there are large numbers of gays and lesbians and their friends in this country who support us," he concluded.

Jeff Levi, executive director of the National Gay and Lesbian Task Force, agreed that grassroots direct action has increased visibility of gay and AIDS issues.

"I think it is very hard to quantify [the] impact [of direct action], but what I think you can show is that all of us, whether it be those doing mainstream work or [those] who may be direct-action–oriented, are providing more vehicles for people to become involved with gay-identified community activities. And I think that, in and of itself, is of measurable value," he said.

Levi said he initially was uncomfortable with the militant tactics being employed by a growing number of gay organizations. But he said he changed his mind during the past year and now sees value in direct-action groups.

"I think the direct-action groups are serving three functions," Levi said. "One is to be an outlet for the rage that I think a lot of people feel. [Another] is to more directly confront the Establishment in ways that prick [its] consciousness a little bit more than those of us who do more mainstream work. And I think the third is to keep those of us who are doing the mainstream work more honest."

Gays Undermining Gays?

Not all mainstream activists take a charitable view of the new activism. Many believe that militant, often erratic behavior can undermine painstaking efforts by mainstream activists to build access and establish credibility with nongay politicians.

In San Diego, for example, the local gay leaders sharply criticized the city's ACT UP group for its direct attacks on the generally pro-gay mayor, Maureen O'Connor, and the city council.

"They have shouted down the mayor and city council just to embarrass them. These are not the kind of things we should be doing to people who are going to be around for a long, long time," said Tony Zampella, publisher of *Bravo!* a gay weekly that recently challenged the group's tactics in a cover story.

"When the politicians call me," Zampella said, "I can't give them any explanation for [the group's] actions. We don't know what their purposes are. We don't know what their agenda is. We don't know what they can or can't do or what they will or won't do.

"They have alienated not only the people that they are targeting but ...[also] the majority of the gay community. That is why they are ineffective."

Zampella blamed ACT UP for O'Connor's recent decision not to participate in the reading of names on the Names Project Quilt. Albert Bell, chief spokesman for the San Diego ACT UP group, could not be reached for comment.

"If you place yourself on the fringe, you really aren't going to get very far in the long run," said Frank Ricchiazzi, executive director of the California Individual Rights/Civil Liberties PAC, a gay Republican group.

"My sense of political reality is one in which you sit down and negotiate and hammer out some kind of agreement on what you want. That is how the political process really works in the long run," he said.

Most of the new activists "have never really participated in the political process," Ricchiazzi continued. "Being effective in politics requires lots of hard work—picks and shovels. And what we have are these fringe groups [that] don't want to do the hard work. They do not want to work the system."

Still, he said the groups "are effective inasmuch as they make the rest of us…mainstream groups look reasonable to the straight politicians. In a way, they make our job dealing with the politicians easier."

Getting Results With Direct Action

In many communities, though, gay direct-action groups have shown successes in agitating for change.

A notable example is Dallas's Gay Urban Truth Squad, which is credited with results including:

• Effectively barring homophobic psychologist Paul Cameron from local airwaves;

• Confronting supporters of political extremist Lyndon LaRouche at Dallas–Fort Worth International Airport;

• Drawing attention to the city's AIDS epidemic by outlining bodies in chalk on city pavement; and

• Forcing Parkland Memorial Hospital to increase staffing at its AIDS clinic and eliminate its waiting list for AZT.

In its six-month history GUTS has become a force to be reckoned with, said William Waybourn, a GUTS organizer and president of the Dallas Gay Alliance.

"Take Mayor [Annette] Strauss, for example," Waybourn said. "Before, when she first ran for office, she said, 'Well, I'll support you privately but not publicly.' But now the woman is supporting us publicly. Not necessarily on issues of gay civil rights…. She is not at first base yet, but she at last is hitting the ball in the right direction.

"A lot of my negotiating strength on behalf of the gay community comes from the fact, the knowledge, the awareness, that GUTS is sitting out there, waiting to come in and do things [its] way.

"Parkland would never have gone along [with us] if they didn't think there were going to be 2,500 screaming queens at their front door," Waybourn said.

In the case of GUTS, the political impact of direction action can easily be measured, Waybourn said. "All you have to do is look at where we were four years ago—hell, one year ago—and you can see that we are using GUTS now to do all the kinds of things we could not do when we were playing good little boys and girls."

[PART FOUR]

SEX, RELIGION, AND POLITICS: FROM ANTIGAY INITIATIVES
TO THE WHITE HOUSE (1989-1999)

In late 1989 I was hired by editor in chief Stuart Kellogg to replace Peter Freiberg as New York correspondent. Not long after I began work, Andy Rooney, the CBS *60 Minutes* commentator, declared on the air that "many of the ills which kill us are self-induced: too much alcohol, too much food, drugs, homosexual unions, cigarettes. They're all known to lead quite often to premature death." I called Rooney at his CBS office. To my surprise, his secretary patched me through. It was

a little after 10 A.M., and Rooney was already in a talkative mood. After he reiterated his statement—
"I have to say what I think, and I think that homosexuality is inherently dangerous"—I asked him
whether he would make similarly unconventional remarks on the air about other minority groups,
such as African-Americans. "Don't be so sure [I wouldn't]," he responded, again to my surprise.
"Blacks have watered down their genes" because unintelligent members of their race "drop out of
school early, do drugs, and get pregnant." I asked him to send a letter clarifying his remarks. It
turned out to be a rant about female genes, "one man introducing his penis into the anus of another," and his 40-year friendship with gay writer and Truman biographer Merle Miller.

When *The Advocate* published the letter alongside my interview with Rooney, the reaction was
overwhelming. It was the most attention the magazine had ever received for a news story; the
media blackout Dick Michaels had remarked on was clearly a thing of the past. CBS suspended
Rooney for three months without pay, and the curmudgeonly commentator claimed I had taken
his remarks out of context. Kellogg and my news editor, Jim Schroeder, stood behind me
throughout the deluge of media attention.

When Kellogg resigned later in 1990, publisher Niles Merton sought to take advantage of the
media's new eagerness to address gay topics by naming as editor Richard Rouilard, a flamboyant
political columnist. Rouilard's tenure was tumultuous, marked by extravagant spending and high-
profile articles. He set out to take the magazine to mainstream America. Stories could no longer be
sourced from within the gay movement alone; reporters were instructed to incorporate the views
of nongay activists, politicians, and analysts.

Increasingly, the magazine came not just to report the news, but to drive it as well. One of
Rouilard's first scoops was published in the July 17, 1990, edition. "Old Politics, New Bedfellows"
told the story of Marvin Liebman, the prominent 67-year-old conservative who had hidden his homosexuality for fear of rejection by his colleagues on the right. In a rare example of collaboration
between the gay and right-wing press, Liebman, one of William F. Buckley Jr.'s best friends, came
out simultaneously in *The Advocate* and in a letter to Buckley's *National Review*. In a tortured response, Buckley asserted that antigay prejudice is "much more than mere accretions of bigotry,"
though he seemed unable to explain why.

By July 1992 Rouilard's acerbic style had worn out its welcome, and Merton replaced him with
Jeff Yarbrough, a former *People* staffer who was *The Advocate*'s features editor. Eager to maintain
Rouilard's colorful editorial approach as well as to place his own stamp on the magazine, Yarbrough
completed the conversion of the magazine from newsprint to glossy paper that Rouilard had begun.
At about the same time, the magazine received a letter from a man who claimed to have been a sex
partner of Jim McCrery, a Republican congressman from Louisiana.

The man was willing to talk on the record about his relationship with the right-wing politician. Two other men signed affidavits swearing that they knew McCrery to be gay. And since the congressman had been an avid participant in GOP's verbal gay bashing, Yarbrough believed the hypocrisy inherent in his stance made him fair game. Shortly after the Republican convention in Houston, the September 22, 1992, issue of *The Advocate* carried "The Outing of a Family Values Congressman: U.S. Representative Jim McCrery's Double Life." (Though the article received a flurry of press coverage in his district, McCrery was easily reelected.)

In April 1993 Merton sold the company to a group of investors headed by Sam Watters, who bailed the magazine out of what had become dire financial straits. The magazine was subsequently rewarded with numerous national prizes. *Folio/Magazine Week* named *The Advocate* "Best Newsmagazine in America" three years running, ahead of mainstream publications such as *Time* and *Newsweek*.

The backlash to gay gains, less vocal during the Reagan years, picked up steam again in the early 1990s. The movement that Anita Bryant had set in motion more than a decade earlier resurfaced. The religious right mounted statewide ballot measures proposing to ban gay rights bills forever in Oregon (failed), Colorado (passed but struck down by the U.S. Supreme Court) and Idaho (failed). John Gallagher, a former *Time* reporter hired by Rouilard as San Francisco correspondent, wrote lengthy stories on each battle. "For gays and lesbians in Colorado, hell began on November 3, 1992," began one Gallagher story. He went on to explain the "new reality" facing gays and lesbians: "The majority of their fellow Coloradans do not believe they should be protected from discrimination." Gallagher soon assumed the AIDS beat, regularly besting mainstream outlets on stories about HIV treatment and prevention.

The renewed attacks on gay rights brought out new, prominent and sometimes unexpected allies. In an exclusive interview in the September 7, 1993, issue, conservative icon Barry Goldwater explained why he had called for the repeal of the military ban on homosexuals. Goldwater's gay grandson, Ty Ross, the article revealed, had encouraged the former chairman of the Senate armed services committee to speak out. Ross had introduced his grandfather to a friend who had been discharged under the policy. "I've know for three or four years that Ty is gay, and it made no difference in my family," Goldwater said. "That's his right as long as he doesn't do damage to anyone else, and no one has ever convinced me that being gay is damaging to someone else." The article went on to note Goldwater's suggestion that "every good Christian ought to kick [televangelist Jerry] Falwell right in his ass."

In opposing the military ban, Goldwater declared that "you don't have to be straight to shoot straight." Congress did not agree. Six months after his inauguration, President Clinton negotiated a compromise that Barney Frank dubbed "don't ask, don't tell, don't pursue." In "D-Day," published in the August 10, 1993, issue, the magazine detailed a series of strategic blunders by gay organizations that contributed to the failure of President Clinton's promise to lift the ban. And in a November 30, 1993, article, "Friend of No One?" Gallagher looked at David Mixner, a gay activist and friend of Clinton.

February 17, 1994, brought bad news. Almost twenty years after he began work at *The Advocate,* Randy Shilts succumbed to the disease he had chronicled—just days after dictating from his hospital bed the final pages of *Conduct Unbecoming,* his book on gays in the military. Shilts was one of more than two dozen *Advocate* staffers and contributors who succumbed to AIDS. After Brent Harris, there were Robert I. McQueen, Nathan Fain, G. Luther Whitington, and Rouilard, among many others. (For a more complete chronicle of Advocate employees lost to the epidemic, see Mark Thompson's excellent pictorial anthology, *Long Road to Freedom.*)

As far as the movement had come, young gay men and lesbians were sometimes left behind. On May 31, 1994, *The Advocate* ran a cover story, "The Lost Generation," about surging HIV infection rates among young gay men. These were men who had not been reached by HIV prevention campaigns or who had chosen to ignore the messages altogether. The April 5, 1994, issue carried a cover story, "Suicidal Tendencies," about the continuing disparity of suicide rates between gay and nongay adolescents. Anguish over their sexual orientation, researchers believed, was driving some gay kids to suicide. Yet the Department of Health and Human Services had not funded a single study examining the problem.

Marvin Liebman was not the only conservative leader to come out on his own. Dick Cowan, another friend of Buckley (it was becoming a trend) and the head of a drug legalization advocacy group, identified himself as gay in the June 14, 1994, issue. That same issue also brought analysis of the massive celebration of 25th anniversary of the Stonewall rebellion in New York City. The week of events was marked by infighting, as groups vied feverishly to inherit the mantle of the riots. Not long after Cowan came out, Steve Gunderson made history in the October 4, 1994, *Advocate* by being the first Republican to identify himself as gay—sort of. What actually happened is that Gunderson's partner, Rob Morris, spoke to the magazine about their long-term relationship while Gunderson restricted his comments to his views on gay politics. One month later *The New York Times Magazine* distributed a press release taking credit for Gunderson's declaration in an article published in the magazine, even though it had been beaten to the punch. *The Advocate* had come of age.

The Advocate kept up its pressure on public figures. On July 25, 1995, the magazine ran a story under the headline "Closet Case" about the AIDS-related death of Arthur Kropp, the well-known president of People for the American Way, a liberal Washington, D.C., interest group. Kropp, worried that his being HIV-positive would be used against him by his adversaries on the right, told all but his closest friends that he was suffering from cancer, not AIDS. The story illustrated that even in liberal Washington circles, the closet was still a fact of life.

In that same vein, J. Jennings Moss, a former *Washington Times* reporter, contributed a series of articles on the sexual orientation of political leaders, both left and right, before Washington sex scandals became a regular staple of press coverage. In a March 5, 1996, cover story, he wrote about Barbara Jordan, the legendary civil rights leader who died of pneumonia at 59. It wasn't until after her death that people "began openly discussing her lesbianism," Moss reported. Despite the reticence of Jordan's friends and family, Moss was able to paint a compelling portrait of the former Texas congresswoman's complicated feelings about her sexual orientation and her race.

During the heated debate over the federal Defense of Marriage Act, Moss investigated the sexual orientation of several lawmakers who voted for the antigay legislation. "Arguably," Moss wrote, "the marital status and sexual orientation of every member of Congress was at issue when the house voted 342–67 to approve DOMA." Noting that the personal nature of the bill had "changed all the rules," Moss's September 3, 1996, article identified Republicans Jim Kolbe of Arizona and Mark Foley of Florida as gay. The magazine applied a high standard. In both instances three sources with "professional or personal relationships with lawmaker said they considered the lawmaker to be gay." The impact of the story was unmistakable: After objecting to questioning by Moss about his sexual orientation during a phone interview, Kolbe called a press conference to declare that he was gay, making him only the second openly gay Republican to serve in the House. (Gunderson, the first, retired that year.)

In August 1996 Judy Wieder replaced Yarbrough, making her the first female editor in chief. She has relied on her background as *The Advocate*'s features editor to inject a dramatic storytelling style into news coverage. While its readership remains largely male, under Wieder's leadership *The Advocate* has regularly covered women's issues, with articles including a groundbreaking 1997 cover story on lesbians and breast cancer as well as a profile of Sharon Bottoms, a Virginia mother who had custody of her biological child stripped from her by a court because she is a lesbian. Wieder has maintained *The Advocate*'s commitment to news analysis, while expanding coverage of sociological issues. Two examples are "One on One: Monogamy," the best-selling cover story appearing in the June 23, 1998, edition, and "Using Pedro," a tough investigative piece about a financial scandal at the Pedro Zamora Foundation, which appeared in the July 7, 1998, issue.

Editors and reporters may come and go, but *The Advocate,* like the movement it set out to cover, has endured and even prospered. As Randy Shilts said shortly before his death in 1994, the magazine "has been and remains the single most important publication in the history of the American gay and lesbian movement. In fact, no other periodical even comes close."

DALLAS GAYS PROTEST JUDGE'S COMMENTS: JURIST'S NOTIONS ABOUT GAYS MAKE HIM UNFIT FOR THE BENCH, THEY SAY

January 31, 1989

A Dallas judge apologized for a "poor choice of words" when he told a newspaper that he had given a convicted killer a lighter sentence because the man's victims were "queers."

The apology came after the official, state district judge Jack Hampton, drew criticism from national and state politicians as well as local gay activists, church leaders, and other judges. Hampton also said he had received "nasty" phone calls and a death threat after the comment was published.

Formal action against Hampton is possible as well: The Texas Human Rights Foundation filed an ethics complaint against Hampton with the Texas Commission on Judicial Conduct. The commission could censure Hampton or initiate removal proceedings.

Hampton told the *Dallas Times Herald* December 16 that he had sentenced 18-year-old Richard Lee Bednarski to a 30-year prison term instead of a life sentence on November 28 in part because Bednarski's two victims were gay.

"These two guys that got killed wouldn't have been killed if they hadn't been cruising the streets, picking up teenage boys," Hampton told the newspaper. "I don't much care for queers cruising the streets, picking up teenage boys. I've got a teenage boy."

Bednarski, a college student, was convicted of shooting and killing Tommy Lee Trimble, 34, and Lloyd Griffin, 27, after Bednarski and nine friends drove to the Oak Lawn section of Dallas to harass gay men the evening of May 15. Bednarski's friends testified that they had been jeering at passers-by when Bednarski persuaded one of the friends to join him in beating and robbing Trimble and Griffin, who had invited the teenagers into their car.

"Spell My Name Right"

Hampton said that he would have given a harsher sentence to Bednarski if his victims had been "a couple of housewives out shopping, not hurting anybody." Hampton told the newspaper that his views might anger people but said he didn't care: "Just spell my name right. If it makes [people] mad, they'll forget it by 1990," when Hampton comes up for reelection.

Hampton defended his comments the day the newspaper article appeared, despite the alleged threats and hostile telephone calls. "You work hard all your life, and you do what you think is right, and sometimes I wonder if it's worth it. If I can't come down here and say what I think is right, they need to get somebody else for the job," he said.

paign in 1990 against people who have shown themselves to be a bunch of unethical liars. The level of debate from the other side is insulting and, at times, downright filthy."

Nasty Attacks

During deliberations on the bill, state legislators who opposed the measure repeatedly attacked the gay community, and in a bizarre turn of events, opponents tried to schedule a vote on the bill on Halloween in order to make a mockery of it.

The attacks were led by Republican legislators David Locke, who argued that the bill would undermine the nuclear family, and Marie Parenti, who helped distribute a book titled *Are Gay Rights Right?* which equated homosexuals with murderers and child molesters. When the bill received its final senate approval, Sen. Edward Kirby stood up and announced that the bill's passage signaled the end of Western civilization.

But even the bill's opponents remarked on the skill, patience, and passion gays and their advocates in the legislature displayed during the protracted battle over the bill.

"At [Harvard's] Kennedy school of government, when they teach a course on how to get a law through, one of the chapters will be on the gay civil rights law," Locke said.

The bill's passage represented a political victory for pro-gay state legislators Michael Barrett and Mark Roosevelt, who had staked their political careers on the bill. Roosevelt was overcome with emotion when the bill passed and said it was the proudest moment of his life.

A Mixture of Tactics

The strategy gays employed to pass the bill utilized a number of tactics and read like a textbook on social change. Activists crisscrossed the state, mobilizing constituents to lobby their local representatives and building coalitions to support the bill, while pro-gay legislators adroitly maneuvered the bill through committees in the house and senate.

Meanwhile, gay lobbyists worked behind the scenes with undecided legislators, and direct-action groups staged a series of rallies outside the Massachusetts statehouse.

Perhaps the most important factor in the bill's passage was the political fall of senate president William Bulger, an autocratic leader who was able to hold the bill in legislative committee for years despite a majority of support in the senate. Bulger was challenged in the 1998 election by Stephen Holt, a liberal opponent who had strong gay support. It was the first electoral challenge to Bulger in years and contributed to Bulger's subsequent decision to drop his opposition to the rights bill.

Role of 1987 Protest

Another catalyst, some said, was a dramatic act of civil disobedience organized by Mass Act Out, a direct-action group, on the last day of the 1987 legislative session, after Bulger had again allowed the bill to die in his committee during the session. In that demonstration nearly 1,000 people stormed the statehouse, and 14 protesters were arrested after chaining themselves to the columns of the senate gallery.

Several protesters were injured by capitol police officers making the arrests. A lawsuit filed against the officers ended in a settlement requiring the officers to undergo sensitivity training.

"That was the turning point in the history of the bill," LaFontaine said. "It drew attention to what the senat[ors were] doing and publicly embarrassed them. We won a lot of respect that day. Two years after that demonstration, legislators are still talking about it."

ANDY, WE HARDLY KNEW YE: AND NOW, A FEW HOMOPHOBIC MINUTES WITH ANDY ROONEY

by Chris Bull

February 27, 1990

Television commentator Andy Rooney said he believes that "blacks have watered down their genes" because unintelligent members of their race "drop out of school early, do drugs, and get pregnant."

The commentator, who was already under fire from gay groups for making remarks that were allegedly antigay during a December 20 television special, made the comments about blacks in an interview with *The Advocate*. He also made several other unconventional statements about gays and people with AIDS.

Rooney writes and narrates short human-interest essays for CBS's *60 Minutes*, the only news program that regularly ranks as one of the country's ten most popular evening television programs. Rooney is known for his puckish wit; light topics like airline food or taxi drivers are the usual subjects of his commentaries.

In his interview Rooney said, "I've believed all along that most people are born with equal intelligence, but blacks have watered down their genes because the less intelligent ones are the ones that have the most children. They drop out of school early, do drugs, and get pregnant."

"Not Normal"

About gays, the commentator said, "I generally feel sorry for you guys. I've been around long enough to know about homosexuality, but I still don't think it's normal."

Homosexuality, he said, "seems to have something to do with genes. I realize everyone has male and female genes, but maybe homosexuals have too many female hormones. I realize that gays face a lot of prejudice, and if I have added to that, I'm sorry, but I have to say what I think, and I think that homosexuality is inherently dangerous."

Reports that new transmissions of HIV, the virus widely believed to be associated with AIDS, are down among gay men are "gay propaganda," Rooney said. "I know you people can't help yourselves, but it's crazy to go on engaging in this behavior in this day and age." Rooney also indicated he believes there is no such thing as safe sex.

"Don't Be So Sure"

Asked whether he would make similarly unconventional remarks about other minority groups, like blacks, on the air, Rooney said, "Don't be so sure [that I wouldn't]. He then made the remark about "watered-down" genes.

After the interview, Rooney sent a letter clarifying his position to the New York City office of *The Advocate.* Rooney said he wrote the letter to address complaints he received from gays about allegedly antigay comments he made during *The Year With Andy Rooney,* the December 20 television special.

"Do I find the practice of one man introducing his penis into the anus of another repugnant? I do," Rooney wrote in the letter. "Is it ethically or morally wrong and abnormal behavior? It seems so to me, but I can't say why, and if a person can't say what he thinks, he probably doesn't have a thought, so I'll settle for thinking it's merely bad taste."

Television Special

The comments and the letter are almost sure to intensify a fire storm that has surrounded Rooney since the airing of *The Year With Andy Rooney.* On the program, Rooney said, "There was some recognition in 1989 of the fact that many of the ills which kill us are self-induced: too much alcohol, too much food, drugs, homosexual unions, cigarettes. They're all known to lead quite often to premature death." Gays complained that the statement blamed gays for AIDS and identified gay relationships as a vice.

Gays also said that during the broadcast, Rooney suggested that the public was tired of subsidizing health care for people with AIDS because they brought the disease on themselves.

In the same broadcast Rooney said a "lovesick homosexual" was responsible for last year's explosion on the U.S.S. *Iowa,* a Navy battleship. Although widely published reports said the explosion was set by a gay sailor as part of a murder-suicide plot, Navy investigators said last September that they had no hard evidence, only strong hunches, that the man whom they believed set the explosion was gay.

Gays and Smokers

The television special was not the first time Rooney made a statement that irritated gays. Last October, in his syndicated newspaper column, Rooney wrote, "I feel the same way about homosexuals as I do about cigarette smokers. I wouldn't want to spend much time in a small room with one, but they don't bother me otherwise."

Alan McClain, the coproducer of Community Action Network News, a gay television show in San Francisco, said he interviewed Rooney after *The Year With Andy Rooney* was aired and found his conversation with the commentator "unbelievable. The amazing thing is that he doesn't even know he's a bigot."

McClain said he was not surprised to hear that Rooney made statements that many people would consider racist. "It's clear to me that bigotry is part of the way he thinks. He has these strange genetic theories…. It's funny, because I've watched him all these years, and he was one of the last people I thought would turn out to be such a bigot."

Letter-Writing Campaign

After the December 20 program, the Gay and Lesbian Alliance Against Defamation, a national media watchdog group based in New York City, began a letter-writing campaign to have Rooney suspended or fired from his job at CBS News.

During a meeting with GLAAD officials, CBS News vice president David Corvo agreed to allow GLAAD to conduct gay-sensitivity seminars with CBS News staffers, said GLAAD assistant director Karen Schwartz. Corvo also said he would consider GLAAD's request that CBS News punish Rooney for his statements in the December 20 broadcast.

Schwartz said that "if [Rooney] had said something [like this] about any other minority, he would have been fired immediately. It points out the double standard of the networks regarding bigotry…. They still tend to take racism more seriously than homophobia."

Antigay commentary from Rooney is particularly dangerous, Schwartz said, because his wit inspires trust. Steve Miller, the chairman of GLAAD's media committee, said Rooney has considerable influence because *60 Minutes* is so popular. "He is a showcase figure for CBS News," he said. "To have a bigot in such a position of power is intolerable."

OLD POLITICS, NEW BEDFELLOWS: CONSERVATIVE MOVEMENT LEADER MARVIN LIEBMAN COMES OUT, ONE STEP AT A TIME

by Dave Walter

July 17, 1990

For as long as the modern conservative movement has been around, gays have played key roles in shaping it, funding it, and seeking to make it more ingrained in society. However, with few exceptions, gay conservative movers and shakers have kept their homosexuality partially or totally hidden. Marvin Liebman, one of the founders of the conservative movement, has long been one of them. Now Liebman has decided that, for him at least, the silence must end. He came out in a letter to his close friend and conservative stalwart William F. Buckley Jr., who agreed to publish the letter, along with a response, in the July 9 issue of the *National Review*. Liebman chose to come out simultaneously to the gay population in *The Advocate*.

Born in Brooklyn, N.Y., in 1923, Liebman first became politically involved at the age of 15, when he joined the Young Communist League. When the leader of the Communist Party of the United States was ousted in the mid 1940s, Liebman quit the party in protest. He remained associated with liberal yet noncommunist causes, raising money for them in the late 1940s in California. However, after his return to New York in the early 1950s, his politics moved to the right and he teamed up with Buckley, Robert Bauman, and others to found the modern conservative movement. He helped pioneer direct-mail fund-raising (right-wing direct-mail wizard Richard Viguerie was his protégé). And Liebman, an ethnic Jew, became a Catholic. Buckley served as his godfather.

From 1953 to 1969 Liebman helped establish and raise money for numerous permanent and ad hoc conservative organizations, including the American Conservative Union, Young Americans for Freedom, the Conservative Party of New York, and the Committee of One Million (Against the Admission of Communist China to the United Nations). He was involved in the presidential campaigns of Barry Goldwater and Ronald Reagan and assorted other conservative political races.

Liebman took a six-year break from conservative politics when he moved to London in 1969 to produce plays and films. Upon his return to the United States in 1975, he resumed his fund-raising work for conservative causes until the early 1980s, when he became a federal employee. With the help of conservative political contacts he'd made through the years, particularly his friendship with Buckley, Liebman landed positions at the National Endowment for the Arts and other government agencies. He is currently a public affairs officer at the Federal Trade Commission.

Liebman spoke to *The Advocate* in his folk-art–filled condominium at Dupont Circle, the District of Columbia's gayest neighborhood.

What made you decide to come out now?

I have been reading about more and more public homophobia. A lot of it has been focused around the [Robert] Mapplethorpe controversy. I am not particularly fond of Mapplethorpe, and I'm not particularly fond of those photographs that caused great concern, but I saw it as leading to other antigay stuff.

So I started being more aware of homophobia. All I could think about was feeling like a [secret] Jew in Berlin in 1937: Nobody knew he was a Jew; his friends who did know protected him. Nobody spoke about it. Meanwhile, everybody else was being taken off to the concentration camps. How did he feel? How did I feel?

Then some incidents over the last three or four months made it more pointed for me. I read *Borrowed Time,* and that bothered me a little bit. Then I saw the movie *Longtime Companion.* I was struck by the very manipulative last scene, where all the boys came off the boardwalk and down to the beach, and they danced and were happy and joyous and wore colorful bathing suits. I thought, *My God, these are butterflies. We're all butterflies, and why are people trying to step on us?*

So I figured, *Fuck it, I'm just sick and tired of it.* That's why I decided to come out. The way I've done it is through Bill Buckley, who's my best friend in the world, and *National Review,* because my main thrust, I think, was to the conservative movement, which was guilty of this sort of antigay stuff and will become even guiltier no matter what we do. But maybe I can stop it a bit, because I was basically one of the founders [of the conservative movement]; I deserve some respect, and they should listen to me. If they don't, fuck them too.

Are you wary of the consequences of coming out publicly?

No, I feel exhilarated. I have no qualms. Whatever comes is good. This is a terrific, exciting time. For the first time in my life, I'm really facing myself without any worry. God knows I have a lot of flaws in character and things that I'm ashamed of, but the one big burden I've carried—being gay— is not a burden anymore. I feel liberated.

Many years ago, you were kicked out of the Army for being gay. What led to that?

I was stationed in Cairo in 1944, when I was summoned to see Captain Ripley, who was my commanding officer. In public, in the C.O. office, with five or seven people around, he said, "You-all a cocksuckah?" I said, "I beg your pardon, sir?" He said, "You sound like a cocksuckah to me." Everyone was looking at me; I was dying of humiliation and shame.

He had seen a campy letter I'd written, and I knew that all the letters were censored, but who'd care about "I pinch your claws good night," which was a line from a funny little story written by Dorothy Parker? There was no reference to anything homosexual; it was a campy letter, probably talking about the Arabs' caftans or something like that.

At this time I was just really coming out as a gay person. I was 21 years old and was very naive about the whole idea. I was really very depressed. It was a nightmare. So, in the process of getting a blue discharge, which is neither honorable nor dishonorable but for the good of the service, I was sent for two weeks or so to an Army Air Corps hospital in Cairo and put in the Section 8 ward, where all the lunatics and people trying to get out were. It was frightening, because there were real nuts there, including one who said he was Superman. In the middle of the night, he would leap from one bed to another, and it terrified everyone.

Then I got out of there, but while waiting for passage home, I was sent back to my original squadron with Captain Ripley, who made my life a misery for several weeks. He publicly humiliated me. He made me march in front of the whole squadron and made fun of me. He said this was a New York queer Jew. It was one of the most traumatic experiences of my life, to be brutally treated as a gay person. It was true gay bashing.

When I came back, I lied about it; I said I'd had sunstroke of something. I never told anybody the truth, not even my family. They knew something happened, but they never questioned it. That was the conspiracy of silence.

Then you moved to Greenwich Village and got married to an artist, even though you knew you were gay. Why?

She was everything I dreamed the Village was. She was very bohemian; she was terrific. I fell in love with her; I just adored her. The reason I got married was to prove that I was a man. What else is new? We found a place, 73 St. Mark's Place. It was very Village-like and bohemian, and we used to hang out. I never told her that I was gay. It's a thing I still feel guilty about. The marriage lasted about nine months.

Have you had male significant others?

Always young people. Very rarely live-in. My own preference was always straight people, and I was always the aggressor. If anybody came toward me, I'd just get freaked out. And if I thought he was gay, I'd get freaked out. I was attracted to straights. Even now. I've never found people who I knew were gay sexually attractive.

How did you meet William F. Buckley?

In about 1951 a man named Harold Oram, a public-relations fund-raiser in New York, hired me, and by '54 I was vice president. He called me in and said, "Listen, I just got a letter from this kid who wrote *God and Man at Yale*. He wants to set up a magazine."

It was a year before *National Review* was founded, and Bill had written to a number of fund-raisers in town to see if they could help him raise money. Harold said, "Well, go over and see him." And I did. We clicked right away. It took us about four years, though, to get to be good, close friends.

But aren't both Buckley and his wife, Pat, antigay?

No. Pat is a very sophisticated woman, and she has no antigay feelings whatsoever. Bill's feelings are really based on theological matters, which sometimes go over my head. His thinking becomes convoluted sometimes, but that's his thing. Socially, some of his best friends are gay, and he'd rather die than do a disservice or do anything mean or rude or unkind to people because they are gay. That's just the way he is.

The tattooing thing [where Buckley said that people with AIDS should be tattooed] was something he thought would protect gays from other gays who didn't have the sense to say, "I have AIDS." His idea of gay sexuality is, You shove your prick up somebody's ass. He figured that the best way of telling them was that they [see the tattoo on the buttock] and they don't go in—they save themselves from getting killed. That's really the reason. It had nothing to do with marking them. That's why he didn't say to tattoo them on their cheek; he said on the buttocks. He is not antigay.

How did you come to know the Reagans?

I was in Hollywood in 1950. A woman I met, Mildred Allenberg, called me and said, "Darling, come out by the pool. I have a wonderful girl for you to meet. She's in the industry, but she's not trashy like the rest. She's a nice girl, a well-brought-up girl, and I think you'd like her. I know she'd like you. And I think she's Jewish, because her father's a dentist." So I met Nancy Davis. We saw each other a couple of times afterward, but then we lost track of each other.

Then, through Bill, who knew everybody, I met Ronald Reagan and Nancy again before I went to England. I was part of the first movement of Ronald Reagan for president at the Miami convention in 1968. I didn't launch his political career, but I was very much part of it. He's a nice man, Ronald Reagan. I like him.

Over the years, whenever there was a conservative thing that I was part of, he was part of it. As he got more and more famous, I was quick to remind Nancy Reagan of our old relationship. And they knew I was friends with the Buckleys. When you're up there, it's a very in group.

I worked, whenever I was around, on Reagan's campaigns. I helped on the '80 campaign, not in a big-shot way but in the delegate race in New York, that sort of thing. But the very fact that I was friends with Bill has been very helpful. He's a very important man. And Pat Buckley, the social butterfly—I was there many times at their place in Stamford [Conn.], and Nancy would call up; she'd call constantly. She's a telephone woman. For hours she'd speak on the phone.

You helped Robert Bauman found the American Conservative Union, and you yourself founded Young Americans for Freedom and other groups, all of which later became antigay. How do you answer your critics on this point?

Never while I was involved, from 1953 to 1968, did one of them do any public gay bashing that I was aware of. The young people who were in Young Americans for Freedom and so forth at that time never did anything like that—certainly not in front of me. Publicly, to the best of my knowledge, it just didn't happen.

I left the country in 1969 for England, and when I came back in '75, I had lost control and lost touch with those organizations, except I was considered one of the great leaders. I needn't apologize. Never was I any part of, nor did I ever condone, gay bashing or anti-Semitism or racism or anything like that.

What about Richard Viguerie? You taught him how to raise money, which later he did for antigay groups.

I'm very fond of him; he's a very bright man. What he's done that's antigay I really don't know. If I ever saw Viguerie saying that homosexuals should be burned or whatever, I would do something about it; I would write to him or call him. Howie Phillips [chairman of the Conservative Caucus] I have seen antigay things from, and I've told him, "You should be ashamed of it." But I've never done it publicly, because I'm not in the movement anymore.

You implied in your coming-out letter to Buckley that the conservative movement is likely to become more antigay.

Oh, I think so, because there's nothing to keep it going—there's no intellectual leadership anymore outside of Bill Buckley. And he's getting tired; he's being doing it for a long time. So what is going to keep it going?

This is the thing to be wary of: You have the right wing in America without focus. You have the Bush administration, which is like the Eisenhower administration—it's easygoing, middle-of-the-road. On the left, they have no leader either. So you have the right-wing functionaries, the bureaucracy, the religious groups, the money-raising element. America is ripe for a hate thing now. As an ethnic Jew and a Catholic and as a gay person, I've very worried.

Doesn't your criticism of hypocritical conservative homophobes suggest Buckley is a hypocrite as well?

No, no, no. I'm suggesting he's so set in his ways that he won't change. I can say nothing [negative] about Bill Buckley. I adore him.

Why?

Because he was one of the people who helped to open my eyes intellectually. He opened my eyes spiritually and has been my dear and good friend for 35 years. What can I say?

What do you think about his response to your letter?

I really can't say anything on the record.

In working closely with Bauman in setting up conservative groups, did you know he was gay before he was publicly exposed?

I didn't have a clue. Of course, I wasn't close with him in Washington; I didn't live here. But even though closeted, I was gay and went out of my way to be as friendly and open and helpful to him as possible. He's still my friend.

When did he find out you were gay?

The minute he came out, I let him know. I had no fear. You know, we were brothers.

What about Roy Cohn?

I always loathed and detested him, as did everybody in the world who had any sense. I knew he was gay. When I came to Washington, I asked him for a number of favors to help me get jobs, because he was very much in with Helene Van Damme and the Reagan White House. The very first job I wanted was with the United States Information Agency. Whatever I asked him, he did. We never once discussed [being] gay or anything like that.

I was once in Bermuda with Pat Buckley, waiting for Bill's boat, and there was Roy; he was ghastly-looking—he was really a worm. He was with this gorgeous young man. He was wearing—in Bermuda, which is the height of WASP gentility—something like a LOVE ME BECAUSE I'M A JEW T-shirt. Outrageous he was. I was not friends with him, not because of the gay issue. I just didn't like him much.

And what about Terry Dolan, the gay leader of the National Conservative Political Action Committee?

Dolan came along after I left for England, and when I came back, NCPAC was very much going. I was never buddies with him, nor did we ever discuss the gay thing whatsoever. I was aware of it, but we never discussed it. I made some overtures to him through a gay friend, because I thought it would be fun, but he never picked it up. I don't know why. I've never known any gay Washington people except my friends, and they are not important types.

Some right-wingers seem to think a homosexual cabal has existed in the recent administrations. Do you know of closeted gay conservatives in such a position of influence?

No. Frankly, even if I knew, which I don't, I wouldn't say.

You promote conservative values for gays, yet the gay movement has made inroads mostly among liberal Democrats. Conservatives and Republicans more often than not push gays away.

Yeah, but the break in the dike, if you'll forgive the expression, is Marvin Liebman. I'll lead my troops to victory [*laughs*]. Give the Republican Party a chance. Move in on them. Shake them up. If they won't be shaken, leave them. But don't leave the field to the enemy. With the Democratic Party, the liberals, you've got a home. [You should] go where they *don't* want you.

Gay activists have long lashed out against Republicans and conservatism. Do you think they're off base?

Activists are always *on* base in attacking anybody they want to, because they make things happen. They focus people's attention on something. If you just sit back and do nothing, nothing happens. So I'm all for it. That's why I'm for kids being active in college. I don't care whether they're right-wing or left-wing; I just think it's terrific for kids to be activists—and not to be stuffy activists like a lot of the right.

Although I object to Young Americans for Freedom screaming, "No rights for sodomites!"—ghastly, hideous—I would hope that there would be gay kids screaming, "Fascist pigs!" at them. It's good for kids to do that. That seems contradictory, but I really believe activism is very good. To do nothing is very bad.

So gay activists are fine, but for years they embarrassed me. The [gay pride] parade right here on P Street, when transvestites march, or the Sisters of Perpetual Indulgence in San Francisco—I've always felt a little embarrassed by that. I shouldn't because it's part of the whole thing. And when gay men are affectionate in public, I find it very embarrassing. I don't know why, I just do.

What do you think of "outing"?

I'm against it altogether. I just really respect people's privacy. There was a Chinese intellectual philosopher named Hu Shih, whom I knew. He was a great thinker. He made a speech once, during the days of mainland China when they made people confess publicly. He said, "They've taken the final freedom away from us, the freedom of silence." And outing is taking the final freedom away.

Now that you're out, what comes next?

I'm not sure; I have no idea. I know that it's going to change my life, hopefully for the better. If I can be of any real service, anything to do to help, I will. For instance, a friend wants me to write a fund-raising letter for a gay youth organization. If I can do anything like that, I will.

Would you recommend that other long-closeted conservatives come out?

Absolutely. It's exhilarating—I promise that. Even if they are shunned by a certain group, they'll be embraced by another group. They will have real love, and I don't mean sexual love but love of community and family. And if their own families reject them, which is unlikely, they'll have another family.

THE NEA's LATEST BOUT OF HOMOPHOBIA: FOUR REJECTED ARTISTS TALK QUEER

by Doug Sadownick

August 14, 1990

In an unprecedented attack on artists dealing with gay themes, National Endowment for the Arts chairman John E. Frohnmayer barred grants totaling $23,000 to four of 18 performance artists last month after they had been selected by the endowment's own panel of peers. Each of the rejected "Gang of Four"—Karen Finley and Holly Hughes of New York and John Fleck and Tim Miller of Los Angeles—deals frankly with gender politics. Three of the artists (Fleck, Hughes, and Miller) are leading figures in gay culture.

National arts groups are soft-pedaling allegations of homophobia in an attempt to save the NEA, which is currently up for congressional reauthorization. But the four artists are now calling on the gay community to see the controversy as part of a trend toward silencing homosexuals.

Last year conservative legislators, led by Rep. Dana Rohrabacher (R–Calif.) and Sen. Jesse Helms (R–N.C.), assailed the NEA for spending taxpayers' money to fund a traveling exhibit of photographs by the late gay artist Robert Mapplethorpe. However, neither the gay community nor the art world extensively rallied around the Mapplethorpe issue at that time.

Most recently the NEA has been crippled by the restrictions that Helms has insisted come attached with each grant, which say that NEA funds may not be used to produce work considered obscene, including depictions of homoeroticism. Dozens of artists have rejected their grant money in protest. The newest NEA obscenity-control measure, released July 11, still requires recipients of NEA grants to certify that anything created with the funds will not be obscene, although the wording is no longer overtly homophobic.

It is widely held that Frohnmayer's June 29 rejection of the four performance artists was an appeasement to conservatives in exchange for less restrictive obscenity guidelines. For 20 years the NEA's only stricture was artistic excellence. Now politicians like Helms and Rohrabacher have become the nation's chief art critics, using homosexuality as a political football to dictate moral standards for Americans.

The Advocate recently caught up with the Gang of Four to discuss the NEA censorship, their attempts to rally gay people around the issue, and the larger implications of the controversy.

Do you perceive the NEA rejection as a personal gay-bashing attack?

Holly Hughes: Gays are the scapegoats du jour. While there are tons of closeted lesbian and gay artists who get funded, my problem is that I have visibility as an artist. I've made it so that the media have to use that word *lesbian* when they talk about me. I've had interviews not run in papers because they would not use the *L* word.

When applying for an NEA grant, I wrote this letter to John Frohnmayer—my friend and yours—and to the NEA and President George Bush, and I talked about my work being homoerotic with a capital HOMO. My play *The Well of Horniness* was running in a Washington, D.C., theater when the national council received this letter.

Tim Miller: Last fall the only way I felt I could apply to the NEA was if I was accurate about the themes in my work: gay cultural identity, sex, issues of AIDS activism, and an aggressive critique of the government's response to AIDS. In my artist's statement I told Jesse Helms to keep his Porky Pig face out of the NEA and out of my asshole. These are the materials that went to Premier Frohnmayer.

Obviously, I experience [the NEA rejection] as an attack on me as an out gay person. I just finished a 17-city tour of America, getting a lot of attention in Washington. There's been this incredible open door within performance art for people of color and lesbians and gay men to spout off. Now there's a desire to silence us, especially queer artists criticizing senators.

John Fleck: Even though I am a gay performance artist, a lot of my work doesn't deal directly with that. I deal more with being sexually confused. What I do in therapy comes out in performance—topics like sexual ambiguity.

But yes, this is an attack on me as a gay person dealing with sexual politics. Just by looking at the nature of the four who got axed here, we're dealing with a repression of sexuality.

Karen Finley: Although I am straight, I think it would be wrong to say that the attack on me isn't about homophobia. My work is pro-gay. In one piece I compare America to Nazi Germany in terms of the health care system and [people with AIDS]. I believe the foremost issue here is dread of homosexuality. The other three artists are very out—they are heroes—and here I am saying that homosexuality is natural and should be legal in the eyes of God and society, that I believe in gay families and gay civil rights.

Do you feel that the NEA funding controversy is something that the gay community should take on as its own battle?

Hughes: I want to make a call to arms to the queer community to see this as their issue, seen in the context of the government's continued indifference to the AIDS crisis and in the huge increase in reported gay bashings in the last year. The homophobes in the United States government don't feel that we're dying quite fast enough. They want to shove us all into the closet, where they hope that we will suffocate and die in silence.

Miller: An analogy to McCarthyism is useful. McCarthy began his process with an attack on gay people in the state department way before he figured, *Oh, we can score on the Communists too.* He created this whole idea of the Homintern—this international homosexual Communist conspiracy in the state department. There's a rich history of gay people being the most vulnerable link in this society to use to begin a bigoted attack on the entire society.

Fleck: Probably the only people who are going to back us up are gay people, because the art world is nervous about all this now.

Finley: The gay community has always been supportive of my work, and I welcome the help. I'm concerned that the straight press is using me to avoid dealing with the homophobia issue. Fat chance. I say that the Mapplethorpe attack is just a smoke screen. As a straight woman planning to have children, I'd be happy to show my children those images, because I think homoerotic images are natural and I think it's good to demystify the sex act.

How did you feel when you learned of the grant denials?

Hughes: Depressed. It plays into my internalized censorship. I left this incestuous, abusive family in 1973 where there was this rule of silence: If you spoke out, you were told that you were imagining things. Now I walk outside and discover that the world is my family. Helms is just my father with a different mask on.

Fleck: Scared. I've gone through this range of roller-coaster emotions. It's bewildering how many people pat you on the back and say, "Congratulations!" But then fear creeps in. I've had newspapers asking, "Why do you urinate onstage? Why do you show your penis?" I don't want to talk about it out of context. It's distorting.

Miller: I see this NEA attack in the context of a series of direct attacks on gay people. This was neither more nor less scary than being at the AIDS conference in San Francisco the week before, which our president didn't attend because he was at a Jesse Helms fund-raiser. I was with colleagues and artists, protesting with ACT UP. We were getting beaten on by 400 police with truncheons. It's hard to say the NEA issue is more extreme than that.

Finley: I have been attacked for a long time. It's beginning to take a toll. Last year Scotland Yard told me that I couldn't perform because I promoted buggery. I told them that I was proud to promote buggery. They kicked me out of England. That was upsetting. People said that would never happen here.

Has this controversy, which sent you into the national limelight, helped your career?

Fleck: You could say Helms is opening a can of worms, trying to repress artists yet turning us into a cause célèbre. I've been getting letters from theater groups offering support. We're getting national prominence. If we could just get people to see the work and let them make up their minds, that'd be great.

Miller: I disagree. Their agenda is to dismantle the whole NEA structure. The notoriety in the press is going to die down very soon. We're going to be left without $7,000, and the art world will be concerned about something else.

It's not so much a concern about what happens to us. We all manage to make maybe $11,000 a year, which is to be wildly successful at this racket. But it sends a frightening signal to younger artists: Stay in the closet if you want a grant.

Hughes: I am not profiting from this. The spaces that present us are being attacked. A few weeks ago, W.O.W. Cafe [a New York club that presents lesbian work] got an eviction notice. The Kitchen [another Manhattan performance space] is being scrutinized by the NEA and the Internal Revenue Service for presenting Annie Sprinkle [another artist who deals with gender issues]. When San Diego's Sushi Gallery announced they were going to present the four of us, the Christian right began harassing them. These are just a few examples of what's happening around the country now.

Finley: I'm so busy speaking with lawyers and writing appeals that I can't make art or my living. I am disgusted because Frohnmayer and those who have written libelous articles on me have never seen my work. This is the man who is in charge of the NEA? I am very concerned because I perform all over the country in public spaces and am being seen not as an asset but a hindrance. This is not the kind of recognition I asked for.

Have yours colleagues been supportive?

Hughes: There's a definite split in the New York art world between those who see the seriousness of this and those adopting the "wait and see if it hits us" attitude. It's not unlike the straight world's response to AIDS.

Miller: In the Los Angeles art world, there's been an immediate rallying, an immediate identification among culturally diverse artists that this is a homophobic act.

Finley: I have been working on my own, trying to figure out what my legal options are. I am cautious about my role, because I think Frohnmayer put Karen Finley on this list so he could argue that his rejection wasn't motivated by homophobia.

Fleck: I was asking an administrator how we get the NEA reappropriated for another five years without content controls. That person felt that we couldn't isolate ourselves and say this a gay issue and take this anti–right wing approach.

Hughes: I've heard that same line from arts lobbyists, and I really disagree. I feel that the whole thing hinges on whether the country can accept us as human beings who deserve support as queer artists. If we hide the specificity of the oppression, I think we are guilty of a certain amount of complicity. Of course, there are broader issues. But to all those liberals, I say, "If this were happening to black artists, you wouldn't dare diminish this as a racist attack."

How do you take action? With greater flamboyance? A new militancy?

Miller: It's war. This is only going to make people stronger, more pushy, more ready to challenge this spooky government. We've just formed this group in Los Angeles, ATTACK [Artists Take the Action in Cultural Krisis]. The NEA isn't the ultimate goal. I'm more interested in working toward a society that oppresses people less. The group is based on an ACT UP model, created by artists working for pro-choice and against racism and censorship. The reason the NEA debacle is happening is because artists are getting pushier. The art world used to be a nice abstract place, deeply unpoliticized.

Hughes: I think the parallels to ACT UP are key. If the gay community had sat around and waited for the straight community to formulate a response to AIDS, we'd have had even more deaths. Our only hope of changing this—because straight artists will sacrifice us—is if the gay community gets mad. We can demand that gay culture be acknowledged. But the four of us can't do it alone. So far the dialogue has been to the right, with the artists who play golf thinking Frohnmayer is a great guy. We need to move the debate to the left so that the center gets listened to.

Finley: I feel that individual legal action is important to identify our rights. But I am all for artists forming a movement based on the ACT UP model.

Fleck: I feel that my destiny has been ordained and I must address the issue of censorship. But I don't know about the militancy. Growing up in a dysfunctional family, I never stated my fucking opinions. I'm just learning how to do that.

What is there in your work that your detractors are calling obscene?

Fleck: I once urinated onstage, but that was in the context of a performance about water and fishes. I deal with personal schizophrenia. I think that we all have male and female tendencies. As men we are taught to repress the feminine, creative, emotional side. And when you are taught to hate something in yourself, you project it out onto the world.

Miller: Recently, for the first time ever, one of my pieces was called pornographic in a newspaper. I talked about jumping up and down on an Irishman's dick, fucking the state of California, and 24 artists having an orgy and bringing down the government. I suppose there are some benighted souls who might consider that obscene. But our work is humane, out to create a moral universe of compassion. In fact, I've always fashioned myself the all-American queer—Jimmy Stewart sitting on a big dick. But this country won't acknowledge the all-American queer. You might think you are that. But when push comes to shove, you're not. Assimilation is not liberation.

Hughes: If any of us were making pornography, we wouldn't need the NEA. We would be making so much fucking money. This is chicken feed, man. But I'm not complaining. I live on chicken feed. A porn maker focuses on sensation and short-circuits any emotional or intellectual response, whereas an artist can make you aware of the way sexuality resonates spiritually.

Finley: I'm being punished because I am a morally concerned artist. By performing onstage in chocolate and alfalfa sprouts, I am making a very clear statement about the oppression of women.

Do you feel a responsibility to bridge the gap that exists between gay artists and the rest of the gay community?

Miller: I think most of the 20 million lesbian and gay Americans in this country would not find it unthinkable that a tiny portion of their tax money should support some cultural representation of them, considering how gays get virtually no services from the government and are illegal in 22 states.

Hughes: I struggle with how to establish greater dialogue with the community and to demystify what it means to be an artist. Sometimes we underestimate what we refer to as Middle America. There are plenty of Jesse Helms–like people who hate anyone who's not a straight white male chain-smoker—but that's not representative.

Finley: At all times I have to realize that I am a heterosexual and that my voice must give way to those whom society would victimize over me. I dream of the day when people of the same sex can show affection to each other freely. But we have a lot of work to do.

Fleck: I just finished three shows at an AIDS hospice. It was a great thing, because I have this fear of doing shows for the already converted. A lot of people don't know what performance art stands for. How do you get more people included?

Miller: I think you need to work onstage and in the community. It is part of our responsibility as artists not to be passive. Performing in a hospice or a church or at an AIDS demonstration is a way to bridge this antiart separation.

Can the NEA be saved?

Hughes: Yes, but we should demand Frohnmayer's resignation immediately. We should also have a say in who gets put in his place. I suggest Liz Taylor. She has the clothes. She's slept with almost everyone in Washington and knows how to make things happen. She's certainly not homophobic. I say Liz for chairman.

Fleck: I second that motion.

MEDIA WATCHERS SAY DAY OF DESPERATION CAUGHT NATION'S EYE

by Chris Bull

February 26, 1991

New York City's Day of Desperation, a series of AIDS protests, succeeded in briefly shifting at least some media attention away from the Persian Gulf war, said media watchers and AIDS activists.

The protests included interruptions of two national network newscasts and demonstrations across the city that resulted in 300 arrests—the largest number of arrests ever made in an AIDS protest in the United States.

"We want people to know that the government is spending $1 billion a day to fight a war but has spent only $5 billion in ten years on AIDS," said Victor Mendolia, a member of the New York City chapter of ACT UP, a direct-action group that helped organize the protests.

"After telling us that they didn't have any money, how did [the federal government] all of a sudden come up with $1 billion per day?" Mendolia said. "I think we got that message out."

The demonstrations began January 22 when activists interrupted nationally televised live evening newscasts at CBS and the Public Broadcasting Service.

At CBS, several activists shouted, "Fight AIDS, not Arabs," during the opening moments of the *CBS Evening News With Dan Rather*. Viewers saw one protester, gay novelist John Weir, appear at the bottom of their television screens for an instant. Weir was pulled off the set while anchorman Dan Rather, visibly shaken, asked for a commercial break.

When the broadcast resumed, Rather said, "I want to apologize to you for the way the program started. There were some rude people in the studio, but they were ejected." The interruption was edited out of the version of the program that aired later that evening in the western part of the country.

At PBS several protesters targeted the *MacNeil/Lehrer NewsHour,* chaining themselves to coanchorman Robert MacNeil's anchor desk. One activist failed in his attempt to handcuff himself to MacNeil. The protesters were not seen by viewers because PBS shifted to MacNeil's coanchorman, who was in Washington, D.C.

Later in the PBS broadcast, MacNeil told viewers that the disruption was caused by activists seeking more media attention for AIDS issues. He said he told the protesters that "this program has spent a lot of time on the AIDS matter and will continue to be interested in it, and we will be covering it more in the future."

Protesters at both networks were charged with criminal trespassing. Activists also tried to disrupt evening news broadcasts at ABC and NBC but were thwarted by security guards at each network.

The network disruptions were followed the next day by a series of demonstrations throughout the city. The day of protests began at 7 A.M. on Wall Street and concluded with a four-hour protest at Grand Central Terminal that ended at 9 P.M. Traffic was slowed throughout the city, and many commuters complained that the Grand Central demonstration caused them to miss their trains.

The CBS demonstration marked the first time protesters had successfully interrupted a network news broadcast since the Vietnam War, said Steven Rendall, director of research for Fairness and Accuracy in Reporting, a national media watchdog group based in New York City. "It was pretty unique," Rendall said. "I have not heard of other protests like it."

ACT UP member Jamie Leo said the protesters eluded security guards by using fake identification cards. He said ACT UP had spies at several networks who helped the activists devise plans to gain entry to broadcast studios, but the plans were complicated by the outbreak of the Persian Gulf war a week earlier.

"The networks' security increased the day the war broke out," Leo said. "They were more guarded than two weeks before the war, when we last checked. The decision to interrupt the broadcasts was not made lightly."

Rendall said he was not surprised that ACT UP targeted the networks. "From watching the networks, you would not know there is a debate raging in this country about the war," he said. "The people who are calling for justice at home—on AIDS, homelessness, health care, poverty—have been completely blacked out. Occupying a newsroom is a profound sign of dissatisfaction with the narrowness of the coverage."

But Rendall said he doubts that activist groups like ACT UP can garner more than small amounts of news coverage for domestic issues while the country is at war. "The networks have reduced all coverage to things that are best left to the war room, like how many Scud [missiles] are left. I'm afraid that until the war ends, there is going to be a tremendous loss in coverage of issues that need attention at home."

CBS spokesman Roy Brunett said his network will continue to cover AIDS and other social issues along with the war. "We feel [the protest] was a misdirected effort to draw attention to a serious health issue," he said. "Certainly we are covering the war because it is an important issue at this time."

Karin Schwartz, assistant director of the Gay and Lesbian Alliance Against Defamation, a media watchdog group, said the CBS interruption was effective because the "four-word sound bite 'Fight AIDS, not Arabs' " was broadcast. "The fact that [that] phrase got into the broadcast made the whole action worthwhile," she said. "Contrast it to [other demonstrations], where some people who read the media accounts couldn't understand [from medical reports] what the purpose was. It was a simple idea, brilliantly conceived and executed, and there was no way the media could ignore it."

Leo said ACT UP members were pleased with the extensive media coverage the CBS and PBS interruptions received but were dismayed that many reporters tried to tie the protests to the threat of war-related terrorism. "The story became part of the war hype," he said. "The reporters tried to use the story to show how vulnerable we are to terrorism. They kept using words like *invasion* and *assault*. We tried to say that this was a classic example of [nonviolent] resistance, but we could just as well have shot Dan Rather as far as [some reporters] were concerned."

The interruptions drew media attention to the series of protests the next day, Mendolia said. "Once the takeover [of the newscasts] happened, coverage the next day was guaranteed," he said. "What really surprised me was the accuracy of the coverage and how pro–ACT UP it was," Mendolia said. Reporters "usually quote commuters bitching about how they missed the train," he said. "This time they didn't do much of that. We saw the news reports and said, 'We could have written that.' "

Mendolia said the protests were planned months in advance, but the onset of the gulf war heightened the resolve of ACT UP members not to allow the media, government, and public to lose sight of AIDS. Shortly before the protest, the group bought a $13,000 quarter-page ad in *The New York Times* that read, 1,175 PEOPLE DIED OF AIDS LAST WEEK, AND YOU MURDERED THEM. Many people who had not planned to risk arrest before the Persian Gulf war changed their minds when fighting began, Mendolia said.

Antiwar activists were pleased with the protest, said Bonnie Garvin, media coordinator of the National Campaign for Peace in the Middle East, a coalition of antiwar groups that includes the National Organization for Women and the Rainbow Coalition.

"It is wonderful that [ACT UP is] making the connection between the lack of AIDS funding and the war," she said. "We all have to make it clear we are opposed to the war not just because we are antiwar but because the government is ignoring every social ill that exists in this country."

HYPOTHALAMUS STUDY AND COVERAGE OF IT ATTRACT MANY BARBS

by John Gallagher

October 8, 1991

A new study suggesting that gay men have brain structures that differ from those of heterosexual men drew praise from some observers but criticism from others, who said the media glossed over the study's weaknesses and misinterpreted its findings.

The study was conducted by Simon LeVay, a researcher at the Salk Institute for Biological Studies in La Jolla, Calif. Its results were reported in an article in the August 30 issue of *Science,* the journal of the American Association for the Advancement of Science. In the article LeVay concluded that differences in size between the hypothalamus of heterosexual and gay men "suggest that sexual orientation has a biological nature."

A statement by the Lambda Legal Defense and Education Fund, a gay rights group, described LeVay's finding as "intriguing. If, as some have suggested, there is a biological basis for homosexuality, it is difficult to fathom on what moral, ethical, or religious basis one can reasonably discriminate" against gays and lesbians.

But John DeCecco, a psychology professor at San Francisco State University who edits the *Journal of Homosexuality,* a scholarly publication, called LeVay's study "19th-century nonsense" that could have "dangerous" political ramifications.

"The Holocaust was not that long ago," he said. "If the AIDS epidemic got more severe, we wouldn't be far off from people looking for a cure for homosexuality and aborting fetuses that have abnormal brain structures."

The study received intense media attention when it was released. Many of the country's major daily newspapers published front-page articles about it, *Time* mentioned it on its cover, and it was the subject of a broadcast of *Nightline,* ABC television's nightly news interview and analysis program.

Steve Morin, a clinical psychologist who is a member of the board of directors of the American Psychological Association, said that the research "has been, by and large, misunderstood by the media. It is only a very small part of the understanding of the function of the hypothalamus and of the biological basis of sexual arousal and behavior."

LeVay, who is openly gay, agreed. The study "does not tell us what contributes to people's sexual orientation and development," he said. "I'm just saying there is a new way to study the topic."

The hypothalamus is a region of the brain that is known to control male sexual behavior. LeVay studied the hypothalamuses of 35 men and six women. Eighteen of the subjects were gay men who had died of complications from AIDS, as had a 19th subject who was a bisexual man.

LeVay said that his research presumed that the remaining men, six of whom had died of complications from AIDS, were heterosexual and that all six of the women were heterosexual. LeVay said he was unable to obtain brain samples from deceased lesbians.

In his *Science* article LeVay said that the size of a specific area of the hypothalamus was twice as large in the presumed heterosexuals as it was in the openly gay men. Researchers had previously observed that the area was twice as large in heterosexual men as it was in women.

As a result, LeVay concluded that "sexual orientation in humans is amenable to study at the biological level." However, he cautioned that "further interpretation of the results of this study must be considered speculative."

Still, LeVay said he believes that there is an inevitable trend toward finding biological explanations for behaviors that were once thought to have psychological origins. "Something as relatively fixed as sexual orientation should have a basis in brain structure," he said.

Critics of the study contended that both LeVay's premise and his research methodology were faulty. Anne Fausto-Sterling, a professor of medical science at Brown University in Providence, R.I., noted that LeVay's study used an unusually small sample of test subjects and that its "entire sample of gay men consists of men who died of AIDS. It is well-known that AIDS affects the brain."

LeVay noted both weaknesses in his *Science* article, stressing that his findings are tentative and must be verified by other researchers before they can be considered conclusive. But Fausto-Sterling said the project is also flawed by its overall view of homosexuality.

"I think that the idea that homosexuality is defined only on the basis of sexual-object choice is a very bad idea of what homosexuality is in any culture," she said. "It completely ignores the work done in gay history in the past 15 years and ignores the work done locating homosexuality in a historical moment." LeVay's research, she said, "takes a complicated, intricate gender system and reduces it to whom you want to screw."

DeCecco agreed. "Homosexuality is not one thing," he said. "It's had many, many different meanings over the centuries." DeCecco said that even today, the definition of homosexuality is changing as young adults "cross gender boundaries" to experiment sexually with members of both sexes.

"As young people find out what it is to be sexual and erotic, they find that these categories of sexual orientation are terribly crude and stigmatized," he said. LeVay's study feeds homophobia by "still saying something went wrong to cause homosexuality," he added.

But Morin said allegations like DeCecco's are off the mark. "It's important to note that the size difference is not presented as pathological in LeVay's paper," he said. And LeVay said he never suggested that "gay men are straight men with holes in their heads. There has been a lot of misinterpretation of my findings on both sides."

LeVay said he was surprised that the articles received so much attention. "I've been doing science all my life without any news media paying attention to what I was doing," he said. "It was a topic close to people's hearts."

Although LeVay praised some coverage of the study, such as that on the Public Broadcasting Service's *MacNeil/Lehrer NewsHour*, he said that much of the reporting "raised this huge issue of what it means to be gay in a circuslike way. It makes it hard to keep your eyes on the significance of what I did and did not do."

David Perlman, science writer for the *San Francisco Chronicle*, said the media paid attention to the report because readers want to know the cause of homosexuality. "Everybody is interested in homosexuality, even more so since the AIDS epidemic," he said.

Perlman said that LeVay's research provided an opportunity to further destigmatize homosexuality. The study says "that gay sexual orientation is not such a terrible choice," he said. "The more I can do to diminish the prevalence of homophobia, the more useful I can be."

But some activists said that even the well-intentioned coverage was still misguided. Hollie Conley, the response chairwoman of the San Francisco Bay area chapter of the Gay and Lesbian Alliance Against Defamation, a media watchdog group, said, "A lot of liberal media say that this proves what we've been saying, as if that's been in question for decades."

As for those who are not well-intentioned, she said, "When you're talking about hard homophobes, it's not going to change their arguments. It may make them even more adamant."

Similarly, Tim Drake, director of the privacy project at the National Gay and Lesbian Task Force, a lobbying group, said, "We received a phenomenal number of calls about this story from straight publications that couldn't care less about gays and lesbians otherwise."

Another reason for the intensive attention LeVay's article received was the advance information about it that *Science* made available to reporters. The magazine regularly uses news releases to alert the media to stories in its forthcoming editions, and a summary of the LeVay study filled the entire first page of the news release *Science* prepared to publicize its August 30 edition. The news release also included a series of articles about gender differences, including one that was tied to LeVay's research.

"They packaged LeVay's article so that it would get attention," said one reporter, who requested anonymity. "It did."

Colin Norman, *Science*'s managing news editor, defended the publicity effort. LeVay's report "is clearly a paper that, if its findings are correct, would have important implications," he said. "We decided it was newsworthy."

But Fausto-Sterling said that *Science* is "enamored of any piece that is biologically determinist. It is willing to publish something very preliminary if it shows that a behavior or a quality is lodged in the brain."

Unfortunately, she said, the media fall prey to *Science*'s inclination. "The sort of gay study that usually gets done wouldn't show up in *Science* and wouldn't get the publicity *Science* gets," she said. "The research about what homosexuality is, how it comes into existence, and how we understand it is far more complex than LeVay's study, but there hasn't been a *Time* magazine article on those gay studies."

TALES OF A REPUBLICAN SCION: DEE MOSBACHER, DAUGHTER OF THE SECRETARY OF COMMERCE, COMES OUT ON CAPITOL HILL

by Robert Julian

October 22, 1991

With one notable exception, George Bush's cabinet has the charm and glamour of a JCPenney white sale. The exception is Secretary of Commerce Robert Mosbacher, a multimillionaire Texas oil baron whose family history reads like an eyebrow-raising season on *Dynasty*. Handsome, charming, and well-educated, Robert is the perfect Blake Carrington, right down to his thick head of silver hair. The Mosbacher entourage includes a glamorous and ambitious third wife, Georgette Mosbacher, who is approximately the same age as Robert's eldest daughter, Dee. Showing no patience for closets—even of the gilded variety—this daughter is openly lesbian.

The distaff Steven Carrington of this *Dynasty* equation is a psychiatrist who lives in San Francisco with her lover of 16 years, Nanette Gartrell, also a psychiatrist. In late June Mosbacher took on the Steven Carrington mantle by going public in *The Washington Post* with her 20-year involvement in the gay rights movement.

"I'm a strong advocate of coming out," Mosbacher says. "As a physician and psychiatrist I really do believe that our mental health suffers more than we'll ever know by maintaining that kind of secrecy. It just chips away at us." At 42, Mosbacher, known for her frankness and occasional intransigence, is a petite woman who laughs as she unequivocally describes herself as the butch partner in her long-term relationship.

Her oil-rich father did not find himself in philosophical agreement with his offspring. But instead of punching out his daughter's lover in front of the fireplace in true *Dynasty* fashion, he provided personal support in an arguably un-Republican way. "She is my daughter, and I love her," Robert stated in a prepared statement this summer. "I am proud of her for what she is, and I hope she feels that way about me."

Falling Far From the Tree

Dee Mosbacher's public honesty on controversial subjects sends shock waves through Establishment circles, especially when it comes from the scion of a family that has been socially prominent for most of this century. Mosbacher's paternal grandfather, Emil, became a millionaire through stock market investments by the time he was 21. Wisely cashing out of the market before the crash of '29, he remained wealthy enough to raise his sons, Robert and Emil Jr., on New York's Park Avenue. After college Robert moved to Houston and amassed his own $200-million fortune as an oil and gas prospector.

With the Mosbacher millions came political connections of the Republican kind. Emil Jr. was Richard Nixon's first chief of protocol. An old friend and adviser of George Bush, Robert raised $75 million for Bush's 1988 presidential campaign while working as his national finance chairman, a gesture that helped earn him the appointment as secretary of commerce.

Robert's paternal blessing may be reassuring, but without it Mosbacher would hardly be out in the cold. In 1988 she paid $1.65 million for a house she shares with Gartrell in San Francisco's exclusive Presidio Heights neighborhood. Comfortably ensconced in the living room of her home, Mosbacher smiles as she describes the unexpected outcome of her father's response to her coming-out. "Dad told me he's gotten only positive, supportive letters about having said what he said—from both inside and outside the Bush administration," Mosbacher says. "I think it may be the most unanimous approval he's received about anything since he's been at the commerce department."

Robert's busy schedule makes regular communication difficult, but he manages to speak with his daughter every three or four months. According to Mosbacher, her father is not privy to inside information on the Bush administration, but she points out, "my father prefers to keep me in the dark about what goes on behind closed doors in Washington, D.C., especially regarding lesbian and gay issues. He knows how I feel, and he probably knows what I'd do with any inside information if he passed it on."

Capitol Hill heavies have managed to keep the wayward heiress—and her politics—at a safe distance. "My only firsthand experience with Washington's power brokers came in the early '70s, when I was demonstrating against them, organizing marches, and picketing the White House," Mosbacher admits. "I sent a letter to *The Washington Post* saying I support of abortion rights while my uncle was Nixon's chief of protocol—it was before *Roe* v. *Wade*. In the letter, I identified myself as Emil Mosbacher Jr.'s niece, and when the paper called my uncle to confirm our relationship, he said he'd never heard of me."

Coming Out on the Hill

In 1971, one year after her mother died of leukemia, Mosbacher moved from Houston to Washington, D.C., leaving behind a life she portrays as "privileged, protected, insular, and segregated."

Describing herself as a lifelong "jock," Mosbacher says she played volleyball and field hockey at Houston's private Kinkaid High School. An all-conference basketball player, she also won many trophies racing her 14-foot sailboat on Galveston Bay. But Mosbacher reveals that her sexual orientation did not come into focus until she moved to the nation's capital.

"I really was a lesbian, but I was unconscious about it," Mosbacher recalls. "One day I ran across this ad for an abortion rights meeting that listed a whole bunch of speakers—a lawyer, a leftist political activist, an antiwar activist, and a lesbian. I thought, *Wow, I've never seen anything advertising a lesbian speaker.* I decided to go see what a lesbian looked like.

"I went to this meeting, and I got really fired up about the abortion issue," she continues. "But I got even more fired up and interested when they didn't announce who the lesbian speaker was. I was so disappointed that I had to investigate further. I got involved in the abortion movement and later found out that every speaker that night was a lesbian. *Everybody* was a dyke. I saw they were all regular people like me, and then it just clicked. It was really quick for me. A few months after I moved to Washington, I came out."

Although Mosbacher would often bring a lover along to family get-togethers to meet her father, she did not come out to him in a formal way. "We didn't talk about it per se," she explains. "In that period I was fairly radical politically. I sort of got away from the family and was living with four or five friends—comrades, as we called each other—in an apartment where my share of the rent was $15 a month. I was involved in the Young Socialists Alliance, antiwar movement, and women's movement.

"When Nanette and I got together, we called my brother after being out of touch for several years," Mosbacher recalls. "And he said, 'I'm really glad you called. I thought you were upset with me for some reason, that I might have said something antigay.' Then I realized all my family knew I was a lesbian. When my father learned I was a lesbian, I think he went through the things most parents go through—questions like 'What did I do wrong?' and 'Is it my fault?' But he tried to understand it, and now we have a mutually loving relationship. He adores Nanette, and he's been really supportive and wonderful to both of us. My father is always there when I need him, and I love and appreciate this."

Mosbacher continues to visit her father on occasion, but their meetings rarely occur in the company of his third wife, Georgette, owner of La Prairie cosmetics. Profiles in various publications, including *Vanity Fair,* portray the 44-year-old, thrice-married Georgette as a graduate of the sultry vixen school of social climbing, not unlike the infamous Alexis Carrington Colby.

"We're not close," Mosbacher remarks in reference to her stepmother. "We don't see a lot of each other. Uh, well…" she stammers uncomfortably, "I really don't want to talk about it." The Mosbacher silence speaks volumes.

Political Aspirations

Putting family tangles aside, Mosbacher is more at home with serious topics like her job as regional medical chief for San Mateo County, Calif., where she deals with mental health issues. Her psychiatric specialty is schizophrenia, and she works with the severely mentally ill who can't afford private services. She also maintains a private practice and serves on several boards, including San Francisco's Lyon-Martin Clinic, which began as a lesbian health service but now serves all poor and working-class women who can't afford health care. A graduate of Houston's Baylor College of Medicine, Mosbacher completed her residency in psychiatry at Harvard University. She also holds a Ph.D. in social psychology from Union Graduate School in Cincinnati.

Yet Mosbacher reserves her greatest intensity for the subject of politics. "Politics is definitely in the blood," Mosbacher declares. "I would consider running for office someday, but I'm not sure if I could run on the Democratic Party ticket or if it would have to be something farther to the left. I would like to make the Democratic Party more honest and true to itself. I think some of the values liberal Democrats used to hold have been lost, and that's sad."

In spite of the positive letters her father received when she came out, Mosbacher is even more pessimistic about the ability of the Republican Party to accommodate the lesbian and gay agenda. "Individually, people can be receptive to the needs of lesbians and gays, but I worry about pressure from the right wing of the Republican Party," she says. "Lesbian and gay issues will be sacrificed to keep the party together. I'm concerned about our ability to receive institutionalized support. Why haven't we had more major changes? It's because of the conservative elements of the Republican Party."

Mosbacher is particularly disappointed by the failure of the Bush administration to reverse the defense department policy requiring the discharge of lesbian and gay soldiers. "This policy is not supportable in any way," she says. "There's certainly no evidence to support that gays and lesbians are any less capable of doing the job required by military service. We've always been in the military, that's clearly documented, and we have generally conducted ourselves with honor."

When asked to describe what needs to be done to change Washington's conservative climate, Mosbacher responds with her own call to arms. "I want more people to do what I'm doing," she says. "There have to be more gay relatives of people who hold high office, and they have to come out. Look at the recent outing of Pentagon official [Pete Williams]. I have mixed feelings about the outing, but when it comes to those who make policy, who are responsible for carrying out a policy that is harmful to us, who are actively involved in destroying our lives, then I'm pushed to say we have to take that step."

Showing her true activist colors, Mosbacher goes even further. "When people in Congress are ruining our lives by their homophobic actions and those people are closeted gays and lesbians, I have very little patience," she asserts. "We need to hold them accountable for their actions. I feel people deserve a right to privacy, but I strongly advocate coming out. At every level, anybody who thinks they can't afford to come out needs to think again. People don't understand the price that's being exacted from them by staying in the closet."

CALIFORNIA EXPLODES AFTER GOVERNOR KILLS WORKPLACE BIAS BAN

by John Gallagher

November 5, 1991

A series of demonstrations of such size and intensity that they surprised even gay and lesbian political leaders greeted California governor Pete Wilson's veto of a measure that would have banned antigay employment discrimination.

The effect of the veto, which Wilson announced on September 29, a Sunday, could spread beyond the protest to produce long-term changes in California politics and the role of gays and lesbians within it, observers said.

"This is Stonewall II," said Torie Osborn, executive director of the Los Angeles Gay and Lesbian Community Services Center. "The veto tapped into a well of anger and pain fed by ten years of AIDS. Its energizing and mobilizing people like you wouldn't believe."

Many gays and lesbians charged Wilson with betraying them out of political expediency. As recently as last April, Wilson, a Republican, told reporters that he was "likely" to sign the bill, but beginning in August, he faced increasingly vocal opposition from conservative members of his own party. The day before Wilson announced his veto, Sen. John Seymour (R-Calif.), whom Wilson appointed to replace him in the U.S. Senate in January, dropped his support for the measure and publicly urged Wilson to veto it.

John Duran, Southern California chairman of the Lobby for Individual Freedom and Equality, a gay group that worked for passage of the measure, said that when Wilson was running for governor a year ago, both he and his opponent, former San Francisco mayor Dianne Feinstein, told LIFE officials that if elected, they would support any sort of antidiscrimination legislation. "We sent the message that either one was OK, and we got fucked," Duran said.

In his four-page veto message, Wilson said he rejected the legislation because it was "a complex statutory proposal of remedies and procedures" that would impose unfair burdens on businesses, particularly small ones, and unleash a flood of litigation. He also argued that gays and lesbians were already protected from employment discrimination by a number of state laws and court decisions.

The measure had already been stripped of a ban on antigay housing discrimination. State assembly member John Burton, a Democrat, called Wilson's statement "sophistry meant to hide the fact that Pete made a political decision based on internal Republican politics."

Angry gays and lesbians responded to the veto message with a series of protests across the state. The day after the veto was announced, Los Angeles activists held rallies at two government office buildings, one of which was damaged when protesters splattered red liquid on it and broke a glass door. Subsequent rallies, most of which were peaceful, attracted thousands of lesbians and gays in West Hollywood, San Diego, Sacramento, and Garden Grove.

One of the most dramatic protests occurred September 30 in San Francisco, where a rally and peaceful march by 7,000 protesters ended with a small group of demonstrators breaking away from the crowd and doing $250,000 in damage to a state office building. The protesters threw newspaper vending racks through the building's windows, set fire to offices, shattered a glass window that was created by openly gay artist Albert March, and pinned a handful of police officers inside the building.

Meanwhile, another splinter group surrounded mayoral candidate Frank Jordan, a former San Francisco police chief who had appeared at the rally to condemn the veto. Jordan was thrown against a plate glass window but escaped with only cuts after losing a shoe. Activists have criticized Jordan since 1989, when he presided over a violent police crackdown on an AIDS protest.

Willis Casey, Jordan's successor as police chief, said the outpouring of gay and lesbian rage at the protest was the most intense display that San Francisco had seen since 1979, when gays and lesbians rose up to protest the conviction of supervisor Dan White, who had killed Mayor George Moscone and openly gay supervisor Harvey Milk, of manslaughter instead of murder.

For a week after the veto, protesters dogged Wilson at his public appearances around the state. Protesters rallied outside the opening of a museum exhibit in Los Angeles September 30 because Wilson was there, and the next day about 300 demonstrators drowned out Wilson's speech at Stanford University's centennial celebration. They showered him with eggs, papers, and oranges, and at the end of his speech, Wilson assailed the demonstrators for using "fascist tactics."

Eighteen protesters were arrested in San Francisco outside a hotel where Wilson was attending a fund-raiser October 2. Wilson's aides denied that the protests caused Wilson to cut back on public appearances but had refused to confirm that he was present at the dinner until after he had left.

Activists said that Wilson's public appearances may attract protesters indefinitely. "Wherever the governor goes, wherever there's an organized gay community, he's going to be confronted and challenged," said Robert Bray, a spokesman for the National Gay and Lesbian Task Force, a political group.

"Even is his appearances are limited to high-security, high-dollar, black-tie–donor events, I wouldn't be surprised if a few people didn't stand up and challenge him," Bray said. Activists may infiltrate the events, he added.

The outburst of large demonstrations every day for more than a week in Southern California surprised many activists, who had long complained about apathy in the region. "In Los Angeles, which never was very political before, we've been getting hundreds of people at rallies," said Richard Jennings, executive director of the Los Angeles chapter of the Gay and Lesbian Alliance Against Defamation, a media watchdog group. The protesters "include bankers and, one assumes, gay Republicans and lots of members of the previously silent majority," he said.

Duran said, "I didn't think that we had it in us in Los Angeles. Nothing has ever pulled people in Los Angeles off their bar stools, but I'll be damned if they didn't put their Cape Cods down and join us." And Mickey Wheatley, a civil rights attorney who is a member of the Los Angeles chapter of the direct-action group Queer Nation, called the Southern California rallies "an explosion of creative energy unlike anything we've ever seen."

Nonetheless, media coverage of the protests centered on only a few violent incidents. "The mainstream media don't understand social movements," Osborn said. When people take to the streets, the activity "becomes renegade, random, chaotic, and uncontrollable to them," she said.

Jennings alleged that some reporters encouraged violence. "The TV crews were applauding when plate glass windows were broken at the state building," he said. But police attacks on protesters in Los Angeles received little notice, he added.

Osborn said that the energy created by protest may lead to a renaissance of gay political power in the state. "The righteous anger that people feel will translate into something," she said. "When momentum happens at the grassroots level in a broad-based way, it always changes the face of things."

Matthew Coles, director of the Northern California gay rights chapter of the American Civil Liberties Union, added, "Five or ten years from now, when we've got the legislation enacted and we have an extremely powerful political movement in California, we can say that Wilson did us a favor without even knowing it. If that is the case, I'm sure he didn't intend it."

But others said the momentum must be skillfully directed to be effective. "If it's not transformed into something, it will lead to violence," Duran said. "The challenge to the gay and lesbian leadership will be to channel the momentum into something productive."

The most immediate political effects are likely to be on the local level. On the day after Wilson announced the veto, Mark Zapalik, a conservative organizer who is spearheading a campaign to overturn a ban on antigay discrimination in Concord, Calif., urged the city's voters to "duplicate the governor's action" by repealing the ban through an initiative. But Robert Birle, cochairman of the Contra Costa Alliance of Gay and Lesbian Organizations, said that the veto will "motivate people in Concord, more on our side than the other."

Activists elsewhere said they may file initiatives that would ban antigay discrimination locally. Ken Yeager, a board member of the Bay Area Municipal Elections Committee, a gay group in San Jose, said that his organization is considering proposing a nondiscrimination or domestic-partnership ordinance there. "All of us feel the need to have a victory," he said.

Several prominent openly gay Republicans in the state said they would leave their party to protest the veto. Among them were Ray Chalker, editor of a gay newspaper in San Francisco, Cliff Anchor, a Wilson appointee to the state Selective Service board, and Tom Larkin, a former Republican party official and state senate candidate.

Frank Ricchiazzi, executive director of the political action committee of the Log Cabin Republican Clubs of California, a gay political group, said his group's members are "bitter" about the veto. Although the group has withdrawn its endorsement of Seymour, Ricchiazzi said that its members would continue to work with Wilson on other issues.

"He's still got three more years in office, and we have a lot of issues that deal with AIDS funding and other things, and we can't cut off communication," Ricchiazzi said. "The gay community had better know that when it comes to fighting in the system, we have a hard-core committed group of Green Berets in the Log Cabin clubs. We have a group of people who are like dogs. They put their jaws around the ankle and will not let go."

Some activists noted that at least two other Republican governors are staunch opponents of antigay bias. One of them, Massachusetts governor William Weld, publicly urged Wilson to sign the ban, and in Minnesota, Gov. Arne Carlson served as honorary cochairman of a Minneapolis fundraiser for the Human Rights Campaign Fund, a gay lobbying group.

Carlson "has said if there were a gay rights bill on his desk, he would sign it," said Ann DeGroot, executive director of the Gay and Lesbian Community Action Council in Minneapolis. "I'm not a Republican, but I have a sense that he would support efforts against discrimination," she said.

Rich Tafel, a Weld aide who is president of the Log Cabin Clubs of America, said that Wilson "jumped in bed with the political right wing" but predicted that other California Republicans will "rise up to take the role" of promoting gay rights.

But Larkin said he left the Republican Party because "I felt we don't have a chance there anymore. The religious right controls more than half the votes on the state central committee. All you hear about is religion." Larkin asked gays and lesbians to boycott the party "so that we can knock the superconservatives out and then go back and clean up."

At a state Republican convention two weeks before Wilson announced his veto, delegates demanded that Wilson reject the measure, and the Rev. Lou Sheldon, head of the Traditional Values

Coalition, a right-wing group, repeated his pledge to challenge the measure with a ballot initiative if Wilson signed it into law.

Sheldon's initiative was likely to hurt Seymour's chances in the Republican primary next June, since it was expected to spur a high conservative turnout that would benefit Seymour's principal opponent, conservative U.S. representative William Dannemeyer. "Pete is overly concerned about returning Seymour to the Senate," Larkin said.

Other insiders said that Wilson is considering running for president in 1996 and was told by Stuart Spencer, a onetime consultant to former president Ronald Reagan, that he would be hard-pressed to explain his support of the antidiscrimination bill in conservative states during the presidential primaries. Duran said, "I don't think we could have done anything that would have overcome his presidential ambitions."

But in the short term, at least, the veto won Wilson few political points. Although he earned the antagonism of the gays, lesbians, and other supporters of the antidiscrimination ban, his veto apparently failed to placate conservatives. Sheldon said after the veto that Wilson "is not family-friendly and has not been sufficiently rehabilitated to warrant reelection."

Sheldon also demanded that Wilson apologize for saying in his veto message that he regrets "any false comfort that may be derived from the veto by the tiny minority of mean-spirited, gay-bashing bigots."

The veto also seemed to be unpopular among moderates. By a 2-1 ratio, respondents to a *Los Angeles Times* poll of more than 1,000 Californians said they believed that Wilson killed the measure "mainly because of political pressure from Republican conservatives," rather than because "it's bad and unnecessary legislation."

In a California Poll that was conducted shortly before the veto was announced, 62% of respondents said they wanted Wilson to sign the bill. The only group in which a majority of respondents said they wanted Wilson to veto the bill were those who identified themselves as "strongly conservative" Republicans. The California Poll results were announced the day after Wilson's veto message, and activists alleged that Wilson hurriedly scheduled the announcement for a Sunday so he would not appear to be influenced by the survey's findings.

Duran said that Wilson "has no friends on the Right, and now he has alienated the Middle and the Left. It's so dumb." However, he said he fears that Wilson may continue to try to appeal to conservatives by giving in to them on other issues. "How many times will this come up on AIDS education, sex education, or the arts?" Duran said. "Every time the right wing raises its ugly head, will he capitulate?"

Whatever the real reason for the veto, activists agreed that the justification Wilson gave for it—opposition from businesses—was a smoke screen. "The veto message is stunningly dishonest and so incoherent that I'm surprised he put his name on it," Coles said.

Activists noted that just two days after rejecting the antidiscrimination measure, Wilson signed a parental-leave bill that was strongly opposed by the state chamber of commerce and the California Manufacturers Association. Both groups had taken a neutral position on the antibias bill.

And civil libertarians disputed Wilson's claim that antigay employment bias was already forbidden by state law and court rulings. Although an executive order forbids antigay discrimination in state employment, Coles said that the state agency that processes bias complaints from public workers recently complained that it has no power to enforce its rulings.

Wilson also cited a 4–3 state supreme court decision that forbids antigay bias against gay and lesbian private-sector workers who had already disclosed their sexual orientation to employers, but Coles noted that the decision has never been tested since it was issued in 1979.

"While it's true that the court decision is the law, it's also true that no one who watches these things would say that it would stay law if it goes before the current court," Coles said. "For the great mass of employees, there's just no support in the law to the contention that people are already protected for antigay discrimination."

Just a week after vetoing the discrimination ban, Wilson signed a measure that would stiffen penalties for some crimes if they are shown to be motivated by antigay hate or bigotry toward other minority groups. Activists said Wilson's support for the measure was ironic, since several gay organizations reported that the veto of the antibias measure had spurred an upswing in antigay violence.

Osborn said that on one day during the week after the veto, her facility received more than 100 hate calls, all of which were linked to the veto. "We've had to double security," she said.

Los Angeles community center's legal director Roger Coggan added, "When the governor of California refuses to protect the basic rights of gays and lesbians to work, what message does it send about the government's willingness to protect our other basic rights? It's a message that resonates in the actions of gay and lesbian bashers."

State assembly member Terry Friedman, a Democrat who sponsored the vetoed measure, said he would reintroduce the bill when the legislature reconvenes in January, but insiders gave the measure little chance of success next year. Many activists said the most promising method for reviving the ban may be a ballot initiative. Duran said that LIFE has raised $40,000 to conduct a survey of voter attitudes toward an antidiscrimination initiative.

But Duran said that promoting the ballot initiative could cost at least $5 million, and he warned that its failure would be a serious setback to gay and lesbian organizing efforts. "If we put an initiative on the ballot and lose," he said, "we lose everything we have gained in 20 years, and we will have no say for ten years."

VERMONT LAWMAKERS APPROVE BIAS BAN; ENACTMENT IS LIKELY

by Chris Bull

May 19, 1992

Vermont's legislature approved a statewide ban on antigay discrimination April 15, due to aggressive backing from Gov. Howard Dean, a lack of strong opposition from religious conservatives, and six years of lobbying by activists.

"Support for gay rights legislation did not turn out to be the big political liability that many legislators had anticipated," said Susan Sussman, executive director of the state human rights commission, the agency that enforces Vermont's antidiscrimination laws. "Some legislators who had opposed the bill in the past changed their minds after hearing a lot about bias against gays and lesbians."

The measure, which is scheduled to take effect July 1, was approved 32–5 by the state senate and 76–68 by the state house of representatives before it was sent to Dean, who pledged to sign it by the end of May. The approval made Vermont's legislature the fourth state legislature since early 1991 to approve a ban on antigay discrimination. Bills in Hawaii, Connecticut, and New Jersey were signed into law, while a measure in California was vetoed by Gov. Pete Wilson.

William Schneider, a political analyst for the American Enterprise Institute, a Washington, D.C., policy group, said that the accelerated passage of the measures is evidence that "in many states, the gay and lesbian community is now a political force. It's clearly a well-organized constituency, and all organized constituencies get attention paid to them."

Schneider said that even though most Americans oppose discrimination, "they don't yet know the extent of discrimination against gays and lesbians. In the states that have enacted bills, the gay community has been able to demonstrate that."

Vermont's bias ban was first introduced in the state legislature in 1986. It forbids antigay discrimination in housing, employment, public accommodations, and provision of services, and it contains exemptions for religious organizations and for multiple-tenant residences if they contain fewer than three apartments and have an owner or a member of the owner's family living on the premises.

Sussman said that support for the bill was bolstered by the state legislature's debate in 1990 over enactment of a hate-crimes bill and by public testimony in favor of the antibias bill last February. In both cases, she said, debate demonstrated that antigay discrimination is widespread in Vermont.

"Four years ago, it didn't really get through to legislators that gay people actually suffer from violence and discrimination," she said. "This time, we had the facts solidly demonstrated, and there was more testimony about specific incidents."

The bill also benefited from strong lobbying by Dean, a Democrat who was elevated to the governorship in August 1991 when Gov. Richard Snelling, a Republican, died unexpectedly of a heart attack after eight months in office. Although Snelling had endorsed the bill shortly before his death, Sussman said that questions remain about whether he would have worked as aggressively for the bill's passage as Dean did.

Both Republican and Democratic Party leaders in the legislature worked hard for passage of the bill, activists said. When the state house was nearing a vote on the measure, political leaders singled out the house for special attention when majority whip Sean Campbell said publicly that the bill was "going to be a tough one to get passed" by his colleagues.

And in an incident that was uncommon in Vermont politics, house speaker Ralph Wright took aside state representative Robert Starr for what Wright called "a man-to-man talk about morals" when Starr introduced a motion to reconsider the house's approval of the bill just a day after it had been approved.

Starr had voted to approve the bill, saying during debate that he had learned firsthand about discrimination as a child, when he was taunted by classmates because he had not grown up in a French-speaking home. But he called for the reconsideration after receiving about 70 telephone calls from constituents who opposed his support for the bill. Although Wright was not able to persuade Starr to drop the motion for reconsideration, the motion failed, and Starr acknowledged while asking for the reconsideration that "inside, I am not comfortable with what I'm doing."

Activists said that several legislators who had taken no position on the bill were swayed by an emotional speech given by openly gay state representative Ronald Squires during debate on the measure April 10. Squires said that "even conservatives who voted against the bill came up to me and said that I should not take their votes personally. Some of the stereotyping that creeped into previous debates over the bill was not able to come up this time around."

Most of the lobbying against the measure originated with two antigay groups, Vermonters for Constitutional Preservation and the Committee on Public Health Concerns, but Sussman said that efforts backfired. "They were responsible for a lot of hateful testimony that made discrimination all that much more evident," she said.

State representative Megan Price, who had voted against the ban in previous years, said during debate on the measure that the "misinformation and fear" expressed by the two groups' lobbyists "convinced me of the need for this bill" and caused her to vote in favor of approving the ban. "This bill is a matter of fairness," she said. "I am tired of my own bigotry, and I am wondering what happened to the swell people I knew in high school who were a little different."

Price added, "I have heard men say, 'If I hire these gay men, what if they make a pass at me?' Well, welcome to the world of women. You can be the sickest heterosexual on the block, but you've got all the rights."

Schneider said that in Vermont, as in the five states that have already enacted bans on anti-gay bias, lobbying from well-organized religious groups was largely absent from the debate. When opposition from religious groups is present, he said, its strength often overwhelms lobbying by gays and lesbians.

"When both sides in the fight are well-organized, it's a question of politicians figuring out which side will give them the most trouble," Schneider said. "In Vermont the decision was easy, but in other states the religious right is so single-minded on the issue that it's hard for politicians to go against them. Most people who support gay rights don't want to be single-issue voters, but the religious right is not uncomfortable with that at all."

THE NEWSROOM BECOMES A BATTLEGROUND: IS THE MEDIA'S SIEGE ON LESBIANS IN THE WOMEN'S MOVEMENT A DESPERATE ATTEMPT TO UNDERMINE FEMINISM?

by Donna Minkowitz

May 19, 1992

Since last fall the media have generated an unprecedented blitz of stories on the women's movement. But the majority, most notably novelist Sally Quinn's widely syndicated column attacking movement leaders, emphasize divisions between heterosexual and lesbian feminists, focusing on the supposed danger lesbians pose to the movement. Does media homophobia skew their coverage so dramatically that they are unable to report objectively on the movement? Many journalists and feminists—chief among them, Gloria Steinem—say yes.

"They would only listen to me after they established that I had a boyfriend," says Naomi Wolf, author of *The Beauty Myth: How Images of Beauty Are Used Against Women,* a 1991 feminist best-seller that has garnered widespread attention in the nation's print and electronic media. "You could almost see their relief that I happen to be sleeping with a man." For a recent article in *People* magazine, editors even asked Wolf to pose for a photo with her boyfriend. (She refused.) While the media were "bending over backward to establish that I and other feminist authors are heterosexual," Wolf complains, "reporters covering the resurgence of feminism have totally left out lesbians, except as a tactic to fundamentally discredit certain feminists. It's divide and conquer—you know, 'You, mother of two, having nothing in common with this scary, fetus-crucifying seducer of Girl Scouts.'"

Beginning in October with Anita Hill's confrontation with Supreme Court justice nominee Clarence Thomas and an all-male Senate judiciary committee on national TV, this country has seen a nonstop explosion of media coverage about the women's movement. The threat to abortion rights and the highly publicized rape trials of William Kennedy Smith and Mike Tyson only increased the media bonanza. Suddenly feminism was on the cover of every major magazine and the new bumper crop of best-selling feminist authors were guests on every interview show. Pundits surveying the upcoming presidential election suddenly found it necessary to examine the women's vote, and Democratic presidential candidates argued loudly about who had the best records on women's rights. But the rash of coverage about the movement has either not mentioned lesbians at all or brought them up only to suggest that they embarrass or endanger organized feminism.

In a column in *The New York Times* last October, essayist William Safire amplified the hinted accusations of Sen. Alan Simpson (R-Wyo.) that Hill, who alleged she had been sexually harassed by Thomas, was a lesbian, and the smear was later picked up by Richard Johnson, a gossip columnist at the New York *Daily News*. But the main media foray against lesbians was sparked by National Organization for Women president Patricia Ireland's decision to come out in an *Advocate* interview last December. From a *Los Angeles Times* article accusing NOW of being "out of touch" because its leader has a woman companion to a *New York Times Magazine* piece questioning whether Ireland can legitimately represent American women, the press suggested over and over again that Ireland and lesbians as a whole taint the movement. In a firestorm of blatant homophobia, the media revived the specter of the man-hating lesbian extremist in the guise of protecting feminism's best interests.

"They present us this way because the media always want to bolster what they see as a kinder, gentler feminism," Wolf says. "It's political propaganda on their part, dividing feminists into 'ugly, man-hating' lesbians on the one hand and supposedly 'gentler' heterosexuals on the other. Women are granted no chance to unite across differences of sexual affiliation, because we'd be zillions times more powerful if we did."

Men Reporting on Women

Many newswomen and some newsmen have become increasingly critical of what they say is the antilesbian bias of their colleagues. Says Pulitzer Prize–winning *Boston Globe* columnist Ellen Goodman: "There's a great deal of homophobia in the media. And that, combined with the fact that the media have always marginalized the more demanding forms of feminism, is why journalists call lesbianism a fringe issue and say it threatens the movement."

Village Voice media critic James Ledbetter explains, "One of the favorite ploys to attack the movement is to set up a division between 'fringe' and 'mainstream.'"

While a growing number of journalists echo Goodman's and Ledbetter's views, they are usually not the ones given space to write about lesbians in the movement. Only two newspapers ran opinion columns defending Ireland in the wake of her disclosure, but dozens ran commentaries accusing her of tainting the movement with lesbianism.

"It's no wonder the media have trouble covering feminism and lesbians fairly, when most of the country's newspapers are owned and operated by men," says *San Francisco Chronicle* reporter Elaine Herscher, a board member of the National Lesbian and Gay Journalists Association, a professional group.

The American Society of Newspaper Editors, the association for top editors, reports that only 9.7% of its membership is female. In a recent study by Women, Men, and Medicine, a project of the University of Southern California in Los Angeles, only 34% of front-page stories in the nation's major newspapers had female bylines, and only one quarter of opinion pieces on editorial pages were by women.

National Public Radio reporter Maria Hinojosa says, "The gay angle in stories is mostly conceptualized in terms of men. My editors will never say to me, 'Be sure you talk to lesbians and gays,' for a particular story, but they will say, 'Be sure you talk to other groups'—such as African-Americans, Latinos, or Jewish voters." A few years ago, Hinojosa says, "there was one person at NPR saying 'We have to cover lesbians,' but there was some tension around it, some resistance to it. There was this attitude like, 'Just give us a break.'"

Peg Byron, an openly lesbian United Press International reporter, says, "Among the men who have power in the media, there's a general skepticism around women's accounts of our own experience. But they perceive lesbians as even more threatening and less credible because of the way we challenge male entitlements."

Perhaps the best indication of biases in the media's coverage of the women's movement has been many editors' choice of author Camille Paglia as a feminist spokesperson. Paglia, who has called lesbians "pathological" because they are not attracted to men, has been the subject of admiring profiles in *New York* magazine, *Esquire*, and elsewhere. "Her calling herself a feminist is sort of like a Nazi saying they're not anti-Semitic," says Steinem, a veteran woman's rights activist whose new work, *Revolution From Within: A Book of Self-Esteem,* has been on *The New York Times* best-seller list for over three months. "She's not a feminist. She's Phyllis Schlafly with sex added." Why would editors choose Paglia as a principal source for feminist viewpoints? Steinem, who has worked in journalism for over 30 years, cofounding the magazines *Ms.* and *New York,* where she was a political columnist, answers unhesitatingly: "Some of the press seizes on any woman who will accuse other women."

New York Post columnist Amy Pagnozzi, cofounder of the Post Minority Sorority, an organization for women, gay, and nonwhite journalists at the paper, adds, "It's always been a tactic of people in positions of power to take a token from the group they want to keep out and use them to guard the gate."

A Gatekeeper on the Edge

One such guard who sounded alarums on lesbians is Quinn, a former reporter who is married to Benjamin Bradlee, the recently retired editor in chief of The Washington Post. Quinn penned a volatile opinion column, which was subsequently syndicated to newspapers around the country. Setting the tone for many articles to follow, Quinn warned, "The movement today is more and more perceived as a fringe cause, often with overtones of lesbianism and man-hating. This notion was hardly dispelled by Patricia Ireland's announcement of a 'love relationship with a woman'... What kind of standards is she espousing?"

Quinn concluded the essay with a harangue that read like a ringing endorsement for a renewed effort to purge lesbians from the leadership of the women's movement. (The most infamous purge was engineered by Betty Friedan while serving as president of NOW in the early '70s.) Quinn asserted, "It is impossible to read the Ireland declaration and argue that the movement she leads is still in touch with the majority of women. The truth is that many women have come to see the feminist movement as antimale, antichild, antifamily, antifeminine. And therefore it has nothing to do with us." In her conclusion she called for "new leaders" who can "speak to the real issues confronting most women."

Quinn's commentary unleashed a torrent of anger among women journalists, many of them feminists of a decidedly mainstream bent. Martha Southgate, an editorial writer for the New York Daily News, says, "The column became sort of a myth among women journalists" because of the way it attacked feminism in the guise of saving it. Columnist Judy Mann, a Washington Post writer since 1972 and a colleague of Quinn's, admits, "I must say that I, along with a great many of my colleagues, had a great deal of problems with the piece. Sally is a very well-known journalist and author, but she has no historical standing within the community of people who have followed feminism. Her credentials on the subject are a bit sketchy. I don't see any reason why lesbians shouldn't be considered part of mainstream feminism."

"It was nauseating," says Susan Faludi, author of the best-selling Backlash: The Undeclared War Against American Women. "The only time she ever weighs in on feminism is to attack it." Faludi, a Pulitzer Prize–winning Wall Street Journal reporter whose book's principal subject is the media's coverage of the women's movement, disputes Quinn's conclusion that lesbians threaten feminist gains.

WHAT AMERICA THINKS OF YOU: THE MORE THINGS CHANGE, THE MORE THEY STAY THE SAME

by John Gallagher

October 6, 1992

When *The Advocate* published its first issue 25 years ago, gays and lesbians were almost universally the target of public disdain or, at best, perplexity. Reflecting their readers' attitudes, newspapers had few qualms about describing gays as "perverts" or "pansies"—if they bothered to refer to them at all. In the process, the media reinforced a hostile environment that few gays and lesbians were willing to confront openly.

Although the Stonewall riots in New York City in 1969 imposed the idea of gay liberation on the public's consciousness, journalists straining for sensitivity did little to shatter stereotypes. Thus, a 1969 *Time* cover story titled "The Homosexual: Newly Visible, Newly Understood" included a handy catalog of "homosexual types." Included among them was "the blatant homosexual...the eunuch-like caricature of femininity" who may be "the catty hairdresser or the lisping, limp-wristed interior decorator." Back then, the guide was presented as a public service.

Today, of course, such sentiments seem ridiculously dated and offensive in a way that few educated people could miss. "I think that there has been a major positive change in the public's perception about homosexuality," says June Reinisch, head of the Kinsey Institute, which studies sexual behavior. Surely, gays and lesbians must agree that the public's attitude has changed. And it has.

But in some ways, it hasn't.

It is true that the gains made by gays and lesbians in the past 25 years are varied and impressive. By mid 1992, six states had enacted laws protecting gays from discrimination in employment or housing. From the local to the federal level, political candidates court the gay vote. Indeed, some of the candidates themselves are gay or lesbian, winning election in districts that are predominantly heterosexual.

But while there is demonstrable support for the belief that more and more people support gay rights, the vast majority of the population continues to view homosexuality as just plain wrong. In a June 1992 Gallup Poll, 57% of respondents said that homosexuality was "not an acceptable lifestyle." Responses collected in the 1991 general social survey conducted by the National Opinion Research Center at the University of Chicago were even more negative: About 75% of respondents said homosexuality is "always wrong."

Perhaps what is most surprising—or depressing—is the revelation that, despite activists' massive public education efforts, the perception of gays and lesbians appears to have changed little over the years. In 1982 51% of Gallup Poll respondents said homosexuality was "not acceptable." Nineteen years ago, 73% of the respondents to the NORC survey characterized homosexuality as "always wrong," a difference from the 1991 figure that is statistically insignificant. "The data," concludes Milton Mankoff, a professor of sociology at Queens College in New York City, "show a fair amount of stability."

Of course, some people dislike homosexuality more than others do. In NORC's surveys the typical respondent was more than twice as likely to think homosexuality is never wrong than were people above the age of 65.

Similarly, people who identify themselves as fundamentalists take a dimmer-than-average view of gays and lesbians. In a 1987 poll conducted by the *Los Angeles Times,* six out of ten fundamentalists surveyed said that relations between gays and lesbians in the privacy of their own homes should be illegal. Only 35% of respondents who were not fundamentalists took the same position.

Sometimes it's not a question of age or faith but of gender. Poll results suggest that men look askance at homosexuality more often than women do. In the June 1992 Gallup survey, for instance, 63% of the male respondents rejected homosexuality as acceptable, while 52% of the female respondents did.

"Men in general are more intolerant than women are," Mankoff says. "It may be a question of identity. But men are also more preoccupied with the idea that the normal order of things can't be violated. Women are looser in this regard."

Surveys also indicate that levels of tolerance toward gays and lesbians tend to vary according to race, with blacks more likely than whites to consider homosexuality wrong. An average of 72% of white respondents to the NORC survey over the years said they disapprove of homosexuality, while the figure for black respondents is 82%.

"There's still not full acceptance" of homosexuality in the black community, says Alvin Poussaint, a professor of psychiatry at the Harvard University medical school. "But there is an acceptance of the fact that homosexuality exists."

Of course, societal changes seldom come rapidly. "I don't think it's easy or going to happen quickly, but it's going in the right direction," says Reinisch. She points out that the public didn't have to learn just some things about homosexuality in the past 25 years—it had to learn *everything*. "People are coming out of an incredible well of ignorance," she notes.

And occasionally, the masses tumble back down the well. At the beginning of the AIDS epidemic, public acceptance of gays and lesbians remained about where it had been. But when the fear that heterosexuals might be at risk for the disease took hold in the mid '80s, acceptance of homosexuality dropped. Only at the end of the decade did the figure begin to rise again.

In a long-running survey of more than 200,000 college freshmen conducted at the University of programs, some school boards are abandoning gay-positive curricula. In New York City, for in-stance, city schools chancellor Joseph Fernandez attempted to end a bitter months-long debate No-vember 10 by threatening the 32 school districts under his jurisdiction with disciplinary action if they do not adopt some form of gay-positive curricula. Fernandez issued the ultimatum after five of the districts rejected *Children of the Rainbow*, a curriculum prepared by the city, because it includes favorable representations of gays and lesbians.

Janice Irvine, a professor of sociology at Tufts University in Medford, Mass., says that the growing in-fluence of the religious right "has changed the entire sex-education landscape. I'm not sure that advocates of sex education realize the insidiousness of the kind of education the religious right is fostering."

Advocates of nonsectarian sex education say that abstinence-based curricular damage AIDS edu-cation and family-planning efforts targeted at sexually active adolescents. In addition, they say, stu-dent are being denied crucial information about gays and lesbians that has the potential to reduce antigay discrimination and violence.

"Gays and lesbians are already marginalized in most high school curricula, and some of the absti-nence-based curricula are overtly homophobic," says SIECUS executive director Debra Haffner. "The presumption of the religious right's program is that all young people will grow up to be monogamous married adults, who actually are only a small percentage of Americans."

Irvine, Haffner, and other proponents of nonsectarian sex education say that schools should present abstinence and heterosexual marriage as two of many options available to teenagers. Such an approach, they say, allows students to make decisions based on knowledge rather than fear. In contrast, abstinence-based curricula stress the dangers of abortion and sexual activity, making them "fear-based," Haffner and Irvine say. Typically, such curricula discuss homosexuality only in connection with AIDS, they say.

For instance, *Sex Respect: The Option of True Sexual Freedom,* a federally funded outline that is the nation's most widely used abstinence-based curriculum, describes AIDS as "the sexually transmitted disease most common among homosexuals and bisexuals" and as nature's way of "making some kind of comment on sexual behavior." A review of the curriculum that was conducted by the federal Centers for Disease Control last year concluded that the curriculum's approach to AIDS attempts "to make a devastating disease even more frightening in order to more clearly limit behavioral choices to that which is being advanced."

In another review of he curriculum conducted last year, education researchers Bonnie Trudell and Marianna Whatley of the University of Wisconsin-Madison concluded that the curriculum "re-lies on scare tactics." Reporting their conclusions in the *Journal of Sex Education and Therapy*, Trudell and Whatley wrote that *Sex Respect* "ignores the reality that not all students are heterosexual. Some may be certain of a gay, lesbian, or bisexual orientation, whereas others may be confused at this point about their sexual preference."

Teen-Aid, another federally funded abstinence-based curriculum that is widely used, attempts to demonstrate the dangers of homosexuality by citing a study of gay men in San Francisco in which 74% of respondents tested positive for antibodies to HIV, the virus believed to lead to AIDS. Even though analysts have warned against extrapolating from the study because its sample is small, Carole Chervin, a senior staff attorney for the Planned Parenthood Federation of America, says that *Teen-Aid'*s reference to its results is "just about the most specific citation in the entire curriculum. The whole thing is loaded with inaccurate and outdated sources, except in the one instance where they believe a study makes their point. It just doesn't give a balanced presentation of the facts."

In New York and New Jersey, nearly all of the opposition to gay-positive sex education curricula has come from conservative parent groups and officials of the Roman Catholic Church. In some cases, even minor, seemingly innocuous references to gays and lesbians have incurred the wrath of this coalition. For instance, only two of the 442 pages in the *Children of the Rainbow* mention gays and lesbians, but the fracas over the curriculum has centered around those two pages.

Among the passages that have drawn fire are the instruction that educators "be aware of the changing concept of *family* in today's society" and notations that "children of lesbian/gay parents may have limited experience with male/female parental situations; if there is no representation of their lives in the classroom, they may suddenly be made to feel different" and that "educators have the potential to help increase the tolerance and acceptance of the lesbian/gay community and to decrease the staggering number of hate crimes perpetrated against them."

Even stronger criticism has been hurled at the school system's decision to include in *Children of the Rainbow'*s bibliography three children's books that are intended to promote respect for gay and lesbian parents. The books—*Daddy's Roommate, Heather Has Two Mommies,* and *Gloria Goes to Gay Pride*—have been widely praised by educators, but Mary Cummins, president of the Queens school board, said in a letter to 22,000 parents in the borough that the books must be excluded from the bibliography because "we will not accept two people of the same sex engaged in deviant sex practices as a 'family.'"

In New Jersey, meanwhile, a conservative parents group succeeded earlier this year in persuading the New Providence school district in Union County to reject *Learning About Family Life,* a Rutgers University Press curriculum for use from kindergarten through 12th grade. The parents group argued that descriptions of reproductive organs and the rectum that were contained in the first-grade portion of the curriculum could lead to masturbation and homosexuality.

Faced with such complaints, many school boards turn to *Sex Respect, Teen-Aid,* and other abstinence-based curricula. These curricula have been developed under the Adolescent Family Life Act, which was signed into law by President Reagan in 1982 and provided $10 million in federal funding for the creation of abstinence-only sex education curricula. In 1983 the American Civil Liberties union filed a court challenge to the Adolescent Family Life Act, saying that the legislation illegally broaches the constitutionally mandated separation of church and state. Nine years later, the challenge is still pending in federal court.

Irvine says that the enactment of the Adolescent Family Life Act marked a sea change in the religious right's approach to sex education. Prior to the act's passage, she says, conservative groups, led by the John Birch Society, expended much of their energy on unsuccessful attempts to bar sex education from schools altogether. But after passage of the act, the groups turned their attention to influencing the content of sex education curricula in schools.

"The Right lost the battle to keep sex education out of the schools," Irvine says. "But advocates of sex education have gotten complacent and said, 'Well, at least we have some kind of sex education in the school.' They don't realize quite how destructive fear-based education can be."

Carole Vance, an associate research scientist at the Columbia University School of Public Health in New York City, says that the emphasis on abstinence that the religious right espoused in the early '80s is more appealing to parents than its attempts to keep sex education out of school were in the '60s and '70s. "It's very difficult to tell parents that its OK to teach kids that sex is pleasurable," she says. "Parents are very nervous about their children's developing sexuality. It's much easier to promise, as the religious right does, to lower pregnancy rates."

The change in strategy was masterminded by a tight network of right-wingers, and one of the most influential among them is Simonds, who founded CEE in 1983. Simonds declined to be interviewed for this article, but in a fund-raising letter mailed in October, he alleged that public schools routinely encourage students to experiment with gay sex.

"Children are taught that one in ten children born are genetically and irreversibly homosexual," the fund-raising letter said. "On this presumption, homosexuals are allowed to enter the classrooms and describe their life-styles to innocent children [and] then hand out hot-line phone numbers to call for help in enjoying their new life-styles. This is open recruitment!"

Fred Clarkson, a journalist who has written extensively about the religious right, says that Simonds is widely though to have focused the religious right's attention on school curricula. "Public education epitomized the religious right's problem with a non-Christian society," Clarkson says. "Public schools serve the function of mainstreaming people—making them into decent, tolerant adults. For Simonds, that makes public schools the enemy, and he has been able to make this case to a lot of fundamentalists."

Much of Simonds's energy has been devoted to engineering the religious right's efforts to recruit fundamentalists to run for local school boards. In his pamphlet *How to Elect Christians to Public Office,* Simonds writes, "An average school [board election] gets 13% to 15% voter turnout. A 1% to 3% shift of the vote can turn the election to your candidate. Most school districts have ten or more churches comprising 75% to 85% of the voters. You CAN win."

Nonetheless, the religious right's gains are spurring a backlash in some school districts. The percentage of CEE-backed candidates who won their election in San Diego County this year declined to one third from two thirds in 1990, according to People for the American Way. In Duval County, Fla., Planned Parenthood filed a lawsuit on behalf of seven families against the use of *Teen-Aid* in the public schools. The lawsuit alleges that the curriculum violates a state law that requires schools to adopt "accurate, complete, unbiased, nonsectarian information on human sexuality."

Parents in Shreveport, La., made similar arguments in a lawsuit they filed November 10 to attempt to stop the local school board from adopting *Sex Respect*. In Wisconsin, the Sheboygan school board rejected *Sex Respect* last year after parents waged a two-year campaign against it. In announcing its decision, one member of the board said that the curriculum amounted to "Christian fundamentalism in disguise."

Jay Sekulow, chief counsel for the American Center for Law and Justice, the legal arm of televangelist Pat Robertson's Christian Coalition, says that the grassroots efforts to stop school districts from adopting *Sex Respect* and *Teen-Aid* amount to censorship of religion. "This has nothing to do with homosexuality as a lifestyle and everything to do with censoring a legitimate philosophical standpoint," he says.

But People for the American Way vice president Mike Hudson says that increased public awareness is the real reason for the religious right's setbacks. "It's pretty clear that once a broad part of the citizenry understands what the religious right is up to in these local elections, the likelihood of getting elected decreases," he says.

As the public awareness spreads, Haffner says, the battle over sex education curricula will intensify. In the meantime, she says, the real losers are students. "While the battles go on, students are deprived of crucial information," she says. "We just can't continue to teach young people that sex is bad and dirty and then expect them to grow up to be sexually healthy adults."

COLORADO GOES STRAIGHT TO HELL

by John Gallagher

February 23, 1993

For gays and lesbians in Colorado, hell began on November 3, 1992. On that day, to the surprise of practically everyone, 806,846 Colorado citizens—54% of the electorate—went to the polls to approve Amendment 2, an addition to the state constitution that would prohibit the passage of gay rights laws and repeal existing antidiscrimination ordinances in three cities. Since then, gays and lesbians in the state have been slowly adjusting to a new reality—that the majority of their fellow Coloradans do not believe they should be protected from discrimination.

That would be painful enough. But the passage of Amendment 2 unleashed a torrent of rage and hostility, not all of it directed at the measure's sponsors. Recriminations aimed at practically everyone involved in the effort to stop or to undo Amendment 2 have been growing.

On January 15 Denver district judge Jeffrey Bayless issued a temporary injunction that blocks the measure from taking effect until a lawsuit challenging it is settled, preserving—for a time—bans on antigay discrimination that are on the books in Aspen, Boulder, and Denver. But the fear and ill will that the passage of Amendment 2 has left in its aftermath will not be as easily stopped. Although Bayless says there is a good chance that the measure will be found unconstitutional, gay rights opponents have pledged to appeal any decision that voids the amendment, and it is sure to be years before the issue is finally resolved. In the meantime, Colorado's gays and lesbians are left to fend for themselves in a poisonous atmosphere.

"There's an increasing degree of distrust, blaming, and Monday-morning quarterbacking," says Patrick Steadman, a gay attorney in Denver who is involved in the effort to overturn the amendment in the courts. "It's pretty vicious."

The rift has widened to encompass not only the gay community but also the entire state. Negative publicity surrounding the passage of the amendment has left the measure's opponents as well as its supporters defensive and uncommunicative. "It really is causing a social fissure," says Robin Miller, a lesbian attorney in Colorado Springs. "It's a tragic outcome. The battle lines have hardened, and we really are in a warfare situation at this point."

The war may be spreading. Thad Tecza, senior instructor of political science at the University of Colorado, says that "Amendment 2 is a reflection of broader trends. We're seeing a nationwide movement by conservative groups to press for a social, moral agenda in the Republican Party and for more direct initiatives."

Emboldened by the passage of Amendment 2, right-wing groups in at least 12 other states, including California, Georgia, Idaho, Iowa, Maine, Minnesota, Montana, Ohio, and Washington, are poised to mount drives to enact similar initiatives by 1994. Says Sue Larson, a lesbian activist in Boulder: "This is the issue of the '90s, and it's going to get pretty hot."

Even Oregon, where voters beat back an antigay measure last November, will not be spared. The Oregon Citizens Alliance is laying the groundwork to put Colorado-style proposals on that state's November 1994 ballot and on municipal ballots in 32 Oregon cities and towns. OCA head Lon Mabon calls the rash of proposed initiatives "a national referendum" on gay civil liberties protections.

William Schneider, a political analyst at the American Enterprise Institute, a Washington, D.C., policy research group, says, "The religious right's view is that after abortion and the fall of Communism, homosexuality is the next item on the agenda."

Given those political dynamics, Colorado's example does not bode well for other states. "Even in a state like Colorado, where people are fairly well-educated, unless you explain how much people suffer from discrimination, people will vote for an antigay measure," says Schneider. "You can't assume that unwillingness to support discrimination will apply to gay rights anywhere." Adds Andrew Dunham, a political science professor at Colorado College in Colorado Springs: "Most states in the country would probably be like Colorado. There's at least a chance that this referendum would pass in other states."

Indeed, it was probably the gains made by gays and lesbians in Colorado that attracted the right wing's attention to gay rights issues in the first place. "We're getting beaten up because we tried" to secure gay rights, says Denver city council member Cathy Reynolds. Adds Larson: "We had done good work here. We were just sitting duck."

But in other respects, Colorado was an ideal testing ground for an antigay ballot measure. The state has had a strong Ku Klux Klan presence throughout its history. Because it is home to the U.S. Air Force Academy and a sizable number of military retirees, Colorado Springs in particular has long been dominated by conservative politicians, and in recent years the city has become a base for right-wing political groups. Citizens Project, a Colorado Springs group that monitors the right wing, says that the city is home to about 50 conservative groups; Colorado for Family Values, the group that sponsored Amendment 2, is one of them.

The schism between progressive communities like Aspen and Boulder and conservative ones like Colorado Springs has given the state a schizophrenic political nature. In elections, it swings between very conservative candidates and decidedly liberal ones. As a result, during the '80s the state's voters found themselves represented in the Senate by both liberal Democrat Gary Hart and archconservative Bill Armstrong. (Now retired, Armstrong donated $4,500 to CFV's efforts on behalf of Amendment 2.)

"There's no homogeneity, which is part of an ongoing political dilemma," says Tecza. "The state is divided very, very closely between Democrats and Republicans. You have pockets of extreme liberalism, like parts of Boulder, and you also have pockets of extreme conservatism, such as El Pas County, where Colorado Springs is."

Thus, before Election Day, Amendment 2 was neither a sure winner nor an obvious loser, Dunham says. "With slightly different publicity, it wouldn't have passed," he says. "It was almost a flip of a coin."

Publicity made the difference, agrees Bruce Loeffler, an openly gay political science professor at Colorado College and a member of Ground Zero, a gay group in Colorado Springs. CFV members

tence and declared EPOC the successor," she says. "They lost the election because they fractured gay and lesbian unity with the statewide community."

Steadman says he does not believe that EPOC campaign officials were racist, but he acknowledges that "they've alienated people and have done nothing to acknowledge it."

Other activists say that the campaign's Michael Dukakis-like decision to try to absorb attacks without responding to them left a bitter legacy. "It reinforced all the existing stereotypes," Loeffler says. "All the good Christians came forward [and made unanswered allegations against gays], and then people say, 'Aha, they *are* child molesters, and they *do* eat shit.'"

However, Marchione says that any attempt to place blame on EPOC is misplaced. "We're honestly of the belief that if the campaign had not been run the way we ran it, the result would have been far worse," he says. "During the campaign, a lot of people who are now naysayers were saying, 'Great job; keep it up.' It's the nature of things."

Larson, who was an EPOC field organizer, agrees: "The campaign wasn't run by a bunch of idiots. They were professional campaign people." The postelection criticism of campaign staffers by gays and lesbians has stunned EPOC workers, she says. "Our eyeballs just popped out of heads, partly from the loss but also from the insane cannibalism," she says.

The national boycott of Colorado, which sprang up days after the election, further divided gay and lesbian Coloradans. Scores of cities across the country, including Atlanta, New York City, Chicago, and Los Angeles, signed on to the boycott early; so did celebrities, including Barbra Streisand and Whoopi Goldberg. The nation's two largest gay political groups, the Human Rights Campaign Fund and the National Gay and Lesbian Task Force, endorsed the boycott December 23.

But Evans says that few people outside Colorado "realize how divided people in Colorado are about the boycott." Morgan says that her group, GLCCC, has "gotten grief" because it supports the boycott. "We may lose some money," she says. "People who don't support the boycott won't support us." Morgan says that a bar owner canceled a fund-raiser to be held at his bar for GLCCC because he disagreed with the group's stance on the boycott.

And the boycott has caused rifts between the state's gays and lesbians and other minority groups. Jorge Amaya, former president of the League of United Latin American Citizens, told the *Colorado Springs Gazette Telegraph* in an article published January 8 that "with the boycott, gays are putting their needs in front of everyone else's." Dunham says that the boycott is "hurting the minority coalition because many hotel workers who bear the brunt of the boycott are Hispanic or black. It's splitting the alliance."

In an effort to restore the fractured coalition, a self-styled statewide "human rights summit" January 10 spurred the formation of an ad hoc human rights commission based on a model proposed by the People of Color Coalition. "Unlike many models, it is grassroots-based, striving for equal representation and ethnic and gender parity," Flores says. Many activists applaud the idea of the coalition but privately express concerns about its ability to organize effectively in the current divisive atmosphere.

For rank-and-file gays and lesbians, the blame and self-examination that permeate the winter air only add to their dread of Amendment 2's effects. "For a lot of people, the impact of Amendment 2 is the realization that we live in a place that is not supportive," says Morgan.

There is danger in the air too. "It was like a switch was thrown November 3, and suddenly after then people could be intolerant," Ogden says. "I put up a NO ON 2 sign every day, and it gets torn down every day."

Even gays and lesbians who live in parts of the state that were not particularly gay-friendly before November 3 now feel the amendment's chill, Larson says. "A lot of people are not losing an ordinance, but they feel it every bit as much," she contends. Middleton says that passage of the amendment "makes it harder to recruit for the university, particularly for graduate students." There are persistent but unconfirmed reports that some people were told in the dark days after the election that they would lose their jobs once the amendment took effect.

Other people fear for their personal safety. GLCCC antiviolence coordinator Jody Andrade says the number of bias-crime complaints made to her group increased 275% after the passage of Amendment 2. "Part of it is because of increased awareness," she says. "The other part is when you create a hostile environment that gives license to people to bash queers. Half of our calls in November were directly related to people's displaying NO ON 2 buttons or bumper stickers."

Andrade says that most of the increase has been in death threats and phone harassment. But several incidents involved personal assaults, she says: A lesbian in the Denver suburb of Lakewood was attacked on a bus December 3 by two young men shouting "Fucking lezzie;" a heterosexual psychotherapist in Colorado Springs who opposed Amendment 2 was assaulted in her office at 6:40 A.M. January 2 by assailants who attacked her and painted slogans, including STOP EVIL, SEEK GOD, and REPENT, throughout her office.

Sometimes the slurs are generalized. When Denver was hit with an outbreak of hepatitis A during the holiday season, local radio talk show host Bob Enyart prompted a flood of supportive telephone calls by suggesting that the illness had been spread by "promiscuous homosexuals." Public health officials say the outbreak was the result of poor food-handling practices at a local catering firm.

Faced with such overt hostility, many gay and lesbian Coloradans are returning to the closet. But activists say that the election results have convinced others of the need for gay visibility. "A lot of people have come forward in what is a very hostile, increasingly dangerous environment to say, 'We are lesbians and gay men,'" Loeffler says. Adds Larson: "Amendment 2 was a wake-up call before November 3 for some, but it was a wake-up call for a lot more after November 3."

That belated awareness has left some activists both wistful and grateful. "I wish we had the people then that we have now," says Ground Zero member Bobby Mone. Marchione concurs: "A lot of people were asleep the first time around."

But despite Judge Bayless's injunction, the climate is unlikely to improve in the near future. "The fight over the amendment is something the state is going to be stuck with for a while," says Tecza. Attorneys say that the legal challenge to the law will take years to wend through the courts. Once the state district court rules on the legality of the measure, its decision is likely to be appealed to the state supreme court and from there could be taken to the U.S. Supreme Court.

"We think that the Colorado courts are our best audience," says Lynn Palm, a member of the board of directors of the gay legal group Lambda Legal Defense and Education Fund and an attorney who is helping prepare the legal challenge to the amendment. "We really tried hard to avoid federal court." But Steadman doubts that even a legal success would change attitudes. "You can have a judge correct what people have done," he says, "but you can't have a judge educate people."

Still, the alternative options present even greater risks, others say. "If the vote of the people is the remedy, we can't go right back to the ballot," says Reynolds. Dunham is even more blunt: "A repeal campaign would be folly."

Dunham's stance is supported by the results of a *Denver Post* survey that was published in the newspaper's January 3 edition. About 94% of the 606 Coloradans who were surveyed said they would not change their vote on Amendment 2 if they were asked to consider the measure again, even though only 13% of respondents said they believe that gays and lesbians are "really different from anyone else."

Rather than weakening Coloradans' resolve, the boycott appears to have hardened their positions, the poll indicates. About 43% of those surveyed say the boycott made them less likely to support the repeal of Amendment 2; only 25% said the boycott had made them more likely to support reversing the measure.

Tecza says that "the majority of the people in the state feel that the amendment doesn't reflect who we are, but they also feel that the reaction to it is also wrong and out of proportion. There's almost a garrison mentality in Colorado. We don't want outside groups telling us what to do."

If history is any guide, Dunham says, voters are likely to rally around Amendment 2. "This has happened before in Colorado politics—an amendment barely passes but a repeal effort is rejected overwhelmingly," he says. "Voters say that they may not have wanted it in the first place, but they will not change it once it has been approved."

After initially pushing to head off the boycott in December, the state's politicians are now trying to ignore it. Denver mayor Webb crisscrossed the country in December, appearing on the *The Arsenio Hall Show* to discuss the boycott and then jetting to New York City to try to deter Mayor David Dinkins from pushing the U.S. Conference of Mayors to cancel a meeting scheduled for Colorado Springs this summer. (Dinkins rebuffed the attempt, and the conference moved the meeting.)

Webb called the trip off early, saying he was emotionally and physically exhausted. Many observers said that instead of nipping the boycott in the bud, Webb's trip drew the nation's attention to Amendment 2 and actually gave the boycott a shot in the arm. Days after Webb ended his visit to New York, *The New York Times* published an editorial throwing the newspaper's support behind the boycott. *The Advocate* requested an interview with Webb for this article; he refused.

However, in a speech to the City Club in Denver on January 5, Governor Roy Romer—who opposed passage of the amendment but after Election Day said that he would sign the measure into law—sought to downplay the importance of the boycott. "We in Colorado want to do what's right and then communicate to the rest of the world what we think is the right thing to do," he said in the speech. "If the rest of the world wants to boycott, that's up to them."

But Romer conceded that the passage of the amendment had already jeopardized the state's efforts to attract businesses to Colorado. The state had been courting a unit of the Ziff-Davis Publishing Co. for relocation to Colorado, but Romer acknowledged that since the passage of the amendment, Ziff-Davis's interest in Colorado had cooled. The company was said to be looking to move to Utah instead. Had the amendment not been passed, Romer said, "we'd have that one in the bag."

The possibility that the amendment might lead Ziff-Davis to relocate to another state with few gay rights protections, such as Utah, strikes some gay rights supporters in Colorado as ironic. Indeed, some of the cities, such as Atlanta, that led the Colorado boycott are in states that have sodomy laws. Colorado repealed its sodomy law in 1977.

"If people want to boycott," Reynolds says, "they should look at states where people are in jail for sodomy. There's a lot of posturing involved. The idea is to provide equal rights for everyone, not bolster political careers or make the national press."

Legislative remedies have also been proposed. "The key now is to start laying the groundwork for national gay rights legislation," says Marchione. But insiders say that President Clinton is unlikely to push vigorously for such a law.

In Colorado, state senator Bill Owens, a Republican who is widely believed to be preparing a run for governor in 1994, is considering proposing a measure that would bar employees from being fired for activities outside of work that are unrelated to job performance. Owens says that the measure would be a compromise.

"A lot of people who voted for Amendment 2 did so because they did not want to give people protections based on sexual preference," Owens says. "A lot of other good people voted against Amendment 2 because they oppose any discrimination based on sexual preference. So the question is, Can we bring those two groups of well-meaning people together to form a majority?"

But the possibility of any compromise worries many gay rights supporters. "I don't know how

AIDS charities; and the Red Ribbon Foundation, working with Project Angel Food, serves 400 meals in Los Angeles every day to people with HIV or AIDS.

Another remarkable offshoot of the ribbons' popularity is the proliferation of ribbons denoting different diseases and political causes. At the Academy Awards, Geena Davis wore a red ribbon for AIDS and a pink ribbon for breast cancer. Both Denzel Washington and Morgan Freeman wore purple ribbons in protest of police brutality perpetrated on members of the African-American community. And a recent trend on college campuses had made white ribbons popular among men concerned about violence against women.

The ribbons have become a cultural icon prone to cynical abuse by presidents' wives, merchandising strategies, and political manipulation. There may be no end to their disease-of-the-month possibilities. The colostomy ribbon? "I don't want to think of the one for prostate cancer," Rudnick worries, nevertheless suggesting, "the clear ribbon,"

In short, the ribbons are frivolous. But the only thing more annoying than a major star mindlessly wearing a red ribbon to an awards show is a celebrity who is mindlessly, or mindfully, not wearing one. I sat through the last Academy Awards ceremony with a roomful of gay men at a photographer's studio in Hollywood. Everyone had a piece of paper to write down his predictions; having contributed a few dollars each to the Oscar pool, we were competing for 20-odd dollars and a petite gold-threaded shirtwaist with fur cuffs and collar. But the score that no one recorded was one we kept out loud throughout the evening—the ribbon score.

Unforgiven was the ribbonless movie. Since neither its Oscar-winning producer and director, Clint Eastwood, nor its Oscar-winning supporting actor, Gene Hackman, was wearing a ribbon, we took its victories personally. On the other hand, Liza Minnelli wasn't wearing a ribbon, and neither was Barbra Streisand, and we made excuses for them. It seemed our attitude toward the ribbons was flexible and ambivalent. We didn't want to be pandered to, but at the same time we did not want to be ignored.

We were a bunch of nice Hollywood homos, after all, grown accustomed to little attention from an industry in which gay men and lesbians have always worked, perhaps in numbers disproportionate to their presence in the rest of society. Ironically, though we were the Oscars' ideal audience, familiar with all kinds of drag, responsive to camp, credulous, skeptical, enthralled, and eager to identify with stars, we were among its most reviled and/or ignored.

We were a roomful of dupes. Perhaps I should speak for myself. I am confusing red ribbons with pink triangles now, as if gays and AIDS were the same. Nevertheless, as my experience with AIDS has been exclusively with gay men, I consider statements about AIDS to be references to my life. And my personal feeling about the red ribbon is that its presence almost guarantees that the person wearing it has never had contact with anyone with AIDS.

People who are truly living with or dying of AIDS or caring for sick lovers of friends don't need gentle reminders about their situation. "I don't have to see a ribbon in order to think about AIDS," says Larry Kramer, who has lost hundreds of friends to the disease. Novelist and AIDS activist Paul Monette agrees. "My *life* is a red ribbon," he says ironically, emphasizing the contrast between evening-gown activism and his own continual battle against AIDS. "In fact," he continues, "sometimes I feel like a big red ribbon with a little Paul Monette pinned to the lapel." For people infected with HIV or sick with AIDS, bland reassurances of caring and awareness are still not enough.

Nor are unfulfilled campaign promises. Health care president Bill Clinton is apparently considering an appearance at the April gay, lesbian, and bisexual civil rights march in Washington. If he shows up wearing a ribbon, he will have to explain why he still hasn't addressed AIDS in a major speech or policy meeting. And we will need to face the possibility that we traded a president who does nothing for one who does nothing except wear ribbons.

How useful is the ribbon in the fight against AIDS? It's like stanching a massive blood flow with a Kleenex. Less a Broadway bauble than a tiny funereal wreath, pinned to the breast like a pallbearer's boutonniere, the ribbon is the smallest possible reminder of a disease that devastates on an epic scale. Its message is conciliatory, its intent is to pander and assuage, its presence is ubiquitous, and its effect, like any constant, droning reminder, is to induce hypnosis, silence, and inaction—to maintain the status quo rather than to mandate change.

IN THE NAME OF CHARITY

August 10, 1993

On June 3 there were almost as many stars in the aisles as there were in the sky when AIDS Project Los Angeles honored marketing whiz and fashion designer Calvin Klein at its annual fashion benefit. The event, which raised $600,000 for the AIDS service group, included dinner, cocktails, a fashion show featuring 300 models, and a Tina Turner concert. It was just another of the spectacular pull-out-the-stops expenses-be-damned this-is-show-business kind of affairs that have become the hallmark of AIDS fund-raising, especially in Los Angeles.

But now everyone was happy, particularly about the selection of the event's honoree. "It makes my skin crawl," says Rodger McFarlane, executive director of Broadway Cares/Equity Fights AIDS. "I'm one of the founders of GMHC [Gay Men's Health Crisis, a New York City AIDS service group], and Calvin was one of the first people we asked and asked most often for support. I was caring for so many people around him, and he was bitterly ungenerous, vicious, and unresponsive. Part of me believes there is no such thing as clean money. I wanted Calvin's money too, and I still want it, but another part of me is saying, 'I will not give absolution to people who colluded in genocide.'"

In selecting Klein, APLA unwittingly catalyzed a long-overdue examination of AIDS group's dependency on event-based fund-raising where big-name celebrities are honored despite having done relatively little in the fight against AIDS. In the case of Klein, for instance, no major AIDS organizations described the honoree as a force in AIDS advocacy. Prior to the benefit, his only known example of meaningful largesse came just last year, when he made a five figure donation to APLA to purchase a ticket to the group's Commitment to Life awards ceremony. The event honored record producer David Geffen, a close friend of Klein's who rescued Klein's company from bankruptcy, and insiders at APLA insist that Klein's ticket was in fact paid for by Geffen. (APLA spokeswoman Nicole Russo would not disclose the source of the money for Klein's ticket.) In the wake of the APLA benefit, GMHC announced that Klein had made a donation, but the group's officials refused to disclose the donation's size, saying only that it was at least $25,000.

Klein spokeswoman Suzanne Eagle declined to provide details about any of Klein's charitable activities, and Klein declined several requests for interviews. Also following the APLA event, Eagle was replaced by the powerful Hollywood public-relations agency PMK. Publicists from PMK said they were surprised and outraged by the criticism of Klein, but they fared no better than Eagle in securing Klein for an interview.

McFarlane says he doesn't care whether Klein bought the Commitment to Life ticket himself. Even if Klein had bought it and several more, McFarlane says he would not be moved. "A couple hundred grand from Calvin Klein is an obscene joke. He is independently wealthy, and it's pocket change he's come up with! Honoring him is one of the most cynical moments in fund-raising history."

Longtime AIDS activist Larry Kramer agrees. "It's beyond gross," he says. "It just makes me puke. Here we have a man who's done so little to fight AIDS but is being given a major award, solely—I would imagine—because he is David Geffen's close friend. It's like the Jews honoring David Duke."

Insiders say APLA's connection to Hollywood is the real reason Klein was selected. The presence of big-name celebrities in the organization is the proverbial double-edged sword—it provides money and visibility but can give rise to a mentality more appropriate for producing a blockbuster movie than a fund-raiser that has meaning for those most impacted by AIDS. Says Kevin Garrity, a major APLA donor who sits on several of the group's committees: "APLA cannot be run like Geffen Records or MCA or Disney." Although Garrity purchases tickets to almost all of APLA's events, he says he chose to sit out the Klein benefit.

Lenny Bloom, APLA's outgoing executive director, acknowledges that the group's choice of

Klein was controversial. "I am not unaware that there are people who felt that Calvin has not been supportive of the AIDS community or the lesbian and gay community," he says. "Hopefully, we're seeing him emerging as the kind of leader we all would like him to have been years ago."

However, Bloom says many people "misunderstand what the fashion event is about. This is not about honoring somebody who has demonstrated a commitment to this organization and to this community. As you go through the list of our honorees, you are going to find that they are fabulous designers who put on great shows, and that is what they are recognized for."

APLA events manager Diane Connors says that prior AIDS advocacy has never been a consideration in the selection of an honoree for the fashion event. "This is not a noble thing, but these events are fund-raisers, and maybe not everybody is as deserving as somebody else," she says. "But if someone more deserving can't afford to do this event for us and can't sell the tickets for us, the they can be deserving all they want. If we're not raising money, then we've missed the boat."

Yet such distinctions were lost in the publicity surrounding the event. The invitation to the event read, "The California Fashion Design Industry Friends and APLA honors Calvin Klein." In the event's ad journal, a glossy book given to attendees, a letter signed by Bloom and APLA board chairman Steve Tisch read in part, "We thank Calvin Klein for his commitment and concern."

Kramer says the fact that the benefit raised a great deal of money is no excuse for honoring Klein. "That APLA is expecting us to swallow it with pride is a farce," he says. "It is hypocrisy writ so large that you wonder what has happened to reason, intelligence, and morality."

Prior to the Klein event, Bloom hung a good deal of APLA's defense on what Klein would say at the benefit, challenging naysayers to wait and see. "This is Klein's chance to make people see he does care about AIDS and that he does care about the lesbian and gay community," Bloom said before the event.

But on that count, those in the audience at the benefit could only have been disappointed. In accepting the APLA honor, Klein made a rambling address, thanking scores of people and sounding more like he was accepting an Oscar than addressing an AIDS fund-raiser. The word "AIDS" was mentioned only twice, almost in passing, and Klein did not once say "gay" or "lesbian." When asked after the event, Bloom demurred from commenting directly on the content-free speech and instead chose to underline that Klein's presence in and of itself "showed him to be gay- and lesbian-friendly and AIDS-supportive."

Tom Viola, managing director of Broadway Cares/Equity Fights AIDS, characterizes the fundamental event fund-raising dilemma like this: "If you are going to hang one of these events on honoring someone, you have to balance the sublime with the ridiculous—who really should be honored with who can sell the event."

Despite the public-relations brouhaha surrounding it, the Klein benefit was a success from a revenue standpoint. Including funds derived from ad journal sales and the event's silent auction, it brought in a little more than $1 million, making it APLA's second-largest event of the year, out-paced only by Commitment to Life. Indeed, the Klein benefit raised twice as much money as any previous fashion benefit, APLA officials say.

But the event also cost a great deal of money to stage. APLA risked $400,000; underwriters, including Klein, brought another $500,000 to the table. By comparison, $900,000 exceeds the entire 1992 operating budget of the Cascades AIDS Project, which provides services to people with AIDS in all of Oregon.

Acting GMHC development director Ken Moore says that "event fund-raising is expensive, time-consuming, and fraught with all sorts of hazards and liabilities. I know of events that were supposed to raise a whole bunch of money for AIDS, but when all the expenses were taken, they didn't. That kind of thing frustrates me and everyone involved with AIDS fund-raising."

The National Community AIDS Partnership estimates that 75% of all money donated to fight AIDS is raised through event fund-raising. And no one seems angrier about AIDS service groups' dependence on big-name event-based fund-raising than the people who actually organize the events. Mike Anketell, who received $45,000 for producing the Klein benefit, says, "I would much rather pick up the phone to call donors and say, 'Can I get $10,000 just because we need it?' Yes, people like to feel like they are contributing, but they also like to be treated to something for making that donation. I don't know if that's human nature or if it's just the way things have gotten, but it's gotten out of hand."

APLA development director Bill Jones agrees. "We are stuck on event fund-raising," he says. "Our donors have gotten into the habit of giving this way. You can say that's unfortunate, but that's reality."

However, Garrity says at least some of the responsibility belongs to the AIDS organizations themselves: "Because they have limited development resources, maybe enough attention isn't paid to cultivate major donors into writing checks for the endowment." Dependence on event fund-raising, he says, "exists because we have allowed it to exist."

Michael Seltzer, executive director of Funders Concerned About AIDS, a nonprofit group that evaluates AIDS fund-raising, says the job of fighting AIDS is too big for the private sector alone. The federal government, he says, should take a cue from the federal response to polio. "Franklin Delano Roosevelt said the fight would be a national priority and called on people to support the March of Dimes in finding a cure. He said to the American people, 'Help fight this terrible disease.'"

Big corporations also deserve blame, Bloom says. "Had the government decided it wasn't going to condemn so many hundreds of thousands to death and instead taken a leadership role, we wouldn't be where we are today," he says. "But corporate America has also expressed zero interest in this crisis. We spend a lot of money on their products, and they've told us, 'We don't care if you die.' It's time to start holding them accountable."

The dearth of business and government support led to the creation of thousands of community-based AIDS groups across the country. Sometimes the groups are forced to develop a top-this-if-you-can mentality to compete for limited AIDS funding. "You did not have thousands of polio organizations," Seltzer says. "Because the president anointed one, you had the American people getting behind one national charity."

But with AIDS charities, says Viola, "there begins to be competition among events. Don't think that just because it's a benefit, people are going to show up. They show up if they want a ticket for your event—it's then they are happy to be there for AIDS." Adds Bloom: "The events are becoming more important than the message. People are forgetting that the issue is AIDS."

Groups that monitor charities say that AIDS groups are far more dependent on big-name event fund-raising than groups that raise money to combat other diseases, and almost without exception, officials of AIDS service organizations admit that event fund-raising is out of control. Yet in the same breath, they fret over the dangers of publicly disclosing the expense, risk, and moral dilemmas of the practice. By making such disclosure, they say, they would shoot themselves in the foot.

Nationwide it's easy to keep the inefficiency of event-based fund-raising a secret because non-profit organizations are not regulated by either the Federal Trade Commission or the Internal Revenue Service. Less than half the states require charities to register with them, and those states that do lost much of their regulatory powers when the Supreme Court ruled during its most recent term that states could not require fund-raisers to disclose the percentage of proceeds that actually went to charity.

Los Angeles, where APLA is based, is one of the few cities in the country with a department overseeing charitable fund-raising. For fund-raisers staged in the city, the department issues cards disclosing information about the proceeds. But the information on the cards is an estimate based on past fund-raisers; it can be misleading: In the case of the Klein event, for instance, expenses were officially filed at a little less than $190,000, a figure that in hindsight represents only 47% of what APLA actually spent and 21% of what the event actually cost.

What can be done? The answer, insiders say, is for AIDS agencies to diversify their fund-raising sources. Earlier this year, for instance, Broadway Cares/Equity Fights AIDS signed a deal with Turner Entertainment to put on a pay-per-view special. The show will be underwritten in its entirety; and regardless of the special's performance, Broadway Cares/Equity Fights AIDS is guaranteed at least $1 million. Not every organization has the kind of assets that would allow it to make such a deal, but every organization can take some percentage of the time, effort, and money spent on special events and allocate it to cultivating major donors, exploring entrepreneurial opportunities, and writing grants.

There is, Bloom says, no other choice. "Events have become so much a part of who we are that it's tough to back away from them," he says. "Perhaps it's because the entertainment industry stepped forward so early. But I do not believe they are the future. We need to find ways to raise dollars that are less work-intensive and that cost less money."

D-DAY: ON THE MILITARY ISSUE, GAY GROUPS REACHED FOR THE BRASS RING BUT HIT A BRICK WALL

by Chris Bull

August 10, 1993

In its final days, the six-month standoff between President Clinton, Congress, and the Pentagon over the military's ban on gay and lesbian service personnel was almost an anticlimax. For weeks Clinton had carefully courted the military, praising its leadership and charming the troops. In leaks to the media, the White House had repeatedly detailed Clinton's intention to back off his campaign pledge to unequivocally lift the ban and stressed the president's growing impatience with the issue. The hints were so frequent and so pointed that there were no surprises left for July 15, President Clinton's self-imposed deadline for settling the issue.

For gay lobbying groups that had for months made the battle against the ban their number one priority and spent hundreds of thousands of dollars on the effort, there was a sense of finality. The stream of news releases from the groups dried up as media attention to the issue plummeted. Despite their hard work, the groups were largely outside the debate at the end, watching from the sidelines as the heavy hitters—defense secretary Les Aspin, Senate armed services committee chairman Sam Nunn, and joint chiefs of staff chairman Colin Powell—ironed out a settlement behind closed doors.

"It was all over except the crying months ago," says Larry Sabato, a professor of political science at the University of Virginia. "Even if the gay groups had been able to do more, I wonder if it would have made any difference."

Adds Craig A. Rimmerman, associate professor of political science at Hobart and William Smith Colleges in Geneva, N.Y.: "The gay groups were never much of a factor in the debate. They were caught off-guard and were up against the most formidable forces they had ever faced. They lacked the resources to really crystallize the issue as one of civil rights."

During his campaign for the presidency, Clinton had been clear about his intention to issue an executive order lifting the ban. "On several occasions, he announced he was going to sign an executive order, and no one said anything, not even the Republicans," says William Schneider, an analyst for the

American Enterprise Institute, a policy research group. "It may not have astonished Clinton, but it sure astonished me. I thought that it could give the Republicans an opening on the family-values issue."

But just days after Clinton's election in November, storm clouds gathered on the horizon. Powell, still popular from Operation Desert Storm, and Nunn, smarting after being passed over by Clinton to be secretary of defense, voiced opposition to Clinton's plan to eliminate the ban. When Clinton acted within a week of his inauguration to begin implementing his campaign promise, he met with immediate and vehement opposition in Congress and quickly agreed to delay a final decision until July 15. By April, Clinton was floating the idea of a compromise that would segregate gay and lesbian troops from their heterosexual counterparts and declaring that his opposition to the ban did not mean he condoned "the homosexual lifestyle."

How did the ban's opponents lose control of the debate so quickly? "The whole problem was bad timing," says Schneider. "The debate never really became one about gay people serving in the military. It was always about the fact that a lot of Americans still simply do not want to say, 'It's OK to be gay.' You can provide book after book of evidence, but in the end the debate never got away from fears."

The three gay groups that did most of the lobbying on the issue—the Human Rights Campaign Fund, the National Gay and Lesbian Task Force, and the Campaign for Military Service—were hampered by infighting and their inability to respond quickly to the attacks from Nunn, Powell, and Senate minority leader Robert Dole. Indeed, CMS, an umbrella organization composed of HRCF, NGLTF, and more than a dozen other political, religious, and civil rights groups, was not formed until early February, when the pro-ban congressional firestorm was well under way. CMS prepared a $100,000 television advertising campaign to respond to the charges but did not launch it until Memorial Day weekend, long after most politicians had taken a stance on the issue. Similarly, HRCF's response—a $60,000 full-page ad in *USA Today*—did not reach the public until July 2.

Alexander Robinson, chief military lobbyist for the American Civil Liberties Union, acknowledges that no strategy was in place to mount a campaign to lift the ban until long after Nunn and Powell gained control of the debate. Caught up in euphoria generated by Clinton's election, many veteran gay and lesbian activists assumed that lifting the ban was, as Clinton had said during his campaign, as easy as issuing an order.

"We did not begin to have a substantive dialogue about strategy until after the inauguration," Robinson says. "That was probably a mistake. Political veterans like [openly gay U.S. representatives] Barney Frank and Gerry Studds should have been brought in earlier."

HRCF executive director Tim McFeeley says he convened an emergency meeting in November to discuss Clinton's election. In attendance were openly homosexual Clinton campaign advisers Bob Hattoy and Roberta Achtenberg as well as David Mixner, a fund-raiser for gay political causes who was an early Clinton backer. "The military issue was raised, and Mixner said, 'Don't worry, it's a done deal,'" McFeeley says. "We figured the president of the United States was powerful enough to get it done with an executive order if he really wanted to. With Democratic majorities in both houses of Congress, we didn't think it would be a problem. There were a lot of things we didn't anticipate."

Mixner says Clinton stumbled just days after his election, when in response to a reporter's question at a news conference, he said that shortly after taking office, he planned to issue an executive order lifting the Pentagon ban. "Clinton put the issue on the front burner without consulting anybody," he says. "From that moment on, it set the agenda for the gay community, because it became a prime issue for the press. We had little input into how it happened."

On December 22, Frank sent a strongly worded memo to HRCF and NGLTF advising them to brace for a touch fight on the ban. "I begged them to get a letter-writing campaign going," he says. "Inauguration week was an anguished time for me. The groups were making a fundamental error. They thought that having a president on your side means you've won. Having the president on your side is a necessary condition, but it's not a sufficient condition. I told the groups, 'You're deciding what to have for dessert when we haven't even killed the chickens for dinner yet.'"

The campaign against the ban was also set back by dissent about the role of CMS, the new kid on the block. McFeeley says that NGLTF and HRCF, the already-established groups, argued that CMS should simply raise funds and coordinate HRCF's lobbying with NGLTF's grassroots organizing and the ACLU's legal work. But gay attorney Tom Stoddard, who headed CMS on a volunteer basis, saw the group as leading the charge.

"It looked to us like CMS was saying, 'Move over and let the pros take over,'" McFeeley says. "It angered people at the established groups who had been working on the issue for years. It just wasn't fair. I know Tom didn't intend to send that message, but that's how it felt. We got off to a slow start because we were spending a lot of time and energy patching up hurt feelings."

Stoddard agrees that competition between the groups hurt their lobbying efforts. "Some disagreements are inevitable, but it did take us a while to achieve a degree of unity," he says. "It almost always had to do with turf and who was going to take credit for what. HRCF, for instance, created a fund-raising entity called Operation Lift the Ban. HRCF didn't go public with it until after we were created. It has certainly raised a lot of money, but CMS has never had any portion of it. HRCF was competing with CMS even though it was part of it."

CMS was also hurt by unrealistically high expectations, Stoddard says. At the time of its inception in February, the group said it expected to raise nearly $3 million to undertake the most ambitious media campaign ever on behalf of a gay rights cause. Adding legitimacy to the claim were media reports suggesting that the group would be funded by Hollywood multimillionaires David Geffen and Barry Diller. Although Geffen and Diller each donated $25,000 to CMS, the group fell nearly $2 million short of its fund-raising goal.

"*The New York Times* reported that both Geffen and Diller had given to the campaign," Stoddard says. "Because they are both exceptionally wealthy men, people imagined that they were bankrolling our campaign. That impression impeded our fund-raising. The truth is that a few wealthy people should not be asked to do this kind of funding alone. We would not want to end up as the fully owned subsidiary of Geffen and Diller."

Many other big-name donors were reluctant to identify closely with CMS, Stoddard says, recalling a Los Angeles fund-raiser that many celebrities sat out. "We can get celebrities to come out to AIDS fund-raisers, but they have stayed away from the military issue," he says.

As a result CMS's media assault was far more limited that Stoddard had hoped. Besides the $100,000 television advertising campaign, the group's other major media initiative was a 26-state bus tour in April that featured gay and lesbian veterans. While the effort generated local news coverage in cities along the tour route, it did little to drum up public support for ending the ban.

Frank says that CMS erred by behaving as if it were in an electoral campaign rather than working to engineer a political victory. "CMS kept saying, 'We have until July 15,' and I said, 'No, we don't.' Members of Congress don't wait until the week before a vote to lock in their positions. They had to figure out their positions right away to answer the hundreds of letters they were getting. A majority had locked in against us in January. You can't turn that around later. CMS's strategy would have been right if it had been running a campaign for office, because voters can think one thing in May and change in July. But members of Congress can't."

However, media consultant Robert Schrum, who ran an advertising campaign for the successful 1991 Senate bid of Sen. Harris Wofford (D-Pa.), disagrees. Television advertising campaigns, he says, should be scheduled for late in a campaign to "build for a strong finish," he says.

In fact, in June the gay groups did gain momentum, succeeding, for instance, in pushing Clinton to resist the temptation to defuse the issue by announcing his decision on the ban early. And on June 10 the gay groups received a major boost when former Arizona senator Barry Goldwater, a strident conservative, sided with them in a *Washington Post* opinion piece. But Northwestern University military sociologist Charles Moskos says that while Goldwater's stance was a blow to Nunn, the retired senator alone couldn't turn the tide so late in the game.

The gay groups' efforts to win support from prominent politicians other than Goldwater were largely unsuccessful. For instance, former president Jimmy Carter, who had advocated lifting the ban during an appearance on Cable News Network's *Larry King Live,* declined the groups' pleas to lobby Congress on the ban. "We were turned down by President Carter and Mrs. Carter after a long and deliberate process to get to them," Stoddard says. "This was played out again and again. People who supported us quietly just didn't want to be out front on this."

Thus, one of the few bright spots in the campaign was its support from civil rights groups, such as the National Association for the Advancement of Colored People and the Leadership Conference on Civil Rights, that had signed on as CMS sponsors. Such backing allowed CMS to arrange for array of civil rights leaders, including Coretta Scott King, the president of the Martin Luther King Jr. Center for Nonviolent Social Change, and Joseph Lowery, president of the Southern Christian Leadership Conference, to declare their opposition to the ban at a June 30 news conference. But Robinson says the impact of the news conference was weakened by its proximity to the July 15 deadline, and the support from the civil rights groups was diluted by their unfamiliarity with gay rights causes and internal dissension over the endorsements.

"The good news is that traditional civil rights groups came aboard like never before," he says. "The bad news is that those groups were not in place when we began. Our preexisting relationships with civil rights groups were weak. We have never had in-depth discussions with the NAACP, for example, about its structure and what the best way is to use it to our advantage. If the NAACP is going to go out on a limb for us on this issue, can we deliver for them when they need us?"

LCCR executive director Ralph Neas says the military ban forced many civil rights groups to begin a "learning process" on gay rights. "We did pretty well putting together a lobbying apparatus on behalf of gays in the military in just a few months," he says. "For a lot of civil rights groups, it was really the first time they were involved in a gay rights cause. That bodes well for the future."

Stoddard says that in many ways the gay groups were victims of events that were beyond their control. "In just a few months, we had to try to move the entire political process against decades of fear and ignorance," he says. "That has never even been tried in the history of our movement."

Frank agrees. "We're talking about gays and lesbians—a group of people who have been mistreated by society," he says. "Yet what we have been saying to them is that this system, which is denying you your rights and mistreating you, works—write them letters and they will listen. Now I know that it's true, that it does work, but I understand why that's a hard thing for gay people to believe. That's what the gay groups are really up against."

But such problems were exacerbated by the White House's lack of a coherent political response to congressional and Pentagon opposition. "We're a new presence on the national scene, and no one seems to know how to deal with us," Mixner says. "The Administration wanted not to seem beholden, not appear to be the captive of what might be perceived as a special-interest group, so it denied itself access to people with enormous knowledge on this issue who could have helped save it from lots of mistakes and lots of pain."

From the beginning of his administration, Rimmerman says, Clinton "failed to articulate a clear position on the issue because he has been caught between his personal and apparently genuine desire to lift the ban and his approach to politics, which is to govern by consensus rather than principle. As a compromiser, Clinton comes across as muddled. When the president is muddled on a controversial issue like this, you can't expect the public and Congress to buy it. This is an issue in which neither side is willing to compromise. Ultimately, no compromise is possible. Either openly gay people are allowed to serve or they are not."

But James Carville, Clinton's chief political strategist during the presidential campaign, says the blame doesn't lie with Clinton. "The primary problem was Congress and the fact that it's a problematic issue with the American public," he says. "The president has made great strides on the issue by promoting the idea that people ought to be judged by what they do and not who they are. It's not really the president's fault that the message was submerged in Congress and the Pentagon."

Washington, D.C., attorney John Holum, who was Clinton's principal adviser on the ban during the period between Clinton's election and his inauguration, says his efforts to line up congressional and military support for Clinton's position were torpedoed by a news leak from the Pentagon in the Administration's early days.

"I wanted to figure out the best way for Clinton to fulfill his campaign promise with a minimum of disruption to the military mission," he says. "The leak made the issue a public matter before we were ready. It meant that the president was not able to consult properly with military leaders and with Congress, and it meant that the opposition had an opportunity to mount a campaign against lifting the ban. It also gave the joint chiefs of staff a reason to be angry because they had not been consulted fully."

But while the effort to lift the ban was marked by missteps and infighting, the campaign to retain it appeared flawless. In congressional hearings, Nunn deftly shifted the debate from discrimination to concerns about morale, discipline, and privacy.

"Nunn and Powell played the right cards from the beginning," says Moskos. "They never made moral arguments, and they left the wild-eyed religious right out of the debate so that they could focus on privacy."

A key turning point in the public-opinion battle was the Senate armed services committee's fact-finding mission on a Navy aircraft carrier. Reporters tagged along, and in photos published across the country, committee members surveyed cramped living quarters and communal showers. Moskos called the idea of taking the trip to the carrier "brilliant."

Powell, who is black, blunted the gay groups' argument that the ban on gays and lesbians is analogous to the racial segregation of the armed forces that was ended by a presidential executive order in 1948, says Lawrence Korb, a senior fellow at the Brookings Institution, a policy research group. "Colin Powell is the most significant military leader in this country since Douglas MacArthur," Korb says. "He is very articulate, and he made the racial argument almost impossible to make." Adds Frank: "Powell said that you don't have to be a bigot to be against gays in the military."

While Nunn and Powell dominated the debate on the Pentagon ban, the House armed services committee held only two days of hearings on the issue. The committee's chairman, Ronald Dellums, was an outspoken opponent of the ban, but he was also new to his post, having been elevated to it when Aspin left the House of Representatives to become secretary of defense. While the Pentagon brass was comfortable with Nunn, it mistrusted Dellums, regarding him as an antimilitary left-winger. Still, gay groups that had hoped that Dellums would counter Nunn by championing their cause were disappointed.

Cynthia Enloe, a professor of government at Clark University in Worcester, Mass., acknowledges that Dellums faced the difficult task of "earning legitimacy in the eyes of the Pentagon, and it is certainly understandable that such a well-known critic of the Pentagon would have to choose his battles carefully to be effective in his new role." But because Dellums kept a low profile in the debate, she says, "the public and the White House were left with the fantasy that the Senate gets to call all the shots. That gives Nunn more authority to protect the military than he should rightfully have."

David Vershure, legislative assistant to House armed services committee member Patricia Schroeder, agrees. "Dellums was at the bottom of a learning curve, and that allowed Nunn to fill the leadership vacuum created by Aspin's departure," he says. "No matter who was chairing the committee, it would have been difficult to keep up with Nunn."

Dellums spokesman George Withers says that Dellums was unwilling to compete with his Senate counterpart for media attention. "Senator Nunn's hearings were one-sided and tended toward the overdramatic," he says. "The sensationalistic nature of some of the testimony in the Senate is what interested the media. Ron was more interested in elevating the debate. He will continue to disappoint anyone who expects a dog-and-pony show."

Despite the end of the six-month standoff, nearly everyone agrees that the battle over the ban is far from over. "We have no idea where the culture will be on homosexuality in five years," says Moskos. "Maybe the culture will be more restrictive then and the ban will stay in place. Or maybe homosexuality will be no big deal and it will be lifted completely."

But in the meantime, gay groups say they will now turn their attention to a wide range of issues, including fighting antigay initiatives on the ballot in many states and obtaining federal antidiscrimination protections. Former HRCF lobbying director Joseph Grabarz says such issues should have been where the gay groups' attention was all along. "One of the problems from the beginning of the military issue is that it didn't have support among the rank and file of the gay community," he says. "The antigay initiatives and AIDS are much closer to most gay people's hearts."

In the short term, those battles may have been made more difficult by the fight over the military ban, because it has created tension between gay and lesbian activists and the White House. "It means our struggle will be a longer one," Mixner says. "But if we can't be a long-distance runner on this, we have no business being in the arena."

Stoddard agrees. "We understood from the beginning that this fight was a proxy for future battles over gay rights," he says. "The military issue is a referendum on gay rights. All other issues will be affected by this."

But Frank is more optimistic. "We are not losing to homophobia in general," he says. "We are losing to some clever homophobes who figured how to manipulate public opinion on this one particular issue. In five years there will be gays and lesbians all over the place, with very few restrictions. And this battle will have helped propel us to that place."

RIGHT TURN: ARCHCONSERVATIVE BARRY GOLDWATER'S SURPRISING STANCE ON GAY AND LESBIAN RIGHTS

by Chris Bull

September 7, 1993

On July 15, the day President Clinton had once set aside for lifting the Pentagon's ban on gay and lesbian service personnel, Barry Goldwater, the godfather of American conservative politics, sits in a hotel room in suburban Washington, D.C., watching television. A CNN reporter is documenting growing military and congressional opposition to lifting the ban—a clamor that just four days later will push Clinton to announce a policy leaving nearly all of the ban in place.

Clicking off the television in disgust, Goldwater thunders, "The president of the United States is the commander in chief of the armed forces, and if he says to drop the ban, by God, everybody should do an about-face or get out of the service. If the commanders can't take orders from the commander in chief, they should submit letters of resignation. Clinton called me up one day about this, and I told him just that—give the order and then shut up about it."

Goldwater, 85, has plenty of experience with commanders. A retired Air Force major general who served in World War II, he was a staunch advocate for the Pentagon as a member of the Senate armed services committee before retiring from Congress in 1986. Until recently he taught at the Pentagon's air-war college in Alabama.

Such a cozy relationship with the Pentagon brass seems only natural for Goldwater, who as the Republican presidential nominee in 1964 espoused such hawkish foreign policy views that his opponent, incumbent president Lyndon Johnson, suggested in television ads that Goldwater's election would spark nuclear annihilation. Goldwater lost in one of the biggest landslides in American politics, but the campaign made him a conservative icon.

It was during his nomination acceptance speech at the 1964 Republican convention that Goldwater uttered the fighting words that galvanized a generation of anticommunist conservatives, frightened the nation, and are today still those most closely associated with him: "Extremism in defense of liberty is no vice… Moderation in the defense of justice is no virtue." It is a maxim, Goldwater says, that should be applied today to the struggle of gays and lesbians to overturn the Pentagon ban.

"People don't seem to be able to understand how important this is," he says. "Look, the Constitution says that all men are created equal, and it doesn't say that all men are created equal except for gays. Just like everyone else who is born in this country, gays are endowed by their creator, God, with inalienable rights, and among those are life, liberty, and the pursuit of happiness. At birth, whether you are born in Russia, Cuba, South Africa, or New York, you are born equal. The difference is that our [American] babies can grow up to live free."

Almost in the same breath, Goldwater comes close to calling the ban's opponents hypocrites, saying they know that gays and lesbians have always played a significant role in the military. He also accuses many members of his party of both gay baiting and race baiting.

"There has always been homosexuality [in society and the military] ever since man and woman were invented," he says. "I guess there were gay apes. So that's not an issue. The Republican Party should stand for freedom and only freedom. Don't raise hell about the gays, the blacks, and the Mexicans. Free people have a right to do as they damn well please. To see the party that fought Communism and big government now fighting the gays, well, that's just plain dumb."

Although such assessments win him few valentines from the Republican right, Goldwater insists that his views on the military issue are consistent with and molded by the hands-off conservative philosophy he has espoused throughout his entire political career. Still, for Goldwater there is another dimension—a human face—to gay rights issues: One of his ten grandchildren, Scottsdale, Ariz., interior designer Ty Ross, is openly gay.

Ross, 31, says he never had to hide his sexual orientation from his family. "I was able to come out when I was 16 because my mother is really cool about these things," he says. "Paka—I call my grandfather 'Paka'—just kind of found out about it, and I never had to tell him."

Ross says his grandfather was "always more concerned that I was a good citizen and doing well in my life than with my sexual orientation. He was pleased, for instance, that I had my own business. I'd bring my boyfriends around to his house, and he never said anything about [my homosexuality]. I think it was then that he realized that there are normal people out there who are gay and it's just a regular occurrence."

Says Goldwater: "I've known for three or four years that Ty is gay, and it made no difference in my family. That's his right as long as he doesn't do damage to anyone else, and nobody has ever convinced me that being gay is damaging to someone else. My brother has a granddaughter in San Francisco—a delightful girl—who is gay. It's up to her who she loves." (Citing Goldwater's grand-niece's wishes, family members declined to identify her.)

Ross says he believes his homosexuality helped influence Goldwater to speak out on gay rights issues. "Barry would never admit this, but this is part of the way he shows his love and respect for his family," Ross says. "He can see how important I am to my mom and my three sisters. He doesn't really express his emotions very often, so this is a way for him to do what's right for me and for his family."

Goldwater acknowledges that "when you have two gays in your family, you don't go around knocking [homosexuality]" but says that Ross's sexual orientation did not spur his opposition to the ban. "I would support any of my children and grandchildren," he says. "If they were in jail, I would try to get them out. They are my blood. I want to support Ty, but I'm doing this because it's a question of doing the right thing."

Whatever his motivation for supporting gay causes, Goldwater's blunt style and impeccable conservative credentials made him a compelling proponent of lifting the ban. A commentary he wrote for the June 10 edition of *The Washington Post* in which he advocated lifting the ban because "you don't have to be straight to shoot straight" was reprinted in 21 newspapers across the country, and he followed the commentary up with a series of print and broadcast interviews on the subject.

For his effort Goldwater was honored July 10 at a dinner in Phoenix by the Arizona Human Rights Fund, a statewide gay rights group. In remarks to the attendees, Goldwater said, "Someone once came up to me and asked, 'Would you fly with a man you knew was gay?' 'Hell yes,' I say, 'as long as the son of a bitch could fly.'"

David Smith, spokesman for the Campaign for Military Service, a now-defunct group formed in February to fight the ban, says that Goldwater was "a real winner for us. Because of his credentials with the military, he has been able to make the point that this is about freedom in a way that very few other public figures, even if they were willing, could achieve."

A pivotal event in Goldwater's development as a leading opponent of the ban occurred in April, when Ross introduced his grandfather to Tom Paniccia, who was discharged as a staff sergeant at Davis Monthan Air Force Base, near Tucson, in October after disclosing that he was gay on the ABC television program *Good Morning America*. Goldwater and Paniccia hit it off instantly.

"We developed a kind of friendship," Paniccia says. "I told him my story and said, 'Sir, is there anything you can do to help me out?' He said he would think about it and talk to some friends in Washington." In truth, Paniccia says, Goldwater's kindness helped him through one of the most difficult disappointments of his life—the estrangement from his father, a Navy veteran who lives in up-state New York, that developed after Paniccia made his television appearance.

"My father and I had already begun to drift apart, but I thought I should tell him that I was gay before he saw me on television," Paniccia says. "I told him that I knew it would hurt him to see me on television like that but that it was something I just had to do. Well, he just let me have it, saying I wasn't his son anymore or something to that effect. I said, 'What about love and family?' and he said there was no love and no family. That's the last I have heard from him. I called him three times, and he hung up each time."

As a result, Paniccia says, Goldwater became a sort of surrogate father figure for him. "I asked the senator if he thought I had done the right thing," he says. "I was pretty depressed about my discharge and my father, and he said, 'Give 'em hell. You're doing the right thing.' It sounded like something a father would say, and it gave me a boost in confidence. For a man of Barry Goldwater's stature to say something like that meant a lot to me."

Goldwater says he doesn't object to Paniccia's characterization of him as a father figure. "That's all right with me," he says. "I don't like what happened to Tom at all. After all these years and all these causes, I suppose I'm a father figure to a lot of people."

Eventually Goldwater agreed to introduce Paniccia to the Senate armed services committee in late June, when Paniccia was scheduled to speak to it on behalf of lifting the ban. The night before Paniccia was scheduled to speak, though, committee member Edward Kennedy phoned Goldwater to tell him that his appearance had been canceled and that retired general Norman Schwartzkopf, a supporter of the ban who commanded the allied forces during Operation Desert Storm, would replace him.

Goldwater says he was not bothered by the cancellation and that he still counts committee chairman Sam Nunn, who led the opposition to lifting the ban, among his friends. "When Ted [Kennedy] told me that [my appearance had been canceled], I just figured I wasn't scheduled and that was it and I would just go home," he says. "I've talked to Nunn about this, and I respect his position. He's from the Deep South, and he comes from a family that served in the military back to the [American] Revolution. I think that way down in his heart he's not convinced that he's right, but that's up to him, not me."

Smith, though, says that in private conversations with CMS officials and members of his family, Goldwater was justifiably "seething" about the cancellation. "Nunn showed Goldwater very little respect," Smith says. "He was so afraid that Goldwater would upstage Schwartzkopf."

Adds Bill Lewis, a gay activist who worked with Goldwater on questions related to the ban: "No question about it—Nunn screwed us. Barry was ready to go, but Nunn got scared."

Although the military issue was the first of Goldwater's breaks with Republican right-wingers to receive widespread media attention, it had been foreshadowed by a series of smaller partings of the way. In December 1991, for instance, Goldwater shocked many Arizonans by endorsing a proposed Phoenix city ordinance that would have prohibited antigay bias in employment, housing, and public accommodations. Under attack from conservatives and religious fundamentalists, the ordinance had been killed by the Phoenix city council. Goldwater, though, staged a one-man lobbying campaign to resurrect it.

"Barry called a press conference with the head of the local Episcopal Church, but the press couldn't see anyone but Barry," says Charles Harrison, a Phoenix gay activist who is a member of AHRF's board. "It was big news that the living legend of Arizona would endorse gay rights. The next day it was on every news broadcast and on the front pages of the newspapers. The city council immediately voted to reconsider. We didn't get everything we wanted, but what we did get was 100% because of Barry." Eventually, a watered-down version of the ordinance—one forbidding antigay discrimination in municipal employment—was enacted.

Ross says he actively encouraged Goldwater to throw his backing behind the gay rights ordinance. "The religious fanatics were on one side, and gays and lesbians were on the other side, and there was no one to speak out for the ordinance who was not in either camp. Barry came back from one meeting with the mayor on the issue and said to me, 'You shouldn't be treated any differently than other minorities. It shouldn't be an issue at all.' That was really great. It was his first acknowledgment to me that my sexual orientation was OK with him."

Such a stance seems to be a far cry from Goldwater's unsuccessful, passionate fight in the Senate against the Civil Rights Act of 1964, a landmark piece of legislation that prohibits racial discrimination in employment, housing, and public accommodations. "I think he may have some guilt about that vote," Ross says. "I know he doesn't want to be seen as a bigot."

Goldwater says he continues to oppose the Civil Rights Act of 1964 because he believes it violates the constitutional rights of property owners. But he says that in the Senate, he worked hard to secure the rights of Arizona's Native Americans and notes that as the owner of a chain of department stores in the Southwest in the '50s, he broke rank with many of his competitors by hiring black salesclerks. In the late '80s, during Arizona's long, mean debate over declaring a state holiday to honor civil rights leader Martin Luther King Jr., Goldwater crossed swords with then-governor Even Mecham, a Republican, by quietly letting the state's politicians know that he supported the holiday.

In addition to Ross, Goldwater's wife, Susan, also played a role in gently encouraging Goldwater to go public with his support for the antidiscrimination ordinance and opposition of the military ban. Ross describes Susan Goldwater as a "catalyst" for gay rights issues, and his grandfather agrees, saying that in that respect she is similar to his first wife, Margaret, a Planned Parenthood activist who died of emphysema in 1986. (Susan Goldwater declined to be interviewed for this article, saying she prefers that the spotlight be focused on her husband.)

"My wife is very concerned about the rights of gays, and I think she's right to be concerned," Goldwater says. "She probably talks to me about it more than anyone else. If my wives weren't an influence on me, I wouldn't have married them. You don't marry a woman just because she's pretty or well-built. You marry one because you love her and can get along with her."

Less than a year after speaking out on the Phoenix gay rights ordinance, Goldwater again ran afoul of Arizona's Republicans, this time by endorsing the congressional bid of Democrat Karan English. Her Republican opponent, former White House political aide Doug Wead, was tied to the religious right and had moved to Arizona from Washington, D.C., to run for the seat, which was created when the size of Arizona's congressional delegation increased due to reapportionment.

Goldwater says Wead had angered him by calling himself a Goldwater Republican during campaign appearances. "I'd endorse a Democrat anytime over a religious-right Republican who came to Arizona because there was a new seat and figured he would just pick it up," he says. "That's not my idea of what it takes to be in government."

Indeed, it is on the role of the religious right that Goldwater most sharply parts company with the Republican Party. A staunch supporter of abortion rights, Goldwater has been openly critical of the religious right's influence on the party and on the country's politics in general. During the early '80s, when televangelist Jerry Falwell's political star was on the rise, Goldwater told a reporter that "every good Christian ought to kick Falwell right in the ass."

More than ten years later, Goldwater, an Episcopalian who is descended from Polish Orthodox Jews, says he stands by the sentiment. "I don't have any respect for the religious right," he says. "There is no place in this country for practicing religion in politics. That goes for Falwell, [Pat] Robertson, and all the rest of those political preachers. There are a detriment to the country, and the sooner they get their asses out of politics, the better. I look at these religious television shows, and they are raising big money on God. One million dollars, 3 million, 5 million—they brag about it. I don't believe in that. It's not a very religious thing to do."

E.J. Montini, a political columnist for *The Arizona Republic,* a Phoenix newspaper, says the split between Goldwater and the Republican Party has more to do with the party's swing to the right than with any philosophical change on Goldwater's part. "On almost every issue he's a standard right-wing guy," Montini says. "What's happened is that as far right as he can be, the right wing has gone beyond him. There was a time when people thought it was not possible to go beyond Goldwater in conservatism, that it would be like falling off the edge of the earth."

Many of the right-wingers who now find themselves at odds with Goldwater's positions, such as *National Review* editor William F. Buckley, syndicated columnist Patrick Buchanan, and Family Research Council head Gary Bauer, started their political careers in Goldwater's 1964 presidential campaign. Sen. John McCain (R-Ariz.), a Vietnam veteran who was elected to replace Goldwater in the Senate largely on the strength of Goldwater's endorsement, was one of the most outspoken opponents of lifting the ban.

The Nation magazine associate editor Andrew Kopkind says Goldwater "was really taken for a ride by the ideologues in the party who later became the religious right and the Reaganites. I don't think Goldwater understood that any of this was happening. He really thinks of himself as a libertarian conservative who just talks about what he wants to talk about. He's not dumb, but his lack of political sophistication allowed a lot of these ideologues to get started in his name. Now they are hard to stop."

Montini says that despite his maverick political views, Goldwater remains popular in Arizona and continues to command respect among conservatives across the country. "People respect him even when he takes unpopular positions because he says what he honestly believes instead of doing what most politicians do, which is to say what they honestly believe people want to hear," he says. "One of the reasons he got so many people upset about his position on the [gays in the military] issue is precisely because he commands so much respect."

But with the gays in the military issue, even Goldwater may have gone too far. After his *Washington Post* commentary was published, callers to radio talk shows in Arizona frequently called him senile, doddering, and a fag lover. And the commentary drew criticism from Buckley, who complained that by speaking out forcefully on the issue, Goldwater "invites polarization."

Goldwater says he's not surprised by Buckley's barb and responds to it diplomatically and graciously—like a politician. "I know Bill Buckley as well as I know my own brother, and if he hadn't said what he said, I'd have thought something was wrong with him. He's writing like Bill Buckley, and he's a hell of a good writer. But when you're 85 years old," he adds with a smile, "criticism doesn't mean a damn thing to you."

DAVID MIXNER: FRIEND OF NO ONE?

by John Gallagher

November 30, 1993

A year ago gay power broker David Mixner was basking in the glory of Bill Clinton's impending inauguration as president. After raising an estimated $3 million from gays and lesbians for Clinton's presidential campaign, Mixner was eagerly awaiting the time when the new president would fulfill the campaign promises he had made on gay rights and AIDS issues.

The most prominent of the promises, of course, was Clinton's pledge to lift the Pentagon's ban on gay and lesbian military personnel. Of all gay rights concerns, Mixner says, "it was the issue Clinton was most comfortable with. He had no problem understanding that kind of blatant discrimination."

But what followed was not what Mixner expected. A week into his term, Clinton's efforts to lift the ban spurred furious opposition in Congress and at the Pentagon. Clinton delayed and then waffled. Within weeks Mixner was berating Clinton, a man who just months earlier he had repeatedly and publicly called a personal friend.

In a speech in March, Mixner pleaded with Clinton not to "negotiate our freedom away." In the weeks that followed, as the Administration gradually backed off its pledge to lift the ban, Mixner's disillusionment deepened. He upbraided Clinton on he ABC television news interview program *Nightline,* repeated his criticisms in a letter to the president, and spoke to the predominantly gay Metropolitan Community Church congregations in Dallas and Phoenix of the betrayal he felt. In July Mixner was arrested for participating in acts of civil disobedience during a ban-related protest outside the White House.

"In many ways the past year has brought me some of the most difficult decisions I have ever made," Mixner says. In particular, he contends, the decisions to appear on *Nightline* and to protest outside the White House were "extraordinarily painful." Last spring *Vanity Fair* had noted Mixner's close ties to Clinton in giddily dubbing him "the undisputed leader of the latest wave of the gay movement," but by summer his welcome at the White House was worn out, and his currency among gay rights activists was seriously devalued.

"He unjustly criticized the president," fumed White House political director Rahm Emanuel in an interview in *The Wall Street Journal* in June. "If somebody criticizes the president, then I think he is persona non grata."

Says Michael Petrelis, who last year was a member of ACT UP's presidential project: "Gays and lesbians thought Mixner's friendship with Clinton equaled power for the gay community. Of course that wasn't true. Mixner's friendship with Clinton blinded them to Clinton's dismal record on gay rights and AIDS issues as governor of Arkansas. If we had evaluated Clinton in a realistic way, we would have been prepared to wage a successful battle to lift the ban."

Many other activists feel just as strongly, acknowledges William Waybourn, executive director of the Gay and Lesbian Victory Fund, a donor network that funds the campaigns of openly gay and lesbian political candidates. "A lot of people don't like Clinton, and that's fine," he says. "They don't have to."

Mixner says that he has not talked to Clinton since his arrest but is not worried about clout he may have lost. "My mother used to say that whenever you close a window, a door opens somewhere," he says.

Despite appearances to the contrary, Mixner's window at the White House may not be altogether closed. "A lot of people think David has been marginalized because of what has happened," Waybourn says. "Nothing could be further from the truth. There is no question that David continues to play a major role in the direction of our movement." Others, though, say privately that Mixner has a chronic weakness for hyperbole and may have exaggerated not only the amount of access he lost with Clinton after the arrest but also the amount of access he had to the president in the first place.

Still, there is little question that Mixner retains access to many Administration officials as well as Democratic National Committee chairman David Wilhelm. It's that access, says Torie Osborn, former executive director of the lobbying group National Gay and Lesbian Task Force, that allows Mixner to redefine gay politics by fusing Democratic Party politics with street activism.

"There's nobody in his league," she says. "When you have someone who is a first-rate, nationally prominent campaign-manager type like David Mixner, it is rare to have in that person someone who also knows that the civil rights movement wouldn't have been anything without street tactics. He understands that it's about organizing and power honchoing in Washington at the same time."

However, Mixner's most visible Washington power play—creation of the Campaign for Military Service, a coalition group that led the effort early this year to repeal the ban on gay and lesbian service personnel—was notable for its failure. By Memorial Day, when CMS attempted to mold public opinion on the military issue by launching a television advertising campaign, both Congress and the Administration were already set in their intention to retain the ban, at least in large part.

After the setback, several activists, such as Tim McFeeley, executive director of the Human Rights Campaign Fund, a gay political group, accused Mixner of creating a false sense of security about their ability to win on the issue, though congressional opposition to lifting the ban had begun to crystallize even before Clinton was inaugurated.

But Mixner says the entire Clinton campaign shared his belief that the ban would be easy to lift. "We made mistakes," he says. "If you want someone who doesn't make mistakes, I'm not the person." It is the Administration, he says, that deserves the blame for the loss on the military issue. Clinton's transition team, he charges, took "a very patronizing attitude" toward gays and lesbians. "We hard from them after decisions were made," he says. "They were saying, 'We'll take care of you. Don't get in the way.'"

Still, when Clinton took office in January, Mixner agreed to support the Administration's decision to delay a decision on the ban for six months. He withdrew his support three months later, when Clinton hinted he might be willing to segregate gay and lesbian troops from heterosexuals.

Mixner says his promise to support the delay is his "biggest political regret"; it was Clinton's passion on the subject that caused him to make it, he says. "When you have someone as visionary as Bill Clinton was on the issue," he says, "it builds faith."

Mixner says he has learned his lesson: "Our biggest mistake was unconditionally believing in them, believing that they were really not lying to us, placing too much power and too much faith in them." As for Clinton, he says, "We should never have put our fate in one individual's hands, especially in a nongay individual's hands."

Petrelis says if Mixner had objectively examined Clinton's record in Arkansas, he never would have trusted Clinton in the first place. "After all our movement has been through with AIDS and homophobia, it is not OK to say, 'Let's trust this Democratic candidate simply because he's not George Bush,' " he says.

Yet, unlike openly gay U.S. representative Barney Frank (D-Mass.) and many other gay and lesbian political insiders, Mixner says that with proper backing from the White House, the military issue could have been won. "I still believe it could have been done," he says. "If the White House would have gone all out, it certainly would have had the votes needed to sustain a veto" of legislation reinstating the ban.

The military debate was not the first brush with political failure for Mixner, who cut his activist teeth during the civil rights and antiwar movements of the '60s and '70s. His outlook was so shaped by those experiences that his conversation is still liberally sprinkled with references to civil rights leaders Dr. Martin Luther King Jr. and Mohandas Gandhi.

In 1985 Mixner organized the Great Peace March for Nuclear Disarmament. His plan called for 5,000 people to march from Los Angeles to Washington, D.C., to protest the arms race, and the march was to conclude triumphantly with a million-person rally in Washington. But the march only drew 1,500 people, and two weeks after it began, Mixner had to tell the marchers, who were in the Mojave Desert, that the event had run out of money.

The next year Mixner played a behind-the-scenes role in efforts to defeat a California initiative that would allow people with AIDS to be quarantined. Osborn, who worked with Mixner on the disarmament march, says the work was his "way of doing penance" for the failure of the march.

Despite its negative image, Mixner says the Clinton administration may be able to rehabilitate its relationship with gays and lesbians. Clinton, he says, "is not an evil man. He's a good man with the right instincts who blundered badly. I like him. He's a friend. Friends make mistakes. You might point out the mistakes, but you don't immediately hate him. If you do, what kind of friend are you?"

Responsibility for helping the Administration redeem itself, he says, falls on gay and lesbian political organizers as a group. "My main goal is not to be the sole access" to the White House, he says. "My job is not to be the kingpin, the honcho. It's to open as many doors as possible to as many people as possible. I want them to keep their good relationships with the president. Let me take the heat."

If gay and lesbian political organizers "do our job right, by 1996 this will be the most enlightened administration around," he says. "Practical considerations tell us it can't ignore us. Somewhere along the line Clinton will have to sign something. It's important to know when to express outrage in the streets and when to sit down and talk."

Meanwhile, Mixner says he will go "wherever I can be helpful. I'm a volunteer, truly. I'm certainly willing to go to jail again. If I can help with fund-raising, I will. I still have many, many friends in the Administration, and I think part of my job is to keep the heat up in the kitchen there."

SUICIDAL TENDENCIES: IS ANGUISH OVER SEXUAL ORIENTATION CAUSING GAY AND LESBIAN TEENS TO KILL THEMSELVES?

by Chris Bull

April 5, 1994

Above the entrance to the office of Out Youth, an Austin, Tex., group for gay and lesbian teenagers, hangs a framed photograph of Bobby Griffith, a California man who killed himself at age 20 in 1983 after years of anguish over his homosexuality. For the members of Out Youth and for gay-youth advocates across the country, Griffith—whose death received considerable media attention—is a national symbol of the plight of gay and lesbian teenagers.

But Out Youth's teenage members need not look all the way to California to find a symbol of the link between gay and lesbian teenagers and suicide: Last August 20-year-old Out Youth member Guy C. Sterling hanged himself with a belt in his apartment after several years of fighting with his parents about his homosexuality. His death prompted so many suicide attempts by other members of the group that Out Youth's adult counselors stepped up their practice of asking members to sign pledges promising to seek out a counselor if they became depressed.

"A lot of these kids have absolutely nobody in the world," says Out Youth program director Lisa Rogers. "They are hated and despised everywhere they go. They are so isolated that it's not surprising that a lot of them don't see a future. Since Guy's death we have had to be even more conscientious about talking about suicide and depression."

For gay-youth advocates the connection between suicide and sexual orientation is far too strong to ignore or even question. But a growing number of prominent researchers who study youth suicide contend that gay and lesbian youths are no more prone to suicide than their heterosexual counterparts. Indeed, some of the researchers have accused gay-youth advocates of manipulating the issue for political gain. The conflict is complex and emotional, pitting youth advocates—who blame the problem on homophobia and the isolation experienced by gay and lesbian teenagers—against some scientists who contend that in the overwhelming majority of cases, youth suicide is caused by a history of mental illness, regardless of the victim's sexual orientation.

"It boils down to a debate over whether social or psychological factors are more prevalent in youth suicide," says Bill Bailey, legislative and federal affairs officer for the American Psychological Association. "Most kids who commit or attempt suicide have a history of mental illness, but we shouldn't ignore the clinical evidence that tells us that some kids are struggling with their sexual orientation and are taking their own lives because of that struggle."

The debate centers on a report prepared by the youth suicide task force of the youth suicide task force of the Department of Health and Human Services in 1989 and suppressed by the Bush administration under pressure from right-wing groups and conservatives in Congress. Based on interviews with 500 gay and lesbian youths in San Francisco, the report alleged that 30% of those interviewed had attempted suicide at least once and recommended a series of initiatives aimed at ending discrimination based on sexual orientation.

None of the task force's recommendations has been implemented to date, but under Clinton administration HHS secretary Donna Shalala, the report has taken on new significance because another federal task force is moving toward designing the first government-sponsored large-scale study of youth suicide and sexual orientation. A task force composed of officials from the federal Centers for Disease Control and Prevention and the National Institute of Mental Health, is scheduled to make a recommendation on the study by July. Says HHS deputy assistant secretary for public affairs Victor F. Zonana: "Secretary Shalala is interested in addressing the problems faced by gay youth, and we plan to have something to say on it in the future."

But despite the changing political climate at HHS, the combination of right-wing pressure and the methodological questions raised by suicidologists—researchers who explore the psychological forces that lead to suicide—causes some observers to wonder whether the link between gay and lesbian youth suicide and antigay discrimination can ever be adequately addressed by the federal government.

"I'm well aware that we're stepping into a political minefield," says Lloyd Potter, a behavioral scientist at the National Center for Injury Prevention and Control at the CDC who is coordinating the new HHS gay teen suicide task force. "I'm cautiously optimistic about our ability to conduct research on sexual orientation, but just because I have some optimism doesn't mean it's going to happen."

Adds Herbert Hendin, president of the American Suicide Foundation, a private research group: "There is no question that suicide has become politicized and that politicization is making calm and rational debate about the issue difficult. Every group from Vietnam veterans to gays and lesbian feels it has a stake in establishing high suicide rates among its members, as if they are not facing enough problems as it is. That is making it very difficult to conduct good science on the topic."

Teenage suicide has been the topic of intense federal concern since 1982, when a government-funded survey found that the incidence of suicide among adolescents between the ages of 15 and 19 had jumped from 2.7 per 100,000 in 1950 to 9.3 in 1982. (The incidence of youth suicide stands at 11.3 per 100,000 today.) The Reagan administration made research into youth suicide prevention a priority, commissioning dozens of studies on the subject that examined every problem from alcoholism to child abuse and the roles each can play in suicidal behavior.

But the federal government did not follow the 1989 HHS report with any major studies looking at the role of sexual orientation in youth suicide. "It's a vicious cycle," says University of Minnesota assistant professor of pediatrics Gary Remafedi, author of the forthcoming book *Death by Denial: Studies of Attempted and Completed Suicide in Gay and Lesbian and Bisexual Youth*. "Without government funding the basic research can't possibly be done because, through funding, the government more or less controls what can and cannot be done."

Remafedi says politics causes the neglect. "It's simply not expedient for government researchers to study gay youth," he claims. "The government doesn't want to be seen as undertaking studies that could benefit the gay and lesbian community in any way. There is a constant fear of Congress's stepping in."

The absence of a comprehensive study of the role of sexual orientation in youth suicide means that the federal government's official youth suicide prevention guidelines make no mention of sexual orientation and that few local prevention programs are equipped to care for adolescents who are struggling with their sexual orientation. In compiling statistics on suicide for its survey on youth risk behavior, for example, the CDC addressed the role of race and gender but left out sexual orientation altogether.

"Prevention campaigns are designed for the general population because there is no awareness that gay and lesbian youths are at high risk," says Joyce Hunter, a behavioral researcher at the New York State Psychiatry Institute's HIV center in New York City. "That sends an even stronger message to gay kids that there is no one out there for them."

In the absence of government-commissioned research, most studies on gay and lesbian youth suicide have been conducted by private researchers, social workers, or advocates for gay and lesbian youths. The fieldwork that formed the basis for the 1989 HHS report was conducted by Paul Gibson, a San Francisco social worker with a sizable number of young gay and lesbian clients. In a 1991 study published in the journal *Pediatrics*, Remafedi also found that nearly 30% of the gay and lesbian youths he surveyed had attempted suicide. Studies by the Hetrick-Martin Institute, a New York City service and advocacy group for gay and lesbian youths, have also found high rates of attempted suicide by gay and lesbian youths.

Conservatives are determined to keep the federal government from researching the topic. After the findings of the 1989 HHS report were published, William Dannemeyer, who was at the time a Republican member of the House of Representatives from California, called for then-president Bush to "dismiss from the public service all persons still employed who concocted this homosexual pledge of allegiance and sealed the lid on these misjudgments for good." HHS secretary Louis Sullivan chimed in as well, writing in a letter to Dannemeyer that Gibson's work "undermined the institution of the family." In 1991 complaints from Sen. Jesse Helms (R-N.C.) led HHS to cancel what was to be the nation's largest-ever study of the sexual behavior of teenagers. Helms had complained that the study would invade the privacy of young people by asking them about private sexual matters.

The atmosphere surrounding federally funded research relating to teen sexuality has relaxed little during the Clinton administration. On February 4 the Senate voted 93–0 in support of an amendment to an education bill that prevents federal surveys from asking public school students about "sexual behavior and attitudes" without prior written consent from parents.

Despite the change in administrations, Bailey says a number of scientists who depend on federal funding are still reluctant to explore the role sexual orientation plays in many social problems. "There are numerous examples of studies or programs that get killed just because the phrase *sexual orientation* is in them," he says. "There are a whole range of social issues and problems where the role of sexual orientation has not been looked at. There are all kinds of examples of misplaced sensitivities that have affected our ability to save lives."

Adds Potter: "Asking a general population sample questions about sexual orientation is politically sensitive. We are doing research in a very conservative time. We have to be an innocuous as possible in asking questions. We can't afford to offend anyone, and that makes getting accurate information difficult."

As a result many of the studies being done are open to scientific criticism on methodological grounds. In a controversial May 3, 1993, editorial in *The New Yorker,* David Shaffer, professor of child psychiatry at the Columbia University College of Physicians and Surgeons, argued that because Gibson's work focused on gay and lesbian teens staying at youth centers and homeless shelters rather than on a scientifically selected sample, the 1989 HHS report is seriously flawed. The teenagers Gibson interviewed, he wrote, "can be expected to have high rates of suicide attempts."

Shaffer, considered one of the country's leading authorities on youth suicide, accuses advocates for gay and lesbian youth of politicizing the youth suicide issue because they cite the 30% figure while knowing full well that the methodology that produced it is flawed. "Suicide is usually a story of misperceptions and misunderstandings, of feelings of despair and lack of control; it cannot be attributed to simply having a difficult life," he wrote. "It has no place on anyone's political agenda."

In the article Shaffer referred to his own research, carried out over several years in the '80s, into the suicides of 120 teenagers in New York City. His study found that only 2.5% of the victims could be identified as gay or lesbian, a figure in proportion to the suicide rates for all youths. The study was based on interviews with the victims' relatives and friends about the sexual orientation along with other characteristics of the deceased, a research technique called a "psychological autopsy." Shaffer cites two other psychological autopsy studies to back up his own. One, conducted in St. Louis in 1959, found no gays or lesbians in a group of 1,333 suicides. The other, conducted in 1986 in San Diego, found a gay suicide rate of 7% among suicides under the age of 30.

But Shaffer's critics, including advocates for gay and lesbian youths and researchers who believe that social forces play a determining role in teen suicide, say that Shaffer's research methodology is also flawed. Even if family members and friends had been aware of the victim's sexual orientation, according to the critics' analysis, they would have been unlikely to disclose it out of either guilt over the death or shame over the sexual orientation or both. "The youths who are at the greatest risk for suicide are the ones who are least likely to reveal their sexual orientation to anyone," Remafedi says. "Suicide may be a way of making sure that no one ever knows."

The reluctance of family and friends to identify the sexual orientation of the victims may have been exacerbated by the questions Shaffer used, the critics allege. In Shaffer's study interviewers asked a series of questions, including "Did he ever say that he wished that he was a girl or insist that he was a girl?" or "Did he think it would be better not to have a penis?"

Hendin says the use of such questions can affect the outcome of a psychological autopsy. "If it were me asking the question and I thought that parents would attach stigma to it, I would probably ask it at the end of the interview," he says. "And I would be sure to make allowances for the fact that it would be hard to get an honest answer. Sometimes, if the questions are presented in terms of helping others, people will be surprisingly forthcoming. Other times there is a great need to deny everything. It's very unpredictable."

According to Hendin, the 1959 study is likely to have undercounted the actual suicide rate of gays and lesbians as well. "That study is undoubtedly subject to concealment of sexual orientation," he says. "If we accept a male homosexual rate of 4% in the general population, the statistical possibility of finding no homosexuals in a survey of 120 suicides is very, very low. The problem is that in the 1950s, there was even more concealment of sexual orientation than there is today."

Shaffer disagrees. "At the time of the study, the St. Louis researchers were thought to be among the finest in the world," he says. "The authors were obsessed with accuracy. And it was undertaken at the time of the Kinsey report, which means that researchers were probably comfortable with studying homosexuality."

Magnifying the complexity of the debate is another, more widely publicized debate over the percentage of American youths who are gay or lesbian. "Every study about sexual orientation is speculative at this point because we don't have an accurate baseline number yet," Hendin says. "If Kinsey's 10% figure is accurate, then Shaffer's numbers look very low; but if the actual proportion is closer to 1%, then his numbers look much higher. We're trying to measure the ground while it is shifting."

The debate over youth suicide and sexual orientation is taking place in the context of an even larger debate among scientists about the causes of suicide. Mainstream suicidologists argue that research indicates that in the overwhelming majority of suicides, the victim has a history of severe mental illness. Social factors like homosexuality, race, or poverty may play a role, they say, but are unlikely to prompt a suicide attempt by themselves.

In fact, Shaffer says that because mental illness is the cause of most suicides, by arguing for a direct link between homosexuality and suicide, gay-youth advocates are unwittingly arguing that homosexuality is a disease. "The idea that mental illness is the cause of suicide is based on an enormous amount of research," he says. "The bottom line is that kids have to be pretty disturbed to kill themselves, and most—gay or straight—just don't do it."

By alleging that 30% of gay and lesbian youths attempt suicide, he adds, activists are shooting themselves in the foot. During the debate over the military ban on gay and lesbian service personnel, he notes, military officials repeatedly invoked the high suicide rates of gays and lesbians as an example of the threat gays and lesbians pose to military order and discipline. "Mental illness is a very bad metaphor for gay youth," he says. "It could very well backfire if the advocates insist on using it."

The view that sexual orientation is rarely the sole cause of suicide is underscored by the stories of some gay youths themselves. In letters, calls, and visits to gay youth groups across the country, teens cite a litany of ills, from abusive parents to drug and alcohol abuse, some of which are unrelated or only partially related to their sexual orientation, making the exact cause of their distress difficult to determine.

In a letter received last year by the Indiana Youth Group, an Indianapolis gay and lesbian support group, an anonymous 17-year-old boy wrote about being verbally abused by his father even before his parents realized he was gay. "One night two months ago, my dad was cutting me down as I was getting ready to go out to the movies," he wrote. "My dad started saying stuff like 'Look how you're dressed like a fag, little faggot boy.' I got so upset that night that it was the first time I tried to kill myself. As I was getting my room in order and planning the way I was going to kill myself, I stopped and cried so hard: 'Why am I killing myself because of my dad?' So I said, 'The hell with him.'"

IYG member Jim Deckard, 20, is another case in point. After attempting suicide three times in his teens—twice by slashing his wrists and once by driving his car off a cliff—he finally overcame his suicidal feelings by joining IYG. Deckard says that while the struggle over his sexual orientation was a source of great unhappiness throughout his teenage years, he also struggled with a number of other problems, some—but not all—of which were related to his homosexuality.

"I came from an alcoholic family and was drinking a lot myself," he says. "My family was a mess, so I more or less had to raise myself. I had to go to work at age 14 to buy myself clothes for school. The combination was pretty hard. It's still hard for me to sort it all out."

Others, though, trace their suicidal thoughts almost exclusively to their struggle with their sexual orientation. Jason Curry, another 20-year-old member of IYG, says he also attempted suicide three times during his teenage years. "I very clearly remember feeling depressed and isolated because I was the only one who was gay," he says. "I thought I would never have any friends and would have to give up my family. The fact is that we are a minority group like no other. A black person would have other black friends, but gay kids can't even count on having other gay friends."

Shaffer says the psychological autopsy studies showing a relatively low number of gay youth suicides demonstrate the strength of gay youths in the face of great adversity and should be welcomed by gay advocates. "I actually take it as a very positive finding," he says. "In some ways it speaks to the positive mental health of gay youth. They can withstand the stress and grow up to be happy adults without resorting to suicide at a significantly higher rate than heterosexual youths."

But Remafedi says ignoring the role of sexual orientation in youth suicide is a mistake. "There clearly are social factors at work, and we have to do everything we can to alleviate them," he says. "Underlying mental illness simply can't account for the high suicide rate of gay and lesbian youth. We are raising the possibility that social factors rather than psychological factors may account for many suicides. It's a mistake to underestimate how powerful factors like homophobia can be in a young person's life."

Remafedi says that because the study of suicide has long been dominated by researchers with training in mental health, the profession has largely ignored the social and political aspects of suicide. "The findings of the studies indicating a high incidence of suicide among gay youth are a break from traditional thought because the researchers are looking for a psychological diagnosis where there is none," he says. "It's homophobia that's killing these kids."

Still, Shaffer's approach to youth suicide is the one that prevails among federal researchers who have been instrumental in thwarting studies examining the sexual component of suicide. In a little-noticed December 1990 article in *The Journal of the American Medical Association,* Susan J. Blumenthal, who at the time was serving as chief of behavioral medicine at NIMH and was regarded as the government's top suicide expert, outlined the government's suicide prevention efforts without mentioning sexual orientation.

In a response to the 1990 article in the June 1991 edition of the *Journal,* Yale University School of Medicine researcher Linda Snelling accused Blumenthal and other government suicide researchers of putting gay and lesbian youth "at risk of being ignored to death." In rebuttal Blumenthal said gay youth suicide has "been inadequately studied" but homosexuality "generally do[es] not provide sufficient cause for completed suicide."

But under Blumenthal, NIMH did not undertake a single study or prevention campaign aimed at gay and lesbian youths, despite her belief that the issue has not been sufficiently studied. And when the Clinton administration promoted Blumenthal to assistant deputy secretary for women's health at HHS last December, advocates for gay and lesbian youth were left wondering how deep Shalala's commitment to addressing the gay youth suicide issue really is.

"Having worked with gay and lesbian youth for more than 20 years, I don't understand how one of the government's top people can write an article that leaves out sexual orientation," Hunter says.

"It's really disturbing that government scientists are willing to overlook the evidence, however imperfect, that gay and lesbian youth are at great risk for suicide."

Blumenthal says that in 1990 she may have underestimated the severity of gay youth suicide. "I believe that mental illness is the major factor in 90% of youth suicide cases," she says. "Other stresses or losses have to come into play, whether they be genetic factors, because suicide runs in families, or biological factors, like a serotonin deficiency, or impulsiveness, to name just a few possibilities. If one or more of these factors are present along with access to a lethal method like a gun, suicide may take place. But there is also no question that the more accepting the social milieu, the less risk young gays and lesbians will have. Homophobia may be one of the many things that lowers the barrier to youth suicide."

As for NIMH's failure to commission a study of sexual orientation and youth suicide, Blumenthal says, "We didn't get any grant applications on that topic that I can remember. It is an important issue to address, and I certainly hope it will be the focus of some future studies."

Still, Blumenthal says she sees only a small role for mention of sexual orientation in HHS suicide prevention campaigns. "I'm an advocate for new forms of health education that take place early on and focus on promoting healthy social behavior," she says. "Fighting antigay attitudes could be a component, but I think the bigger issue is giving young people a great sense of mental-health skills."

The relationship between youth suicide and sexual orientation is further complicated by AIDS. A 1989 study conducted by researchers at Cornell University Medical Center in New York City found that people with AIDS are 36 times more likely to attempt suicide than those without AIDS at a comparable age. Little systematic research has been conducted on gay youth, but advocates say HIV infection and the risk of it dramatically magnify the likelihood that gay youths will contemplate suicide.

In a study of HIV-positive youths published as a chapter in the 1992 book *Living and Dying With AIDS,* New York City researcher Hunter found that fear of AIDS, whether real or imagined, adds to the burden gay youths experience. "Gay teenagers already have so much to deal with that when they find out that they are HIV-positive or even that they are going to have to live in a world where HIV is prevalent and a constant threat, they become overwhelmed," she says. "It's just another factor that can add to their suicidal thoughts."

Whatever the outcome of the federal task force's efforts, advocates for gay and lesbian youth say they desperately need assistance and direction from the federal government. After the ABC television newsmagazine *20/20* ran a segment on gay and lesbian youth last March that included a profile of IYG, the group received more than 100,000 phone calls and letters from gay and lesbian teens across the country but was able to assist fewer than 1,000.

In one of the letters, a 15-year-old boy from Jackson, Miss., pleaded with the group for help. "If you refuse me, all I will have left is suicide," he wrote. "I am a gay teen. When my friends found out, they all disowned me. Some even come together to beat me up. I am not afraid or ashamed to say that I have never hurt or cried as much as I am doing right now. I am so alone. Even my own father will have nothing to do with me. My mother does not know, and I plan to keep it like that for as long as I can. Right now she is the only person talking to me. You guys are my only hope. I beg of you to help."

Even though IYG received the letter more than a year ago, executive director Chris Gonzales says it still haunts him. "We sent the young man some information," he says. "But there's not much more we can do for these kids. We just don't have the resources. It keeps you wondering what became of him. The letter is a desperate cry for help. Is he still alive?"

San Francisco social worker Gibson, who now works with people with AIDS, says the same kind of thoughts motivated him when he wrote a summary of his research for the 1989 HHS report. "I wrote it not as a political tract but out of concern for the youths with whom I was working as a way to get the country to understand their needless suffering," he says. "It's tragic that we have allowed politics to get in the way of helping them. Gay and lesbian youths are one of the easier groups to help. Many times it's just a matter of giving them accurate information, support, and an accurate understanding of who they are. How many times do we have an opportunity to help people so easily?"

THE LOST GENERATION: A SECOND WAVE OF HIV INFECTIONS AMONG YOUNG GAY MEN LEAVES EDUCATORS WORRIED ABOUT THE FUTURE OF THE EPIDEMIC

by Chris Bull and John Gallagher

May 31, 1994

When Kevin received the results of his HIV antibody test last year, he wasn't surprised to learn he had tested positive. The 27-year-old gay man, who says he became sexually active six years ago in Washington, D.C., recalled several instances of unprotected intercourse and feared the worst. "I'd made my mistakes," he says, "and it was time for my reckoning."

Kevin is hardly alone. According to recent surveys and anecdotal reports, a sizable number of young gay men who became sexually active well after the onset of the AIDS epidemic are testing HIV-positive despite a barrage of educational messages. A 1993 survey of gay men aged 17 to 22 in

San Francisco, for example, found that nearly one third had engaged in at least one instance of un-protected anal intercourse—the riskiest form of sexual activity—in the prior six months.

For these young men, testing HIV-positive may be even more devastating than for those who contracted the virus before scientists had even identified its existence. "All I could think of was how I had done something terribly wrong and thrown my life away, like all those nasty things conservatives have been saying about us were true," Kevin says. "I remember my mom, who has always been really cool about my being gay, saying, 'How could you have been so stupid?' I was asking myself the same question."

More than a decade into the epidemic, educators are frantically reevaluating prevention strategies in the wake of what public health officials have dubbed the "second wave" of HIV infections among gay men, many even younger than Kevin. A 1993 report from the San Francisco Health Commis-sion found that almost 12% of 20- to 22-year-old gay men surveyed were HIV-positive, as were 4% of 17- to 19-year-olds. If those figures are not quickly reversed, health officials say, the current gen-eration of young urban gay men will have as high an infection rate by the time they reach their mid 30s as middle-aged gay men are thought to have today—close to 50%.

"The data is absolutely unacceptable," says Columbia University professor of public health Ronald Bayer, author of *Private Acts, Social Consequences: AIDS and the Politics of Public Health.* "AIDS education has failed an entire generation of gay men who are going to be wiped out if the current trajectory continues. The challenge is to put a renewed emphasis on prevention campaigns that work."

Although the epidemic has killed more than 100,000 gay men, educators still lack basic demo-graphic and psychological information about the sexual behavior and attitudes of gay men that would allow for the design of effective prevention campaigns. Even worse, educators often can't agree on how best to design prevention campaigns based on what they do know.

"AIDS has been marked by a search for a technological—with a heavy emphasis on biomed-ical—solution when there may well be none," says Harvard University history of science profes-sor Allan M. Brandt, author of *No Magic Bullet: A Social History of Venereal Disease in the United States Since 1880.* "As a result, we don't know nearly enough about sexual behavior change, which is the only sure way to save lives."

Further compounding the problem is opposition from conservatives in Congress and right-wing groups, which are using the high infection rates as one of their primary arguments against govern-ment funding for sexually explicit AIDS education campaigns. In its final report before it closed its doors in 1993, the National Commission on AIDS blamed antigay conservatives for the lack of a serious national prevention campaign that it said could cut the annual rate of new infections in half. "The specter of male homosexuality has repeatedly been used to circumscribe prevention efforts," the report maintained. "Continuation of this situation is morally indefensible."

In many ways AIDS education is the victim of its own success. After annual new infections of gay men in San Francisco and other major urban areas declined from a rate of close to 25% in 1983 to less than 1% by 1987, some AIDS educators declared victory, closed up shop, and went home. Public health experts were widely quoted in the media lauding the gay community's AIDS prevention campaign as one of the most successful examples of behavior modification in the history of public health. The accomplishment was even more impressive because it involved sex, which public health experts have long identified as perhaps the most difficult behavior to change because it is linked to deep-seated emotional and social taboos.

"What is true is that by 1987 in San Francisco, people honestly believed that the battle had been won," says Dan Wohlfeiler, education director of Stop AIDS Project San Francisco, an HIV prevention group that briefly closed its doors three years after its founding in 1984. "The feeling at that time was that we could shut down and allow our resources to be used at other agencies that really needed them. We had no idea how difficult our task really was."

Those optimistic projections proved to be a fatal miscalculation. The annual rate of new infection among gay men is now almost 3%—a far cry from earlier figures but still alarming to educators. "By 1989 it was apparent that a couple of things were happening," Wohlfeiler says. "The community is not under a bell jar. A lot of new people moved in, and younger people came out. These people were not part of the community that was mobilized against AIDS in the '80s."

The early optimism was based in part on the mistaken assumption that AIDS was a temporary affliction that scientists would eventually learn to cure or prevent with a vaccine. "It was ten years ago that [health and human services secretary] Margaret Heckler stood up and said that we have discovered the virus and would have a cure by the end of the decade," says David L. Kirp, a professor at the graduate school of public policy at the University of California, Berkeley. "It was seen as just a matter of having a little less sex with fewer partners and learning how to make safe sex sexy. The understanding now is that some form of HIV will be around as long as there are human beings on this planet. All of a sudden gay men have to learn how to change the way they relate to one another permanently."

In the case of young gay men, educators say the key is getting them started practicing safe sex as soon as they become sexually active. But if the experience of older gay men—some of whom are reverting to unsafe practices—is any indication, establishing a lifetime commitment to safe sex is easier said than done. Moreover, the heavy prevalence of HIV infection among gay men in major urban areas makes every unprotected sexual experience fraught with risk.

"In the early '80s you really did need to have a lot of partners to acquire a partner with HIV infection," says Jeffrey A. Kelly, director of the Center for AIDS Intervention Research at the Medical College of Wisconsin. "Now in the big cities, if you have sex with two men, you have a 50% chance of meeting someone who is HIV-positive."

Researchers have identified many reasons gay men of all ages engage in unsafe sex, including depression, alcohol and drug use, survivor guilt, and sexual shame. Lack of knowledge about how to prevent transmission, though, is not one of them. "Typically, knowledge about how HIV is transmitted and about condoms is very high," says Roger Roffman, director of Project ARIES, an AIDS prevention service developed by the University of Washington's School of Social Work. Instead, the problem is "feeling kind of lonely and kind of horny on a Friday night, drinking too much, feeling attracted to someone, and fearing rejection if you take out a condom."

But educators disagree—often sharply—about whether AIDS prevention should focus narrowly on safe-sex practices or on larger issues of communal and personal responsibility. Walt Odets, a clinical psychologist in Berkeley, Calif., who has written extensively about sexual behavior and HIV prevention, contends that many AIDS education campaigns have failed by not taking into account the emotional content of gay men's sex lives.

"Some educators forget that sex often takes place on a sensual and irrational level," Odets says. "We try to pretend there's no reason gay men would want to have unprotected sex with each other, because sex is just a big game. But people practice unsafe sex for emotional reasons—it brings you closer to your partner. This exchange of semen is one way to displaying affection for one another."

Contrary to what some conservative critics believe, research indicates that lust is not the only factor that incites unsafe sex among gay men. "When love and affection come into the picture, people tend to forget what they know," says Kelly. "Finding someone special can make you feel an illusion of safety."

That illusion is especially troubling in the case of young gay men, who often engage in what educators describe as serial monogamy. "With the younger guys what we observe is a pattern," says Tom Coates, director of the Center for AIDS Prevention Studies at the University of California, San Francisco. "They are doing OK, then they get into a relationship and practice unsafe sex, and that relationship may not last very long. People who are just starting to date have a more rapid turnover, but it's a situation that's perceived as safe. In a desire to be more intimate with a partner, safety is dropped. That can lead to infections."

The problem is further complicated by the inability of educators to reach a consensus on what constitutes safe sex, leaving gay men unsure of exactly how to protect themselves. Studies indicate that unprotected anal intercourse is by far the most dangerous activity, but research is inconclusive about anal sex with condoms and unprotected oral sex. As a result, safe-sex guidelines often vary from city to city.

But as some educators turn their attention to the emotional aspects of sex, others fear that prevention efforts are becoming too squeamish just when gay sex clubs are reemerging across the country. Most clubs mandate that patrons engage only in safe sex, but public health officials in New York City complain that the mandates are often poorly enforced and have periodically threatened to shut the clubs down. In San Francisco the Coalition for Healthy Sex, a group of sex club owners, has established a system to monitor the clubs.

"A lot of times you will hear educators say things like 'When you go to bed with a man, use condoms,' implying a one-person-per-night kind of thing when the reality is that a lot of people are out leaning against a tree in a park having sex with lots of people," says Christopher Wittke, public-sex outreach coordinator for Boston's AIDS Action Committee. "We're telling people to protect the one they love rather than to love and protect the one they're with."

Wittke's view is bolstered by some preliminary research. In an unpublished study conducted by Bayer and his associates at Columbia University, gay men surveyed were more likely to practice safe sex in committed relationships than during anonymous sexual encounters. "In sexual encounters in bars, parks, or bathrooms, there is a tendency for people to care less about one another," says Bayer. "The unspoken calculus is that one's partner is dispensable because he is engaging in casual sex. In an ongoing relationship we found that the idea of not telling a partner about HIV infection is usually considered morally outrageous."

In an article in a forthcoming edition of *American Journal of Public Health,* Bayer argues that this evidence demonstrates that AIDS educators should stress the positive role personal and communal responsibility can play in HIV prevention. "For a long time," Bayer says, "AIDS campaigns have stressed protecting yourself, but a sense of moral responsibility would indicate that you should be concerned about your partner as well."

But Steve Humes, director of HIV prevention at New York City's Gay Men's Health Crisis, the country's largest AIDS service group, says he fears that many gay men don't care enough about themselves to care about others. Educational messages, he argues, fall short when they fail to address the intense psychological burden of living in the midst of an epidemic. "You can hardly put an entire community in therapy," Humes says, "but we have to find ways for gay men to value themselves enough to protect themselves. The question for educators today is, How do we build up gay men's self-esteem?"

Indeed, the widespread despair among gay men caused by the overwhelming horror of AIDS has itself become an obstacle to AIDS prevention. Many have seen their entire community of friends decimated by the disease and wonder how long they themselves may be able to hang on. To combat this situation several AIDS groups are featuring an educational campaign titled "Be Here for the Cure," an attempt to remind gay men that, despite the toll AIDS has taken, there is hope for the future.

"For many people this does feel like a hopeless period," says Coates. "We've reached a wave of the epidemic where lots of people are dying, so it's hard to pay attention or even want to pay attention to protecting yourself. So now AIDS education is going to have to deal with issues of hope, caregiving, and survival beyond AIDS."

This approach is a far cry from early prevention efforts, many of which used fear as a motivator. One notorious advertising campaign in San Francisco, for instance, depicted a man's legs covered with Kaposi's sarcoma lesions. "Fear was very motivating," says Tom Lindsay, a Stop AIDS Project educator. "But at this point in the epidemic, it doesn't work. People who have AIDS are around long enough so that AIDS is now part of the milieu. They don't want to be presented with the downside of it. They want to have a productive and fun life. Prevention can't be a downer."

But activists' switch to make campaigns more upbeat was tempered by the changing face of activism itself. Young gay men today lack some of the political and social support groups—ACT UP and Queer Nation in particular—that dominated the gay community's early activist response to the epidemic and helped establish safe-sex practices among their older counterparts by fostering a sense of purpose and belonging. ACT UP's New York chapter, for instance, designed its own educational materials as a way of making safe sex fashionable. One celebrated poster depicted an erect penis over the words MEN: USE CONDOMS OR BEAT IT.

"Some young gay men don't even know what ACT UP and Queer Nation are anymore," says Kirp, who is the author of *Learning by Hearth: AIDS and Schooling in America's Communities*. "The assumption was that for gay men who came into gayness in the age of AIDS, safe sex would be a way of life. But that's not based on the reality of their lives."

Race further complicates AIDS education. According to a February report by the Centers for Disease Control and Prevention, gay and bisexual men of color constitute 20% of the total number of people with AIDS in this country. And because many minority gay men travel in different circles than their white male counterparts, educators are designing new methods of reaching them. In the New York City borough of Queens, which has a large population of Latino gay men, educators from GMHC have established a program to identify and train community leaders to serve as peer educators.

But Ernest Andrews, an educator at the National Task Force on AIDS Prevention, a minority AIDS groups, says GMHC's efforts are too little, too late. "I'm glad they're finally dealing with black and Latino gay men, but it's been a very long time coming," he says. "For too long gay men of color have faced racism from white-dominated gay AIDS organizations and homophobia from AIDS organizations run by people of color."

Racial barriers are not the only target of the peer-education approach. The tack has also worked well in smaller cities, where AIDS prevention campaigns have often been less intensive, says Kelly. Since 1985 CAIR has been using peer-education and community-building techniques to educate gay men in more than 20 cities with populations of less than 250,000.

"We're finding a lot of high-risk behavior in the smaller cities because AIDS is perceived as a big-city problem," Kelly says. "We identify people who are key to a community and quite popular; we call them opinion leaders. We have bartenders watch the crowd in their bar for ten days and tell us who is popular. We approach these people and teach them ways they can personally endorse the desirability of risk aversion among their friends and acquaintances. You can change the attitudes of the entire gay community in a city this way."

At times, though, peer education may actually be too successful for its own good. Acknowledgment of engaging in unprotected sex became tantamount to admitting to criminal behavior, increasing the difficulty educators already faced identifying trouble spots among gay men. "Some say we did too good a job at promoting a peer norm for safe sex," says Wohlfeiler. "It put unsafe sex in the closet, a dirty little thing you can't talk about."

Indeed, the unspoken idea that the risk of HIV infection is itself erotic and one of the motivations for unsafe sex underscores the difficulty facing AIDS educators. "Sex and risk have long been linked together even when it involves death," says Bayer.

Securing the massive resources necessary to effectively take on such issues, though, ultimately depends mainly on the larger political climate, over which AIDS educators have little control. With the rate of increase of new AIDS cases among heterosexuals exceeding that of gay men for the first time last year, federal, state, and local governments are shifting already limited prevention resources toward heterosexual transmission. In California, for instance, the state is spending just 10% of its prevention funds on gay men even though they still make up close to 80% of the total number of AIDS cases. Nor has the Clinton administration delivered on its promise to significantly increase funding for prevention. The biggest increase in this year's AIDS budget was for medical research, while AIDS prevention remained unchanged.

But James Curran, associate director of HIV prevention at the CDC, insists there is a light at the end of the tunnel. Since 1991 federal regulations have required that two thirds of the CDC's AIDS prevention funds go toward HIV testing and surveillance. Starting in 1995 those regulations expire, freeing up millions of dollars for direct outreach to high-risk groups. "What we have to do is get young gay men to age 25 safely," Curran says. "More than half the gay men who are becoming infected are infected by the time they are 25. If we can get them to 25 safely, they are not home free, but it gets much easier. The new regulations will help make this happen."

Activists maintain, however, that these relatively minor changes in the CDC's AIDS prevention program are not nearly enough, given the current political climate. Despite a new administration with a professed sympathy for AIDS prevention efforts, right-wing groups and conservatives in Congress continue to exert pressure to curtail government funding for gay-friendly educational efforts. In March the House narrowly turned back legislation that would have denied federal funding to local school districts if their curricula portray gays and lesbians in a positive light.

Such attacks on AIDS prevention make it more difficult for gays and lesbians to acknowledge that it is not the success it once appeared to be, says Benjamin Schatz, executive director of the American Association of Physicians for Human Rights, a gay group that is organizing a summit on AIDS prevention in Dallas in July. "The way we have been able to get prevention funding—indeed, any funding—for AIDS services at all was historically to say that prevention is working fine: 'We're all being really good boys and deserve funding,'" Schatz says. "It's considered deeply embarrassing to admit that is not always the case. There's a fear that it will make us look bad or jeopardize our funding."

Humes agrees that politics and public health are a deadly mix. "Gay men have been able to make changes that are unique in the history of public health, but they are still subject to a barrage of messages that they are responsible for the epidemic," he says. "Gay men have the weight of the world on their shoulders. This is no way to build the kind of self-esteem gay men need to maintain safe sex."

But the self-esteem of gay men has never been a particular concern of right-wing groups. In fact, many of these groups are stepping up their efforts to use AIDS as a component of their antigay campaign. For instance, an April report by the American Family Institute, an antigay research group, alleged that as a result of AIDS, the life expectancy of gay men is just 42.

Although public health officials immediately denounced the study as inaccurate and biased, potential Republican presidential candidate William Bennett said on a conservative cable-TV talk show that it provided evidence that homosexuality is unhealthy. "If I gave you a subset of the population that died at the age of [42], you would say, 'Stop these three-pack-a-day-smokers,'" he said. "When gays talk about the joys of the gay lifestyle, they are lying. We know they are lying, and they know they are lying."

But Brandt says Bennett's analogy underscores the depth of the public's ignorance about the emotional and psychological complexity of AIDS prevention. As a former smoker himself, Bennett "should understand how difficult behavior modification is for some people," Brandt says. "If the press reports I read were correct, Bennett had enormous difficulty giving up smoking, which could have proved as fatal as unsafe sex. Here's an intelligent and well-educated man who had trouble modifying his own destructive behavior. Imagine the difficulty when you bring sexuality, not to mention race and class, into the equation. Changing people's behavior, especially when it comes to sex, is an enormously complex task, and blaming people only makes things more difficult."

Meanwhile, educators in the trenches say they have little choice but to make the best of a climate dominated by prejudice and ignorance. "The metaphor in public health is a river," Wohlfeiler says. "You're standing on the side of the river, and people are screaming for help as they're swept away by the waters. You go in and pluck them out. You keep pulling people out of the water. Finally, you have to go upriver and figure out why people fell in. We've got a lot of people downriver helping folks, but we have to get people to go up the river and stop people from falling in."

JUST A NORML GUY: RICHARD COWAN, THE NATION'S LEADING ADVOCATE OF MARIJUANA LEGALIZATION, IS A STAUNCH CONSERVATIVE—AND A GAY MAN

by Chris Bull

June 14, 1994

In September 1986 the conservative political journal *National Review* published a long article titled "A Conservative Speaks Out on Gay Rights" from an anonymous writer who used the pseudonym John Woolman. Not long before, the magazine's high-profile editor, William F. Buckley Jr., had advocated tattooing warnings on people with AIDS, and Woolman took Buckley and other leading conservatives to task for their "unseemly obsession with homosexuality, totally disproportionate to its significance as either a phenomenon or a problem compared with the disastrous state of heterosexuality."

For years the magazine's readers wondered aloud about Woolman's true identity, especially after the magazine published a second article, this one titled "AIDS and Right-wing Hysteria," two years later. In truth Woolman is Richard C. Cowan, a conservative and friend of Buckley's who is a well-known *National Review* contributor. A month after the first Woolman article appeared, Cowan used his own name on a controversial cover story he wrote for the magazine that attacked the Reagan administration's war on drugs.

Only now—eight years after the first Woolman article appeared—has Cowan publicly acknowledged that he is gay and the author of the Woolman articles. "I wrote the gay articles in the *Review* under the Woolman name because I had already written on the drug issue, and I didn't think it was fair to either issue to use my name," he says. "I could hear people saying, 'No wonder he's in favor of drug legalization—he's a pervert' or 'No wonder he's a pervert—he's a pothead.'"

Cowan—who is now the national director of the National Organization for the Reform of Marijuana Laws, a Washington, D.C., advocacy group—had reason to be cautious. The two causes closest to his heart—marijuana legalization and gay rights—are anathema to many traditional conservatives. Nor is his advocacy of a libertarian political philosophy and his association with conservatives like Buckley likely to win him many fans among gays and lesbians.

"Dick makes the best case one can make for drug legalization, but it's a very hard case to make among conservatives like Rush Limbaugh and William Bennett, who are dead set against it," says *National Review* senior editor Richard Brookhiser. "As for gay rights, conservatives are unlikely to buy it, even coming from Dick."

Adds Dennis Peron, a longtime gay rights and marijuana legalization advocate: "As far as I'm concerned, Dick is a saint sent to the marijuana movement to articulate our issue, but a libertarian political philosophy does not do any of us much good outside the criminal justice system. It doesn't really address the need for progressive change across the entire political system for gay and lesbian people."

But while Cowan faces criticism from both ends of the political spectrum, his conservative credentials make him an ideal spokesman for gay rights and marijuana legalization—causes that have traditionally been dismissed in part because of their association with liberalism.

"Dick certainly doesn't fit the stereotype of the leftist political activist," says NORML founder Keith Stroup, now executive director of the National Association of Criminal Defense Lawyers. "During the '70s we in the marijuana movement decided to lock arms with every left-wing group out there as part of an overall social revolution movement. The problem with that approach is that it makes it easy for everyone to oppose you. As part of the political establishment, Dick is making a much narrower—and more effective—argument for legalization."

Indeed, Cowan's advocacy for marijuana legalization has found success in unusual places. Not only has Buckley published Cowan's two *National Review* articles on drug legalization, but he also endorsed Cowan's arguments as "tough-minded and analytically resourceful" in a column in 1992. And since Cowan took over the helm at NORML that same year, media attention to the group has skyrocketed.

"The whole thing has certainly gotten us a lot of coverage because of my man-bites-dog kind of appeal," Cowan says. "[The media] would say, 'Here's a conservative for marijuana, and not only a conservative, but a bald-headed conservative.' Invariably I would explain why it is not at all exceptional for a conservative—bald-headed or not—to smoke pot, and invariably they would say it anyway."

Cowan's case for marijuana legalization centers on the argument that the government has no business regulating the private drug-using habits of its citizens. NORML argues that the estimated 370,000 marijuana arrests every year unnecessarily clog the already overburdened criminal justice system with harmless pot smokers.

In recent years, though, the campaign for legalization has been bolstered by a growing recognition among health care workers and people with AIDS and a wide range of other illnesses that marijuana has medicinal applications. For instance, the Cannabis Buyers' Club, an underground group that provides marijuana to people with AIDS, now has 32 chapters nationwide.

"The buyers clubs have put the narcs in a double bind," Cowan explains. "They can go out and arrest a bunch of sick people or allow these people to openly break the law. They have chosen, with a few exceptions, the latter course. That works in our favor because it allows us to show the hypocrisy of the policy." (In January Clinton administration officials said they were considering allowing marijuana to be made available for medicinal purposes.)

Cowan, 53, first articulated his live-and-let-live political philosophy as a founding member—along with Buckley—of the conservative group Young Americans for Freedom while a student at Yale University in 1960, where he also served as president of Yale Republicans. It was during his undergraduate years at Yale that Cowan fell under the sway of libertarian philosopher Ayn Rand, whose work Cowan says gave intellectual sustenance to his own budding libertarianism.

The seeds for Cowan's political ideology had already been sown during his comfortable upper-middle-class boyhood in Fort Worth, Tex. "It was an *Ozzie and Harriet* sort of world, where every one had 'colored help,'" Cowan says. "But my parents were a little different from most. My mother was very antiracist for as long as I can remember, and my father was fond of gambling as a hobby. My parents danced, drank, smoked, and played cards, so I was never very concerned about whether someone approved of what I did or not. That visceral liberalism evolved into libertarianism when I was older."

Such libertarianism, he says, led him to select the Woolman pseudonym to pay homage to an early antislavery advocate. "Woolman worked as a clerk for merchants and one day was making out a bill of sale for a slave and suddenly said to himself, 'This doesn't seem right,'" Cowan says. "From that point on, he refused to fill out bills of sale for slaves. No man can own another man, and that is the basis of my political work. I don't own you, and I cannot tell you how to lead your life. I can tell you how I think you ought to lead your life, but whether you choose to follow my wise advice is none of my business."

In the '60s, as YAF and the conservative movement took an increasingly reactionary bent, Cowan took a hiatus from politics, returning home to Fort Worth to run his father's manufacturing business. It wasn't until 1972, after selling the business and traveling to Washington, D.C., that Cowan sought to renew his political ties.

"I was considering going to work for Nixon's reelection campaign or in [Vice President Spiro] Agnew's office," he says, "but as I like to say now, I went to work for a nicer class of criminals instead. I had read an article in *Playboy* that talked about the huge number of people being arrested for marijuana possession. So I started going by the NORML office, and I just got more and more absorbed in the cause. I called all my Republican friends and said, 'Stop looking. I found something to do,' and they asked what I was going to do. My answer was met with long silences on the other end of the line."

Cowan then returned to Texas, where he lobbied on behalf of NORML to liberalize the state's notoriously stiff antidrug laws. He also started a new business venture, this time in the petroleum industry. Cowan stayed in Texas until 1992, when he accepted the top job at NORML, which had fallen upon hard times in the just-say-no '80s. Independently wealthy, Cowan does not draw a salary from NORML's $400,000 annual budget.

Cowan says the passage of years and a desire to "reach out to my gay and lesbian brothers and sisters" has lessened his concern about speaking publicly about his homosexuality—but only to a point. "My general view is someone's sexual orientation shouldn't matter to anyone," he says. "It's just part of the way I was brought up—with a sense of decorum. If I were a porn star, maybe my sex life would be something to talk about."

Cowan is less tight-lipped when it comes to his marijuana use, though. Asked if he fears prosecution for publicly acknowledging that he smokes the drug, Cowan grabs his interviewer's tape recorder and, speaking directly into it, says, "I have smoked marijuana every day for the past 26 years, and that's for the record. According to the marijuana critics, I should be dead or vegetative at least, but I'm in good health, and I seem to be reasonably coherent."

Although Cowan's sexual orientation has been the subject of rumors for years, Cowan admits to some trepidation about how Buckley and his conservative colleagues will react to his declaring that he is gay. "I guess I'm afraid I might lose some friendships," he says. "I'm concerned about causing them pain. I know that sounds kind of old-fashioned, but I'm just not the 'I'm here, I'm queer, get used to it' sort."

As a result, Cowan says that he is largely undaunted by the antigay views regularly expressed in *National Review* and by conservatives in general. "American conservatism didn't invent homophobia," he says. "But sometimes I think that if I could afford it, I would like to endow the editors of *National Review* with a cold shower every time they get the urge to write about sex. It's not something they do very well." (Buckley decline to be interviewed for this article.)

Although some might consider moving among often radically different (but occasionally overlapping) groups of friends and colleagues—conservatives, gays and lesbians, marijuana users—a bit of a strain, Cowan handles it with ease. In fact, he insists it is one of the most enjoyable, though sometimes confusing, aspects of his life. "I've always had a very eclectic groups of friends," he says. "I've had big parties where the pot smokers were all in one room and the drinkers in another, and that's just where the differences begin. Maybe that's where my politics help me. We all need to learn to tolerate each other's eccentricities."

"For Transsexuals, 1994 Is 1969:" Transgendered Activists Are a Minority Fighting to Be Heard Within the Gay and Lesbian Community

by John Gallagher

August 23, 1994

As organizers for the Stonewall 25 march were completing their preparations, they found themselves facing a potentially embarrassing threat from an unexpected source. Angry at having been excluded from the march's formal title—the International March on the United Nations to Affirm the Human Rights of Lesbian and Gay People—transgendered activists were planning to stage civil disobedience actions on the march route.

"It was a symptom of the mainstream [gay and lesbian] community's trying to get civil rights passed by not accepting the whole community," says Denise Norris, a member of Transexual Menace, a direct-action group in New York City.

The protest was called off less than 24 hours before the march, but not until the activists felt their point had been made. "We caused the Stonewall people a lot of stress for not including us in the title," says Phyllis Randolph Frye, executive director of the International Conference on Transgender Law and Employment Policy, a Houston-based group.

The dispute signaled the beginning of a newfound political activism. "It was our own Stonewall this year," contends Riki Anne Wilchins, a member of Transexual Menace. "For transsexuals, 1994 is 1969."

But the political emergence of the transgender community, defined by activists to include not only transsexuals but also individuals who dress in drag or cross-dress, may not be a smooth one. As the contretemps over Stonewall 25 indicated, the gay community may find the proposed alliance an uneasy one at best.

"We've already seen the mixed feelings," says Ann Northrop, a lesbian activist from New York City. "Conservatives want a homogenous image and are afraid to embrace the transgender community because they think that's going to screw up our ability to gain civil rights."

The increased notice given to transgender concerns has been nurtured by a growing societal interest in gender issues, argues Eve Sedgwick, a professor of English at Duke University who writes about gender theory. "The work of the [transgender] community has kept those issues visible," she says. "It has made them seem real to people and not just theoretical."

The events surrounding Stonewall 25 indeed marked a turning point, and not just because of the march gaffe. Gay Games IV also became a focus of controversy, adopting a detailed policy for transsexual participation that dealt with such matters as legal name changes and the length of time the athlete had been taking hormones. But when one transsexual inquired about participating in the games, recalls Norris, the event's representative addressed her as "mister" and "sir." "A few of us got very upset," she says.

Transsexual activists subsequently distributed flyers reading GAY GAMES TO TRANSSEXUALS: DROP DEAD. After meeting with transgendered activists, the Gay Games board voted to drop the guidelines and to allow athletes to participate in events under whatever gender they declared.

"People were concerned that the system would be abused, but as far as I know, there were no problems," says Northrop, a member of the Gay Games board. "Everybody seemed happy, and I'm proud the Games took a progressive step."

"The transgender community is very much more activist and more organized as a result of [the Stonewall controversy]," insists Frye. "We've been organized for a long time for social and support events, but as far as demanding our rights, it's still in the early stages."

Buoyed by their successes and by the explosion of books by transgendered authors, activists are expanding their strategies. In New York City organizers are developing a big brother/big sister outreach to gay street youth, many of whom are transgendered. In addition, a national political and health conference is being planned for next year.

Some activists also intend to mount an action at the Michigan Womyn's Music Festival this summer, where a three-year debate has been raging about whether transsexuals should be allowed to participate. One transsexual was barred from the festival in 1991, while five more were excluded two years ago, ostensibly for security reasons. This year transgendered activists plan to have their own encampment near the festival—Camp Trans, which will be the site of 18 to 20 workshops over a four-day period.

"It's not about forcing them to bow to our terms," says Norris. "If they're nice enough to gather 7,000 women together for us, we're going to be nice enough to camp across the street and have a hell of a good time with everyone who wants to join us."

The increased visibility also includes at least one transgendered candidate seeking political office. Karen Ann Kerin, a Vermont Republican, is seeking election to the state's house of representatives. An engineer who travels frequently to Muslim countries on business, Kerin says that her political activism began when she tried without success to change her sex legally in order to avoid the apparent discrepancy on her passport.

"I determined that the only thing to do is to get elected and make noise from a higher platform," she says. "People who know me know all about it and have no problem with it. I don't go out of my way to enunciate it on the platform at large."

Frye maintains that individuals beginning sex reassignment are often subject to discrimination, particularly in the workplace. Most nondiscrimination ordinances provide little relief from such problems.

"We need to stress to lawmakers and activists that the phrase *sexual orientation* does not include transgendered people unless it is specifically defined to include us," says Frye. Of the eight states with sexual orientation nondiscrimination laws, only Minnesota provides protections for transsexuals.

While transgendered activists may feel ignored by government, they could be drawing attention from less welcome sources. A proposed antigay initiative in Washington also includes a clause that defines an individual's gender as fixed at birth.

Dallas Denny, executive director of the American Educational Gender Information Service, a national clearinghouse, believes that such proposals by the religious right underscore the connection between the transgender and gay communities. "Those people don't distinguish between us," she argues. "We have to come together to work for the common good because if we're fragmented, we'll be easy to pick off."

"The emergence of the transgender movement has forced the hand in the card game," notes activist Leslie Feinberg, a drag king and author of the novel *Stone Butch Blues*. "Are we going to be estranged from one another, or are we going to fight together and still have autonomy as movements? What's escalating the urgency is that we're up against the same enemies."

But if past attempts to forge a coalition are any indication, the effort will not be easy. Frye recalls an unsuccessful battle in the mid '80s to have the word *transgendered* included in the title of a local gay group in Houston.

"It was a very bitter fight from people I had marched with for ten years," she says. "I consider myself a lesbian, but these people were saying that transgendered had nothing to do with the [gay] movement. It was really ugly and very hurtful." As a result, continues Frye, "I've pretty much become a transgendered activist only, which is sad. I'm having to fight with my natural allies."

The push for transgender rights developed in the '80s as support and social groups for transsexuals began to form, says Denny. "It's not like we weren't there," she says. "We were just incommunicado."

It has been only in the past decade that transsexuals have been talking among themselves. Previously, says Denny, "doctors thought we should go back into society. It was a state of being in two closets. One was similar to that of gay people, the closet of self-acceptance. The other was the closet at the end of the rainbow, where people were assimilated. It's only recently that people have taken a stand after the process."

But the struggle within the transgender community may be uphill as well. To begin with, not all its members identify with gay activism. "Within the transgender movement not everyone is gay, lesbian, or bisexual," observes Feinberg. "There is certainly a huge heterosexual population that is transgendered." Even some segments of the gay community claimed by transgendered activists, such as drag queens, may not always agree with the designation.

Moreover, not all transgendered individuals welcome the high profile of Christine Jorgensen, the pioneering transsexual who lectured extensively and became a media celebrity in the early '50s. "There's a lot of assimilationist attitude among transgendered people," says Denny, who is also the author of *Gender Dysphoria: A Guide to Research,* which she describes as the first scientific work on gender issues by someone who is transgendered. "One friend of mine told me, 'I can't afford to be seen at these kind of events.'"

"There are segments in both the [transgender] community and the gay community that want mainstream acceptance and perceive these other segments as doing harm to their chances of being accepted," says Norris. "They eagerly point fingers at the other community and say it's not part of our community."

And the activists themselves are engaged in a debate about whether the old norm of trying to appear nontranssexual is valid. "There's a real split going on in the transsexual community," says Wilchins. "The younger cohort coming up says passing does not work. 'I don't have to be a real woman; I can be a transsexual woman.' Older transsexuals says that's not what they're about."

Denny regards the emphasis on passing as a nontranssexual as a form of "internalized transphobia." She says, "It was very damaging because many people didn't have the physical attributes to do it successfully. Now people are saying it's all right to be this way, that in fact it's a fine way to be."

"The idea of passing is essentially a way of saying, 'I am not OK, I have to fool you,'" argues Wilchins. "Every transsexual does not have to get surgery. Transsexual women sometimes have penises, which are entirely appropriate genitals. Some have vaginas, and those are equally appropriate. Neither one is any less female."

Although not everyone accepts such views, says Denny, disagreements are to be expected. "It's not any worse or any better than any other group of people," she points out. "It's like the leather issue in the gay community, or when gay liberation started and there was lesbian self-exclusion. We're just thrashing those things out because we're new and just getting into the dialogue."

Despite such potential pitfalls, Frye remains optimistic. "Five years ago I was pretty disillusioned," she says. "Now so many leaders and activists are coming up, I see nothing but progress ahead."

OUTWARD BOUND: WISCONSIN CONGRESSMAN STEVE GUNDERSON TALKS ABOUT HIS PRIVATE LIFE—AT LAST

by Chris Bull

October 4, 1994

When Rep. Robert Dornan (R-Calif.) accused his Wisconsin counterpart, Steve Gunderson, of having a "revolving door on his closet" during a House debate on an education bill in March, the bluntness of the charge shocked House members. But the allegation gave voice to a whispered assessment that had long rumbled through political circles—that Gunderson, a Republican who is running for his eighth term representing a rural district, is a gay man who contends that his sexual orientation is a private affair but drops hints about it in public.

For instance, after a widely reported incident in 1991 in which AIDS activist Michael Petrelis threw a soft drink in Gunderson's face in a gay bar, Gunderson, 43, told the *La Crosse* [Wis.] *Tribune* that he is "married to my job. I don't really have a personal life." But late last year when he was addressing a fund-raiser for the Human Rights Campaign Fund, a gay political group, Gunderson spoke at length about sharing a house at a gay resort area with a man he identified as Rob—a disclosure that led *The Milwaukee Journal* to report that Gunderson "now appears comfortable at least leaving the impression that he is gay."

Says Doug Mell, who as city editor of the *Eau Claire* [Wis.] *Leader-Telegram* has followed Gunderson's career: "It sure looks as though Steve is trying to have it both ways. He keeps saying that the whole sexual-orientation issue is being forced on him by the press, but the facts don't really bear him out."

Noting that Gunderson brought Rob to the HRCF fund-raiser, Mell says, "Bringing his boyfriend to a speech when he knows there is a reporter from *The Milwaukee Journal* there is not exactly being in the closet. But then when someone asks him a direct question about it, he says it's none of anyone's business. I don't think people really care if he is straight or gay, but they do want him to be straightforward."

But Gunderson says he has what he considers valid reasons for refusing to say publicly whether he is gay. "People are obsessed with sex," he says. "Quite frankly, I thought the whole goal of equal rights in this country was to make parts of your life over which you have no control, like your sexual orientation, and some over which you do have a choice, like religion, irrelevant. I come from a small-town family, from a 100% Norwegian-American background, and we are very private people."

And he says he's paid a price for the disclosures he's made. "The Dornan episode was very difficult for my family," he says. "At the same time I was standing on the House floor defending gay youth and being attacked for it by Dornan, my dad was in the hospital for heart bypass surgery. My sister told me recently that she was with my dad in the hospital when a newscast showed Dornan attacking me. As she was holding his hand, my dad said to her, 'Why is this man attacking Steve? Just because my son is different doesn't make him a bad person.' "

In a series of interviews with *The Advocate,* Gunderson still refused to answer when asked whether he is gay. However, he invited an *Advocate* reporter to visit the Washington, D.C., town house he shares with 34-year-old architect Rob Morris, who has been his lover for 11 years. During a taped, on-the-record Sunday lunch in August, the two men described their relationship in intimate detail.

Says Morris: "Steve is tired of being hounded. Elements of the gay community have waged an all-out war on Steve. If you look at some of the activists' comments, you'll see that they don't care if he is reelected. The activists live in gay communities in New York and D.C. and have no idea what it's like for a gay congressman to survive politically in Middle America."

Indeed, Gunderson's political career has been marked by conflict between gay rights activists, who have encouraged him to speak frankly about his sexual orientation, and his campaign advisers, who have counseled him to play down the issue. On the same day that Morris lent *The Advocate* personal photos of him and Gunderson to accompany this article, Morris Andrews, a top strategist for Gunderson's current reelection campaign, summoned an *Advocate* reporter to his office. Andrews strenuously argued that publication of this article would harm Gunderson's campaign and repeatedly asked that its publication be delayed until after November, even though Gunderson had already agreed to a September publication date.

Scott Evertz, a gay Republican candidate for the Wisconsin state assembly, says that Gunderson—acting on Andrews's advice—backed out of a commitment made in June to appear at a fund-raiser in Milwaukee for a Wisconsin gay Republican group August 24. "Andrews indicated he was concerned that Gunderson was appearing to be too much of a single-issue [gay rights] candidate in a district that doesn't want to hear too much about the issue," Evertz says. Andrews declined to be interviewed on the record for this article.

Last year, after Gunderson spoke against the Pentagon ban on gay and lesbian service personnel, La Crosse County board member Mike Huebsch reneged on his promise to emcee a Gunderson fund-raiser, saying that "if he's going to use his position as our representative to be the advocate for the gay rights movement, that steps over the line." And Doug Knight, chairman of the Republican Party in Gunderson's congressional district, warned Gunderson that he could support gay rights causes only as long as he did not "cross the line" into public discussion of his sexual orientation.

Milwaukee Journal political columnist Craig Gilbert says many voters don't mind suspecting that Gunderson is gay but at the same time don't want him to confirm it. "It would force voters to consider something they would rather not think about," he says. Adds Evertz: "The blue-haired lady in his district who does not necessarily want to know whether Steve Gunderson is gay can continue to believe he is not until he actually comes out and admits that he is."

But some say Gunderson's reticence is merely self-destructive. "When someone who is in the public eye guards his personal life—especially in the convoluted way the Steve has—a mystery is created that everyone wants to solve," says Tammy Baldwin, an openly lesbian member of the Wisconsin state legislature. "Sometimes it's much better to just let it out and then say, 'OK, let's get on with the business of the district.'"

And Mell says Gunderson may be selling Wisconsin voters short. In a two-part series of articles published by the *Leader-Telegram* in August, a large majority of the residents of Gunderson's district who were interviewed say they don't care whether Gunderson is gay. According to the articles, Mell says, "the district doesn't give two rips about Gunderson's sexual orientation." Still, he acknowledges that sometimes "people will tell a reporter one thing and then go into a voting booth and end up doing the opposite."

Openly gay U.S. representative Barney Frank, a Massachusetts Democrat, believes that as a gay Republican, Gunderson is in a political no-man's-land. "I admire his courage in speaking up in a party that's moving quickly to the right," Frank says. "But who does Steve Gunderson have to turn to for support? There are not enough gay Republicans around to provide him any kind of base of support to work from."

As a result, Gunderson says he must avoid being perceived as a single-issue candidate interested only in gay rights. "Let's be honest," he says. "I'm not running for reelection to advance the gay cause. The reasons I'm running are the issues that happen to be very important to my district—the farm bill, passing and implementing a health care bill, and supporting vocational education. Everyone seems to think I'm consumed by gay issues, but I have probably given close to 100 speeches on health care, 50 on education, and only three on gay rights."

Indeed, Mell points out that Gunderson is regarded by his district's voters as being a very effective legislator who is an expert on federal milk-price support legislation. "He is a hell of a hard worker who has a reputation as a real honest guy," he says. "He's a genuinely nice guy. There's never been any hint of scandal around him, and people in this district really appreciate that."

Gunderson is the eldest son in a large, socially prominent family in Osseo, where his father owned a Chevrolet dealership, and he has been in politics for virtually all of his adult working life. Shortly after graduating from the University of Wisconsin-Madison and briefly attending a sports broadcasting school, Gunderson was elected to the state assembly in 1974 at age 23. He was just 29 when he was elected to Congress in 1980.

While Gunderson's perception of his district's politics has pushed him to de-emphasize his sexual orientation as a member of Congress, the increasing prominence of antigay activists in the Republican Party has compelled him to speak out increasingly within the party on gay rights issues.

Soon after the 1992 Republican National Convention in Houston, for instance, Gunderson resigned his leadership post as a deputy to Newt Gingrich, House minority whip, to protest the antigay tone that was prevalent at the convention.

"I took a big step politically a couple of years ago when I voluntarily left the leadership because I was concerned about the movement of the Republican Party to the very hard right," Gunderson says. "It was clear to me at the time that the party needed tension from the center, and in the absence of others willing to provide that tension, I had to do something. The only way Republicans are ever going to become the majority party is by focusing on the issues that unite Americans—such as economic and foreign policy issues—rather than on those that divide them. Opposition to gay rights and abortion or support for school prayer should never become the centerpiece of the Republican domestic agenda."

Similarly, Gunderson says that during congressional debate over the Pentagon ban last year, he felt compelled to speak out, comparing the ban to activists' attempts to out him. "I have experienced what it feels like to have my life—who I am, what I am, and what I have accomplished—reduced to a single irrelevant factor," Gunderson wrote in a speech published in the *Congressional Record*.

Says Gunderson: "There was so much disinformation being disseminated that I felt I had to find some way to rise above the members of Congress who were giving these divisive speeches. I wanted to challenge the prevailing notion that the only people who had a place in the debate were conservative military men. I wanted people to know exactly what it is like to be the victim of a witch-hunt."

Gunderson says that if he appears inconsistent, it is because he attempts to place issues in their proper context. "The speech on gays in the military was a thoughtful attempt to deal with the very legitimate concerns of Middle Americans," he says. "Contrast that with the HRCF speech in Baltimore, where I was primarily addressing gay people. It would have been improper there not to talk about friends who have died of AIDS or not to say that Rob was there with me. There were issues important to the audience that had touched me personally, just as there were other issues that were important for members of the House to hear on the gays in the military issue. Somehow the contexts of my speeches have been lost in the media's translation of them."

Gunderson has said that if he is reelected this fall, he will leave the House of Representatives when his next term expires in 1996. As a result, Morris says, he has been gently encouraging Gunderson to address his sexual orientation more openly and consistently. "Whether Steve wins or loses this next election, it's essential that he be able to look back on this campaign and say that he remained true to himself," Morris argues. "He's got to be able to say, 'I maintained my own dignity and didn't bend to the left or to the right. I was honest with myself and my constituents.'"

Gunderson calls Morris, whom he met at the Washington, D.C., gay bar Badlands in 1983, "my best political counselor." Morris, he says, "comes from outside the political world and has a very good gut political sense, yet he brings great concern and commitment to it. He and I discuss every political strategy we make more than you can imagine, especially on an issue as big as gay rights."

Morris says that when he began dating Gunderson, he never imagined he would become what he laughingly calls a "political wife." In fact, he recalls that at first Gunderson did not even tell him he was in politics. "He wasn't very forthcoming," Morris says. "So I took the lead and said there are just three things I don't like to talk about—politics, religion, and sports, kind of in that order. Given that he didn't have anything else to talk about, I said, 'OK, let's just talk about architecture. That will be something fun to talk about.' For the first four years or so of our relationship, I re-sented his involvement in politics immensely. The hours are unpredictable and long. You are led to believe that it is a glamorous life, but believe me, it's not glamorous. You give up all your privacy."

But Morris says he eventually grew accustomed to a political life. "One day about three years ago, I answered the phone while I was half asleep," he says. "I had Beethoven blaring on the stereo to wake me up, and Steve was already in the shower. Some guy was saying something about a pack-age, and I couldn't figure out what he wanted. So I finally said, 'Look, buddy, I don't know who you are or what you want, but I don't know anything about a package.' So the person on the other end of the line says, 'Is this Congressman Gunderson?' It turns out it was Vice President Quayle calling to lobby Steve about the 1990 budget package. So I said, 'Yo, Steve, it's the vice president.' "

In part, Gunderson's long unwillingness to discuss his sexual orientation—even in the face of such inadvertent disclosures—may reflect his resolve not to give in to pressure from gay rights activists who have dogged him on the issue since his run-in with Petrelis in the gay bar. "I felt that target-ing Steve Gunderson was justified because he was not being asked about gay political issues in the context of his own sexual orientation," says Petrelis. "His voting record was not that great, and he had failed to sign on to federal gay rights legislation."

Such pressure has succeeded in prompting newspapers in Gunderson's district to ask him about his voting record on sexual orientation issues. When he was asked by the La Crosse Tribune, for in-stance, about his position on federal legislation prohibiting employment discrimination on the basis of sexual orientation, Gunderson said, "To be honest, I have not studied the issue. I have been con-cerned with the dairy bill and higher education bill."

Still, Daniel Zingale, director of public policy for HRCF, says that in the wake of the run-in with Petrelis, Gunderson has become a "reliable ally" and has begun to cast more pro-gay votes. "Gun-derson is very important to us," he says, "because as a Republican from a moderately conservative district, he has clout with his fellow Republicans."

Petrelis suggests that it is his outing campaign that was responsible for Gunderson's turnabout. "He certainly hasn't been very good at keeping his private life private since we started after him," Petrelis says. "All of a sudden he's all worked up about lifting the military ban on gays and lesbians, but it's too bad he wasn't pissed off about gay men dying of AIDS in the '80s. He just wasn't there for his own community when it needed him most."

But Gunderson counters that the outing campaign made it difficult for him to be an effective congressional advocate for gay rights. "Everybody in America thinks that their congressmen and congresswomen go to Washington and live disrespectful lives," he says. "And now some of my constituents were thinking that I was living a double life—one by day and another by night. I could no longer speak out—as I had done throughout my entire political career—on social issues without people suggesting that it was because of some sort of personal agenda."

Instead, Gunderson says his approach to gay rights issues actually evolved with Congress's and the nation's. "I didn't choose the issue of gays in the military, but when it came along I had to speak up," he says. "I didn't schedule an amendment on AIDS education and counseling in the education bill, but when it happened I had to speak up. The issue for me is whether I should have remained silent when the big gay issues came up in Congress in recent sessions for the first time. Do I think I would have spoken up five years ago had they come up then? The answer is yes, absolutely. You would be hard-pressed to find that Steve Gunderson has ever been hypocritical on any of these issues."

LUNATIC FRINGE: AFTER THE OKLAHOMA CITY BOMBING, AN ANGRY NATION FOCUSES ITS FURY ON RIGHT-WING MILITIAS. BUT THEIR BIZARRE ANTIGAY MESSAGE IS LARGELY IGNORED

by Chris Bull

May 30, 1995

For years gay rights activists have pleaded with federal authorities to thwart antigay violence by stepping up their monitoring of right-wing hate groups. But antiterrorism legislation proposed by President Clinton days after the horrific bombing of the Alfred P. Murrah Federal Building in Oklahoma City on April 19 left them fearing that the government's get-tough policy will ultimately be directed against them.

"It been very rewarding watching the country finally wake up to the threat posed by extremist groups," said Russ Bellant, a journalist for Political Research Associates, a Cambridge, Mass.-based clearinghouse of information on right-wing political groups and trends. "But it's not going to help our cause to give the FBI free rein to stomp out political groups." Added Phil Gutis, media relations director of the American Civil Liberties Union: "Once you give the government too much power, it is not just going to shut up the white guys [allegedly involved] in the bombing. It is going to go after ACT UP and Queer Nation as well. When you target the enemy, you end up targeting yourself."

The proposed federal response to the bombing includes hiring more than 1,000 new federal law enforcement agents, easing a ban on military involvement in federal policing, and allowing agents to more easily obtain approval to wiretap suspected terrorists. At an April 27 Senate judiciary committee hearing, FBI director Louis J. Freeh said federal authorities are currently at an "extreme disadvantage" in dealing with an estimated several hundred violent white supremacist groups and antigovernment militias—armed paramilitary groups—around the country.

Timothy J. McVeigh, accused by federal authorities of helping plant the Oklahoma City bomb, is allegedly linked to militias across the country, including the Michigan Militia—one of the nation's largest—and militias in Arizona. While these groups are concerned primarily with gun control issues, they are also vehement in their opposition to civil rights for minority groups, especially gays and lesbians. The mix of angry people involved in the loosely affiliated militia movement includes survivalists, skinheads, white supremacists, and Christian fundamentalists.

"The membership and ideology of these groups is very fluid and overlapping," said Mary Ann Mauney, research assistant for the Atlanta-based Center for Democratic Renewal, which monitors conservative groups. "Some of the groups are just a bunch of guys playing war games in the woods. Others have a very serious political agenda that they plan to carry out at any cost."

At their meetings members of the Michigan Militia have angrily decried gay rights, said Jeffrey Montgomery, president of the Triangle Foundation, a gay political group in Detroit that has monitored the confabs. "A central aspect of their litany is what queers are doing to tear this country down," he said. "They seem to think that homosexuals, along with women's groups and blacks, have taken over the federal government and are going to destroy their own families and communities." (Michigan Militia founder Norm Olson has said that McVeigh was expelled from the group because his views were too extreme.)

However, George Matousek, the sponsor of an antigay initiative that failed to qualify for the November 1994 ballot in Michigan, is a self-professed member in good standing of the Michigan Militia and is closely associated with the Michigan Wolverines, an offshoot of the militia. In a 1993 interview with the [Detroit] Metro Times, an alternative weekly, Matousek blasted gays and lesbians as a key element of "the new world order," an alleged conspiracy hatched by international bankers and the United Nations to take over the government of the United States.

"The homosexual movement will destroy the military," Matousek said in the interview, which was conducted as the nation was grappling with the gays in the military issue. "Soon half the troops will be gone. They don't want to serve next to the queers. And the half that's left will be useless—

women and homos, people who can't fight their way out of a paper bag. When that happens we'll be doomed. Clinton, or whoever's in office, will turn all our troops over to the United Nations. And this country won't exist anymore."

Asked how he planned to fight the new world order, Matousek replied, "Armed revolution. I believe we're headed there someday. But right now we have to deal with the military—and take back control. That means stopping the queers."

But in a telephone interview with *The Advocate* days after the bombing, Matousek—a fish farmer in Bentley, Mich.—contended that he and other members of the Michigan Militia spend little time discussing gay-related issues. "The real problem is the federal government's corrupt crusade to bring down patriotic Americans like myself with gun control and other meddling in our lives. The queers are just one small part of a big problem."

Matousek also denied that he or the Michigan Militia has targeted gays and lesbians for violent attacks. "I'm a friend of Norm Olson, and many times I don't think he goes far enough," he said. "But we are really just a defensive group that is trying to keep people out of our lives. We're just a bunch of pussycats trying to make the country a better place to live."

But Jerry Sloan, cochair of Project Tocsin, a Sacramento-based group that monitors the right wing, warned against blindly accepting such characterizations. "These groups are expanding all across the country, and no one really knows who they are and what they are doing," he said. "If the federal government were more sensitive to actual and threatened antigay violence, it would have been able to sniff these people out more easily long ago."

But at the same time, civil libertarians are dead set against reviving the all-powerful FBI of the '60s and '70s, when the agency routinely infiltrated and kept files on gay, lesbian, and left-wing political groups. Information obtained by *The Advocate* under the Freedom of Information Act indicates that the FBI kept close tabs on ACT UP throughout the '80s, and in 1989 agency officials sent memos to 57 field offices sayings that it suspected ACT UP of plotting violence at an international AIDS conference in Montreal and calling for surveillance of the group. (No such violence occurred at the conference.)

Brian Glick, author of *War at Home: Covert Actions Against U.S. Activists and What We Can Do About It,* said the FBI has traditionally been more likely to monitor left-wing groups rather than right-wing ones. "The FBI has a tendency to confuse militants with terrorists," he said. "ACT UP may be militant at times, but it's laughable to think that it poses any terrorist threat. The fact is that many times the FBI is ideologically more hostile toward gay groups than toward militia-type groups. That's why the FBI's counterintelligence on extremist groups have never been very good."

But in at least one case, FBI infiltration of a right-wing group foiled a planned antigay attack. In May 1990 three members of the Aryan Nations, a heavily armed white supremacist group with a compound near Hayden Lake, Ida., conspired to detonate several bombs in a crowded alley outside

Neighbors, a Seattle gay disco. FBI agents taped conversations in which the members discussed the details of the plan. When two of the three members showed up in Seattle just days before the date they had planned to carry out the attack, they were arrested.

Robin Kane, media director for the National Gay and Lesbian Task Force, a political group, said federal officials are sometimes hampered in their efforts against groups such as the Michigan Militia and Aryan Nations by the lack of federal gay rights legislation. In 1994, for instance, the FBI was stymied in its efforts to monitor threats against Brenda and Wanda Henson, a lesbian couple in Ovett, Miss., because federal law does not explicitly prohibit antigay discrimination.

"We had to do a lot of extra groundwork because the FBI's legal mandate does not include sexual orientation," Kane said. "The Justice Department's civil rights division basically told us their hands were tied when it came to gays and lesbians." Justice Department officials did not return telephone calls seeking comment.

But ultimately, said those who watch the radical right, blunting the growth of the extremist groups will come not through legislation but through solving the underlying social and economic ills that periodically swell the ranks of hate groups that use gays, lesbians, and other minorities as scapegoats for the country's problems.

"Short of turning the country into a police state," said Sloan, "there is not much we can do about angry people on the fringes of society. But we can make this a place where citizens are not so afraid for their economic future and don't feel that gays and lesbians are trying to destroy them and their way of life."

THE ROYKO AFFAIR: COLUMNIST DISPLAYS A WAY WITH WORDS DURING A DRUNKEN-DRIVING ARREST

by John Gallagher

June 27, 1995

Nationally syndicated *Chicago Tribune* columnist Mike Royko—a longtime gay rights foe—repeatedly hurled vulgar antigay epithets at cops while being arrested on drunken-driving and resisting-arrest charges in Winnetka, Ill., December 17, 1994, *The Advocate* has learned.

A police description of the arrest, which received only scant coverage in Royko's newspaper, gives details of an agitated and intoxicated Royko, 62, berating police officers and ambulance attendants with antigay slurs at least four times in the hours he was in custody after being involved in an auto accident.

At one point during his detention, Royko—who won a Pulitzer Prize for his writing in 1972—shouted at the arresting officer, "Fuck you, fag. Get your fucking hands off me. Jag off, you queer." When an ambulance crew arrived at the scene, the journalist told attendants, "Get away from me. What are you—fags? Why are you wearing those fag gloves for?"

Royko, whose column is syndicated in about 650 newspapers nationwide, did not return telephone messages left with his assistant at the *Tribune,* and his home telephone number is not listed. Chicago attorney David Pritikin, a partner in the firm of Sidley and Austin who was identified as Royko's lawyer in arrest reports, said it "would be inappropriate for me in any way to comment" on the incident.

Royko pleaded guilty to the drunken-driving and resisting-arrest charges May 16. At that time he apologized for his behavior. Associate court judge Daniel Gillespie fined Royko $1,600, placed him on probation for two years, and ordered him to perform 80 hours of community service at the Blind Service Association in Chicago.

Royko's contrition during the court appearance contrasted sharply with his belligerence during the arrest. Almost from the start of the incident, when Winnetka police officer John Manella arrived at 4:38 P.M. at the scene of the accident involving Royko's Lincoln and another car, the columnist was, in the words of police records, "very verbally abusive."

Royko "did not have a whole lot of nice things to say about anybody that night, including the officers," said Winnetka deputy police chief Eric Bennett. "He was highly intoxicated when he was saying that stuff."

Shortly after arriving at the scene, Manella smelled liquor on Royko's breath. He asked Royko for his driver's license on three occasions, only to have Royko give the office his American Express card each time. When Manella told Royko he was under arrest for driving under the influence of alcohol, police reports say, Royko responded, "I'm not going anywhere with you…you motherfucking asshole."

Manella then called for a backup officer and an ambulance crew to look at an injury to the head that Royko sustained during the crash. But Royko kept shouting at Manella, telling him, "You cocksucker, I bet you'd like to beat the living shit out of me, goddamn it!"

When the paramedics arrived at the scene, Royko refused their help and screamed antigay slurs at them. Royko also resisted officers' attempts to handcuff him—refusing to walk and saying he was "paralyzed" and punching officers. In addition, Royko made a motion that police interpreted as an attempted punch, which led officers to cite him for resisting arrest. Royko then struggled with officers while they put him in a squad car to take him to the police station.

Officers had to carry Royko into the Winnetka police station, where in the processing room he repeatedly slammed the back of his head against a wall and punched his head with his fist. He gave officers a fake phone number and told them that his place of birth was "Warsaw, Poland" (Royko is a native Chicagoan).

When Manella and another officer offered to obtain medical assistance for him, Royko began yelling at them, shouting, "What are you, Croatian? You fucking loser! What is your ethnicity, you fag?" When Pritikin arrived at the station, Royko told him, "Get the fuck out of here. I don't want any attorney."

Royko then told police, "I've gotta take a piss." But when the officers uncuffed Royko so he could go to the bathroom, he declared, "I'm gonna go right here," apparently unzipping his pants, until officers convinced him to change his mind.

Royko then refused to have his mug shot taken and stuck out his tongue at the point that the photo was snapped. He was eventually released on $100 bond into the custody of his sister-in-law and Pritikin.

Royko's curmudgeonly writing style has earned him a loyal following among readers, but he has also incurred the enmity of gay rights activists over the years. In a 1974 column in response to the American Psychiatric Association's decision to remove homosexuality from its list of mental disorders, Royko wrote a thinly veiled parody of the gay rights movement. Called "Banana Lib," the column discussed the problems facing men who had relationships with monkeys. Its publication led to protests outside the offices of the *Chicago Sun-Times,* where Royko was working at the time.

"He was comparing gay people to monkeys without really saying so," said William B. Kelley, a gay rights activist involved in the protest. "It aroused a great deal of uproar."

A 1993 *Washington Post* profile of Royko described the columnist as "a lunchbucket laureate" who "doesn't mind telling people off." In the profile Royko appeared to back off his previously combative stance vis-à-vis gays and lesbians.

"You call someone a wacko, and you hear from the mental health people," Royko was quoted as saying. "Feminists get mad at me sometimes. Blacks get made at me. Whites get made at me if I write anything sympathetic to blacks. Gays get mad at me—not lately, because I don't write anymore about gays. I've heard from gays and parents of gays. Maybe I could have been a little more considerate."

Former CNN reporter Ed Alwood, author of the forthcoming book *Straight News: Gays, Lesbians, and the News Media,* said Royko's use of antigay epithets during his arrest "does undermine the comments he made in the *Post,* where he sounded repentant."

But gay and lesbian activists in Chicago said that while Royko's column seldom directly addresses gay rights issues, it often alludes negatively to them in asides. "It crops up a lot," Kelley said. "Homophobia has been a constant undercurrent when he is talking about San Francisco sports teams, for instance."

Such columns, Alwood said, are typical of "an underlying, unacknowledged homophobia in the media." The bias, he added, "may not come through completely clearly, but its message is still there."

Closet Case: Up to the End, People for the American Way's Arthur Kropp Kept His Sexuality Separate From His Politics

by Chris Bull

July 25, 1995

As president of the liberal lobbying group People for the American Way, Arthur Kropp was a gay man who lived for politics. But you wouldn't have known it from his memorial service in Washington, D.C., June 15. AIDS, the cause of Kropp's death at age 37, was never mentioned in eulogies. Only a few of the mourners—who included the nation's liberal elite—even wore red AIDS awareness ribbons. Kropp's lover, Chris Bobowski, spoke movingly about Kropp's life but addressed his homosexuality only obliquely.

This is exactly how Kropp would have wanted it. Until just weeks before his death on June 12, Kropp—who was hailed in obituaries as turning his group's attention to gay rights issues—told all but his closest friend and associates that he was dying from cancer, with which he had been stricken twice before. PAW had reportedly even prepared an obituary listing cancer as the cause of Kropp's impending death; it wasn't until a few weeks before his actual death and after firm prodding from friends that Kropp relented and allowed group officials to reveal that he had AIDS—but only after he died.

"He did have a very complex relationship with his identity as a gay man and a person with AIDS," said PAW national field director Mary Jean Collins, who is a lesbian. "Ultimately, he did reveal his HIV status to those closest to him on the staff. We did talk about the issue over several months, but I never believed he would die without publicly revealing his illness."

In the final analysis Kropp was more concerned about his work than about how he would be remembered after his death, Collins said. "Art realized that his life would be short and that he would have to make the most of it," she said. "He felt very strongly that he did not want to be seen as a dead person before his time. I honestly believed his silence was a sincere attempt to make the most of his short time on earth."

Kropp was familiar to most Americans through his frequent appearances on national television and radio programs, and by the time of his death, his commentaries had been published in nearly every major American newspaper. He led his organization through a series of congressional battles in the '80s and early '90s, most notably against the Supreme Court nomination of conservative jurist Robert Bork and against a proposed constitutional amendment to ban flag burning.

In announcing his death June 12, PAW credited Kropp with leading the group "into a range of new issues and activities [including] protection of equal rights for gay men and lesbians." But gay men and lesbians who knew Kropp best said that under his leadership PAW often shied away from gay rights issues for fear of creating suspicions about Kropp's sexual orientation and diminishing his impact on mainstream politics.

Indeed, the organization never threw its weight completely behind gay rights causes until January 1993—13 years after it was founded—when its board passed a resolution calling for it to become "an active voice against the discrimination and intolerance faced by gays and lesbians in America."

Sue Armsby, who served as the group's associate director for public policy from 1986 to 1992, said Kropp personally blocked her efforts to work on federal gay rights legislation in 1992 after PAW had built a coalition with gay rights and liberal groups on behalf of the federal Hates Crimes Statistics Act. "Art made it very clear that he felt it was safer for the organization to work from a broad civil rights perspective than to focus on gay issues," said Armsby, who now works for the Boulder, Colo., public school district. "I argued that because gay rights issues had been ignored for so long, they needed a lot of remedial work.

"It didn't help that he was a closeted gay man," Armsby continued. "I'm sure his internal mental calculus was something like, *Only gay people care about gay issues, and if we are too closely associated with those issues, people will realize that I'm gay.*"

But PAW's education policy director, Deanna Duby, laid the blame at the organization's structure. "Sue felt we were not moving fast enough in jumping into the larger gay rights arena," she said. "But what she doesn't understand is that Art had to go to the board to get its backing before going forward. The issue had to be presented in a way that would persuade the board to be supportive. It just took some time."

As for Armsby's allegation that Kropp feared a close association with gay rights causes for personal reasons, Duby said, "I've been privy to a lot of meetings here where decisions were made on gay issues, and I've never heard anyone, including Art, be less than totally supportive of pursuing the issue to the best of our ability."

Bob Hattoy, who is the White House's liaison to the Department of the Interior and who is open about being gay and having AIDS, said Kropp confronted him last year at the Washington, D.C., gay bar Trumpets about Hattoy's disclosure of Kropp's sexual orientation to a female friend. "Someone at a Democratic Party function had asked me about him in an admiring way, and I said, 'Don't bother to ask him out, because he is gay,'" Hattoy said. "I figured that most people in town knew that Art was gay anyway. Well, it got back to him, and he was really annoyed."

During the confrontation, Hattoy said, Kropp asked him not to tell anyone else that he was gay. "I thought it was a little odd to be in a gay bar with him and have him tell me not to tell people he's gay," Hattoy said. "I know what it's like to have psychological fears about coming out, but I always think that unless the situation is physically unsafe, it's much better to be out."

Many liberal activists in Washington political circles "still have a subtle homophobia about them," Hattoy said. "The fact that Art could be in their midst and still think he needed to live a lie is an indictment of them, not Art. Their discomfort created his silence. The questions the liberal establishment should be asking itself right now are, What could we have done to make Art's life easier for him? and How could we have helped him come out?"

Part of the reason for Kropp's reticence was political strategy, said PAW board member John Buchanan. "Arthur was a very private person by nature," he said. "But he also really wanted to make sure that his personal life did not detract from the organization, especially when the religious right has sown so much hatred about gays and lesbians. They would use it against us in any way they could. Personally, I think Arthur did the right thing by putting the welfare of the organization first and not doing anything that would increase our vulnerability."

Added Collins: "We have a political enemy [the religious right] whose key issue is homosexuality. One of that enemy's most disgusting characteristics is that it treats AIDS as a moral rather than medical problem. I understand why Art did not want to hand these people ammunition."

Hattoy, who was a friend of Kropp's, said that Kropp often called or wrote notes when Hattoy's name appeared in right-wing direct-mail campaigns. "He sent me copies of Jerry Falwell's letter denouncing me that said a gay man with AIDS was hiring lots of gay people at the White House. Art would write little notes on it like, 'This could be me if I were out.'

"It was very sweet, partly," Hattoy added, "because I knew his interest was as much personal as political. But there was something very sad about it too. He would always ask those of us in the AIDS community who knew about his secret to respect his privacy. We all did that, of course, but it meant that he suffered alone a lot."

The Glamorization of AIDS: Everywhere You Look, the Media Send the Message "It's Sexy to be HIV-Positive"

by Todd Simmons

November 28, 1995

He's the chiseled-to-perfection god in the movie *Jeffrey,* the smiling hunk in magazine ads for nutritional supplements, the sinewy marathon runner just doing it for Nike, the flawless *Playgirl* centerfold smoldering on the cover of *Poz*. He's the public image of AIDS, and some say he's too good to be true. Worse yet, some charge that by glossing over the realities of the disease, such images can lull the young or impressionable into a false sense of security.

"We've tried so hard to remove the stigma of HIV that we're not sending the right message to young people who are HIV-negative," says Jim Key, spokesman for the Los Angeles Gay and Lesbian Community Services Center. "We've taken away the reality of the disease and taken away the fear."

Leaders of the center were so concerned by what they saw as the sanitization of AIDS's public image that they launched an ad campaign in the summer featuring graphic, sometimes provocative photos of people in the final stages of AIDS. The ads, which ran on city buses, were intended to steer the public back to reality by providing frank reminders of "what the disease actually is," says Key. The need for such reminders is underscored, center leaders say, by the fact that more than 200 newly infected people under the age of 25 have come to the center during the past year. Those infections reflect a national rise in the rate of infection for gay teens and young adults—a group that lacks the personal experience of AIDS common to older gay men and that is often denied frank and realistic information from other sources.

Former *Playgirl* model Thom Collins, who has been HIV-positive for more than a decade, says it's important for the public to understand that life doesn't end once one is infected. But the 28-year-old— who has also been featured in the International Male catalog, *Poz* and *Men's Workout* magazines, and most recently in fellow model Dirk Shafer's film *Man of the Year*—is also troubled by what he calls the "illusion of physical appearance" perpetuated by media that trade exclusively in youth and beauty.

"Just because you look beautiful on the outside, you still could be deadly on the inside," says Collins. "You can look like me and be infected and infect other people."

Some media have occasionally used starker AIDS imagery—and endured sharp criticism in the process. Italian clothing giant Benetton came under fire in the early '90s for running ads featuring a dying AIDS patient, male body parts branded HIV-POSITIVE, and a doctored photo of Ronald Reagan that showed his face covered with lesions from Kaposi's sarcoma, an AIDS-related cancer. Some of the ads were banned in Great Britain and Germany. On its October/November cover, *Poz,* a magazine aimed at people affected by the epidemic, featured a frank photo of a drawn Tom Stoddard—a well-known Washington insider and activist for gay and AIDS causes—his hair thin and his smiling face dotted with remnants of KS lesions.

But such representations are the exception rather that the rule. In advertising people with AIDS or HIV are usually fit, handsome, and happy—if sometimes saddled with short-term difficulties that can be resolved with the purchase of a product or service. Even entertainment and soft-news reporting tend to emphasize appealing and politically correct images such as that of heartthrob Pedro Zamora in MTV's *The Real World*. Fans watched the evolution of his touching romance with Sean Sasser as part of the television program but never witnessed his decline in 1994 into illness and death.

While it's important to show that people with HIV or AIDS can be sexual and attractive, such images can have unintended consequences, especially for vulnerable gay youth, says Michael Davis, former coordinator of Rainbow's End, a support group for young gays at the Tampa AIDS Network in Florida. "There's such an emphasis in our community on great bodies, on beauty," says Davis, 20. "And there's a great fear among gay youth that they're not good-looking enough." Insecure and fixated on the importance of being attractive, some young men come to associate seropositivity with unfading good looks. "They have a fear of getting old," says Davis. "I hear kids who are HIV-positive say, 'At least I'll be dead before I become a troll.'"

Some even say that the adoration showered on glamorous, attractive stars with AIDS—such as Zamora, Greg Louganis, and Magic Johnson—may lead some young gays to believe that HIV infection is a valid way to get love and affirmation. "In one of my focus groups, one of the guys was talking about how a lot of kids in his age group are really starved for attention," says Salvatore Daino, youth outreach worker for the Colorado AIDS Project's Boy2Boy Program, which focuses on prevention efforts for Denver-area gay youth. "He said if contracting HIV is what it takes to get attention, that's what they'll do. I was kind of shocked."

But others say that by depicting people with AIDS or HIV as seemingly healthy and usually attractive—by refusing to let AIDS be defined by symbols of victimization, decline, and defeat—image makers accomplish something empowering. That's the idea behind Proof Positive. Opened in 1993 as a division of the Morgan Agency, a Costa Mesa, Calif.–based modeling agency, Proof Positive is a representation service exclusively for models who are HIV-positive or who have AIDS, says agency owner Keith Lewis.

"It started because we noticed an increase in castings from companies marketing products to the HIV community," says Lewis. "It was a wonderful thing. They wanted people who were HIV-positive [for their ads]." The first to join the Proof Positive stable was Chris Crays, the original model for print media ads for Advera, a nutritional drink. Crays—who still models and is a spokesman for Advera as well as a lobbyist for a California AIDS organization—has since been joined by 60 other models.

It's virtually impossible today to leaf through a copy of any gay magazine without seeing a Proof Positive model, many of whom are identified as HIV-positive in their ads. And while their bodies and faces are most often used to promote products aimed at people with HIV and AIDs, the models work for a broad range of other campaigns too, says Lewis. "Proof Positive has been a wonderful experience for us all," says Lewis. "It provides work for people who can still be productive. And it provides self-esteem for people whose self-esteem is often stripped in the process of living with HIV and AIDS."

Poz founder and executive editor Sean Strub shares Lewis's views. In the October/November issue, Strub responds to criticism *Poz* has received for its consistent portrayal of HIV-positive people as "attractive." "That criticism comes from those who have a firm idea of what AIDS looks like: grotesque, desperate, terminal," charges Strub. "Anything that does not fit their denial-driven stereotype is challenging. Depictions of people who look like them (read: not obviously ill) are threatening. They hit too close to home."

Strub says the magazine also uses images of people who are obviously sick, though editors "respect the privacy of those who don't want to be seen on a respirator in a national magazine." But "like any magazine, we try to make everyone in *Poz* as attractive as possible, using the best photographers, stylists, hair and makeup people," Strub writes.

Like those photographed for *Poz,* Proof Positive models are usually transformed into perfectly coiffed, artfully lit manifestations of physical beauty hardly representative of most people with AIDS—a fact Lewis readily concedes. But that, he says, is simply a reality of the marketplace. "People wouldn't expect companies selling toothpaste with tartar control, for instance, to show people with really ugly teeth," Lewis says. "We're talking about marketing products."

Indeed, the exploitation of beauty is hardly unique to gay or to AIDS culture, says Michael Isbell, deputy executive director for public policy at New York City's Gay Men's Health Crisis, an AIDS service group. "[Gay men] don't live in a vacuum. We live in a society that's obsessed with youth and good looks. So I'm not sure whether there's a purposeful sanitization of AIDS or whether it's part of an overall obsession with physical beauty."

Isbell sees no reason why advertisers marketing to HIV-positive people should use models who are anything less than very attractive. While hundreds of thousands have died from AIDS-related complications, hundreds of thousands of others are HIV-positive and living healthy, productive lives. And while the issue of AIDS imagery is important, Isbell sees it as only one part of the strategies needed to help HIV-negative gay men stay negative.

"If the only images of AIDS that a young man sees are beautiful ones, it may make it more difficult for him to grapple with the choices he has to make," Isbell says. "But I'm more concerned with whether this young man has ever been engaged in a serious conversation about the decisions he's making. Many never deal with these issues until they have to confront the fact that they're HIV-positive."

Safer-sex campaigns may be part of the answer—and yet these campaigns also rely on sexy images of attractive young men, the impact of which is also controversial. The models featured in safer-sex ads are not presumed to be HIV-positive, but some say the use of sexual imagery often overpowers the ads' primary message. After all, text that urges people to use precautions can seem comparatively subtle when attached to a photo of a sweaty, lithe torso.

Often, too, safer-sex messages "aren't frank enough or real enough to be absorbed," says Juan Ledesma, director of health services at the gay and lesbian center in Los Angeles. Ledesma predicts that if the way we depict and talk about AIDS with young people doesn't become more candid and explicit, "we'll se a new wave of the epidemic among youth."

Davis shares that concern, pointing to the almost complete lack of AIDS education in the public schools. "We need to mandate this from the federal level and make sure explicit literature is provided," he says. "Otherwise, schools are not going to provide what kids need. There's very little discussion of gay sex and almost no depictions of people with AIDS."

But Lewis doubts whether images of people with AIDS—glamorous or otherwise—would ever make anyone with even a passing knowledge of the epidemic forget that it involved disease and death. "I don't think anyone who's actually living in a community being affected by HIV or AIDS can miss the point," he says. "I'm reminded every time I go through my address book at the beginning of the year and cross through the names of friends I lost over the course of the past year."

Lewis admits that his industry is often accused of being exploitative, but he prefers a more transcendental notion of physical appearance. "I view the body as just a container. It doesn't last," says Lewis. "It doesn't matter what it looks like. It's what's inside that counts."

Then why not increase the representation of images of "obviously sick" people with AIDS in the media? "If I went to Advera or Marinol and said, 'I'm going to give you this person who's in the latter stages of AIDS to market your product,' I don't think they'd agree to it," Lewis says. "I wish I could change the world, but that's just the reality."

But Isbell wonders whether quibbling over how people with AIDS are depicted ultimately misses the point as the epidemic continues to expand around the world and temptations to dabble in risky sexual behavior grow strong with each passing year. "Rather than overconcern ourselves with these representations, we need to create a range of programs serving both people who are HIV-positive and people who are HIV-negative," he says. "We need to care for people with AIDS. But we also need to care for people who are HIV-negative and find powerful ways to stress that staying negative is a very important thing."

Barbara Jordan—The Other Life: Lesbianism Was a Secret the Former Congresswoman Chose to Take to Her Grave

by J. Jennings Moss

March 5, 1996

"Do you really have to write this story?" asked an anguished friend of Barbara Jordan. "This is not what Barbara would have wanted." What Jordan would have preferred, say those close to the trailblazing Texas congresswoman—who died of viral pneumonia January 17 at age 59—was to be remembered for her devotion to the U.S. Constitution and for the lives she touched during her teaching career at the University of Texas at Austin.

What she didn't want was to be pigeonholed. "I really do not have much interest in being a symbol," Jordan said in 1976 when her name popped up on Jimmy Carter's list of potential vice presidential running mates. But for those inspired by her, she was a monument. She was the first black woman to be elected to the Texas state senate, the first black Southern woman to be elected to the House of Representatives, and the first black woman to deliver to a keynote address to a Democratic national convention, in 1976.

Those were parts of Jordan's profile that were public knowledge. But other aspects of her life were not, and she tried to keep them that way. It wasn't until after her death that people began openly discussing her lesbianism, a topic she had never addressed during her life. The silence was not broken until the *Houston Chronicle* included Nancy Earl, whom it called a "longtime companion," among survivors in an obituary of the congresswoman.

Associates say Jordan was straightforward about her sexual orientation in private but did not think it should be fodder for public consumption. "She never denied who she was," said a friend who, like nearly everyone who knew her personally, asked not to be identified. "It just was not the public's need to know."

"I know I am not alone in feeling less respect for Barbara Jordan for not coming out in death," wrote an *Advocate* reader to the magazine shortly after Jordan's death. "But I am especially anxious for all those of every community who idolized Jordan to know she was a lesbian."

Austin American-Statesman reporter Juan R. Palomo, who is gay, says he was bothered by Jordan's silence: "If anybody had the luxury to say, 'By golly, I'm a lesbian, and this is the woman I love,' it was Barbara Jordan. She could have done it, and her stature would not have been diminished one bit."

Many Texas gay rights activists declined to discuss Jordan's sexual orientation even after her death. "She never announced that she was a lesbian, and I go by the rule that if I wasn't in the bed or under the bed, then I don't know," says Pat Gandy, president of the Houston Gay and Lesbian Political Caucus. Adds Dianne Hardy-Garcia, executive director of the Austin-based Lesbian/Gay Rights Lobby of Texas: "Her sexuality was not something that was discussed." Still, she acknowledges that the topic fueled "a great deal of speculation."

A friend of Jordan's says that Jordan's attitude about discussion of her sexual orientation paralleled her attitude about talking about her health. Jordan long suffered first from multiple sclerosis and then from leukemia—the pneumonia that felled her was a complication of the leukemia—but she often denied she was having health problems. In Congress, for example, she complained of a bum knee when in fact multiple sclerosis was forcing her to walk with a cane. "For years she would refuse to tell people what she had," the friend says. "She was not defined by her physical conditions, her sexual orientation, or the color of her skin. If you were to define her by any of those areas, Barbara Jordan would roar."

A Baptist minister's daughter, Jordan was born February 21, 1936, in Houston, the youngest of three sisters. As a young adult she joined the National Association for the Advancement of Colored People and decided to become a lawyer, earning an undergraduate degree from the all-black Texas Southern University and a law degree from Boston University before returning to Houston.

Jordan's interest in politics was piqued during the 1960 presidential campaign, when she volunteered to work for the Kennedy-Johnson ticket in Texas. Two years later she made her first stab at elected office when she ran for the Texas house of representatives. She lost, ran for the same seat two years later, and was again defeated. But in 1966 she ran for a state senate seat and won.

Concern about how Jordan's lesbianism might affect her political career surfaced during those early races, according to one of her political advisers. The adviser, who has requested anonymity, says Jordan had a female companion in the early '60s who had joined her on the campaign trail. At one point, either shortly before the 1964 house election or as Jordan prepared to run for the state senate, a small group of advisers warned Jordan that the image of two women being so close could damage her political aspirations. Jordan listened and, without putting up a fight, agreed to impose a public distance between herself and the companion. The adviser could not remember the woman's name but said the relationship did not last long after that.

After Jordan arrived in Austin to begin her legislative career, she met the woman who would be her close friend and companion for the rest of her life. Jordan first encountered Earl while on a camping trip with a group of women friends. The encounter is described in Jordan's 1979 autobiography, *Barbara Jordan: A Self-Portrait:* "At some point in the evening Nancy Earl arrived, and that was the first time we'd met face to face. Nancy and I sat there playing the guitar; we had just met but we were singing and drinking and having a swell time.... I had had a great time and enjoyed myself very much. I remember I thought: This is something I would like to repeat. I'd like to have another party like that. Nancy Earl is a fun person to be with. We all did have other parties. There were many other occasions where I could relax and enjoy myself.... I liked to be part of those parties. I had discovered I could relax at parties like that where I was safe."

In 1972 Jordan ran for Congress in a new House district that state lawmakers created especially for her. And for the next six years Jordan left an indelible mark on Washington. She served on the House Judiciary Committee, which adopted articles of impeachment against President Richard Nixon, and she made sure her deep, resonant voice was heard.

"My faith in the Constitution is whole, it is complete, it is total," she said during nationally televised impeachment hearings. "I am not going to sit here and be an idle spectator to the diminution, the subversion, the destruction of the Constitution."

Earl, who has a master's degree in educational psychology, remained close to Jordan during the lawmaker's years in Washington, D.C., though she lived in Texas and, for a short time, in upstate New York. Jordan's autobiography described her as "tanned and tow-haired, she wanted to pick watercress in the shade of cypress trees, plant grass on the back slopes, be outdoors when she was not in the professional situation of her job."

In 1976 she and Jordan began building a home together on five acres of land near Austin. The couple threw a bash to celebrate the Bicentennial, with friends and family taking part. After the fireworks ended and Jordan's two sisters returned home, they sent Earl a letter: "Dearest Nancy, Barbara is our most precious possession: our sister, our congresswoman, and our friend. We shall be eternally grateful to you for your providing such a picturesque setting for our celebration of the nation's birthday and our friendship."

On December 10, 1977, Jordan shocked the nation by announcing she would not run for reelection. Her "internal compass," she said, told her to "divert my energy to something different and to move away from demands which are all-consuming." But Jordan had also been diagnosed with multiple sclerosis, which forced her to walk around the Capitol with a cane. At the time, though, she adamantly denied that she had a chronic health problem or that the ailment was partly responsible for her departure.

A month after Jordan said 1978 would be her last year in Congress, Earl went to work in Jordan's office in Washington, D.C. Congressional records show that Earl had the title 'special assistant" and was the second-highest-paid person in Jordan's office. Another staffer at the time recalled that Earl wrote speeches for Jordan and occasionally dealt with reporters. Upon her retirement from Congress, Jordan and Earl returned to Austin, where Jordan taught at the University of Texas's Lyndon B. Johnson School of Public Affairs. In 1994, however, she briefly reentered public life to chair a presidential task force on immigration.

In private life Jordan rarely granted interviews. Earl remained largely in the background–with one notable exception. In 1988 Jordan nearly drowned in her backyard swimming pool while performing physical therapy. Earl, who had left Jordan alone briefly, returned to find her floating and jumped into the pool to revive her. Media accounts at the time identified Earl as Jordan's "housemate."

Reached at her home for this article, Earl declined to discuss her life with Jordan in much depth. Asked about being labeled Jordan's longtime companion by the *Houston Chronicle,* Earl said, "I was her good friend. I was there morning and night to help her get up and get showered and get dressed and go to work. She had lots of companions. People can say whatever they want. She was a friend of mine. You can write what you want."

But if people in Texas did not know the exact nature of Jordan's relationship with Earl, its depth was well understood. On January 20, during Jordan's funeral at the church where her father had preached, former Texas governor Ann Richards began her eulogy by speaking directly to Earl.

"Well, Nancy," Richards drawled, "I always thought Barbara would preach at *my* funeral." Rep. Sheila Jackson Lee, who now represents Jordan's old district, also mentioned Earl by name.

Before the funeral Jordan's sisters turned to Earl, who was sitting behind them, and hugged her. Later, during Jordan's burial at the Texas State Cemetery in Austin, they motioned for Earl to sit with them in the front row, under the cedar tree that would forever shade Jordan's grave. Earl shook her head and pointed to the back row. That was where the friends sat.

ON THE RECORD: HEATED DEBATE OVER HOUSE APPROVAL OF THE ANTIGAY DEFENSE OF MARRIAGE ACT SHINES A WARY SPOTLIGHT ON THE CONGRESSIONAL CLOSET

by J. Jennings Moss

September 3, 1996

They spoke to their colleagues—and the nation—from experience. They argued that by passing a bill that defines marriage strictly as a union between a man and a woman, the House was trampling on the civil rights of gays and lesbians. They were talking about their own rights as gay men. And everybody knew it.

Steve Gunderson, Barney Frank, and Gerry Studds made their status as gay men relevant to the debate that took place in July. Arguably, the marital status and sexual orientation of every member of Congress was at issue when the House voted 342–67 to approve the Defense of Marriage Act, a bill that would allow states to avoid recognizing same-sex marriages granted in other states. (Hawaii could be the first to legalize such unions.)

Reporters quizzed Rep. Bob Barr, a Georgia Republican and a chief sponsor of the bill, about his three marriages. But they stayed away from approaching lawmakers long thought by many to be gay to ask why they voted the way they did. Gay rights activists, however—including many who abhor the practice of outing—argued that given the current climate and an issue as crucial and controversial as gay marriage, such questions were fair.

"If it's relevant to the issue, why not ask?" said Mindy A. Daniels, founder and executive director of the National Lesbian Political Action Committee. Or as Torie Osborn, former head of the National Gay and Lesbian Task Force, put it: "Anything's a fair line of inquiry that's involving a public debate about morality and politics."

However, gay opinion makers were far from consensus on the issue. Frank, the Massachusetts Democrat who disclosed his sexual orientation in 1987, was among those who expressed reservations. While Frank had threatened to out closeted House Republicans if the GOP tried to reinstate sexual orientation as a reason to deny someone government security clearance and while he conceded that gay marriage opens the door to asking lawmakers questions about sexual orientation, he argued that boundaries remain. "If you're not a hypocrite or misleading people," he said, "you have the right to be quiet about [being gay]."

The Advocate has a policy against outing, which the magazine defines as "the initial disclosure in a public medium or forum of someone's sexual orientation without his or her permission." For this story *The Advocate* followed up on prior reports in other media and on the Internet about closeted lawmakers where their names were mentioned. If these reports could be independently verified—that is, if at least three sources with professional or personal relationships with a lawmaker said they considered the lawmaker to be gay—the next step was to approach the lawmaker in question. They were verified, and *The Advocate* contacted Rep. Jim Kolbe of Arizona and Rep. Mark Foley of Florida, both Republicans, to ask them to explain their votes in favor of DOMA as well as to talk about their sexual orientation.

Both men objected to the latter line of questioning. "Even members of Congress should be allowed to have personal lives," Kolbe, 54, said in a telephone interview. "The issue of my sexuality has nothing to do with the votes I cast in Congress or my work for the constituents of Arizona's fifth congressional district." Upon reflection, however, Kolbe decided to come out soon after talking to *The Advocate,* saying the magazine's questioning of him was a chief factor. Foley, in written answers to *The Advocate*'s questions, stated his belief that "a lawmaker's sexual orientation is…irrelevant."

But while Kolbe and Foley told *The Advocate* that a member of Congress's sexual orientation should not be an issue, activists were saying otherwise. Michael Petrelis—who gained notoriety for throwing a drink on Gunderson at a gay bar in 1991 and then publicizing the incident in an attempt to force the congressman to come out—used his computer to raise questions about several lawmakers he said were in the closet. Petrelis sent his own reports or forwarded others to a mailing list that included more than 100 activists, writers, and publications.

Shortly afterward a gay broadcast journalist in New England, Kurt Wolfe, discussed both Kolbe's and Foley's sexual orientation publicly. In late July, in a story on the congressional closet, Wolfe reported on WBAI radio in New York and on the cable television program *Out in New England* that Kolbe is gay. In a follow-up report August 8 on his television show, Wolfe also reported that Foley is gay.

In the past both Kolbe and Foley probably would not have experienced the kind of scrutiny now thrust upon them. Activists used the standard that if a lawmaker or senior government official acted in a hypocritical way and was actually gay, then he or she was fair game for outing. What changed the rules for some activists was the gay marriage issue. Gays and lesbians shuddered when Republicans introduced DOMA, threatened to rebel when President Clinton backed it, and demanded accountability when the House passed it. All eyes now are on the Senate, which is expected to take up the measure in September.

Apart from their controversial votes on DOMA, however, Kolbe and Foley are two of the most pro-gay Republicans in the House. They have voted consistently in the minority of their party to support gay rights and efforts to fight AIDS. Both signed pledges saying that their congressional offices would not discriminate based on sexual orientation, and Kolbe is cosponsor of a bill to outlaw antigay discrimination in the workplace.

Among those who were particularly pained by the House debate on gay marriage was Tracy Thorne, a former Navy lieutenant who made history in 1992 when he disclosed his homosexuality on national television. Thorne's family lives in Foley's district and has helped Foley in his political career. While Thorne said he respected the rights of people who choose to remain in the closet, he said a different standard applies to people who hold positions of power: "What I cannot respect or tolerate is one who makes that choice and then, in the name of self-promotion, climbs on the very backs of those who need help the most."

Both Kolbe and Foley defended their votes in favor of DOMA. Kolbe said he backed the measure because he wanted to preserve a state's right to decide whether to accept gay marriages. He noted that he had also backed an effort to conduct a government study about the legal problems same-sex couples face. Foley criticized those who used the debate to "bash" gays and lesbians but added that "there were many people who voted for this legislation—myself included—because they have genuine reservations about tampering with an institution many Americans regard as sacred."

As to how their personal lives influenced their votes, neither man offered explanations. "That I am a gay person has never affected the way I legislate," Kolbe said in a written statement in which he came out to his constituents on August 1. "I am the same person, one who has spent many years struggling to relieve the tax burden for families, balance the budget for our children's future, and improve the quality of life we cherish in southern Arizona."

Coming out was a relatively short step for Kolbe, a six-term lawmaker from Tucson who four years ago ran against an openly gay Democrat and who was arguably the most open closeted member of Congress. He held parties at his home attended by such prominent gay men in Washington as Rich Tafel of the national gay group Log Cabin Republicans and Daniel Zingale, political director for the Human Rights Campaign, a gay lobbying organization, according to guests who attended the events. He occasionally visited Trumpets, a gay bar in Washington.

For Foley, questions about his sexual orientation first surfaced publicly when he ran for the House of Representatives in 1994. His conservative primary opponent John Anastasio implied that Foley was gay, but the strategy received little attention, and Foley won the primary with 61% of the vote. In interviews for this story, several people close to the 41-year-old representative from West Palm

Beach said they knew him as a gay man, although one also said he dated women.

"Frankly, I don't think what kind of personal relationships I have in my private life is of any relevance to anyone else," Foley said without defining how he characterizes himself. "I know one thing for certain: When I travel around the district every weekend, the people who attend my town meetings and stop me on the street corner certainly are a lot more concerned with issues like how I voted on welfare reform or whether or not Medicare is going to be there when they need it—not the details of whom I choose to have a relationship with."

The very thought of a return to outing angered some gay political operatives. "I don't think it's ever appropriate," said Zingale. Even though a vote for DOMA was a "disgrace and a moral failure," Zingale said, the vote was not grounds for outing. Mark Agrast, legislative aide to Representative Studds, said he could "think of many circumstances when outing is a great temptation but none in which it is morally acceptable. It is a form of psychological terror."

Others tried to turn the spotlight on the congressional closet without naming names. "To all closeted gay and lesbian members of Congress," read a full-page ad in the July 26 issue of *The Washington Blade,* a gay weekly. "We call upon you to end your silence and defend your community in this time of unprecedented hostility."

Said Joel Lawson, a former staffer on Capitol Hill who helped create the ad: "Someone has got to call them on this. There is no excuse for their vote. They might lose an election. They might not be as popular as they were. But these are tough times, and courage is never easy or risk-free."

Some of the 29 people who signed the ad, like Jeff Coudriet, a congressional staffer and president of Washington, D.C.'s Gertrude Stein Democratic Club, said they fully supported outing. "I think we are at war up here," said Coudriet, "and if you hold back some of your troops, you're colluding with the enemy."

William Waybourn, managing director of the Gay and Lesbian Alliance Against Defamation and a signatory of the ad, said that while he is opposed to activists' outing people, he believes the press has a different responsibility. "There are no unfair questions for anyone in public life," Waybourn said. If lawmakers go to gay events, patronize gay businesses, live in a gay environment, but vote in an antigay way, Waybourn believes that should be called on it. "They're asking to be outed," he said. "They're not leading a secret life. They're fooling themselves."

Reporters routinely ask Catholic lawmakers to justify votes in favor of abortion rights. They question African-American legislators who back an end to affirmative action. They ask small-business owners now in Congress to shed light on tax legislation that would benefit entrepreneurs. So scrutinizing closeted gay members about their voting records on gay and lesbian issues just seems to follow, Waybourn said.

Other prominent gays and lesbians interviewed for this article agreed. "We're approaching a time when the closet is no longer respected," said Osborn. "Fifteen years ago the closet was OK, even for gay people. The closet used to stand for privacy. Now the closet stands for prison."

Daniels also argued that members of Congress have chosen to live by different standards than private citizens. "They put themselves out there as public figures," she said. "You're taking all your stuff with you, including your skeletons. If you're not ready for that, don't go out there."

Tackling the NFL Closet

by Anne Stockwell and J.V. McAuley

December 24, 1996

In the high-profile world or professional sports, our gay and lesbian heroes have all been individual participants: Martina Navratilova, Greg Louganis, Rudy Galindo. Perhaps that's not surprising. For these athletes, the decision to come out affects only their own performance. But in team sports the ramifications extend far beyond the solitude of one psyche. That might be why, in the macho world of contact sports, we don't see any openly gay icons suiting up.

Gay and lesbian sports fans have waited too long for a football superstar to call our own. And it looks as if we'll be waiting a while longer. "The pressures working against a superstar coming out are powerful," says NBC Sports commentator Bob Costas. "Despite the changes in attitude that have taken place in society, it's still a macho environment. If a superstar came out, I think it wouldn't have that much effect. But the *possibility* that it would might frighten somebody." So fear of the unknown still rules.

However, there are signs that the fear is easing. In exclusive interviews with *The Advocate,* players, newscasters, and reporters predicted gay-friendlier times ahead. But others described a world where "gay" is still an insult—and a "homo" is still a guy on the other team.

Take the case of Dallas Cowboys star quarterback Troy Aikman. He's led his team to three Super Bowl wins over the past four years. He's also been the ongoing subject of the gay rumor mill. Those rumors hit the mainstream in a big way in sports journalist Skip Bayless's book *Hell-Bent: The Crazy Truth About the "Win or Else" Dallas Cowboys,* published in September, which tells of the football team's wild ride to the top.

Whether these rumors are true—and Aikman has flatly denied them—they certainly haven't come his way via rainbow flags and freedom rings. In fact, Bayless tells *The Advocate,* he suspects that the rumors might have stemmed from the bitter and well-known feud between Aikman and the team's head coach, Barry Switzer. In his book Bayless reveals the coach's antagonism with such quotes as "I have to take so much shit off that kid, and he's *gay*"—as if that added insult to injury.

What's more, according to Bayless, Switzer wasn't the only one tossing those rumors around. "You have to understand how widespread the gay rumors about Troy Aikman have become in the Dallas-Forth Worth area," Bayless goes on to say. "Somehow it got out on the talk-show rumor mill, spreading like wildfire. I could be wrong, but I think Barry Switzer and his cohorts had something to do with it."

"Last December," Bayless continues, "it was so bitter between the two and Switzer was so convinced that Aikman was trying to get him fired that he and his *compadres* came to me and other media people, saying, 'Why don't you have the courage to stand up and tell the truth about this guy,' as in, *he's gay*."

Before long, says Bayless, "Aikman got wind that the book was going to be an outing of Troy Aikman. After he heard this rumor he called me for an interview, and his opening remark was, 'I want you to know that I am not gay.'"

But what if an athlete of Aikman's stature said not only "I'm gay" but also "I'm proud to be gay"? According to Costas, that would be a big story. "In some quarters it would be greeted with signs of relief as a breakthrough," he offers. "That person would receive a backlash but also a great deal of support."

Veteran ABC Sports reporter Dick Schaap agrees. "People have been surprised enough by who is and isn't gay, so that they'll be less surprised in the future. If the meanest player in NFL were gay, I doubt people would think, *Oh, my God, I can't believe that.*"

At least one gay observer disagrees. "They're dreaming. Otherwise, why hasn't anyone come out?" says Dan Woog, author of a book about gay athletes and coaches in high schools and colleges tentatively titled *It Takes Balls*. "The reason people aren't coming out is because they are petrified of the reactions of the Bob Costases of the world. They celebrate hypermasculinity. The film clips they show, the way they refer to athletes when they're broadcasting games, how tough they are, how masculine they are. They never, ever open the door for anyone who is different."

Schaap himself admits he knows no pro football players who are gay and says no one has come out to him. Asked how long until someone does take the plunge, he says, "All I know is that it's a hell of a lot closer than when Dave Kopay came out."

Though Kopay didn't come out until after he had retired from football, gay fans count him as a genuine hero. The former NFL running back came out in 1976, when it was far less fashionable to be gay in this society. "While I was playing, I was out to a number of my teammates and to my wife," Kopay tells *The Advocate*. To this day he's the only openly gay athlete to emerge from the sport.

In his 1977 memoir Kopay told the truth about himself. But he wasn't rewarded. "I couldn't even get a job," he remembers. "There were big corporations where I knew I could be a good sales rep, but they were worried about my identifying them as a gay company." Finally Kopay found a career in the retail linoleum business.

But if coming out didn't reward Kopay in material ways, he found other satisfactions. "I think my teammates mostly really cared for me," he says. "I wasn't out when I was in college, but I was elected cocaptain of the team when we went to the Rose Bowl. After I spoke out and there was a big fuss, I went back to play in the alumni game. They still elected me captain of the team."

Both Costas and Schaap echo Kopay's point: At the end of the game, team sports are about being part of a *team*. "There are people who have done a hell of a lot worse who've been accepted because they help a team win," says Schaap. "And I'm not implying that being gay is bad. I think if Emmitt Smith, Troy Aikman, and Michael Irvin were to announce that they were gay, Deion Sanders might be tempted to say, 'I'm gay too'—if he thought it would help the team win."

But what about those awkward moments in the locker room? For Schaap, that concern is out-of-date. "Athletes are so vain, they figure they're immune to anything," he says, laughing. "With that old fear 'There's a gay person in the locker room,' I think their attitude now would be 'So what?' "

If it's not a problem for teammates, what about the publicity-conscious National Football League? "I don't see where the NFL would perceive coming out as being in their interest," speculates Costas. "At the same time, I think that if a player came out, the NFL's official position would be one of tolerance and support because that's an enlightened position now."

But wouldn't a gay player lose out on endorsements? Probably, Costas acknowledges. "I think it would be naive to believe that coming out wouldn't diminish a player's endorsement potential."

With teammates, the league, and endorsements accounted for, there's only one unknown left: the fans. "Fans can be brutal about anything," says Woog, "about someone who's ugly or someone who was involved in a drunk-driving accident. And they can be real, real brutal about sexuality."

That doesn't mean we won't get our gay football hero, he adds. Just not yet. "There are a number of openly gay athletes at the high school and college level," he says. "All over the country athletes are coming out, and it's not a big deal. As this trend continues, they're going to make their way into the pros. It's going to happen from someone coming up through the ranks, not an NFL star suddenly saying, 'By the way, I'm gay.' "

SILENT BUT DEADLY: THE RELIGIOUS RIGHT HASN'T DISAPPEARED

by John Gallagher

March 4, 1997

They lost the presidential election. They saw the Supreme Court overturn Amendment 2. They watched while IBM and other major companies joined the trend to offer gay employees domestic-partner benefits. Surely, after the hits they took in 1996, the religious right must be in decline.

Think again.

Despite the hurdles the Christian right failed to clear over the past year, its major organizations and players remain steadfastly on track, continuing to win new converts to their cause and to hawk their political agenda, including attacks on gay rights.

"The death of the religious right has been announced numerous times since the movement got off the ground in the late 1970s," says Robert Boston, a spokesman for Americans United for Separation of Church and State, a group that monitors right-wing organizations. "They've probably had their obituary written more times than any other social movement. Like any other political force, they have setbacks, but that doesn't mean they're going away."

Indeed, below the surface—beyond the range of the mainstream media and under the radar even of many gay activists—the religious right continues its campaign against gay rights unabated. "We don't see the virulent antigay activism that we saw with 1994's antigay state ballot initiatives, but the religious right is stronger than ever," says Donna Red Wing, national field director for the Human Rights Campaign, a gay lobbying group. "We can pretend they're not there, but I think they're getting much more substantive."

In fact, even though the religious right is waging no battles that are currently attracting attention at the national level, its leaders are laying the groundwork for future fights. Moreover, brushfires continue to break out at the local level over such issues as school curricula, nondiscrimination ordinances, and library books. "They're avoiding the major-headline statewide issues," says Frank Whitworth, executive director of Ground Zero, a gay group in Colorado Springs, Colo. "They're picking small things, building foundations for the bigger issues. What I fear is that all of a sudden we're going to find that from a lot of little skirmishes, they've won the war."

Much of the perception that Christian conservatives are reeling from last year's election, observers say, can be traced to the defeat of Republican presidential candidate Bob Dole. Dole had been embraced by such conservative Christian leaders as Ralph Reed, executive director of the Christian Coalition. However, concentrating on the results of the presidential election alone is a mistake, says William Martin, a professor of sociology at Rice University and the author of *With God on Our Side: The Rise of the Religious Right in America.*

"Because Dole didn't win, many people believed the religious right proved themselves to be impotent," says Martin. "But when they saw it was clear that Dole would not win, they spent more time on state and local elections. It wasn't a sweep, but Republicans are in control of both houses of Congress."

Moreover, Dole was never the choice of rank-and-file Christian conservatives. Many of them preferred far-right Republican candidates Pat Buchanan and Alan Keyes—in part because of Dole's equivocations on abortion early in the campaign, in part because he failed to exhibit the uniformly antigay attitude of a true believer. He alternately accepted and rejected money from gay Republicans, and he also stated in an interview that he opposed antigay discrimination. Still, after complaints from conservatives, Dole said that he opposed "the special-interest gay agenda."

If nothing else, religious right leaders have taken the line that the election results weren't as bad as they looked. "Bill Clinton may have enjoyed a triumph, but *Liberalism* did not," Gary Bauer, president of the Family Research Council, a conservative think tank, wrote in "an open letter to conservatives" published as a full-page ad in "The Christian American," the newsletter of the Christian Coalition. If anything, Bauer argued, Dole failed because he was "afraid of our values."

Those values, religious right leaders have indicated, are what prevented a Democratic sweep in Congress. "Reed in particular has been saying that evangelical Christians stopped what might otherwise have been a liberal rout," says Matthew Freeman, senior vice president of People for the American Way, a lobbying group that tracks the religious right. While that claim may seem an exaggeration, the new Congress is still conservative and in some ways even more to the liking of the religious right than its predecessor.

"If you look at the results they had in some Senate races, they did get some people who are going to be quite favorable to them," says Boston, pointing to Republican freshmen Jeff Sessions of Alabama and Tim Hutchinson of Arkansas. According to an article in the January 6 issue of *Christianity Today,* the religious right "is moving to concentrate its influence over federal legislation" in Congress. Among its goals are to keep at bay the Employment Non-Discrimination Act, a bill that would ban antigay job bias and that failed by one vote in the last Congress.

But special efforts to push conservative issues could seem less noticeable, given the influence that conservative Christians already wield in the Republican Party. "Take a look at the agenda that the Republican Party is focused on these days," says Freeman. "Just because these issues have been taken up by the Republicans, I wouldn't give them a free ride by identifying them as Republican Party issues. These are religious right issues, front and center."

Red Wing suggests that many gay men and lesbians have become so inured to the religious right's clout in mainstream politics that it no longer registers with them: "Has the religious right become so mainstream that we don't recognize it for what it is anymore? Are the wolves looking more like sheep?"

One sign of the religious right's continuing clout in the Republican Party was the election January 17 of Colorado businessman Jim Nicholson as Republican National Committee chairman. While Nicholson, who is Catholic, has not had a high profile on gay issues, observers say he could never have won the party chairmanship had he not been acceptable to Christian conservatives.

Yet concentrating on the impact the religious right has at the national level alone is misleading. "When people look at the religious right, they tend to focus on Congress and the president, forgetting that there are 50 state governments and tens of thousands of local governments as well," Boston notes. "The religious right is interested in all of them." Indeed, perhaps especially at the local level. "They have said they are more interested in school boards than the White House," Martin adds, "because government near where people lives is more likely to affect the culture more. It's also easier to win local elections."

Without doubt the greatest opportunities for conservative Christians to score political points are around the issue of same-sex marriage. Last year 16 states passed anti–gay-marriage bills, and activists expect a slew of anti–gay-marriage bills to reappear in state legislatures this year.

"They're bringing the measures, they're generating them, they're using them as an organizing and fund-raising tool," says Freeman. In January Concerned Maine Families, a conservative group that has sponsored antigay ballot measures in the past, presented 62,000 signatures to put a measure on the 1997 ballot banning same-sex marriage or to have the legislature ban such unions outright. "We believe it has plenty of bipartisan support," Larry Lockman, vice president of the group, told the *Portland Press Herald*. "It's a mainstream issue."

Although such battles continue to erupt around the country, Martin believes that in the long term the religious right may begin to modify its virulent condemnation of homosexuality, if ever so slightly. "I think there has been a softening of the resistance as people recognize that we have gays in our churches, gays in our families," he says. "To treat them as pariahs is a difficult position to support from scripture." However, Martin adds that antigay rhetoric "is an evergreen. It may be less green gradually, but this is not going to go away quickly."

Reed has already tried to present a benign countenance of the religious right movement to the public. However, Bauer and other conservative leaders have stressed the need to articulate principles clearly and not soft-pedal the goals of conservative Christians, creating a potential rift between two strains of religious right thought. Disregarding Reed's message of compassion, Reed's boss, televangelist Pat Robertson, still regularly slams gays and lesbians. In a January 7 episode of Robertson's television program *The 700 Club*, the Christian Coalition founder declared, "There's a natural aversion in people who are heterosexual to the, quote, homosexual lifestyle, unquote. That does not mean that you are a hater of homo—or whatever that word is. That doesn't mean that. And I'm tired of being characterized by politically correct people because we stand for the Bible."

A prime reason such antigay attacks will continue throughout the foreseeable future is that, as Freeman suggests, antigay rhetoric is a profitable mainstay of the religious right's fund-raising appeals. "It's a cash cow for them," says Boston. "It's almost replaced their bashing of public education."

Clinton's reelection allows conservative Christian groups to play up the gay "threat" even further. In a January fund-raising letter, Beverly LaHaye, chairwoman of Concerned Women for American, raises the specter of ENDA's passage to plead for contributions. "ENDA was a blatant attempt to destroy our society's moral foundations," LaHaye wrote. "This bill would have forced Christian businessmen and women and other decent Americans to hire homosexuals and those with a variety of 'sexual orientations,' including transvestites and pedophiles."

In the end, Martin says, 1997 may indeed be a quiet year for the religious right—on the surface. "Without an election, without big legislative issues, this may be a year of consolidating and trying to strengthen their own numbers in local organizations," he says.

There could be some exceptions, however, One large event, at least in terms of numbers, is a planned gathering of the Promise Keepers in Washington, D.C., this fall. Critics have complained that the group has a strong antigay and antifeminist agenda. The group, which promotes creating "godly" men, swears that it has no political agenda. However, Promise Keepers was founded by Bill McCartney, a former University of Colorado football coach and a vocal supporter of Amendment 2. "It's not so much that they are overtly political but that their message has obvious political implications," says Freeman. "They're certainly building an enormous infrastructure out there." In the first five years of its existence, Promise Keepers grew to have an $11 million budget and a staff of 300.

Red Wing says the success of Promise Keepers underscores the problem facing gay activists in their attempt to remain vigilant. "Maybe some people are lulled into thinking the radical right is somehow dormant because they are evolving into something much more mainstream and much more palatable," she says. "That's where they're dangerous. Their work doesn't have the edge that it used to, but I think it cuts much more deeply."

If the religious right is becoming more mainstream, it could be because they have tapped into genuine concerns among many Americans. "It's important to understand that they are concerned about real issues, however one comes down on them," Martin says. "They are a relatively permanent and important force on the American political landscape, and those who think they are going away are just wishing it."

"HOMICIDAL HOMOSEXUAL:" THE MEDIA LEFT THEIR MARK: CUNANAN WILL BE REMEMBERED FOREMOST AS A GAY KILLER

by Harry Crowley

September 2, 1997

Hours after Miami police identified Andrew Cunanan's body, ABC's *Ellen* received five Emmy nominations. It was an ironic coupling of events. While Ellen DeGeneres may eventually be re-garded as one of the greatest public relations representatives the gay community has ever seen, Cu-nanan will undoubtedly considered one of the worst.

For three months this spring, the media were captivated by *Ellen* and its star. They seemed to care about gay men and lesbians, and when the coming-out episode garnered extremely high ratings, it seemed the public cared too. But then Gianni Versace was killed on the steps of his South Beach mansion, and things changed. The media still cared, that's for sure. But instead of cute blond actresses who make re-freshingly honest jokes, they wanted to hear about sick men who sell their bodies for fun and profit.

The media are supposed to hold up a mirror to reflect whom they're reporting on; in the Cu-nanan case, however, the mirror seemed to reflect the media's own confused perceptions about who gay men are. When the *Los Angeles Times* wrote a news article on how the media covered the Cu-nanan story, it arrogantly proclaimed, "The issue is less ill will on the media's part than its struggle to adjust to the rapidly changing mores of the gay community"—as if there's an annual gay and les-bian convention where mores are voted on or a collective gay consciousness capable of arriving at a consensus for such a diverse group.

Maybe it's just the way the media deals with sordid slayings. Whatever the reason, gays were de-monized once again. The point is not that there wasn't good reporting or that every bit of the om-nipresent, obsessive coverage of the shooting was laced with a vicious homophobic subtext. To the contrary. Many of the journalists did a better job uncovering clues than the FBI, and much of the mainstream press was vigilant about not treating the case like a faggot hunt. Nevertheless, ugliness seeped into the newsprint like blood into limestone.

"Homicidal homosexual" is the way Tom Brokaw described Cunanan on the *NBC Nightly News*. On *CNN & Company,* anchor Mary Tillotson asked her guests whether serial killers have a "pro-clivity" for "sexual dysfunction."

"My visceral sense is that the coverage says gayness is all about sex, that sex is perverted and leads to horrible murder," says Leroy Aarons, former president of the National Lesbian and Gay Journal-ists Association. Cunanan was, after all, the "gay serial killer" (occasionally he was "allegedly" one).

While letter writers and a few pundits have said, "You'd never call him a Filipino serial killer," no one ever gets to the point: Linking Cunanan's sexual identity to his violent actions is a specious act. By suggesting (or sometimes blatantly saying) that his sexual orientation somehow informed the hideous crimes Cunanan was accused of committing, the media implied that anyone's homosexual-ity can cause them to run around the country blowing off heads, slashing necks, and pounding faces with crowbars. In some reports the message became clear: Violence is just part of the "lifestyle." It was *The Great Gatsby* meets *Cruising*.

"It's been a mixed bag," says Liz Tracey, associate communications director for the Gay and Lesbian

Alliance Against Defamation, a media watchdog group. "Some of it's actually been really good. But a lot of outlets have been taking things without much evidence and just going with them." And it wasn't just the *New York Post*, which almost daily printed something that deserved an angry press release from GLAAD. Just about every major news organization added to the stack of misinformation.

For many in the media, truth wasn't nearly as important as what they perceived the public expected: wondrous and effervescent stereotypes of serial murderers (one victim was wrapped like a mummy—was Cunanan playing out a sexual fantasy?), spree killers (did AIDS set off his rage?), gay men (many news organizations headed straight for the discos and gay ghettos to profile the community), drag queens (is *that* how Cunanan's eluding police?), and Filipino altar boys (Cunanan's own father fueled this one, telling the Associated Press, "He is not a high-class male prostitute...He was an altar boy").

Sadly, another of those expectations is that gay men don't have long-term relationships, let along life partners. Antonio D'Amico, Versace's lover of 11 years, didn't exist in most of the press until the end of the first week following Versace's murder. Would Ralph Lauren's wife go unmentioned? Or Donna Karan's husband? Elton John's partner got the silent treatment was well. In a widely printed photograph from Versace's funeral, a weeping John is comforted by Princess Diana and a dark-haired man. When the image appeared in the *Los Angeles Times* and many other papers, the photo captions made no reference to the mysterious man, who happened to be David Furnish, John's longtime partner.

In its story on how the media covered the Versace slaying, the *Los Angeles Times* explained the omission of Furnish's name by stating, "Until recently, the vast majority of gays did not want to come out publicly; many still don't. Over the past few years, however, a repeated theme within the gay community has been the importance of coming out as a political and social statement."

To ignore information is one thing, but to create it is another. And even the venerable *Economist* did it. The first newsweekly to appear on the stands with a story about Versace's death declared that the suspect was "a male prostitute." While Cunanan's mother has famously described him as a "high-class homosexual prostitute," there is no reliable evidence that he ever turned tricks. He may have been a gold digger—a "kept boy," even—but he was no whore.

Even quotes from male prostitutes in San Diego who claimed never to have seen Cunanan turning tricks failed to quell the rumors. The *San Francisco Chronicle* referred to Cunanan as a hooker in a headline. *New York Post* gossip columnist Cindy Adams even went so far as to devote a whole article recounting the dubious story of a "friend of a friend" who was propositioned by a man who looked vaguely like Cunanan about the time the fugitive was supposedly hiding out in New York City. According to the story, a man with "Oriental" eyes asked if he could get paid for sex. Must have been Cunanan!

Adams again raised ire the day after the shooting when she wrote a piece insinuating that Versace's lifestyle somehow contributed to his downfall. She referred to his favorite haunts as what "the uptight might refer to as dens of iniquity...joints where a *second date* was only a phrase, not a reality." It was at places like these or maybe at parties in the Hamptons (a weekend getaway spot on New York's Long Island) or in the VIP lounge at the San Francisco Opera—as *Vanity Fair* seems to think—that the media wanted Versace to have met his killer.

The newshounds were desperate to find a way to connect Cunanan to the supposed sleazy world of Versace and other rich gay men who make up what is called the Velvet Mafia. When *Newsweek* reported that Cunanan had attended a "small party" at Versace's house two days before the killing, that seemed to prove that the two were sinisterly connected. The magazine's source was proved false a day after the article appeared on newsstands, but such mistakes didn't seem to matter. Even as the days wore on and it became more clear that Versace had led a much more subdued lifestyle, not one news organization apologized for what they had assumed: that gay men with money inhabit a highly secret underworld rife with shady drug dealers, flamboyant boy-buying fashion designers, and sadomasochistic sex, sex, sex.

Even lesbian writer Achy Obejas, of the *Chicago Tribune,* had a part in it, filing a fascinating but sordid report from Miami Beach describing leather-clad genitals, the tweaking of nipples, and hustlers who weren't losing any business because of the incident. "I tried to capture the scene," she says. "The scene is wild and over-the-top." But whether the scene had anything to do with the killing has yet to be proved.

If party boys and disco balls are the first things Americans think of when they hear the word "gay," certainly AIDS is the second. The media went after that angle too. Even before the rumor was given a tidbit of credibility by the AIDS counselor who said he had talked with Cunanan in the spring, several "experts" were speculating in print and on television that Cunanan's discovering he was HIV-positive may have led to his rampage. In the mystical netherworld inhabited only by news editors, somehow the speculation was transformed into fact. (The loopiest headline was the *New York Post*'s "AIDS Fuels His Fury.")

The problem with this is obvious: When was the last time you heard about a heterosexual serial killer raping the headless bodies of cheerleaders just because he had AIDS? As Jim Graham, executive director of the Whitman-Walker Clinic, an AIDS service organization in Washington, D.C., told *The Washington Post*—in one of the few tempered, smart analyses of this story—"It is as conceivable that he has a sixth toe." *The Miami Herald*'s health writer wrote, "It was a naked reminder that 16 years after AIDS seeped into the national consciousness, the virus is still seen through a prism of fear and misunderstanding." The speculation continued until August 1, when the *Herald* quoted anonymous law enforcement officials as saying that an autopsy of Cunanan's body showed he was HIV-negative.

Equally misunderstood, it seemed, were the clues Cunanan left behind. When the police found clippers and hair shavings in Cunanan's abandoned hotel room, they concluded he was shaving off his body hair. Then a tourist gave the police a videotape of a man in drag standing outside Versace's home several days after the shooting. ("I saw the tape," Tracey says. "It looked nothing like him.")

Those two events together made law enforcement officials conclude that Cunanan may have been posing as a woman to escape capture. Those same officials changed their minds within two days—he was probably in casual men's clothing, they then said—but by that time the media were too fascinated with the prospect of a serial killer wandering around in a wig and a print sundress to stop talking about it.

Sightings of a cross-dressed Cunanan became progressively bizarre. "Someone…spotted Mr. Cunanan in a peach dress in the Publix supermarket, pushing his cart along the narrow aisles, eyeing produce and cereal boxes," reported *The New York Times*. One CBS morning news telecast showed pictures of what Cunanan might look like as a woman. The images were later reprinted in the *Chicago Tribune,* looking very much like "before" and "after" shots from some makeover gone terribly wrong.

For the record, Cunanan was found dead in a pair of boxer shorts. He still had dark hair, according to the caretaker who spotted him aboard the houseboat.

The media bumbled along to the bitter end. MSNBC was the only national news channel to cover the stakeout of the houseboat where Cunanan's body was eventually found, but neither the anchor nor the correspondent on the scene noticed the SWAT team storming the boat. The viewers saw it, but the talking heads didn't mention the event for ten minutes. They spent the time interviewing the host of TV's *America's Most Wanted,* John Walsh, who in a July 24 interview with *Entertainment Tonight* made the chilling statement, "[Cunanan] crossed the line from killing gay people for revenge and started killing innocent bystanders."

It was a fitting finale for the saga. For in the end this story wasn't about a crazed killer and his five victims. For much of the news media, it was about giving Americans a glimpse into a world they've never understood—and perhaps understand even less now. America has shown an interest in the lives of gay men and lesbians, and the media has an obligation to put them into the mix of everyday coverage. To take the actions of one disturbed individual and use it as a news peg to report on an often misinterpreted group is dangerous and irresponsible.

LESBIAN PLAGUE?

by John Gallagher

September 30, 1997

Having someone assume you're heterosexual can be annoying, frustrating, and alienating. If you're a lesbian, it can also be life-threatening.

For women—one in eight of whom face the prospect of developing breast cancer—visits to the doctor often lead to questions about birth control and sexuality. That leaves many lesbians with a dilemma: Should you out yourself to a straight doctor or ignore the lump in your breast?

Whether lesbians are at greater risk for the disease—the second leading cause of cancer death among women—is still a subject of debate. But on the eve of National Breast Cancer Awareness Month in October, experts say the bigger issue is that lesbians are not getting into the health care system for early screenings.

"The piece that should stand out is that lesbians don't get screened as often as heterosexual women because we're not in the family planning or child health care system," says Donna Knutson, a section chief in the cancer division of the federal Centers for Disease Control and Prevention in Atlanta. "It's not necessarily the sexual orientation that puts you at risk, but for whatever reason we don't go to providers as often."

The reasons, according to lesbians who have had bad experiences with health care providers, are all too clear. "When you get to a health care provider, the first thing they do is an intake of medical history," says Beverly Baker, executive director of the Mautner Project, a lesbian cancer service organization in Washington, D.C. "You get to questions like, Are you married? and you have to decide whether to say you're in a life relationship. Then, Are you sexually active and are you on birth control? If you say no, you get a big, long lecture from the person doing the intake asking if you are crazy."

Tania Katan, who was diagnosed with breast cancer four years ago at age 21, says her treatment, while impersonal, was not affected by her being openly lesbian. Still, she adds, the assumption was that she was heterosexual. "[The topic of] birth control was always on the questionnaires you had to fill out," she says, "and when I said I didn't use any, it always made them cock their heads."

Katan used the moment to come out to her physician. But many lesbians, says Liza Rankow, a physician assistant and lesbian health advocate, find it easier to lie. "We tend not to walk in the door, and if we do, a lot of women tend to be dishonest," says Rankow. "Lots of lesbians will leave the doctor with prescriptions for birth control pills rather than say their partner is a woman."

No wonder. Physicians often refuse to acknowledge that female partners exist. "Partners are crucial, but they tend to be left out," says Linda McGehee, a cofounder of the Atlanta Lesbian Cancer Initiative and a professor of nursing at Georgia State University who has studied lesbians with breast cancer. "One survivor said the only thing that made her uncomfortable was when she went to the physician's office. He would look at her all the time and not at her partner. When her partner asked questions, he would look at her as if to say, What are you doing here?"

Beverly Saunders Biddle, executive director of the National Lesbian and Gay Health Association, which represents gay clinics and providers, adds, "It is such an ordeal for a lesbian to even consider health care, because we have to figure out, Do we or do we not come out? Do I have to educate another provider? What happens to my records once I come out? What impact is coming out going to have on the care I receive? Because breast cancer is such an emotionally laden issue for women, it compounds any fear or distrust of the medical system in general."

For many heterosexual women, access to the medical system is through birth control; indeed, the system seems geared toward that purpose. Without the need for birth-control measures, however, many lesbians can easily neglect contact with a health care provider and subsequently neglect their health. The problem is not only breast cancer; lesbians may be less likely to get Pap smears to detect cervical cancer because doctors may not feel they need the test.

Without a doubt, breast cancer among lesbians has attracted attention the likes of which it barely had five years ago. "There's been a huge explosion," says Nancy Lanoue, 45, a founder of the Lesbian Community Cancer Project in Chicago and herself a breast cancer survivor. "It's something that is not a secret anymore. The activism has resulted in creating visibility for the disease." The effort even attracted the attention of the federal government, which declared lesbians an underserved population in 1994 and provided money for four pilot screening projects to perform outreach to lesbians at local YWCAs.

"We surveyed women in the lesbian community about different issues—whether or not they were being screened, those kinds of things," says Connie Winkle, director of women's health services at the YWCA in Dallas. Last year 190 women, most of them lesbians, were screened for breast cancer through the project.

But that funding ran dry in August. Meanwhile, for many lesbians, the disease remains all too visible. Too many women can provide a long list of friends and acquaintances who have the disease and in some cases died of it. "I was first diagnosed five years ago," says Dennie Doucher, 45, a cofounder of the Atlanta Lesbian Cancer Initiative. "There was only one other woman we knew at the time [who also had breast cancer], and we weren't real close to her." That quickly changed. "In the same year I was diagnosed, three other lesbians I knew were diagnosed," she says. "I would say at least ten, if not more, have been diagnosed since."

Still, the evidence of just how widespread breast cancer is among lesbians remains primarily anecdotal. Even the most rudimentary information about breast cancer among lesbians is hard to come by. "The one thing we know is that lesbians have breasts," says Rankow. "Our risk for breast cancer is not as lesbians but as women."

Part of the reason so little data exists is that doing research on lesbian (or, for that matter, gay) health issues is fraught with methodological difficulties. "Of all the people who get breast cancer annually—which is 180,000-plus women in this country—we don't know how many of them are lesbians because it's not a question usually on the history that is taken by a physician or nurse-practitioner," says Dr. Caroline Burnett, investigator for the Lombardi Cancer Center at Georgetown University. "We don't approach that issue."

Still more controversial is the question of whether lesbians are at increased risk for breast cancer. Susan Love, a professor of medicine at the University of California, Los Angeles, and author of the best-seller *Dr. Susan Love's Breast Book,* says, "To know more about increased risk, you'd have to get more accurate data about the lesbian lifestyle. That's almost impossible to get because by definition the information you get is from people who are self-identified. Any sampling you do get is going to be very biased." Baker agrees: "We can speculate, we can try to extrapolate from the data that does exist, but we just don't have those numbers."

However, among many lesbians—and several media outlets—at least one set of numbers has achieved widespread currency, no matter how inaccurate it may be: that lesbians have a one-in-three risk for breast cancer. That higher rate, experts say, came from figures presented at a health care conference in 1992 that a reporter misinterpreted.

Still, there may be reason to believe that lesbians have particular risks that increase their chances of developing the disease. "The factors for breast cancer in lesbians may be higher, generally speaking, because they don't have children," says Love, noting that not bearing children or delaying childbirth until late in life has been found to increase the risk of breast cancer. "Apart from that it gets harder." Love says she is leery about relying on other supposed lesbian characteristics—such as obesity, smoking, or heavy drinking—that could increase risk. Even an assumption of childlessness is questionable. "More lesbians are having children," says Burnett. "What is going to be the effect of that?"

There may eventually be a better answer to the question of whether lesbians are at greater risk for breast cancer. The Women's Health Initiative, a study of 160,000 women, has included questions about sexual orientation, allowing researchers to assess lesbian health.

Other study projects are tracking a variety of lesbian health care issues. "Lesbians are a hot research topic right now," says Knutson. Still, says Biddle, "there are these openings, but there needs to be more, certainly."

To counter the problems they have faced, lesbians are becoming increasingly self-reliant, forming their own breast cancer groups and outreach programs to educate other lesbians. "There are a lot more community groups, a lot more local activism," says Knutson. "We have support groups in a lot of major cities for lesbians with cancer." Among the goals of the groups is compiling a list of lesbian-friendly health care providers and educating other providers about the need for such sensitivity.

"We got together around kitchen tables, in living rooms, talking about the needs for providing lesbians with support," says Andrea Densham, a board member of the Lesbian Community Cancer Project in Chicago, recalling the group's formation in 1990. "It's a grassroots organization still run by volunteers."

McGehee says her research indicated that what lesbians with breast cancer wanted besides partner involvement and respectful health care providers was emotional-support services. While many breast cancer services exist, they often are not cognizant of a lesbian presence.

Katan's experience confirms that. She says the shock of her diagnosis was compounded by the lack of lesbian visibility she found in cancer support groups. "I was actively seeking a community of lesbian breast cancer survivors, and I didn't find a lot of lesbians coming to those meetings," she says. "I had nothing in common with these women at the meetings other than the fact that we all had breast cancer." Katan dropped out of the groups and wrote a play about the disease to come to terms with it.

"I was in support groups that were straight; I was very uncomfortable," says Doucher, who had a recurrence of the disease in 1994 and again in 1996. "I felt it was inappropriate to come out, and therefore I could not share a lot of the things that were going on in my life."

"My partner and I were not comfortable with some of the support services that existed," says Lanoue. "We went to a few different cancer agencies, and they were very well-meaning, but it wasn't a comfortable place for my partner. And most of the people had very different concerns."

In their efforts to get the message out about the need for screening, activists were happy to have found an ally in the federal government. And although U.S. funding of the four pilot projects ran out in August, activists hope those programs will be a springboard for a new era in lesbian health care. "It's our hope and desire that lesbian health advocacy can be done on a broader scale," says Jeanne Barkey, project coordinator for the Minnesota Lesbian Health Care Access Project. "In the grand scale of things, this was a teeny, tiny project, but it was a starting point. It's an effort from lesbians saying we should do something about lesbian health now."

Rip van Revolution

by Donna Red Wing

October 14, 1997

Whoever has traveled through Oregon must remember the beautiful city of Portland. It is nestled between the Cascade and Coast ranges, intersected by the mighty Columbia and Willamette rivers. This mist and mountains create magical hues of blues, pinks, and purples, seemingly suspending Mount Hood's perpetually snow-capped peak on the southeast horizon.

Before the millennium I lived in that city. My partner, Sumitra, and I moved to Portland in 1989 so I could work as a grassroots organizer with the Lesbian Community Project. We were almost immediately challenged by the antigay initiatives of the radical right and played a role in keeping their bigoted agenda from becoming law. From there I moved into national gay movement work, always from a place informed by Tip O'Neill's adage "All politics is local" and insisting on a commitment to grassroots organizing.

It was a later summer evening in 1997. We were on vacation. While Sumitra visited friends, I had stopped at the Brew Sister's Pub and then drove on to the Oaks on Sauvie Island. We loved the ancient oak grove and the river waters that surrounded the island. Our dog, Wolf, could run and swim and chase squirrels for hours.

It was a beautiful evening. I scrambled to the top of a green knoll and from the precipice could see both rivers. Huge purple clouds reflected on the rippling waters. I lay back and closed my eyes. "Hey, hello, wake up," I heard a voice say. "What are you doing, girlfriend?" I blinked, looked around, and saw a lone crow circle the grove. Wolf growled from the back of her throat. I felt some apprehension but walked toward the sound. Where I thought I saw the crow land, I saw an old woman dressed in a black cotton dress. She beckoned with a crooked finger.

I walked to a clearing where a dozen women were seated around a fire pit. They were dressed in black; some in long dresses, others in trousers. Some wore boots; others were barefoot. There were old crones and young women. There was no doubt that they were all dykes. Each played a percussion instrument: congas, drums, shekeres. The rhythms were unfamiliar, exciting, hypnotic. I thought I heard thunder in the eastern sky and could detect the sulfuric odor of lightning. The women smiled. I fell into a deep sleep.

On waking I found myself on the hill where Wolf and I first saw the old woman. I rubbed my eyes. *Damn, have I slept here all night?* I wondered. *Those women, who were they?* I looked around for my backpack and wondered if the women had taken it. Wolf too had disappeared. She may have strayed away chasing a duck or squirrel. With some difficulty I walked back toward the road. My truck was gone. And the dirt road seemed more overgrown than I remembered—blackberry bushes had begun to wind across the path. The Columbia River seemed much cleaner than I had ever seen it. I called for Wolf and was answered by a murmur of idle crows that seemed to look down from an old dead oak and scoff at my dilemma.

My watch had stopped. And where was Wolf? I quickly walked toward St. John's Landing. I'd call home from there. My appearance—baggy Levi's and Doc Martens—soon attracted the attention of everyone at Coffee People. I stared back, feeling out of place and out of time. I glanced at the hologram calendar and trembled when I saw *2027*.

An older woman with a familiar face worked the ancient espresso machine. When I asked for a double Velvet Hammer, she laughed and said, "I haven't made one of those in years. The gal who used to order these disappeared a long time ago. Her dog came back without her." I had one question. "What happened to her girlfriend, Sumitra?" "Well, she's still living in their old house….says she's waiting for the old girl to come back." I smiled and paid for my coffee with crumpled old bills. She looked at me, looked at the bills, and said, "Sit down, honey: I'm calling Sumitra."

It didn't take me long to establish myself again in Portland. Most Portlanders understand that

Sauvie is a place of magic and fairies and things that can't be explained. I was so pleased to be home. And I was amazed and delighted by the changes that had occurred. Sumitra and I were married almost immediately. The bishop of Portland's Catholic diocese said she was honored to marry us at the cathedral.

I was astonished at the political changes. It seems that the Employment Non-Discrimination Act, legislation I had worked on, was passed by the 105th Congress in April 1998. A groundswell of local support had moved fair-minded members of Congress to vote the right way. And every member who did was returned to Washington with unprecedented gay support. What's more, the elections of 1998 returned a Democratic Senate.

The gay community had begun to organize, person by person. In 1998 Hawaii's voters approved same-gender marriage and overwhelmingly voted to protect their constitution. Success was possible because a coalition of labor, social justice groups, and religious communities united to support the rights of gays and lesbians, all in the spirit of *aloha*. More than a million couples married in Hawaii that year, and thousands brought suit against those states that refused to recognize those marriages. A Supreme Court decision two years later supported the rights of same-gender couples to marry. In 2003 the U.S. Congress voted to protect the rights of gays, lesbians, bisexuals, and transgendered individuals in housing, credit, and public accommodation. Again, it was constituency-based advocacy and lobbying that pressured Congress.

I was not surprised to learn that the Christian Coalition began to crumble after Ralph Reed's departure in 1997. With its demise most radical-right organizations had no strategy or center. The Rutherford Institute and the Heritage Foundation closed their doors in 2005. Reed joined the board of Parents, Families, and Friends of Lesbians and Gays in 2015, when his son finally came out to the family. Reed's youngest daughter married the niece of HRC's longtime executive director, Elizabeth Birch in 2019, cementing two political dynasties. Reed and Birch cowrote a best-selling book on family values in 2025.

After the great and solemn march on Washington in the year 2000, the gay movement took on a political profundity that matched its political muscle, and today gay politics are at the heart of mainstream politics. Sumitra and I have become an old couple enjoying shared pension and Social Security benefits. We also enjoy the basic human and civil rights that our nongay friends have always taken for granted. Gay politics have moved into the mainstream.

The great-great-granddaughter of Wolf, a large red and black canine, has begun to follow me wherever I go. She is a fierce dog who tenderly protects my grandchildren and has become my best traveling companion. Someday soon, I think, she'll follow me back to the Oaks on Sauvie Island. This time, Sumitra will come with us.

BLACKS AND GAYS: THE UNEXPECTED DIVIDE

by John Gallagher

December 9, 1997

A right-wing radio host railing against the Walt Disney Co. for being pro-gay. Alveda King, Martin Luther King Jr.'s niece, describing gay rights as an affront to the civil rights movement. Nation of Islam leader Louis Farrakhan preaching against the gay "lifestyle." Gospel singers Angie and Debbie Winans setting the condemnation of homosexuality to music.

Under most circumstances none of these antigay tirades, or others like them, would make headlines. But because in each instance the critics are African-American, the incidents suddenly seem more astonishing. The underlying message behind such attacks—that gays are unfairly comparing their struggle for civil rights with that of blacks—creates an impression of competing minority groups. It is, say some black gay men and lesbians, a false impression. "It shouldn't surprise people," says playwright Brian Freeman, who is on tour performing *Civil Sex*. The play, inspired by Bayard Rustin, a gay black man credited with organizing the 1963 civil rights march in Washington, D.C., speaks to the black gay experience. "There are a whole gang of black conservatives out there," he says. As for Alveda King, he adds, "She's the LaToya Jackson of the King family."

Some African-Americans say comparing the black and gay civil rights struggles somehow taints or belittles the black struggle. But Mark Johnson, communications director for the National Gay and Lesbian Task Force, believes blacks should feel honored if gays want to pattern their movement after the 1960s civil rights movement. "[The black] community has written the book," says Johnson, who is black. "Why wouldn't that get to be a textbook for others? For people to say 'This is ours; it's demeaning our struggle to adapt it' is a little shortsighted. What's really being said there, whether they're saying it or not, is a tribute to the black community. It's more a fraternal issue than a fractious issue."

Still, the attacks play on a recurrent fear among some minorities. "On some level we really do believe that equality and justice are matters of choices," says Phill Wilson, founder of the National Black Gay and Lesbian Leadership Forum. "We don't believe it's possible for all of us to be treated fairly. What black people see is if gays and lesbians use the language of the civil rights movement to fight for their civil rights at the same time that our civil rights are being eroded, there is a connection between one group ascending and the other being attacked. That's a myth."

There's also a religious component to some of the antipathy, one example of which are the Winanses, who made a publicity splash with their song "Not Natural." Among the forums the sisters have won for themselves have been two appearances on the Black Entertainment Television cable network. Keith Boykin, executive director of the National Black Gay and Lesbian Leadership Forum, criticized the network for giving the sisters "not one but two televised opportunities to spew out their bigotry." Boykin appeared on one of the BET shows as a counterpoint to the sisters' argument.

Conservative activist Alveda King would not have attracted much attention if it weren't for her uncle. In the past several months, King has been making appearances around the country condemning gay rights. While she said during a Seattle appearance in September that she was not representing her uncle, she added, "I am very familiar with how he felt about the Bible and the standards of the Bible, and he upheld those." Gay people, Alveda King said, lack the "innate and immutable" characteristics of racial minorities.

Talk-show host Alan Keyes, failed Republican presidential candidate in 1996, regularly attacks gay rights. In a June program about the Southern Baptists' Disney boycott, Keyes put the company "squarely in the camp of those who are tearing down the moral fabric of this country, culminating in their hoopla over the coming-out episode of Ellen 'Degenerate.'"

Of course, the vast majority of antigay attacks come from white conservatives, many of them affiliated with the religious right. But while the Winanses, King, and Keyes also are affiliated with the religious right, it is usually their race that becomes the focus of attention.

"It's this black thing, not a religious-right thing," says novelist Jewelle Gomez. "That's a problem around all issues with African-Americans. It's not put in relation to anything else. You end up feeling singled out, as if there is a special way that black people are homophobic or that we have an extra power in our homophobia."

Gomez notes that the views of conservative blacks are often held separate from those of conservative whites. "Within the context of the religious right, Alveda King is just one of them," she says. In fact, overwhelmingly white religious-right groups—such as the Traditional Values Coalition and Colorado for Family Values, which promoted that state's antigay Amendment 2—have regularly recruited blacks to help deny the validity of the gay rights movement. By comparison, gays have been more lax in their outreach, Wilson argues. "The gay and lesbian community has not strategically looked at that," he says. "Our separate ethnic communities are drifting further and further apart instead of coalescing in any strategic way."

If anything, says Freeman, the antigay outbursts are in their own way a blessing in disguise. "When people go there they provide us an opportunity to speak out," he says. "A lot of times, the problem of dealing with homophobia in the African-American community is the silence. Anytime someone like this pops up, it provides us the opportunity to have a discussion in public, which is the only way it's addressed."

Unfortunately, the efforts of pro-gay African-Americans fail to garner much attention. Coretta Scott King, widow of Martin Luther King Jr., has endorsed both federal nondiscrimination legislation for gays and same-sex marriage. Other black leaders, including the Rev. Jesse Jackson, have been equally supportive. "Who has the best voting record on gay rights in Congress, 100 times better than the next group?" asks Freeman. "The Congressional Black Caucus."

Gomez says King and the Winanses have the spotlight in part because there are no openly gay African-Americans of comparable stature. "We as a black queer community don't have anyone who gets up and talks for us on that level, who has been brave enough to come out to be active," she says. "Until that happens the black conservatives and the religious right are always going to get the headlines."

Yet while black gay men and lesbians in general have been increasingly visible within the gay community, it often takes a controversy, such as those generated by King or the Winanses, to get white gays and lesbians to take notice. "The gay and lesbian movement is a microcosm of the society in which we live," says Johnson. "How could it not be? People never focus on people-of-color issues unless there's a crisis. It's not something the culture thinks about, knows about, cares about or is interested in discussing.."

"I don't think, generally, that there is a lot of dialogue on race issues," says A. Cornelius Baker, executive director of public policy and education for the National Association for People With AIDS, a Washington, D.C.–based advocacy group. "The times we talk about it most in the gay community, I find, is when we get to meetings and there is not enough diversity in the room. Then we have an hour's discussion about how we can get more diversity in the room."

Johnson says the gay movement has come to a greater appreciation of black gays but still has a ways to go. "The mainstream gay community does realize that the black gay community has a stronger sense of self and has taken on more power," he says. "I think they see us now as teenagers, as opposed to babies. There's a certain respect—often distant, but still respect. Everybody is usually invited to the table, but sometimes when you get there the old ways of operating don't stop."

For all the gains made by black gay men and lesbians, they remain underrepresented in gay leadership. "Heading NAPWA and being a black gay male, I look at the landscape, and with the exception of the Leadership Forum, all the other organizations are headed by nonblacks," notes Baker. "One of the things we have to recognize is that we are part of the leadership. Part of the challenge is for white people to be able say that we're not just that thing that's black and gay but that we are part of the leadership of our community, irrespective of our color."

Some gay African-Americans have already written off the larger gay community. "One of the cutting-edge issues is about separatism and identity," says Boykin. "*Gay* is considered a white, Eurocentric, culturally imperialistic term that doesn't represent the values of African-Americans." Other black gays, while not going quite so far, feel their connections to the larger gay community to be tenuous, citing poor representation not just in the gay leadership but also in the gay press.

At the heart of the debate lies the belief of many white gays that homophobia in the black community flies in the face of that community's own history. "There's a sense in the white community that the black community is somehow more homophobic," says Freeman, "a sense that 'How could it be homophobic, because it had to face its own discrimination?' "

As Johnson notes, the issue is not that gay people don't experience discrimination but that their experiences often differ from those of African-Americans. "You have a whole group of gay people—white gay men—who, save for being gay, have never known discrimination," he says. "Because they now know what it's like to be discriminated against, they don't have the patience or heart to hear anybody else's anger. That's what people of color get upset about. To hear a white gay man say 'I've been discriminated against' is hard for some people of color to fathom because he looks like the people who discriminated against *them*. Until white people understand that the oppression they see is probably never like the oppression people of color see, it's going to be hard for people to get along."

ONE ON ONE: MONOGAMY

by Dan Woog

June 23, 1998

One of the hottest debates in today's gay world involves the *m* word. Is it for us, we wonder, or is it just aping straight society? Is it a basic human drive or a dumb social construct? And, of course, each of us wonders, Is it for me?

But this *m* word is not marriage. It's monogamy. Etymologically, the word means "one marriage." So how can it possibly apply to a group of people who are not legally allowed to wed?

It applies because at least some of us want it to. "The fact that so many gay and lesbian couples settle down and nest despite the lack of societal support indicates it's an important need," says Aleta Fenceroy, a 49-year-old computer programmer in Omaha who has spent seven monogamous years with Jean Mayberry, a factory worker. "We just found ourselves and knew that we wanted to be together. It might not be for everybody, but it's always been around. We know couples who have been together and monogamous for 20, 30, even 40 years. Maybe it's more prevalent in the Midwest!"

"The fact that gays can't be married shouldn't change anything," adds Buff Carmichael, 50, editor of *Prairie Flame,* the gay newspaper in Springfield, Ill. He and Jerry Bowman, 43, who works for the state of Illinois, have been in a monogamous relationship for six years. "A commitment is something made by two people, not by a minister or license," Carmichael says.

But, in fact, two men or two women making a commitment is different from a man and a woman doing it. Evolutionary scientists say males and females set different standards for sexual partners. They argue that since sperm is cheap, males instinctively want to spread their seed among many partners, but eggs are precious, so females seek copulation with one mate who will be a good provider. Socially, that results in compromises—marriage and adultery—but what happens when two people of the same gender don't have to meet in the middle?

One result might be the old joke: What do two lesbians take on their second date? A U-Haul. What about two gay men? What second date?

Thus, says neuroscientist Simon LeVay, gays and straights can be seen as biologically similar: The males share an interest in casual sex, while the females want to settle down. He cites studies from San Francisco in the pre-AIDS 1970s showing that the average gay male had had 500 partners up to the time of the survey interview; the average lesbian, fewer than ten.

But those are averages, and Dean Hamer, a molecular geneticist at the National Institutes of Health, believes the reason some males are more monogamous than others is genetic. His lab has discovered a gene for a dopamine receptor, which influences a personality trait called "novelty seeking." Those with a strong tendency for novelty seeking are more apt to bungee jump, enjoy abstract art—and have multiple sexual partners—than those with a lesser tendency. (No comparable data exists for women.)

Yet life is more than genetics, and the monogamy debate is about more than getting off. The real issues, says Betty Berzon, a Los Angeles–based psychotherapist who has written extensively on monogamy, are "intimacy, commitment, planning your life—things most gay people are not very good at." The reason, she believes, is that society does not provide gays with the same blueprints or models it gives straights. Because no one expects gay relationships to last, gay people think the only solution to trouble is to run out and find a new partner. This "antigay myth" begins in straight society, Berzon says, but gays internalize it until it becomes self-fulfilling.

Michael Cohen, a psychotherapist in Hartford, Conn., thinks monogamy is a social construct derived from religion and may or may not be natural. But he knows from his experience with clients that it is something many gay people strive for. "It's an unconscious desire to be like our parents and to be assimilated," he says. "Some people get beyond that—and see monogamy as an emotional challenge—to find the intimacy required of a close relationship. Lots of gay men can't dig deep inside to reach the emotional foundation needed to achieve sexual intimacy. When we're nonmonogamous, our emotional presence is not required as much."

Others disagree. Frances Donovan, who has "experience on both sides of the monogamy fence" and conducts workshops on that topic at educator and youth conferences, believes *nonmonogamy* is a negative definition. She prefers *polyamory*—the ability to love more than one person at a time—and says the key to successful polyamory is open, honest communication. At one workshop, participants listed several benefits of polyamory, including freedom, love, happiness, and trust.

Which brings us to two specific types of polyamory: threesomes and open relationships. Perhaps surprisingly, some of the strongest advocates for monogamy view threesomes with equanimity.

"They can be shared experiences that couples go through together," Berzon says. "The key is that it has to be both partners' choice. If it is, my job becomes helping them think about the best ways to make it work."

"There's a difference between emotional monogamy and sexual monogamy," argues Cohen. "If a couple have threesomes occasionally and are still committed to each other, they can usually separate the two."

Yet not everyone can do that. "For me, intimacy is so complicated and scary," says Sara Schley, a faculty member in special education at New York City's Hunter College. She and her partner, carpenter Terry Barrett, firmly believe that two is enough; three would be an unacceptable crowd. "Adding another person into my life would make me shut down, not feel more erotic or excited," Schley says.

Part of monogamy's power flows from its uniqueness. It is the ultimate form of privacy, yet it also requires sharing, no easy feat. "I'm a very private person," Mayberry says, "and I've never wanted 'just anyone' to know me that well. I'm not very open and trusting in that way. But I trust Aleta completely—heart, soul, and body."

Open relationships, on the other hand, are not shared experiences. Cohen warns that such arrangements are an enormous challenge, requiring great inner security. "You need to negotiate together," he advises, "and allow that your partner might have separate needs you can't always meet. It also means separating sex from love. But if you're out in the open about it, it can actually be a means of accomplishing intimacy."

During their three years together, Rebecca Scott, a 20-year-old from Tallahassee, Fla., and her partner devised four ground rules for an open relationship: Always let each other know what's going on (including who you're sleeping with and who you'd like to); always have safer sex outside the relationship; if the other person has a partner, always obtain her permission; be there for your partner when she needs you.

Some gay people cannot understand that point of view. "Open relationships seem like insecurity or codependency," says 26-year-old Brad Bergman, a production finance coordinator at the Walt Disney Co. "I don't want to share Mr. Right with anyone, and I hope he wouldn't want to share me."

Most people draw the line at cheating—that is, having outside relationships without the knowledge or consent of one's partner. "The rules are simple: If you are in a monogamous relationship, you don't cheat," says Jeffrey Denke, 26, a video producer. "It is a matter of self-control and will." The best way to combat the desire to cheat, he says, is to "explore a variety of sexual encounters together. Third partners and other couples are a great way to add variety to sex."

Even the most committed monogamists admit that boredom is a dangerous enemy. However, says Berzon, monogamy can still be sexy. "The quality of a relationship changes with time," she says. "It's uncommon for the thrill to remain over decades, but deeper love and caring replace that. Love is more than lust, but you have to talk about what's happening. You need 'relationship skills' or else you'll just do the same thing over and over and only on Saturday night."

Liam Miller, 30, and Dan Wine, 27, have been together for six years. They share more than their home life: Both work at *The Herald-Sun* newspaper in Durham, N.C., as news copy editor and assistant sports editor, respectively. Yet such closeness does not breed boredom. "Monogamy can be very sexy," Wine says. "We use candles!"

"We make sure we have plenty of 'alone' time," Miller adds. "We do things together, just the two of us, and that makes our relationship even more intimate."

The two men have discussed the importance of monogamy to their relationship. "We're both like-minded, introverts, and unlikely to prowl," Miller says. "We feel lucky to have found each other. When I first met Dan I was 24, and people told me to sow my wild oats. But I didn't want to throw away a great thing, and thankfully he felt the same way. Now we don't want to do anything to burst this bubble."

For Jerry Bowman, Buff Carmichael's partner, monogamy signals comfort. "I don't feel right except with Buff," he says. "With him, I feel secure. There's something closer about a monogamous, one-to-one relationship that you can't get anywhere else."

Mayberry finds joy and sustenance in her monogamous relationship with Fenceroy. "We're like an old pair of slippers, kind of worn-down and raggedy," she observes. "There are certainly better-looking shoes out there, but none quite so comfortable. Nobody would laugh at my stupid jokes the way Aleta does. I can't imagine being with anybody else, and I don't want to imagine it."

Barrett sees monogamy as one of the most important elements in keeping a relationship stable. "Personally," she says, "in every legitimate long-term relationship I know, the people are monogamous." Her partner, Schley, describes the changing role sex has played over the years they have been together: "Hot passion is great, but if it stayed that way for 20 years, we'd be exhausted! Sex now is different."

They continue to find new ways to please each other—and they say that with monogamy and trust comes an ability to communicate that enhances their pleasure. "We do things with each other that we might have been hesitant to try before," Schley says. "We're constantly surprising each other. That apprehension level is gone."

For two partners intent on maintaining a monogamous relationship, Cohen recommends replacing the words "hot" and "sexy" with "comfortable" and "creative." Monogamy can be boring, he admits, but so can nonmonogamy: "Going from partner to partner can get old hat too."

But the fact remains that society celebrates heterosexual monogamy with legal weddings, newspaper announcements, and unquestioning joy, while gay marriage is so controversial that its very existence must be decided by the courts. If we are, as has been said, "sexual outlaws" or, at least, men and women pushing the boundaries of sexual norms, why should we want to settle down for life, the same way straight folks do? Isn't that slavishly following a society that often shuns us?

"That's the silliest argument there is," blasts Berzon. "We have exactly the same needs as straights: intimacy, connection. Is the only way to maintain our uniqueness through sex? I hope not. We are unique, but there are many different ways to express uniqueness beyond sex."

Yet Ann Northrop, a lesbian activist and coanchor of the Gay USA cable TV news show, sees the debate about monogamy as "a window of opportunity" for gays to be honest about our behavior—far more honest, in fact, than straights, who from U.S. presidents on down have never been paragons of monogamy.

"We don't have the hypocritical, hierarchical heterosexual system of rewards" that flow to folks in monogamous, committed relationships, she says. "However, we also have not talked openly about what we want from a relationship, where sex and intimacy fit in, and what may or may not work for us." Now, Northrop believes, is the time.

Ultimately, of course, choosing monogamy or polyamory is an individual's—and a couple's—decision. The results are as varied as the entire gay population, and each situation is as unique as each of us. There are people who are nonmonogamous because they fear intimacy and growing up, and couples whose 40-year relationships are as loving and unexciting as any straight pair's. There are gays who are "serially monogamous," and couples who seek new partners every weekend.

But for couples like Barrett and Schley, monogamy is the only way to go—and the *m* word need not stand for mundane. Their sex life is more varied than ever, thanks to their deep trust and heightened communication, but there is more to their commitment than physical pleasure.

"The emotional piece of our relationship is so important," Barrett says. "Sex is fun, but how much time can you spend on it? If you focus just on sex, you'll miss out on the emotional connection. Monogamy is about more than sex; it's really about fulfillment, joy, sharing, love, and life."

USING PEDRO

by Lee Condon

July 7, 1998

A year before he died of complications from AIDS at the age of 22, Pedro Zamora, the AIDS activist and star of MTV's third installment of *The Real World,* asked legislators on Capitol Hill who would carry on his efforts to educate the nation's youth about HIV and AIDS. "I wonder now as I look around me, Who is going to pick up my torch?" he asked.

Since his death in November 1994, four entities have been named for Zamora: a memorial fund run by AIDS Action, a Washington, D.C.–based advocacy group that represents more than 2,400 local AIDS service organizations; a youth health clinic at the Los Angeles Gay and Lesbian Center; a second health clinic, Boston's Pedro Zamora Center; and the West Hollywood, Calif.–based Pedro Zamora Foundation. While the memorial fund raises money for AIDS Action's fellowship program for young people and the clinics provide HIV and AIDS services, it is the foundation that was created specifically to continue Zamora's crusade.

"The Pedro Zamora Foundation was established by Zamora family members, friends, and MTV *Real World* cast members to continue Pedro's work of educating America's youth about HIV/AIDS," reads the foundation's mission statement.

But now, just two years after the foundation was created, Pedro's sister Mily Zamora, his *Real World* roommates Judd Winick and Pamela Ling, and his lover, Sean Sasser, say they want the Pedro Zamora Foundation shut down. The problem, they say, is Brian Quintana, 32, president and chairman of the foundation's board of directors. They say he is running the foundation against their wishes and with no supervision by anyone. In essence, they charge, Quintana is using Zamora.

Winick and Ling, who became a couple after their stint on *The Real World* and still live together in San Francisco, are among the original five members of the foundation's board (the others are Quintana, Mily Zamora, and Alex Escarano, a longtime Miami friend of Pedro's who died of AIDS complications in the fall of 1997). They claim Quintana has ignored all of their directives, has kept basic financial information from them, and has failed to carry out the foundation's mission to educate America's youth. Making matters worse, they say, Quintana has spent a good deal of the past year fighting felony criminal charges that he sexually assaulted another gay man in October 1996.

"If Brian Quintana tells you he's working in the best interest of Pedro Zamora, don't you believe it, because he's not," Winick says. "The foundation has nothing to do with anything Pedro would have been interested in. Brian was a friend for a long time, someone we thought we could trust with Pedro's name. At every turn there was a lie."

Quintana, meanwhile, denies the charges by Winick and Ling—who, he says, were removed from the foundation's board March 26—and says he will continue using Zamora's name to educate young people. "Pedro would be the first person to say, 'Use me, exploit me, put my name out there, put my picture out there if it's going to make a difference in the lives of young people,' " Quintana says. "This is not about any one individual or any one person involved. This is about making a difference."

But what started out as an effort to make a difference by picking up Zamora's torch has devolved into an acrimonious exchange of charges and countercharges. And today those who created the Pedro Zamora Foundation disagree on just about everything connected with it—down to such elementary points as how Quintana met Zamora in the first place.

In the Beginning

Quintana says he first met Zamora in 1989 at a party given by Zamora's uncle. "As two young Latinos, we clicked," he says. "He was really excited to meet another Latino who was doing something with his life." Five years after that initial meeting, when Zamora was dying in the hospital, Quintana organized a fund-raiser—at Zamora's request, he says—at a Methodist church in Hollywood. He raised $45,000 to help pay some of Zamora's medical bills.

Winick believes Quintana did not meet Zamora for the first time until he was near death and barely able to speak. Winick and Ling say they were grateful for Quintana's work on the benefit. "We were very impressed by his ability to do an event like that," Winick says. "Brian made it his job 24-7."

After the fund-raiser Winick and Ling started talking to Quintana about plans for the Pedro Zamora Foundation. While they were interested in creating a foundation, the couple didn't have any fund-raising experience. Quintana, on the other hand, had worked on political campaigns and fund-raisers, had boundless energy, possessed connections in Hollywood and Washington, D.C., and seemed like the right guy at the right time.

The Pedro Zamora Foundation was created in May 1996, 18 months following Zamora's death. In the paperwork submitted to the California secretary of state's office, Quintana listed himself as president of the board and Winick as secretary.

In a biography he wrote shortly after the foundation's creation, Quintana lists impressive credentials, including his work with various AIDS charities, both Clinton-Gore campaigns, and campaigns for California senators Dianne Feinstein and Barbara Boxer. In addition, he had experience as a candidate, running unsuccessfully for the California assembly in 1992, then entering but dropping out of the assembly race in 1994.

Quintana also once worked for the William Holden Wildlife Foundation, run by Stefanie Powers, star of the TV series *Hart to Hart*. However, that relationship ended badly. In the spring of 1995, Quintana obtained a temporary restraining order against Powers, claiming that a person who he says worked for her had called him and threatened his life. He also claimed Powers had forced herself on him sexually and had refused to pay him $4,500 in foundation commissions owed to him. As a result of his charges, the *National Enquirer* ran a story with a headline that screamed "Young Assistant Tells All: Stefanie Powers Forced Me to Make Love to Her."

But Powers, in a written statement to the Los Angeles County superior court on June 2, 1995, said of Quintana: "We may bring our own claims against him for the damage we believe he caused our fundraising effort by…forging the signature of an executive of one of the Walt Disney companies on a letter pledging a $15,000 'sponsorship' of the event.'" Ultimately, Powers denied all of Quintana's allegations, and a judge ordered that the temporary restraining order be vacated "not just by the preponderance of the evidence, but by the overwhelming weight of the evidence."

A year later Winick and Ling agreed to let Quintana take a leading role at the time of the foundation's inception. However, they say he was supposed to be helping them find a professional executive director and additional board members with experience running a nonprofit. "We were more concerned about getting people in to do nonprofit work, and that just wasn't happening," Winick says. By November 1997 Quintana was still at the helm, and, the couple say, they were very concerned about the activities of the foundation.

At this point they started asking Quintana for copies of the foundation's bylaws and for financial information, including how much money he was taking in and how it was being spent. But they say they received nothing but a runaround, while Quintana maintains he "honored every request" they made. Winick says Quintana would answer their requests for information by saying such things as "Yeah, I'm putting it into the mail today" or "Oh, you didn't get it?" and "I don't know where it is."

As for the money, Quintana says that in 1997 the foundation took in $69,767. According to a tax filing he furnished *The Advocate,* $17,560 was spent on "professional fees and other payments to independent contractors," $13,168 was spent on "occupancy, rent, utilities, and maintenance," $3,339 was spent on "printing, publications, postage, and shipping," and $35,518 was spent on "education events, engagements, and programming." After expenses, the group was left with $182, according to the tax document.

Told of Winick and Ling's claims that there have been only fund-raising parties and no education programs at all, Quintana says the foundation's Peer Education Program conducted 110 speaking engagements in 1997 and that 30,000 youths had received "face-to-face" HIV/AIDS education "as participants at these peer education forums and our other awareness events."

But that was a surprise to Ling, who says she had never heard of the Peer Education Program. "Was Brian able to tell who the peer educators are, who's on the speakers bureau?" she asks. "This is how he operates. He'll never provide you with any concrete evidence of these programs."

Indeed, when asked by *The Advocate* to provide a list of speakers who could be contacted to confirm they worked with the foundation or a list of specific speaker events he had set up, Quintana did not do so. He did, however, provide a letter from a nonprofit group called the Peer Education Program of Los Angeles, which details its involvement with the Pedro Zamora Foundation education programs. But a secretary at the program's office said the director was out of the office for health reasons and could not confirm the program's connection with the foundation.

"All proceeds have been spent correctly on programs," Quintana says. "Because [Winick and Ling] have not been actively involved [in the foundation], they don't know how many engagements we've done and what expenses are incurred."

When the couple called Bank of America in April, they were told there was only about $40 left in the foundation's account. "The fact that there is no money in there makes us sick beyond words," Winick says. "We always thought the money going in was sitting there. We were told everything was being donated. As far as we knew, the money wasn't being spent."

Quintana says it is "conceivable that there was less than $100 [in the account] at the time they checked it. We don't have a huge cash reserve."

Winick and Ling's frustration is understandable, according to Kathleen Enright, director of public relations at the National Center for Nonprofit Boards. Enright says denying records to board members is unacceptable: "The board has to be fully up-to-date on financial information. They need access on a quarterly basis to anything and everything they ask for. If I were a member of a board that was denied access to financial information, I would immediately resign."

Zamora's lover, Sean Sasser, whose romance with the young activist was chronicled on *The Real World* and who since has served as an infrequent adviser to the foundation, says Quintana was able to run the foundation without oversight because Zamora's family and Winick and Ling don't live in the Los Angeles area. "He took direction from himself," Sasser says. "He didn't get board approval to do anything. It's a clear case of someone taking advantage."

The Events

While Quintana is proud of the support he has secured among Hollywood celebrities and local politicians, Winick and Ling say the foundation's history is marked by a series of debacles. The first, they say, was the Concert to Benefit the Pedro Zamora Foundation, which was to be held at Los Angeles's Great Western Forum and was to feature acts such as Jewel, Joan Osborne, Soul Asylum, the Presidents of the United States of America, and Extra Fancy. After three separate dates were announced in local newspapers and then canceled, the idea was dropped.

The next black eye, Winick and Ling say, was Quintana's arrest on three charges of sexual assault and a charge of assault with a deadly weapon, just five months after the foundation's incorporation.

The charges stemmed from an October 1996 encounter with another gay man on the porch of a private residence near the leather bar Cuffs in the Silver Lake district of Los Angeles. Soon after he met Quintana on the street, the alleged victim said in court testimony, the two of them started engaging in sex on the porch. The alleged victim charged that when he decided to cut the sex short, Quintana twice shoved his fingers up his anus.

"I did not want something like that to happen," the alleged victim testified in court last January. "I know that when I pulled away, I pulled away. That's when he placed his hand inside me." When the alleged victim tried to leave the scene, he said, Quintana threatened to hit him with a brick. Quintana pleaded innocent to the charges.

After she heard about the sexual assault charges, Mily Zamora sent Quintana a letter, dated December 9, 1996, asking him to "immediately separate yourself from leadership positions in any activities carried on in Pedro's name, pending the resolution of the sexual-assault case against you." In addition, she asked that the foundation be dissolved and that Quintana "cease representing yourself as an adviser to the Zamora family or anything similar."

Quintana says Mily Zamora privately supports his efforts but was embarrassed by his arrest. "People who are involved—certainly those with public profiles—feel a need to distance themselves from me, if not outright, certainly publicly," he says.

Winick and Ling, however, stood by Quintana when he was hit with the charges. Believing Quintana when he said he was innocent and that the charges would soon be dropped, Winick says, "We basically were going to try to stick with the foundation to salvage it. We felt by resigning right then and there it would create a bigger mess."

Pedro Goes Hollywood

In July 1997 Quintana held a grand opening party for the foundation's new headquarters at the Pacific Design Center in West Hollywood. At the event the Design Industries Foundation Fighting AIDS presented Quintana with a check for $10,000. For the event Quintana secured proclamations congratulating the foundation from a wide range of public officials, from President Clinton to California lieutenant governor Gray Davis. Those accolades now line the walls of the foundation's offices.

In November 1997 the Actor's Fund of America and the United Way organized a benefit performance of *Rent* in Los Angeles, and Quintana signed up such young celebrities as Neil Patrick Harris, Kiefer Sutherland, and Brendan Fraser for the event.

Quintana says the foundation netted about $23,000 from the benefit, but to Winick and Ling the parties were meaningless. "I think he's using Pedro's name to speak to people in Hollywood," Ling says. After more than a year and half of existence, the foundation had thrown only fund-raising parties; it had done no AIDS education, the couple says. "It was papier-mâché," Winick says of the foundation. "There was nothing there."

But it wasn't until the postparty for the *Rent* benefit, when Quintana introduced a board member Winick and Ling had never even heard of, that they realized how out of the loop they really were. "Brian was now acting unilaterally," Ling says.

The Morning After

Winick and Ling say Quintana is supposed to be a volunteer and that there has never been any deal for him to be paid by the foundation, an allegation with which Quintana takes issue. Court transcripts show that Quintana told a judge he used at least $2,500 he earned from the *Rent* fundraiser to hire new lawyers to fight the sexual assault charges.

On November 3, 1997, the morning after the *Rent* benefit, Los Angeles superior court judge Rodney E. Nelson granted a motion at Quintana's request to substitute lawyer Charles Lindner for the public defender assigned Quintana for the case.

"We had a huge fund-raiser last night on which I was getting a commission," Quintana told Nelson, according to the transcript. "I would like to proceed with the counsel of my choice. It was totally impossible prior to this date to give them any sort of fee."

Today, Quintana says he ultimately did not use money from the fund-raiser to pay his lawyers and that his parents paid for his defense—which he estimated in court testimony cost about $30,000. Regardless, he says Winick and Ling are "outright lying" if they say they did not know he was being compensated for his work with the foundation. He says he was paid $15,400 in 1997. "First of all, it's not Pedro Zamora Foundation money," he says. "It was money paid to Brian Quintana."

But Winick insists, "We never approved anyone being paid any salary at any time. At one point we asked him point-blank, 'You're not paying yourself a salary, are you?' "

After the *Rent* benefit, the couple decided to attempt a coup—specifically voting as board members to oust Quintana and dissolve the foundation. "If we stayed on, we had some hope of using our power as board members to do something about this," Ling says. "If we resigned, it was pretty clear that Brian had no intention of stopping."

The Trial

Quintana went to trial in January on the sexual assault charges. On the stand he acknowledged he had had a tryst but said it was the alleged victim who was the aggressor. Quintana said it was he who tried to walk away and that he pushed the other man only because the man would not let go of him.

Los Angeles County superior court judge Carlos Moreno threw out all three felony sexual assault charges. He did, however, find Quintana guilty of the charge of assault with a deadly weapon (the brick)—reduced from a felony to a misdemeanor. He sentenced Quintana to serve 180 days in jail, with the option of work furlough, and up to three years probation. Under the original charges he had faced 18 years in state prison.

"It was the worst experience of my life," Quintana says of the ordeal. "I'm sorry for any negative impact it had on the foundation." In May Craig Levy, a spokesman for the Los Angeles County probation department, said Quintana was under house arrest and that his location was being electronically monitored through an ankle bracelet.

While Quintana says the arrest and the foundation have nothing to do with each other, the trial did reveal an inconsistency regarding a key issue for an official of an AIDS organization: his HIV status. During testimony Quintana stated he is HIV-negative. Later deputy district attorney Steve Meister confronted him about an eviction proceeding against Quintana years earlier. Meister asked Quintana to read a declaration he had filed in Los Angeles municipal court in 1994 in opposition to the eviction. It read, "I have not been able to vacate the premises by the date set forth on the notice to vacate for the reason I've been diagnosed HIV-positive and am unable to move." Meister asked, "So you lied...to a court?" And Quintana replied, "Yes."

And then there was the matter of the letter. At the time of Quintana's sentencing, Moreno received a letter on Pedro Zamora Foundation letterhead urging him to be lenient. "Mr. Quintana's direct leadership and personal involvement have been key to the success of this organization," the letter read. "His absence would adversely impact the success of the Pedro Zamora Foundation and the educational programs we provide to youth across America." It was signed by vice chair Brett Ratner and board secretary Judd Winick.

Ratner, a film director, says the letter is a fake and that he didn't even know Quintana had been arrested. "This guy is obviously exploiting me and my name," he says. Ratner's lawyers sent a letter to Quintana, dated March 10, saying that Ratner had never "consented to or accepted any position with the foundation as a board member or otherwise" and requesting that Quintana stop using Ratner's name in connection with the foundation "Vice chair, that's ridiculous," Ratner says. Winick also says the letter is a forgery and that he is in the process of making a formal complaint to police. Quintana would not comment on the forgery allegations.

The Future

In April Winick and Ling held a conference-call board meeting with former member Mily Zamora. They voted to remove Quintana from the board and started the process of dissolving the foundation. The couple also have hired a lawyer in an attempt to have the foundation stripped of its nonprofit status.

But Quintana does not recognize their actions, saying he and a new board voted to remove

Winick and Ling two weeks earlier, on March 26. "We acted first," he says. He also points out that Mily Zamora quit the board in December 1996. Quintana says the new board consists of U.S. state department official Andre Lewis; record company executive John Dukakis; Seth Warshavsky, president of Seattle-based Internet Entertainment Group; and medical marijuana activist Jay Schurman. Lewis, Dukakis, and Warshavsky did not return phone calls seeking comment. Schurman, however, confirms he is on the board and that he voted to remove Winick and Ling. But he says he cast his vote during a one-on-one phone conversation with Quintana and that he has never met the other new board members.

So now the Pedro Zamora Foundation is in the difficult position of having two boards of directors, each of which denies the legitimacy of the other. Quintana says he has learned from his mistakes and promises he will document foundation endeavors better in the future. "We are taking measures to document everything a lot more thoroughly now because in the past it was just like 'Let's do it and move on,'" he says. In April the foundation launched its new Web site, www.pedrozamora.com, and received a donation of 250,000 condoms from Trojan, which the foundation is now distributing—as part of a safe-sex kit sporting Zamora's picture—at pride events and to small nonprofits. In May the foundation held a concert at the University of California, Los Angeles, featuring the band Wank. Dean Cheley, a student volunteer with UCLA Campus Events, says Quintana assembled the whole event. "We rarely get an opportunity to put something like this together," he says. And Quintana says the foundation is continuing its Peer Education Program, will start showing public service announcements in movie theaters this fall, and even has the backing of another one of Zamora's former *Real World* cast members, Dave Puck. However, that alliance is sure to raise eyebrows among MTV viewers who remember Puck's antagonism toward Zamora on the show. While Puck says he supports AIDS education, he still has little good to say about the foundation's namesake: "I thought, personally, he was kind of a dick."

However, there are still some problems. The foundation may have to move its offices, and the group is still having difficulties pulling off events. Michael Anketell, a fund-raising producer, says he stopped working with the foundation after talking to Winick and after Quintana wrote him a $1,500 check on a closed bank account.

Quintana says he remains dedicated to the group's mission. Asked how he justifies continuing this work, he says, "To the extent that we are still providing a valuable service, this foundation will continue. That's how we justify it."

Quintana has his defenders. Yesenia Alonso, a 25-year-old teacher who has known Zamora since grade school, says Zamora's wish for a foundation is more important than all the squabbling. "I know Brian has the best interests of the foundation in mind," Alonso says. "This is what [Zamora] wanted."

As for the opposition board, Winick has been calling people to discourage them from getting involved with the foundation. He says his lawyer is contacting the California secretary of state and attorney general and the Internal Revenue Service to ask them to investigate Quintana and the foundation.

Sasser says he hopes the government agencies will help Winick and Ling in their quest to stop Quintana. "I would really like to see justice bite Brian in the ass," he says. "I'm definitely for the burn-him-at-the-stake option."

Meanwhile, Mily Zamora says she has given up on Brian Quintana, but she has a simple request for everyone else. "The only thing I ask is that people respect my brother's memory," she says. "Respect means there is nothing that can hurt my brother."

THE LOST BROTHER: MATTHEW SHEPARD WAS A GENTLE OPENLY GAY MAN IN A STATE WHERE BEING OUT ISN'T EASY

by Jon Barrett

November 24, 1998

On the night of Tuesday, October 6, the members of the Lesbian, Gay, Bisexual, and Transgendered Alliance at the University of Wyoming got together for dinner at the Village Inn, a popular student hangout in Laramie. The group had a lot to be excited about. The students were planning a gay awareness celebration for the following week, which was to include a screening of *In & Out* and a discussion of "safe zones" for gay and lesbian students.

After dinner most of the group wanted to retire for the evening. But Matthew Shepard was aching to go out. "He wanted to go to the Fireside [Lounge], and he begged every single one of us to go with him," says Hauva Manookin, one of Shepard's friends. "But it was a weeknight, and we didn't want to. We figured he wouldn't go by himself." But in a fateful decision, Shepard did go by himself to the Fireside, a campus bar where he was a regular. The next day his battered body was found tied to a fence outside of town.

While he was alive, Matthew Shepard was a cheerful young gay man known only to his friends and family. In death Shepard became the lost brother of gay men and lesbians across the country who were suddenly united in a devastating grief for a man they had not heard of just a week before.

At hundreds of vigils held across the country—from Pittsburgh to Pasadena to Portland, Ore.— tens of thousands of people burned candles in Shepard's memory and angrily demanded action on hate-crimes legislation. But underneath their chants was an element of fear and the enduring question of "How could this happen?"

Most of all, how could it happen to Matthew Shepard? A native of Wyoming, Shepard was nonetheless new to the state's gay scene. He went to high school in Europe, attended Catawba College in Salisbury, N.C., and Casper College in Wyoming, and had worked in Denver for a while before moving to Laramie last summer to study political science and foreign relations at the University of Wyoming. By all accounts, Shepard was a gentle, fun-loving person whose slight build (5 feet 2 inches, 105 pounds) and ebullient disposition made people feel protective toward him, not threatened by him.

Kurt Scofield, a friend of Shepard's from North Carolina, called him "little Matt." Scofield recalls his friend as a "marathon shopper" who also read a lot—Old West–themed books were his favorite. The 21-year-old also says Shepard was the first to take him to a gay bar (bars in North Carolina are allowed to admit patrons 18 or older). "He just stood by me the whole time and made sure I was OK," he says. "He was a very wonderful person who thought everybody was as pleasant as he was."

Shepard made quite an impression during his short time in Laramie too. Manookin remembers first meeting him at dinner several months ago. "We shook hands, and he just gave me this heartfelt smile," she says. "I don't remember anything we said; we just had fun. And I remember how captivating his smile was."

Manookin and Shepard became fast friends. Most Fridays they would caravan with other friends to one of Fort Collins, Colo.'s two gay bars, the Tornado Club. As much fun as he had dancing in Fort Collins, Shepard was cautious about being openly gay. "When he left Wyoming, he had just started dealing with being gay. So he was very concerned about the attitudes when he first came back," says his friend Walt Boulden.

"He didn't wear a shirt that said, I'M GAY," Manookin says, "but if you were someone who looked safe, he would tell you." People also sometimes made their own assumptions. "He fit a stereotype," she says. "He talked effeminately, and while that doesn't mean someone is gay, he fit it."

At a Washington, D.C., vigil on October 14, Boulden told the thousands gathered how a forlorn Shepard used to come to his house after someone had called him a "faggot." "We'd talk about how this touched Matt at the core of his heart and that he needed to feel safe again," Boulden said.

But there is some indication that Shepard let some of his defenses down when he went out, even when he wasn't at a gay club. The Cody [Wyo.] Enterprise reported that he was punched in the face last August by a bartender turned off by his advances. According to a Park County, Wyo., sheriff's incident report, Shepard was in Cody with his parents and younger brother on their way to Yellowstone National Park, and he contacted police the morning of August 19 to report that he had been sexually assaulted by three men the night before. Deputy Scott Steward told the weekly newspaper that a rape test was conducted on Shepard and that it showed no signs of sexual assault. He also said that Shepard, whose only visible injury was a bloody lip, decided not to press charges because he couldn't remember details of the incident due to having been drunk.

The investigation found that Shepard had been at a local bar and had accompanied a group of people, including the bartender, to a nearby lake. "He kept asking the perpetrator to go for a walk, and when he put his hand on the perpetrator's arm and asked him to go around to the back of the car, the perpetrator hit him in the jaw," Steward said. The late-summer incident wasn't reported in the Cody newspaper until after that night at the Fireside Lounge in Laramie—October 6.

As much as he pleaded and pleaded with his friends that night, Shepard could not persuade any of them to join him at the bar. "My friend took him home," Manookin says, "but somehow he got back to the Fireside."

And somehow he struck up a conversation with 21-year-old Russell Henderson and 22-year-old Aaron McKinney, who, according to police, lured Shepard out of the bar by telling him they too were gay, robbed him, pistol-whipped him with the butt of a .357 Magnum, and then left him to die, tied up to a fence just outside of town.

"What if all of us had gone with him?" Manookin asked two days after Shepard's death. "What if we had him just come over to our house? That's the hardest part, the 'what if.' "

Shepard's death crystallizes the risk and fear that gay men and lesbians in small-town America are forced to live with every day. A city of about 27,000 people that, Manookin says, takes only ten minutes to drive across, Laramie doesn't have many places where gays can hang out comfortably. In fact, Wyoming—a vast state whose landscape comprises the towering Teton Mountains, high desert plains, and a smattering of small cities and towns connected by slim ribbons of highway—has only 475,000 residents and no gay hangouts whatsoever. The gay bars closest to the University of Wyoming are in Fort Collins, 65 miles south by way of a pass through the Rocky Mountains that is closed by snow several times a year.

To compensate, gay men and lesbians in the state have arranged an extensive schedule of dinner parties, dances, casino nights, and camp-outs. It's a setup that works well, according to Terry Summers, the 26-year-old executive director of the Lambda Community Center of Northern Colorado and Southern Wyoming. Summers says he found enough support as a college student in Laramie that in 1995 he was able to come out in the *Casper Star-Tribune* under the headline "Laramie Man Attends National Gay Conference."

"I never received one piece of hate mail or [a negative] phone call [as a result of the story]," he says. "What I did receive were messages from people saying, 'Thank God there are people like you in the state.' "

Even the strongest support networks have fissures, though. The dinner party circuit, for example, is riddled with what the Rev. Mark Lee, a Metropolitan Community Church minister in Cheyenne, Wyo., calls the "incest taboo." It's either "everybody's already dated everybody" or "sisters don't sleep with sisters," he explains. While restless young men or women who find themselves in a similar situation in another state might venture out to a local gay bar to meet somebody new, that isn't as easy an option in Wyoming. "Gaydar is not infallible," Lee says. "You run the risk of hitting on the wrong guy. That's why most of the linking up here takes place in parks and rest stops. And those aren't necessarily safe."

Jim Muir, 32, who grew up in Casper but now lives in Sheridan, Wyo., with his partner, Tim, says that when he was single, he "spent a lot of time at one of the cowboy bars in Casper picking up 'straight' men who were way in the closet." Most of them were married, he says.

Often called a "live and let live" state, Wyoming—like much of the United States outside the gay ghettos—might better be described as the "don't ask, don't tell" state, Lee says. "You wouldn't walk down the streets of Laramie or Cheyenne holding your boyfriend's hand—never," he says. But Shepard, of course, was not holding his boyfriend's hand when he was attacked.

The horrific murder undoubtedly has changed Wyoming forever. The university football players now wear decals symbolizing nonviolence on their helmets; Jason Marsden, one of the *Casper Star-Tribune*'s top reporters and himself a friend of Shepard's, came out in a column in the newspaper; and Manookin reports that the gay student group had trouble keeping up with demand for STRAIGHT BUT NOT NARROW buttons during Gay Awareness Week. "If this changes things even for a while, then something positive came out of his death," says Manookin. "If nothing positive comes out of his dying, it's going to be that much harder."

Meanwhile, Shepard's friends are left to remember Matthew. Summers recalls that Matthew enjoyed the clubs in Fort Collins so much that one night he hired a limousine to take him and his friends on the 130-mile round trip. When asked why he would spend so much money just to go dancing, Summers remembers Shepard had a simple reply: "Because life is too short."

A MOTHER'S MISSION: JUDY SHEPARD TALKS ABOUT HER SON MATTHEW, HIS LEGACY, AND HER OWN NEWFOUND ACTIVISM

by Jon Barrett

March 16, 1999

As Judy Shepard drives through Casper, Wyo., on a brisk Sunday morning, she points out the way things used to be. Before she and her husband moved the family to Dhahran, Saudi Arabia, for his job as an oil safety engineer. Before her two sons left for boarding school. And, of course, before her elder son, Matthew, was left to die on a fence in Laramie, Wyo., about 180 miles south of Casper.

She passes through a subdivision on a bluff outside the town of about 50,000 to look at her family's old home. It's the two-story one on the ridge—the nicest on the block. On a clear day like today, you can see the white tops of the Bighorn Mountains from the backyard.

She points out Matthew's junior high school and Casper College, where Matthew performed in several productions. Was he a good actor? "You're asking the wrong person," she says, admitting the bias of a proud mother. Shepard was clearly close to her son; on her last visit to Wyoming before the fatal attack, she and Matthew spent five hours together in a restaurant just talking and enjoying each other's company.

On this day not all of Judy Shepard's memories are as happy as that one. At the family's church, St. Mark's Episcopal, she drives past the black fence in the park across the street that corralled the Rev. Fred Phelps and his antigay clan during Matthew's funeral. In the same park is a tree planted a month ago by some of Matthew's former classmates.

The 46-year-old Shepard looks different today than she did in October, when the world first saw her on the day of Matthew's funeral. Her shoulder-length hair is longer and redder—the water in Saudi Arabia bleaches it. But she still looks like a mom. And at only 5 feet, 2 inches, she looks like Matthew's mom.

Someone meeting Judy Shepard for the first time might think her naive. It's an impression her understated voice and demeanor don't belie. But if you spend time with her and listen to her story, it's clear that any naïveté she may have had has been elbowed away by bewilderment, loneliness, and the determination that something good come from her son's death.

While 18-year-old son Logan is away at boarding school and husband Dennis is in Saudi Arabia earning the family's keep, Shepard is back in Casper after six years. She's here to lay the groundwork for the Matthew Shepard Foundation, which she says will be "dedicated to the principle of helping people move beyond tolerance to embrace and rejoice in diversity." In an exclusive interview with *The Advocate,* she discusses her plans for the foundation, talks about the effort to maintain privacy for herself and her family, and remembers the joys and struggles of Matthew's life.

Until now, I know a lot of the contact you've had with people with regard to Matthew has been through the Internet. Were you an Internet person before this?

No. Living in Saudi Arabia, we had no live Internet. So I had no experience with the Internet at all. But I have a niece who's a computer nerd, and she was showing me how to find things on the Web. I had been hearing so many things about the Web sites dedicated to Matt that I wanted to see them. There were so many E-mail letters we got that I knew there must have been a lot of discussion on the Internet about it.

How did the E-mail make you feel?

At first I found reading the messages very hard. The same with the cards because it brings up such an emotional reaction. But as I go through them all, it's very cathartic to share that hurt, to know that so many people cared about him—and about us—and actually took the time to take a pen to paper or type out a message on the E-mail. It's really very touching, very strengthening to me.

Were you surprised by the mail?

Oh, totally, totally amazed. Still am when I look at all of it. It's just overwhelming how many people responded in a positive way—very, very few otherwise; they're in my weird file. But it's been a very overwhelming, amazing, and totally wonderful—in an odd sense—experience to know that so many people would care.

How many total letters would you say you've received?

About 10,000 letters and 70,000 E-mails. We received letters, cards, gifts, stuffed animals, blankets, food. Some people just sent a card and signed their names, and some wrote amazing 20-page letters—just whatever the spirit moved them to write. I'm going to read them all, and they will be answered, but not personally.

Can you tell me a little bit about the Matthew Shepard Foundation and your plans for it?

Well, we've only begun laying the groundwork. So I don't have a mission statement. We only have a basic idea. And the idea is that we will be a foundation that will have fund-raisers, seminars, and symposiums based on education about tolerance and diversity. But I will not be developing one of my own education programs. There are so many already in existence—some struggling—that if I find them meeting what my ideas are, then we will be helping them.

So you're very much at the beginning stages?

Oh, absolutely, absolutely.

Do you have ultimate goals in mind?

Actually, we're so far in the beginning that I don't even have those yet. I just want to make a positive difference. Even if it only lasts a year, I feel we will have affected more people than already have been—that we will reach people somehow.

Are you hoping to reach those like Matthew or those like the people who hurt Matthew?

I guess I'm trying to reach them all. Everybody has a right to live a life free of fear. The people like Matthew have a right to live their lives and be true to themselves. And the people [like those] who hurt Matthew also have a right to live their lives, as long as they do it without hurting other people. What happened to the days of just being nice to each other? Why do we have to feel that we need to express every bit of everything all the time? You know? I'm just trying to reach everybody. And to show people with the phobias and the fears that they're groundless. I don't know if that's possible, but I'm going to try.

Are you surprised to find yourself an activist?

Oh, totally. I've always been an activist in my own mind, but I so dislike the public eye that I would not be out there doing anything. Among my friends or those who see us, I'm opinionated, and I speak out. But doing it in front of people—I just couldn't ever do it. So I'm amazed at my role right now. I feel Matt sitting here [*points to her shoulder*], just pushing me, just going, "I know you can do it. I know you can." Even though he knows I hate it.

Is this the kind of thing he would have wanted to have been doing?

Yes. He's not a rostrum beater. He doesn't get up there and pound his fist and say, "This is the way it should be." But he would love to be out there sharing ideas and talking and debating the issues and trying to make a difference.

And you're kind of doing this for him.

Yes, I owe it to him.

When I heard about the foundation and I started seeing your name, I was just amazed that you were able to be doing this so soon.

[Deep breath]

Does everybody say that?

Yes.

People would assume that you would have to retreat and be by yourself for so long. Where do you find the strength to do something like this?

I find I can deal with it better…if I could retreat, I would retreat. [*Crying*] Sorry. I need to stay busy. I don't know—I don't know how to put it in words. I feel that it's something I have to do. So many people have asked us to do something to not let Matt be forgotten, and we have to give them the opportunity to do something. Dennis, Logan, and I felt that I would be the one who would have to do it. And it's not easy. To be here alone and doing it. [*Crying*] But Matt's with me, and together we'll make a difference.

Do you have family out here?

No, my family is all scattered. I have a lot of friends here, though. And they're wonderful. I also find that in order to deal with everything and to talk about Matt every day, I have to build a little pocket to put my emotions away in and deal with it in a sort of a third-person detachment. Sometimes I can't. Sometimes it sneaks up on me, like right now. But I know it's something I have to do, so I'll take it just a day at a time.

Have you talked to other parents who have been in similar situations?

No, but I've received a lot of correspondence from those parents and from victims themselves.

Does that provide support?

Oh, yes. Actually, it also supplies a reason to go on—thinking maybe it wouldn't happen again if we're really successful at what we're doing.

What other kinds of people have you met since Matthew's death?

The only people who come up to me are people who already knew me. My face really hasn't been publicized, so they don't really know who I am. I get an awful lot of mail, but I really have not had direct contact because I've had so many people protecting me.

Have there been a lot of people looking for you?

Yeah. Media people mostly.

Are they successful in finding you?

No.

Did the press make it more difficult for you?

Yes. When we first got to the States, we picked up our son Logan and went to Colorado. That's when we found out the events surrounding Matt's attack had been in the national newspapers. And it was very upsetting. We felt something had been taken from us—our privacy, our own lives. We immediately had the idea of total exploitation—*National Enquirer*-type, horrific exploitation—and it was very upsetting. When we realized how many people were positively responding because of the news reports, we realized our take on the media had been wrong.

But at first...

The press made it very difficult for us to maintain anonymity in that we had to secretly be led in and out of the hospital. But if they had really tried to find us, they could have. They were, as we look back now, really respectful of our wishes to be left alone. Even when we came to Casper—especially when we came to Casper—because we just couldn't be that secret here. But for about a day we felt it was a total invasion. We got some pretty strange requests mediawise too. But overall, the media were really pretty fair to us.

Requests like what? To appear on 20/20?

Yeah, and *Larry King*—and I'm thinking, *Oh, jeez, there's just no way.*

Within the same time as the funeral?

Yeah, yeah.

Were you able to follow the press at that time?

Only our local newspapers. We were so busy planning the funeral and trying to make sure that only our friends and family could get into the church and not a bunch of reporters. Our time was taken up with burying our son. And in the hospital we didn't care about anything else. We just devoted all of our time and attention to Matt, and that was it.

I had heard there was some resentment on your and your husband's part regarding people who went on Larry King to talk about Matt. Was that true?

Kind of. We felt that, in particular, some individuals were hopping on the media wagon, and not to Matt's benefit. Maybe they had his best interest at heart, but there was some resentment.

Many people made the connection between his death and the national campaign saying that people can be cured of homosexuality—that it is something that should be cured. Was this a valid connection? Do you think the campaign in some way incited hatred?

I don't know anything about the campaign. I don't want to comment on that. I didn't know anything about it until I read your piece ["From Soft Words to Hard Fists," November 24 issue of *The Advocate*]. I think it's ridiculous that anybody thinks that there's a choice to be made. I guess that's all I really have to say about that…. It's just one of those things I don't pay attention to. It's just so stupid. It just makes me mad.

Were you surprised by the level of hatred, like that from Fred Phelps, for example? Did that affect you in any way? Did you see it?

No, we never saw it. We were very protected from it. We did, of course, hear about it and see the pictures that appeared in the national media. At the time it was like, *OK, they've accomplished just what they wanted to—they got national exposure; they're being talked about.* And they still are being talked about. But a friend pointed out to me that what they are doing is showing people the depths of their hatred and their ignorance. But as far as my personal reaction to them? It wasn't worth one. Nothing is going to change their minds, and that's just the way they are.

Would you say anything to them?

Oh, no. They're not worth that energy.

Did you know about all the demonstrations? I'm talking about the positive ones now.

I knew of a few. The one in Fort Collins [Colo.], of course, because we were there for part of that one. The one in Laramie. But as far as across the nation, no.

When did those come to your attention?

Well, we started reading the newspapers after the funeral, and that's when we found out about them—like the one in New York that got so out of hand and then the smaller ones at colleges. They started sending us photos and newspaper articles and placards with signatures and cards, and that's when we we really found out about the magnitude and the quantity worldwide.

Obviously Matthew struck a chord with a lot of people, especially with gays and lesbians. Even though people didn't know him, they felt that they did. Did this surprise you?

No, it didn't. In the two or three press releases Dennis and I did, we tried to explain the kind of person Matt was. And as I reread them I realized that they really painted a pretty full picture of who he was and that people would identify with everything we said. He was just a kid who liked everything. He wasn't different from anybody. And I think it was just so easily identifiable for everyone, gays and straights alike.

There have been so many other people who have been attacked and killed, and for some reason, this time everything came together and took everybody's attention. Was Matthew an everyman sort of kid? Or was there something about him that made people feel particularly close to him?

I can't answer that, other than to say that it seems the photo released at that time just so showed his youth and his…just showed him, just showed how trusting and youthful and naive he was. And so full of promise and a future and just a regular kid.

How did he come out to you?

He called me on the phone from North Carolina and told me that he was gay. And I said, "And that means I'm supposed to have some reaction?" I had known for a long time.

Had you ever talked to him about it?

We sort of talked around it. I wanted to give him the opportunity to tell me face-to-face, but he wouldn't do it. He wasn't ready, and I wasn't going to ask him. If he wasn't ready, he wasn't ready.

How did you know?

I don't know. I had known for a long time. I think I knew before he did.

When he was a little kid?

I think I did.

You could tell a difference between him and his brother?

Yeah. And I can't explain it, so don't even ask me to. I just knew.

How old was he when he told you?

Eighteen. He was very afraid to tell his dad. And he built up this worst-case scenario, and that was the one he always carried around. So it was longer than that before he told his dad, even though his dad knew because I had told him. There was no reaction from him either. There was a sense of loss in that you're not going to have that traditional wedding, daughter-in-law, children, grandchildren kind of thing, but he was still our son, and we still loved him. Everything about him that we loved was still him. That didn't change. But Matt was more afraid to tell his dad, thinking that—actually, I don't know what he thought. But Dennis was always very accepting, and I think Matt had a hard time understanding that he was.

Did he ask you to keep it a secret from his dad?

No. They talked around it for a long time before Matt finally just said "I am."

Was that over the phone too?

No, it was in person.

After he came out to you, was he more comfortable being out in public? Did he come out to other people then?

I think he came out to his friends in high school before he did to me. In fact, they have told me they knew in high school he was gay. That was one of the things in articles that wasn't true—that he was openly gay. He was confident in who he was, but he was also confident in knowing who he should not tell. I thought he was. So if people asked him, he would say yes. But he didn't put a sign around his neck saying I'M GAY. He was fearful.

Did he tell of instances where he'd had a problem?

No. I have a feeling there were a lot of things he didn't tell us because he didn't want to worry us.

Were you concerned about his personal safety?

Oh, yes, and for a lot of reasons—one of them being that he was so small but his mouth was so big. He just never, ever let the fact that he was small ever get in the way of his expressing his opinion. And that worried me.

What kind of things would he do?

He would stick up for himself and others—just jump right in there. And that really concerned me because he was so small. He had no idea how to defend himself. He just knew things were wrong, and he wasn't going to let it go by. He was never, as I recall, ever hurt by that physically—emotionally but not ever physically.

Where did he go to boarding school?

Switzerland. There are no high schools for Western kids in Saudi Arabia, so they all have to go to boarding school.

Have you met a lot of his friends?

I have met none of his friends in Laramie, but I've met his older friends from school here, in Casper, and his boarding school friends.

Did he have boyfriends?

You know, that was part of his life he never shared. I knew he had one in North Carolina, but I don't want to talk about him. He was on the Internet with someone he evidently felt quite close to as well. I've heard about him, but I've not met him yet. Other than that, I don't know.

None have come forward to talk to you?

No. And his other friends have said that he was just really careful about forming a relationship, again because he was fearful. He felt that if he made a friend and they didn't know he was gay and if they found out later he was and it was a problem, he had just wasted all that time. "Why do that?" he told us. "Why start a relationship on false grounds?"

So, in between the time you kind of figured out he was gay and when he told you he was, was there a learning process for you about gay people?

Yes, there was. I knew several gay people in my own personal life. And I guess the learning process was about my own ignorance and trying to come to terms with Matt. I was so ignorant about the kind of community life he would need to be safe. I didn't join any support groups or anything because I never felt I needed to. I never had a problem accepting him. That was not a problem for me or with Dennis or even with Logan. None of us were surprised.

Since his death, has that learning curve continued?

I was always very afraid for Matt's personal safety, and I knew there were attacks going on everywhere, all the time. I don't think I was aware of how many really severe ones there were until this happened to Matt. Because now I've heard about so many. And I don't think they make the news the way Matt's did. And I've heard from several people who didn't report incidents because they weren't ready for it to be known that they were gay. I find that very sad, very sad.

But do you understand that?

Yes, I do understand that. Yes, I do.

What would you say to those people?

I don't want to say anything. I wouldn't know what to say. It's a matter of choice. And they have to come out when they're ready. And if they don't feel comfortable doing it…I mean, it's a travesty that they feel that they need to be hidden. But things will never change until everybody takes a stand.

When he moved back to Wyoming last year, did you think he would be safer?

I did feel he would be safer. I also felt that he would be lonelier because I felt the gay scene in Laramie would be much smaller than what he was used to.

But he wanted to come home?

He wanted to come home. He was ready. He wanted to experience the nature of Wyoming—the mountains and the things he had left behind. He wanted to come back to where it was small enough that he could get around, where there were people he already knew, and where there was still the environment of a university and an international student presence.

He was majoring in political science—what did he want to do with that?

He wanted to go into the foreign service and work with human rights issues overseas—all human rights.

His story has certainly changed some people's opinions regarding human rights, but do you have any fears that he'll be exploited for political purposes?

Yes, I do. Matt was a human rights activist who happened to be gay. I don't think—and this is only my opinion—I don't think he would want to be the poster child for gay activists because there were some points in their doctrine that he didn't agree with. He was more a believer in that if there was better care in what's already here…yes, there are some specifically needed…I can't go there. Sorry. I'm digging myself a hole I know I'm not going to get out of.

Can you tell me some of the things he didn't agree with?

He felt that the same rules should apply to everyone and that there shouldn't have to be a separate set of rules for specific groups. Because we're all people. But he also knew that just wasn't going to happen. So specific laws that said you can't fire gays, you can't discriminate in housing for gays, gay marriages—he was for that. But I can't really say what he did not support. I guess we talked more about what he did agree with. But I know there were some things that he thought were too…isolating. I'm just really hesitant to talk about the hate-crimes legislation, though. I just don't know enough about it to really put forth my own opinion.

Is it something you want to educate yourself about more?

Oh, yes, definitely. And at some time I will have things to say about it. But also because of the charitable nature of the foundation, I really can't have a political stand.

There were some things about gay people that embarrassed him, though, right?

Yes. I can only think of one specific instance. In general, it was the stereotypical gay bars with sex going on rampantly in the bathrooms. But there was one specific instance in a park, and it really angered Matt.

He said, "That's just whoring, and it sets back people's views on gay relationships so far that it brings forth the stereotypical view of gay men and that they're incapable of having a committed relationship—a monogamous, committed relationship." He was really upset about it.

Are you talking about George Michael?

I don't want to name names. That's burning bridges, in my opinion, and I don't want to do that.

Where do gay people meet each other in a place like Wyoming?

I suppose I really can't answer that either, except that they meet at organizational meetings, and Matt used to call it gaydar. You just sort of know, and you tentatively begin a conversation and sort of decide whether each other is gay or not. But there are no social gathering places. When you move to a place, you hear about it underground, you know? But there are no gay clubs in Wyoming.

Was the Fireside Lounge supposed to be gay-friendly?

Gay-friendly? Oh, they were all gay-friendly, I think, to a point. It was a bar that welcomed everyone. College students, everyone felt comfortable there.

Had he talked about the bar?

Oh, yeah. I know he went there quite a lot. In fact, I was beginning to worry that he had a drinking problem. He went there too often, especially with the medications he was on.

For depression?

Uh-huh. He shouldn't have been drinking at all.

What kind of medications?

He was taking Effexor for depression and something called Klonopin for anxiety.

Did that have anything to do with his being gay?

I think it was a factor.

One of several?

Yes.

Was he lonely out here?

Matt could have a million friends and still be lonely. He was just really insecure in his friendships. He could have a bazillion friends and always feel that he needed more. He just liked everybody to be around all the time.

Is that why he went out a lot, do you think? To meet new people?

Well, I guess.

I'm struck by your talk about gaydar and the discrepancies in the stories of that night as to whether he tried to pick up those two guys or not. Do you think faulty gaydar played a role that night at all?

Oh, I have no idea. I think Matt did have a tendency to overcompensate for his fear. He would say, "Oh, I'm being irrational." You know? "Why am I afraid of them?" And he would do things that maybe he wouldn't do ordinarily. And that's only supposition. I'm just grabbing at straws to figure out why he went with them. I don't know.

Is that a question that's going to always bug you?

Yes.

Do you hope an answer will come out at one of the trials?

Oh, I'm sure it won't. I'm sure it won't.

He was hurt before, right? In Morocco? Can you tell me about that?

He was on a school trip his senior year, and he was in Morocco and had gone out to a coffeehouse alone, and he was speaking to other exchange students. And on the way back to the hotel, some [male] locals grabbed him, and he was raped and robbed.

How many people were there?

I don't know. He never told us the details.

How did you find out about it?

He called me in Saudi Arabia from Morocco to tell me. And I could not go to him any sooner than he could come to me. It would have taken me longer to get the proper paperwork to get out of Saudi Arabia and into Morocco. So I think he was there one more day, maybe two, before he could leave and come to Saudi Arabia.

Was he hospitalized?

He was examined and released to the police to help find the attackers.

Was this what triggered his emotional problems?

Well, in high school, as we talked about before, he suffered a little depression, but this Morocco incident was certainly a major factor in his current medical condition. He suffered anxiety attacks, panic attacks, and depression. He just felt that as time went by he wasn't getting any better at being able to deal with the attack. He was still afraid of groups and strangers. There would be times when it didn't bother him at all, and sometimes he would be paralyzed by his anxiety.

So much so that he had thoughts of suicide and considered checking into an assisted living facility, right?

Yeah, he did consider that for a while. That was when he lived in Denver and he felt very isolated. He thought a smaller community would be better for him, so he moved to Laramie.

Then there was a report in The Cody *[Wyo.]* Enterprise *that last August he befriended some people in a bar, accompanied them to a nearby lake, and then later was punched in the face by a bartender. Did that happen?*

I really can't say. He felt safe with these people, and he didn't know what happened. He couldn't remember. He had blackouts—and he didn't remember anything other than flashbacks from Morocco. He said he liked those people and felt that they liked him. I think he felt safe when he left with them.

Did they say what happened?

I believe in the newspaper report the bartender said Matt had made a pass at him.

And do you believe that?

Well, it's not Matt. It's not the Matt I know, and it's not the Matt other people know.

When you first heard about the October 6 attack, you were in Saudi Arabia, right?

Uh-huh.

Did you automatically assume he was attacked because he was gay?

Yeah, I assumed it. I just couldn't think of another reason why anybody would beat him. In fact, every time the phone would ring and you'd hear that long-distance ping, you just say this silent prayer to yourself, *Oh, please let Matt be OK.*

How long did it take you to get here?

It was 4 a.m. Thursday our time when we received the call, which would have made it about 6 p.m. Wednesday Wyoming time. We got in at 4 p.m. Friday. It was horrible. It just drug on and drug on and drug on.

You were able to get your other son?

We called him at school and told him that we were picking him up and we were going to Colorado.

Did he know before you got him?

I don't think so. I went one direction when we got to the airport, and Dennis went the other direction with Logan. I called Colorado to check on Matt, and Dennis was talking to Logan, and I'm pretty sure that's when he told Logan.

Were you able to get updates on Matthew's condition when you were coming back to the States?

No. We had no idea until we got here.

The first trial begins March 22. Will you be there?

Yes. I'll be at all of them.

Is your husband going to attend too?

No. The company told him he could have unpaid leave. But we can't afford to do that because we have a son getting ready to go to college and we can't go without pay for six months.

Are you afraid? Do you anticipate a feeling of anger or fear?

No. We went to the preliminary hearings, and I didn't experience any of that. I have no feelings toward the defendants at all. To acknowledge their presence requires some kind of emotion, and I don't want to expend any of that on them. The fear I have is of just being there and hearing what happened. I just have to do that.

Are you afraid you'll hear something that you haven't heard before?

Oh, sure. I mean, he didn't live with us for six years, and he had a very private life, other than what he would tell us. And no child tells his parents everything. And I'm sure the defense is doing everything they can to find ways to make Matt a less sympathetic individual. So I'm sure things will come out that I've not known before. I don't know necessarily that it will be bad, but I'm sure I'll hear things I don't know. It would be difficult for my parents to learn about things I did! So I'm sure something will come out.

But today, knowing your son as only his mother could, what do you think his legacy will be?

Oh, gosh, just that he opened people's eyes. I hope to make it a long-lasting one. If he's changed anybody's mind in any way, it's been a successful legacy. Far-reaching, I have no idea. I hope I can see it in my lifetime.